THE **FRONTIERS**
OF **PROJECT MANAGEMENT RESEARCH**

The **FRONTIERS**
of **Project Management Research**

Editors

Dennis P. Slevin, Ph.D.
David I. Cleland, Ph.D.
Jeffrey K. Pinto, Ph.D.

Project Management Institute • Newtown Square, Pennsylvania

ISBN: 1-880410-74-5

Published by: Project Management Institute, Inc.
Four Campus Boulevard
Newtown Square, Pennsylvania 19073-3299 USA
Phone: +610-356-4600 or Visit our website: www.pmi.org
E-mail: pmihq@pmi.org

10   9   8   7   6   5   4   3   2   1

TABLE OF CONTENTS

ACKNOWLEDGMENTS

The Project Management Institute (PMI®) and the volunteer co-editors are indebted to each other for their encouragement and support of the conception, development, and delivery of this new unique book on project management research. Both parties are also indebted to the authors of the chapters for the voluntary sharing of their knowledge and wisdom about specific topics of project management research. Finally, recognition is given to the practitioners, researchers, and academics that attended *PMI Research Conference 2000* in Paris, France during June 2000. Their enthusiastic receptivity to the conference provided the encouragement to the co-editors to undertake this endeavor.

PREFACE

Advancing its body of knowledge is a cornerstone and hallmark of any profession. The Project Management Institute (PMI®), the world's leading project management professional association, recognizes the importance of this role by including *the expansion of the body of knowledge of project management* within the *Ends Policies* of the Institute. As further evidence of its awareness of this important role, PMI supports a vigorous research program into professional knowledge and practices. No profession can survive long term without a continuous effort on knowledge management, especially both knowledge generation and knowledge transfer.

Both the general literature and the research literature about project management have grown significantly since the field became a point of professional focus fifty or so years ago. There are over 500 books on project management topics and a few thousand books on closely related subjects. In the past forty years, over 3,500 research articles have been published within the project management field in the English language.

The dynamic advancement of a profession's body of knowledge requires focus on several areas. These areas include the expansion and exploitation of generally known, proven and accepted project management knowledge and practices along with the identification, demonstration and verification of innovative and advanced knowledge and practices. In fulfilling this critical mission of aiding the advancement of knowledge and practices, a professional association must encourage the continuing generation, refinement, and broad dissemination of new material. It is in support of this important goal, that this book, *The Frontiers of Project Management Research*, has been published.

The book contains twenty-eight chapters of research information about the theory and practice of project management. The chapters are divided into four key sections discussing:

- Background research in the field
- Effective practices and success factors
- Organizational and team relationships
- Project management techniques.

Each chapter is written by a well-known and established researcher in the discipline of project management and is based on their original work or critical judgment. The book's genesis is the highly successful *PMI Research Conference 2000* (Paris, France). The co-editors selected twenty-eight of the papers for refinement, updating of the underlying research, and incorporation of the latest thinking by their authors.

The Frontiers of Project Management Research focuses on the current state of the art in project management research and application. The Project Management Institute is proud to make this learning available to everyone with an interest in understanding and using project management as a professional discipline and as a methodology for executing the strategy of businesses and other enterprises.

Rebecca Ann Winston, Esq.
PMI Chair

A LOOK AT BACKGROUND RESEARCH IN THE FIELD

Introduction

Section one contains a set of papers whose theme is an attempt to position the current state of project management research. Each of the papers addresses some aspect of the overall nature of research, including lessons learned, future directions, and missing pieces.

- Timothy Kloppenborg and Warren Opfer (primary authors) present the results of their comprehensive analysis and literature review of the past forty years of project management research. Their perspective points to a number of important trends and predictions for future streams of research. Chapter 1—Forty Years of Project Management Research: Trends, Interpretations, and Predictions.
- Peter Morris uses the current state of the project management body of knowledge developed in the United Kingdom as a framework for examining the research in project management over the decade of the 1990s. He suggests a number of areas in which the literature is underdeveloped and in need of additional research and theory building. Chapter 2—Research Trends in the 1990s: The Need Now to Focus on the Business Benefit of Project Management.
- David Wilemon draws on his extensive experience in project management research and practice to point to some current important research topics, as well as future areas that will require additional work. He suggests that project management is subject to enormous external pressures that require future research to focus on the new stressors and demands project managers will face to be successful. Chapter 3—Project Management Research: Experiences and Perspectives.

- Christophe Bredillet focuses on the fact that current project management research represents a paradigm that is not well defined. Theory building, based on the synthesis of dynamic models of human behavior, is vital for developing the sorts of lifelong learning models that are the key to effective knowledge transfer and future theory building. Chapter 4—Proposition of a Systemic and Dynamic Model to Design Lifelong Learning Structure: The Quest of the Missing Link Between Men, Team, and Organizational Learning.

- Owen Gadeken brings his years of experience in project management with the United States Defense Systems Management College to address the key lessons he has learned from project leadership. He offers a number of key suggestions for developing and nurturing effective project leaders. Chapter 5—What the United States Defense Systems Management College Has Learned from Ten Years of Project Leadership Research.

- Mark Nissen, Keith Snider, and Ira Lewis address an important subset of the United States program management function: the area of defense acquisition research and practice. They point out that the current state of research in defense acquisition management is still in its infancy and in need of more formal theory development and empirical research. Chapter 6—United States Defense Acquisition Research Program: A New Look.

- Christophe Midler creates an important view for the future in project-based research. He identifies some of the key external environmental shifts and pressures on project-based organizations and the need for project practice to take these changes into consideration when managing project development. At the same time, he argues, these changes offer some important opportunities for project management research at the start of the 21ST century. Chapter 7—Project Management for Intensive, Innovation-Based Strategies: New Challenges for the 21ST Century.

CHAPTER 1

FORTY YEARS OF PROJECT MANAGEMENT RESEARCH: TRENDS, INTERPRETATIONS, AND PREDICTIONS

PRIMARY AUTHORS:
Timothy J. Kloppenborg, Ph.D., PMP—Xavier University
Warren A. Opfer, MBA, PMP—The Dayton Group

CONTRIBUTING AUTHORS:
Peter Bycio, Ph.D.—Xavier University
Julie Cagle, Ph.D.—Xavier University
Thomas Clark, Ph.D.—Xavier University
Margaret Cunningham, Ph.D.—Xavier University
Miriam Finch, Ph.D.—Xavier University
James M. Gallagher, PMP—The Dayton Group
Joseph Petrick, Ph.D., SPHR—Wright State University
Rachana Sampat, MBA—Xavier University
Manar Shami, Ph.D.—University of Cincinnati
John Surdick, Ph.D.—Xavier University
Raghu Tadepalli, Ph.D.—Xavier University
Deborah Tesch, DBA, CDP—Xavier University

Introduction

The discipline of project management is currently being used as a key strategy to manage change in contemporary organizations. Consequently, the project management profession is undergoing tremendous growth worldwide as corporations, governments, academia, and other organizations recognize the value of common approaches and educated employees for the execution of projects. Research into the management of projects has had an important role in the previous growth of the profession and should have a significant role in the future growth. Because of the growth of the profession and of the interest in advancing the body of knowledge in project management, the Project Management Institute (PMI®) commissioned this project for presentation at the *PMI Research Conference 2000*. A source selection process was conducted by PMI, and in October 1999, Xavier University, Cincinnati, Ohio, and their strategic partner, The Dayton Group (TDG), Dayton, Ohio, were selected to perform the English language portion of this research activity. In this chapter, the researchers are referred to as the Xavier/TDG Project Team.

Scope of the Research

Scope

This research study project covers research published in the English language in the period from 1960 through 1999. A search of the current literature, utilizing automated and manual reference library capabilities at Xavier University and the United States (US) Air Force Institute of Technology, Dayton, Ohio, and numerous Internet-based literature and research databases, was conducted utilizing a PMI-approved keyword search list. From the material generated by these searches, a refined annotated bibliography was developed by applying the "Project Management Research Definition" jointly developed by the Xavier/TDG Project Team and the *PMI Research Conference 2000* Project Team.

Among the materials searched in the project were scholarly periodicals and journals, conference proceedings, research papers, theses, and dissertations. Research sponsored or published by the US Department of Defense (DoD), the National Aeronautics and Space Administration (NASA), other US government agencies, and the Canadian Aeronautics and Space Institute (CASI) were also included where the material was unclassified and available to the general public. Additionally, the Xavier/TDG Project Team conducted a one-day workshop with fourteen professors and over fifty project management practitioners to assist in identifying and interpreting trends and areas for future research.

Limitations

Textbooks were specifically excluded from the material reviewed. This was due to the volume of texts published and because the Xavier/TDG Project Team and the *PMI Research Conference 2000* Project Team felt that most research was covered in the other literature sources. Therefore, it is felt that this research project has captured approximately 85 percent of all research material published in English since 1960 that met the project research definition. Limitations of time and financial resources prohibited further study into the subject at this time, although we propose a plan to continue and expand the study in the future. (See Recommended Follow-On Work section.)

Assumptions and Research Citation Selection Criteria

The research team developed a list of assumptions and selection criteria during the project that relate to the selection criteria of a specific research citation. These assumptions and research citation selection criteria appear in Table 1.

Source and Citation Exclusion Assumptions and Criteria

During the course of our study, the research team came across several periodicals wherein citations were very technical in nature and not within the scope of our research. Hence, such journals and similarly identified citations have been deleted directly, without review, if they satisfy any of the conditions enumerated in Table 2.

Assumptions Relating to Trends

The following three assumptions were made regarding the identification of trends.

1. Trends have been identified based on a sample of all citations. The words "project management" and the respective knowledge areas have been searched for in the title, keywords, and abstract fields and the resulting sample has been used to identify citations in each knowledge area.

2. Each researcher or workshop facilitator was given a list of thirty-six specific search criteria to provide a common starting point in trend investigation. After that, each researcher was given the liberty to identify trends in their own fashion. Therefore, no consistency in trend identification between knowledge areas can be implied.

3. The verification of trends is based upon the experiences of each Project Management Professional (PMP®) participant in the workshop and those of the researchers and workshop facilitators. The validity of these has been ascertained solely upon their inputs and no statistical inference can be derived from this information.

Methodology

The Xavier/TDG Project Team performed a thorough literature review of English language periodicals, doctorate dissertations, and publicly available government reports from 1960 through 1999. We also included PMI Seminars & Symposium papers and easily available masters theses. A total of ninety-two people worked approximately 6,000 hours on this research project between September 1999 and April 2000. The project team is listed in Table 3. Timothy J. Kloppenborg, Ph.D., PMP, served as the principal investigator. Tim is an Associate Professor of

- If a citation measures project success only by generalizations and lessons learned were not explicitly mentioned, they have been excluded.
- Only citations including real-life case studies have been included.
- If the citation mentions some kind of new technique being examined, it has been included.
- Citations relating to the trends in project management have been included only if they refer to other research citations or are based on substantial data. They have been excluded if they state only the authors' point of view without substantial data to support it.
- Citations based on the *PMBOK® Guide* or any other citation, book, paper, or published work which apply the concepts used in *PMBOK® Guide* or another citation have been excluded unless the lessons learned were specified or the data was in the form of testimonials from clients, etc., as in a real-life case study.
- Citations based on surveys of practitioners, experts, or people involved in project management have been included. However, citations that have only a marketing flavor have been excluded.
- Citations based on models (either ones already in use or created by the author) have been included, if they otherwise satisfied the research definition.
- Citations based upon the experiences of authors have been excluded unless they have resulted in the invention of a new concept or technique.
- Citations based on empirical data, even if only part of the work was data based, have been included.
- Citations that were very technical in nature, but not dealing with the management of projects directly, have been excluded.
- Citations on book reviews, industry reviews, etc., have been excluded.
- Citations that relate a concept from any field to project management have been included.
- Citations have been retained or deleted only on the basis of the abstracts written. There has been no attempt to locate the full text of citations except in the case of manually researched citations.
- Citations that did not have an abstract at all have been deleted.
- Conference proceedings have been researched separately and if they have appeared as an article in a journal, they have not been retained.
- Books have been specifically excluded from the scope of the study.

Table 1. Assumptions and Research Citation Selection Criteria

Management at Williams College of Business, Xavier University. He led the effort, coordinated with all stakeholders, recruited the team, and was involved in making all major decisions. Warren A. Opfer, MBA, PMP, served as the co-principal researcher. Warren is a principal with The Dayton Group. He led the research on government sources, led much of the technical effort, and was involved in making many of the decisions. James M. Gallagher, PMP, served as contributing investigator. He is President of The Dayton Group. Jim recruited Warren and Tim, was instrumental in securing and organizing this research effort, and was involved in making many decisions. John Stemmer, MLS, is Xavier's electronic librarian. John

- Citations from computer journals.
- Citations from regional papers or magazines.
- Citations that had keywords such as "Book Reviews," "Software Reviews," "Industry Reviews."
- Citations that relate to only the technical aspects of logistics, quality, and configuration management.
- Citations from newspapers.
- Editorial notes, brief articles, and news reports.

Table 2. Source and Citation Exclusion Assumptions and Criteria

was involved in making many of the technical decisions and led the day-to-day efforts of the students throughout the investigation. Rachana Sampat, MBA, was a graduate student at Xavier. Rachana was the principal assistant on all phases of the research and was involved in making many decisions.

The deliverables included an annotated database of project management research and a final written report, resulting in the research conference paper and this chapter. This chapter includes trends found in the research, reasons for the trends, "potential best article candidates," and predictions for the future. The tasks accomplished on this project can be described in the following twelve areas:

1. Determine what project management research is.
2. Identify sources of data.
3. Determine formats for our outputs.
4. Acquire data.
5. Input data.
6. Identify records to be retained.
7. Plan and conduct the workshop.
8. Identify and interpret trends.
9. Identify "potential best article candidates."
10. Predict future directions.
11. Advise the French language team.
12. Construct the final database.

Determine What Project Management Research Is

Our first critical task was to define project management research. After much coordination and discussion among the Xavier/TDG Project Team and the *PMI Research Conference 2000* Project Team, the following definition was agreed upon:

Project Management Research Definition: For the purposes of this study, project management research is defined to include published works that are based upon data (either primary or secondary) and that make generalizable conclusions drawn from the data where the data and conclusions are focused on either the project

Principal Investigator:	Timothy J. Kloppenborg, Ph.D., PMP
Co-Principal Investigator:	Warren A. Opfer, MBA, CDP
Contributing Investigator:	James M. Gallagher, PMP
Electronic Librarian:	John Stemmer
Principal Graduate Assistant:	Rachana Sampat

Other Student Assistants:

Luis Barriga	Matthew O'Connor
Julie Butz	Megera O'Donnell
Christopher Debrunner	Priya Patel
Kimberly Dulin	Michael Sigg
Michelle Groetzinger	Greg Walker
James Krallman	

Knowledge Area Facilitators:

Bycio, Peter	XU, Management	Integration
Cagle, Julie	XU, Finance	Risk
Finch, Miriam	XU, Communication Arts	Communications
Clark, Thomas	XU, Management	Communications
Cunningham, Margaret	XU, Management	Quality
Petrick, Joseph	WSU, Management	Human Resources
Shami, Manar	UC, Construction Science	Scheduling
Surdick, John	XU, Accounting	Cost
Tadepalli, Raghu	XU, Marketing	Procurement
Tesch, Deborah	XU, Information Systems	Scope

Workshop Arrangements:
Debra Miersma, PMP
Lynn Mills
Alan Dulin

GroupWare Consultants:
Teresa Frank, PMP
Patrick Sepate, PMP
Ryan Belt

Workshop Volunteers: 51 Senior Project Executives (mostly PMPs)

Other Database Workers:
Cathy Heuing
Chris Schenck
Laura Opfer
Jennifer Voelker, PMP
Thomas Youger, PMP

PMI Research Conference 2000 Project Team:
Lewis Gedansky, Ph.D.
David I. Cleland, Ph.D.
Jeffrey Pinto, Ph.D.
Dennis Slevin, Ph.D.

Table 3. Xavier University/TDG Project Team

management context or the management activities (not the technical activities) needed to complete a project successfully; where:

1. *Published* means that the works are in public distribution or through publicly available government sources (i.e., DoD, NASA, and such).

2. *Data* means information organized for analysis.

3. *Generalizable* means able to draw inferences beyond the individual case.

4. *Conclusions* mean judgments or decisions made after deliberation.

5. *Project management context* means the environment in which projects/programs operate.

6. *Management activities* mean all the processes used to manage the nine project management knowledge areas as described in *A Guide to the Project Management Body of Knowledge* (*PMBOK® Guide*) and other information dealing with project management knowledge, skills, and attitudes.

7. *Technical activities* mean project specific tasks such as writing code, digging a foundation, and so on.

Research can include both theory and practice in the field of project/program management. Examples include:

1. Summaries and critical analyses of research results.

2. Surveys of current practices.

3. Critical analyses of concepts, theories, or practices.

4. Developments of concepts, theories, or practices.

5. Analyses of successes and failures.

6. Comparisons and/or analyses of case studies.

Identify Sources of Data

The second task was to identify the useful sources of data. We explored various commercial databases and selected those shown in Table 4 because collectively they covered the various disciplines (management, engineering, computers, and so forth) that may be interested in project management, covered many journals both from North America and elsewhere in the world, and covered all doctoral dissertations.

We also manually researched selected journals by either paper or microfilm, both to ensure we covered the time period before the electronic databases started and to include specific journals we felt were important but were not included in the electronic databases. These selected journals are shown in Table 5.

We initiated contact with various other professional associations to inquire about alternative sources of project management research. While this effort resulted in interesting phone calls and emails, the sources identified were already included. Examples of these organizations are Institute of Industrial Engineers, Academy of Management, Institute of Electrical and Electronic Engineers, and Construction Industry Institute.

We also initiated contacts with various government agencies to locate publicly accessible government reports that qualified as project management research. These sources are listed in Table 6.

ABI Inform (1971–present)
Provides coverage of business, management and related topics.
Includes over 1,000 leading business and management publications.
Includes over 350 English language titles from non-US sources.

Compendex (1980–present)
A comprehensive interdisciplinary, engineering database.
Covers engineering, manufacturing, quality control, and engineering management issues.

Infotrac General Business File (1980–present)
Includes business and management topics in over 900 journals.
Includes information on finance, trade, new technologies, trends, etc.

Digital Dissertations (1861–present)
Dissertations from over 1,000 North American graduate schools and European Universities.
Post 1980 includes abstract written by author.

Table 4. Sources of Data

- *PM Network* (1989–1999)
- *Business Horizons* (1960–1972)
- *Operations Research Journal* (1960–1972)
- *Omega* (1981–1992)
- *PM Quarterly* (all issues)
- *California Management Review* (1960–1972)
- *Harvard Business Review* (1960–1972)
- *Sloan Management Review* (1960–1972)
- *Management Sciences* (1960–1972) (microfilm)

Table 5. Selected Journals

1. US Air Force Institute of Technology	AFIT
2. Scientific and Technical Information Network	STINET
3. Defense Technical Information Center	DTIC
4. US Defense Systems Management College	DSMC
5. Research on Ongoing Acquisition Research (in DSMC)	ROAR
6. Canadian Aeronautics and Space Institute	CASI
7. US National Aeronautics and Space Administration	NASA
8. Dudley Knox Library—Naval Postgraduate School (NPS)	DUDLEY
9. The Rand Corporation	RAND

Table 6. Government Sources

Determine Formats for Our Outputs

The third major task was to determine the reporting formats for the project working documents and deliverables. These needed to be decided early so we did not lose time redoing work. Many of our project tasks were on the critical path and the ones that were not had very little slack time. We needed to select bibliographic software and design a database quickly. For this a product called Reference Manager® (ISI ResearchSoft; previously Research Information Systems) was selected, as it appeared to have all the necessary features that are required to create a comprehensive database with the added advantage of allowing the user to create different databases based on various criteria. It also provided the option of exporting the database records to Microsoft® Access® for ease of use and portability.

The database design we developed is included as Table 7. We determined that we would use the abstract from any entry that had one, regardless of the length or format. These vary widely since they come from thousands of primary sources. We also decided that any abstracts we would write would be simple, descriptive, and approximately five lines in length. An example of a citation in the database format is included as Table 8.

An analysis and research taxonomy based on the *PMBOK® Guide* nine knowledge areas was developed. This provided the basis for the development of the search keywords and facilitated the categorizing and cataloging of the research, allowed for the verification of observed trends in the previous research, and assisted in the identification of major research opportunities for advancing the body of knowledge in project management.

We identified three sets of keywords that would be used as the taxonomy and would be used in the review, classification, and cataloging of the citations. These keyword sets are summarized below and described in Table 9.

1. The *first* set of keywords relates to the nine knowledge areas of project management as defined in the *PMBOK® Guide*. It has been useful in identifying citations relating to the different aspects of project management.

2. The *second* set of keywords relates to the application of project management to different industries.

3. The *third* set of keywords relates to the process aspect of project management. Fifteen process areas, including project life-cycle stages such as plan and close, as well as management processes, such as organize and motivate, have been established.

Acquire Data

The fourth major task was to actually acquire the data. This included selecting search terms, searching electronic databases, and downloading files. Our selection criteria for searching the online databases were based on the list shown in Table 10.

Reference Type: Generic

Reference ID: 1

Authors Primary: Author Name

Title Primary: Sample Record

Author Secondary: if needed

Title Secondary: if needed

Periodical: Periodical Name

Volume: Volume Number

Issue: [Issue Number]

Starting Page: 1

Ending Page: 999

Date Primary: 12-3-1999

Publication Place: City, State, and Country of publication (optional)

Publisher: Name

Title Series: Optional

Authors Series: Optional

Keywords: These are from the Citation

Reprint: Not in File

Abstract: From the resource database or written by us (initial ones we write)

Notes: As you need them. Add editors/reviewers comments here also

Knowledge Area Keywords: Knowledge Area Keyword

Application Area Keywords: Application Area Keyword

Process Area Keywords: Process Area Keyword

User Defined Field #4: Not Used

Status Codes: Status Field (blank/E-<initials>/?[flag for review]/R-<initials>) {entries are separated by;}

ISSN/ISBN: from the resource database

Availability: from the resource database

Source Code: resource database source name

Misc. Field #2: not used

Misc. Field #3: not used

Address: from the resource database—optional

Web URLs: from the resource database or entered by us (can be used to link to full text files stored on hard drive)

Table 7. Database Record Design

Reference Type: Generic
Reference ID: 26
Authors Primary: Baumgardner, C.R.
Title Primary: An Examination of the Perceived Importance of Technical Competence in Acquisition Project Management
Author Secondary: AIR FORCE INST OF TECH WRIGHT
Starting Page: 243 PAGES Report Number: AFIT/GSM/LSY/91S-4
Date Primary: 9-1-1991
Keywords: *Program manager/*PROJECT MANAGEMENT/ACQUISITION/Acquisition managers/ADDITION/ADMINISTRATION/Attributes of project managers/DETERMINATION/LIFE CYCLES/LIMITATIONS/MANAGEMENT/Management skills/PHASE/Project management/PROJECT MANAGER/Project managers/RATES/SCHOOLS/SKILLS/TEAMS (PERSONNEL)/Technical competence/THESES/TRAINING/TRAINING
Reprint: Not in File
Abstract: This research examined the importance Air Force acquisition project managers attribute to technical competence, and several individual and situational factors which might affect their perceptions of the importance of technical competence: extent of acquisition experience, degree of technical academic training, level of project technology, caliber of technical project team, and acquisition phase. A review of the literature revealed that previous studies of project and program managers suffered from several limitations with regard to a direct examination of the importance of technical competence. No single study has empirically supported a clear determination on the importance of this attribute to project managers. Considering the nature of today's projects and the ongoing dramatic rate of technological advancement and change, an investigation of the potential importance of technical competence in managing projects seems particularly critical for prospective project managers and those with little experience. In a study of 228 acquisition managers, the findings show a majority consider technical competence as extremely important or absolutely essential, even though they may rank the attribute low in terms of use when compared to other skills. Further, the results indicate the importance of technical competence among acquisition project managers varies significantly as a function of technical project team capabilities and phase of the acquisition life cycle. In addition, the research suggests technical competence is an important contributor to project managers' ability to communicate.
Notes: AD Number: ADA246682
Descriptive Note: Master's thesis
Monitor Acronym: XF
Monitor Series: AFIT
Imitation Code: APPROVED FOR PUBLIC RELEASE
Source Code: 012250
Knowledge Area Keywords: 5;6;7;9
Application Area Keywords: 9
Process Area Keywords: 1;14
Status Codes: E-LMO; R-WAO
Source Code: DTIC

Table 8. Sample Database Record

Knowledge Areas:

1. **Integration:** Citations about general project management, i.e., those citations that are not focused on any one or two knowledge areas. For example, a citation may be about one whole project, beginning from the determination of the scope, and have almost all knowledge areas explained, without placing emphasis on one or two areas.
2. **Scope:** Citations relating to the scope of the project may have a particular case that talks about what the project seeks to accomplish.
3. **Time (Schedule):** Citations that clearly emphasize time or schedule. Citations relating to the Critical Path Method (CPM) or any other scheduling techniques; Costs/Schedule Control Systems Criteria (C/SCSC).
4. **Cost:** Citations about the economics of an organization; profit centers; financial models in some cases; budgets; expenses; citations discussing how contract management reduces costs; Earned Value; Costs/Schedule Control Systems Criteria (C/SCSC); forecasting costs; resource planning.
5. **Quality (Performance):** Citations about Total Quality Management; new concepts in quality management; explanation of the importance of quality in a project; quality control.
6. **Human Resource:** Citations about education; training; ethics in project management; anything to do with employee motivation, hiring, firing; type of organization structure-matrix etc.; career; cultural aspects of Project Mgmt; teams; stakeholders.
7. **Communications:** Any form of communication technique, e.g., electronic meetings, Statement of Work (in some cases); interaction.
8. **Risk:** Citations about Crisis management; Return on Investment; contingency planning; insurance.
9. **Procurement:** Citations about supply; supply chain management; contractors; outsourcing; acquisition; purchasers or purchasing; vendor; litigation about procurement.

Application Areas:

1. **Aerospace (Defense):** Air Force, Army, Navy, aerospace engineering and manufacturing.
2. **Construction (Design):** Engineering projects, architectural projects.
3. **Information Systems (Information Technology):** Selecting right kind of software, different kinds of software packages, hardware, Internet, software quality management, Y2K, supplier-vendor, outsourcing, outside contractors, various IT companies.
4. **New Product Development (Research and Development):** Mainly in Pharmaceutical, Medicine, IT. Could be other industries also.
5. **Pharmaceutical:** Drug or medical device or supplies development or certification projects.
6. **Utility (Energy):** Power Projects, Nuclear Energy, about the Department of Energy.
7. **Government:** Dept. of Transport, other non-DOD government departments not related to any other application areas.
8. **Telecommunications (Electronics):** Citations about telecommunication companies, e.g., AT&T.
9. **Defense:** DOD, Defense documentation.
10. **NASA:** Citations about Apollo 13, other space missions, any citation that is directly related to NASA project management.

Table 9. Project Management Keywords

11. **Consulting:** About consulting firms or consulting projects. This could have been done by a company in any of the application areas.
12. **Manufacturing:** Manufacturing related development of construction projects.
13. **Education:** Any education-related projects or projects conducted by educational institutions.
14. **General:** Any citation that does not fit into the above application areas.

Process Areas:
1. **Life Cycle:** Any citation that describes the beginning to the end of the project, feasibility studies.
2. **Initiate:** Beginning of the project, how it started, launch of a project, how it originated how it was introduced.
3. **Plan:** Project planning, work breakdown structure, any other planning tool.
4. **Execute:** Carrying out of the project: in most cases, this will have to be implied from the abstract or the citation.
5. **Control:** Monitoring, control measures, Enterprise Process Control.
6. **Close:** End of the project, discussion about the success/failure of a project after it has been completed.
7. **Organize:** Organize the processes, project teams.
8. **Motivate:** Employee motivation.
9. **Direct:** Direct project or business related activities.
10. **Lead:** Team leader, project manager, importance of the leader/manager, role of leader/manager, how a project succeeded or failed because of leader/manager.
11. **Benchmark:** A process, criteria, model, or standard for which others are measured.
12. **Reengineer:** A process, procedure, or practice that is modified, replaced, or eliminated in response to changing business requirements.
13. **Concurrent Engineering (Simultaneous Engineering):** Product design team composed of members from all disciplines, projects related to concurrent engineering.
14. **Teams:** How teams have succeeded or failed, role of a team member.
15. **Improve:** Product improvement or process improvement related projects.

Table 9. *Continued*

The commercial databases were downloaded en masse. Ensuring that individual citations met the research definition occurred later. Reports in the government databases were verified for inclusion first and then downloaded. Many entries from both traditional and government sources were only available in either paper or microfilm format. These needed to be copied individually. Some entries, such as PMI Seminars & Symposium papers, were available on CD-ROM.

Input Data

The fifth major task was to input the data into Reference Manager. To accomplish this we first had to write a unique filter for each electronic database from which

1. Project Management
2. Program Management
3. Acquisition Management
4. Systems Acquisition Management
5. Systems Management
6. Logistics Management
7. Performance Management
8. Configuration Management
9. Financial Management
10. Program Control
11. Human Resource Management
12. Integration Management
13. Scope Management
14. Cost Management
15. Quality Management
16. Communication Management
17. Risk Management
18. Procurement Management
19. Contract Management

Table 10. Selection Criteria

we wanted to import files so they would be compatible in Reference Manager. Even with these filters, some files needed to be manually manipulated for correct format. We then needed to develop Reference Manager procedures and train everyone who used it to maintain consistency. We wrote abstracts when necessary and typed entries that came from old paper and microfilm sources. At this point, we imported files into Reference Manager.

Identify Records to be Retained

The sixth major task was to apply the research definition to all of the citations and eliminate those that did not meet the criteria. Due to the volume of citations, that was a very substantial task. The first step in this was to remove duplicates from the imported records. As records often appeared in more than one source, duplicate citations could be deleted. Since records were identified through queries of commercial databases, there were often citations and papers included that did not apply. When counting all sources, over 100,000 total entries were considered for inclusion. Very quickly it became apparent that it would be impossible to locate all 19,000 books that were identified using our keywords. Therefore, the assumption was made that most research that is included in books has also appeared in an article or paper somewhere, and books were deleted. We noticed certain publications

Advertising Age	*Marketing*
American Medical News	*Marketing News*
Automotive News	*New York Times*
Business Insurance	*PC Week*
Business Marketing	*PC World*
Computer Technology Review	*PC Computing*
Computer World	*PC Magazine*
Financial Times	*Publishers Weekly*
InfoWorld	*Wall Street Journal*

Other items were deleted because of a readily identifiable indication that they were not research such as:

- Brief citation
- Company profile
- Column
- Financial profile
- Editorial
- News briefs
- Book reviews
- Software reviews

Table 11. List of Publications Not Used

were not research oriented and, as such, we deleted them en masse electronically. A list of these publications appears in Table 11.

Other items were deleted because of a readily identifiable indication that they were not research. Examples of these indications are also contained in Table 11.

Based on further review of the materials kept, additional items that were quickly deleted included authorless citations, abstractless citations, certain proceedings, and systems and computer type journals.

Finally, the primary method of deleting unneeded records was to manually look at the abstract of every single entry and make decisions on whether it met the definition of project management research stated above and whether it was really on topic. Many, many articles, papers, and government reports were deleted because they did not qualify as research. The most common reason was that the entry was based on opinion instead of data. More than half of the identified dissertations failed the test of being on topic. Most of these included the term project management in their abstract to describe the efforts of their dissertation as a project such as "this butterfly-collecting project." While they are research, they are certainly not project management.

Plan and Conduct the Workshop

The seventh major task was to plan and conduct a workshop so we could utilize the collective judgment of nine additional professors and the experience of over fifty project management practitioners to assist in identifying and interpreting the trends and identifying areas for future research. Each professor acted as a facilitator and was an expert in one of the nine knowledge areas; however, not all were experts in project management. These professors were from Xavier University, Wright State University, and the University of Cincinnati. These professors are listed in Table 3.

We assembled a book for each workshop participant that included an agenda, a table of contents, a summary of the trends uncovered in each *PMBOK® Guide* knowledge area, a list of approximately twenty-five "preliminary best article candidates" from each *PMBOK® Guide* knowledge area, and a special section on government reports. We arranged for a computer network with groupware software to support the workshop. This included loading a great deal of information into the groupware, conducting a technical setup with the software consultants, and conducting a dry run with the facilitators and online scribes.

The actual workshop started with several people representing PMI setting the stage. Then the workshop facilitators of each group quickly overviewed the trends discovered in the nine *PMBOK® Guide* knowledge areas, as well as in the government reports. The practitioners were divided into the nine *PMBOK® Guide* knowledge areas based on their specialization and preferences. The professors facilitated breakout sessions for each of the nine *PMBOK® Guide* knowledge areas asking the practitioners to comment on why they felt each identified trend in research developed the way it did. The next activity in the workshop was for the practitioners and professors to vote on the "top ten" articles in their respective knowledge area. That was followed by a prediction within each knowledge area of research trends likely to be seen in the future. The practitioners were then challenged to identify what potential research they would find most useful in the future in each knowledge area. Finally, all workshop participants identified best practices they would like to see repeated in future workshops and lessons learned to improve future workshops. The groupware downloaded workshop results into several documents totaling fifty-five pages of text. Since this was so voluminous, each professor wrote a two to three page summary of the results of his respective knowledge area.

Identify and Interpret Trends

The eighth task was to identify and interpret trends in the research. To accomplish this, each of the professors was furnished with their respective portion of the working database (this ranged from several hundred to several thousand citations), the results of thirty-six simple queries (each of the knowledge area, application area, and process area keywords defined above), and a student to assist them with more complex queries.

Once the professor identified the citations of interest, she reviewed their abstracts to identify trends. We then imported these trends into the groupware software for the workshop. The professor briefly described the trends to all workshop participants, and then asked the experts in her area detailed questions concerning the trends. The answers to these questions were captured electronically. Finally, when the workshop was over the professors each wrote a summary of the results of their respective areas. We then compared these results and have included an overall summary in the results section of this paper. The working database at that point in time did not include PMI Seminars & Symposium Papers and a few articles prior to 1980 that were manually added later. This working database did include some articles that were later deleted because they did not satisfy our research definition.

Identify "Preliminary Best Article Candidates"

The "best article candidates" list made up the ninth task. Each professor also identified (just from abstracts) approximately twenty-five citations that they thought had important research findings and/or ideas. The citation and abstract of each of these was printed and included in the workshop book. The professors used these abstracts to facilitate discussion aimed at interpreting the identified trends. After a morning of discussion on the trends identified and some time to review the abstracts, the participants voted on up to ten citations that they thought made the most meaningful contribution to their personal understanding. These lists of "preliminary best article candidates" are listed in the results section of this chapter. They are not meant to be an authoritative list. They are meant to generate discussion among project management researchers concerning what is important project management research.

Predict Future Directions

The tenth task was to predict future directions for project management research. The professors and practitioners did this for each knowledge area toward the end of the workshop. One interesting note is that while there is some overlap between what the practitioners predict will happen and hope will happen, there are many differences. A summary of both of these lists is included in the results section. We believe researchers should make careful note of the areas in which these senior project management experts say research is needed.

Advise the French Language Team

The eleventh task was to provide guidance to the French language team to ensure that both efforts would yield results that could be consistently compared. The English language team started first and had many more records to consider. As we developed procedures, we wanted to ensure the French team knew what we were doing.

Construct the Final Database

The twelfth, and final task, was to construct the final database. For this, we constructed individual, "clean" databases of journal citations from electronic database sources, PMI Seminars & Symposium papers, dissertations, government reports, and a miscellaneous database of journal citations that came from paper and microfilm. These were then combined and one final check for duplicated citations was performed.

Results

We are confident that the vast majority of publicly accessible project management research that has been published in the English language between 1960 and 1999 is included in this annotated database of 3,554 records. The methods used to construct the database are described above, as well as the limitations to its completeness. We feel that it is as complete as possible given the amount of time and money we had to use. Another part of the research was to begin analyzing the database contents. The research team makes no claim that this is a comprehensive analysis; rather it is a starting point for other project management researchers. Our fervent hope is that the trends, the comparisons among *PMBOK® Guide* knowledge areas, and the predictions made serve to inspire other researchers to dig deeper. This, after all, represents forty years worth of research and it would be presumptuous for us to attempt to identify and interpret every important trend.

The Xavier/TDG Project Team utilized a number of techniques in analyzing the data gathered for determining trends and interpreting the data. The team members spent many hours compiling and evaluating the data to identify, catalog, and classify the research citations, extract the issues and trends, and understand the message in the data. However, in addition to determining major issues and finding trends in the literature, the team wanted to involve more academics and practitioners in the interpretation process to validate the information from a "real-world" perspective. Our goal was to understand the environment and circumstances surrounding the past research and to develop an understandable portrayal of how the theory and practice of project management has evolved, where it is going, and in what direction it should be going. To that end, the *Project Management Current and Future Trends Executive Seminar* was held. This seminar was the first of its kind. The event was more of a workshop than a seminar, in that the participants actively made the process flow and were the source of the output from the process. The team provided the raw material input, acted as a catalyst and process facilitator, and the participants took it from there. It was a very rewarding effort. The following discussion specifically addresses the results from the seminar. The research results are reported as trends, commonalties between knowledge areas, differences between knowledge areas, predicted future directions, recommended future directions, and "potential best article candidates."

Trends

Some very important trend information emerged as we went through this process. Most notably was the lack of research, and for that matter, lack of literature on project management in the 1960s. We found only 1 percent of the research citations occurred during that decade. See Table 12 for more detail on this and other trends.

In the 1970s, there was a trend toward the development and use of automated project management software. Also during that period, there were a number of research citations related to the use of the Program Evaluation and Review Technique (PERT). The focus of research during this period was on cost and schedule control,

As observed with each individual knowledge areas, research in project management has increased substantially over the decades.

The break-up percentage of citations in each decade is as follows:

1960s	1%
1970s	7%
1980s	29%
1990s	60%

The number citations in each knowledge area have also followed the trend available in the seminar results with the greatest number of citations being in Time and Cost. The break-up is as under:

Integration	5%
Scope	5%
Time	24%
Cost	28%
Quality	12%
Procurement	4%
HR	4%
Communications	8%
Risk	10%

For the process areas, planning has the maximum number of articles, with the least importance on execution.

Plan	29%
Lead/Direct	17%
Control	23%
Execute	1%
Improve	14%

If we consider the industry-wise distribution, construction, and information technology are the most written about by far.

Construction	21%
Information Systems	21%
Utilities	3%
R&D	4%
Manufacturing	5%
Education	8%
Telecommunications	1%

In the Government area, the following is the breakout of articles:

NASA	3%
Defense	11%
Aerospace	1%
Military	3%
Government	7%

Note:
- The total number of articles used to derive these figures is 3,554. The database may have been negligibly modified after these trends have been developed.
- Most of these figures will overlap with one another, when used in conjunction with other parameters.
- Due care has been taken to ensure accuracy of figures. However, due to the enormous possibilities of keywords in the abstract for one topic, a small margin of error may be possible.

Table 12. Observed Trends from the Final Database

performance measurement, the use of Work Breakdown Structures (WBSs), and life-cycle management. Government still sponsored a large number of the research projects in the literature, but the number of projects sponsored commercially or by educational institutions increased. Toward the end of the 1970s, the concept of design-to-cost and life-cycle costing first appeared in the research literature. This became very common in the 1980s particularly in the government and defense sectors. In addition, the research literature included several research studies in the late '70s related to leadership and conflict management in projects.

In the 1980s, the volume of research projects in the literature increased significantly (29 percent of the total articles). The research literature continued to focus on design-to-cost and life-cycle costing, plus a number of studies were reviewed on project management computerized systems. Research on project risk management and the Cost/Schedule Control Systems Criteria (C/SCSC) and earned value appeared in the literature. Additional research subjects included team building and quality management. The initial reporting on the use of Artificial Intelligence (AI)/Expert Systems and Knowledge-Based Systems (KBS) appeared.

In the 1990s, a large number of research projects focused on the human resource aspects including team building, leadership development, and motivation. There were also quite a few articles concerning the risk management, quality management, and communications knowledge areas of the *PMBOK® Guide*.

Commonality between Knowledge Areas

Perhaps the single most important trend that was observed as a commonality among all the areas of project management was the increase in literature on project management issues. For most knowledge areas, there was a paucity of research in the 1960s and the 1970s. The research increased significantly in the 1980s and expanded in the 1990s. One reason for this is that the importance of project management as a profession started to be widely realized only in the l980s. Also, more and more companies have been coming out of the regulated mode of functioning. As non-regulated companies, they now face stiffer competition, which requires the use of project management, and they are now able to disclose more information than they could previously.

The dominant application areas described in the project management literature are construction, information systems, and the utilities industries. This result is not surprising, since engineering and construction firms have long been the masters of project management. However, in the case of information systems, the literature has started expanding only in the 1990s. The influx of hundreds of computer software programs that address the issues of project management in general, and each knowledge area specifically has been observed.

The government was an early adopter of project management and, hence, we found numerous articles about the government in the different knowledge areas. In the period of 1960 through 1990 the following trends were observed:

■ Cost/Schedule Emphasis
■ Systems Analysis/Structured Design

- Systems Management
- Procurement/Contract Administration Focus
- Value Engineering
- Earned Value and C/SCSC.
  In the period of 1990 through 2000 the following trends have been observed:
- Increased focus on competency and commitment
- Increased focus on interpersonal/behavioral aspects
- Increased emphasis on stakeholder identification and management
- Increased emphasis on communications and communications planning
- Increased emphasis on performance measurement to specifications/objectives and benefits
- Change to project management as a career path
- Increasing focus on standards and certification
- DoD certification (Acquisition Management)
- Defense Extension to the *PMBOK® Guide*
- Interest in PMI Certificates of Added Qualification (CAQ)
- Increased interest in using the *PMBOK® Guide* as a basis for training (American National Standard—American National Standards Institute [ANSI])
- Broad interest by government agencies besides the DoD.

In regards to the processes in project management, the trend was toward planning and control. This was attributed to the complexity of project management and the need to plan efficiently and carefully each aspect of the project and then monitor it to ensure it functions as planned.

Some studies also focused on the relation of one knowledge area of project management with several other knowledge areas, specifically how they would work in conjunction with each other. For instance, many authors have emphasized how important it is that time and cost management work in synergy, while keeping in mind the risk factors.

Differences among Knowledge Areas

There were various differences spotted among the project management knowledge areas. There were very few research-based articles dealing with project integration management. Most of the articles we originally found in integration were opinion based. There were also very few articles concerning project procurement management. The opposite was found in project scope management. As firms have become more competitive, an increased demand for quality has led practitioners to recognize the importance of developing solid scope statements before they perform any other function. Hence, a great deal of literature relating to scope can be found. Project cost and project time management were also widely investigated areas.

Also, the types of articles found differed for each knowledge area. In the case of project human resource management, most of the project management publications are case studies or "expert accounts" rather than empirical studies based on systematic data gathering and analysis. In the case of time and cost, most articles relate to the tools, techniques, and methodologies adopted. For procurement, there is an emphasis on the operational aspects, such as contracting. Large numbers of articles were found for each of the management functions that are traditionally associated with quality such as planning, control, and improvement.

Predicted Future Directions

Based upon the identified trends, the project management practitioners and professors predicted future directions for project management research both in each specific *PMBOK® Guide* knowledge area and for project management in general. A few of the predictions are listed below:

- The most frequently considered future trend was support for increased standardization. Standardization of processes and tools, as well as standardization of terminology, are expected to contribute to project management success.
- Practitioners predict a greater use of web technologies for enterprise communication and collaboration.
- Contracts will contain specific language requiring the use of generally accepted project management practices and philosophies.
- There will be more outsourcing of project management by major companies.
- Nontraditional projects dealing with volunteers, resources, and fundraising campaigns will increase.
- The project manager's role will evolve to demonstrate more leadership than project management. Advanced training for project managers will be offered through companies, universities, and professional organizations.
- There will be movement away from super projects.
- There will be refinements in how project scope is defined and related to business requirements and measurable benefits.
- Project selection and prioritization of projects will continue to evolve as a large issue for both government and industry.
- There will be increased emphasis on formal project management training and certification, and verification of what training really works.
- There will be more emphasis on risk management in general and specific training for project managers on risk identification, contingency planning, risk mitigation, and managing risk events.
- There will be increasing focus on communications and communications planning, particularly as it relates to stakeholder management and communications in times of project crisis.

Recommended Future Directions

The project management practitioners were then asked to consider their work demands and identify additional research that they felt would be useful to them. These are listed below:

- Case studies that illustrate the application of knowledge-based systems for project management should be developed.
- Standards and benchmarks should be developed similar to the ANSI standards in the computer industry.

- More universities should create programs that allow students to major in project management and there should be methods to coordinate and benchmark between these universities.
- Techniques and presentation methods for determining and reporting return on investment analysis and measurement should be developed.

"Preliminary Best Article Candidates"

The professors who facilitated the workshop sessions identified articles that they felt potentially were very useful in project management research. This was a very subjective screening based solely upon abstracts. There was no attempt to define what a "seminal" or even "best" article should entail. Neither was there any effort to rank order the importance of these articles. There may be other articles that deserve to be on a best article list. The professors used these articles to stimulate discussion among the practitioners during the workshop. Toward the end of the workshop each practitioner was allowed to vote for up to ten articles that he felt were the most useful. The five articles that received the most votes in each knowledge area are listed in Table 13. Where there was a tie for fifth place all articles receiving the same number of votes were included. This list is absolutely not meant to be a definitive list. Rather it is meant to encourage project management researchers to identify additional articles they feel should be on a best article list and state the contribution made by that article that they feel merits consideration. Even more fundamentally, we hope this preliminary work will serve as a catalyst for discussion aimed at defining the contributions an article should make to be considered a "best project management research article." Our hope is that this simple start will generate a great deal of discussion and even controversy.

Recommended Follow-On Work

We strongly feel that additional effort should be focused in the future on the interpretation of the data and how the information derived from the data can be used to assist practitioners. All of the nine *PMBOK® Guide* knowledge areas are important, but some subjects stand out as areas of keen interest for project management practitioners and executive management. Questions like "How do I select projects?" and "What is the true return on investment for competing projects?" come to mind. In addition, questions about effective means to identify risks and develop strategies to mitigate the risks are common. These are areas that have a major impact, not only on project resource allocation decisions, but also on how effective and successful the business unit is going to be. We believe that part of our focus needs to be on finding practical answers to these questions.

We hope this research effort is merely the start in documenting the field of project management as a discipline. We feel that there are many fruitful avenues to refine and update this beginning. First, in addition to completion of the investigation of project management research published in the French language, similar investigations should be conducted for other languages. Second, we feel there

Knowledge Areas	Title	Author	Journal Name	Year
Communication	A Personal Perspective of MRM	D. Cleland	Project Management Journal	1994
	What It Takes to Be a Good Project Manager	B. Z. Posner	Project Management Journal	1987
	Influence of Project Concurrency on Project Outcomes	O. Hauptman and K. K. Hirji	IEEE Transactions on Engineering Management	1996
	Relationship Building: A Key Technical Skill	Cliff Vaughan	Project Management Journal	1999
	Project Management and the Worldwide Web	J. G. Questore	NA	1996
	Cultural Analysis in IS Planning & Management	Jeff Butterfield	Journal of Systems Management	1996
Cost	Benchmarking in Construction Industry	D. Fisher, S. Miertschin, and D. R. J. Pollock	Journal of Management in Engineering	1995
	Earned Value Reporting Earns Its Keep	R. Mahler and M. Mazina	Cost Engineering	1982
	Development of a Knowledge-Based Schedule Planning System	N. B. Yunus, D. L. Babcock, and C. O. Benjamin	Project Management Journal	1990
	Component-Based Work Breakdown Structure (CBWBS)	R. E. Luby, D. Peel, and W. Swahi	Project Management Journal	1995
	CPM Use in ENR Top 400 Contractors	A. Tavakoli and R. Riachi	Journal of Management in Engineering	1990
Human Resources	Human Resource Practices in Project Management	Bruno Fabi and Normand Petterson	International Journal of Project Management	1992
	Developing an Incentive Scheme for a Project	S. Globerson	Project Management Quarterly	1983
	Business Globalization—The Human Resource Management Aspect	Yehuda Baruch	Human Systems Management	1995
	Ethical Considerations in Merger and Acquisition Management: A Human Perspective	Anthony Buono and James Bowditch	SAM Advanced Management Journal	1990
	Human Resource Planning: A Business Necessity	Stanley Schrager and Chester Delaney	Information Systems Management	1995
	Reward and Recognition for Teams Managing Two Fits of Strategic Human Resource Management	Lloyd Baird and Ilan Meshoulam	Academy of Management Review	1988
Integration	Examples and Characteristics of Shared Project Models	M. Fischer and T. Froese	Journal of Computing in Civil Engineering	1996
	Mega Project Management: The Need for Support Systems	R. Venkatesan	ASCI Journal of Management	1983
	Enterprise-Wide Project Management	D. McFarlane	IIE Solutions	1993
	Intranet and Internet Tools for Project and Knowledge Management	M. Hoynalanmaa, R. Rahkonen, and H. Martikainen	NA	1998
	Product Design Teams: The Simultaneous Engineering Perspective	D. Cleland	Project Management Journal	1991
	Benefits and Pitfalls of Software for Project Management	J. Katzel	Plant Engineering	1999
Procurement	Materials Management: The Key to Successful Project Management	D. U. Kini	Journal of Management in Engineering	1999
	Demystifying the Local Agency Procurement & Selection Process for Professional Engineering Construction Services	E. A. Avila	Journal of Management in Engineering	1997
	Empowering the Construction Project Team	R. Newcombe	International Journal of Project Management	1996
	Web Management and Integrative Procurement Communications	A. M. Barry and S. Pascale	Project Management Journal	1999
	A Study of the Management and Procurement of Building Services Work	D. R. Shoesmith	Construction Management and Economics	1996
	Early Involvement of Purchasers Saves Time and Money	E. E. Scheuing, I. Wirth, and D. Antos	NA	1996
	Role of Procurement in Liabilities Management	R. D. Nicole	Nuclear Energy	1998
	Supply Chain Management: Developing Visible Design Rules across Organizations	NA	NA	NA
Quality	Setting and Meeting Requirements for Quality	A. W. Saarinen and M. A. Hobel	Journal of Management in Engineering	1990
	Assuring Success of the Total Quality Process through QITs	M. I. M. Sangrey	NA	1991
	Concurrent Management of Total Cost and Total Quality	B. R. McConachy	NA	1996
	Fabrication of Steels—A Designers Viewpoint	E. V. Lockney	NA	1988
	Project Controls and ISO 9000	D. G. Pellicena and G. J. Hill	NA	1994
	Importance of the Planning and Specification Phases of a CIM Project	R. Lawley	NA	1992
	Considering Quality in Management of Software-Based Development Projects	R. J. Redmill	Information and Software Technology	1990
	TU Electric Generating Division Fossil Construction Quality Management Program	C. C. Clark	NA	1991

Table 13. "Best Article Candidates"

Knowledge Areas	Title	Author	Journal Name	Year
Risk	Techniques for the Analysis of Risk in Major Projects	S. Baker, D. Ponniah, and S. Smith	Journal of Operational Research Society	1998
	Planning for Crises in Project Management	L. A. Mallak, H. A. J. Kurstedt, and G. A. Patzak	Project Management Journal	1997
	Empowerment vs. Risk Management	T. M. Williams	International Journal of Project Management	1997
	The Role of Project Risk in Determining Project Management Approach	J. Couillard	Project Management Journal	1995
	Risk-Management Infrastructures	T. M. Williams	International Journal of Project Management	1993
Scope	Scope Management Using Project Definition Rating Index	P. R. Dumont, G. E. Gibson, Jr., and J. R. Fish	Journal of Management in Engineering	1997
	Reengineering the Capital Development Process	Albert A. Badger, Donald R. Hall, and Joseph P. Murray	NA	1994
	Determinants of Construction Project Success	D. B. Ashley, C. S. Lurie, E. J. Jaselskis	Project Management Journal	1987
	Estimating?—Yesterday, Today, and Tomorrow	Kul B. Uppal	Transactions of the American Association of Cost Engineers	39th Meeting
	Knowledge-Based Approach to Construction Project Control	J. E. Diekmann and H. Al Tabtabai	International Journal of Project Management	1992
Time	Cost and Schedule Control Integration. Issues and Needs	W. J. Rasdorf and O. Y. Abydayyeh	Journal of Construction Engineering and Management	1991
	Innovative Distributed Project Control Approach: A Case Study of Cassini	M. W. Hughes and R. E. Wilcox	Engineering Management Journal	1996
	The Role of Project Management in a Fast Response Organization	M. K. Starr	Journal of Engineering and Technology Management	1990
	Why Project Fail: The Effects of Ignoring the Obvious	M. W. Hughes	IIE Solutions	1986
	Computerized Inquiry-Feedback Knowledge Engineering System	J. K. Yates	NA	1992
	Development of a Knowledge-Based Schedule Planning System	N. B. Yunus, D. L. Babcock, and C. O. Benjamin	Project Management Journal	1990
	The Denver Airport: Managing a Mega Project	G. S. Evans, R. F. Haury, and G. M. Stricklin	Civil Engineering	1993

Table 13. *Continued*

should be a working session of other researchers to offer advice on refining the methods used. Specifically, we feel a broader collection of researchers could evaluate the definition of project management research, the choice of journals and databases that are included, the choice of keywords used, and the methods of analysis. The results of this working session of project management scholars could serve as the guide for an annual update of the database to include the most current research and to retroactively add any sources that might not be included in this first edition.

We suggest that articles, doctoral dissertations, and government reports that meet the research definition should definitely be included in any updates. We further suggest that PMI conference papers and masters theses be considered for inclusion (however, we do not feel strongly about these). Finally, we suggest proceedings from other conferences and books not be included at least until such time that electronic means make it easy to systematically locate all of them.

We feel the database should be updated either annually or biannually. We feel interpretation workshops should be conducted at least twice annually. Each interpretation workshop should build upon the results of the previous one. Participants should receive, in advance, results of the previous workshop, pre-reading, and a list of discussion questions.

A presentation should be made each year at the PMI Seminars & Symposium and an update should be sent to *PM Network*® so the broad PMI membership can stay informed. A presentation and a workshop should be conducted biannually at the PMI Research Conference and a manuscript should be submitted to *Project Management Journal*® biannually so the PMI research community can stay informed and participate in the continuing development.

Summary

This project followed a very carefully thought out plan and methodology. Since the team had not worked together before and, to our knowledge, no project of this nature had ever been attempted previously, we had to develop our own blueprint. The team came together quickly and worked together very well. This was important because we had a very large task and limited resources, especially time, to accomplish our objectives. Sounds like most projects, doesn't it?

The team utilized sound project management techniques and methodology strategy. The use of Reference Manager as a tool for gathering, cataloging, categorizing, and analyzing the citations worked very nicely and we believe will be an asset for future researchers and authors. The research methodology worked well, but the real beneficial aspect of that strategy was to hold the workshop. We gained invaluable assistance and insight from the professors and practitioners that participated. We believe this to be a significant means to obtain, define, and validate information about what is really happening in the field of project management and feel more of these workshops are needed in the future.

This research proved to be a monumental effort involving nearly 100 people who worked about 6,000 hours (much of it on a volunteer basis) over the short time period of seven months. When we identified over 100,000 documents that were related to project management, we were overwhelmed. We are proud to say that we greatly exceeded our expectations for this project. There are some sources that are not included, such as books, and time did not permit us to include as many conference papers as we would have liked. However, we do feel that the vast majority of important project management research published in English is included in the annotated bibliography of 3,500 articles, dissertations, government reports, and conference papers that resulted from this research effort. We are also very pleased that we persuaded over fifty senior project managers to help us interpret the trends we identified, state their opinions on the articles that they felt were most useful to them, and predict future directions for project management research. Our hope is that the combination of the database and these interpretations will encourage other project management research.

Trends that emerged from our analysis showed that in the 1970s there was a trend toward the development and use of automated project management software. The use of the Program Evaluation and Review Technique (PERT) became widespread. The focus of research during this period was on cost and schedule control, performance measurement, the use of WBSs, and life-cycle management. The government still sponsored a large number of the research projects in the literature, but the number of projects sponsored commercially or by educational institutions increased. As the decade closed, the concept of design to cost and life-cycle costing first appeared in the research literature, as did leadership and conflict management issues. In the 1980s, the volume of research projects in the literature increased significantly with focus on project risk management and the Cost/Schedule Control Systems Criteria (C/SCSC) and earned value. The research literature also continued to focus on design to cost and life-cycle costing, plus a number of studies were published on team building, quality management, and project management computerized systems. The initial reporting on the use of Artificial Intelligence (AI)/Expert Systems and Knowledge Based Systems (KBS) also began appearing in the literature. In the 1990s, a large number of research projects focused on the human resource aspects including team building, leadership development, and motivation. Other research topics included project risk management, project quality management, and project communications knowledge areas of the *PMBOK® Guide*.

Our findings based on our research literature search were borne out for the most part by the practitioners in the workshop. We determined that in the early years in project management (1960–1970) most of the research and focus in project management centered on large government programs in the DoD. Over time the commercial use of project management techniques in construction, information systems development, and new product development have become much more prevalent. Project management is now used in virtually all aspects and areas of commerce and industry. Today, as in the foreseeable future, this trend is likely to continue. As government research and development (R&D) budgets have declined in real terms and our economies turn global, the use of project management in enterprises has risen sharply. We believe this is more than just an issue of numbers; it is a genuine focus by executive management to improve their chances for success in both return on investment and in the quick and economic development and release of new products and services to the marketplace. Therefore, we would say that project management now has a very strategic role in industry and is not just being used as a means to mitigate corporate risk. We think this is an important distinction because project managers are now, more than ever, being looked to as the people who are going to implement the corporate strategies and objectives rather than just being a reporter of status or the messenger of a disaster. We as project management practitioners are now being viewed as a needed and important profession and we are of strategic importance to the corporation or the government agencies we work for and to the executives who run them. We see a distinguished past, a current world of opportunities, and a bright future.

RESEARCH TRENDS IN THE 1990S: THE NEED NOW TO FOCUS ON THE BUSINESS BENEFIT OF PROJECT MANAGEMENT

Peter W. G. Morris, Ph.D.—University College, London, UMIST, and INDECO Ltd.

It is notable how little impact project management has either in the business schools or indeed in the business management literature. Yet speak to many managers, particularly of engineering-based organizations, and typically they will wax strong and enthusiastic about the importance of the effective management of projects. Why the disconnect?

One reason often given is that project management is pre-eminently a practical discipline, whereas much of general business management is more knowledge based. Another, however, is that project management is too often inadequately focused, concentrating on middle management tools and techniques and organizational issues and not sufficiently on the things that deliver real business benefit.

Neither point necessarily precludes the other. Both can be right. Nevertheless, it is the contention of this chapter that the subject as it is too often presented is insufficiently connected to the question of business success; and that its conceptual framework is inadequate to the job it should really be addressing. Since there is not a lot of benefit, on this basis, for doing research, it is not surprising that most of what gets done is seen as "techy" and of little interest to project management practitioners.

This chapter prosecutes this argument by:
- Reviewing recent evidence of project-related concerns in major enterprises.
- Proposing a new model of project management.
- Reviewing recent publications in the principal project management research journals.
- Suggesting a refreshed research agenda for the discipline.

Contemporary Issues in the Management of Projects

Some modesty is necessary before attempting such a catalogue. Who, after all, can lay claim to speak authoritatively on *all* the contemporary issues that are of concern in the management of projects?

Indeed it is worth pausing here for a moment, for this question goes to the very heart of the issue being addressed. If project management is to be really relevant to the big picture of organizational performance then its scope is going to be broad indeed. Are *all* the issues that are relevant to all organizations involved in projects to be potential candidates? Is this practicable? Can it be correct?

A project can be characterized as a *unique* endeavor—in the sense of a one-off—undertaken to accomplish a defined objective. Yet in reality the most fundamental characteristic of a project is something that is a direct result of this uniqueness, namely the project life cycle. Although there are several detailed versions of this life cycle, as shown in *A Guide to the Project Management Body of Knowledge* (*PMBOK® Guide*) – 2000 Edition all projects, no matter how small or complex, follow a similar life cycle. Roughly this is something like Agree Concept; Prepare Definition/Design; Build; Complete (see Figure 1).

To develop a broad understanding of the generic discipline of the management of projects, scholars will therefore have to address the broad range of issues affecting all stages of the life cycle in all kinds of projects. This is certainly a tough challenge: it will require a substantial breadth of analysis and understanding. Maintaining a coherent conceptual view of the discipline at this broader level is genuinely difficult. But this, this chapter argues, is what the discipline's research agenda should be about.

Critically, however, the discussion must be about more than merely tools and techniques, processes and structures, people, or decisions. It has to relate to some measure of performance and success.

The Management of Projects

Initiating and accomplishing projects successfully should be the aim of the discipline.

Success is both an important concept and a difficult one. *The Anatomy of Major Projects* (Morris and Hough 1987) addressed the topic at length. It showed that:
- Success is a slippery concept to measure—and that it has different definitions depending on who you are and what your role in the project is (and when you attempt to measure it).

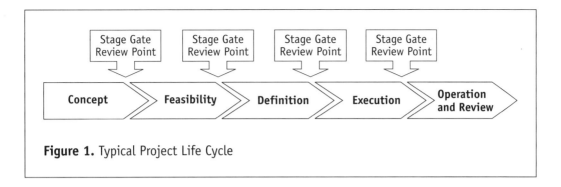

Figure 1. Typical Project Life Cycle

- Defining the project is critically important. Defining what the targets are is a major part of delivering a successful project.
- Many of the issues that caused projects to go wrong were not even addressed in most of the simpler, generic project management textbooks, not the least of these being those of technology, design, environment, and finance.
- A more holistic model of project management was needed—one that focuses on delivering successful projects rather than simply completing a task "on time, in budget, to scope." This model is called "the management of projects" (Morris 1997).

Figure 2 was an attempt, now somewhat dated, developed in *The Anatomy of Major Projects* to capture the factors that were seen to contribute to project success (and failure). At the heart of the model is agreeing on a robust definition of what it is that we are trying to achieve. (For if you cannot define this effectively, don't be surprised if you don't achieve it.) Developing this definition is not easy and is itself, of course, part of the process of managing a project. The definition interacts with a number of key factors: the sponsor's objectives, the financing available, the socio-political and environmental context of the project, and the scheduling requirements and possibilities. Optimizing all these so that the best value, most realistic definition is obtained is a real management skill. And just as project management has traditionally thought that delivering "on time, in budget, to scope" requires commercial, organizational, people, and systems (control) skills—as it does—so too does developing the project definition.

Within this framework of the world of managing projects, then, what are the issues that concern today's managers?

Current Issues in the Management of Projects

Table 1 categorizes issues that are typically current in a range of project-based industries. The examples are not scientifically derived but are drawn from current personal consulting and academic experience. The key point is, however, that any reading of the technical press, or interviews with executives in these industries, would, I believe, validate that it is issues such as these that are typically dominating management's attention in the projects' field.

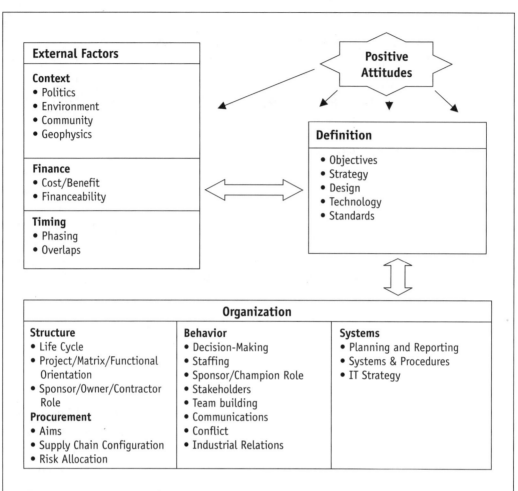

Figure 2. The *Anatomy of Major Projects* Framework of Issues Affecting Project Success

Generalizing, issues in today's world of project management might, therefore, typically include the following:

■ How do we ensure that our projects develop and deliver successful products?

■ How do we accurately capture requirements and effectively manage project development against them?

■ How can we develop products more quickly (time-to-market, concurrent engineering) and securely (avoiding overruns and poor performance) and for better value (lower cost, better functionality)?

■ How can we better manage design, including requirements capture (briefing), technology selection, documentation/information technology (IT), integration with manufacturing and marketing, and testing?

■ What is the appropriate procurement strategy for our projects? Should we be using partnering and if so, where and with what financial incentives? Are we getting the best value for money from our procurement and contract management practices?

Industry	Issues	Examples
Construction	Partnering, E-commerce, Design management, Standardization, VM and VE, Project management as a discipline, Finance/BOT, Continuous improvement, IT contracts, Organizational learning (OL)	European and US construction majors; Changing roles of UK quality surveying companies and construction management
Transport	Systems engineering, Design management, Program management, Health, safety, and environment (HSE), Partnering, Procurement strategy, Overruns	Railtrack; US Program management; Architecture and engineering firms; British airport authorities
Oil and Gas	Front end loading, Benchmarking, Partnering, E-commerce, Procurement strategy, HSE, Project management competencies	Shell; BP; DuPont; Chevron
Power and Water	BOT, Cost competitiveness, Competencies and joint venture relationships	Enron; PowerGen; Thames Water
Electronics	Requirements management, Time-to-market, Risk management, Systems engineering, Marketing, Technology	Nokia; Ericsson; British Telecommunications; WorldCom; Bowthorpe; Dell
Pharmaceuticals	Time-to-market, New product development, Project management as a discipline, Role of the project manager, Competencies, OL, Risk management, Portfolio management, Benchmarking	Pfizer; GlaxoWellcome; AstraZeneca; Merck
Finance/Banking	Project management as a discipline, Change management, Project support office, Project management methodologies/processes, E-project management (portal support), Benefits management	National Australia Bank Group; Lloyds TSB; Legal and General
Software	Requirements, Estimating, Change control, Overruns and poor performance, Competencies, Processes, Testing, Project management methodologies, Change control, Project management role and authority, Maturity models	Unisys; EDS; Andersen Consulting; Microsoft
Defense/Aerospace	Requirements, Systems engineering, Partnering, Integrated project teams, Overruns, Concurrent engineering, Processes, IT, Competencies, Processes, Configuration management	BAES; Rolls-Royce; Thomson CSF; Boeing; Lockheed Martin

Table 1. Examples of Current Project Management Issues in Leading Project-Based Industries

■ Are we getting optimum productivity throughout the life cycle?
■ What is the Internet doing to project management practice? What is e-project management? How will e-commerce affect us? What is e-learning?
■ What really are the roles and authorities that we should have in our project management people? How do we build these competencies?
■ Do we have the right project management processes and practices in place?
■ How does our organization learn and continuously improve?
■ Is project management really giving us business benefit? How do we know this?

And so on. The point is that answering these questions is not easy. Sometimes advice can be found that will help in moving things forward. Sometimes, however, research is needed to understand the issues, formulate the proper questions, and begin to get the answers.

Research Issues in the Management of Projects

Research is the practice of discovering information that was not previously available. Note that in this definition, it is a practice—a set of processes, techniques, and competencies—and that its product can be represented as information. Also, although the pun is unintended, it is best practiced rather than just occasionally attempted. The practices are better if performed frequently.

Research can be the collection of survey data, for example on markets, usage, performance, and so on. On the other hand, it can relate to building our conceptual and theoretical understanding.

Information can be defined as interpreted data. At a more subtle level, knowledge can be distinguished from information by the ability to predict through the application of theory (cognate models). At another level then, research is about interpreting data or information, and this requires a theoretical (conceptual) base.

The more challenging research is that which tries to build or extend our theoretical models. It is primarily with this kind of research that this chapter is concerned.

In some areas research is a very important and popular activity. In life sciences and new materials, for example, the current pace of research is feverish. The tide of knowledge is rolling back at a huge rate: lives and fortunes hang on research outcomes. Even in management, research answers can significantly affect companies' well being and performance. Management research is certainly alive and thriving. But what about research in project management? What kinds of issues are candidates for this kind of research in project management, and what in fact *is* being researched?

Project Management Research Areas

It is not the intent of this chapter to delve too deeply into suggesting such topics but a few might usefully be extended from Table 1. These are shown in Table 2.

Though specialized to the project management field, an important aspect of this list is that it is squarely about how project management can best contribute to improved business performance.

- What is the so-called body of knowledge of project management; in what areas do we in fact expect project managers to be knowledgeable?
- What then are the competencies that we expect of our project management staff (taking competencies to comprise knowledge, skills, behavior, and aptitude)? Are there "core" competencies in addition to role-specific ones? How should we best be developing project management competencies?
- What are the measures of project success? What are the critical factors that cause projects to be successful or to fail? (And how useful a measure is project overrun?)
- What contribution has project management made to business performance?
- When, and how, should life-cycle costs be factored into project optimization?
- What is the core [set of] project life-cycle processes? Why does the life cycle vary between project types and what does this tell us about the generic practice of project management?
- What is the relationship between project management, systems engineering, and design management? What is best practice in requirements management (and why does it vary between industries)?
- What is project management's role in effecting fast track/concurrent engineering?
- Is procurement the responsibility of project management? Do we know where and when partnering is best applied and under what commercial conditions? How do different procurement strategies affect project management's roles, responsibilities, and processes (partnering, firm price, BOT, etc.)?
- Can we honestly say that we understand the basic project management toolkit? Do we understand why the various project management methodologies differ?
- What is the real difference between program management, portfolio management, and project management? How generic are these terms? How generic is the PSO?
- What are current changes in CIT—not least the intranet—doing to project management's abilities? How does these changes affect, for example, project modeling and design, data management and configuration control, commercial practices, and organizational learning and competency development?

Table 2. Current Examples of Research Issues in Project Management

Research, surely, will be seen as more relevant when it is more evidently addressing business-driven issues such as these rather than being primarily middle management, tools, and techniques oriented.

But is this fair? Is this a valid portrait of contemporary project management research? To test this thesis the Centre for Research in the Management of Projects (CRMP) recently reviewed all the papers and book reviews in *PM Network®* and the *Project Management Journal®* and in *The International Journal of Project Management* (*IJPM*) from 1990 to 1999.[1] Papers were classified against the Body of Knowledge (BoK) framework developed recently by CRMP that has now

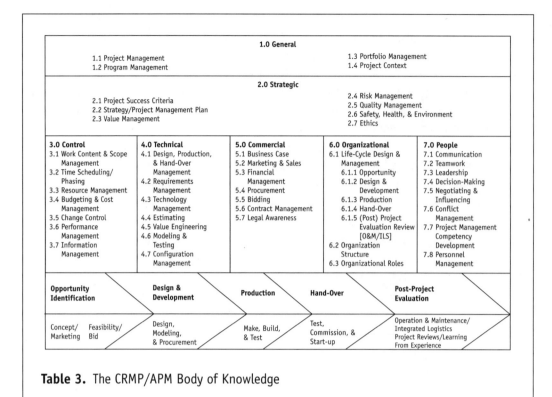

Table 3. The CRMP/APM Body of Knowledge

become the basis of the new *Association for Project Management* (APM) *Body of Knowledge* (and is likely to influence the revisions to the *International Project Management Association* [IPMA] *Body of Knowledge* when these are made in a year or two's time). The current CRMP BoK framework is shown in Table 3.

Before discussing the classification of project management research we should spend a moment considering the BoK model(s) and why they are so important in shaping our thinking on project management research.

The Body(s) of Knowledge and the Relevance to Project Management Research Paradigms

Between 1998 and 1999 the CRMP at UMIST conducted research sponsored by industry and APM to determine what topics project management professionals feel that project management practitioners should be knowledgeable in. A "straw man" framework was developed—admittedly based on the existing APM BoK but revised with some items omitted and some other topics added. Data was collected from over 117 companies. A very high degree of agreement was achieved on what topics companies believed project management practitioners ought to be knowledgeable in (Urli and Urli 2000). These topics are shown in Table 2.

It was the UMIST team's intent not so much to deliver a new BoK "model" but to determine genuinely (a) whether those polled considered it important that project management practitioners be knowledgeable in these areas or not and (b) what in fact is meant by these topics.[2] A structure for the new BoK only became necessary toward the end of the research when it became very apparent that reviewers wanted the topics grouped into a model containing a limited number of major elements (Morris, Wearne, and Patel 2000). The research team therefore developed a BoK model, a slightly revised version of which is shown in Table 3. (The initial version was published in April 1999.)

Why wasn't the Project Management Institute (PMI®) Project Management Body of Knowledge (PMBOK®) structure used, and why is the CRMP BoK so much broader than PMI's?

APM's BoK was developed in the early '90s (1990–95), PMI's essentially between 1981 and 87 with a revision in 1996 and further refinement in 2000. APM's model was strongly influenced by research then being carried out into the issue of what it takes to deliver successful projects (Miller 1956). The question being asked was the "management of projects" one referred to earlier: "What factors have to be managed if a project is to be delivered successfully?" APM considered this to be crucial because it goes to the heart of what the professional ethos of project management is. Put simply, is it to deliver projects "on time, in budget, to scope," as the traditional view has had it (Morris and Hough 1987; Project Management Institute 1986; Pinto and Slevin 1987, 1988, 1989; Pinto and Prescott 1988), or is it to deliver projects successfully for the project customer/sponsor? In essence, it was felt it has to be the latter, because if it is not, project management is ultimately a self-referencing profession that in the long-term no one is going to get very excited about.

The APM BoK therefore incorporated knowledge on the management of topics that the work of researchers had identified as contributing to project success—such as technology, design, people issues, environmental matters, finance, marketing, the business case, and general management (Archibald 1997; Meredith and Mantel 1995)—in addition to the traditional PMBOK® areas of scope, time, cost, human resources, quality, risk, procurement, and so on.

The resultant BoK is indisputably a broader model than PMI's. The PMBOK® focuses on ten areas of project management, nine of which are "knowledge areas" (Figure 3) with another being general to project management. These ten areas overlap, but essentially are distinguished from "General Management Knowledge and Practice" and "Application Area Knowledge and Practice." General management is referred to as relating to management of the ongoing enterprise; recognized as "often essential for any project manager," it addresses leading, communicating, negotiating, problem solving, and influencing, together with a note on standards and regulations and culture. Application areas are described as categories of projects with common elements that may be significant in some projects but not in all. The paradigm is thus proposed that everything generic to project management is covered by the ten knowledge areas, with extensions where appropriate for general management and application areas.

The flaw in this model, I would suggest, is its failure to recognize and elaborate on the critically important responsibilities project managers have, and the generic functions they perform, in:

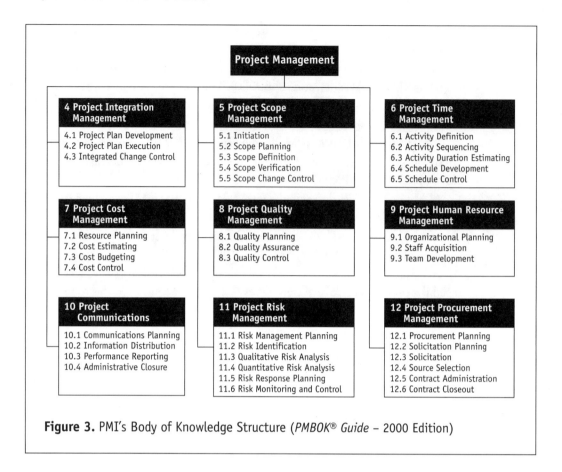

Figure 3. PMI's Body of Knowledge Structure (*PMBOK® Guide* – 2000 Edition)

1. Ensuring that the project's *requirements* and *objectives* are clearly elaborated.

2. Defining the relation of the project to the sponsor's *business* objectives.

3. Developing the project's *strategy*.

4. Managing the evolution of the proposed *technical* solutions to the project requirements.

The key point is that, as research and practice have demonstrated (Lim and Mohamed 1998; Baker, Green, and Bean 1986; Baker, Murphy, and Fisher 1974; Cleland and King 1988; Cooper 1993; Morris and Hough 1987; Might and Fischer 1985; Pinto and Slevin 1989; General Accounting Office; National Audit Office; World Bank Operations Evaluation Department; www.standishgroup.com), there *are* generic practices and processes that all competent project management practitioners may have to call on and should be familiar with in these areas. Project management work in these areas is [very] often critical to project success, yet the PMBOK® either totally or virtually ignores them. The result is that a huge swathe of the profession is led to ignore these dimensions; the discipline is downgraded from its real potential; and researchers are encouraged, tacitly, to overlook many of the issues that are most critical to the discipline's real effectiveness.[3]

The intent in making these points is not to argue that one BoK is "better" than another—hopefully the different models will slowly converge—but that as it stands the PMI model is unnecessarily, and even dangerously, delimiting the scope of the discipline. And one casualty of the paradigm it creates of project management is research in the subject. The broader CRMP model provides a better tool; it is proposed for mapping the range of research published in the *Project Management Journal®*, *PM Network®*, and *IJPM* and comparing this research with contemporary concerns in the management of projects.

Research in the '90s in Project Management

Table 4 shows the number of papers published in the *Project Management Journal®* and *PM Network®* between 1990 and 1999 classified against the fifty CRMP BoK topics.

The most popular topics are papers or books dealing with:
- Examples or issues relative to particular project contexts (application areas): 38
- Time scheduling/phasing: 22
- Project success criteria: 14
- Control: 12
- Project management in general: 12
- Teamwork: 12
- Performance management: 10
- Project management competency development: 10
- Organization structure: 9
- Procurement: 9
- Estimating: 7
- Financial management: 7
- Information management: 7
- Resource management: 7
- Risk management: 7
- Design & production management: 6
- Communication: 5
- Contract management: 5
- Quality management: 5

These 204 papers or book reviews on these nineteen topics account for 83 percent of all the papers published in the *Project Management Journal®* and *PM Network®* during this period. The large number of papers (17 percent) dealing with contextual issues certainly attests to an interest in the practical application of project management. Of the twenty-two papers on scheduling, seventeen are on operational research [technique] based issues; of the remaining five, only three[4] relate overtly to business performance. Indeed of the total 204 papers, arguably only nineteen (approximately 10 percent) refer explicitly to business-related performance at all.[5,6] (Note, however, how the number increases in frequency post-1996.) There is little on strategy, nothing on value management (VM), none on requirements management, none on the business case, and just one on value engineering (VE). There are however, nine on procurement and four others on bidding and contract management.

1.0 General: 12
- 1.1 Project Management
- 1.2 Program Management
- 1.3 Portfolio Management: 2
- 1.4 Project Context: 38

2.0 Strategic
- 2.1 Project Success Criteria: 14
- 2.2 Strategy/Project Management Plan: 3
- 2.3 Value Management
- 2.4 Risk Management: 7
- 2.5 Quality Management: 5
- 2.6 Safety, Health, & Environment: 1
- 2.7 Ethics

3.0 Control: 12
- 3.1 Work Content & Scope Management: 3
- 3.2 Time Scheduling/Phasing: 22
- 3.3 Resource Management: 7
- 3.4 Budgeting & Cost Management: 2
- 3.5 Change Control: 3
- 3.6 Performance Management: 10
- 3.7 Information Management: 7

4.0 Technical
- 4.1 Design, Production, & Hand-Over Management: 6
- 4.2 Requirements Management
- 4.3 Technology Management: 1
- 4.4 Estimating: 7
- 4.5 Value Engineering: 1
- 4.6 Modeling & Testing
- 4.7 Configuration Management: 2

5.0 Commercial
- 5.1 Business Case
- 5.2 Marketing & Sales: 2
- 5.3 Financial Management: 7
- 5.4 Procurement: 9
- 5.5 Bidding: 2
- 5.6 Contract Management: 5
- 5.7 Legal Awareness

6.0 Organizational: 1
- 6.1 Life-Cycle Design & Management
- 6.1.1 Opportunity
- 6.1.2 Design & Development
- 6.1.3 Production
- 6.1.4 Hand-Over
- 6.1.5 (Post) Project Evaluation Review [O&M/ILS]: 1
- 6.2 Organization Structure: 9
- 6.3 Organizational Roles: 9

7.0 People: 3
- 7.1 Communication: 5
- 7.2 Teamwork: 12
- 7.3 Leadership: 4
- 7.4 Decision-Making: 3
- 7.5 Negotiating & Influencing: 1
- 7.6 Conflict Management: 1
- 7.7 Project Management Competency Development: 10
- 7.8 Personnel Management: 4

Table 4. The Number of Papers Published in the *Project Management Journal*® and *PM Network*® between 1990 and 1999 Classified against the CRMP BoK Topics

The exact numbers should not be treated too definitively—for example, Cleland's 1991 paper *Product Design Teams: The Simultaneous Engineering Perspective* (a) could be classified as being under design, phasing, or teams (we took the latter) and (b) is related, via improved cycle times, to business performance. However, the point basically is demonstrated that the overwhelming majority of papers do not make any real connection between project management and business performance.

Table 5 shows the number of papers published in *IJPM* between 1990 and 1999 classified against the CRMP BoK topics. Here the situation is a little better, though not much.

The most popular topics are:
- Examples or issues relative to particular project contexts: 100
- Project management in general: 47
- Risk management: 42
- Time scheduling/phasing: 30
- Control: 24
- Project management competency development: 21
- Information management: 19
- People: 19
- Procurement: 19
- Quality management: 19
- Project success criteria: 11
- Bidding: 10
- Financial management: 10
- Organization roles: 10
- Contract management: 9
- Portfolio management: 8
- Teamwork: 8
- Program management: 7
- Performance management: 6
- Communication: 5
- Configuration management: 5
- Estimating: 5
- Decision-making: 5
- Leadership: 5
- Organization structure: 5
- Program management: 5
- Resource management: 5

These 459 papers or book reviews on these twenty-seven topics account for 93 percent of all the papers published in *IJPM* during this period. *IJPM* is much more clearly research focused than *PM Network®* and (even) the *Project Management Journal®*. The number of papers is greater and its coverage, on the whole, broader. The large number of articles makes it virtually inevitable that there is considerable "techy-ness" for many of the papers—the forty-two on risk management being a

1.0 General: 47
1.1 Project Management
1.2 Program Management: 7
1.3 Portfolio Management: 8
1.4 Project Context: 100

2.0 Strategic: 3
2.1 Project Success Criteria: 11
2.2 Strategy/Project Management Plan: 4
2.3 Value Management
2.4 Risk Management: 42
2.5 Quality Management: 19
2.6 Safety, Health, & Environment: 3
2.7 Ethics: 1

3.0 Control: 24
3.1 Work Content & Scope Management: 6
3.2 Time Scheduling/Phasing: 30
3.3 Resource Management: 3
3.4 Budgeting & Cost Management
3.5 Change Control: 3
3.6 Performance Management: 5
3.7 Information Management: 19

4.0 Technical: 3
4.1 Design, Production, & Hand-Over Management: 5
4.2 Requirements Management: 3
4.3 Technology Management: 2
4.4 Estimating: 7
4.5 Value Engineering: 2
4.6 Modeling & Testing
4.7 Configuration Management: 5

5.0 Commercial: 2
5.1 Business Case: 2
5.2 Marketing & Sales: 1
5.3 Financial Management: 10
5.4 Procurement: 19
5.5 Bidding: 10
5.6 Contract Management: 9
5.7 Legal Awareness: 2

6.0 Organizational: 3
6.1 Life-Cycle Design & Management
6.1.1 Opportunity
6.1.2 Design & Development
6.1.3 Production
6.1.4 Hand-Over
6.1.5 (Post) Project Evaluation Review [O&M/ILS]
6.2 Organization Structure: 5
6.3 Organizational Roles: 10

7.0 People: 19
7.1 Communication: 1
7.2 Teamwork: 8
7.3 Leadership: 5
7.4 Decision-Making: 5
7.5 Negotiating & Influencing
7.6 Conflict Management: 1
7.7 Project Management Competency Development: 21
7.8 Personnel Management: 2

Table 5. Papers Published in *IJPM* between 1990 and 1999 Classified against the CRMP BoK Topics

case in point. There are twenty-five papers in the technical area, compared with the *Project Management Journal*® and *PM Network*®'s seventeen, with a more even coverage. (Seven of the *Project Management Journal*® and *PM Network*® papers were on estimating.) There is a strong emphasis on procurement and related contract matters (forty-one, with a further ten on financial management). There *are* papers on business case and marketing and sales though, at two and one respectively the proportion is minute. In fact, of the 501 papers published in *IJPM* during the decade, we would estimate only thirty-eight as explicitly relating project management and business performance.[7] Even doubling this number to allow for an over-harsh classification, the percentage is still less than 15 percent.

Table 6 presents the combined numbers of papers from the three journals.

The most popular topics are:

- Examples or issues relative to particular project contexts: 148
- Project management in general: 59
- Risk management: 49
- Control: 36
- Project management competency development: 31
- Procurement: 28
- Information management: 26
- Project success criteria: 25
- Quality management: 24
- People: 22
- Teamwork: 20
- Performance management: 18
- Financial management: 17
- Contract management: 14
- Organization structure: 14
- Bidding: 12
- Estimating: 12
- Design & production management: 11
- Organization roles: 11
- Portfolio management: 10
- Work content & scope management: 10
- Leadership: 9
- Decision-making: 8
- Configuration management: 7
- Program management: 7
- Strategy: 7
- Personnel management: 6
- Communication: 5
- Resource management: 5

1.0 General: 59
1.1 Project Management
1.2 Program Management: 7
1.3 Portfolio Management: 10
1.4 Project Context: 148

2.0 Strategic: 3
2.1 Project Success Criteria: 25
2.2 Strategy/Project Management Plan: 7
2.3 Value Management
2.4 Risk Management: 49
2.5 Quality Management: 24
2.6 Safety, Health, & Environment: 4
2.7 Ethics: 1

3.0 Control: 36
3.1 Work Content & Scope Management: 10
3.2 Time Scheduling/Phasing: 52
3.3 Resource Management: 10
3.4 Budgeting & Cost Management: 2
3.5 Change Control: 2
3.6 Performance Management: 18
3.7 Information Management: 26

4.0 Technical: 3
4.1 Design, Production, & Hand-Over Management: 11
4.2 Requirements Management: 3
4.3 Technology Management: 3
4.4 Estimating: 12
4.5 Value Engineering: 3
4.6 Modeling & Testing
4.7 Configuration Management: 7

5.0 Commercial: 2
5.1 Business Case: 2
5.2 Marketing & Sales: 3
5.3 Financial Management: 17
5.4 Procurement: 28
5.5 Bidding: 12
5.6 Contract Management: 14
5.7 Legal Awareness: 2

6.0 Organizational: 4
6.1 Life-Cycle Design & Management
6.1.1 Opportunity
6.1.2 Design & Development
6.1.3 Production
6.1.4 Hand-Over
6.1.5 (Post) Project Evaluation Review [O&M/ILS]: 1
6.2 Organization Structure: 14
6.3 Organizational Roles: 11

7.0 People: 22
7.1 Communication: 6
7.2 Teamwork: 20
7.3 Leadership: 9
7.4 Decision-Making: 8
7.5 Negotiating & Influencing: 1
7.6 Conflict Management: 2
7.7 Project Management Competency Development: 31
7.8 Personnel Management: 6

Table 6. The Combined Numbers of Papers from the *Project Management Journal*® & *PM Network*® (1990–99) and *IJPM* (1990–99)

As one would expect, the very great proportion of the combined set of papers is focused on *intra*-project management topics—though with the obvious proviso of the 148 (20 percent) on the project context. Even procurement and the related areas of finance and contracts, which together provide fifty-nine papers, only account for 8 percent of the total. And project success criteria (twenty-five) is, overall, very low (3 percent). Strategy is even lower (seven: 1 percent). VM is zero! (VE is three—not much better.) Requirements management equally scores a dismal three.

Discussion and Relevance to Today's Research Agenda

It must be emphasized that this analysis can only be taken at a broad level of generalization. It is more than easy to claim that a paper has really been misallocated or wrongly classified. (Several papers deal with issues from more than one BoK topic: one analyst could say that in their opinion a paper should really be classified under another topic. Similarly, another analyst could say that in their view a paper *did*, say, address business needs where here we have said that it did not.) The analysis is made not to prove an ineluctable truth but to make the following points via the survey data.

Even allowing for errors in categorization, the data shows the following.

1. Project management research has not been particularly oriented to demonstrating business relevance.

2. There is almost nothing at all relating expenditure on project management to business benefit.

3. There is significant mismatch between current research priorities and published research.

Let us take the first point as now made. The second point, which is quite extraordinary, seems to be a matter of record, at least as far as these journals are concerned.[8] (And would seem to point to a major research need in its own right.)

The third point is worth looking at further. First it needs acknowledging from the outset that the list of topics given in Table 2 is both personal and very generalized. Perceptions of research priorities are bound to differ depending on the role one occupies and the issues being faced at the time. Second, the survey is bound to show a mismatch: the data shows the published results of research that was conducted during at least the last three or four, to fourteen or more years ago. It takes time for research to be initiated, carried out, and then published. Nevertheless, if we accept the list in Table 2 as a valid set of high-level generalizations, it is worth comparing the Table 2 list, and extensions thereof, with the findings of Table 6. This is Table 7.

Again, due note needs to be made of the inaccuracies inherent in such a high level comparison. There are whole research communities busy in just single areas of the table (for example in IT and procurement). The table is presented for indicative purposes.

Topic	No. of Papers	Table 2 Type "Current" Issues	Comment
1.0 General	59	Benchmarking; Maturity models	Benchmark processes and practices as well as metrics.
1.1 Project Management	0	Definition as a discipline; Methodologies; Business benefit	Several industries are seeking to understand better and introduce PM as a core discipline.
1.2 Program Management	7	Business benefit; Methodologies (PRINCE, etc.); Practice as super PM-as with US A/Es (Bechtel etc.)	
1.3 Portfolio Management	10	New product development/Project management	
1.4 Project Context	148		New product development generally failing to appreciate management of projects perspective. Engineering management/PM linkage could be strengthened.
2.0 Strategic	3	Linkage between project and corporate strategy	
2.1 Project Success Criteria	25	Overruns; High failure rate of IS projects, Key performance indicators and critical success factors; Business benefit; Scorecards	A crucial area. Links with 5.1, 5.3, and others.
2.2 Strategy Plan	7	Strategy formulation	Project strategy, though central, is inadequately understood.
2.3 Value Management	0	Evidence of application and benefit	
2.4 Risk Management	49	Perception of risk	Already exhaustively covered?
2.5 Quality Management	24		
2.6 Safety, Health, & Environment	4	New legislation	
2.7 Ethics	1	Reasons why important	
3.0 Control	36	Scorecards (e.g., balanced)	

Table 7. Current Research Areas of Interest with the Record of Past Papers

Topic	No. of Papers	Table 2 Type "Current" Issues	Comment
3.1 Work Content and Scope Management	10		WBS, PBS still causing terminology difficulties.
3.2 Scheduling and Phasing	52	Concurrent engineering	More has been published outside *IJPM* and *Project Management Journal*® and *PM Network*®.
3.3 Resource Management	10		
3.4 Budgeting and Cost Management	2	Treatment of whole life [operating] costs	BOT/private finance; relates also to 5.3.
3.5 Change Control	2		
3.6 Performance Management	18		EVA still unpopular.
3.7 Information Management	26	IT tools, intranet, e-project management; Role of IM strategy; Knowledge management	An enormous area with whole networks of researchers active- e.g., Construct IT, Stanford University CIFE, etc. Link with processes and practices (i.e., business benefit) important.
4.0 Technical	3	Need to establish more clearly the generic role of PM	This area is not well "mainstreamed" yet in project management, though research shows that its management is vital to project success.
4.1 Design, Production, etc. Management	11	Identification of generic practices; Simultaneous design; Systems engineering/PM and design management/PM linkages.	
4.2 Requirements Management	3	Best practice; applications; tools	Still weakly recognized as fundamental to PM.
4.3 Technology Management	3	Strategy; Introduction of not-yet-proven technology	
4.4 Estimating	12	Software	Still difficult to get s/w estimating reliability.
4.5 Value Engineering	3	Non-construction applications	A powerful area of business benefit not well applied outside construction.

Table 7. *Continued*

Topic	No. of Papers	Table 2 Type "Current" Issues	Comment
4.6 Modeling and Testing	0	CAD and virtual modeling	
4.7 Configuration Management	7	Relation to Information Management	
5.0 Commercial	2		
5.1 Business Case	2	Business benefits of PM; Link with corporate measures (See 2.1, etc.)	
5.2 Marketing & Sales	3	Linkage to PID; Concurrent engineering	
5.3 Financial Management	17	BOT, etc.; Financial measures for project management benefit (2.1 and 5.1)	BOT has figured strongly in *IJPM*.
5.4 Procurement	28	Partnering; Supply chain management; E-commerce; Procurement strategy; Target setting in partnering	A huge area with still an enormous amount to be clarified.
5.5 Bidding	12	Rebid on repeat contracts	
5.6 Contract Administration	14	New forms of contract	
5.7 Legal Awareness	2		
6.0 Organizational	4		
6.1 Life Cycle	1	Generic models; role of ILS	
6.2 Organization Structure	14	Processes; Impact of procurement/supply chain configuration on (a) organization (b) project management practices-e.g. design/build vs. independent designer models	Continued need to clarify and refine processes.
6.3 Organization Roles	11	PSO; Role of sponsor-particularly in inexperienced organizations	
7.0 People	22		

Table 7. *Continued*

Topic	No. of Papers	Table 2 Type "Current" Issues	Comment
7.1 Communication	6	Impact of telecoms/Internet	
7.2 Teamwork	20	High-performance teams; IPTs; Virtual teams	A key area, but well covered in research.
7.3 Leadership	9		
7.4 Decision-Making	8		
7.5 Negotiating & Influencing	1		
7.6 Conflict Management	2		
7.7 PM Competency Development	31	BoK topics; Competency; E-learning; Learning mechanisms; Organizational learning; Certification	A very important area, consistently receiving attention, and needing to with new technology and pressures on competency and external certification.
7.8 Personnel	6	PM as a career	PM often not a core career: how then to build best practice professionalism?

Table 7. *Continued*

The following points would seem to stand out.

- There has, surely, to be research initiated as soon as possible on the business benefits of investing in project management. There has been hardly any to date.
- Benchmarking results have in general been poorly covered so far.[9]
- The role of "the management of projects" as a paradigm in new product development ("Project Context") would seem to offer a link into the general business management writing that should be exploited.
- Engineering management ("Project Context") is in general not a well-covered area. Project management could make a significant contribution to improving understanding of this area.
- Strategy is widely seen as of fundamental importance in projects and their management. There is virtually nothing published on it.
- VM has nothing published on it in *IJPM* or the *Project Management Journal®* and *PM Network®*. VM and VE both have significant potential to business benefit; neither is formally well practiced outside construction.
- There has been a vast output on risk management: is there really that much more to be researched? (Yet the public's perceptions of risk continue to be poor; often intuition does not fit well with probability theory.)

- Much of what has been published in *IJPM* and the *Project Management Journal®* and *PM Network®* on concurrent engineering is anecdotal, and tends more to be about fast tracking projects. There is little on the theoretical underpinning, little on technology support, and little on business benefit. More is published in general engineering management literature.

- There is no research published in these journals on ethics in project management.

- The traditional areas of project control—the basics of much of the literature, training, and teaching in project management—would seem to offer little significant scope for research.[10]

- Information management—already well served—is a strong area for continued research.

- There are several areas in the technical arena that are currently weakly served: requirements management, systems engineering, and design management, for example, all need more robust analysis and exposition.

- There is next to nothing published in *IJPM* and the *Project Management Journal®* and *PM Network®* on the relation between marketing and project management.

- Build Operate Transfers (BOT)—private finance—have been well covered in *IJPM* but the whole area is creating profound changes in the practice of project management—and not just in construction (power, water, transport, and so on). IT and defense/aerospace for example are both significantly affected. The impact extends through organization, financing, supply chain, people, process, metrics, and so forth. There is much research opportunity here still.

- Procurement and supply chain configuration continues to offer major research opportunities. Partnering and e-commerce are currently extremely hot topics. Arguably our overall theory of procurement is not as robust as it could be.

- Organization and people issues continue to cause major challenges in the effective implementation of projects. How much new theoretically-based research is still to be accomplished is questionable. Organizational learning is an example, however, of where there is genuinely new theoretical ground to explore.

- Project manager competency development—particularly of the knowledge [BoK] elements and the issue of certification, and the relationship with knowledge management and organizational learning—has rightly been, and will continue to be, a major area of research enquiry. This also links to business benefit and to career development (personnel).

Validity of Project Management as a Research Area and Research Funding

However arguable the shape and details of the above analysis, there would seem to be little doubt that the subject area is (a) important and (b) alive and full of potential. Much is on going, both in industry—competencies, BOTs, concurrent engineering, and so on—and in research groups. Much, however, is industry specific (construction, software, defense, and so forth). How valid a research field is generic project management as such? How strong a theoretical basis does it have? Are we fooling ourselves by proposing that there is such a thing as a research agenda in project management?

The above analysis suggests that the traditional core of project management (tools and techniques—and to a lesser extent, middle management organizational issues) is now well understood. Though they often pose challenges in implementation, their theoretical bases and application have limited (though still some) research needs.

There has been much published on the contextual application of project management (20 percent of all the papers). This is excellent and much needed. Project management, though a generic discipline, is contextual.

The results of this chapter's analysis suggest that the major research needs of project management are now to demonstrate, within a theoretical context, how the overall discipline works coherently to deliver projects successfully. This finding, I believe, is supported not just by the above analysis but also by current business experience.

Validity of the Findings

A potential criticism of the analysis behind this view is that it is overly self-referencing. After all, the criticism could go, the analysis is based partly on a personal and quasi-subjective presentation of project management issues and research needs, and partly on a more objective (but still very questionable) categorization of papers classified against a framework that stems from a particular view of the discipline (the "management of projects"/APM BoK view).

There is some validity in such a criticism. There is also much that could be said to counter it. Tables 1 and 2 undoubtedly *do* represent contemporary issues. The APM/CRMP BoK models *are* based on research (first on the causes of project success and failure; second on what project management professionals believe project management practitioners need to be knowledgeable of).

Funding and Theoretical Coherence

Who will pay for this research? Is there a strong enough theoretical basis for at least some of it to be funded by the traditional academic research funding agencies?

This is where we came in. Many enterprises are willing to pay for work to be done to provide answers to as yet unanswered questions in project management. Often they call this consulting support—and this is indeed research of a kind, as we said at the outset. The challenge for research, which has a stronger theoretical basis, is precisely the perceived weakness of the discipline's theoretical base. Partly because project management *is* so practical, many practitioners find it difficult to get enthusiastic about introducing theory. And from the academic side, the subject—at least as it has been presented here in this chapter—is so large, cross-sectional, and multi-dimensional that the traditional funding agencies often (though not always) consider it too tenuous. Project management does not hit square onto many of the traditional academic funding agencies. Academic work is typically funded by agencies looking at a particular aspect of the overall subject.

There are exceptions—and we should look to the professional institutions to be leading them: PMI's sponsorship of the "Return on Investment" study undertaken by Ibbs, Reginato, and Morris is just such an example (www.berkely.edu/pmroi)—but generally it is up to us, the researchers, teachers, scholars, and enthusiasts of the discipline, to work on building the overall theoretical basis to the subject. I genuinely see this still as the major challenge.

Conclusions

Research into project management is alive and well. *IJPM* is having to increase the number of its issues per year to cope with rising demand. The *PMI Research Conference 2000* itself attests to this fact. But there is still far to go.

It is inevitable that an analysis such as that carried out in this chapter will show that published research lags today's research issues: three to four years is a typical cycle time from research topic conception, through raising funds, performing the research, to publishing it. Yet there is a need, fundamentally, to refocus the discipline and its research paradigm. We need to understand better, in particular, the linkages between project management and business performance, and project management's generic responsibilities and actions in the whole area of technology and design. Information technology and procurement/supply chain management remain as key areas, in many sectors, of project management business leverage. And the way we deal with and build knowledge, learning, and competency development is key, and with today's human resource concerns and technologies, is an important area of research.

The challenge of research in project management today, I contend, is to build a broad, multi-industry, theoretically grounded explanation of what is required to initiate and accomplish projects successfully. Research has a fundamental role to play in building this theoretical framework.

Notes

[1] This makes the fourth such analysis. Martin Betts and Peter Lansley classified *IJPM* papers for the period 1982–92 (Betts and Lansley 1995). The topics they used to classify the papers (with the percent of papers over the period shown in parenthesis) were: human factors (15 percent), project organization (15 percent), project environment (12 percent), project planning (12 percent), conceptual models (10 percent), project information (9 percent), project performance (7 percent), risk management (7 percent), project startup (6 percent), project procurement (4 percent), and innovation (3 percent). Professor Stephen Wearne, at UMIST, has recently analyzed *Project Management Journal*® and *IJPM* papers and PMI and IPMA conference papers using an early version of the CRMP BoK as the basis of classification (Themistocleous and Wearne 2000). Urli and Urli analyzed all the papers relative to project management in the bibliographic ABI-INFORM database from 1987 to 1996 using an "associated word" method (scientometric analysis) (Urli and Urli 2000). Their findings are interesting and relevant: the field appears to have broadened in scope during the review period while the themes seem to have become less and less linked—

not surprising perhaps given the breadth of source material. Apropos the opening paragraph of this paper they reported, "Even though there is considerable professional interest in project management, one is forced to conclude that this interest is not as visible among university academicians, at least in North America" (Urli and Urli 2000).

[2] Apropos research: interestingly the APM review team, while welcoming whole-heartedly the empirical basis now provided by the CRMP data, was adamant that the APM version should not refer to abstruse, difficult-to-understand research papers, such as those published in *IJPM*!

[3] For example, the 2000 New Zealand Project Management Conference streamed all papers under the ten PMBOK® topic areas. QED.

[4] Those by Thamhain (1993), Ibbs, Lee, and Li (1998), and Leach (1999).

[5] Those of Mark (1992), Feney (1992), Christensen (1993), Ryder (1993), Thamhain (1993), Ingram (1994), Blanchard (1995), Tan (1996), Jiang (1996), Pascale et al. (1997), Shenhar et al. (1997), El-Najdawi and Liberatore (1997), Jannadi (1997), Robinson (1997), Christensen and Gordon (1998), Leach (1999), Lidow (1999), Baccani (1999), and Chang (1999).

[6] The ten on performance management refer predominantly to earned value.

[7] Tighe (1991), Rhyne and Whyte (1991), Gyeszly (1991), Barnes (1991), Leong (1991), Ireland (1992), Frizelle (1993), Tiong et al. (1993), Lisburn et al. (1994), Mansfield et al. (1994), Reijners (1994), Wearne (1994), Kayes (1995), Wateridge (1995), Sunde and Lichtenberg (1995), Belassi and Tukel (1996), Ongunlana (1996), Quartey (1996), McElroy (1996), Jafaari et al. (1996), Laufer et al. (1996), Kirby (1996), Chan (1997), Gabriel (1997), Voropayev (1998), Love et al. (1998), Gupta (1998), Eden et al. (1998), Wateridge (1998), Lopes and Flavel (1998), Grundy (1998), Clarke (1999), Archer and Ghasemzedah (1999), Tam (1999), Lim and Mohammed (1999), Hendricks et al. (1999), Kog et al. (1999), and Atkinson (1999)—no doubt there are others: the list is intended to be indicative, not exhaustive.

[8] Ibbs, C. W., and Y. H. Kwak (1997), published by PMI—and somewhat in the *Project Management Journal*® and *PM Network*®—is an exception. Interestingly the United Kingdom (UK) project management monthly magazine *Project Management Today* (*PMT*)—not as research or technical as the other three—tends to have more on business benefits. Every issue in the first half of 2001 had at least one feature. (This may well be due to the influence of the Projects in Controlled Environments [PRINCE] methodology which is pervasive in the UK and which exerts a significant impact on *PMT*'s editorial content.)

[9] This includes the contribution of the PMI Fortune 500 Benchmarking program. The Construction Industry Institute's (CII) work for example, though still relatively weak, is much more robust.

[10] As an example of the danger of such generalization, research under way at UMIST is currently looking at linguistics as a basis for time recording and estimating in software projects instead of the more traditional product breakdown structure (PBS). The method has been successfully adopted in the old British Aerospace (BAES).

References

Archibald, R. 1997. *Managing High-technology Programs and Projects*. Chichester: John Wiley & Sons, Inc.

Baker, N. R., S. G. Green, and A. S. Bean. 1986. Why R&D Projects Succeed or Fail. *Research Management* (November–December): 29–34.

Baker, N. R., D. C. Murphy, and D. Fisher. 1974. *Determinants of Project Success*. National Technical Information Services N–74–30392.

Betts, M., and P. Lansley. 1995. International Journal of Project Management: A Review of the First Ten Years. *International Journal of Project Management* 13 (4): 207–218.

Cleland, D. I., and W. R. King. 1988. *Factors Affecting Project Success. Project Management Handbook*. New York: Van Nostrand Reinhold.

Cooper, R. G. 1993. *Winning at New Products*. Reading, MA: Addison Wesley.

General Accounting Office: Various reports on United States defense projects' performance.

Ibbs, C. W., and Y. H. Kwak. 1997. *The Benefits of Project Management—Financial and Organizational Rewards to Corporations*. Newtown Square, PA: Project Management Institute.

Lim, C. S., and M. Z. Mohamed. 1998. Criteria of Project Success: An Exploratory Re-Examination. *International Journal of Project Management* 16 (4): 243–248.

Meredith, J. R., and S. J. Mantel. 1995. *Project Management: A Managerial Approach*. Chichester: John Wiley & Sons, Inc.

Might, R. J., and W. A. Fischer. 1985. The Role of Structural Factors in Determining Project Management Success. *IEEE Transactions on Engineering Management (EM)* 32 (2): 71–77.

Miller, G. A. M. 1956. Processing Information. *Psychological Review* 63 (1): 81–97.

Morris, P. W. G., and G. H. Hough. 1987. *The Anatomy of Major Projects*. Chichester: John Wiley & Sons, Inc.

Morris, P. W. G. 1997. *The Management of Projects*. London: Thomas Telford.

Morris, P. W. G., S. H. Wearne, and M. Patel. 2000. Research into Revising the APM Project Management Body of Knowledge. *International Journal of Project Management* 18 (3).

National Audit Office: Various reports on United Kingdom defense projects' performance.

Pinto, J. K., and J. E. Prescott. 1988. Variations in Critical Success Factors over the Stages in the Project Life Cycle. *Journal of Management* 14 (1): 5–18.

Pinto, J. K., and D. P. Slevin. 1987. Critical Factors in Successful Project Implementation. *IEEE Transactions on Engineering Management (EM)* 34: 22–27.

———. 1988. Critical Success Factors across the Project Life Cycle. *Project Management Journal* 19 (3): 67–75.

———. 1989. Project Success: Definitions and Measurement Techniques. *Project Management Journal* 19 (1): 67–75.

Project Management Institute. 1986. Measuring Success. *Proceedings of the 1986 Project Management Institute Seminars & Symposium*, Montreal.

Themistocleous, G., and S. H. Wearne. 2000. Project Management Topic Coverage in Journals. *International Journal of Project Management* 18 (1): 7–11.

Urli, B., and D. Urli. 2000. Project Management in North America, Stability of Concepts. *Project Management Journal* 31 (3): 33–43

World Bank Operations Evaluation Department: Various reports on World Bank project performance.

www.berkely.edu/pmroi

www.standishgroup.com

Zobel, A. M., and S. H. Wearne. In Press. Project Management Topic Coverage in Recent Conferences. *Project Management Journal* (available from CRMP: www.UMIST.ac.uk/CRMP).

CHAPTER 3

PROJECT MANAGEMENT RESEARCH: EXPERIENCES AND PERSPECTIVES

David Wilemon, Ph.D.—Syracuse University

The purpose of this chapter is to share one researcher's perspectives and experiences on project management research. The chapter begins by identifying some of the early issues researched and how these studies helped identify and explain some of the underlying managerial and theoretical foundations of project management. The chapter also discusses four areas of research currently under way, which hopefully will add to the growing knowledge base in project management and help those charged with managing today's complex projects.

Building a Research Platform

Project management became part of my life in the late 1960s when I was asked to join a multidisciplinary team to study the National Aeronautical and Space Administration's (NASA) Apollo Program (Moon Landing Program). James Webb, the administrator of NASA at that time, believed that NASA was doing something remarkable and worthy of scholarly research attention. Syracuse University, Massachusetts Institute of Technology (MIT), and Northwestern University, among other universities, were invited to participate and "use NASA as a living laboratory." I was asked to join the, "Management of the Apollo Program," study team at Syracuse University, consisting of three aerospace and mechanical engineers, a sociologist, a political scientist, and two researchers from our school of management. For the next four years we studied NASA's project management system extensively, e.g., NASA's Headquarters in Washington D.C.; Houston (spacecrafts and the Lunar Excursion Module Program [LEM Program]); Huntsville (engine/rocket programs); Cape Kennedy (launch programs); and several supporting contractors—Boeing, McDonald-Douglas, Rocketdyne, IBM, North American Rockwell, and so on. My specific responsibility was to study the role of the NASA project manager.

Some of the major highlights resulting from our work on NASA's Manned Spaceflight Program follow (Syracuse University/NASA Research Program 1973a and 1973b):

- NASA project managers faced major challenges garnering support for their projects. Many of the experts who could contribute to specific projects were often located in other functional groups, other NASA organizations, as well as in the companies (the contractors) who supported NASA. Project participants often had to deal with conflicting agendas, priorities, multiple bosses, diverse political agendas, and so forth.

- Intense conflicts often occurred over schedules, priorities, administrative procedures, budgets, and technological choices. NASA project managers often spent considerable time negotiating with people and organizations beyond their project teams.

- Team performance and dynamics varied greatly.

- Project control systems were often crude and labor-intensive.

- Problems were often required to be resolved in "real-time."

- There was a massive amount of experimentation and learning involved in each major project.

- The concurrent management of multiple projects was, perhaps, the major managerial challenge.

This initial experience in studying one of the most complex programs ever undertaken helped provide this author with a foundation and the desire to research a number of issues associated with the field of project management. During the next several years we, and many other researchers around the world, continued our efforts to add to the emerging project management knowledge base.

Contemporary Project Management Research Issues

Using these earlier experiences as a platform, we have continually reinvented our research agenda and are currently focusing on four areas, which will be briefly explored in this chapter, and our research plans and results to date examined. These research areas include, project team performance assessment, stress in project management, project partnering, and project team member experiences. The context and setting for each research area discussed are new product development project teams. The purpose is to share the thinking and research processes used with colleagues interested in conducting research on project management issues.

Project Team Performance Assessment

Managing project performance has traditionally focused on how well a team met its intended objectives, e.g., cost, schedule, and performance targets. Although much work has been conducted on these traditional performance appraisal methods, there are many opportunities to assess a project's performance during the project as well as at its completion (Lynn and Reilly 2000). While there are several instruments that can help evaluate project performance, a fairly comprehensive assessment approach is discussed in *Project Skills* (Elbeik and Thomas 1998). A similar instrument can be found in *Project Leadership* (Brier, Geddes, and Hastings 1990). Elbeik and Thomas (1998) have devised an instrument that measures how well project managers perform in six areas:

1. Managing Senior Management Expectations and Meeting the Business Needs of the Project

2. Managing Stakeholder Relationships

3. Managing Progress and Reviewing Achievements

4. Planning and Managing the Future

5. Managing the Project Team

6. Self-Management—Managing Individual Effectiveness.

Project leaders in completing this instrument respond to several items under each of the above groupings on a scale of: "often," "sometimes," and "rarely."

While the above self-analysis offers many supplemental advantages over many of the more traditional means of assessing project performance, there are important limitations of the Elbeick and Thomas instrument. First, their instrument focuses primarily on the project leader and his activities. While such a focus is helpful, a more robust approach would involve all team members and all key functional interfaces that participate in the project. Second, the authors do not stress the importance of benchmarking a project's progress over time. Assessment of a project, for example, needs to be accomplished several times during a project. The scores can be posted on a project website or bulletin board and the results studied and corrective action taken as needed. Such data can also be useful in team development sessions. These periodic team assessments give a more dynamic, accurate assessment of capabilities and concerns (Lynn 1998). The notion of multiple assessments during a project aligns well with the notion of continuous improvement programs. This is far better than when the evaluation comes at the end of a project when little corrective action can be taken. Third, there is little or no assessment of learning in the Elbeick and Thomas instrument. Fourth, a critical factor in project success is how customers perceive the progress of a project team. It is suggested that customers, and in some cases suppliers, need to be involved in the ongoing assessment of project teams.

Another limitation of the Elbeik and Thomas instrument is that the role of the project leader as "entrepreneur" is ignored. While some of the dimensions of this role may be implied in the Elbeick and Thomas instrument, more emphasis is needed on how well the leader performs as entrepreneur and as business manager. Dimensions of this role might include how well the project leader is able to sell and build support for the project. Also, how well is the project leader able to garner and efficiently use scarce organizational resources? And, how effectively does the project leader use her capabilities to build future business opportunities with customers?

In using similar instruments in several in-company and public programs for project managers, we have observed that many project leaders may have two or three strong areas and lack capabilities in others. When asked if these strong areas are ones where they enjoy working, the response most often is "yes." In a similar vein, project managers often will have two or three areas where they do not score well on the instrument. More often than not, the low-scores are in areas that project leaders feel less confident in and enjoy less. These insights can be important since project leaders can actually see how they "invest" their time and energy in their projects.

Research on Performance

The focus of our research is to improve upon existing instruments and methods in order that project managers and their teams can engage in continuous improvement activities. Our research approach involves a review of the literature on performance assessment; interviews with senior managers who manage project managers; and a field study of project leaders and members of their teams. The project leaders are all responsible for managing high-technology based projects, e.g., telecommunications equipment, medical devices, and electronic components. We are using a multiphase design as follows:

Phase 1—Review of Literature

Our first task is reviewing the literature and identifying the various metrics discussed in the literature to measure project performance (Brown and Eisenhardt 1995; Levi and Slem 1995; Cordero, Farris, and DiTomaso 1998; Elbeik and Thomas 1998). In addition, we are reviewing the measures used in the commercially available project management assessment tools. We are currently classifying and assessing the various performance measures we identify from these sources.

Phase 2—Senior Management Interviews

Our second task is conducting interviews with senior managers who manage, supervise, and/or sponsor project managers in the three industries previously noted. The purpose is to identify the metrics these senior managers actually use and the measures that they see as potentially useful, but which are not formally used. Based on these interviews we will develop a ranking of the actual and desired performance metrics used by these senior managers. Thus, in Phase 2 we are searching for "gaps" that may occur between actual and desired performance metrics.

Phase 3—Project Leader/Team Member Interviews

This phase entails interviews with project leaders and two or three members of their teams to identify how they perceive they are actually evaluated and what type of assessment metrics would be most useful to them. As with the senior managers, we will obtain a ranking of performance metrics—actual and desired—for team leaders and team members. We also are having project leaders, team members, and senior managers evaluate various commercially available team assessment instruments. In this phase we also are examining how project leaders and their team members experience project evaluation processes. What types of feedback are helpful and what feedback forms are not helpful, perhaps even destructive?

Phase 4—Performance Assessment Instrument

Based on the results of Phases 1, 2, and 3, a performance assessment instrument will be developed that can be used to evaluate project leader performance, project team performance, and overall project performance. As noted, this instrument will help various stakeholders assess and contribute to project performance at multiple points during the life of a project.

Stress in Project Management

There has been considerable anecdotal evidence that project managers and their teams often experience high degrees of stress in carrying out their assignments. My colleague and I have been studying stress and its potential impact on project team members (Kim and Wilemon 2000). Project-oriented stress is likely to increase in the future due to the emphasis on shorter project life cycles, technological changes, rapidly changing customer demands, and increasing project complexity (Millson, Raj, and Wilemon 1992; Ivancevich and Matteson 1980).

In our study of stress in project teams, we conducted an extensive review of the general literature on stress (Driskell and Salas 1996) and performed exploratory interviews with several project team members. In this process, we identified fifteen potential stressors. We then had the members and project leaders of four different product development teams evaluate the stressors on a five-point scale ranging from strongly agree to strongly disagree regarding the extent that each stressor created stress for the respondent. Fifty-eight project team members and their leaders participated. What we found was that "lack of clear objectives," "poor communication among team members," "schedule pressures," "lack of information to perform adequately," "poor intergroup cooperation," "failure of others to perform," "lack of resources to carry out tasks," lack of senior management support," "work overload," "changes to the scope of the project," "personality conflicts," and "participation on multiple projects" were the stressors most commonly experienced.

While difficult to ascertain, we also wanted to know if and how stress affects performance. Using a five-point scale, which ranged from "a very great extent" to "not at all," 69 percent of the project team members indicated that stress affected performance from "some" to "a very great extent." When we probed how stress impacted performance, project members noted that high stress levels often affect concentration, decision-making performance, productivity, and that it can negatively impact interpersonal relations. Some respondents noted that stress also could lead to "burn-out," "negative attitudes toward work," and "nervousness."

We also studied how the degree of stress experienced changes over a project's development cycle. We used a framework, which we have used in prior research projects, to denote a generalized project development life cycle (Thamhain and Wilemon 1975). This framework defines a project as consisting of four phases, namely 1) *Project Formation*—the project is just getting started and the team is being assembled; 2) *Build-Up*—the project is under way and prototypes are often developed during this phase; 3) *Main Phase*—the majority of the work occurs here and much integration is required; and 4) *Project Phaseout*—the project comes to closure. We asked our respondents to identify the degree of stress experienced in each of the four phases and give examples of typical stressors by project life-cycle phase.

In the *Project Formation Phase* stressors included creating the plan for the project, team development issues, gaining goal and role clarity, dealing with incomplete and, in some instances, conflicting information, and lack of resources to carry out the project's requirements.

In the *Build-Up Phase*, we found that gaining team member cooperation was particularly stressful, as was communicating with other groups and departments. Dealing with unanticipated problems and schedule pressures were also frequently mentioned stressors.

Lack of authority, resources, and management support were examples of major stressors in the *Main Phase* of projects. Several project team members noted that firefighting, crisis management, and keeping the project focused were also important stressors in this phase. In addition, attempts to maintain a team's energy and motivation were found stressful in this phase.

The final stage, *Project Phaseout*, revealed several stressors. Performance concerns and doubts, for example, were frequently noted sources of stress. As expected, bringing closure to a difficult project, documentation, and project performance assessments were also stressors.

Stress Research Questions

Based on our work and others' research, there are several questions about stress and its impact, which warrant further study (Jex and Boehr 1991).

1. What role does stress play in project performance? Can stress be a positive contributor to individual and team performance? When is stress a barrier to performance?

2. Can measures be developed to assess a team member's tolerance for stress? If so, can these measures benefit team leaders and their project teams? Can such a measure be useful in making project assignments?

3. How useful might periodic checks on stress levels be for project teams and their members?

4. Since many project teams devote considerable energy and time to team-building activities, how, if at all, does team building affect the capabilities of individuals and teams to deal with stress and its potential consequences?

5. Do different types of development projects influence the degree of stress experienced by team members? For example, do more complex projects (radical innovations, disruptive, or new venture projects) increase the stress team members' experience (Bodenstein, Gerloff, and Quick 1989)? How functional/dysfunctional is the stress experienced in these complex projects?

As noted, we suggest that the potential for project-related stress is likely to increase in the future (Driskell 1996). As several recent articles have acknowledged, this topic is too important for managers and organizations interested in maximizing project management performance to ignore (Cole 1998; Driskell, Salas, and Johnson 1999).

Project Partnering/Alliances

While partnering has been practiced for many years, empirical work in alliance management in new product development (NPD) projects has been somewhat limited. We have recently begun a research program to study the process of partnering in NPD. Usually, when two companies or two organizations partner, an individual or a team will be charged with the responsibility of accomplishing the goals of the partnership. Our unit of analysis is the project team responsible for managing and maintaining the partnering relationship. When a project team is established to manage an alliance, it offers the advantage of having a group with the expertise to solve problems as they develop during the life of a project.

Companies engage in partnering NPD projects and programs for a variety of reasons (Eisenhardt and Galunic 2000). Some companies simply lack the resources to undertake a major development program. Examples of resources may include technological capabilities, financial, marketing, managerial, or time. By engaging in a partnered NPD program companies can often:

- Become more agile
- Cut development time
- Develop synergies not otherwise available
- Save development funds
- Reduce capital costs, e.g., new plant equipment
- Build long-term relationships
- Manage complexity.

In an earlier study we identified a number of steps/phases that partnering companies often follow in creating and developing a relationship with another company (Millson, Raj, and Wilemon 1996). We are using this framework in our current study on project partnering. These phases include:

Awareness Phase

Firms may realize that in order to develop a new product, they require capabilities that they do not currently possess and it is too costly or takes too long to develop them. For example, a smaller high-technology company may have great technology yet it lacks access to the market. In another case, a technology-based company lacks the managerial and industry knowledge to successfully enter a new market. Another example is when a company has an idea but lacks the manufacturing and marketing capabilities to successfully commercialize the idea. The discovery of these missing capabilities and how a partner might help resolve the identified limitations occurs in the awareness stage. In addition, the types and characteristics of potential partners are considered.

Exploration Phase

Once limitations have been acknowledged and potential partners identified, the exploration phase begins. When each partner sees the potential benefits of cooperating together, scenarios are developed that help identify how each partner can "win" by establishing a productive relationship. As we noted in our earlier work, issues around expectations, alliance leadership, power, control, and reporting relationships are identified and discussed. Plans for executing the new product project are discussed even though these may be preliminary plans. In effect, they are "scenarios" of the NPD process envisioned by the allying partners. As the above issues are discussed and debated, the level of trust between the parties is likely to increase. If not, it can be a harbinger of future problems. Also, perceptions of the risk involved in successfully accomplishing a new project usually decline as the communication increases between partners and trust builds (Millson, Raj, and Wilemon 1992).

Commitment Phase

If the exploration phase proves satisfactory and clear potential mutual benefits arise from partnering, then the alliance enters the commitment phase. Here the actual day-to-day management of the alliance begins. The front-end investment makes "switching costs" very high. This can be a major motivator in making a partnership work.

Research Issues

There are several research issues involved when two or more companies partner their development efforts. While some of these issues have been explored via various research projects, more systematic, holistic studies are needed. Our work is focusing on three industries, namely, telecommunications equipment, medical devices, and biotechnology. Companies in these industries often rely on partnering in order to develop new products and achieve their business objectives.

Our objective is to obtain a total of approximately fifty "sets of alliance partners" in the three industry grouping. We will primarily focus on the project team responsible for managing the partnership. In some cases there will be more than the simple model of a partnership between two companies since complex development projects may require several partners. Our goal is to interview a minimum of fifteen sets of partners in each of the three industries. Examples of the types of questions we will use in our interview follow:

1. What challenges occur as two different project teams attempt to coordinate their development efforts?

2. What senior management actions are most helpful in supporting partnered projects?

3. What issues are likely to arise when two organizations of unequal size work together in accomplishing a development project?

4. What issues arise in sharing core competencies?

5. What communication challenges develop when allying project teams carry out their work?

6. What issues are encountered when the two allying project teams attempt to achieve a common vision for the project?

7. What conflicts are likely to occur between allying project teams? What resolution approaches do participants find most constructive?

8. What role does trust play in project performance and in the quality of teamwork?

9. What "processes" appear especially helpful in accomplishing joint development projects?

10. What problems are encountered when computer technology (information technology [IT] systems) are integrated to help manage partnered projects? What, if any, are the legal implications of linked IT systems in the case of performance failures, accidents, and so on?

11. What methods do partnering teams use to capture, store, and retrieve the learning that occurs during the project? How effective are these methods?

12. How are stakeholders involved in partnered projects? What issues are likely to occur in managing multiple stakeholders?

13. What processes are used to identify and manage risks in partnered projects?

Based on our interview results, a questionnaire will be developed and administered to focus on our most important findings. The aim of our research on partnering projects is to shed new light on how this process can be conducted more efficiently and effectively. All indications are that we are likely to see even more partnering in the future. The teams that manage these relationships are important to partnering success.

Project Team Member Experiences

A review of the literature on project management reveals that many of the studies that have focused on the human aspects of project management (Barczak and Wilemon 1992) reveal a focus on project leader behaviors, e.g., project leadership effectiveness, conflict management, performance outcomes, communication, and team building. Such a focus is clearly important as project managers play such a pivotal role in the success of projects. The focus has also been fruitful in uncovering insights into the issues project leaders encounter in carrying out their assignments (Gemmill and Wilemon 1994). A limit of the project leader centric approach is that project team members and their experiences have often been ignored by researchers. The consequence is an incomplete perspective regarding what occurs within project teams. One project we have undertaken to look more closely into project team members involves a study of seventy-one team members in a variety of technology-based organizations (Barczak and Wilemon 1999). Using an interview protocol, interviews were conducted with team members about their experiences as members of product development project teams. The interviewees represented a variety of functions and had been with their companies for an average of ten years. The average length of the NPD project was 1.8 years. We used a qualitative research approach and used a semi-structured protocol. This allowed us to probe in-depth the responses of the project team members. Two individuals working independently coded the resulting data and themes from the interviews.

Positive Team Experiences

One of the areas we were interested in is how team members viewed "successful" and "unsuccessful" team experiences. In our interviews, we asked team members to respond on the basis of their overall experiences—not a single project or the latest project completed. We found that team members viewed "successful experiences" as largely derived from team characteristics. Team characteristics included having very clear project goals, clear roles and responsibilities, an appropriate skill mix within the team, and effective, undistorted communication. We also found that team members valued the learning and professional development opportunities and new learning opportunities offered by project assignments (Keller and Kedia 1996). Such work gave them the opportunity to see the "big picture" versus a more narrow functional perspective, which often develops when working primarily in a functional area.

Team members also noted the importance of achieving specific project accomplishments. These team members wanted their project assignments to be meaningful in terms of accomplishing the goals of the project.

When we asked team members what contributed to their least successful project experiences, the perceived lack of support from senior management was noted. Others noted that senior management support for their projects often waned over time. This created a perception that the work they were performing was of limited value. We also found that a lack of clear goals was the second most important determinant to the organization of an unsuccessful experience. The third reason for an unsuccessful experience related to teamwork problems, e.g., having to work with people who did not have the experience or skills. Finally, the lack of teamwork contributed to an unsuccessful project experience.

Selection, Evaluation, and Reward Issues

We wanted to see how clear team members were regarding how they were selected, rewarded, and evaluated for their efforts. While some research has been conducted on these issues in various project team settings, it has been limited. We found that team members were clear in terms of how they were selected (approximately 90 percent). The method of selection, however, varied considerably. Some team members asked for their assignments; the project team leader selected others; some were assigned by their manager; while others were placed on teams by default.

While team members were generally clear on how and why they were selected/assigned to a project they were far less clear on how they were evaluated for their project work. In fact, while 44 percent were clear on how they were evaluated, an almost equal number (41 percent) were unclear on how their personal performance on the team was assessed. The remainder was clear on some aspects of their evaluation and unclear about other dimensions. Several team members expressed their lack of knowledge about evaluation processes at both the team and at the organizational level.

Regarding rewards, only 46 percent of our respondents were clear about how they were rewarded for their project performance. We found it interesting that 44 percent noted that, other than keeping their jobs, they received no special rewards for their project work.

Project Leader Effectiveness

We were particularly interested in determining how project team members viewed their project leaders. What are the qualities of an effective team leader from the perspective of a team member? We found several factors team members experienced with regards to their leaders. First, nearly 58 percent noted that "team management skills" were the most important quality of an effective project leader. Our probes into this issue revealed that project leader activities such as motivating, coaching, and leading were the most important factors. Second, nearly 52 percent noted that the personal qualities of the team leader were especially important. Examples of personal qualities included motivated, easy to work with, and respected. The third quality found was the ability to manage the process/project (42 percent). The skills involved here included setting goals, assigning/negotiating roles, project planning, meeting management, dealing with stakeholders, and assessing performance.

Conflict Sources and Impacts

Many studies have been conducted on the sources of conflict in project-oriented work environments (Thamhain and Wilemon 1975; Pelled and Alder 1994). We found, however, that few specific studies focused solely on how team members experienced conflicts, e.g., the sources and impacts. We found that nearly 54 percent of team members found that company policies, systems, and procedures were the major sources of conflict. These team members often noted that these were senior management issues and responsibilities and were beyond their control. Yet, their projects could be significantly influenced and impacted by these issues (Pinto, Pinto, and Prescott 1993).

Interestingly, the second most important source of conflict noted by 48 percent of the interviewees centered around "teamwork issues." Examples included interpersonal conflicts, communication breakdowns, personal agendas, and intergroup conflicts.

The third category of conflict noted by 32 percent of the team members focused on "task issues," which created conflict and disagreements. Examples of task issues included changing project requirements, shifting priorities, and schedule slippage.

We found that these conflicts often had a negative impact on team members. Nearly 50 percent of the team members noted that conflicts affected them personally and in a dysfunctional manner, e.g., creating frustration, attitude problems, stress, and in some cases, apathy.

Development Process Clarity

One of the most interesting findings in our study of project team members is that only about 42 percent were clear about how their company's NPD process functioned; 28 percent were unclear; and about 30 percent were both clear and unclear about their development processes (Barczak and Wilemon 2000). Respondents noted that in some cases their company had an NPD process but it was not used, others noted that their company did not have a development process and, in some cases, the respondents noted that each new development team had to devise their own process. This is a surprising finding since so many companies invested in total quality management (TQM) approaches, International Organization for Standardization (ISO) Programs, and development acceleration programs in the 1990s (Cooper 1996, 1999).

Development Process Effectiveness

We also found that only 50 percent of the team members believed that their process was effective while approximately 32 percent viewed their development process as ineffective. Effectiveness was defined as being useful and helpful to the project team. Regarding ineffective processes, our interviewees often made such comments as, "our development process is too complex," "our development process is too outdated to be useful," and "we don't emphasize processes in our development areas."

Project Clarity Issues

We found that while 66 percent of the project team members were clear on the objectives for their development projects, another 34 percent were not clear or somewhat clear. Project clarity resulted from the efforts of the project leader to effectively articulate the goals of the project to all involved team members and stakeholders. Without a clear focus, team members can become frustrated and demotivated. An important part of gaining project clarity is clearly articulating what customers want and what the project must achieve in order to fully satisfy the customer's requirements. In some cases, we found the customer intimately involved in a team's development efforts.

Team Member Research Issues

There are several research questions that have developed during this project that warrant additional study. Examples of these questions include:

1. What is the impact of project team experiences on team members' perceptions of project work? For example, how does a "negative experience" shape one's view of project work, particularly in the early phases of one's career?

2. What "motivators" are particularly important for young, inexperienced team members? Which motivators are especially important for experienced, senior team members?

3. What mechanisms can project managers use to ensure proper skill-blending and generational-blending within a team?

4. What is the impact of a project team's "internal culture" on a team's ability to work with other supporting functional groups, customers, and other stakeholders?

5. What can management do to ensure that all project participants are clear on team selection methods, evaluation procedures, rewards, and development processes?

Summary

The purpose of this chapter is to share one researcher's perspectives and experiences regarding research on project management. This author's early exposure to project management within NASA clearly shaped his perceptions regarding what project managers do and the issues they encounter in carrying out their work. What is particularly surprising is that many of the problems that the NASA project leaders faced are very similar to the issues today's project managers encounter. Project leaders continue to deal with issues that test the ablest of managers, e.g., dealing with new technologies; operating in a global environment; dealing with multiple, complex organizations; and operating under stringent performance, schedule, and cost targets. In addition, there are numerous interpersonal challenges involved in achieving successful project performance. It is hoped that the issues examined in this chapter like project team performance assessment; stress in project management; project partnering/alliance management; and the experiences of project team members will encourage further research and managerial thought.

It is estimated that approximately 75 percent of companies use cross-functional project teams in their NPD programs (Cooper and Kleinschmidt 1994; Griffin 1997). These teams clearly can have an important impact on cycle time and project performance (Gupta and Wilemon 1990). The experiences of organizations in implementing these teams, however, have been mixed. Some organizations have created high-performing project teams with impressive development performance. Other organizations have found achieving authentic teamwork difficult at best. As one researcher noted, "teamwork collaborations are often tentative, fragile, threatened by confusion, stressful, conflictful, and skeptical" (Donnellon 1992). It appears that we have much more to learn about implementing and creating successful project teams (Denison, Hart, and Kahn 1996).

In summary, the purpose of this chapter is to highlight some ongoing research areas that may prove helpful in further understanding the purpose and function of project management. As a field of study, project management continues to evolve. The research that has been conducted has strengthened the field. The challenges that project management faces in the future will be even more daunting as projects become more complex and increasingly sophisticated. Researchers can help by focusing on issues that help increase the effectiveness of project managers, their teams, and make their work lives more productive and satisfying. Conferences such as the *PMI Research Conference 2000* conducted by the Project Management Institute (PMI®) are an excellent venue to share ideas and approaches that offer the potential increases in project management effectiveness.

References

Barczak, G., and D. Wilemon. 1992. Successful New Product Team Leaders. *Industrial Marketing Management* 21 (February): 61–68.

———. 1999. Perspectives of Team Members in New Product Development Projects. Working Paper, Innovation Management Program, School of Management, Syracuse University.

———. 2000. Project Team Members and Their Experiences with New Product Development Processes. Working Paper, Innovation Management Program, School of Management, Syracuse University.

Bodensteiner, W., E. Gerloff, and J. Quick. 1989. Uncertainty and Stress in an R&D Project Environment. *R&D Management* 19 (4): 309–323.

Briner, W., M. Geddes, and C. Hastings. 1990. *Project Leadership*. New York: Van Nostrand Reinhold.

Brown, S., and K. Eisenhardt. 1995. Product Development: Past Research, Present Findings, and Future Directions. *Academy of Management Review* 20: 343–378.

Cole, Joanne. 1998. De-Stressing the Workplace. *HRFocus* (October): 9–11.

Cooper, R. 1996. Overhauling the New Product Process. *Industrial Marketing Management* 25: 465–482.

———. 1999. The Invisible Success Factors in Product Innovation. *Journal of Product Innovation Management* 16: 115–133.

Cooper, R., and E. Kleinschmidt. 1994. Determinants of Timeliness in Product Development. *Journal of Product Innovation Management* 11: 381–396.

Cordero, R., G. Farris, and N. DiTomaso. 1998. Technical Professionals in Cross-functional Teams: Their Quality of Work Life. *Journal of Product Innovation Management* 15: 550–563.

Denison, D., S. Hart, and J. Kahn. 1996. From Chimneys to Cross-functional Teams: Developing and Validating a Diagnostic Model. *Academy of Management Journal* 39 (4): 1005–1023.

Donnellon, A. 1992. Cross-functional Teams in Product Development: Accommodating the Structure to the Process. *Journal of Product Innovation Management* 10 (5): 375–392.

Driskell, J., and E. Salas. 1996. *Stress and Human Performance*. New Jersey: Lawrence Erlbaum Associates Publishing.

Driskell, J., E. Salas, and J. Johnston. 1999. Does Stress Lead to a Loss of Team Perspective? *Group Dynamics: Theory, Research, and Practice* 3 (4): 291–302.

Eisenhardt, K., and C. Galunic. 2000. Coevolving at Last, A Way to Make Synergies Work. *Harvard Business Review* (January–February): 91–101.

Elbeik, S., and M. Thomas. 1998. *Project Skills*. Oxford, England: Butterworth-Heinemann.

Gemmill, G., and D. Wilemon. 1994. The Hidden Side of Leadership in Team Management. *Research-Technology Management* 37: 25–32.

Griffin, A. 1997. The Effect of Processes and Teams on Product Development Cycle Time. *Journal of Marketing Research* 34 (February): 24–35.

Gupta, A., and D. Wilemon. 1990. Accelerating the Development of Technology-Based New Products. *California Management Review* 32 (2): 24–44.

Ivancevich, J., and M. Matteson. 1980. *Stress and Work: A Managerial Perspective*. Glenview, IL: Scott, Foresman Publishing.

Jex, S., and T. Boehr. 1991. Emerging Theoretical and Methodological Issues in the Study of Work-Related Stress. In *Research in Personnel and Human Resources Management* (311–365). Edited by K. Rowland and G. Ferris. Greenwich, CT: JAI Press 9.

Keller, R., J. Scott, and B. Kedia. 1996. A Multinational Study of Work Climate, Job Satisfaction, and Productivity of R&D Teams. *IEEE Transactions on Engineering Management* 42 (February): 1.

Kim, J., and D. Wilemon. 2000. Managing Stress in Product Development Projects. *Proceedings of the International Association of the Management of Technology*, February, University of Miami, FL.

Levi, D., and C. Slem. 1995. Teamwork in Research and Development Organizations: The Characteristics of Successful Groups. *International Journal of Industrial Ergonomics* 16: 29–42.

Lynn, G. 1998. New Product Team Learning. *California Management Review* 40 (1): 74–93.

Lynn, G., and R. Reilly. 2000. Measuring Team Performance. *Research-Technology Management* 43 (2): 48–56.

Millson, M., S. P. Raj, and D. Wilemon. 1992. A Survey of Major Approaches for Accelerating New Product Development Projects. *Journal of Product Innovation Management* 9 (1): 53–69.

———. 1996. Strategic Partnering in Developing New Products. *Research-Technology Management* 39 (3): 41–49.

Pelled, L., and P. Adler. 1994. Antecedents of Intergroup Conflict in Multifunctional Product Development Teams: A Conceptual Model. *IEEE Transactions on Engineering Management* 41 (1): 21–28.

Pinto, M., J. Pinto, and J. Prescott. 1993. Antecedents and Consequences of Product Team Cross-Functional Cooperation. *Management Science* 39 (10): 1281–1297.

Syracuse University/NASA Research Program. 1973a. *Apollo Project Management: An Interdisciplinary View*. Syracuse, New York: Syracuse University.

Syracuse University/NASA Research Program. 1973b. *Manned Spaceflight in Transition*. Syracuse, New York: Syracuse University.

Thamhain, H., and D. Wilemon. 1975. Conflict Management in Project Life Cycles. *Sloan Management Review* 12: 31–50.

CHAPTER 4

PROPOSITION OF A SYSTEMIC AND DYNAMIC MODEL TO DESIGN LIFELONG LEARNING STRUCTURE: THE QUEST OF THE MISSING LINK BETWEEN MEN, TEAM, AND ORGANIZATIONAL LEARNING

Christophe N. Bredillet, D.Sc.—UTS, ISGI Lille Graduate School of Management

Background

Strategy: Management of/by Projects, to Deal with Complexity and Irreversibility

For the past forty years, project management has become a well-accepted way to manage organizations. The field of project management has evolved from operational research techniques and tools to a discipline of management (Cleland 1994; Bredillet 1999). Many authors emphasize the evolution in the way to manage projects: "this book traces the development of the discipline of project management," writes Morris (1997). Project management becomes *the* way to implement corporate strategy (Turner 1993; Frame 1994) and to manage a company: "… value is added by systematically implementing new projects—projects of all types, across the organization" (Dinsmore 1999). Management of projects—the way to manage projects within the same organization—(Morris 1997) and management by projects—projects as a way to organize the whole organization—(Gareis 1990; Dinsmore 1999) are both a good example of that tendency. To go further in the strategic issue, we can point out that strategic processes, in other words focused actions, implement strategy, defined in its dynamic dimension. These processes aim to modify the conditions of insertion of firms in their environment. Through them, resources and competencies are mobilized to create a competitive advantage and a source of value. As resources are easily shared by many organizations, competencies are the relevant driver. Thus, through processes or projects, past action is actualized as experience, present action reveals and proves competencies, and future action, discounted as a project, will generate and experiment with new competencies (Lorino and Tarondeau 1998). Lastly, projects are a form of organization that puts a company in relation to its environment. As projects are the vectors of the strategy (Grundy 1998), project management is a way to deal with the characteristics of the whole environment: complexity (Arcade 1998), change (Voropajev 1998), globalization, time, and competitiveness (Hauc 1998). Thus, with the help of project management, strategic management really becomes the management of irreversibility (Declerck and Debourse 1997), concentrating on the ecosystems project/company/context, operation/company/context, and their integrative management (Declerck, Debourse, and Navarre 1983).

Competencies: Source of Competitive Advantage and Creation of Value

Thus, competencies (both individual and organizational) are at the source of competitive advantage and creation of value: some research programs are working on this. For example, Lynn Crawford, directing the Project Management Competence Research Project, writes that "interest in project management competence stems from the very reasonable and widely held assumption that if people who manage and work on projects are competent, they will perform effectively and that this will lead to successful projects and successful organizations" (Crawford 1998). The Project Management Institute (PMI®) Standards Program project "Project Manager Competencies" puts forward in the project overview that "The Project Manager Competency Framework will be based on the premise that competencies have an impact on outcomes indicative of effective performance. The degree or extent of this impact is expected to vary depending on certain contingencies (such as project types and characteristics). At a more specific level, the framework will identify and define some of the key dimensions of effective performance, the competencies that likely impact performance, and the contingencies likely to influence the extent to which a particular competency has an impact on performance." These projects and the development of professional certifications contradict former findings. For example, Pinto and Prescott (1988) conclude that the "personnel factor," even if designated in theoretical literature as a crucial factor in project efficiency, is a marginal variable for project success at any of the four project life cycles. For a criticism of their findings, see Belout 1998. A working paper (Turner 1998) shows the influence of the project managers on value of shares: "Projects are undertaken to add value to the sponsoring organization. In the private sector this ultimately means increasing the value of shares to the holders of equity in the company." But performance also comes from the maturity of an organization to deal with projects, especially through the aspects of learning. The Organizational Project Management Maturity (OPM3) project with the PMI Standards Program and others papers (Remy 1997; Saures 1998; Fincher et al. 1997) explore the relations between maturity of the organizations and success of the projects. The issue is important in a context of the globalization of the profession (Curling 1998).

Project Management: A Knowledge Field Not That Clear

To develop competencies, a knowledge field is needed. But both in academia and the business world, the field of project management is not clearly defined. To that, there are numerous reasons: the field evolves in breadth and in depth. In breadth, embracing information systems, human resources management, change management, strategic management, economic value management, psychology, management of technology, quality, sociology, multicultural management, systems thinking, knowledge management, organizational learning, team management, temporary group, systems engineering, and so on. In depth, going further into cost engineering, finance, specific aspects of risk management, earned value management, scheduling methods, resources allocation, project life cycle, processes, studying phases, types of projects, projects portfolio management, and so on. Over the last twenty years the profession has been working on its recognition and standards; certifications arose from professional associations. They work on the definition of the field and on the recognition of project management as a profession. Definitions of standards, bodies of knowledge (broad range of knowledge that the discipline encompasses plus some behavioral characteristics), certification and assessment of project management competence models and maturity models, and best practices reflect this trend (Toney and Powers 1997; Hobbs and Miller 1998; Hobbs 1997; Gareis 1997; PROJECT 2000 1998).

We can identify three main points of view among the attempt to clarify the field (International Project Management Association [IPMA] GWG 1999). A first one relates primarily to the management of projects (International Organization for Standardization [ISO] 10006, *A Guide to the Project Management Body of Knowledge [PMBOK® Guide]*). A second one is designed primarily as a standard and guideline to define the work of the project management personnel and a basis for the assessment of the project management competence of people. The *IPMA Competence Baseline (ICB)* from IPMA and the *Australian National Competency Standards for Project Management (ANCSPM)* are good examples, albeit different in their perspectives and coverage (Turner 2000a; 2000b). A third one is directed at the project management practices of organizations (such as the current PMI OPM3 project mentioned previously).

One main point is the ongoing adaptation of the different standards according to the change in project management. The theory of conventions can enlighten this, as socioeconomical constructs (Gomez 1994), standards are the result of negotiation enabling reduction of complexity and uncertainty in the relations between the stakeholders of projects. But since the global evolution of the environment will change the bases of the negotiation, the standards need to evolve in a dynamic perspective.

On the other hand, numbers of books and papers give both depth and breadth to points of view across several dimensions: technical, methodological, and managerial. They aim to fill a long-standing need for a comprehensive, unified, and practical description of the field (Archibald 1992; Forsberg and Mooz 1996; Harrison 1992; Cleland 1994; Kerzner 2000; Pinto 1998; Dinsmore 1993; Kerzner 1997). But the quest for key success factors, best practices, and other "best ways" doesn't prevent failures and waste of money. The present development of bodies of knowledge and the reengineering of certifications show that the current situation is not that clear and a number of practices are hindering growth and quality of the field.

Thus, we have to note that:

1. Project management is becoming the way to manage the development of organizations.

2. Competencies and learning (both individual and organizational) are the source of competitive advantage and of the creation of value (Stata 1989; de Geus 1988).

3. The project management knowledge field is not that clear because it evolves in depth and breadth, so that standards, as social constructs, need ongoing adjustment.

Considering the definition, the assessment, the development of competencies, and the certification processes, we have to note that they are all built from standards both in a synchronic and diachronic perspective. There is a synchronic perspective because they need to answer to "hic et nunc" requirements for current projects. And, there is a diachronic perspective because the development of competencies, both for individuals and for organizations (developing maturity implies time), takes time and it is a necessary condition for future performance to forecast and anticipate the needs for future projects. For example, people who want to pass the different degrees of the IPMA Certification have to consider time. According to the development of their ability to manage bigger and more complex projects, they will be able to get a higher recognition. Some companies like IBM Global Services, Bull, or Unisys use this process (appropriate degree of certification plus continuous education) to manage the competencies (and the career) of their project managers.

It is unfortunately not a sufficient condition because the future is not predictable. That means the capacities to deal with uncertainty and risk are fundamental. And the link(s) between individual competencies, team competencies, and organizational competencies is (are) neither that clear nor is the way to develop it (them).

Thus, we see the rapid implementation of project management in organizations and great efforts spent to train people in project management (Parker 1999).

The National Aeronautical and Space Administration (NASA) trains one-third of its workforce (18,500) in one way or another in project management each year and its Center of Excellence changed its name from Project/Program Management Initiative (PPMI) to NASA Academy of Program and Project Leadership (APPL): "Initiative" has become "Academy" (NASA 1999).

We see many papers and books about individual competencies, the way to develop them, about organizational learning, about lessons learned, about knowledge management, and about communities of practice. But many companies reach a limit in terms of efficiency and effectiveness while using traditional approaches (seminars, business games, teamwork, and university degrees) and find it very difficult to simultaneously combine individual and organizational development in a coherent way while using approaches like total quality management (TQM), 5S, and 6σ. We lack an integrated perspective of individual, team, and organizational learning, where systemic and dynamic aspects of learning are taken into account.

This is the reason why we would like to propose a systemic and dynamic conceptual framework to answer the following question: *How to design a learning process enabling concurrent development of individual competencies and maturity of organization in a perspective of creation of value?*

Before giving some insights and elements of response we have to clarify our vision of project management and what approaches we are going to mobilize.

Some Insights on Research Issues and Method

An Epistemological Perspective of Project Management

I would like first to adopt Terry Cooke-Davies presentation of research issues and approaches in his International Research Network on Organizing by Projects (IRNOP IV) Conference paper as mine (Cooke-Davies 2000). Quoting Michael Polanyi (1959), he proposes an alternative epistemology both to positivism and constructivism. We do not want to separate personal judgment from scientific method.

We think that, especially in project management, knowledge has to integrate both scientific and mathematical aspects (operational research in network optimization for example) and fuzzy or symbolic aspects. A "reality" can be explained according to a specific point of view and be considered as the symbol of higher order (Guenon 1986) and more general reality (for example, a 2-dimensional form can be seen as the projection on a plan of a n-dimensional figure). We think that the "demiurgic" characteristic of project management involves seeing this field as an open space, without "having" but rather with a *raison d'être*. This is because of the construction of reality by the projects. Project management can be seen as a means to realize different purposes as Boutinet shows in his compass rose: technical/existential project and individual/collective project (Boutinet 1996).

Our vision of project management would be one of an integral function: the knowledge field is made up of differential elements, each of them being able to be defined (for example, cost control, scheduling, communication, quality, information system, temporary group) but seen as a whole. It is a transition to the limit. In mathematics the result of an integral is both quantitatively and qualitatively more than the sum of the parts. In another way, it is what we can call a system effect: parts A, B, and C form a system S, keep some of their properties and potential performances, lose some others, but gain some entirely new performances (Legay 1996).

Discourse on the Method ...

"... of rightly conducting the reason, and seeking truth in the sciences" (René Descartes 1637).

> I am in doubt as to the propriety of making my first meditations in the place above mentioned matter of discourse; for these are so metaphysical, and so uncommon, as not, perhaps, to be acceptable to every one. And yet, that it may be determined whether the foundations that I have laid are sufficiently secure, I find myself in a measure constrained to advert to them (Part IV).

The method we chose is the integration of inputs coming from several fields according to two dimensions. The first dimension is what we call the individual/organizational dimension. The individual level includes the aspects of project management having an impact on the person: bodies of knowledge, certifications, standards, best practices, and all project management tools, techniques, experiences, competencies, changes, and task performances. The organizational level includes the aspects of project management having an impact on the team, the organization: bodies of knowledge, maturity, standards, norms, best practices, all project management tools and techniques, project success and performance, and creation of value. The second dimension is what we call the synchronic/diachronic dimension. The synchronic dimension is made up of what has an immediate or short-term impact or effectiveness. It's the level of optimization, stability, predictability, and control. The diachronic dimension is composed of what has to be considered over a long period of time. It is the level of complexity, fuzzy logic, influence rather than control, creation of value, project performance, performance of the organization, and change of culture.

We are considering a map figuring only the first level of the inputs (fields). For example at a lower level knowledge management would include: Anthropology, Artificial Intelligence (Individual), Artificial Intelligence (Collective), Artificial Intelligence (Other), Cognitive Psychology (Individual), Cognitive Psychology (Collective), Complexity and Adaptive Systems, Linguistics, Organizational Learning and Management Science, Philosophy, and Sociology of Knowledge (Knowledge Management Consortium International [KMCI] website, last updated 06/18/99).

We have to note that we want to keep a general perspective according to the definition of the inputs; the different perspectives of each input are sources of pluralities of meaning.

1. Standards: Standards (including all organization standards: for example NASA 7120-5A, NSIA EVMS, United States Department of Defense (DoD) 5000, bodies of knowledge, best practices, norms, maturity models, and professional certifications) represent the social construct of the project management knowledge field mainly accepted at a time (Bredillet 1998), but as we put it forward higher they evolve according to changes in the global context (Gomez 1994).

2. Learning aspects: We will consider the different levels of learning: individual learning (Hawrylyshyn 1977), organizational learning (Senge 1990), single loop learning, and double loop learning (Fiol and Lyles 1985; Kim 1993). They represent both the structure and the process of learning (Romme and Dillen 1997).

3. Performance, value: The performance measurements have to be done at the different levels and according to the different time perspectives. Normative, prescriptive, or threshold definitions can be considered. The creation of value includes here all the developments on intellectual capital, intangible assets, and the different perspectives developed in this field (Sveiby 1998; Kaplan and Norton 1992, 1996).

4. Knowledge management: Knowledge management (KM) is "The art of creating value from an organization's Intangible Assets" (Sveiby 1999). With Sveiby we can define KM by looking at what people in this field are doing. "Both among KM researchers and consultants and among KM users there seem to be two tracks of activities—and two levels. The tracks of activities are 1) Management of information: Researchers and practitioners in this field tend to have their education in computer and/or information science. They are involved in construction of information management systems, artificial intelligence (AI), reengineering, group ware, and so on. To them knowledge equals objects that can be identified and handled in information systems. This track is new and is growing very fast at the moment, assisted by new developments in information technology (IT); 2) Management of people: Researchers and practitioners in this field tend to have their education in philosophy, psychology, sociology, or business/management. They are primarily involved in assessing, changing, and improving human individual skills and/or behavior. To them knowledge equals processes, a complex set of dynamic skills, know-how, and such, that is constantly changing. They are traditionally involved in learning and in managing these competencies individually—like psychologists—or on an organizational level—like philosophers, sociologists, or organizational theorists. This track is very old, and is not growing so fast.

The two levels are 1) Individual Perspective: The focus in research and practice is on the *individual* (AI specialists, psychologists) and 2) Organizational Perspective: The focus in research and practice is on the *organization* (re-engineers, organization theorists).

Crossing these two dimensions, we can capture one essential issue: There are paradigmatic differences in our understanding of what knowledge is. The

Figure 1. Mapping the Four Fields (Inputs) According to the Individual/Organizational and the Synchronic/Diachronic Dimensions

researchers and practitioners in the "knowledge equals object" column tend to rely on concepts from Information Theory in their understanding of knowledge. The researchers and practitioners in the column "knowledge equals process" tend to take their concepts from philosophy, psychology, or sociology. Some development including KM and measurement of performance can be found in Bontis (1999) showing that creation of value and knowledge are closely linked, see Figure 1.

The Interrelation between the Fields

As many books and papers show it, the four fields we consider are in interrelation: for example Sveiby (1998) and Bontis (1999) integrate KM, intellectual capital, and measure and management of intangible resources. Some others (Morten et al. 1999) put forward the role of standardization to manage knowledge. Individual learning and organizational learning are the heart of numerous books and papers (Senge 1994, 1999; Kim and Senge 1994; Kim 1993; Morecroft and Sterman 1994; Garvin 1993). Many standards include the management of knowledge through the lessons learned (*ICB* 36, PMBOK® 9.3, NASA 7120-5A, see "capture process knowledge" in each step), training, and building communities of practice (Wenger 1998). But these fields not only interrelate, they share the same fundamental way of seeing the world. To take into account complexity, one needs

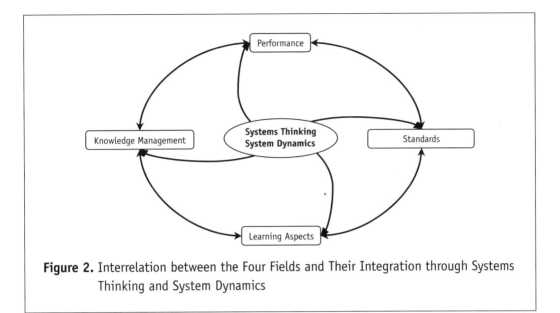

Figure 2. Interrelation between the Four Fields and Their Integration through Systems Thinking and System Dynamics

systems thinking and a system dynamics perspective. Thus, we have the integral function of the four fields, as seen in Figure 2.

After these short insights on research issues and method, we are going to propose some insights and elements to define a systemic and dynamic conceptual framework to design a lifelong learning process enabling concurrent development of individual competencies and the maturity of the organization in a perspective of creation of value.

Proposition of a Systemic and Dynamic Model to Design Lifelong Learning Structure

At this stage we have to clarify what kind of model we would like to build. Then we will give some insights and elements on the conceptual framework and assumptions supporting the construction of the model. Lastly, we will propose a generic model to design a lifelong learning structure.

Clarification on Modeling

Our purpose is not to rewrite all the work and research done on this subject, but to focus on specific aspects useful for our purpose. (For more details see, for example, MIT Sloan School of Management System Dynamics Group, URL: http://web.mit.edu/sdg/www/.) Let us specify the key points.

The Purpose of the Model

"A model must have a clear purpose, and that purpose should be to solve a particular problem. ... Beware the analyst who proposes to model an entire social or economic system rather than a problem. Every model is a representation of a system—a group of functionally interrelated elements forming a complex whole. But for the model to be useful, it must address a specific problem and must simplify rather than attempting to mirror in detail an entire system .... The usefulness of models lies in the fact that they simplify reality, putting it into a form that we can comprehend .... The art of model building is knowing what to cut out, and the purpose of the model acts as the logical knife. It provides the criterion about what will be cut, so that only the essential features necessary to fulfill the purpose are left .... The resulting models would be simple enough so that assumptions could be examined" (Sterman 1991).

The specific problem we address is how to design a learning process enabling concurrent development of individual competencies and maturity of organization in a perspective of the creation of value. The assumptions will be explained in the following.

The Type of Model

The distinction between optimization and simulation models is particularly important since these types of models are suited for fundamentally different aspects. 1) Optimization. "The output of an optimization model is a statement of the best way to accomplish some goal. Optimization models do not tell you what will happen in a certain situation. Instead they tell you what to do in order to make the best of the situation; they are normative or prescriptive models" (Sterman 1991). Limitations of Optimization: "Specification of the Objective Function, linearity, lack of feedback, and lack of dynamics" (Sterman 1991). 2) Simulation. "The purpose of a simulation model is to mimic the real system so that its behavior can be studied. The model is a laboratory replica of the real system, a *microworld*. Simulation models are descriptive. A simulation model does not calculate what should be done to reach a particular goal, but clarifies what would happen in a given situation. The purpose of simulations may be *foresight* (predicting how systems might behave in the future under assumed conditions) or *policy design* (designing new decision-making strategies or organizational structures and evaluating their effects on the behavior of the system). In other words, simulation models are 'what if' tools. Often such 'what if' information is more important than knowledge of the optimal decision. Every simulation model has two main components. First it must include a representation of the physical world relevant to the problem under study. In addition to reflecting the physical structure of the system, a simulation model must portray the behavior of the actors in the system. In this context, behavior means the way in which people respond to different situations, how they make decisions. The behavioral component is put into the model in the form of decision-making rules, which are determined by direct observation of the actual decision-making procedures in the system. Given the physical structure of the system and the decision-making rules, the simulation model then plays the role of the decision-makers, mimicking their decisions. In the model, as in the real world, the nature and quality of the information available to decision-makers will depend on the state of the system. The output of the model will be a description of expected decisions. The validity of the model's assumptions can be checked by comparing the output with the decisions made in the real system" (Sterman 1991). Limitation of Simulation: "Most problems occur in the description of the decision rules, the quantification of soft variables, and the choice of the model boundary" (Sterman 1991).

The model we plan to build is a simulation one with a "design" purpose in an "insight modeler" perspective (we mean using systems thinking diagramming and not, at that time, a complex quantitative model) (Graham and Sharon).

Conceptual Framework and Assumptions Supporting the Construction of the Model

First, we would like to formulate some preliminary remarks, and then, indicate the approaches, models, and assumptions supporting the construction of the model.

Preliminary Remarks

In spite of a different perspective, we wish this to be based on the contributions of the research and work in progress dealing with the three main aspects we mentioned previously. 1) Project management (ISO 10006, *PMBOK® Guide*), 2) standard and guideline to define the work of the project management personnel and a basis for the assessment of their project management competencies (*ICB* and *ANCSPM*), 3) project management practices of organizations (current PMI project OPM3 on project management maturity model).

In the same way, we will adopt a viewpoint of assembler, i.e., initially at least, we will seek to put together existing models, but with the concern of giving it a system dynamics perspective.

The fact of relying on existing or under development standards is coherent with the quality seen from the perspective of theory of conventions (Gomez 1994): as socioeconomical constructs standards are the result of negotiation enabling reduction of complexity and uncertainty in the relations between the stakeholders of projects. (Visible demonstration of the socioeconomic adjustments produced by a convention of qualification [relation of customer-provider] on the one hand, and a convention of effort [relation of manager-project team] on the other hand, whose conjunction characterizes social and technical division of work.)

This implies the following issues:

1. The model proposes a theoretical framework to the problem of the training of the "project" teams. It does not pose it as obviousness, but exposes the logic of its development.

2. It is impossible to find measurements of competence that are not "deus ex machina" and invented for a special case, and this generates uncertainty and explains the existence of conventions of quality, i.e., standards that provide the elements of calibration.

Types of Models	Dimensions S = Synchronic D = Diachronic I = Individual O = Organizational	Fields K = Knowledge Management L = Learning Aspects S = Standards P = Performance	References
Simulation-Design	DO	KLP	Widemon 1998
Simulation-Design	SDO	KLP	Declerck & Debourse 1997
Simulation-Design	SDIO	KLP	Romme & Dillen 1997
Simulation-Forecast	DO	SLP	Alarcõn & Ashley 1993
Optimization	SO	SP	Griffith & Gibson 1997
Optimization	DO	P	Milosevic 1990
Optimization	DO	SP	Hartman & Ashrafi 1996
Optimization	SIO	SP	Beale 1991
Optimization	DI	L	Thamhain 1991
Optimization	SI	SP	Pettersen 1991
Optimization	SO	L	Globerson & Ellis 1994
Optimization	DIO	L	Communier 1998
Optimization	DIO	KLP	Peters 1997
Optimization	DIO	LP	Belout 1998
Optimization	DO	KLP	Hubbard 1990
Optimization	DI	LP	Turner 1998

Table 1. Models: Some Examples of Combinations According to the Different Dimensions and Fields

3. The whole of the model constitutes a complex system: there is no causal linearity (such competence leads to such result), but permanent adjustments between competencies and their use.

4. We put at the same level of importance, the standard as built in the exchange, and the standard as a result of an effort of production. That means that we will pay detailed attention to the way in which the profession or the field of the management of projects evolves. The standard is thus not seen as a fixed fact.

Models and Approaches Taken into Account

As mentioned above, the construction of the conceptual model will be based on various models and approaches. (We indicate only some of them, but the list is not exhaustive.)

We have previously presented the four fields and basis of the work: knowledge management (Sveiby 1999; Bontis 1999), performance (Sveiby 1999; Bontis 1999), standards (*ICB*–IPMA, *PMBOK® Guide*–PMI, *ANCSPM*, Maturity Model [OPM3]; Remy 1997; Saures 1998; Fincher and Levin 1997), and learning aspects (Senge et al. 1990, 1994, 1999; Kim 1993, 1994; Morecroft and Sterman 1994). These fields may be combined together through different ways to give different kind of models. Table 1 shows examples of combinations according to the different dimensions and fields.

Approaches integrate the different models into a coherent whole.

1. A systemic vision of the management of a project (Declerck and Debourse 1997; Wideman 1997, 1998; Leroy 1998).

2. An approach that highlights the links between competencies of the managers of projects and success of the projects (Project Manager Competency Development Framework under development by PMI).

3. An integrated model of development of competencies in management of project (Development Assessment of Project Management Competence–Crawford 1998).

4. The model of education of the leaders proposed by Hawrylyshyn (1977).

5. Design for learning in teams seen as communities of practice (Wenger 1998).

6. Principles of organizational learning according to a systems dynamic perspective (Kim 1993; Romme and Dillen 1997).

Assumptions

Before presenting the general system in which the model is included we need to clarify some assumptions.

Increasing competencies (individual, team, and organizational) leads to improved performance (Crawford 1998). Implementing standards and best practices (PMI, IPMA) leads to increased performance. But without a double-loop learning system, increasing competencies and implementing standards and best practices leads to limited performance if not poor performance (Kim 1997). We consider that general environment, context of the project, and contingencies affect the performance of people, tasks, project, organization, and stakeholders. They also affect the learning aspects (individual, team, and organizational) (Communier 1998; Wideman 1998). The systemic and dynamic model enables us to deal with different time horizons (from short-term to long-term).

The integration of these different elements leads us to propose the general system and the learning subsystem shown in Figure 3 and Figure 4.

Thus, the model suggested will have to allow the design for learning to answer three series of objectives:

The objectives of individual learning (project managers, project "people"): They are dependent on the gap between their present level (performance, experience, and knowledge) and their expected level. For example, if they need to reinforce their project management capacities, they will have to get Project Management Professional (PMP®) certification or prepare for IPMA project management certification according to their responsibilities, their experiences, and the nature of project they manage or are involved in (Hawrylyshyn 1977)—see Table 2.

The objectives of team training: The development of team competencies depends on many aspects—participation/reification, designed/emergent, local/global, identification/negotiation, engagement, alignment, and imagination (Wenger 1998)—and has a great influence on both individual performance and

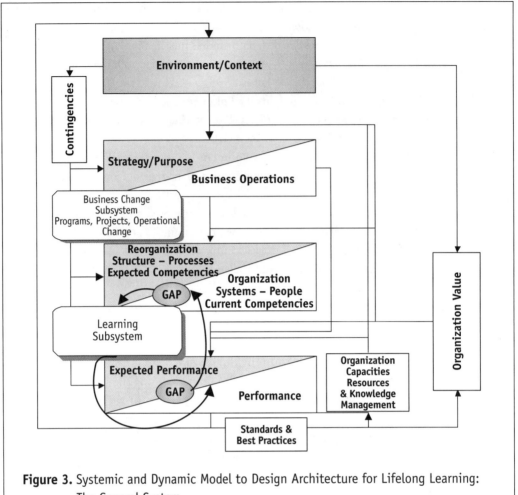

Figure 3. Systemic and Dynamic Model to Design Architecture for Lifelong Learning: The General System

organizational performance (maturity levels, lessons learned). The level is the key of the learning process; it makes the link between individual learning and organizational learning. It integrates all the aspects developed in the other levels and represents a kind of mirror between them. This is also the level of the link between project team members and operational team members (Table 3).

The objectives of organizational learning: They are dependent on the disturbances in organizational learning (Kim 1993; Romme and Dillen 1997) and on the degree of maturity reached by the organization (Figure 5).

The architecture for lifelong learning proposed has to be coherent between the different learning levels. It integrates both single-loop and double-loop learning. It considers the factors of contingencies, the characteristics of the organization, the context, the environment, and the state of the standards and best practices.

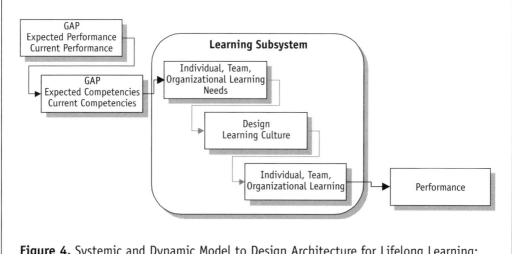

Figure 4. Systemic and Dynamic Model to Design Architecture for Lifelong Learning: The Learning Subsystem

Individual Needs	Learning Categories	Learning Process	Learning Methods
	Performance = f (Competence, Motivation, Occasion) Competence = f (a-Knowledge, b-Attitudes, c-Aptitudes) a, b, c Weightings = Functions of the position in the hierarchy of decision-making, nature of company, dimension, political, economic and social context, particular functional field, ...		
Competence	Knowledge	Cognitive	Lecture or based on the didactic media, reading, conferences, discussions, films or audio-visual methods, programmed learning, CAL, exercises
	Attitudes	Emotional	Socio-economic, short speeches, speech in public, group dynamics, confrontations
	Aptitudes	Practical	Participating, real studies, exercise of the "basket-entry," method of the incident, method of the cases, exercise of simulation of decision-making, role play, consultancy work

Table 2. Individual Learning Level: A Design Framework (Hawrylyshyn 1977)

At this stage we will stay on a general pattern because of the nature of learning. With Wenger (1998) we think that learning cannot be designed. Learning happens, by design or not by design. One can design curriculum but not learning, process but not practice. Learning can only be designed for. Which implies a contextualization of the architecture. There is not a "one best way" architecture.

Components: Three Infrastructures of Learning ⇨ Four Dimensions of Design for Learning ⬇	Engagement ✔ Mutuality: interactional facilities, joint tasks, peripherality ✔ Competence: initiative and knowledgeability, accountability, tools ✔ Continuity: reification, memory, participative memory	Imagination ✔ Orientation: location in space, in time, in meaning, in power ✔ Reflection: models, patterns, comparisons with other practices ✔ Exploration: play, simulations, prototypes	Alignment ✔ Convergence: common focus, leadership, persuasion ✔ Coordination: standards, methods, communication, boundary facilities, feedback facilities ✔ Jurisdiction: policies, contracts, mediation, conflict, resolution	⇦ Educational Design ⬇
Participation/ Reification	Combining them meaningfully in actions, interactions, and the creation of shared stories	Stories, playing with forms, recombination, assumptions	Styles and discourses	Learning as negotiation: how much to reify learning, its subject and its object
Designed/ Emergent	Situated improvisation within a regime of accountability	Scenarios, possible worlds, simulations, perceiving new broad patterns	Communication, feedback, coordination, renegotiation, realignment	Teaching and learning: the relation between teaching and learning is not one of simple cause and effect
Local/Global	Multi-membership, brokering, peripherality, conversations	Models, maps, representations, visit, tours	Standards, shared infrastructures, centers of authority	From practice to practice: educational experiences must connect to other experiences
Identification/ Negotiability	Mutuality through shared action, situated negotiation, marginalization	New trajectories, empathy, stereotypes, explanations	Inspiration, fields of influence, reciprocity of power relations	Identities of participation: there are multiple perspectives on what educational design is about; its effect on learning

Table 3. Team Learning Level: A Design Framework of a Learning Architecture (Wenger 1998)

An Example of Application: The Design of an International Master in Project Management Program

The model has been used to design a new academic program in project management. The objective was to meet several purposes. One was to provide cutting-edge education in project management, based on international standards and on the main development in the field. Another one was to build a common platform between

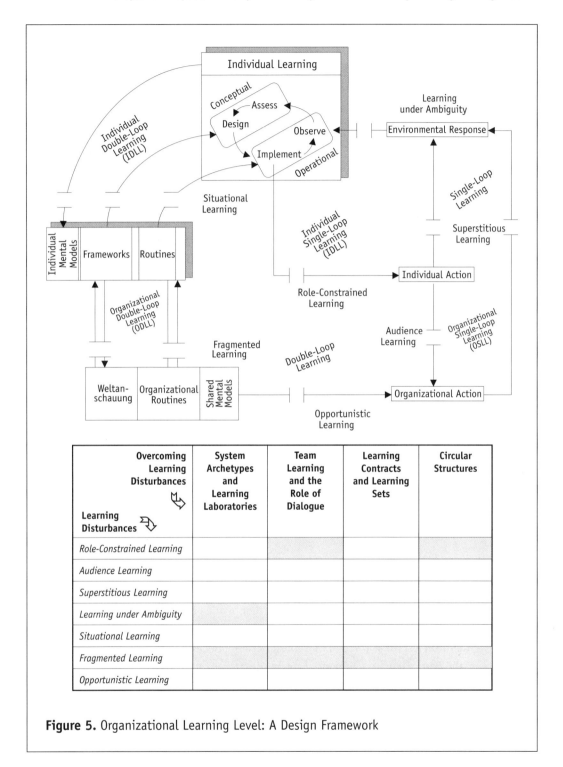

Figure 5. Organizational Learning Level: A Design Framework

the academic partners (ESC Lille, France; University of Washington, Seattle USA; University of Technology, Sydney Australia) with a flexible design enabling each partner to meet its local constraints and enabling future new partners to join. Another one was to give the opportunity to the students to work on real-life projects and to involve their companies, including companies on the same "value chain" or competitors looking for creation of value through common projects.

Thus, the design framework (see Figure 6) was used on a global basis to build a common platform in terms of competencies to develop (knowledge, attitudes, aptitudes) and apply them according to three dimensions (people, team, organization) based on common principles, international standards, and best practices. The underlying idea was that the architecture would promote a self-improvement cycle (innovation-implementation-integration-invention) between the organizations involved (academic and companies) and between the different groups of students (from one year to another). To ensure the lifelong learning aspect, both former students and their companies are part of the learning network.

In practical terms, students have a mix of self-training (online basis, but also research and course development on specific topics) and tutorials, work on a real project (or several) as part of a project team, usage of collaborative tools (Internet-based software and tools) and shared methodologies to work with their international project team, attendance at workshops around the world (USA, Europe, Australia, Asia), and both educational (for them) and business (for their companies) objectives. The steering group of the program includes the academic staff involved, but also top management of the companies involved, and some experts who are lecturers. (This is a very good way to provide organizational learning within the companies involved.)

The assessment of the first three years for this organization provides an excellent feedback both from students, building strong competencies and networks, and from companies testing new paths to project excellence, having projects developed in a very competitive way, and receiving a high return on their education investment. For example, one of the projects was to develop a recycling water shower for business jets. A company has just been created to produce and sell this product.

By Way of Conclusion ...

We tried in this work to demonstrate that, while project management has become a well-accepted way to manage the organizations and to deal with complexity and uncertainty, the source of competitive advantage and creation of value are the competencies (individual, team, organizational). But developing competencies means that we need to have a clear view of the field. It is the reason we tried to give some insights on this emergent field showing the fundamental role of standards, as social constructs, in its dynamic structure. We showed that, according to the nature of project management, a necessary condition to get project success and organization, and stakeholder performance was to manage member, team, and organizational learning in a systemic, dynamic, and integrated perspective. Standards, knowledge management, learning aspects, and performance and value management provided the basis of the model. As a consequence, the design of architecture had to consider different time periods, factors of contingencies, char-

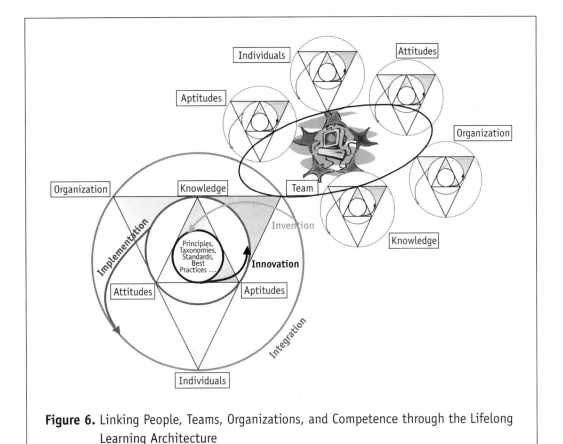

Figure 6. Linking People, Teams, Organizations, and Competence through the Lifelong Learning Architecture

acteristics of the organization, context, environment, state of the standards and best practices, learning curves, and complex interactions between the individual, team, and organizational levels. Systems thinking provided a support to simulate this complex learning process and helped to design architecture for lifelong learning. The result of this work is the proposition of a systemic and dynamic model to design architecture for lifelong learning. In essence, this model has to be generic and "contextualizable." There is not a "one best way" architecture. Further research will lead us to develop computer simulation (a "what if" model) to link design and performance of organizations.

Thus, we hope to have contributed to demonstrate that project management is an emergent scientific field according to Audet's sense (1986), to show that the design and the application of standards are a dynamic way to build a legitimate framework for the profession while recognizing its existence, to put forward, beyond the dynamics of fads, that the profession, by nature, needs a systemic and dynamic learning framework to provide performance and creation of value and to avoid the rise and decline of popularity and the risk to fall quickly to oblivion.

References

Alarcōn, Luis F., and David B. Ashley. 1993. A Modeling Approach to Predict Project Performance. *Proceedings of the 24th Annual Project Management Institute Seminars & Symposium*: 105–110.

Arcade, Jean. 1998. Articuler prospective et Stratégie—parcours du stratège dans la complexité. *Travaux et Recherches de Prospective* 8 (mai): 1–88.

Archibald, Russell D. 1992. *Managing High-Technology Programs and Projects*. 2nd ed. New York: John Wiley & Sons, Inc.

Audet, M. 1986. Le procès des connaissances de l'administration dans. *La production des connaissances de l'administration sous la direction de audet et malouin.* Québec: Les Presses de l'Université Laval.

Beale, Peter. 1991. Successful Project Execution: A Model. *Project Management Journal* 22 (4): 23–30.

Belout, Adnane. 1998. Effects of Human Resource Management on Project Effectiveness and Success: Toward a New Conceptual Framework. *International Journal of Project Management* 16 (1): 21–26.

Bontis, Nick. 1999. The Knowledge Toolbox: A Review of Tools Available to Measure and Manage Intangible Resources. *European Management Journal* 17 (4).

Boutinet, Jean-Pierre. 1996. *Anthropologie du Projet*. 4th ed. Paris: PUF.

Bredillet, Christophe. 1998. Essai de définition du champ disciplinaire du management de projet et de sa dynamique d'évolution. *Mémoire de DEA, USTL—IAE de Lille, Septembre.*

———. 1999. Essai de définition du champ disciplinaire du management de projet et de sa dynamique d'évolution. *Revue Internationale en Gestion et Management de Projets* IV (2): 6–29.

Caupin, Gilles, et al. 1999. *IPMA Competence Baseline.* Bremen: International Project Management Association.

Cleland, David I. 1994. *Project Management: Strategic Design and Implementation*. 2nd ed. New York: McGraw-Hill.

Communier, Jacques. 1998. Apport de la formation dans l'apprentissage des organisations vers le management de/par projets. *Les Mémos de l'IQM* (Janvier): 131–140.

Cooke-Davies, Terence J. 2000. Discovering the Principles of Project Management: An Interim Report on the First Five Years of an Investigation into the Practices of Project Management in Large Projectised Private-sector Companies. *Proceedings of IRNOP IV: Paradoxes of Project Collaboration in the Global Economy: Interdependence, Complexity and Ambiguity,* January 9–12, Sydney, Australia.

Crawford, Lynn. 1998. Project Management Competence For Strategy Realisation. *Proceedings of the 14th World Congress on Project Management*, June 10–13, Ljubljana, Slovenia.

Curling, David. Globalization of the Project Management Profession. URL: http://www.pmforum.org/.

de Geus, Arie. 1988. Planning as Learning. *Harvard Business Review* (March–April): 70–74.

Declerck, Roger P., Jean-Pierre Debourse, and John C. Declerck. 1997. *Le management stratégique: contrôle de l'irréversibilité.* Lille: Les éditions ESC Lille.

Declerck, Roger P., Jean-Pierre Debourse, and Christian Navarre. 1983. *La méthode de Direction générale: Le Management Stratégique.* Paris: Hommes et Techniques.

Dinsmore, Paul C. 1999. *Winning in Business with Enterprise Project Management*. New York: Amacom.

———. 1993. *Handbook of Project Management*. New York: Amacom.

Fincher, Anita, and Ginger Levin. 1997. Project Management Maturity Model. *Project Management Institute 28th Annual Seminars & Symposium*, September 29–October 1, Chicago, Illinois.

Fiol, C. M., and M. A. Lyles. 1985. Organizational Learning. *Academy of Management Review* 10: 803–813.

Forsberg, Kevin, and Haal Mooz. 1996. *Visualizing Project Management*. New York: John Wiley & Sons, Inc.

Frame, J. Davidson. 1994. *The New Project Management: Tools for an Age of Rapid Change, Corporate Reengineering, and Other Business Realities*. San Francisco: Jossey-Bass.

Gareis, Roland. 1990. Management by Projects—The Management Strategy of the 'New' Project-Oriented Company. In *Handbook of Management by Projects*. Edited by R. Gareis. Vienna: MANZ.

———. 1997. Best PM-Practice—Results of a Research Project on Project Management Benchmarking. *Research Workshop within the PM-Research Network*, November 10th, Vienna, Austria.

———. 1998. Best PM-Practice: Benchmarking of Project Management Processes. *Proceedings of the 14th World Congress on Project Management*, June 10–13, Ljubljana, Slovenia.

Garvin, David A. 1993. Building a Learning Organization. *Harvard Business Review* (July–August): 78–91.

Gharajedaghi, Jamshid. 1999. *Systems Thinking: Managing Chaos and Complexity: A Platform for Designing Business Architecture*. Boston: Butterworth-Heinemann.

Globerson, Shlomo, and Shmuel Ellis. 1994. Intensity of Learning in Project Environment. *Project Management Institute 25th Annual Seminars & Symposium*: 701–704.

Gomez, Pierre-Yves. 1994. *Qualité et Théorie des Conventions*. Paris: Economica.

Graham, Alan K., and A. Sharon. Els. System Dynamics and Systems Thinking: It Takes All Kind. Pugh-Roberts Associates, URL: http://www.strategicsimulation.com/pdfdocs/allkinds.pdf.

Griffith, Andrew F., and G. Edwards Gibson. 1997. Alignment of Cross Functional Teams During Pre-Project Planning. *Proceedings of the 28th Annual Project Management Institute Seminars & Symposium*: 38–43.

Grundy, Tony. 1998. Strategy Implementation and Project Management. *International Journal of Project Management* 16 (1): 43–50.

Guénon, René. 1986. *Initiation et Réalisation Spirituelle*. Paris: Editions Traditionnelles.

Hamilton, Albert. 1997. *Management by Projects—Achieving Success in a Changing World*. London: Thomas Telford.

Hansen, Morten T., Nitin Nohria, and Thomas Tierney. 1999. What's Your Strategy for Managing Knowledge. *Harvard Business Review* (March–April): 106–116.

Harrison, F. L. 1992. *Advanced Project Management—A Structured Approach*. 3rd ed. Aldershot: Gower.

Hartman, Francis, and Rafi Ashrafi. 1996. Failed Successes and Failures. *Proceedings of the 27th Annual Project Management Institute Seminars & Symposium*: 1–5.

Hauc, Anton. 1998. Projects and Strategies as Management Tools for Increased Competitiveness. *Proceedings of the 14th World Congress on Project Management*, June 10–13, Ljubljana, Solvenia.

Hawrylyshyn, Bodhan. W. 1997. *L'éducation des drigeants, Aspects méthodologiques*. Université de Genève—Faculté des sciences économiques et sociales, Collection des thèses, édition Peter Lang, Berne.

Hobbs, Brian. 1997. The International Research Programme on the Management of Engineering and Construction Projects. *Research Workshop within the PM-Research Network*, November 10th, Vienna, Austria.

Hobbs, Brian, and Roger Miller. 1999. The International Research Programme on the Management of Engineering and Construction projects. *Proceedings of the 14th World Congress on Project Management*, June 10–13, Ljubljana, Solvenia.

Hubbard, Darrel G. 1990. Successful Utility Project Management from Lessons Learned. *Project Management Journal* 21 (3): 19–23

International Project Management Association. 1999. Documentation of Meeting Global Working Groups, February 27th, East Horsley, United Kingdom.

Kaplan, Robert S., and David P. Norton. 1992. The Balanced Scorecard: Measures that Drive Performance. *Harvard Business Review* (January–February): 71–79.

———. 1996. Using the Balanced Scorecard as a Strategic Management System. *Harvard Business Review* (January–February): 75–85.

Kerzner, Harold. 1997. *Project Management: A Systems Approach to Planning, Scheduling and Controlling*. 6th ed. New York: John Wiley & Sons, Inc.

———. 2000. *Applied Project Management: Best Practices on Implementation*. New York: John Wiley & Sons, Inc.

Kim, Daniel H. 1993. The Link between Individual and Organizational Learning. *Sloan Management Review* (Fall): 37–50.

———. 1997. *Toward Learning Organizations: Integrating Total Quality Control and Systems Thinking*. Waltham: Pegasus Communications Inc.

Kim, Daniel H., and Peter M. Senge. 1994. Putting Systems Thinking into Practice. *System Dynamics Review* 10 (2–3): 277–290.

Legay, Jean-Marie. 1996. *L'expérience et le modèle: un discours sur la méthode*. Paris: INRA Editions.

Leroy, Daniel. 1998. Cours de Systémique de Projet: Mastère Spécialisé en Management de Projets. *ISGI et DESS Gestion de Projets—IAE de Lille*.

Lorin, P., and J. C. Tarondeau. 1998. De la stratégie aux processus stratégiques. *Revue Française de Gestion* 117 (Janvier–Février): 5–17.

Milosevic, Dragan Z. 1990. Case Study: Integrating the Owner's and the Contractor's Project Organization. *Project Management Journal* 21 (4): 23–31.

Morecroft, John D. W., and John D. Sternman. 1994. *Modeling for Learning Organizations*. Portland: Productivity Press.

Morris, P. W. G. 1997. *The Management of Projects*. London: Thomas Telford.

National Aeronautic and Space Administration. APPL URL: http://appl.nasa.gov/.

Parker, Mark. 1999. U.S. Government Rapidly Implementing PM Techniques. *PMI Today* (April): 1.

Peters, Lee A. 1997. Make Project Learning a Learning Project: The Way to Better and Better Project Success. *Proceedings of the 28th Annual Project Management Institute Seminars & Symposium*: 173–178.

Pettersen, Normand. 1991. Selecting Project Managers: An Integrated List of Predictors. *Project Management Journal* 22 (2): 21–26.

Pinto, Jeffrey K., and J. Prescott. 1998. Variations in Success Factors over the Stages in the Project Life Cycle. *Journal of Management* 14 (1): 5–18.

Pinto, Jeffrey K. 1998. *Project Management Handbook*. San Francisco: Jossey-Bass.

Project Management Institute Standards Committee. 1996. *A Guide to the Project Management Body of Knowledge (PMBOK® Guide)*. Upper Darby, PA: Project Management Institute.

Polanyi, Michael. 1958. *Personal Knowledge. Towards a Post-Critical Philosophy*. Chicago: University of Chicago Press.

PROJECT 2000. Norwegian University of Science and Technology. URL: http://www.ntnu.no/ps2000/.

Remy, Ron. 1997. Adding Focus to Improvement Efforts with PM3. *PM Network* (July).

Romme, Georges, and Ron Dillen. 1997. Mapping the Landscape of Organizational Learning. *European Management Journal* 15 (1): 68–78.

Saures, Isabelle. 1998. A Real World Look at Achieving Project Management Maturity. *Project Management Institute 29th Annual Seminars & Symposium*, October 9–15, Long Beach, California.

Senge, Peter M. 1990. *The Fifth Discipline, the Art and Practice of the Learning Organization*. London: Doubleday/Currency.

Senge, Peter M. et al. 1994. *The Fifth Discipline Fieldbook: Strategies and Tools for Building a Learning Organization*. London: Nicholas Brealey Publishing.

———. 1999. *The Dance of Change: The Challenges of Sustaining Momentum in Learning Organizations*. New York: Doubleday/Currency.

Stata, R. 1989. Organizational Learning: The Key to Management Innovation. *Sloan Management Review* 30 (3): 63–74.

Sterman, John D. 1991. A Skeptic's Guide to Computer Models. In *Managing a Nation: The Microcomputer Software Catalo*g (209–229). Edited by G. O. Barney et al. Boulder, CO: Westview Press.

Sveiby, Karl-Erik. 1998. *Measuring Intangibles and Intellectual Capital—An Emerging First Standard*. Internet version August 5.

———. 1999. *The Invisible Balance Sheet: Key Indicators for Accounting, Control and Evaluation of Knowhow Companies*: Konrad Group.

———. 1999. *What is Knowledge Management?* Updated 20 March. URL: http://www.sveiby.com.au/KnowledgeManagement.html.

Thamhain, Hans J. 1991. Developing Project Management Skills. *Project Management Journal* 22 (3): 39–53.

Toney, Frank, and Ray Powers. 1997. *Best Practices of Project Management Groups in Large Functional Organizations—Results of the Fortune 500 Project Management Benchmarking Forum*. Upper Darby, PA: Project Management Institute.

Turner, J. Rodney. 1993. *The Handbook of Project-Based Management*. The Henley Management Series. London: McGraw-Hill.

———. 1998. Projects for Shareholder Value: The Influence of Project Managers. *Proceedings of IRNOP III: The Nature and Role of Projects in the Next 20 Years: Research Issues and Problems*, July, Calgary, Alberta.

———. 2000a. The Global Body of Knowledge, and Its Coverage by the Referees and Members of the International Editorial Board of International Journal of Project Management. *International Journal of Project Management* 18 (1): 1–5.

———. 2000b. The Profession of Project Management: The Role of Professional Institutions and Map of the Body of Knowledge. *Proceedings of IRNOP IV: Paradoxes of Project Collaboration in the Global Economy: Interdependence, Complexity and Ambiguity*, January 9–12, Sydney, Australia.

Voropajev, Vladimir. 1998. Change Management—A Key Integrative Function of PM in Transition Economies. *International Journal of Project Management* 16 (1): 15–19.

Wenger, Etienne. 1998. *Communities of Practice: Learning, Meaning, and Identity*. New York: Cambridge University Press.

Wideman, R. Max. 1997. A Project Management Knowledge Structure for the Next Century. *Proceedings of the 28th Annual Seminars & Symposium*, September 29, Chicago, Illinois.

Wideman, R. Max. 1998. Defining PM Knowledge as a Basis for Global Communication, Learning, and Professionalism. *Proceedings of the 29th Annual Project Management Institute Seminars & Symposium*, October 3–9, Long Beach, California.

CHAPTER 5

WHAT THE UNITED STATES DEFENSE SYSTEMS MANAGEMENT COLLEGE HAS LEARNED FROM TEN YEARS OF PROJECT LEADERSHIP RESEARCH

Owen C. Gadeken, D.Sci., PMP—US Defense Systems Management College

Introduction

The traditional view of project management emphasizes both the technical and management expertise required of project managers. The words by themselves, project and management, imply a technically complex effort for which organization, planning, and control are required. However, an emerging view of the project management profession is that while technical and management expertise are important, the primary role of project managers is to provide the leadership focus on their projects. This is becoming even clearer as current project managers are forced to cope simultaneously with both internal project and external market shifts such as global competition, rapid technological obsolescence, unpredictable organizational transformations, and unstable international political and economic conditions.

Many project managers fail to recognize the shifting role demands over their careers. Most project managers begin their careers with a strong technical or functional focus. By demonstrating their technical abilities, project managers

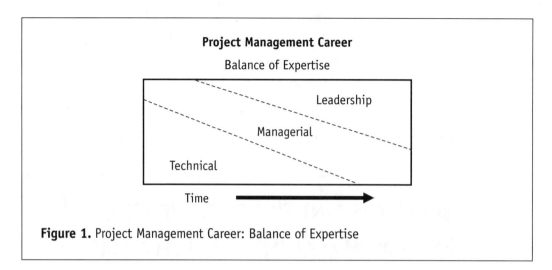

Figure 1. Project Management Career: Balance of Expertise

are frequently promoted to supervise or manage other technical professionals. But when project managers are asked to take on large, complex, or one-of-a-kind projects, technical and management skills alone are not sufficient to ensure success. Leadership skills become the predominant focus. This gradual career evolution toward leadership is depicted in Figure 1. The shifts between the dashed lines from a technical to a managerial and then to a leadership focus are actually quite dramatic and call for significant new skills development. The underlying question to be addressed in this chapter is what are the specific leadership skills required to be successful as a project manager.

While much has been written about leadership in the literature, there is some question about its applicability to project managers. The following excerpt from the classic *War and Peace* (Tolstoy 1993) illustrates the idealized view of military leadership. There would appear to be little here which would apply to project managers.

> Napoleon was standing a little in front of his marshalls, on a little gray horse, wearing the same blue overcoat he had worn throughout the Italian campaign. He was looking intently and silently at the hills, which stood up out of the sea of mist, and the Russian troops moving across them in the distance, and he listened to the sounds of firing in the valley. His face-still thin in those days-did not stir a single muscle; his gleaming eyes were fixed intently on one spot …. When the sun had completely emerged from the fog and was glittering with dazzling brilliance over the fields and the mist (as though he had been waiting for that to begin the battle), he took his glove off his handsome white hand, made a signal with it to his marshalls, and gave the orders for the battle to begin.

Perhaps a more relevant analogy to the project manager's job is found in Dallas, Texas Mayor Erik Jonsson's account of what it is like to be the mayor of a large city (Kotter and Lawrence 1974).

> Being a mayor is like walking on a moving belt while juggling. Right off you've got to walk pretty fast to stay even. After you've been in office a short time, people start throwing wads of paper at you. So now you've got to walk, juggle, and duck too. Then, the belt starts to move faster, and people start to throw wooden blocks at you. About the time you're running like mad, juggling and ducking stones, someone sets one end of the belt on fire. Now, if you can keep the things you are juggling in the air, stay on the belt, put out the fire, and not get seriously injured, you've found the secret to the job.

Although this account matches the crisis management atmosphere of many project management experiences, the question remains as to where leadership can or should be included in the above example.

The nature of the leadership challenge facing defense project managers has been extensively researched by the United States (US) Defense Systems Management College (DSMC) along with other US Defense Acquisition University schools. This chapter summarizes the results of five separate research studies conducted from 1989 to 1999. The first two studies were conducted by DSMC (Cullen and Gadeken 1990; Gadeken 1991). Then, three follow-on validation studies (Best and Kobylarz 1991; McVeigh 1994; Armstrong 1999) were performed by graduate students at the US Air Force Institute of Technology (AFIT) and the US Naval Post Graduate School (NPGS). All of the studies were based on the premise that the best way to find out what it takes to be a good project manager is to analyze a current group of outstanding project managers and identify what they do that makes them so effective. The research studies involved both surveys and in-depth personal interviews of a broad cross-section of project managers as illustrated in Table 1.

This chapter will use the research findings to focus on four key areas which must be considered in developing successful project managers: defining project manager leadership competencies, assessing the leadership competencies, methods of developing these competencies, and selecting project managers who possess the necessary leadership competencies.

The Research Approach

Any job can be considered from two perspectives: tasks and personal competencies. Tasks are a break out of the job itself and are usually defined in terms of the minimum requirements for acceptable performance. By contrast, personal competencies describe what the person brings to the job that allows him to do the job in an outstanding way. These competencies may include motives, traits, aptitudes, knowledge, or skills. For any given job defined as a set of tasks, personal competencies are what superior performers have or do which allow them to achieve superior results.

Year Completed	Conducted by	Target Population	Project Size	Project Interviewed	Managers Surveyed
1990	DSMC	USA (All Services)	Large/Small	52	128
1991	DSMC	UK (All Services)	Large	15	111
1991	AFIT	USA (All Services)	Large	--	53
1994	NPGS	USA (US Army)	Large	7	25
1999	NPGS	USA (US Army)	Large/Small	--	39
			Total	74	356

Table 1. Defense Project Manager Research Studies

A systematic approach to job analysis should consider both tasks and personal competencies, as shown in Figure 2. The inclusion of personal competencies pushes beyond the minimum job requirements to what makes for superior performance. DSMC chose to study personal competencies of project managers rather than use traditional methods like task analysis and expert panels that had been employed in the past. The reasoning is that for more complex jobs, such as project managers in defense acquisition, it is more important to study what each project manager brings to the job that results in outstanding performance. Figures 2, 3, and 4 and Tables 2 and 3 are provided courtesy of Cambria Consulting in Boston, MA who were employed as a support contractor for the initial DSMC research studies (Klemp 1982).

As an example, consider the difference between a capable pilot and a fighter ace. The basic skills of flying can be considered of moderate complexity on the Figure 2 diagram and are probably amenable to a task-analysis approach. On the other hand, a fighter ace or "top-gun" pilot would be difficult to characterize based on tasks alone. This is especially true if you were interested in what differentiates the ace from the other capable pilots in the squadron. This is where the analysis of personal competencies is of most value. One could argue that a project manager's job is on the right side of the complexity scale in Figure 2 along with the fighter ace and, therefore, is also most suitable for analysis of personal competencies.

Using critical incident interviews and detailed follow-up surveys, the selected research process gets beneath espoused theories about what it takes to do a job, to what the best performers actually do. Past studies (Klemp 1982) have shown that job experts are often wrong in their assumptions about what it takes to do a job well. This is illustrated in Tables 2 and 3, which summarize a private sector research

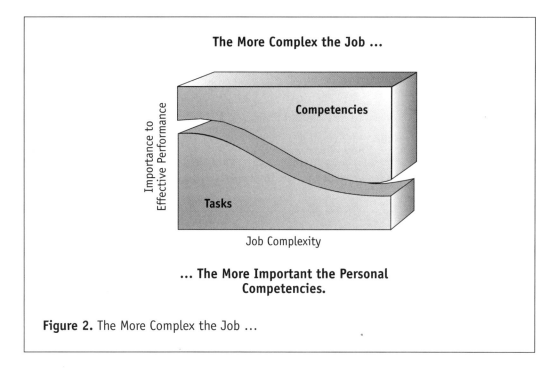

Figure 2. The More Complex the Job ...

study on new product development managers in different divisions of the General Electric Company. At the start of the research project, a panel of company new product development experts was assembled and asked to predict the competencies that would characterize top performers (Table 2). Then, selected top performers from the different divisions (based on results achieved) were interviewed and surveyed. The research findings confirmed only one of the expert panel competencies but found additional competencies the experts had not identified (Table 3).

Even the top performers themselves are often unaware ("unconsciously competent") of what they do that makes them so effective. An interesting example from *Training Magazine* (Gilbert 1988) illustrates this point. Two researchers interviewed the famous American College football Coach Paul "Bear" Bryant at the University of Alabama and asked what he did that made him such a great coach. Coach Bryant stressed recruitment, motivation, and teamwork in his interview. However, instead of immediately writing up the findings from their interview notes, the researchers stayed on for several days and actually observed Coach Bryant in practice sessions and during games. What they found was that Coach Bryant didn't actually do most of the things he alluded to in the interviews. They also discovered other "new" behaviors, such as detailed observation of player performance and immediate feedback, that actually accounted for Coach Bryant's success. As the article states, "exemplary performers differ very little from average ones, but that the differences are enormously valuable" (Gilbert 1988).

The competency research process is outlined in Table 4 and has several benefits. It identifies the characteristics that distinguish outstanding project managers from their contemporaries. The research focuses on the critical few characteristics

New Product Development Managers

What the experts thought:

✔ Senses trends and identifies opportunities

✔ Takes risks

✔ Is creative—able to generate new product ideas

✔ Has knowledge of manufacturing processes

Table 2. The Necessary Competencies (What the Experts Thought)

New Product Development Managers

What the competency research found:

✔ Senses trends and identifies opportunities

✘ Takes risks—but only moderate risks

✘ Is not creative—but recognizes the worth of others' ideas

✘ Knowledge of manufacturing processes did not distinguish top performers

In addition, the research revealed:

✔ Has skill in informal influence

✔ Has skill in facilitating groups

Table 3. The Necessary Competencies (What the Research Found)

that make the most difference in job performance. These characteristics are defined in terms of observable job-related behavior rather than abstract concepts. Finally, the resulting leadership model serves as an excellent communication tool and training model to move organizations toward their goal of creating a cadre of top performing project leaders.

Project Leadership Competencies

With the 1990 DSMC research study as a model (Cullen and Gadeken 1990), the subsequent research studies found a common set of competencies with some variation in rank order. These competencies were characteristics of top performers, and they were not further classified into management or leadership skills. The DSMC study of United Kingdom (UK) defense project managers (Gadeken 1991) validated these same competencies, with UK project managers favoring more of the analytical rather than interpersonal skills. Several underlying themes emerged from the set of competencies found in the research. These themes are

Interviews
- 3 hours focused on 3–5 critical incidents chosen by each project manager
- In-depth reconstruction of actual events
- Emphasis on what each project manager thought, said, and did throughout the process
- Systematic coding of all transcripts for key behaviors

Surveys
- Behaviors grouped into competency themes
- Larger group of project managers asked to rank order competencies
- Extra "dummy" competencies added as distracters

Table 4. Research Process

1. *Are strongly committed to a clear mission.*
2. Have a long-term and big-picture perspective.
3. Are both systematic and innovative thinkers.
4. Find and empower the best people for their project teams.
5. Are selective in their involvement in project issues.
6. Focus on external stakeholders.
7. *Thrive on relationships and influence.*
8. Proactively gather information and insist on results.

Note: Italicized competencies differentiate top performers

Table 5. The Best Project Managers

listed in Table 5 and discussed next along with selected quotes from the project manager interviews.

1. Strong Commitment to a Clear Mission

Top performing project managers are first and foremost mission focused and results oriented. They take personal ownership of their projects in a manner almost approaching the quest of a champion fighting for a just cause. They model their personal commitment with such dedication and enthusiasm that it permeates their project team, external customers, and support organizations. Here is the way one Air Force civilian project manager described the project goal to his team:

> Remember your primary mission. Keep saying that to yourself. Your job is to field a system that will put electrons on the (enemy). Everything else is incidental to that and not important.

In the words of one Army project manager:

> I felt frustrated. But at the same time I feel like it is such good thing we are doing for the Army that it is worth all the frustration and hard work and whatever else we need to do to make it successful.

2. Long-Term and Big-Picture Perspective

The best project managers interpret events from a big-picture (mission) perspective with an eye toward future consequences of immediate decisions. As one Navy project manager said:

> We were heading to a point where, although it was years away from happening, things would start to diverge. But action needed to be taken right then and there, so that ... we would have enough canisters to go around and support the missile base. That was the driving factor in what I was doing.

Another Army project manager stated that as a project manager, you must maintain a:

> big-picture focus—keep the whole effort, along with the people involved, in focus, not letting the day-to-day details and tasks become more important than the overarching goal.

3. Systematic and Innovative Thinkers

Outstanding project managers are both systematic and innovative thinkers. They understand the complex and rapidly changing environment in which they must work. Further, they are able to see through this complexity to provide a structure for sound decision-making as well as a point of departure for more innovative solution options. In the words of Admiral Carlisle Trost, a former Chief of Naval Operations:

> Figuring out what is going on in a complex world is the heart of leadership. Otherwise leaders are defeated by events they do not understand.

Today's project managers are expected to "think outside the box" to provide a better system or better value for money. As one Army project manager adamantly stated:

> If something is not prohibited by law or regulation or can be waivered, and it will benefit your project, then do it! Push the system until it cries out in pain to get what is needed to make your project successful!

4. Find and Empower the Best People

The best project managers are masters of working with and through others. They focus their efforts on finding the best people for their project teams and then let them handle the myriad of decisions and details that epitomize even the most basic projects. As one project manager noted:

> The first thing you do is get the right people. My contractors have made an observation. They told me I don't have many people here but the ones I've got are terrific. And, that's exactly the way they were picked.

Another Army project manager described how he assessed and then leveraged the strengths of his staff:

> I believe that it is imperative for the PM (project manager) to know the unique capabilities of each staff member, and then ensure that each staff member is placed in the position that will make the best use of those capabilities. The PM must then understand what it takes to motivate these individuals to the point that each achieves more than he or she thought possible.

5. Selective Involvement in Project Issues

Effective project managers do not try to do everything themselves. They typically focus on a few strategically important areas, leaving the mass of administrative and technical matters to subordinates. This is most clearly illustrated in the DSMC research interviews, which focused on critical incidents selected by the project managers. Of the 285 critical incidents, over half were concentrated in just four functional areas: contracting (sixty-two), personnel management (forty-two), test and evaluation (thirty-one), and acquisition strategy (i.e., project planning) (twenty-six).

As one Army project manager put it:

> You must realize, you can't do everything yourself. People are your most precious asset!

This Air Force colonel clearly reveals his willingness to delegate:

> My role in the restructuring was to task the organization, to work with the user and with the contractor to come up with this program. I never got involved with the details. That is not my job.

6. Focus on External Stakeholders

While outstanding project managers craft effective project teams, they also spend considerable time networking with external customers and support organizations. The number of external stakeholders who can potentially impact a project is huge. Thus, project managers must determine who the key players are and what is important to them. One Army project manager commented:

> The project manager is always operating outside of his controlled environment. In fact, very seldom is a project manager huddled around with all the people just from his project office.

Another Army project managers stated:

> Without cooperation from the large number of people and organizations who make up the acquisition process no project will go forward.

7. Thrive on Relationships and Influence

Since project managers have no formal power over these external stakeholders, they must rely on their ability to cultivate relationships and use influence strategies to achieve their objectives. This Navy project manager traveled overseas not only to solve a fielding problem, but more importantly to develop an ongoing relationship with his customers in the fleet:

> I made a trip to Scotland as a damage control effort, if you will, to talk to the squadron people and that kind of thing. To talk to them after having spent a lot of time and being kind of a nuisance to everybody ... with these modifications which now didn't work. My credibility was zero. I tried to restore our credibility. We really did want to help them out. I think they were surprised to see a four-striped captain come all the way from Washington DC to talk about their problems.

This UK project manager found himself in a very difficult situation on a joint project with the US Navy and used his political savvy to get out of it.

> I would tread on people's toes because the US project manager didn't want me speaking directly to his folks who are in the Pentagon, although I couldn't work without that. So I got around that by holding the meetings in the British Embassy and inviting him to come to our "foreign territory." Whatever happened, I would just look for a way around it. It was just—it just became a game actually, of trying to unravel all the pressure groups.

To reverse a potentially devastating budget cut, this Army project manager knew who to involve, at what point and why:

> I finally recognized that I needed heavy hitters with more influence and authority than I had, so I set up a meeting with the program executive office, the head of procurement, my staff, an attorney advisor, and the Army's contract policy expert. In other words, I had to go in there and literally stack the deck in terms of influence and independent representatives who would vouch for what I had said.

8. Proactively Gather Information and Insist on Results

The best project managers constantly probe for information and push for results. This project manager used his own questioning technique to insure that information he received was accurate.

At this meeting, I asked the contractor what they knew about the subcontractor status. You know, where precisely are they? What are their plans to do this? With each answer, I would just ask one question, I would just ask one question deeper than that. When they started to stutter, I knew they were in trouble because I shouldn't be able to go that one level deeper and ask a question they can't answer.

Finally, successful project managers must produce results. As this project manager concluded:

Everything you do [as a project manager] has got to be focused on results, results, results.

Relative Importance of the Competencies

The initial DSMC research study (Cullen and Gadeken 1990) was the only one with a large enough interview sample to allow for subgroup comparisons. With the interest in top performers, the research team asked the sponsoring military organizations to identify the very best project managers from those who had been interviewed. An assessment of each project manager by their project team was correlated with the senior rater nominations. This split the group of fifty-two interviewed project managers approximately in half.

Statistical comparisons were then done on the frequency data for each competency (i.e., number of times each competency appeared in the interview transcript). The results of this analysis were that competencies 1, Strong Commitment to a Clear Mission, and 7, Thrive on Relationships and Influence, were demonstrated, with statistical validity more often by the top performing project managers than by their contemporaries. So these competencies were listed in *italics* in Table 5 to denote their greater importance to effective project leadership.

Validation Surveys

An interesting finding from the DSMC study (Cullen and Gadeken 1990) emerged from the comparison of importance rankings of specific competencies by project managers with ranking from other acquisition professionals (functional managers from different specialty areas such as contracting, budgeting, engineering, and logistics). This comparison is illustrated in Table 6. It is clear that there are some significant differences in the competency rankings between the two groups (as noted by the arrows between the columns). The acquisition professionals (functional managers) considered technical expertise, attention to detail, and creativity (defined as developing novel technical solutions) as far more important than did project managers.

On the other hand, project managers rated sense of ownership/mission, political awareness, and strategic influence much higher than functional managers did. An underlying issue emerges from the difference in competency requirements for project managers and functional specialists: the transition from functional specialist to project manager may be conceptually quite difficult. A review of the literature (Gadeken 1986) supports this conclusion, especially for scientists and engineers who currently make up the bulk of defense project managers.

Competency Assessment

Assessing project managers' ability to perform critical management and leadership skills is a difficult proposition. However, assessment techniques have emerged in recent years that are quite useful. Tailored survey assessment instruments can be created and given to the project manager's supervisor, peers, and subordinates asking for their assessment of both past performance and future potential in selected competency areas. This "360° feedback" (from above, at the same level, and below in the organization) has rapidly gained momentum in both US public and private sector organizations. Several commercially developed multi-rater instruments are now available. Most feature computer scoring, automated feedback (report) generation, and even tailoring of items to fit the individuals and organization using the instruments.

Another useful method is the critical incident interview process used in DSMC's competency research. Here, the project manager is asked to recount several significant prior job situations of their own choosing. In each situation, the interviewer listens and probes for detail, seeking to identify which competencies the individual has used (and not used) in the past. Such discussions often cut through generic statements of capability and accomplishment to what project manager actually did in real-life situations.

Experiential exercises and behavioral simulations are ideally suited to assess leadership and management competencies. These exercises vary from short role-playing scenarios requiring minimal preparation, to more elaborate behavioral simulations with several participants, each provided with a detailed in-basket of background information. Project managers can be put into these realistic situations and asked to respond, not by stating what they would do in the situations, but by actually doing it. Participants then step aside and become students of their own behavior through follow-up discussions including feedback from trainers and other participants. Assessment instruments and behavioral checklists can also be used to augment the personal feedback provided.

Clearly, no project manager career development model is complete without a credible competency assessment process.

Competency Development

Even with effective assessment and selection processes, further improvement of critical project manager skills is desirable for all project managers, even the most competent. Efforts to achieve this improvement should be directed both on the job and in the series of professional training opportunities that may be available or sponsored by the organization. Several self-development and training method-

Note: Identical Numbers = Tie Scores	Rank Order of Importance	
	Project Managers	Other Acq. Prof.
COMPETENCIES	(N = 128)	(N = 225)
Sense of Ownership/Mission	1 ←	17
Long-Term Perspective	2	6
Managerial Orientation	3	2
Political Awareness	4 ←	21
Optimizing	5	5
Results Orientation	6	8
Systematic Thinking	7	3
Innovativeness/Initiative	8	11
Focus on Excellence	9	9
Action Orientation	10	10
Relationship Development	10	14
Coaches Others	12	12
Proactive Information Gathering	13	15
Strategic Influence	14 ←	23
Creativity	15 →	3
Self-Control	15	13
Interpersonal Assessment	17	18
Collaborative Influence	18	16
Critical Inquiry	18	24
Positive Expectations	20	24
Technical Expertise	21 →	1
Interpersonal Sensitivity	22	22
Attention to Detail	22 →	7
Assertiveness	24	20
Efficiency Orientation	25	18
Directive Influence	26	26
Competitiveness	27	27

Table 6. Survey Validation of Project Management Competencies

ologies exist which can be adapted for this purpose. These include the competency assessment instrument and critical incident interview described above.

Case studies have also proven effective in addressing project manager competencies when imbedded in established training programs. Case studies based on past projects can bring the real-world dimension to the classroom and provide additional focus on project manager unique skill requirements. Several such real-work cases have been developed by DSMC and are now used in the curriculum.

Experiential exercises can add the behavioral dimension to the classroom environment. Here, understanding is only the first step in mastering the complex set of project manager competencies. In his book *The Competent Manager*, noted management researcher Dr. Richard Boyatzis states (Boyatzis 1982):

> Too often training programs attempt to teach the fundamentals using lectures, readings, case discussions, films, and dynamic speakers to transfer knowledge to course participants. Unfortunately, it is usually not the lack of knowledge, but the inability to use knowledge that limits effective managerial behavior.

To focus on this application of knowledge, DSMC uses several experiential exercises (Gadeken 1989, 1994) in its project management courses. They range from short team-building exercises to the elaborate Advanced Unmanned Ground Vehicle (AUGV) which features development of a small remotely controlled model vehicle with programmable software. This exercise covers the entire project life cycle with student work groups acting as project teams.

Project Manager Selection

Selection of US defense project managers is currently conducted by special panels in the military services. Although future potential is considered, most of the evaluation is, of necessity, based on the candidates' performance in their prior jobs. Project manager candidates are given in-depth training (three courses totaling twenty weeks as a minimum) covering project management functional disciplines. The assumption here is that these project managers have already acquired the necessary leadership and management competencies through their prior work and supervisory experience. This assumption appears to be flawed based on the conclusion made earlier in this chapter that there are several unique project manager competencies not normally developed by more junior project management professionals.

An alternate selection approach might be to use the current selection process based on knowledge and experience and then train the project manager candidates in the critical leadership and management competencies. While this approach appears attractive, it ignores basic limitations of the training process (Figure 3). Specialized knowledge can easily be imparted in a training environment even under time constraints (a few days). However, leadership and management competencies are by their nature complex and are generally developed only with time and experience perhaps over an entire career.

Thus, the preferred alternative for project manager selection is to assess which candidates have or can more readily develop the critical leadership and management competencies identified in this research. Training can then be provided or tailored in project management functional disciplines (knowledge areas) to augment the candidates' prior knowledge and experience base. This training is much more likely to succeed than a training program to develop critical leadership and management competencies in candidates lacking such skills.

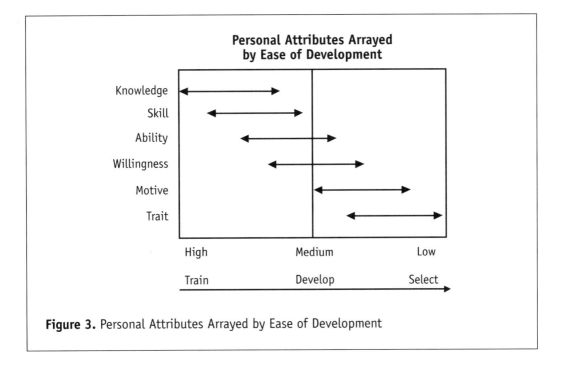

Figure 3. Personal Attributes Arrayed by Ease of Development

A project manager selection process focused on the critical leadership competencies should have a multiplier effect on project results over time as illustrated in Figure 4. Although candidates possessing the critical personal competencies (but lacking experience) may start off as less productive, they will rapidly overtake their less competent but more experienced counterparts in the organization.

Future Research and Applications

As this research has shown, defense project managers require a unique set of competencies focused extensively on managerial and leadership skills. Future research should be done to confirm that these competencies apply equally to other public and private sector project-based organizations. Further research is recommended to investigate the relevance and distribution of these competencies among the members of successful project teams. Additional research is also suggested on how to apply these competencies within the framework of organizations' human resource and career development programs.

This research could be of considerable value for those organizations that wish to move beyond basic certification of project managers to create a talent pool of top performing project management professionals. These research results could aid in setting up the criteria for both selection and professional development of this more highly skilled workforce.

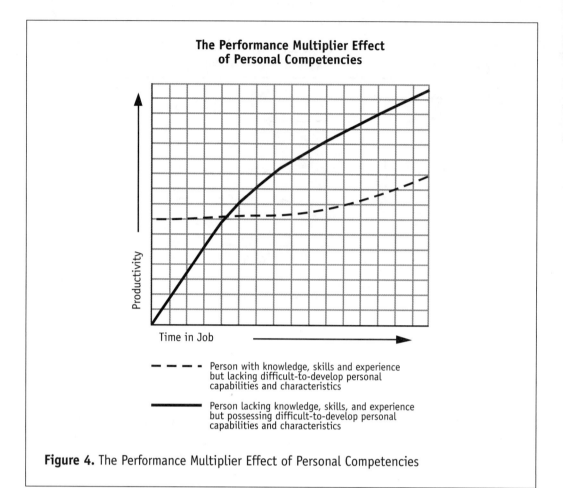

Figure 4. The Performance Multiplier Effect of Personal Competencies

Conclusions

The role of the project manager has and will continue to be the corner stone of effective project-based organizations. From an organizational perspective, considerable planning and attention must be applied now to ensure that future project managers will have the prerequisite skills. This includes carefully structuring processes for selection, assessment, and development of project managers with the specialized management and leadership skills required to succeed in the complex global environment that awaits them.

References

Armstrong, Scott C. 1999. *A Reassessment of Army Program Manager Competencies*. Master's thesis, Naval Post Graduate School, Monterey, CA.

Best, Gregory D., and Korina L. Kobylarz. 1991. *Establishing a Department of Defense Program Management Body of Knowledge*. Master's thesis, Air Force Institute of Technology, Wright-Patterson Air Force Base, OH.

Boyatzis, Richard E. 1982. *The Competent Manager: A Model for Effective Performance*. New York: Wiley-Interscience.

Cullen, Bernard J., and Owen C. Gadeken. 1990. *A Competency Model of Program Managers in the DoD Acquisition Process*. Fort Belvoir, VA: Defense Systems Management College.

Gadeken, Owen C. 1986. Why Engineers and Scientists Often Fail as Managers (and What to Do About It). *Program Manager* (January–February): 37–45.

———. 1989. DSMC Simulations (Games That Teach Engineers and Scientists How to Manage). *Program Manager* (May–June): 29–39.

———. 1991. *Competencies of Project Managers in the MOD Procurement Executive*. Shrivenham, England: Royal Military College of Science (Technical Report).

———. 1994. Developing Project Leadership Skills Using Behavioral Simulations. *Proceedings of the 1994 Project Management Institute (PMI) National Conference*, Vancouver, Canada.

Gilbert, Thomas F., and B. Marilyn. 1988. The Science of Winning. *Training* (August): 33–40.

Klemp, George O. 1982. Job Competency Assessment: Defining Attributes of the Top Performer. *Pig and the Python and Other Tales*. American Society for Training and Development, Research Series No. 8.

Kotter, John P., and Paul R. Lawrence. 1974. *Mayors in Action: Five Approaches to Urban Governance*. New York: Wiley-Interscience.

McVeigh, Bryan J. 1994. *Army Program Managers: A Competency Perspective*. Master's thesis, Naval Post Graduate School, Monterey, CA.

Tolstoy, Leo. 1993. *War and Peace*. Reprint. New York: Barnes & Noble Books.

CHAPTER 6

UNITED STATES DEFENSE ACQUISITION RESEARCH PROGRAM: A NEW LOOK

Mark E. Nissen, Ph.D.—Naval Postgraduate School
Keith F. Snider, Ph.D.—Naval Postgraduate School
Ira A. Lewis, Ph.D.—Naval Postgraduate School

Acquisition represents a critical process to the United States (US) Department of Defense (DoD), but the acquisition process suffers from neglect. Although acquisition in the DoD is moving to reflect best commercial practices, we face a novel and rapidly changing military environment that calls for new acquisition processes. But the current DoD is ill equipped to develop such new acquisition processes, as they require new knowledge. This condition calls for research, as the researcher's primary motivation is knowledge creation. The DoD Acquisition Research Program addresses this condition directly. Sponsored by the US Defense Acquisition University, and managed by the US Naval Postgraduate School (NPS), this program explicitly targets top researchers from leading institutions to engage in high-level, high-quality acquisition research. Taking a broad, multidisciplinary approach, this research program—now in its third year—is effectively engaging prominent academics to address topics of interest to the acquisition practitioner, policy maker, and researcher. This chapter outlines key aspects of the DoD Acquisition Research Program.

Introduction

Acquisition may be viewed as a process that transforms user needs into products, services, and the information required to satisfy those needs. It pertains to the strategy, planning, procurement, contracting, program management, logistics, and other activities required to develop, produce, and support systems and other materiel required to accomplish the mission of an enterprise (Nissen, Snider, and Lamm 1998). A more concise description is simply the process employed to satisfy enterprise materiel requirements.

Although in the US acquisition is often described in the context of weapon system development (e.g., in support of the defense mission), the breadth of this term indicates it does not apply solely to the US Department of Defense (DoD). Rather, we consider it axiomatic that the acquisition process occurs in similar ways in the various domains of defense, the broader public sector, and the private sector. Thus, though there may be some differences in the ways it is manifested in a particular domain, acquisition's theories and practices are generally relevant for enterprises in the public and private sectors alike.

The field of project management has strong historical ties to acquisition, and many consider it to represent the most important acquisition area. Many writers locate project management's roots in the large, highly complex weapons projects, such as the Manhattan project and aerospace projects that were undertaken during and following World War II (Acker 1993, 4–5; Przemieniecki 1993, 13). Project management concepts, methods, and organizations became the means by which DoD attempted to exploit and integrate scientific and technological advances in increasingly capable and complex weapon systems that often took many years to design, develop, and produce. And project management soon became the focus of DoD training programs in acquisition. Today, the design, development, and production of almost all major defense systems proceed under project or program management.

Because acquisition and project management are so closely connected, researchers in each area have many concerns in common. In this chapter we describe the origins, purpose, and operations of the DoD External Acquisition Research Program (EARP). Our purpose is to inform project management researchers of the details of this program in order to facilitate the exchange of ideas among scholars of both communities on the pressing research needs of the new millennium.

Acquisition Criticality

Acquisition represents a process that is critical to the survival of commercial and defense enterprises alike. Despite this critical role, however, acquisition has long been subordinated to other processes with respect to executive attention, funding, innovation, and other key enterprise attributes. In the DoD, funding and prioritization arguments have relied on the "tooth vs. tail" metaphor. That is, under financial constraints, organizations give priority to combatants and weapons (the "teeth") over procurement, program management, and even logistics. Corporate America has also relied on this same argument. In the past, few corporations would hesitate to shift discretionary spending from Quality Assurance to Manufacturing, from Customer Service to Marketing, or from Purchasing to Research and Development (R&D).

Now, progressive firms are shifting their emphasis and priorities as they recognize the criticality of traditional "tail" processes. For example, industry discovered in the '80s that quality represents a critical performance factor, and that emphasizing quality can actually *save* cost and *reduce* cycle time. The need for change is particularly evident in R&D, the fundamental mechanism for new product and service development for the hierarchy (see Williamson 1985 for a comparison of markets and hierarchies). Drucker (1998) claims product innovations may take as long as fifty years to reach and affect the market. Such a lengthy period of time clearly limits a firm's agility, flexibility, and responsiveness to unforeseen changes in the environment and competitive arena (Porter 1985). Thus, we now observe strategic networks between organizations, decreased process cost and cycle time, increased flexibility and agility, and a host of other signals that radical change has indeed occurred.

Progressive firms have made radical changes in acquisition processes due to widespread supply-chain integration, just-in-time inventory practices, virtual organizations (Davidow and Malone 1992), electronic markets (Malone et al. 1987), mass customization (Pine et al. 1993), and other contemporary business practices. For example, the procurement focus has shifted away from short-term transactions and toward strategic relationships. Although price is still vitally important, it is no longer necessarily more so than capability, quality, reliability, and trustworthiness. In today's era of hypercompetition (D'Aveni 1994), global operations, and exploding information, progressive companies realize the environment has shifted abruptly and are effecting radical change where called for.

The DoD is also now recognizing acquisition's criticality, as evidenced by a new emphasis on commercial off-the-shelf (COTS) equipment and software, simplified regulations, and a preference for commercial specifications and standards (FASA 1994, FARA 1996). And the DoD acquisition regulation is modeled on "sound business practices" (Department of Defense 2001). Increasing partnerships with industry (see Cole 1997), less reliance on a shrinking defense-unique industrial base (Gansler 1998), process reengineering (Nissen 1997), electronic commerce, and other advanced initiatives are now occurring in the DoD (Bryan 1998) with much the same intensity as in industry a few years back. Indeed, realizing the importance of acquisition, a former Secretary of Defense challenged the acquisition workforce to effect a 50 percent reduction in the cycle time required to develop and field major weapon systems (Perry 1994). This represents a call for radical change of reengineering proportions (Hammer and Champy 1993).

The "tooth vs. tail" argument from above is clearly outdated. Regardless of the number and size of one's teeth, one can run only as fast and as long as one's tail allows. Notwithstanding the success in the Gulf War, for example, armored units were restrained by the logistical chain. Even the theater information systems were critically dependent on relationships with commercial vendors for equipment, software, and bandwidth in the region. A former Secretary of Defense recently acknowledged that acquisition (especially procurement and logistics) now limits battlefield information, mobility, and speed (Cohen 1997). Thus, in much the same way that the scope and pace of change have elevated acquisition to a level of strategic importance in industry, the acquisition process has become strategic to the military. This represents a radical concept for the DoD, a concept that calls for revolution in defense acquisition as well as in military affairs. To manage such radical organizational change, it is clear to the authors that simplistic, "quick-fix" approaches or recirculating old ideas under new labels will not suffice. Rather, substantial new acquisition knowledge is required, and it is required now.

Acquisition Research

At present, we perceive a critical need to catalyze a quantum increase in the quality and quantity of new acquisition knowledge produced through scholarly research. Although research represents only one of several important knowledge sources—others include, for example, professional practice, trial and error, lessons learned—it is arguably the most neglected at present and the most critical for the future, particularly at this time when "out of the box" thinking and radical process redesign are called for.

Need for Acquisition Research

In his classic work, Kuhn (1970) describes the idea of "revolutionary science" as exemplified by the "paradigm shifts" from Newtonian to Einsteinian physics, or from Ptolemaic to Copernican astronomy. Such revolutions can occur, according to Kuhn, as evolving conditions lead to situations for which the extant paradigm simply cannot account. It seems likely to us that acquisition stands on the threshold of such a paradigm shift. Earlier we noted the heritage of US defense acquisition in the post-World War II, Cold War environment. Recent acquisition reform initiatives notwithstanding, many of the laws, policies, regulations, and practices that govern present-day acquisition are products of the Cold War mindset. Given the fundamental changes of the past decade, we question whether that particular paradigm can long endure.

As the US enters the twenty-first century, it confronts a new military environment characterized by expanding mission requirements, declining defense funds, and the absence of a monolithic superpower threat. This environment has drastically changed the face of acquisition. For example, policy initiatives associated with "reengineering" and "downsizing" are blurring the traditional distinctions between the public and private sectors' acquisition roles in several ways. First, new public-private partnerships may be radically reshaping our view of the proper relationship between government and industry. To illustrate, recent plans called for a government weapons facility at Rock Island Arsenal, Illinois to produce items, in effect as a subcontractor, to United Defense Limited Partnership, the industry consortium under contract to develop the Army's new Crusader howitzer system. Second, the nature of government contracting is changing in significant ways. The government now relies far less on detailed and restrictive specifications and standards, choosing instead to communicate only broad objectives with the details left to industry discretion. We even see evidence of a trend away from strict reliance on contracts in the increased use of simplified agreements—so-called "other transactions"—between government and industry. Perhaps most significantly, functions that previously were performed almost exclusively by DoD—logistics support for weapon systems, for example—are now increasingly being "contracted out" to private industry.

Such changes call for new acquisition processes. The nature, scope, and pace of change required to effectively transform these acquisition processes imply that new knowledge will be required. Change of such magnitude and speed is unprecedented within the defense acquisition system; hence leaders cannot simply reuse old ideas and techniques. Rather, these new processes require new knowledge—theoretical knowledge to guide high-level policy and decision-making; applied knowledge to support transition and execution in the new acquisition environment; reliable, generalizable, cumulative knowledge to leverage problem solutions across many defense programs and avoid redundancy or duplication. New acquisition knowledge such as this calls for research, as the researcher's primary motivation is knowledge creation (e.g., discovery research).

Without research of a relatively fundamental, loosely applied nature, it is next to impossible to achieve paradigm shift, and it would be inconceivable that such a shift could occur through incremental changes in acquisition practice alone (i.e., without research). Researchers provide a unique ability to generalize from experiences. They build cumulatively upon the work of others (what Kuhn calls "normal science") and employ rigorous methods to ensure high validity and reliability of their results. Indeed, only research that stretches the boundaries of current knowledge can be used to leverage solutions across entire *classes* of problems (e.g., through new theory) and to adapt effective solutions induced from one process or program to many others. And academics are trained to design experiments and employ rigorous research methods that isolate effects and minimize the cost of knowledge creation. Such research requires careful planning and preparation and is time-consuming. But it minimizes exposure to failure from trial and error (e.g., as with professional practice, on-the-job training, lessons learned) and maximizes the impact and dependability of results per unit cost. Thus, academic research is efficient as well as effective at knowledge creation. By building on the cumulative work of others, researchers are able to avoid the redundancy, duplication, and waste that plagues many current acquisition reform efforts in practice. Of course, research also feeds education, training, consulting, and ultimately professional practice itself, as new knowledge creation (i.e., research) sits at the top of the knowledge "food chain."

State of Acquisition Research—Quantity

Despite acquisition's critical role and its changing nature in the defense domain, research in acquisition has been sorely neglected. Scholars outside of the DoD community have for the most part simply ignored acquisition as an area of inquiry. To illustrate, a review of titles for the 100-plus panels conducted at the year 2000 annual conference of the American Society for Public Administration revealed no presentations or papers dealing with acquisition. Such inattention may be attributed in part to society's, and hence academe's, historical tendency to draw distinctions between military and civilian matters, and to the separate identity of the military created by its unique role and ethic. These can lead to ignorance— perhaps even a distrust or fear—of military matters among non-government scholars (Jefferies 1977). At the very least, such perceptions indicate to scholars that "defense is different," and thus they inhibit consideration of similarities between the defense and non-defense domains of acquisition.

As for the few civilian scholars who have attended to acquisition, some are highly critical and some take a more balanced perspective. The critics usually focus on the highly politically charged atmosphere of major weapon system acquisition. Their characterizations of acquisition as an often irrational process are evident in their works' titles, such as *The Pentagon Paradox* (Stevenson 1993), *Foregone Conclusions* (Lebovic 1996), and *Weapons Without a Cause* (Farrell 1997). Scholars taking the more balanced approach are represented by Thompson and Jones (1994), Fox (1974, 1988), and Mayer (1991). Other researchers write on topics that, while not "acquisition-specific," are central to acquisition. Aaron Wildavsky's (1969) work in budgeting and policy analysis is but one example.

Within DoD, the potential benefits of acquisition research have long been recognized (Strayer and Lockwood 1975), yet little substantive research has emerged from DoD sources. Past attempts to enhance acquisition research include establishment of the Army Procurement Research Office in 1969, the Procurement Research Coordinating Committee in 1971, the Federal Acquisition Research Symposia in 1972, the Air Force Business Research Management Center in 1973, the Federal Acquisition Institute, and the Naval Center for Acquisition Research in 1977 (Office of Management and Budget 1980). We speculate that the general ineffectiveness of these efforts is attributable to the dominant Cold War acquisition paradigm under which they were all undertaken. That is, because the underlying assumptions regarding threats, missions, budgets, and so on remained stable, new knowledge (as derived by research) received little value and priority.

DoD's institutions for education and training have also contributed little to acquisition research. Dedicated acquisition curricula are relatively new additions to the respective graduate schools of the Navy and the Air Force. In the past, the faculties have focused on the task of preparing students for acquisition jobs, rather than on research. At acquisition training institutions like the Defense Systems Management College, a few programs of research in acquisition are ongoing, such as the biennial Acquisition Research Symposia, the Military Research Fellowship Program, and a program of Research on Acquisition Research (Abellera 1993).

A need for acquisition research in DoD was reflected in the legislation that established the Defense Acquisition University (DAU). The Defense Acquisition Workforce Improvement Act, enacted in 1990, gave DAU the charter to lead the training and education of acquisition professionals, and it also provided for a research function in DAU. Understandably, DAU's focus during its first several years was on training and education, with little attention being given to research. In 1994, DAU began publishing a refereed journal, *Acquisition Review Quarterly*. To date, the great majority of articles have been practitioner-oriented works, such as tutorials, "lessons learned" papers, and opinion pieces, rather than papers with theoretical rigor.

State of Acquisition Research—Quality

Exacerbating this situation of the general lack of acquisition research is the fact that much of what is currently performed within DoD tends to be very applied in nature and lacks research rigor. This is not to imply that applied research is less valuable than basic or exploratory work, but research is governed by a well-understood maxim: the more applied the work, the more narrow the benefits of its results. By contrast, the more fundamental the work, the wider the coverage of benefits. Further, unless research is conducted with the kind of rigor demanded by top academic journals, the results risk duplication with previous efforts (e.g., if not guided by a thorough literature review), confounding of causal effects (e.g., not being able to assess a particular result to decisions made or actions taken), non-generalizability (e.g., results that apply only to the specific case, process, program or system studied), and other threats to validity (e.g., rival hypotheses, concept invalidity, unreliability) (Campbell and Stanley 1973, Yin 1994).

Research that tends to be very applied in nature and which is conducted with little rigor is classified as "1-1" and "2-2" work using the research framework depicted in Figure 1 (Nissen, Snider, and Lamm 1998). Briefly, on the horizontal axis we have the fundamentalism or "basicness" of the research, which corresponds roughly to the standard research categories used in the DoD—management and support, engineering development, advanced development, exploratory research, and basic research (Fox 1974, 22). As depicted by the five-point scale for this axis, work toward the extreme end of the scale characterizes research of a more fundamental and general nature that seeks to solve broad classes of problems in a domain of investigation.

As research moves toward the origin along this dimension (i.e., becomes increasingly applied), the associated research takes on a narrower, more specific, shorter-term character. This helps to depict the natural migration of research from the basic and exploratory development of new knowledge toward management and applied work as research in an area matures. This dynamic pattern also highlights the need for systematic introduction of new knowledge and ideas—that *derive* from more-fundamental investigations—through applied research. Indeed, without such fundamental (e.g., basic, exploratory, developmental) research, a program based solely on applied work will eventually stagnate and regress into a

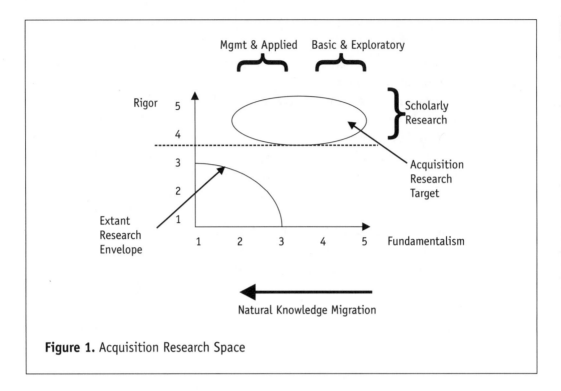

Figure 1. Acquisition Research Space

pattern characterized by recirculation of old ideas. In fact, a number of scholars perceive this pathological pattern exists in the acquisition domain today (Williams and Arvis 1985).

Returning to the research space diagrammed in Figure 1, the ordinate is used to depict the methodological rigor associated with research (in any category, basic or applied). This five-point scale is used to classify the increasing use of high-confidence research methods that leave decreasing margin for refutation of the results. For example, work at level 1 (i.e., lowest level of rigor) may involve an "investigator" who is not even objectively detached from the work being studied (e.g., a knowledge worker simply reporting the results of his acquisition work). At level 2, an *independent* investigator is at least in a position to objectively observe and describe some acquisition phenomenon of interest. At level 3, this independent investigator conducts a thorough *literature review* in a particular area, in order to avoid duplicating previous results and to focus on the kinds of high-payoff research targets and topics that can only be identified through an understanding of, and appreciation for, previous work in a research area. At level 4, this investigator ensures *reliability* and *generalizability* of the results by employing a well-founded research design (e.g., multiple case study, factorial, stratified survey). At level 5, the researcher may even employ *experimental* (or quasi-experimental) methods—like those stressed in the physical sciences—in order to promote the highest levels of confidence in the results.

Two main points emerge from this diagram. First, the majority of extant research in the acquisition domain would be classified near the origin of this

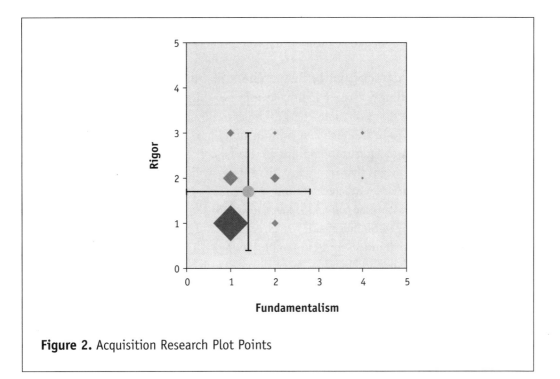

Figure 2. Acquisition Research Plot Points

research space, as depicted by the "extant research envelope" in Figure 1. This tends to represent just POK (plain old knowledge) work and specialized consulting, more than what most academics would even consider to constitute "research," and it suffers from high refutability and lack of generalization. Although the contribution of such work is positive, it is minimal in that it tends to address only one specific problem at a time, is often redundant with previous or parallel work and offers results confounded by poor methodology. This arguably represents a suboptimal allocation of scarce research resources. Second, any acquisition research—whether basic or applied—needs to be scholarly to overcome the refutability and generalization problems from above. These points are used to establish the acquisition target research area depicted above the horizontal, "scholarly research" line in the figure.

As empirical evidence of these claims, we examined some seventy articles published from the Acquisition Research Symposium (Brown 1997). It represents a principal outlet for acquisition research in the US. Using the same two-dimensional research space described above, we present the results from categorizing these papers in Figure 2. Notice the mean (denoted by a small circle icon) falls within the "2-2" quadrant, and the 90 percent confidence ellipsoid (delineated in two dimensions by lines extending outward from the mean) indicates the average acquisition research paper falls within the ("3-3") extant research envelope delineated above. Indeed, only three papers fall outside this envelope, and no paper crosses the "scholarly" threshold at level 4 along the rigor axis. Another point pertains to the modal value (denoted by the largest diamond icon in the chart): it lies squarely at the "1-1" point. In other words, this empirical evidence suggests the characteristic (i.e., modal) acquisition research paper reflects "1-1" research.

How to Attract Quality Researchers in Quantity?

The preceding discussion indicates the pressing need surrounding the current state of acquisition research: to engage scholars who can perform high quality (i.e., at "4" or "5" levels) research in quantities sufficient to generate knowledge and understanding of acquisition appropriate for its contemporary problems. Satisfying this need means that researchers in leading civilian institutions must be actively sought out and attracted by some means to this work. It also implies that these researchers must be convinced that the defense domain of acquisition is not in fact "different," but rather that it represents a fruitful area for study and for extending their research into exciting and important new directions. To these ends, the DAU has established the External Acquisition Research Program (EARP).

External Acquisition Research Program

The EARP is sponsored by the DAU and managed by the NPS. The mission of the EARP is to dramatically increase the quality and quantity of acquisition research, in addition to expanding the base of researchers interested in topics germane to defense acquisition and producing new, relevant knowledge, solutions, and technologies from a variety of disciplines. The program targets the top researchers at leading universities outside the DoD and its customary sphere of influence and support, but is open to all institutions capable of top-quality acquisition research. To summarize, the EARP has been designed to focus on seven principal objectives.

1. Raise the quality and quantity of relevant acquisition research.
2. Catalyze a broad and robust external acquisition research program.
3. Involve top researchers and institutions in research germane to defense acquisition.
4. Augment and complement current acquisition research activities.
5. Disseminate relevant, impactful results to researchers, policy-makers, and practitioners.
6. Integrate research with education, training, and practice in acquisition.
7. Establish and maintain a community of academic and professional acquisition scholars.

University Focus

One obvious approach to the problems noted above is to get trained academics from leading universities involved in acquisition research. Although few universities aside from the NPS have specific groups or departments that are devoted to *acquisition* research today, relevant work can be obtained from a number of potential reference disciplines, including (alphabetically) Economics, Finance, Information Systems, Law, Logistics, Operations Research, Organizational

Behavior, Public Policy, and others; and unlike acquisition, per se, these reference disciplines are represented by established groups and departments at most universities.

The key is that university academics must be *interested* in their topics of research and they must be able to *publish* the results in leading academic journals. Thus, the problem is not so much one of funding acquisition research—although some funding is certainly required to catalyze a robust acquisition research program. Rather, the key is motivating the participation of top academics at leading universities and guiding them to adapt their current research streams to also address the needs of our acquisition community. This represents a problem for which the NPS possesses a unique capability to address.

As a leading research institution itself, NPS experience suggests this kind of motivation and guidance (i.e., leadership) can best be accomplished at the *peer level*, and NPS represents the only DoD institution possessing the research capability, reputation, and personnel necessary to lead the top universities as a peer research organization. This leadership takes on two principal modes: 1) bridging, brokering, and guidance, and 2) leadership by example. Bridging, brokering, and guidance pertains to peer-level assistance with the problem of adapting current research streams at external universities to focus on acquisition research problems, future as well as current; helping to provide relevant context, background, knowledge, and information about the acquisition domain; matching research capabilities with DoD professional needs, and vice versa; and facilitating access to DoD personnel, systems, processes, and tools for purposes of research.

Leading by example requires NPS to remain active in producing scholarly acquisition research and publications. For example, such leadership can be effected by producing some of the key, seminal articles that add to the body of knowledge in acquisition. Through refereed publication, such articles can become widely available to researchers and practitioners, and they may be used to set a standard in terms of high research quality, along with helping to establish prudent topical directions and methods for external research in the university community.

Process and Organization

The process supporting the EARP has a heavy seasonal component coupled with a smaller perennial counterpart. Five seasonal activities are performed each year: 1) establishing and refining a target list of research topics for the year; 2) advertising and soliciting proposals from leading universities and other research institutions; 3) forming an independent, interdisciplinary team to review the research proposals; 4) selecting the subset of research proposals for award and provide feedback on all submittals; 5) evaluating the research results and helping disseminate through the acquisition and academic communities. The perennial activities include: 1) ongoing program management and program marketing, which is perhaps the most important role; 2) grant/contract and office administration; and 3) providing DoD access to researchers along with the kinds of bridging, brokering, and acquisition guidance mentioned above.

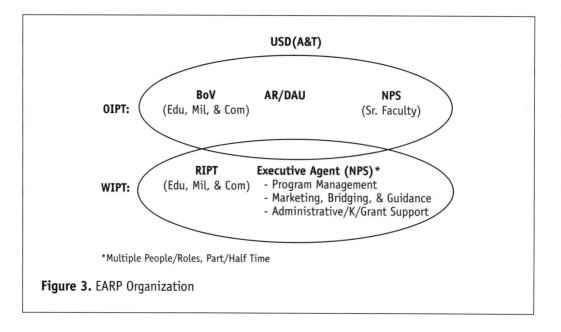

Figure 3. EARP Organization

The organization designed to manage the EARP can be described at two levels: 1) Overarching Integrated Product Team (OIPT) and 2) Working-Level IPT (WIPT), as depicted in Figure 3. The center point of the OIPT, which is responsible for policy and high-level direction of the research program, is represented by the DAU President and the Deputy Under Secretary for Acquisition Reform (AR), both of whom report to the Under Secretary of Defense for Acquisition, Technology and Logistics (USD [AT&L]). This OIPT also includes acquisition executives from research, military, and commercial organizations, with members drawn principally from the DAU Board of Visitors (BoV). The OIPT provides guidance to the WIPT, which centers on the Executive Agent.

The WIPT reports to the DAU President and also includes members from research, commercial, and military acquisition organizations. OIPT members often nominate people from their own organizations to serve on this WIPT, and the BoV has representation through liaison with the WIPT. This OIPT-WIPT structure bears considerable resemblance to the kinds of organizations that now represent the state of the practice in defense acquisition. The Executive Agent is comprised mainly of a few part-time, research-oriented officials, augmented by a host of qualified people from universities, commercial industry, and the DoD. The Executive Agent organization accomplishes the seasonal and perennial activities mentioned above.

Research Topics

The research topics for the program were generated by an integrated group of acquisition researchers, professionals, and executives from leading universities, industry, and government. Topics were categorized as either management, applied, developmental, exploratory, or basic. Following are brief descriptions of each category and selected research topics for each.

Management

This category addresses organizational, policy, and people issues with research topics such as:

1. What processes should an acquisition organization measure in order to reflect efficiency, and how unique are various acquisition activities with respect to the processes measured and tracked?

2. What should be the authority and responsibilities of a Life Cycle Program Manager, and how should horizontal management be maintained in a product-managed organization?

3. How to calculate the impact of cycle time reductions with respect to other project aspects (e.g., cost, performance) in development efforts?

The first question addresses process measurement, a key element of quality. We need to understand which processes in acquisition organizations are crucial to providing quality service and products. Further, since activities of acquisition organizations vary widely (e.g., testing, contracting), each type of organization may likely have a different set of critical processes. The second question addresses the concept of a single individual managing an acquisition program from start to finish. This provides leadership and management continuity through the various acquisition phases, in contrast to the usual 2-3 year tenure of DoD program managers. The corresponding issue of horizontal (e.g., cross-functional) management would likely become more acute if other program participants (e.g., engineers, planners, testers) also remained on a single program for extended periods of time. The third topic relates to the common saying, "time is money." We seek to understand and quantify monetary savings for each increment of cycle-time reduction. And we need to understand the implications in terms of performance, particularly if reducing cycle time requires a corresponding performance compromise.

Applied

The applied category addresses operational application and the study of feasible concepts, processes, and technologies. Topics include:

1. How to adopt price-based acquisition, for example, eliminating cost type contracting and its attendant bureaucracy (Cost Accounting Standards, cost principles, cost-based valuation), and value acquisitions through market and price analysis?

2. How can a customer rely on the market to determine prices when there are only a few large suppliers (e.g., oligopoly) and only one buyer (e.g., monopsony)?

3. How can life-cycle costs be effectively measured and evaluated?

The first question addresses application of a market-based commercial pricing practice to DoD acquisitions, in contrast to the cost-based manner in which defense acquisitions are typically valued. The second question complements the first, in that the defense industry does not reflect true markets throughout. For instance, many large and advanced weapon systems (e.g., aircraft carriers, nuclear submarines, tanks) have only one or two suppliers capable of their design and manufacture, and the government represents the only buyer of most such weapons. This begs the economic question of how market-based pricing can be effected in such an environment. The third research question seeks to apply cost measurement across all phases of the acquisition life cycle and understand how best to evaluate the resulting measures.

Developmental

The developmental category addresses feasibility demonstrations of new concepts, processes, and technologies, but without operational implementation, as with applied research. Research questions in this category include:

1. What are the implications of privatization of acquisition functions?

2. What are the various implications of consolidating defense acquisition processes into a single DoD (or non-DoD) system?

3. How can the life-cycle process be modeled to determine the optimal level of program concurrency?

The first question considers the feasibility and implications of outsourcing acquisition functions (e.g., procurement, contracting, testing) that have traditionally been performed by military and governmental personnel. Such outsourcing is increasingly practiced by commercial firms. Similarly, process consolidation (e.g., eliminating service and geographical differences) seeks economies of scale and scope, but the feasibility of this concept is questionable, thus requiring investigation. The third research question seeks to develop analytical models for various acquisition programs and employ such models to optimize the level of concurrency (e.g., simultaneous development and test, test and production) for each specific acquisition.

Exploratory

Research questions in this category address promising new concepts, processes, and technologies in order to assess their potential in terms of desirability, utility, or payoff, but they do not assess their feasibility, as with developmental research. They include the following:

1. To what extent can (and should) private sector systems/processes be adapted for the public sector?

2. What enterprise activities, strategies, processes, and organizational forms may facilitate more effective government/contractor relationships in today's evolving acquisition environment?

3. What models and process innovations are available to improve the performance of acquisition processes?

One overarching theme of many of the topics above is a focus on commercial practices. Indeed, many of the developmental, applied, and management research questions pertain to the feasibility, adaptation, and employment of commercial practices to defense acquisition processes and systems. But this presumes that commercial practices are inherently better than their DoD counterparts, and they are suitable for defense application. We have yet to identify definitive research to support such putative superiority or suitability; and the first exploratory research question seeks to investigate these aspects of systems and processes from the private sector.

The second question addresses inter-organizational relationships between the military/government and commercial suppliers. In industry, customers are consolidating their supplier bases and forming closer alliances with fewer vendors. In many such cases, performance gains in efficiency, efficacy, speed, and agility have been noted. This question explores how the government may establish and benefit from similar, closer relationships with suppliers.

The third question addresses process innovation and seeks to explore how acquisition processes can reap the benefits of quantum, order-of-magnitude performance gains. Many firms in the private sector have reported such quantum gains through business process reengineering, but it is unclear how to effect such reengineering in the domain of defense acquisition.

Basic

Research questions in the basic category pursue fundamental knowledge, but without promise in terms of potential utility or payoff, as with exploratory research. For example:

1. How can we better understand what "acquisition" is (e.g., its nature, scope, and boundaries)? What are the different dimensions/contexts (e.g., technological, political, military, business), issues, and questions that define "defense acquisition," and how do these interrelate?

2. What are the central research questions to be answered through a program of inquiry in the acquisition domain?

3. Does the acquisition field merit scholarly inquiry?

Despite our simple operationalization of the term *acquisition* above, broad and informal use of the term is accompanied by a wide diversity of definitions and conceptualizations. In order to conduct a program of inquiry in an area such as acquisition, it is important to understand what that area involves and includes. The first basic research question addresses this issue and is somewhat introspective. The second and third basic research questions are even more introspective, as they seek to identify the central acquisition research questions and assess the extent to which scholarly inquiry should even be undertaken for acquisition as a field.

Curiously, most existing research activity is being undertaken on the more applied topics discussed previously. But we have yet to develop a common definition of "acquisition," to identify the central research questions associated with the phenomenon, or to even determine whether it merits scholarly inquiry through research. Clearly, the answers to such basic questions will directly influence and permeate through the entire set of more applied questions, exploratory through management.

Status and Plans

At the time of this writing, EARP is in its third year. After more than a year of planning and preparation, the program was funded beginning in 1999 to solicit and engage top researchers from leading universities in topics of interest to the acquisition community. A Broad Agency Announcement (BAA) is used to formally advertise the program.

During 1999, five research awards were made; twelve grants were approved in 2000; but in 2001, only six awards were made. A leadership change at the DAU shifted its perspective on acquisition research, and many top researchers working on grants in 2000 were not retained in the 2001 program. DAU funding in 2001 is also down considerably from planned levels, which inhibits the EARP's growth potential.

Since the beginning of 2001, the emphasis has been on creating a stronger link between EARP research and DoD acquisition research priorities. A key program goal will be to closely associate the researchers from the six 2001 projects with DoD agencies that have a direct interest in the research being conducted.

A significant improvement for the EARP has been the development and release of a website, at <http://www.nps.navy.mil/earp>. Research reports are now posted as they are received, and reference materials for prospective and current researchers are provided. The creation of the website is part of the effort being made by NPS to build bridges between researchers and DoD agencies.

The complex nature of the BAA, which also does not provide a clear indication of DoD acquisition research priorities to prospective researchers, is a key concern. Thus, the BAA is being rewritten by requesting comments from many interested parties, including current and past EARP researchers. Another planned change will be advertising the BAA in professional and academic publications, rather than only posting the solicitation on CBDNet. This should broaden our exposure and better reach the target academic audience.

We believe that with changes such as those described previously, we will receive a large number of high-quality, relevant research proposals during 2002, the fourth year of the program, and beyond. Furthermore, EARP stands to become a very exciting tool for supporting DoD's acquisition research requirements. We are also closely following the evolving strategic direction of the new administration, which will be reflected in the 2002 BAA. As with any sponsored program, however, the key lies in satisfying the sponsor, whose views may not be congruent currently with the broad goals of the program. Given the recent changes in DAU leadership and acquisition-research perspective, this represents a challenging issue that potentially impacts the EARP.

Conclusion—Research and Reform

It has recently become common in DoD to associate the phase "acquisition reform" with the major policy initiatives of the mid-1990s, for example, the move away from military unique specifications, teaming, Federal Acquisitions Streamlining

Act, and Federal Acquisitions Reform Act. Such a view diminishes perspective of the long history of defense acquisition reform efforts in the US, efforts that are linked to names such as Goldwater-Nichols, Grace, Carlucci, Packard, and Hoover, and which indeed extend back to the Continental Congress' attempts to reform the buying practices of General Washington's Army. Considering this history, "reform" may well be acquisition's defining characteristic.

Of course, acquisition can never be truly and completely "reformed." As a process, acquisition constantly evolves as military and political priorities shift, as economic and business conditions change, and as technology advances. Acquisition reform, then, must also be viewed as a process rather than as an end state. The slogan of 16th century Protestants, *Reformata et Semper Reformandum* (Reformed and Always Reforming), must apply in acquisition.

How may such a perspective take hold in acquisition? Elected and appointed leaders can provide the political will to pursue reform, but reform cannot simply conform to shifting political landscapes. Acquisition professionals have the expertise to implement reform measures, but as "owners" of acquisition processes they often have difficulty challenging the *status quo*. We assert that a process of reform must include acquisition researchers. Only scholars can provide the type of critical and focused inquiry that informs acquisition's policies and practices and thus promotes its reform. It is in such a spirit of reform that the research program described in this chapter seeks to engage scholars in the study of acquisition and its important issues.

References

Abellera, J. W. 1993. National Resources for Defense Research. Proceedings: *Defense Systems Management College and National Contract Management Association Acquisition Research Symposium*.

Acker, D. D. 1993. *Acquiring Defense Systems: A Quest for the Best*. Fort Belvoir, VA: Defense Systems Management College Press.

Brown, C., ed. 1997. Proceedings. *Defense Systems Management College and National Contract Management Association Acquisition Research Symposium*, Washington.

Bryan, T. 1998. Open Systems—Fielding Superior Combat Capability Quicker. *Program Manager* 28 (1): 48–56.

Campbell, D. T., and J. C. Stanley. 1973. *Experimental and Quasi-Experimental Designs for Research*. Chicago: Rand McNally.

Cohen, W. S. 1997. Defense Reform Initiative Report: Leading Change in a New Era. URL: http://www.defenselink.mil/pubs/dodreform/.

Cole, W. E. 1997. *A Case Study on the Relationship Between OPM-Crusader, UDLP, and TACOM-ARDEC in the Development of the Crusader Armament*. Master's thesis, Naval Postgraduate School, Monterey, CA.

D'Aveni, R. 1994. Call for Papers on the Topic of Hypercompetition. *Organization Science*.

Davidow, W. H., and M. S. Malone. 1992. *The Virtual Corporation*. New York: Harper Business Press.

Department of Defense. 2001. The Defense Acquisition System. Directive 5000.1 (with Change 1). Office of the Under Secretary of Defense (Acquisition, Technology and Logistics), 4 January, Washington, D.C.

Drucker, P. F. 1998. The Discipline of Innovation. *Harvard Business Review* (November–December): 149–157.

Farrell, T. 1997. *Weapons Without a Cause: The Politics of Weapons Acquisition in the United States*. New York: St. Martin's Press.

FASA. 1994. Federal Acquisition Streamlining Act. US Department of Defense.

FARA. 1996. Federal Acquisition Reform Act. US Department of Defense.

Fox, J. R. 1974. *Arming America: How the U.S. Buys Weapons.* Cambridge: Harvard University Press.

Fox, J. R., and J. L. Field. 1988. *The Defense Management Challenge: Weapons Acquisition.* Cambridge: Harvard University Press.

Gansler, J. S. 1998. Realizing Acquisition Reform. Keynote address at the Executive Acquisition Symposium. *Program Manager* (January–February).

Hammer, M., and J. Champy. 1993. *Reengineering the Corporation: A Manifesto for Business Revolution*. New York: Harper Business Press.

Jefferies, C. L. 1977. Public Administration and the Military. *Public Administration Review* 37 (4): 321–333.

Kuhn, T. S. 1970. *The Structure of Scientific Revolutions*. 2d ed. Chicago: University of Chicago Press.

Lebovic, J. H. 1996. *Foregone Conclusions: U.S. Weapons Acquisition in the Post-Cold War Transition*. Boulder, CO: Westview Press.

Malone, T. W., J. Yates, and R. I. Benjamin. 1987. Electronic Markets and Electronic Hierarchies. *Communications of the ACM* 30 (6): 484–497.

Mayer, K. R. 1991. *The Political Economy of Defense Contracting*. New Haven, CT: Yale University Press.

Nissen, M. E. 1997. Reengineering the RFP Process through Knowledge-Based Systems. *Acquisition Review Quarterly* 4 (1): 87–100.

Nissen, M. E., K. F. Snider, and D. V. Lamm. 1998. Managing Radical Change in Acquisition. *Acquisition Review Quarterly* 5 (2): 89–106.

Office of Management and Budget. 1980. Results of the Ninth Annual DoD/FAI Acquisition Research Symposium. Office of Federal Procurement Policy, October.

Perry, W. J. 1994. Reducing Cycle Time in DoD. Memorandum from the Secretary of Defense.

Pine, B., B. Victor, and A. C. Boynton. 1993. Making Mass Customization Work. *Harvard Business Review* (September–October): 108–119.

Porter, M. E. 1985. *Competitive Advantage: Creating and Sustaining Superior Performance*. New York: Free Press.

Przemieniecki, J. S., ed. 1993. *Acquisition of Defense Systems*. Washington: American Institute of Aeronautics and Astronautics.

Stevenson, J. P. 1993. *The Pentagon Paradox: The Development of the F-18 Hornet*. Annapolis, MD: Naval Institute Press.

Strayer, D. E., and L. W. Lockwood. 1975. Evaluating Research Needs and Validating Research Results. Proceedings: *Fifth Annual DoD Procurement Research Symposium*, August.

Thompson, F., and L. R. Jones. 1994. *Reinventing the Pentagon: How the New Public Management Can Bring Institutional Revival*. San Francisco: Jossey-Bass.

Wildavsky, A. 1969. Rescuing Policy Analysis from PPBS. *Public Administration Review* 29 (2): 189–202.

Williams, R. F., and P. F. Arvis. 1985. The Possibility of a Contracting Science. Proceedings: *Federal Acquisition Research Symposium*, November, Defense Systems Management College.

Williamson, O. E. 1985. *The Economic Institutions of Capitalism*. New York: Macmillan.

Yin, R. K. 1994. *Case Study Research: Design and Methods*. Thousand Oaks: Sage.

CHAPTER 7

PROJECT MANAGEMENT FOR INTENSIVE, INNOVATION-BASED STRATEGIES: NEW CHALLENGES FOR THE 21ST CENTURY

Christophe Midler—de l'École polytechnique

The issue of growth by innovation is central to current dynamics in the industrialized nations. As Navarre (1992) puts it, we have moved on from "the battle to produce better to the battle to design better." In markets which are saturated, as European markets typically are, gaining competitive edge means differentiating and focusing products with increasing precision ("niche" strategies) by means of more frequent product replacement to anticipate market trends, reacting before others to the often unpredictable signs given out by fluctuating markets, and integrating as quickly as possible technological innovations which make cost savings possible in order to better withstand price warfare in increasingly globalized markets.

Thus, during the '90s we have witnessed a number of changes in various sectors, some radical, in the processes whereby new products are designed. The concept of project management has deeply reshaped the inside organizations of firms with the overhaul of subcontracting systems. In our research we have analyzed how this "projectization" process (Midler 1995; Benghozi, Charue, and Midler 2000) developed in various industrial contexts: auto industry, construction, chemical, and pharmaceutical firms.

But, on the other side, such enlargements in project management application scope, combined with greater expectations for efficiency in projects results, call for deeply and rapidly revisiting the traditional project models. The objective of the present chapter is to characterize these dynamics during the '90s in the French context and point out the main challenges that need to be faced in the following century.

This chapter is based on a research program, which has been ongoing since the beginning of the '90s, conducted by a team at the Management Research Center of the Ecole Polytechnique. The approach adopted has been that of interactive research with manufacturing companies over a long period of time (usually three to five years), against the background of the problematics of contributions to experimentation and the acquisition of knowledge on the dynamics at work in French companies. This kind of in depth inquiry has been, or is currently being, conducted in the armaments, automotive, construction, chemical, electronics, power, pharmaceutical, and steel industries. A common theoretical matrix for analysis has been constructed and regular exchanges of views make it possible to compare the dynamics observed in these different cases.

The general hypothesis behind this research program is a contingency vision of project management models (Lundin 1998), due to the specificity of the activity (with variables such as risk, complexity, and size of the project) and of the social context where the project is embedded. In that perspective, the development of the project management field appears as a combination of contingent organizational and instrumental knowledge creation processes (for example, the program evaluation and review technique [PERT] method for the Polaris program for United States (US) Department of Defense in the beginning of the '60s) with formalization of de-contextualized bodies of knowledge (typically, *A Guide to the Project Management Body of Knowledge* [*PMBOK® Guide*]), intersectoral dissemination via institutional processes (professional associations, education systems, normalization and regulatory authorities, and so on), and the hybridization of these outside contributions with the traditions already in place. The research program is designed to focus on emblematic cases, where the implementation of existing best practices is problematic because of the singularity and novelty of the situation.

After characterizing the projects context of intensive, innovation-based strategies in a first part, we will then analyze the consequences on project coordination processes.

The Intensive Innovation Strategy Context: The "Design Revolution" Beyond Development Projects

After focusing on product development processes, the ongoing "design revolution" reaches a new and more radical step in the 1990s. The performance achieved by development programs, as measured by the yardsticks of quality, cost, and lead-times, is not sufficient to ensure competitiveness if the resulting products are not genuinely and radically innovative. K. Eisenhardt and B. Tabrizi (1995) and Brown (1997) found, when looking at the information technology sector, a new model for the innovative enterprise that explodes the traditional dichotomy between continuous, marginal innovation on the one hand, and rare, singular breakthroughs

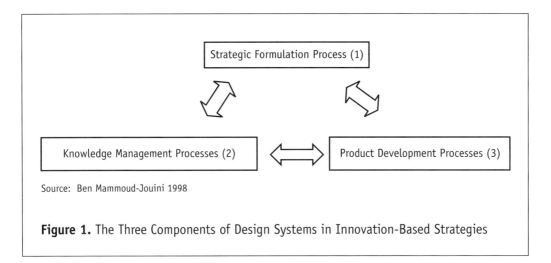

Figure 1. The Three Components of Design Systems in Innovation-Based Strategies

on the other. In this context, the boundary line between research and development becomes less clear. A similar statement can be made in the rather different contexts of mature industries like automobile (Weil 1999) or household equipment industry (Chapel 1996). In upstream industries like chemical and steel, the importance of innovation in French firms' strategies also grew considerably in the 1990s (Charue-Duboc 1998; Lenfle 2001) from the effect of two combined causes: on the customers' side, the accelerating pace of the more or less radical redesign of end products downstream is increasing the opportunities for the substitution of raw materials as part of the never-ending search for better compromises; on the competitors' side, firms from emerging countries get more and more aggressive on commodities markets as they catch up the occidental technological know-how.

Hatchuel (1998) formalized the principles of the "Design-Oriented Organization," which associate knowledge and product development management. On the same line, we (Ben Mammoud-Jouini 1998; Benghozi 2000) have identified the three processes that are at the heart of intensive, innovation-based strategies (see Figure 1).

- The company's strategy: How does it integrate innovation into its strategy? Is innovation a main or a secondary lever for action? Can signs of the dynamics defining the priority granted innovation be seen in changes in budgets allocated to it? How does the company guide the key processes for product innovation defined below? Are explicit structures in place for the management of portfolios of groups of skills and projects? And so on.
- The process whereby key skills are developed for input into the innovation process: not only research, but also learning processes within product development programs.
- The process whereby those skills are coordinated in product development management.

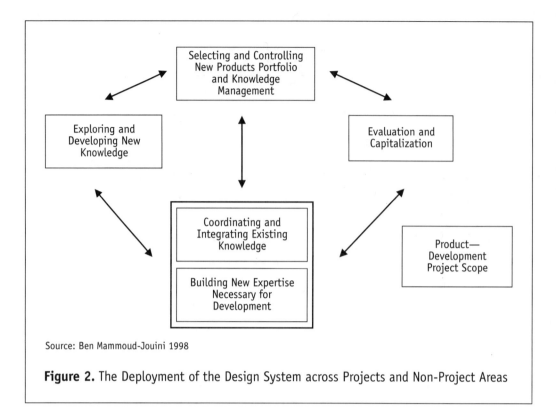

Source: Ben Mammoud-Jouini 1998

Figure 2. The Deployment of the Design System across Projects and Non-Project Areas

Project management is of course a key component of this design system. Figure 2 shows how advanced project management contributes to this global design system of the firm, as it was introduced in the firms in the 1980s and beginning of the 1990s for developing new products (Clark 1992; Midler 1993).

But the transition is still uncompleted within the two other levels (one and two). The importance of knowledge management is increasingly more evident as competitive advantage in product markets comes from more and more radically innovative products with development projects now being a shared competency among firms. At the same time, reducing lead-time and costs in development projects creates a situation where radical innovation and learning are rarely accepted by project managers, because of the resulting risks. Traditionally, depending on their activity, firms developed more on a knowledge-based pattern (typically pharmaceutical and chemical sector) or on the product development side (automobile). What is new now is the necessity to combine the two processes to succeed in creating a track of successive radical and valuable innovations.

How can we make project management fit into these new challenges? We will focus on four points that call for deep revisions in the classical project management paradigm:

- Managing learning and solidarity within risky projects
- From demand-pull projects to design-push projects
- From product projects to platform or knowledge projects
- Managing the learning externalities in project portfolios.

Beyond Contract/Process Dilemma: Management of Convergent Commitment, Collective Learning, and Solidarity between the Project Members

The first immediate consequence of the competition by innovation context is to increase the risk level of projects. Uncertain projects are of course not new in industry. But what is more original is to consider such projects as a normal and repetitive way to sustain survival, and, if possible, growth of the firm. Therefore, the level of efficiency required for risky projects has significantly increased in terms of functional performances, quality, costs, and lead-time. The importance of risk management as a key point in recent project management conferences is a significant reflection of such a trend.

In that context, uncertainty creates many surprises that imply the need for revisions in means and ends of the project. Therefore, the efficiency in such projects depends on:

- First, the efficient collective learning processes that will permit the rapid detection of the problems and generate satisfactory answers.
- Second, the solidarity between the contributors, in order to reallocate the resources, constraints, and performances among the contributors, for the best of the global project.

The classical contractual and standardized coordination model is not adapted to such priorities (Lundin 1995; Söderlund 1998). In that model, the targets are precisely specified and contracted in advance with each contributor. The coordination logic is the fulfillment of these contracts. Revising the initial contracts in order to face unpredicted events leads to difficult and often unproductive debates, because the solution-finding target is put behind the responsibility attribution question. Moreover, the contractual system is a significant obstacle to the creation of collective solidarity on the global objectives of the project: for contributors not directly confronted with a problem appearing to another contributor (a delay for example) it is often taken as a good opportunity to elude their own difficulties.

Modern concurrent-engineering literature insists on the importance of process coordination to ensure project efficiency. Characteristics, such as collocation, mutual understanding, trust, and leadership styles in project teams, problem-solving methodologies, and reactive decision processes, appear as variables of great importance in risky projects, compared to formal, initial detailed contracting. In the case of important projects (such as automobile development), far from neglecting the contractual side, this emphasis on collective design processes has experienced a growing interest in renewed contracting philosophy, to coordinate the contributors inside the firm (internal contracts as studied by Naklha and Soler [1998]) as well as to regulate inter-firm relationships within a partnership relation (Garel and Midler 2001). The role and the form of the contracts are different than in the market-oriented regulation. In the traditional project regulations, contracts are supposed to ensure, by their fulfillment, the coordination of the project. They are supposed to be the "invisible hand" of the project. Adjusted penalties in case of failure are supposed to be the effective defense against the risk of opportunistic behavior and incompetence. In the renewed philosophy, contracts have no such ambition. They appear not as a substitute to the coordination process, but more modestly, as a component of it. In particular, to solve the classical problem of trusting the contributors, other certification processes are called upon. Their specific functions are:

- In the beginning, to force the actors of the project to make their expectations and priorities for the project explicit.
- To formalize, confront, and share the strategies and hypothesis that underlie the commitment of the contributors.
- To negotiate incentives that are coherent with these priorities and strategies.
- To define collective and accepted "warning processes" that will serve as the basis of the collective learning process when surprises occur.

Such an approach to contracting within projects is similar to modern conceptions in the strategic planning of firms (Ponssard 1992). On the contrary, it contradicts in many ways the juridical approach, where the contract is conceived as an instrument to solve contentious business, whereas it is here mainly an instrument to make the project converge and prevent legal dispute.

From "Demand-Pull" Projects to "Design-Push" Projects

The classical project paradigm is a demand-pull design model. It organizes the mobilization of professionals to answer explicit demands from project owners. But in our specific economic context it is more a design-push process than a market-pull one. Innovations like the Walkman® by Sony, Post-it® Notes by 3M, or Navigator by Netscape® were not designed as an answer to an explicit question of existing customers. Generally, innovation strategies are more proactive to market signals than reactive. Thus, implementation of the traditional project management model is problematic in cases of radical breakthrough and emerging phases of innovation. In that situation, the innovation process includes the elaboration of the demand or question, at the same time as the definition of the answer.

Taking the concepts from Simon (1969) and Schön (1983), prominent theorists in the field of design activity, we could say that the "problem setting" side of the design activity is as much (and sometimes even more) important than the "problem solving" side. (The Post-it Note case is typical of an extreme situation. The key question was to find a valuable use for a paste that already existed. In "how" words, the answer existed, what was to be invented was the question that fitted with it.) Therefore, the asymmetry of the economic relation between the owner-customer and the contractor-supplier creates a bias to the need of a symmetric and dialectic exploration of setting and solving of the problem.

What are the consequences of such theoretical arguments on the practical structuring of research and development (R&D) projects in firms? The evolution of the French chemical group Rhône-Poulenc can illustrate this point (Charue-Duboc 1997). Until the '80s, R&D were clearly in a science and technology push logic with central R&D departments. In the beginning of the '90s, the reorientation of the core chemical industry group toward production of innovative, high utilization value chemicals lead to a change in the type of projects conducted: from projects involving heavy industrial production toward product-focused research.

In order to implement this new strategy, a matrix structure with Strategic Business Units (SBU) and a decentralization move of R&D was implemented. The central share of R&D budgets is gradually declining, as budgets allocated by sector or SBU are rising. The philosophy was to "focus research on the market" by adopting the demand-pull traditional project model, with marketing people as project owners and research people as contractors. The limits of such a model for breakthrough projects appeared rapidly. Marketing people from SBUs were more focussed on incremental rather than radical innovations. Many interesting innovative ideas from the researchers could hardly be financed in this situation because the innovation did not fit in with the existing market segmentation and responsibilities (generally, the market gets restructured as a result of breakthrough innovation). Marketing people did not have the skills to help the exploration of new valuable functionalities.

A new step was implemented to overcome these problems. New research units were created, not in order to synthesize products, but to analyze functional and utilization characteristics (application and "applicability" laboratories). The project patterns moved from a demand-pull contractual model to a more design-push model, which emphasized the role of applicability researchers, and also adopted a more symmetrical and integrated vision of the marketing and research part of the project. Let us insist on the fact that this move is not a come back to the science push logic of the '60s, but a new model fitted to meet the modern, proactive strategies of innovative features *and* technologies.

This design-push project model spread beyond the firm's frontier by the setting of exploration partnerships with customers. The goal was to succeed in mobilizing customers' expertise for the exploration of potential utilization values and the final development of new products. We are moving here from a linear view of the downstream value chain towards "customer system concurrent engineering" as represented in Figure 3.

Setting up design-push partnerships is more difficult than demand-pull ones. In the manufacturing sector, the initiative for new design approaches comes from the end firms in the chain. They are able to compel their suppliers to use a concurrent engineering approach by wielding their power as buyers. The situation is obviously different for upstream firms, as projects usually require coordinating downstream customers or specifiers rather than upstream suppliers. How can customers be convinced to take part when, as is usually the case, it is not possible to exercise financial leverage over the downstream part of the chain?

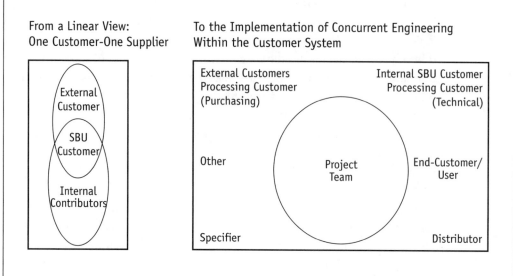

From a Linear View:
One Customer-One Supplier

To the Implementation of Concurrent Engineering
Within the Customer System

External
Customer

SBU
Customer

Internal
Contributors

External Customers
Processing Customer
(Purchasing)

Internal SBU Customer
Processing Customer
(Technical)

Other

Project
Team

End-Customer/
User

Specifier

Distributor

Figure 3. Evolution in Customers System from Linear to Concurrent Approach

From Product Projects to Platform and Knowledge Projects

The third consequence of the ongoing "design revolution" we will discuss is the re-focussing on research and preliminary project design after the focus in the '90s on product development *per se* (Ciavaldini 1996; Cusumano 1998; Midler 1995; Charue-Duboc 2001). In line with the argument developed in the precedent paragraph, the idea is to develop an innovative "generic solution, proven concepts, platform investments" (Kesseler 1998) or a "semi-product" (Weil 1999; Lemasson and Weil 1999) that will be finalized and incorporated in a family of future product developments.

Managing such projects raises difficult and new problems because of the characteristics of the nature of the target (Lenfle 2000):

- One of the major levels for mobilization in project management is the clear identification of the goal that must be reached at the end of the project. In platform projects, the definition of the result is abstract and fuzzy, compared to the "clear" reality of the launching of a new product. In a way, such a project is by definition not finished. An excessive finalization raises the risk of a very contingent solution, which would be contradictory to the objective of extrapolating the concept to a large range of different products and markets.

- Another difficult problem is the long-term nature of such predevelopment projects. This type of project often faces what we call a "hidden urgency" (Lenfle 2000). The effective commercial launching of derived products is far ahead in time. It is often more than ten years for an innovative component or technology in the car business and more than twelve years for a breakthrough concept in pharmaceutics. But irreversibility is created long before, at the beginning of the product development where matured solutions are required and the patents obtained.

■ The evaluation of importance of such platform projects also suffers a decision-modeling conceptual problem. Their value comes from an option-value reasoning (Kogut 1994), which is less developed and formalized in firms than the classical return on investment for product projects. Many economic works on real option themes insist on the systematic, bias favoring, short-term investment linked to oversimplified financial calculations.

■ Last but not least, such projects support a level of risk, which is significantly higher than a product development product. "Properly" closing or radically reorienting an exploration track is important know-how for managing such projects. Never-ending up front exploration is one of the classical burdens of research departments, resulting in a detrimental resource scattering. But the classical myths about project management tend to assimilate a project stop with a failure of the project manager, and then do not encourage such behaviors.

The Emphasis on Portfolio Management: Cross-Learning and Real-Option Market

Finally, intense innovation strategies call for a renewed interest in portfolio management logic as a specific level of analysis to take into account. In the 1990s, modern development project management as "heavy weight project structures" (Clark 1991) emphasized integration and valuation of existing knowledge and energies into projects. The major challenge for intensive innovation strategies is to move from mobilization on single projects, to global management of bunches and series of projects along innovation trajectories (Ben Mahmoud-Jouini 2000) or lineage (Hatchuel 1999) of products. The increase of risk level for each isolated project is another argument for focussing on portfolio management, as observed in the pharmaceutics (Cooper 1998; Sharpe 1998). Last but not least, the increased allocation of resources to R&D and the strategic importance of innovative performance create new constraints in terms of communication on R&D projects portfolios.

This perspective emphasizes the multiple interdependencies and potential externalities of project processes, whereas the single management project view considers only the cash results obtained at the end of the projects. Such an approach focuses on:

■ Reconsidering the evaluation of individual projects with respect to the global portfolio, in terms of global risk and profit profile, continuity, and smoothness of expected revenues as consumption of spare resources.

■ Organizing the cross-project learning of technological aspects and market opportunities (Ayas 1997; Charue-Duboc 1999).

■ Considering the possibility of "trading," buying, or selling projects (wholly or partly) at different stages in their development. The relevant business model is modified to take into account the management of the R&D portfolio.

The Project Funnel: The track is followed through to marketing or the project is killed.

The "Porous" Funnel: Value can be gained from projects other than by bringing them to market. At each stage a project can be halted, pursued, or implemented.

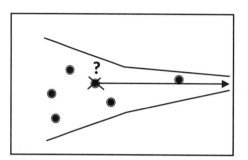 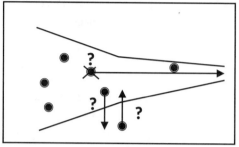

Figure 4. The R&D Process: From "Conventional Funnel" Metaphor to "Porous Funnel"

Conventional Funnel Situation		Porous Funnel Situation
Resource allocation is based on sharing out a fixed overall budget (zero-sum game between projects)	=/=	The overall budget varies according to the decisions reached (nonzero-sum game)
Projects are evaluated according to defined corporate norms	=/=	Each project has an inter-firm trade value that may differ from its value for the originating company
Gaining value from the project is based on the expertise of downstream sales personnel	=/=	Gaining value from the project is an ongoing activity from the outset and is based on R&D expertise

Table 1. Comparison on the Decisional Frameworks of "Conventional Funnel" R&D and "Porous Funnel" R&D

That last perspective forces us to reconsider the traditional vision of the R&D portfolio as a "funnel" to an image that we might describe as a "porous funnel" (Bayart 1999), leaving room for trading with other firms as shown in Figure 4.

The decisional framework for R&D management in porous funnel mode is significantly different from that associated with the conventional funnel, as Table 1 shows.

In that perspective, conventional analysis of project portfolios in a risk/attractiveness "bubble-diagrams" graphic (Cooper 1998) has to be reconsidered because the same project may be positioned at two very different locations, as is shown in Figure 5.

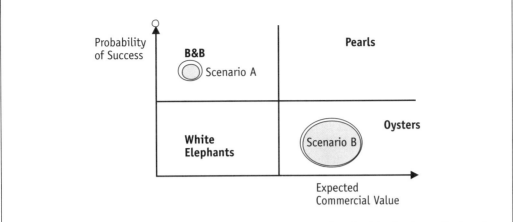

Figure 5. The Representation of Various Scenarios Associated with the Same Project in a "Bubble Diagram" Representation on Conventional Type

In Figure 5, at bottom right, the representation picturing internal development implies high risk and investment, while promising large profits in the event of success. At top left is the assessment of the same project if value is gained from it during development by means of a trade with another pharmaceutical firm. Specifically, the risk and the investment are smaller (because return on the project is immediate and simultaneous with the trade, and the other firm will complete the development), but the profit in the event of success is obviously lower (sale price plus royalties on any future sales for example).

Such an emphasis on a global portfolio management issue is not to be interpreted as a coming back to functional structures that pre-existed to the development of project management structures. It has to be considered, on the contrary, as a new step in order to take into account, and if possible conciliate, the temporary and durable identities of the modern business society.

To conclude, the four above points raise important problems when the traditional project management approach is being implemented to support intensive innovation strategies. In this communication, we have indicated tracks to address these problems by referring to organizational and business theories. Analysis of such issues appears a fruitful opportunity for cross-disciplinary theoretical exchanges as for cooperation between scholars and practitioners. The creation of research networks such as the International Research Network on Organizing by Projects (IRNOP) and PRAMECO help as the research currently under way with major European firms try to materialize this opportunity (A French research network on analyzing the ongoing transitions in R&D practices and professions. It gathers researchers who share an interactive methodology in various scientific fields: organization and management, engineering, sociology, ergonomics, and cognitive psychology).

References

Ayas, K. 1997. *Design for Learning for Innovation*. Delft, Netherlands: Eburon Publishers.

Bayart, D., Y. Bonhomme, and C. Midler. 1999. Management Tools for R&D Project Portfolios in Complex Organizations: The Case of an Iinternational Pharmaceutical Firm. *The 6th International Product Development Management Conference*, Cambridge, UK.

Benghozi, P. J., F. Charue-Duboc, and C. Midler. 2000. *Innovation Based Competition & Design Systems Dynamics*. Paris: L'Harmattan.

Ben Mammoud-Jouini, S. 1998. Stratégies d'offre innovantes et dynamiques des processus de conception. Le cas des grandes entreprises françaises de bâtiment. Thèse de doctorat de gestion, Université Paris IX Dauphine, Paris.

Brown, S. L., and K. M. Eisenhardt. 1997. The Art of Continuous Change: Linking Complexity Theory and Time-Paced Evolution in Relentlessly Shifting Organizations. *Administrative Science Quarterly* 42 (1).

Chapel, V. 1996. La croissance par l'innovation: de la dynamique d'apprentissage à la révéla-tion d'un modèle industriel. Le cas Tefal. Thèse de doctorat spécialité Ingénierie et Gestion, École Nationale Supérieure des Mines de Paris, Paris.

Charue-Duboc, F. 1997. Maîtrise d'oeuvre, maîtrise d'ouvrage et direction de projet: des caté-gories pour comprendre l'évolution des fonctionnements en projet dans le secteur chimie de Rhône Poulenc. *Gérer et Comprendre* (septembre): 54–64.

———. 1998. The Role of Research Departments in Focusing Innovative Projects and Understanding Customer Usage and Needs. *The International Research Network on Project Management and Temporary Organization (IRNOP Conference)*, Calgary, Canada.

———. 2001. What are the Organizational Artefacts Implemented to Foster Learning Processes in a Context of Intensive Innovation? *The 17th EGOS Colloquium: The Odyssey of Organizing*, Lyon.

Charue-Duboc, F., and C. Midler. 1999. Impact of the Development of Integrated Project Structures on the Management of Research and Development. *The 6th International Product Development Management Conference*, Cambridge, UK.

Ciavaldini, B. 1996. Des projets à l'avant projet: l'incessante quête de la réactivité. Thèse de doctorat spécialité Ingénierie et Gestion, Ecole des Mines de Paris, Paris.

Clark, K. B., and T. Fujimoto. 1991. *Product Development Performance. Strategy, Organization and Management in the World Auto Industry*. Cambridge, MA: Harvard Business School Press.

Clark, K., and S. C. Wheelwright. 1992. *Revolutionizing Product Development*. New York: The Free Press.

Cooper, R. G., S. J. Edgett, and E. J. Kleinschmidt. 1998. Best Practices for Managing R&D Portfolios. *Research Technology Management* (July–August).

Cusumano, M., and K. Nebeoka. 1998. *Thinking Beyond Lean*. New York: The Free Press.

Garel, G., and C. Midler. 2001. Front-Loading Problem-Solving in Co-Development: Managing the Contractual, Organizational and Cognitive Dimensions. *Journal of Automotive Technology and Management* (3).

Hatchuel, A., et al. 1998. *Innovation répétée et croissance de la firme*. Paris: Rapport de recherche CNRS.

Hatchuel, A., and B. Weil. 1999. Design Oriented Organisations. Towards a Unified Theory of Design Activities. *The 6th New Product Development Conference*, Cambridge, UK.

Kesseler, A. 1998. *The Creative Supplier: A New Model for Strategy, Innovation, and Customer Relationships in Concurrent Design and Engineering Processes: The Case of the Automotive Industry*. Thèse de Doctorat, spéc. Gestion, Ecole Polytechnique, Paris.

Kogut, B., and N. Kulatilaka. 1994. Options Thinking and Platform Investments: Investing in Opportunity. *California Management Review* (Winter): 52–71.

Lemasson, P., and B. Weil. 1999. Nature de l'innovation et pilotage de la recherche industrielle. *Cahiers de recherche du CGS, Ecole des Mines de Paris.*

Lenfle, S., and C. Midler. 2001. Innovation-Based Competition and the Dynamics of Design in Upstream Suppliers. *International Journal of Automotive Technology and Management* (3).

Lundin, R. A., and A. Söderholm. 1995. A Theory of the Temporary Organization. *Scandinavian Journal of Management* 11 (4): 437–455.

Lundin, R. A., and C. Midler. 1998. *Projects as Arenas for Renewal and Learning Processes.* Norwell, MA: Kluwer Academic Publishers.

Midler, C. 1993. *L'auto qui n'existait pas; management des projets et transformation de l'entreprise.* Paris: Dunod.

———. 1995. "Projectification" of the Firm: The Renault Case. *Scandinavian Journal of Management* 11 (4): 363–375.

Midler, C., J. C. Monnet, and P. Neffa. 2001. Globalization through Projects: The Renault Case. The IXth Gerpisa International Colloquium: *Reconfuring the Auto Industry: Merger & Acquisition, Alliances & Exit*, Paris.

Navarre C. 1992. De la bataille pour mieux produire à la bataille pour mieux concevoir. *Gestion 2000* (6): 13–30.

Ponssard, J. P., and H. Tanguy. 1992. Planning in Firms: An Interactive Approach. *Theory and Decision* (34): 139–159.

Schön, D. A. 1983. *The Reflective Practitioner. How professionals Think in Action.* New York: Basic Books.

Sharpe, P., and T. Keelin. 1998. How Smithkline Beecham Makes Better Resource-Allocation Decisions. *Harvard Business Review* (March–April).

Simon, H. A. 1969. *The Sciences of the Artificial.* Cambridge, MA: MIT Press.

Söderlund, J., and N. Andersson. 1998. A Framework for Analyzing Project Dyads—The Case of Discontinuity, Uncertainty and Trust. In *Projects as Arenas for Renewal and Learning Processes* (181–189). Edited by R. A. Lundin and C. Midler. Norwell, MA: Kluwer Academic Publishers.

Weil, B. 1999. Conception collective, coordination et savoirs. Les rationalisations de la conception automobile. Thèse de doctorat spécialité ingénierie et gestion, École Nationale Supérieure des Mines de Paris, Paris.

Section II

Effective Practices & Success Factors

Introduction

The second section contains papers that address various perspectives on developing more successful project management practices. The papers include profiling successful project managers, assessing project management's value to the corporation, and other aspects of successful project-based organizations.

- Lynn Crawford's research aims at developing a profile of competent project managers. Through extensive research and field study, she has created a framework for analyzing the characteristics of effective project leaders. Chapter 8—Profiling the Competent Project Manager.

- C. William Ibbs and Justin Reginato address one of the most contentious problems in project management—demonstrating the unique value it adds to corporate practices. While many companies have begun initiating project work, Ibbs' research represents one of the few attempts to assign real value to its use in corporations. Chapter 9—Measuring Project Management's Value: New Directions for Quantifying PM/ROI[SM].

- Daniel Leroy chronicles the current state of project management practice in French organizations. By use of a number of key success metrics, he demonstrates the key success drivers underlying the performance of effective project firms. Chapter 10—Project Management Practices in French Organizations: A State of the Art.

- Roger Miller and Brian Hobbs show that large, capital-intensive projects offer their own unique challenges. Through a series of sixty case studies across four continents, the authors draw some integrative conclusions about the successful practices found in organizations implementing these projects. Chapter 11—A Framework for Analyzing the Development and Delivery of Large Capital Projects.

CHAPTER 8

PROFILING THE COMPETENT PROJECT MANAGER

Lynn Crawford, DBA—University of Technology, Sydney

Introduction

A major concern of the field of project management and a recurring theme in the literature is that of project success. There are two major strands to this concern—how success is judged (success criteria), and the factors that contribute to the success of projects (success factors). Closely associated with this is concern for the competence of the project manager. On one hand, the competence of the project manager is in itself a factor in successful delivery of projects and on the other hand, the project manager needs to have competence in those areas that have the most impact on successful outcomes.

The importance of the project manager in the delivery of successful projects has generated a considerable amount of rhetoric and a smaller body of research-based literature dealing with the knowledge, skills, and personal attributes required of an effective project manager. With a few notable exceptions, findings have been based on opinions, primarily of project managers.

At the same time, concern for the competence of project managers has fuelled interest in the development of standards and certification processes that can be used for assessment, for recognition, and as a guide for the development of project management competence. Standards include those relating primarily to what project managers are expected to know; such as *A Guide to the Project Management*

Body of Knowledge (PMBOK® Guide) – 2000 Edition (Project Management Institute 2000), the *International Project Management Association* (IPMA) *Competence Baseline* (*ICB*) (International Project Management Association 1999), and *The Association for Project Management Body of Knowledge* (*APM BoK*) (Dixon 2000) and those that address what project managers are expected to be able to do; such as, the occupational- or performance-based competency standards of Australia and the United Kingdom. The process for development of these standards has primarily involved extensive consultation with industry and participation of experienced project personnel in identifying what they think project managers need to know and be able to do in order to be effective in delivering successful project outcomes. Some attempt has been made in the standards (*ICB* and *APM BoK*) to identify personal characteristics of effective project managers but this has played only a minor role, with the major attention being given to the required knowledge and skills rather than personality characteristics and behaviors.

This chapter presents a review and analysis of research-based literature concerning the criteria by which project success is judged, the factors that contribute to the success of projects; and the knowledge, skills, and personal attributes of project managers that are expected to lead to achievement of successful project outcomes. Analysis of data on the project management practices and perceived performance ratings of over 350 project personnel from three countries are then presented. Analysis suggests that there is little direct relationship between perceived performance in the workplace and the level of project management knowledge and experience reported against either project management standards (*PMBOK® Guide* and *Australian National Competency Standards for Project Management*) or previous research findings.

Project Success Criteria

There is a considerable volume of literature dealing with project success, and this tends to fall into three categories—those dealing primarily with the criteria by which project success is judged; those primarily concerned with the factors contributing to the achievement of success; and those that confuse the two.

Although not strongly supported by empirical research, there are many articles that address the issue of project success *criteria*, including a number of papers presented at the Project Management Institute (PMI®) Seminars & Symposium held in Montreal, Canada in 1986, which focused on this theme.

These papers tend to agree on a number of issues. Firstly, project success is an important project management issue; secondly, it is one of the most frequently discussed topics; and thirdly, there is a lack of agreement concerning the criteria by which success is judged (Pinto and Slevin 1988; Freeman and Beale 1992; Shenhar, Levy, and Dvir 1997; Baccarini 1999). A review of the literature further reveals that there is, in fact, a high level of agreement with the definition provided by Baker, Murphy, and Fisher (1988, 902), that project success is a matter of perception and that a project will be most likely to be perceived to be an "overall success" if:

> … the project meets the technical performance specifications and/or mission to be performed, and if there is a high level of satisfaction concerning the project outcome among key people on the project team, and key users or clientele of the project effort (Baker, Murphy, and Fisher 1988).

Furthermore, there is general agreement that although schedule and budget performance alone are considered inadequate as measures of project success, they are still important components of the overall construct. Quality appears intertwined with issues of technical performance, specifications, and achievement of functional objectives and it is achievement against these criteria that will be most subject to variation in perception by multiple project stakeholders.

Project Success Factors

The work of Murphy, Baker, and Fisher (1974), using a sample of 650 completed aerospace, construction, and other projects with data provided primarily by project managers, remains the most extensive and authoritative research on the factors contributing to project success. Their work has been cited and used in the majority of subsequent research papers concerning project success. Ten factors were found to be strongly linearly related to both perceived success and perceived failure of projects, while twenty-three project management characteristics were identified as being necessary but not sufficient conditions for perceived success (Baker, Murphy, and Fisher 1988).

Important work was conducted on project success factors in the 1980s, notably by Pinto and Slevin (1987, 1988) and Morris and Hough (1993). Both studies draw on the research of Murphy, Baker, and Fisher (1974) and have been regularly cited in later work. While Morris and Hough (1993) drew primarily on literature and case study analysis of major projects, Pinto and Slevin (1987, 1988) based their findings on the opinions of a usable sample of 418 PMI members responding to questions asking them to rate the relevance to project implementation success of ten critical success factors and four additional external factors (Slevin and Pinto 1986).

Further studies aimed at identifying factors contributing to the success, and in some cases the failure, of projects (Ashley, Lurie, and Jaselskis 1987; Geddes 1990; Jiang, Klein, and Balloun 1996; Zimmerer and Yasin 1998; Lechler 1998; The Standish Group 2000; Whittaker 1999; Clarke 1995, 1999) used methodologies similar to that of Pinto and Slevin, with findings based on ratings or in some cases rankings of success factors by project personnel, general managers, or other professionals. Beale and Freeman (1991) identified fourteen variables that affect project success from a review of twenty-nine papers. Wateridge (1996) identified eight most often mentioned success factors from a review of literature reporting results of empirical research relating to information system (IS)/information technology (IT) projects.

Using the ten critical and twenty-three necessary success factors identified by Baker, Murphy, and Fisher (1988) as the starting point, the findings of the twelve other studies listed above were analyzed and compared. Similar factors were grouped and then ranked according to the number of times they were mentioned across the thirteen studies. Factors receiving the least number of mentions were progressively grouped with the most directly related factor receiving a higher number of mentions, and the factors re-ranked. This procedure was conducted iteratively, resulting in the emergence of twenty-four success factors. Rankings were based on the number of mentions identified over all thirteen studies, and calculated separately for those studies relating primarily to engineering and construction projects (n = 7) versus IS/IT projects (n = 6) and for those studies conducted pre-1995 (n = 6) and post-1995 (n = 7). This was done to see whether there was any change in the results concerning the most mentioned project success factors across industries, and with the development and more widespread adoption of project management. The year 1995 was adopted as the break point as reports published prior to that date primarily related to studies conducted in the 1980s. The results of this analysis are shown in Table 1.

In conducting the analysis, the importance of planning, monitoring, and controlling at the integrative level, rather than the detailed levels of specialist scope, time, cost, risk, and quality planning was a strong and interesting result, with monitoring and controlling of risk being the only specialist area to be mentioned within the top three ranking categories. Stakeholder management (other) encompasses stakeholder issues external to the parent and client organizations, including environmental and political issues, and it seems intuitively correct that this would rank highly for the success of engineering and construction projects. The increase in mention of communication, strategic direction, and team selection and decrease in importance of technical performance, post-1995, are of interest and appear attributable, at least in part, to the application of project management beyond its strong engineering and construction origins.

With the possible exception of organizational support, organization structure, and team selection, the factors identified in Table 1 call directly upon the competence of the project manager. Although organizational support is a factor that can be addressed by people other than the project manager, a competent project manager could be expected to understand that support of the organization is required to enhance the likelihood of project success and use interpersonal and other skills to achieve it. Similarly, the competent project manager can exert influence over the way in which the project team is structured and how it relates to the structure of the parent organization and others. Team selection draws together factors relating to capability and experience of the project manager and team for the project and is therefore a factor that is directly concerned with project management competence.

All studies (N = 13)	E & C (N = 7)	IS/IT (N = 6)	Pre-1995 (N = 6)	Post-1995 (N = 7)
Planning (Integrative)	Planning (Integrative), Stakeholder Management (Other), Team Development	Strategic Direction, Team Selection	Planning (Integrative), Technical Performance	Communication, Monitoring & Controlling (Integrative), Organizational Support, Planning (Integrative), Strategic Direction, Team Selection
Monitoring & Controlling (Integrative), Team Selection, Technical Performance	Communication, Leadership, Monitoring & Controlling (Integrative), Monitoring & Controlling (Risk), Technical Performance	Monitoring & Controlling (Integrative), Planning (integrative)	Leadership, Monitoring & Controlling (Integrative), Stakeholder Management (Other), Team Development	Leadership, Monitoring & Controlling (Risk), Stakeholder Management (Client), Team Development, Technical Performance
Communication, Leadership, Strategic Direction, Team Development	Organization Structure, Organization Support	Communication, Leadership, Organizational Support, Technical Performance	Communication, Monitoring & Controlling (Risk), Organization Structure, Strategic Direction, Team Selection	Decision-Making & Problem Solving, Organization Structure, Project Definition, Task Orientation
Monitoring & Controlling (Risk), Organizational Support, Stakeholder Management (Other)	Administration, Decision-Making & Problem Solving, Planning (Specialist-Time), Project Definition, Stakeholder Management (Client), Strategic Direction, Task Orientation, Team Selection	Monitoring & Controlling (Risk), Organization Structure, Project Definition, Stakeholder Management (Client), Team Development	Administration, Organizational Support, Planning (Specialist-Time), Project Definition	Administration, Planning (Specialist-Cost), Planning (Specialist-Time), Stakeholder Management (Other)

Table 1. Project Success Factors Identified in the Literature—Ranked by Frequency of Mention

All studies (N = 13)	E & C (N = 7)	IS/IT (N = 6)	Pre-1995 (N = 6)	Post-1995 (N = 7)
Organizational Structure	Closing (Cost), Closing (Integrative), Monitoring & Controlling (Cost), Monitoring & Controlling (Scope), Monitoring & Controlling (Time), Planning (Specialist-Cost)	Administration, Planning (Specialist-Cost), Planning (Specialist-Time), Stakeholder Management (Other), Task Orientation	Stakeholder Management (Client), Task Orientation	Closing (Cost), Closing (Integrative), Monitoring & Controlling (Cost), Monitoring & Controlling (Scope), Monitoring & Controlling (Time)
Project Definition, Stakeholder Management (Client)		Closing (Cost), Closing (Integrative), Decision-Making, Monitoring & Controlling (Cost), Monitoring & Controlling (Scope), Monitoring & Controlling (Time)	Closing (Cost), Closing (Integrative), Decision-Making & Problem Solving, Monitoring & Controlling (Cost), Monitoring & Controlling (Scope), Monitoring & Controlling (Time), Planning (Specialist-Cost)	

NB: Not all 24 literature-derived factors are listed here. See Appendix A for a full listing of literature-derived constructs and their relationship to Performance Criteria from the *Australian National Competency Standards for Project Management*.

Table 1. *Continued*

This review of research-based literature concerning project success factors therefore clearly demonstrates agreement that the competence, or knowledge, skills, and attributes, of the project manager, are critical to project success.

Project Manager Competence

Interest in the role of the project manager and aspects of competence in that role can be traced back to an article by Gaddis in the *Harvard Business Review* of 1959 (Gaddis 1959) and another *Harvard Business Review* article, by Lawrence and

Lorsch, in 1967, the "New Management Job: The Integrator." Since then, much has been written in project management texts (Kerzner 1998; Meredith and Mantel 1995; Dinsmore 1993; Turner 1993; Pinto 1998), magazines (Dewhirst 1996), and journal articles (Einsiedel 1987; Pettersen 1991) about what it takes to be an effective project manager, culminating with Frame's work on project management competence published in 1999.

The primary research-based reports on the subject began to appear in the early to mid-1970s based on the investigations of Thamhain, Gemmill, and Wilemon into the skills and performance of project managers (Cleland and King 1988; Gemmill 1974; Thamhain and Gemmill 1974; Thamhain and Wilemon 1977; Thamhain and Wilemon 1978). This research and work by Posner (1987) in the 1980s, Gadeken in the early 1990s (1990, 1991), Ford and McLaughlin (1992), and more recently by Zimmerer and Yasin (1998), and a major literature review-based study by Pettersen (1991) constitute the primary research contributions to the understanding of project management competence.

As for studies concerning project success factors, research-based literature on aspects of project management competence draws primarily upon the opinions of project managers and others concerning the knowledge, skills, and personal attributes required by effective project personnel (Posner 1987; Thamhain 1991; Ford and McLaughlin 1992; Wateridge 1996; Zimmerer and Yasin 1998).

Gadeken's work (Gadeken and Cullen 1990; Gadeken 1991) is based on critical incident interviews with sixty United States (US) and fifteen United Kingdom (UK) project managers from Army, Navy, and Air Force acquisition commands. The findings relate solely to personal attributes with identification of six behavioral competencies that distinguished outstanding project managers from their peers; five demonstrated at a slightly lower level of significance; and seven that were demonstrated but with no significant differences indicated between outstanding and average performers. This remains the most important work on behavioral competencies of project managers but the results should be addressed with some caution due to the focus on both acquisition and the armed forces.

Pettersen (1991) conducted a major literature review concentrating on American texts to develop a list of predictors, defined in task-related terms, intended for use in selection of project managers.

Morris (2000) reports on the work of the Centre for Research in the Management of Projects at UMIST, on behalf of the Association for Project Management (APM) and a number of leading UK companies, which focuses on the knowledge required by project managers. Findings are based on interviews and data collection in over 117 companies, seeking their opinion as to the topics they thought project management professionals should know and understand in order to be considered competent.

The same process as outlined for analysis of the research-based literature concerning project success factors was applied to the eight studies mentioned above. Respecting the strong links between project success factors and project manager competence, the ten critical and twenty-three necessary success factors identified by Baker, Murphy, and Fisher (1988) were again used as the starting point. The same twenty-four categories or concepts that emerged from the analysis of success factors emerged from the analysis of findings concerning the knowledge, skills, and personal attributes identified as important to effective project management performance. Only one change was made. Organizational support was renamed stakeholder management (parent organization) in the list of project manager competence factors.

The project management competence factors were ranked according to the number of mentions identified over the eight selected studies, and separately for those studies conducted pre-1995 (n = 4) and post-1995 (n = 4). A breakdown for engineering and construction versus IS/IT is not provided, as there were only two studies that related directly to IS/IT. The year 1995 was adopted as a break point as reports published prior to that date primarily related to studies conducted in the 1980s or very early 1990s. The results of this analysis are shown in Table 2.

It is interesting to note that leadership, a factor that relates almost exclusively to personality characteristics or personal attributes, appears consistently in the highest-ranking category amongst project manager competence factors, whereas it appeared no higher than the second ranking category for project success factors. Similarly, team development appears consistently in the first ranking category for project manager competence factors, but fell as far as fourth ranking in one case for project success factors. Communication and technical performance are consistently stronger for project manager competence than for project success factors. Planning (integrative) is clearly a strong factor, as it appears consistently in the first ranking for both project success factors and project manager competence factors. It is interesting to note that the increased ranking of monitoring and controlling (integrative) that appears in the post-1995 studies of project success factors is supported by post-1995 studies of project manager competence factors indicating an increased concern for control.

Project Management Standards

Concern for the competence of project managers in successfully delivering projects is evidenced not only through research into project success and various aspects of project management competence, but through the development of standards that can be used to guide the development and assessment of project personnel.

Standards relating to aspects of project management competence fall into two main areas—those relating to what project managers are expected to know, represented by project management body of knowledge guides; and those relating to what project managers are expected to be able to do, which primarily take the form of performance-based or occupational competency standards.

There are three widely accepted project management knowledge standards:
- *A Guide to the Project Management Body of Knowledge (PMBOK® Guide)*—PMI (Project Management Institute 2000)

All Factors (N = 8)	Pre-1995 Factors (N = 4)	Post-1995 Factors (N = 4)
Leadership, Planning (Integrative), Team Development	Leadership, Planning (Integrative), Strategic Direction, Team Development, Technical Performance	Leadership, Monitoring & Controlling (Integrative), Planning (Integrative), Team Development, Communication
Communication, Technical Performance	Communication, Decision-Making & Problem Solving, Stakeholder Management (Parent Organization)	Stakeholder Management (Parent Organization), Technical Performance, Organization Structure, Project Definition
Organization Structure, Stakeholder Management (Parent Organization), Strategic Direction	Monitoring & Controlling (Integrative), Monitoring & Controlling (Cost), Monitoring & Controlling (Scope), Monitoring & Controlling (Time), Organization Structure, Stakeholder Management (Client), Team Selection	Administration, Stakeholder Management (Client), Stakeholder Management (Other), Decision-Making & Problem Solving, Monitoring & Controlling (Cost), Planning (Specialist-Cost), Planning (Specialist-Time), Strategic Direction
Monitoring & Controlling (Integrative)	Administration, Monitoring & Controlling (Risk), Planning (Specialist-Time), Project Definition, Stakeholder Management (Other)	Team Selection, Closing (Integrative), Monitoring & Controlling (Quality), Monitoring & Controlling (Risk), Monitoring & Controlling (Scope)
Decision-Making & Problem Solving, Monitoring & Controlling (Cost), Planning (Specialist-Time), Project Definition, Stakeholder Management (Client)	Closing (Integrative), Monitoring & Controlling (Quality)	Monitoring & Controlling (Time)

NB: Not all 24 literature-derived factors are listed here. See Appendix A for a full listing of literature-derived constructs and their relationship to Performance Criteria from the *Australian National Competency Standards for Project Management*.

Table 2. Project Manager Competence Identified in the Literature—Ranked by Frequency of Mention

■ *IPMA Competence Baseline* (*ICB*)—IPMA (International Project Management Association 1999)

■ *Association for Project Management Body of Knowledge* (*APM BoK*)—APM (UK) (Dixon 2000).

Of these, the *PMBOK® Guide* is the most widely recognized and accepted, with over 800,000 copies distributed worldwide. It was approved as an American National Standard (ANSI/PMI 99-001-2000) on 27 March 2001. It defines nine knowledge areas within project management, and claims to "identify and describe that subset of the [Project Management Body of Knowledge] PMBOK® that is generally accepted" (Project Management Institute 2000, 3), providing a "consistent structure" for the professional development programs of PMI including:

■ Certification of Project Management Professionals (PMP®)

■ Accreditation of educational programs in project management.

The *PMBOK® Guide*, which in its current form was published in 2000, was developed through a process of consultation, "written and reviewed by a global network of project management practitioners, working as volunteers" (Project Management Institute 1999a).

Performance based competency standards describe what people can be expected to do in their working roles, as well as the knowledge and understanding of their occupation that is needed to underpin these roles at a specific level of competence.

The first generic performance-based competency standards for project management were the *Australian National Competency Standards for Project Management*, which were developed through the efforts of the Australian Institute of Project Management (AIPM) and endorsed by the Australian Government on 1 July 1996. In the United Kingdom, the Occupational Standards Council for Engineering (OSCEng) produced standards for Project Controls (Occupational Standards Council for Engineering 1996) which were endorsed in December 1996 and for Project Management (Occupational Standards Council for Engineering 1997) which were endorsed in early 1997. The Construction Industry Standing Conference (CISC), the Management Charter Initiative (MCI), and what was then called the Engineering Services Standing Conference (ESSC), now the Occupational Standards Council for Engineering (OSCEng), developed Level 5 NVQ/SVQ (National Vocational Qualifications/Scottish Vocational Qualifications) competency standards for construction project management. A section of the *Management Charter Initiative Management Standards*, titled Manage Projects (Management Charter Initiative 1997), provides a further set of competency standards for project management but in this case, within the general management framework.

Of these standards, the *Australian National Competency Standards for Project Management* and the OSCEng standards for both project management and project controls have attracted the most interest. However, the Australian standards, which follow the same structure as the *PMBOK® Guide* and use the *PMBOK® Guide* as a knowledge base, have attracted the most global interest.

The Australian standards were developed over a three-year period commencing in 1993 and culminating in the endorsement of the standards by the Australian

	Level 4	Level 5	Level 6
Unit 1	Not Applicable at Level 4	Guide Application of Project Integrative Processes	Manage Project Integration
Unit 2	Apply Skills in Scope Management	Guide Application of Scope Management	Manage Scope
Unit 3	Apply Skills in Time Management	Guide Application of Time Management	Manage Time
Unit 4	Apply Skills in Cost Management	Guide Application of Cost Management	Manage Cost
Unit 5	Apply Skills in Quality Management	Guide Application of Quality Management	Manage Quality
Unit 6	Apply Skills in Human Resources Management	Guide Application of Human Resources Management	Manage Human Resources
Unit 7	Apply Skills in Communications Management	Guide Application of Communications Management	Manage Communications
Unit 8	Apply Skills in Risk Management	Guide Application of Risk Management	Manage Risk
Unit 9	Apply Skills in Procurement Management	Guide Application of Procurement Management	Manage Procurement

NB: Level 4 of the standards does not include the Unit relating to Integrative Processes.

Table 3. Units in the *Australian National Competency Standards for Project Management*

Government in 1996. Development was carried out by a consultant working under the guidance of a Steering Committee and Reference Group representing over fifty Australian organizations. The standards development process is well documented (Gonczi, Hager, and Oliver 1990; Heywood, Gonczi, and Hagar 1992) and requires the examination of existing information about the occupation and *analysis of the purpose and functions of the profession and the roles and activities of its members* (Heywood, Gonczi, and Hagar 1992, 46) in order to derive the units and elements of competency that provide the structure for the standards. There are nine units in the standards, described at Levels 4, 5, and 6 as shown in Table 3.

Research Methodology

As outlined previously, both the research-based literature on project management competence and the standards that have been developed to define aspects

Age Category	Study Group Demographics	PMI Member Demographics
31–40 Years Old	31%	30%
41–50 Years Old	43%	40%
All Other Ages	26%	30%
	100%	100%

Table 4. Demographic of Sample—Age

Gender	Research Sample	PMI Member Demographics
Male	74%	75%
Female	26%	25%
	100%	100%

Table 5. Demographic of Sample—Gender

of project management competence have been developed primarily from the collective opinion of project management practitioners and others as to what project personnel need to know and what they need to be able to do in order to be considered competent.

The assumption behind the development and use of project management standards is that the standards describe the requirement for effective performance of project management in the workplace and that those who meet the standards will therefore perform, or be perceived to perform, more effectively than those whose performance does not satisfy the standards. To date, no research has been conducted to validate this assumed positive relationship between project management competence as described in the literature and assessed against standards and perceptions of effective performance in the workplace.

Using two recognized project management standards as described previously, *A Guide to the Project Management Body of Knowledge* (Project Management Institute 2000) and the *Australian National Competency Standards for Project Management* (Australian Institute for Project Management 1996), data was collected to explore the relationship between performance against project management standards and perceived performance in the workplace.

Industry Sector of Organization	Australia	USA	UK	Total
IS/IT & Telecommunications	59	39	19	**117**
E & C	104		50	**154**
Business Services	46	28	7	**81**
Total	**209**	**67**	**76**	**352**

Table 6. Industry Sector of Organization by Region

Five instruments were used in data collection. One instrument was used to gather general demographic information about respondents and their project management role. Two instruments were used to collect information on project management knowledge and practices of participants:

1. A knowledge test, using multiple-choice questions drawn from sample questions for the Project Management Professional (PMP®) certification examinations, with five questions for each of the nine *PMBOK® Guide* knowledge areas.

2. A self-assessment against the nine units of the *Australian National Competency Standards for Project Management* with responses against a five-point scale from 1 to 5 where:

Two instruments were used to gather information on perceived effectiveness of project management performance:

1. A self-rating questionnaire
2. A supervisor-rating questionnaire.

Based on review of the project success criteria literature, the self- and supervisor-rating questionnaires addressed the issue of perceived success according to differing stakeholder perspectives, seeking ratings of the participating project personnel on a 1 (low) to 5 (high) scale of perceived value to clients, value to their organization, effectiveness of relationships in achieving project goals, and ability to inspire and encourage the performance of others.

A deficiency of the perceived performance rating instruments was that information was only sought from the participant and his supervisor (or suitable equivalent). Ideally feedback would also have been sought from other stakeholders, such as clients, but this was beyond the achievable scope of the study. Another problem encountered was in securing completed rating forms from supervisors. Subsequently, although the supervisor rating appears to be a more reliable indicator (Cronbach's alpha 0.8650) than the self-rating (Cronbach's alpha 0.6214), responses are not available for all participants. Difficulties in obtaining supervisor ratings highlighted an interesting dimension of the project manager role. In a number of cases, organizations claimed that there was no one in a position to rate the performance of the participating project personnel.

It must also be noted that the standards do not directly address two important factors identified in the literature review, namely leadership, drawing primarily on personality characteristics, and technical performance, which tends to be application area specific and is therefore not directly addressed in generic standards.

The sample for the study was obtained by asking organizations in Australia, the United Kingdom, and the United States to identify between five and twenty of their project personnel to participate in the study. Data collection was conducted on the premises of participating organizations.

Reluctance on the part of respondents to provide either age or gender, or both, reduced the value of these variables for analysis. However, based on those who did respond, the demographics of the study resemble those of PMI membership (Project Management Institute 1999b) in terms of both age (Table 4) and gender (Table 5).

The industry sector of organization and regional location of the study group is shown in Table 6. As the research was funded by an Australian Research Council grant for conducting it in Australia, the Australian sample is the largest and best distributed. Engineering and construction organizations in the United States were reluctant to participate in the study, largely due to the time commitment required.

Self and Supervisor Ratings—Perceived Performance

Competence is a socially constructed concept (Burgoyne 1993) and studies which have endeavored to identify high performance competencies (Boyatzis 1982; Schroder 1989; Gadeken and Cullen 1990; Cockerill 1989) have encountered difficulties in identifying the best or most effective performers.

As a measure of job performance, Boyatzis (1982), in his study of general managers, suggests three types of performance or criterion measure:

- Supervisory nominations or ratings
- Peer nominations or ratings
- Work-output measures.

Supervisory ratings are, of course, subjective, and it is recognized that subjective measures are excessively prone to contamination, especially by supervisor bias (Campbell 1990). However, Nathan and Alexander (1988) conclude that objective measures are *not* more predictive than subjective measures. The most important issues appear to be awareness of the potential construct validity threats of any measure used (Bommer et al. 1995) and recognition that performance is not a single construct (Campbell 1990).

In the field of project management competence and effectiveness, some studies have used a supervisor's subjective rating of the degree of effectiveness of the project participant under examination. Thamhain and Wilemon (1977) asked superiors to rate project managers relative to their peers on overall project performance on a 0-100 percent scale.

Gadeken (1991) having experienced the problem on a previous occasion in his studies of US defense systems procurement program managers (Gadeken and Cullen 1990) has explained the dilemma of identifying project management effectiveness:

> The first and most difficult step in the job competency assessment process is to identify truly outstanding performers to study. For project managers, this is problematic because there are no clearly objective performance measures that can be applied. Overall assessment of project success and hence project manager success is difficult because of the complexity and extended time duration of most projects. Also many projects are significantly affected by external funding and political factors. Since projects usually involve several project managers over their duration, the current project manager may benefit or suffer from the efforts of his predecessors. Consequently, the only reasonable and acceptable approach for this study was to ask for nominations from senior officials (Gadeken 1991, 7).

For the purposes of this study, scales were constructed to distinguish top from lower performers by taking the total scores for the self- (n = 347) and supervisor- (n = 208) rating instruments, and identifying those above median score as top performers and those below the median score as lower performers. Those cases with scores on the median were removed to ensure a clear split between top and lower performers, leaving a sample size of n = 278 for self-ratings and n = 176 for supervisor ratings.

It is important to note that due to the method of selecting the sample, all participants in this study should be considered to be relatively effective performers. All participants were, at the time of the study, employed in project roles by organizations that recognized the value of project management sufficiently to support the study and valued the participants sufficiently to support the time that they spent in providing data for the study. Therefore, any differentiation in terms of performance must recognize that such performance is relative only. Those who are identified as lower performers are still gainfully employed in project roles.

Using this scoring, and relating self-ratings and supervisor ratings, 31 percent of the sample were rated as having low perceived performance by both themselves and their supervisors. Twenty-seven percent rated their performance as high, and this was supported by supervisor ratings. Twenty-four percent of the sample rated themselves high but their performance was considered low by supervisors, and 19 percent of the sample was rated more highly by their supervisors than they rated themselves.

Project Management Knowledge as a Predictor of Perceived Effective Performance

Analysis of the previous results (independent samples T-Test) on the multiple choice knowledge test using the nine knowledge areas identified in the *PMBOK® Guide* and related to perceived performance as outlined above, provided no direct

1 = I have never done or participated in doing this.
2 = I have done or do this under supervision.
3 = I have done or occasionally do this myself.
4 = I have often done or do this myself.
5 = I have done and managed this across multiple projects or subprojects.

Table 7. Scale Used for Reporting of Use of Project Management Practices

evidence that more knowledge in these areas lead to greater perceived effectiveness of performance. However, investigation using logistic regression methods to explore the relationships between variables, revealed that increasing levels of project management knowledge appear to have a positive rather than a negative effect upon supervisor perceptions, with the possible exception of quality knowledge although this is at a lower level of significance.

Project Management Practices as a Predictor of Perceived Effective Performance

No direct relationship between the use of practices and supervisor perceptions of performance was identified (independent samples T-Test). However, exploratory analysis suggested complex relationships between the use of practices and supervisor perceptions of performance with some practices (e.g., contract finalization, time management) enhancing the odds of being perceived as a top performer while other practices (e.g., communication activities, stakeholder management) were associated with decreasing odds.

Two levels of analysis were applied to the results collected in the self-assessment against the *Australian National Competency Standards for Project Management*.

1. Summary scores were calculated for each of the nine units in the *Australian National Competency Standards*, identifying patterns of use of the practices and then exploring their predictive value relative to perceived effective performance.

2. Summary scores were calculated for literature-derived constructs.

Analysis at Unit Level

Each of the nine units in the *Australian National Competency Standards for Project Management* is made up of a number of elements and performance criteria—integration (11), scope (8), time (9), cost (9), quality (11), human resource management (12), communications (11), risk (9), and procurement (14). Data was collected by asking each respondent to indicate, on a 5-point scale (Table 7), their level of experience in each of the ninety-four performance criteria.

The nine Units have good reliability with Cronbach's alpha ranging from 0.8384 for integration to 0.9494 for procurement. From investigation of pat-

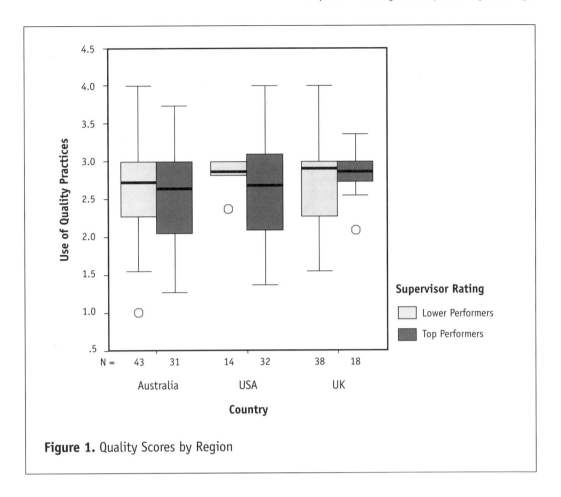

Figure 1. Quality Scores by Region

terns of use of practices, the spread for use of integration, scope, time, cost, and communications practices is fairly evenly distributed across the sample.

Quality, human resource management, and risk practices are not evenly distributed, with fewer people using practices in these units, than those who do not. Procurement is particularly interesting. There are some who use procurement practices extensively, some who don't appear to become involved in procurement practices at all and others in the middle range.

Quality is the only one of the nine items for which there is an apparent distinction between the perceived top and lower performers (Figure 1). Those perceived *as less effective performers* have slightly *more experience* in use of quality practices. Quality results also provide an opportunity to demonstrate an overall tendency for the supervisor scores to be different between countries. The distinction is particularly marked between the UK and the rest, interpretable as a cultural difference where in the UK being understated and "objective" is valued more highly.

The use of communications practices, associated in logistic regression models with decreasing odds of being perceived as a top performer, provides a further example of cultural differences on perception of performance. Analysis (Figure 2)

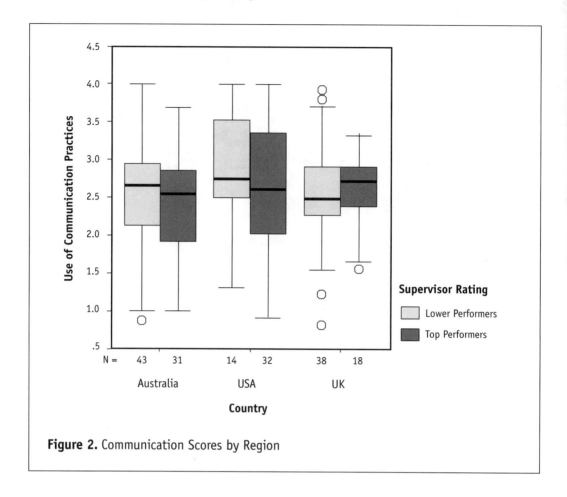

Figure 2. Communication Scores by Region

reveals that those perceived as lower performers have slightly more experience in the use of communications practices for both the Australian and US samples, while the reverse is true in the UK where those perceived as top performers have higher levels of experience in the use of communications practices.

Analysis Based on Literature-Derived Constructs

Each of the ninety-four performance criteria against which data was collected were grouped according to the literature-derived constructs presented in Table 2. A reliability analysis was conducted, identifying those constructs that had a reasonably high value (above 0.80) for Cronbach's alpha. Only a few of the more interesting constructs will be discussed here.

Planning (Integrative) (alpha = 0.8319)

Use of this group of practices, consistently considered in the first rank of importance according to the literature analysis (Table 2), shows that there is a tendency for all self-assessed, high-performing individuals to have a higher rating on the planning (integrative) scale. However, this pattern is not supported by supervisor

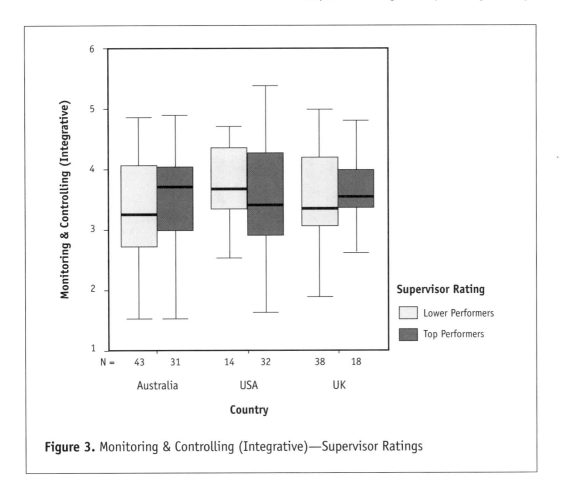

Figure 3. Monitoring & Controlling (Integrative)—Supervisor Ratings

perceptions. In logistic regression models based on supervisor ratings, integrative planning is associated with decreasing odds of being perceived as a top performer.

Monitoring & Controlling (Integrative) (alpha = 0.9005)

This variable represents a consistent construct, based on eleven items. This construct, identified in the first rank of importance according in post-1995 research-based literature for both success factors (Table 1) and project manager competence (Table 2), was also identified in logistic regression analysis as a variable associated with increasing odds of being perceived as a top performer. Examining the supervisor ratings, this tendency is apparent (Figure 3) for both the Australian and UK, but not for the US sample, where those identified as top performers tend to have lower scores for use of these practices.

This construct also provides a useful illustration of the tendency for self-ratings to be less affected by cultural differences than supervisor ratings, with higher scores for use of monitoring and controlling (integrative) practices being more strongly and consistently associated with self-assessed top performers (Figure 4).

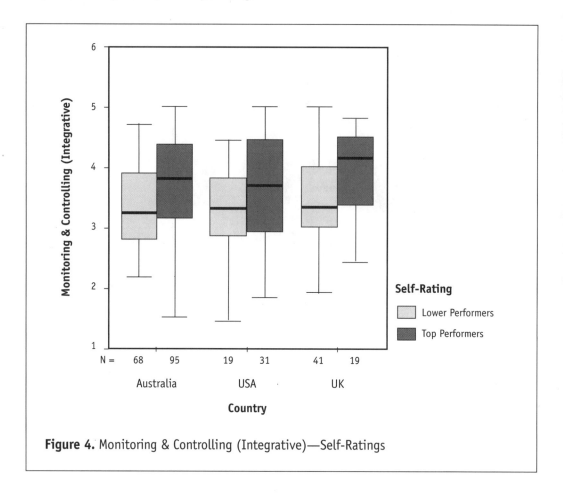

Figure 4. Monitoring & Controlling (Integrative)—Self-Ratings

Monitoring & Controlling (Risk) (alpha = 0.9024)

This is a very reliable construct, even though it is only based on four items. However, the sample is divided between those who use risk management practices and those who don't. There is a tendency for higher scores on this item to be associated with higher self-rating of success. On the other hand, it does not appear to be associated with higher supervisor ratings (Figures 5 and 6).

Team Development (alpha = 0.8974)

There is a very small group scoring highly on this scale, and quite a large group scoring well below 2.5, indicating that there are many people who are not using these practices. This is interesting given the high ranking this construct received based on the literature. Team development is not identified in logistic regression analysis as a predictor of perceived performance.

Lessons Learned (alpha = 0.9351)

Despite considerable rhetoric concerning the importance of capturing, sharing, and utilizing lessons learned, this construct does not appear in the results of the literature review. This may be a result of focus, in research and literature, on man-

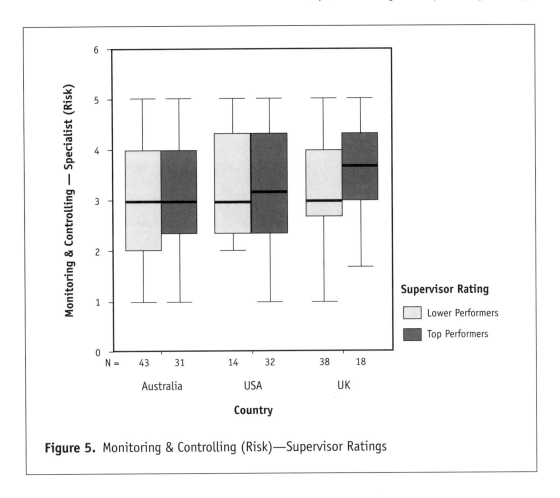

Figure 5. Monitoring & Controlling (Risk)—Supervisor Ratings

agement of single projects. More recently interest has been widened to consideration of organizational project management and multiproject contexts (Engwall and Kallqvist 1999; Turner and Keegan 2000) and further research in this area may justify inclusion of lessons learned as a required area of project management competence. As it stands, there are a number of performance criteria in the *Australian National Competency Standards for Project Management* that relate to lessons learned that could not be grouped with variables identified from the research-based literature. It is interesting however, that this is a very reliable construct, based on fourteen items, but that most people score low on this scale. In other words, most project management personnel in the sample do not use lessons learned practices. There is a slight tendency for those with higher scores to be perceived by supervisors in all three countries (Australia, US, and UK) as lower performers. Higher scores are associated with top performers in self-ratings.

Conclusions

The competence of project managers is clearly a vital factor in the success of projects, yet it remains a quality that is difficult to quantify. The majority of research

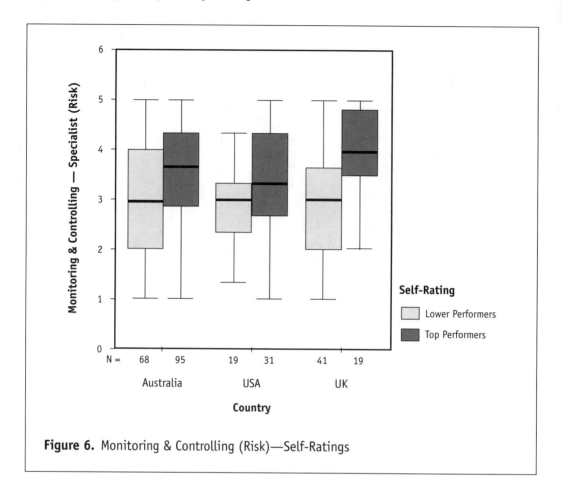

Figure 6. Monitoring & Controlling (Risk)—Self-Ratings

and standards development conducted to date relating to project management competence is based on the opinions of project management practitioners and others. The research reported here has attempted to approach the profiling of the competent project manager from a potentially more objective viewpoint, by gathering data on project management knowledge and practices, using established project management standards, and then relating this to separately derived ratings of perceived workplace performance. Analysis suggests, however, that there is little direct relationship between perceived workplace performance and performance against either project management standards or previous research findings.

The only construct that appears in the highest rankings of both project success factors (Table 1) and project manager competence (Table 2) and is also valued by senior management (supervisors), being identified in logistic regression models as a predictor of supervisor perceptions of high performance, is monitoring and controlling (integrative). While integrative planning is the literature-derived construct most consistently identified in the top rank in the literature analysis as a key factor in project success and project manager competence, the value placed on integrative planning practices by project managers does not appear to be supported by senior management (supervisors). Team development practices, although highly rated in the literature as a factor in project success and project manager competence, are not widely used and higher levels of use do not appear to have any predictive value in terms of supervisor assessment of performance.

Some constructs identified in the research-based literature, such as leadership and technical performance, are not covered by standards, while lessons learned, although included in the *Australian National Competency Standards for Project Management*, are not identified at all in research into project success and project manager competence.

Research results indicate that project management activities valued by project managers are not necessarily the same as those valued by senior management (supervisors), suggesting an important avenue for further research. Associated with this are apparent cultural differences in perceptions and rating of performance between countries, with supervisors in the US significantly more likely to give higher ratings than those in either Australia or the UK. Personality characteristics and application area specific technical issues are not addressed by the standards, suggesting a need for further investigation in these areas.

References

Dixon, M. 2000. *APM Project Management Body of Knowledge*. 4th ed. Peterborough, England: Association for Project Management.

Ashley, David B., Clive S. Lurie, and Edward J. Jaselskis. 1987. Determinants of Construction Project Success. *Project Management Journal* XVIII (2): 69–79.

Baccarini, David. 1999. The Logical Framework Method for Defining Project Success. *Project Management Journal* 30 (4): 25–32.

Baker, Bruce N., David C. Murphy, and Dalmar Fisher. 1988. Factors Affecting Project Success. In *Project Management Handbook* (902–919), edited by David I. Cleland and William R. King. 2nd ed. New York: Van Nostrand Reinhold.

Bommer, William H. et al. 1995. On the Interchangeability of Objective and Subjective Measures of Employee Performance: A Meta-Analysis. *Personnel Psychology* 48 (3): 587–606.

Boyatzis, Richard. E. 1982. *The Competent Manager: A Model for Effective Performance*. New York: John Wiley & Sons, Inc.

Burgoyne, John G. 1993. The Competence Movement: Issues, Stakeholders and Prospects. *Personnel Review* 22 (6): 6–13.

Campbell, J. P. 1990. *Modeling the Performance Prediction Problem in Industrial and Organizational Psychology*. 2nd ed (1). Palo Alto, California: Consulting Psychologists Press.

Clarke, Angela. 1995. The Key Success Factors in Project Management. *Proceedings of a Teaching Company Seminar*. London: The Teaching Company.

———. 1999. A Practical Use of Key Success Factors to Improve the Effectiveness of Project Management. *International Journal of Project Management* 17 (3): 139–145.

Cleland, David I., and William R. King. 1988. *Project Management Handbook*. 2nd ed. New York: Van Nostrand Reinhold.

Cockerill, Tony. 1989. *Managerial Competencies as a Determinant of Organizational Performance*. London: London University.

Dewhirst, Dudley. 1996. Needed: A New Model for Training Project Managers. *PM Network* (November): 25–27.

Dinsmore, Paul C. 1993. *The AMA Handbook of Project Management*. New York: AMACOM.

Einsiedel, Albert A. 1987. Profile of Effective Project Managers. *Project Management Journal* XVII (5): 51–56.

Engwall, Mats, and Anna S. Kallqvist. 1999. The Multiproject Matrix: A Neglected Phenomenon. In *IRNOP IV Conference—Paradoxes of Project Collaboration in the Global Economy: Interdependence, Complexity and Ambiguity*. Edited by Lynn Crawford and Cecelia F. Clarke. Sydney, Australia: University of Technology, Sydney.

Ford, Robert C., and Frank S. McLaughlin. 1992. 10 Questions and Answers on Managing MIS Projects. *Project Management Journal* XXIII (3): 21–28.

Freeman, Mark, and Peter Beale. 1992. Measuring Project Success. *Project Management Journal* XXIII (1): 8–17.

Gaddis, P. O. 1959. The Project Manager. *Harvard Business Review* 37 (3): 89–97.

Gadeken, Owen C., and B. J. Cullen. 1990. *A Competency Model of Project Managers in the DoD Acquisition Process*. Defense Systems Management College.

Gadeken, Owen. C. 1991. *Competencies of Project Managers in the MOD Procurement Executive*. Royal Military College of Science.

Geddes, M. 1990. Project Leadership and the Involvement of Users in IT Projects. *International Journal of Project Management* 8 (4): 214–216.

Gemmill, Gary R. 1974. The Effectiveness of Different Power Styles of Project Managers in Gaining Project Support. *Project Management Quarterly* 5 (1).

Gonczi, A., P. Hager, and L. Oliver, eds. 1990. *Establishing Competency Standards in the Professions*. Canberra: Australian Government Publishing Service.

Heywood, L., A. Gonczi, and P. Hager. 1992. *A Guide to Development of Competency Standards for Professions*. Canberra: Australian Government Publishing Service.

International Project Manageement Association. 1999. *ICB: IPMA Competence Baseline*. Ed. G. Caupin, H. Knopfel, P. Morris, E. Motzel, and O. Pannenbacker. Germany: International Project Management Association.

Jiang, James J., Gary Klein, and Joseph Balloun. 1996. Ranking of System Implementation Success Factors. *Project Management Journal* XXVII (4): 49–53.

Kerzner, Harold. 1998. *Project Management: A Systems Approach to Planning, Scheduling and Controlling*. 2nd ed. United States: Van Nostrand Reinhold.

Lechler, Thomas. 1998. When It Comes to Project Management, It's the People that Matter: An Empirical Analysis of Project Management in Germany. In *IRNOP III—The Nature and Role of Projects in the Next 20 Years: Research Issues and Problems*. Edited by Francis Hartman, George Jergeas, and Janice Thomas. Calgary: Project Management Specialization, University of Calgary.

Management Charter Initiative. 1997. *Manage Projects: Management Standards—Key Role G*. London: Management Charter Initiative.

Meredith, Jack R., and Samuel J. Mantel, Jr. 1995. *Project Management: A Managerial Approach*. 3rd ed. New York: John Wiley & Sons, Inc.

Morris, Peter W. G. 2000. Benchmarking Project Management Bodies of Knowledge. In *IRNOP IV Conference—Paradoxes of Project Collaboration in the Global Economy: Interdependence, Complexity and Ambiguity*. Edited by Lynn Crawford and Cecelia F. Clarke. Sydney, Australia: University of Technology, Sydney.

Murphy, David C., Bruce N. Baker, and Dalmar Fisher. 1974. *Determinants of Project Success*. Boston: Boston College, National Aeronautics and Space Administration.

Nathan, B. R., and R. A. Alexander. 1988. A Comparison of Criteria for Test Validation: A Meta-Analytic Investigation. *Personnel Psychology* 41: 517–535.

Occupational Standards Council for Engineering (OSCEng). 1996. *OSCEng Level 4. NVQ/SVQ in Project Controls*. England: Occupational Standards Council for Engineering.

———. 1997. *OSCEng Levels 4 and 5: NVQ/SVQ in (Generic) Project Management*. England: Occupational Standards Council for Engineering.

Pettersen, Normand. 1991. Selecting Project Managers: An Integrated List of Predictors. *Project Management Journal* XXII (2): 21–25.

Pinto, Jeffrey K., and Denis P. Slevin. 1987. Critical Factors in Successful Project Implementation. *IEEE Transactions on Engineering Management (EM)* 34 (1): 22–27.

———. 1988. Project Success: Definitions and Measurement Techniques. *Project Management Journal* XIX (1): 67–72.

Pinto, Jeffrey K. 1998. *The Project Management Institute Project Management Handbook*. San Francisco: Jossey-Bass Publishers.

Posner, Barry Z. 1987. What It Takes to Be a Good Project Manager. *Project Management Journal* (March): 51–54.

Project Management Institute. 1999a. *A Guide to the Project Management Body of Knowledge (PMBOK® Guide)*. Approved by ANSI as an American National Standard [webpage]. Available at http://www.pmi.org/standards/. (Accessed 13 April 2001.)

———. 1999b. *The PMI Project Management Fact Book*. Newtown Square, PA: Project Management Institute.

———. 2000. *A Guide to the Project Management Body of Knowledge* (PMBOK® Guide) – 2000 Edition. Newtown Square, PA: Project Management Institute.

Schroder, Harold M. 1989. *Managerial Competence: The Key to Excellence*. Iowa: Kendall Hunt.

Shenhar, Aaron J., Ofer Levy, and Dov Dvir. 1997. Mapping the Dimensions of Project Success. *Project Management Journal* 28 (2): 5–13.

Slevin, Denis P., and Jeffrey K. Pinto. 1986. The Project Implementation Profile: New Tool for Project Managers. *Project Management Journal* XVII (4): 57–70.

Thamhain, Hans J., and David L. Wilemon. 1977. Leadership Effectiveness in Program Management. *Project Management Quarterly* (June): 25–31.

Thamhain, Hans J. 1991. Developing Project Management Skills. *Project Management Journal* XXII (3): 39–44.

Thamhain, Hans J., and Gary R. Gemmill. 1974. Influence Styles of Project Managers: Some Project Performance Correlates. *Academy of Management Journal* 17 (2): 216–224.

Thamhain, Hans J., and David L. Wilemon. 1978. Skill Requirements of Engineering Program Managers. Convention Record, *26th Joint Engineering Management Conference*.

The Standish Group. 2000. *Chaos* [webpage]. Available at http://www.standishgroup.com/chaos.html. (Accessed 19 February 2000.)

Turner, J. R. 1993. *The Handbook of Project-Based Management*. Maidenhead: McGraw-Hill.

Turner, J. R., and Anne Keegan. 2000. The Management of Operations in the Project-Based Organization. *Journal of Change Management*. Submitted for publication.

Wateridge, J. F. 1996. *Delivering Successful IS/IT Projects: Eight Key Elements from Success Criteria to Review via Appropriate Management, Methodologies and Teams*. Henley Management College, Brunel University: Henley Management College Library.

Whittaker, Brenda. 1999. What Went Wrong? Unsuccessful Information Technology Projects. *Information Management & Computer Security* 7 (1): 23–29.

Zimmerer, Thomas W., and Mahmoud M. Yasin. 1998. A Leadership Profile of American Project Managers. *Project Management Journal* 29 (1): 31–38.

Construct	Alpha	ANCSPM Ref #	Comment
Leadership		No related performance criteria.	
Planning—Integrative	0.8319	1.1.3; 1.1.4; 4.1.3; 8.1.3; 8.1.4; 9.1.1	
Team Development V	0.897	6.2.1; 6.2.2; 6.2.3; 6.3.1; 6.3.2; 6.3.3; 6.3.4; 9.1.2; 6.2.1; 6.2.2; 6.2.3; 6.3.1	
Communication	0.8715	7.1.1; 7.1.2; 7.1.3; 7.2.1; 7.3.1; 9.2.2	
Technical Performance		5.1.1	Only one item.
Organization Structure	0.5234	1.2.1; 6.1.2	Low reliability as a scale exacerbated by small number of items.
Stakeholder Management (Parent Organization)	0.7329	1.2.2; 1.2.3; 2.1.1	
Strategic Direction	0.7258	1.1.2; 2.2.1; 2.2.2; 5.1.3	
Monitoring & Controlling—Integrative	0.9005	1.3.1; 1.3.2; 1.3.3; 2.3.2; 2.3.3; 3.2.1; 3.2.3; 4.2.3; 7.2.2; 7.3.2; 8.2.2	A scale with strong reliability.
Decision-Making and Problem Solving			No items.
Monitoring & Controlling—Specialist (Cost)	0.7638	1.3.2; 4.2.1; 4.2.2; 8.2.2	
Planning—Specialist (Time)	0.7396	3.1.1; 3.1.2	
Project Definition	0.7971	2.2.1; 2.2.3; 2.3.1; 5.1.1; 9.1.2	
Stakeholder Management (Client)	0.6121	1.1.1; 7.3.3; 9.2.3	
Administration		6.1.4	Only one item.
Monitoring & Controlling—Specialist (Scope)	0.7747	2.3.2; 3.2.2; 3.2.4	
Planning—Specialist (Cost)	0.8166	4.1.1; 4.1.2; 4.1.3	
Stakeholder Management (Other)		7.3.3	Only one item.
Team Selection	0.8954	6.1.1; 6.1.3; 6.2.1; 6.2.2; 6.2.3; 6.3.1	
Monitoring & Controlling—Specialist (Risk)	0.9024	8.1.1; 8.1.2; 8.2.1; 8.2.3	This is a very reliable construct although based on only 4 items.
Monitoring & Controlling—Specialist (Time)	0.6954	1.3.2; 3.1.3; 8.2.2	
Closing Integrative	0.7107	7.4.1; 4.3.1; 9.5.1	
Monitoring & Controlling—Specialist (Quality)	0.6352	5.1.4; 5.3.1	
Lessons Learned	0.9531	1.3.4; 2.3.4; 3.3.1; 3.3.2; 4.3.2; 4.3.3; 5.3.3; 6.3.5; 7.4.2; 7.4.3; 8.3.1; 8.3.2; 9.5.2; 9.5.3	This is a very reliable construct based on 14 items. It is one of the constructs that did not appear in the literature.
Procurement	0.9625	9.2.1; 9.2.2; 9.2.3; 9.3.1; 9.3.2; 9.3.3; 9.4.1; 9.4.2; 9.4.3; 9.5.1	Procurement receives little or no mention in the literature, but this is very reliable construct.
Quality	0.8879	5.1.2; 5.2.1; 5.2.2; 5.2.3; 5.2.4; 5.3.2	Quality is another item that is barely mentioned, directly, in the literature (Section 2.5).

Appendix A. Performance Criteria from *Australian National Compentency Standards for Project Management* (Grouped by Literature-Derived Constructs)

CHAPTER 9

Measuring Project Management's Value: New Directions for Quantifying PM/ROI^{SM}

C. William Ibbs, Ph.D., P.E.—University of California, Berkeley

Justin Reginato, P.E.—University of California, Berkeley

Introduction

Previous research investigated the quantitative value of project management; that is, project management's return on investment (PM/ROI^{SM}). The results, while encouraging, were not statistically significant. A second study is under way that will address that previous study's shortcomings: insufficient sample size (only thirty-eight companies and seventeen projects); an outdated version of the Project Management Body of Knowledge (PMBOK®) (eight knowledge areas rather than the current nine); project data selection by the benchmarked companies (which may interject bias and unreliability into the source data); and variability of project performance metrics.

This chapter outlines some of the issues that have set the foundation for that second study.

Today's Successful Organization

Increasingly the successful business organizational model is taking the form of a loosely coupled confederation of business units. Examples of the loose confederation model include Microsoft® (software), Fidelity and Vanguard (financial services), Genentech and Millennium Pharmaceuticals (bio-engineering and life sciences), and General Electric (in various industries). They are successful because they have grown exponential revenues and profits during the past decade and have achieved remarkable stock market capitalization.

These firms share common characteristics such as devolved power, strong emphasis on intellectual property, powerful brand identification, and a premium on project-driven services. They are all more bottom-line (net profit) focused, as well; whereas many companies in the past had more diffuse goals such as revenue growth, market share, technology leadership, and so on. Companies that have historically attended to "softer measures" such as social responsibility and public welfare, charitable donations, and a satisfied workforce (Ben & Jerry's Ice Cream, various dot-coms, the "old IBM," and universities) are definitely out of vogue these days. Strong, centralized, command-and-control companies (General Motors, the United States [US] Federal Government) are decidedly lagging in today's hyper-competitive environment, as well.

The most important characteristic in the eyes of this readership is that these companies depend on projects for much of their success. Benefits of a project-centric focus and sophisticated project management processes include improving organizational effectiveness, meeting quality standards, and fulfilling customer satisfaction (Al-Sedairy 1994; Boznak 1988; Bu-Bushait 1989; Construction Industry Institute 1990; Deutsch 1991; Gross 1990; Ziomek 1984). However, the senior management of these companies is very demanding in terms of proof in more quantitative terms.

The progress of our research in this area is presented in this chapter.

Prior Research

Previous work in this arena includes the work of Ibbs and Kwak (1997). This study developed and presented the 5-step Berkeley Project Management Process Maturity Model to better understand and locate an organization's current project management process level.

The Berkeley Model is an adaptation from Crosby (1979), the Software Engineering Institute (Paulk 1993), and McCauley (1993). The novel feature is that it incorporates a learning component (Level 5), which many companies profess to support but in reality do not.

The next step was to use this model to benchmark over thirty-eight companies in five different industries. The express purpose of this study was to test the research hypothesis:

H_o: Project management has value to companies that can be quantitatively demonstrated.

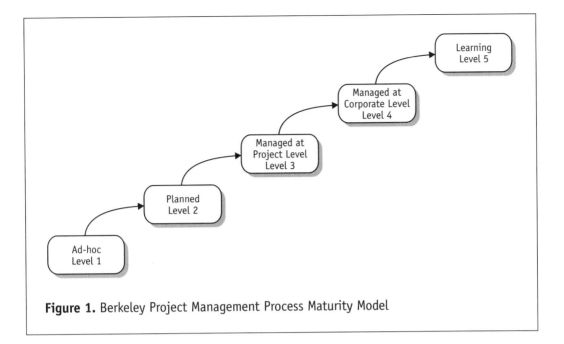

Figure 1. Berkeley Project Management Process Maturity Model

Though the research broke new ground, it did not prove this hypothesis in a traditional, academic sense. Namely, the Berkeley team found that:

- There was an association, but not a statistically significant relationship, between an organization's project management maturity and its ability to execute projects more effectively.
- There was an association, but not statistically significant relationship, between a company's project management expenditures and its project effectiveness.
- There was no meaningful relationship between the number of professionally-trained project managers (including Project Management Professionals (PMP®) and the company's ability to execute projects.

Companies were seen to be relatively weak in the project risk management knowledge area and in the project execution and project support phase areas, which confirmed the suspicions of many industry professionals.

This first study had weaknesses though. Among these weaknesses were:

- The survey population was self-selecting and principally the companies themselves conducted the project management maturity assessment. The Berkeley research team provided some quality assurance of the responses but not as much as ideally desired. Limited resources precluded a more comprehensive study.

■ Project management maturity was contrasted with project cost and schedule indices. One complication was the question of budget and baseline consistencies between companies (e.g., authorized budget at concept versus authorized budget at contract signing). Perhaps more importantly, the cost index was probably of secondary importance for those enterprises whose revenues derived from the project's deliverable were not tightly coupled to the project's costs. For instance, software prices and revenues were more a function of market-driven pricing and perceived value, and not just a markup on project cost (as was the case in the construction industry).

■ Project management cost accounting structures differed radically among companies, to the extent that tracking the cost of project management services was, at best, haphazard in most companies. Companies amortized project management training, for instance, quite differently. Moreover, the line between operations and project management was rarely clearly delineated; so salaries, for one, were quite difficult to apportion. On a more global level, many corporate accounting systems were designed to track functions (marketing, engineering, research and development [R&D]) but not the portion of engineering or accounting that directly, let alone indirectly, supported a project.

■ The value of project management was measured by its return on investment (ROI). Some have argued for different measures. For instance, Knutson (1999) presents a benefit-cost calculation, but ignores the time value of money and ignores subtleties such as how to amortize project-related capital costs. Crawford (Cabanis-Brewin 2000), on the other hand, has proposed a "balanced scorecard approach," but does not specify how to define and cope with the various details. It also puts an artificial and masking weight on qualitative aspects in an attempt to balance them with quantitative factors.

To improve upon the previous study, the Berkeley team has taken a very active role in the assessment process, both in terms of guiding each participant through the assessment process and by performing follow-up interviews to ensure data quality and accuracy. A revamped assessment tool will help organizations to itemize their project management expenditures, lending to increased ROI calculations.

What is Value?

The question of value is almost an epistemological question. It depends very much on whose perspective is being taken. For our purposes, we will assume the perspective of the shareowners of the enterprise. Other perspectives exist, such as those of customers, employees, the public-at-large, and so on. Ultimately though, the first perspective that matters most is usually that of the owners and investors of the company. A shareholder revolution has occurred within the past decade due to the emergence of mutual funds companies and widespread pension plans like 401(k)s. In the past couple of years, we have seen increasingly fickle shareholders reward profitable companies while bludgeoning others. One Wall Street message is once again clear: in the post-Internet bubble economy, shareholder value is vital. And since project management is a corporate asset, managers and investors are seeking an answer to the question "What is project management's return on investment?"

How Should We Measure Value?

There are several approaches to answering this question. One methodology that speaks in "CEO language" is the economic value added (EVA) and market value added (MVA) procedures developed and popularized by the financial consulting firm, Stern Stewart & Company. In simple terms, this methodology requires an analysis of the firm's cost of capital for any new investment (e.g., business line, acquisition, assets) and the true economic gain (in the case of EVA) or the gain in stock market capitalization (MVA) attributable to that investment. Today, MVA is the preferred model if the company's valuation can be measured reliably. Prudent investments have a MVA that is greater than the cost of capital that the firm must expend to make that investment.

One of the difficulties of applying MVA to this field is that project management does not always directly and exclusively contribute to a company's market capitalization (as in the case of companies like Hewlett-Packard). Also, MVA is a very meticulous procedure, where capital costs must be amortized and pooled costs distributed to the appropriate business unit or project.

Benefit/Cost (B/C) analysis is another methodology that has been used for project management investment analysis in the past (Knutson 1999). However, it is largely discounted these days because of conceptual flaws. For instance, when comparing multiple projects, there is ambiguity over whether to select the project with a superior B/C ratio or perhaps another project with a greater B/C difference. Another problem is that B/C comparisons must be discounted for the time value of money, and it is easy to hide the discounting factor. Finally, B/C analysis has acquired a stigma because it has occasionally been used to improperly legitimize the quantification of qualitative factors (Riggs 1984).

Others have suggested balancing tangible and intangible metrics to appraise project management value (Crawford and Pennypacker 2000). They contend that a mix of financial and non-financial measures allow companies to track the metrics that matter most to themselves. Unfortunately, from the standpoint of shareholders, allowing managers to pick metrics that best suit them, particularly non-financial, may be the equivalent of allowing "the fox to watch the henhouse." Organizations must exercise caution when measuring value with non-financial measures. The use of non-financial measures can be disadvantageous because multiple measurements can be time consuming and the cost of measurement greater than the benefits. Bureaucratic measurement policy may degenerate into practices that add little value to the bottom line resulting in "paralysis by analysis." Additionally, unlike accounting measures, non-financial metrics have no common denominator, and thus comparisons between other companies (and even different business units within one company) may be arbitrary. This, in turn, will lead to a lack of statistical reliability. Lastly, while financial measures alone may not paint a complete picture of management performance, a scorecard system with an overabundance of measures can dilute the effects of the measurement process (Ittner 2000).

Crawford and Pennypacker also fail to explain how balanced measures are linked to shareholder value. Combining tangible and intangible measures only works if its implementation moves beyond an ad-hoc collection of financial and non-financial measures (Ampuero 1998). The purpose of a scorecard is to map an organization's overall strategy, comparing individual units on equal footing where financial measures alone may not tell the entire story. However, the strategy must be implemented with a cause-and-effect model that links measures to shareholder value, through a vehicle such as ROI or EVA. In other words, it is not productive to simply measure metrics regarding customer satisfaction, employee satisfaction, quality, EVA, and so forth, but to join each metric in a causal financial relationship that determines how shareholder value is being created or destroyed, a point overlooked in recent applications of balanced measures to management (Kaplan 1996; Kenney).

Lastly, by using non-financial measures to determine value, organizations run the additional risk of reporting values that seem fuzzy to institutional lenders, analysts, and shareholders. Accurate financial reporting is crucial for companies because their cost of capital is tightly linked to the quality of their measurement—the better and more trustworthy the measurement of value, the lower the cost of capital for that organization because of reduced risk to investors. Banks and investors may experience difficulty determining the cost of capital for organizations that use non-financial measures to determine value, but the aforementioned stakeholders can easily grasp rational measures of value such as the ROI. If organizations as a whole use financial measures to report the value of the corporation, then project management should follow suit (Tarsala 2001; Larcker 1999).

The PM/ROI[SM] Trifecta

To best measure the value of project management, we propose and are pursuing a process that combines an organization's project management maturity and its cash flow ROI from a project, what we call PM/ROI[SM]. Benchmarking can determine a company's project management effectiveness and captures the non-quantitative measures that many turn to balanced measures to determine. However, our model is project management-specific, drawing on the PMBOK® and established project management processes for its depth of analysis (see Figure 2). This allows non-financial and qualitative measures to be captured within the PM/ROI[SM] fold.

PM/ROI[SM] has the added benefit of joining project management maturity with a quantifiable financial measure that determines its monetary value. The cash flow ROI, an established and trustworthy financial method, is used to calculate project

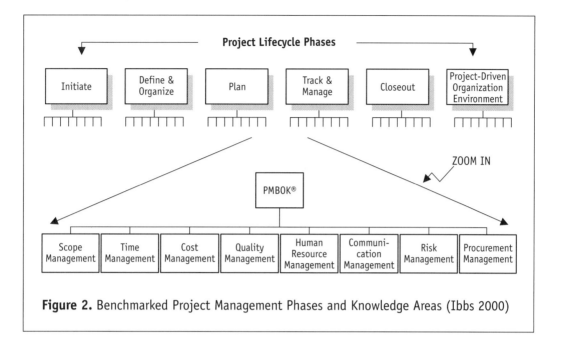

Figure 2. Benchmarked Project Management Phases and Knowledge Areas (Ibbs 2000)

management value. Cash flow ROI calculates the internal rate of return using risk and inflation-adjusted assets, asset life, capitalized operating leases, and so on, and it takes the weighted average cost of capital (WACC) into effect. While seemingly complex, it can be easily calculated with a spreadsheet and yields the most accurate financial measurement of value (Knight). ROI is then compared to a minimum attractive rate of return (MARR). If ROI is > MARR, the investment is feasible.

This method has the advantages of including the time value of money; it is a ratio approach, rather than an absolute number; it is well understand and tractable by chief executive officers (CEO), chief financial officers (CFO), and other senior executive audiences. By including the WACC in its calculation, organizations are able to take financial risk into consideration. ROI is also easily translatable across both companies experiencing rapid growth or those concentrating on capital or market preservation. Positive movements in ROI can be tracked by rapidly increasing returns (growth companies) and by increasing margins and/or decreasing capital (return companies) (Ferracone 2000). However, quantifying the benefits and costs can be tricky. Also, there are always competing requests for investment capital, and a ROI > MARR for project management does not automatically lead to an investment in project management.

Various factors can be used as risk surrogates and must be treated in a proper analysis. Often risk is handled by adjusting the MARR or WACC in line with the presumed and perceived risk of the investment. A pipeline project in Texas has an entirely different risk profile than the same project built in Nigeria. A software project using Microsoft Windows® and Access® is generally less risky than the same software project developed in a less popular software environment.

One way to measure the risk of a project management endeavor or project management department is to measure the ability to consistently deliver good cost, schedule, and quality performance. In other words, how able is a project management team to deliver superior performance and to deliver it reliably? The PM/ROI^{SM} process manages these issues.

The third and final pillar of the strength of PM/ROI^{SM} is that it allows organizations to capture the project management value generated from knowledge management. As previously stated, the fifth and highest level of project management maturity in the Berkeley model is based upon sustainable learning. Value creation, more than ever, is correlated with the knowledge-based organization, and the ability to learn translates into the ability to create seemingly insurmountable business advantages (Holland 1994). The Berkeley model is set up so that organizations with project management maturities approaching Level 5 are constantly adding new knowledge to their base of information, resulting in operations that improve themselves over time. The acquisition of knowledge begets new knowledge, all of which leads to super-competitive advantages (Hamel 2000). Intrepid organizations able to achieve higher project management maturities tend to create better returns on assets invested in project management, relating project management knowledge creation to project management economic value. The knowledge created and used by project management creates an additional lever from which competitive advantage can be exploited.

Summary

This chapter has sketched a few of the issues associated with measuring project management's value. By no means does the chapter prescribe a comprehensive research plan. But the chapter does reflect the current thinking of the Berkeley PM/ROI^{SM} team as it progresses with its second PMI-sponsored research study into project management's value.

The project is scheduled to be completed by the end of 2000. Progress and final results will be published in Project Management Institute (PMI®) forums as the research is completed.

References

Ampuero, Marcos, Jesse Goranson, and Jason Scott. 1998. Solving the Measurement Dilemma. *Strategic Performance Management Series* 2 (September).

Al-Sedairy, Salman T. 1994. Project Management Practices in Public Sector Construction: Saudi Arabia. *Project Management Journal* (December): 37–44.

Boznak, Rudolph G. 1988. Project Management—Today's Solution for Complex Project Engineering. *IEEE Proceedings*.

Bu-Bushait, K. A. 1989. The Application of Project Management Techniques to Construction and R&D Projects. *Project Management Journal* (June): 17–22.

Construction Industry Institute. 1990. Assessment of Owner Project Management Practices and Performance. *Special CII Publication* (April).

Crawford, Kent, and James Pennypacker. 2000. *The Value of Project Management: Why Every 21st Century Company Must Have an Effective Project Management Culture*. Center for Business Practices.

Crosby, Philip. 1979. *Quality is Free*. New York: McGraw-Hill.

Deutsch, Michael S. 1991. An Exploratory Analysis Relating the Software Project Management Process to Project Success. *IEEE Transactions on Engineering Management* 38, no. 4 (November).

Ferracone, Robin, and Bertha Masuda. 2000. It's the New Economy: Who Said Anything About Returns? *World at Work* (Fourth Quarter): 55–60.

Gross, Robert L., and David Price. 1990. Common Project Management Problems and How They Can be Avoided through the Use of Self Managing Teams. *1990 IEEE International Engineering Management Conference*.

Hamel, Gary. 2000. *Leading the Revolution*. Boston, MA: Harvard Business School Press.

Holland, Robert. 1994. *Leadership and Organizational Change*. Philadelphia, PA: Wharton School of Management.

Ibbs, C. W., and Young-Hoon Kwak. 1997. *The Benefits of Project Management-Financial and Organizational Rewards to Corporations*. Newtown Square, PA: Project Management Institute.

———. 2000. Calculating Project Management's Return on Investment. *Project Management Journal* 31 (2): 38–47.

Ittner, Christopher, and David Larcker. 2000. Non-Financial Performance Measures: What Works and What Doesn't. *Financial Times' Mastering Management* (October).

Kaplan, Robert, and David Norton. 1996. *The Balanced Scorecard: Translating Strategy into Action*. Boston, MA: Harvard Business School Press.

Kenney, Joseph, and Marcos Ampuero. Unpublished. *Ties That Bind—Using the Balance Scorecard to Link Compensation to Your Business Strategy*. Unpublished Ernst & Young paper.

Knight, James. Performance Measures and Strategy. *Handbook of Business Strategy*. Publisher and date unknown.

Knutson, Joan. 1999. A 3-part series in *PM Network* (January, February, and July).

Larcker, David, and Christopher Ittner. 1999. *Measures that Matter: Aligning Performance Measures with Corporate Strategy*. Philadelphia, PA: Wharton School of Management.

McCauley, Mike. 1993. Developing a Project-Driven Organization. *PM Network* (September): 26–30.

Paulk, Mark C. et al. 1993. Key Practices of the Capability Maturity Model, Version 1.1. Technical Report. *Software Engineering Institute*, SEI-93-TR-025.

Riggs, James et al. 1984. *Decision Analysis for Engineers*. New York: McGraw Hill.

Tarsala, Mike. 2001. Making the Most of the Market: Companies Should Be Judged By Their Efficiency. *CBS MarketWatch* (May 9).

Ziomek, N. L., and G. R. Meneghin. 1984. Training—A Key Element in Implementing Project Management. *Project Management Journal* (August): 76–83.

CHAPTER 10

PROJECT MANAGEMENT PRACTICES IN FRENCH ORGANIZATIONS: A STATE OF THE ART

Daniel Leroy, Ph.D.—Université des Sciences et Technologies de Lille

Introduction

The purpose of this study came from the discrepancy noticed between the current bodies of knowledge, both American and European—describing what should be effective project management practices—and what we could observe in the real world during our participation in more than one hundred projects in French organizations and in many different sectors. Furthermore, much of the literature in project management is written by field specialists and empirical studies are mainly achieved in sectors dedicated to projects with professionals. With the broadening of project management implementation into every sector of economical activity, it appears important to try to map what occurs in France in order to better know to what extent and how project management is used. So, we decided to conceive a database in order to better understand what happens really in both sectors, traditionally project oriented and not, collecting information from project professionals and others. Like in other management fields, theorization doesn't precede the companies' practices but the contrary. For four years, with the help of our postgraduate program, we have administrated questionnaires, collecting information about the projects' concept understandings and basic parameters, project actors roles and organizational matters, project key factors of success, tools and methods used, and elements of project management culture embedding. Presently, we have collected 621 valid questionnaires corresponding to 1621 projects. We are presenting here only the global results in four main dimensions showing the diversity of project management practices in France and the imperative necessity to better contextualize the way we consider the project management field.

How the Concept of Project is Understood

First of all, because of the random way to collect questionnaires, we realized *a posteriori* a typology according to project's nature. It's obvious that project management is overwhelming every economical sector and covers many different types of projects, although "internal projects" are becoming predominant (Figure 1).

According to a literature review (Leroy 1994), the concept of a project is generally understood by listing its intrinsic characteristics. We selected the definition that seemed to us the most complete, the definition proposed by J. Rodney Turner (1993, 8):

> An endeavour in which human, material and financial resources are organized in a novel way, to undertake a unique scope of work, of given specification, within constraints of cost and time, so as to achieve beneficial change defined by quantitative and qualitative objectives.

In order to know which characteristics are considered as the most important ones by people, we imposed among these ten items the choice of three ones only. As we noticed in our experience the extreme confusion of project perceptions—certainly due to the polysemy of this concept (Boutinet 1992)—we wanted to verify at what scale people could identify that *the essential features of a project are that it is a unique piece of work, undertaken using a novel organization to deliver beneficial change* (Table 1).

Globally, we can notice that the uniqueness of the scope of work and of the project organization are not considered as fundamentals. Beneficial change gets a roughly moderate score also. The allocation of human, financial, and material resources is pinpointed as the most important project feature but, considering also the score of the "set of activities," which managerial fact doesn't encounter these two characteristics? It is interesting to see the very close scores of quality, time, and cost items which constitute the famous triangle of project control still deeply embedded in the mind of French project actors.

Looking more precisely at this data, a general assumption can be proposed: to explain the diversity of project perceptions, it seems that the job function plays a role of being moderately variable. For example, project leaders are well sensitized to cost and time constraints, project experts are aware of the uniqueness of the scope of work and project organization, people from logistics, quality, or production highlight the importance of quality specifications, people from human

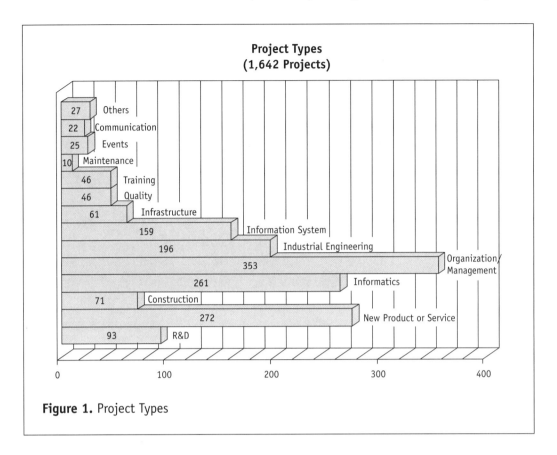

Figure 1. Project Types

relations emphasize the beneficial change, and so on. These ideas deserve further examination to test this hypothesis.

It's also interesting to observe this ranking according to other variables. We did so with the private or public status of companies' respondents. The main deviations are noticed for the cost, quality, and performance characteristics that are notably considered less in public sector (respectively 8.0 percent, 8.5 percent, and 10.1 percent versus 11.8 percent, 12.4 percent, and 11.6 percent) to the benefit of profitable change (15.6 percent versus 11.3 percent). We have also taken into consideration the difference of project perceptions between project-oriented companies and those not project oriented. The same deviations are noticed for the cost and time characteristics with amplified results (respectively 14.9 percent versus 9.0 percent; 16.3 percent versus 9.3 percent). But the position of quality constraint is in reverse order to the benefit of public companies (10.9 percent versus 11.7 percent) certainly due to the preeminent technocratic culture of the French state-owned companies. At the opposite, the uniqueness of the project activities is better considered in project-oriented companies (7.1 percent versus 5.7 percent) but the beneficial change generated by the project is better taken into account by the public sector companies (14.4 percent versus 7.8 percent), similarly for the novelty of project organization (5.8 percent versus 3.8 percent).

Job Functions Project Features	Global	Project Expert	Logis-tics	Top Direction	Human Relations	R&D	Informatics	Project Leader	Quality	Project Consultant	Production	σ
Set of Activities	12.7	10.1	6.1	18.9	17.9	12.7	9.4	15.2	9.4	16.8	8.1	3.72
Resources	22.3	20.8	21.2	26.5	25.6	20	19.5	23.1	22.3	25.2	22.5	2.25
New Organization	5.2	8.7	6.1	6.1	7.7	1.8	4	1.4	7.2	7.5	4.5	2.05
Unique Scope of Work	6.1	8.7	4.5	2.3	10.3	8.2	8.1	5.2	5	8.4	2.7	2.23
Cost Constraint	10.6	10.1	13.6	9.1	7.7	12.7	11.4	15.5	7.2	4.7	11.7	2.83
Time Constraint	11.2	12.1	13.6	10.6	0	13.6	14.8	15.5	10.8	9.3	8.1	4.09
Quality Constraint	11.1	11.4	18.2	11.4	7.7	12.7	10.1	8.6	11.5	8.4	16.2	3.40
Beneficial Change	12.6	12.1	10.6	12.1	20.5	7.3	14.8	9.7	15.8	10.3	15.3	3.90
Quantitative Objectives	4.3	4.7	3	1.5	2.6	5.5	4.7	4.5	6.5	4.7	7.2	1.49
Qualitative Objectives	3.8	1.3	3	1.5	0	5.5	3.4	1.4	4.3	4.7	3.6	2.20

Table 1. Main Project Feature Perceptions According to Functions

The project perceptions ranking is not clearly discriminated by the variable "size of the manpower;" any project characteristic is correlated significantly with it.

Project Metrics

We have collected some basic information about the 1,621 projects performed by the respondents:

Project Duration

The global results indicate that 21.5 percent of the projects have an average duration less than six months, 51.5 percent with an average duration comprised between six months and two years, and 27.0 percent with an average duration over two years. According to the nature of the projects, it's not surprising to notice that infrastructure projects have the maximum duration (53 percent of projects over two years duration) followed by industrial engineering projects, information system projects, research and development (R&D) projects, and construction projects (respectively 34 percent, 34 percent, 33 percent, and 31 percent).

Project Budget

Seventy-two percent of the projects have a budget less than 50 billion French Francs (FF), 18.5 percent a budget comprised from 50 to 500 billion FF, and 9.5 percent with a budget exceeding 500 billion FF. The latter are better represented in infrastructure projects (28 percent), in industrial engineering projects (23 percent), in construction projects (18 percent), and in new product or service projects (13 percent).

Number of External Partners

The sample is divided into five categories according to the number of external partners involved in the projects: none, one to five, six to ten, eleven to thirty, and over thirty. The score obtained by each category gives respectively 14 percent, 42 percent, 15 percent, 15 percent, and 14 percent. The latter category can be found more easily in infrastructure projects (31 percent), construction projects (24 percent), industrial engineering (23 percent), evolutionary maintenance projects (22 percent), and information system projects (13 percent).

Degree of Innovation between Two Successive Projects of Same Nature

We introduce this variable because of its relative importance for many specific recommendations in project management contextualization. Four categories are distinguished: weak, mean, important, and unknown. The global average score for each category gives respectively 14 percent, 37 percent, 42 percent, and 7 percent. It is much more interesting to examine more precisely the results according to the nature of projects as shown in Figure 2.

With this variable, the ranking is more original. R&D, quality, and training project participants consider that the innovation degree between two successive projects is important with respective scores of 65 percent, 58 percent, and 50 percent.

Life Cycle

We used a very traditional five-stage life cycle: initiation, design, execution, finalization, and closeout. We questioned the degree of relative importance (without defining criteria) they gave to each project phase. The average results show an interesting relation of proportionality between each phase, respectively 14 percent, 29 percent, 43 percent, and 14 percent!

More precisely, the initiation stage is considered more important for communication, training, organization and management, and closeout projects with respectively 19.7 percent, 17.5 percent, 16.7 percent, and 16.1 percent. For the design stage, events, training, new product and service, and R&D projects are more represented with a score quite equal to 32 percent. The execution stage is the kingdom of traditional external projects in construction, infrastructure, and industrial engineering (respectively 54.4 percent, 50.9 percent, and 50.2 percent) but also for quality projects (49.2 percent). Finally, it's not so amazing to notice

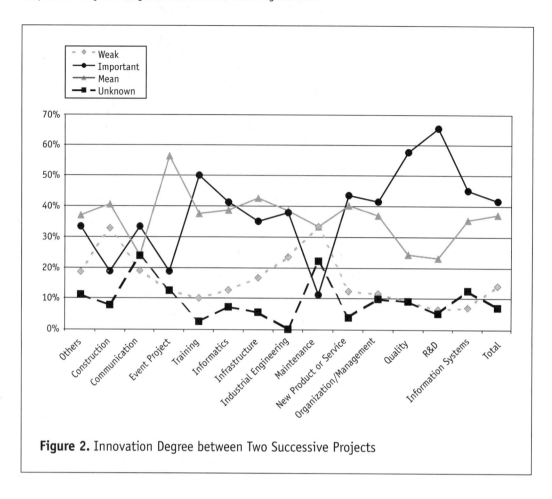

Figure 2. Innovation Degree between Two Successive Projects

the ranking of maintenance, informatics, and information system projects in the closeout phase which is often more problematic in such areas.

Turner and Cochrane's Project Typology

"Projects can be judged against two parameters: how well defined are the goals, and how well defined are the methods of achieving them," as Turner and Cochrane (1993, 93) suggested. We tried to give some statistical validation to this very suggestive typology. Every respondent was invited to map his projects on a goals-and-methods matrix directly on an exhibit included in the questionnaire. We represent on Figure 3 the results concerning four types of projects, considered by these authors to be the archetypes in each of the four sectors of their matrix (industrial engineering, new product or service, R&D, information systems). Our results show the validity of Turner and Cochrane's assumptions clearly for industrial engineering projects and for R&D projects. But it is less evident for product development projects and for information systems projects. The figure is conceived with a scale showing the relative density of the localization of the answers in proportion with the darkness of the areas, from the white one (0 to 2.5 percent) to the black one (more than 10 percent) with intermediate levels of gray every 2.5 per-

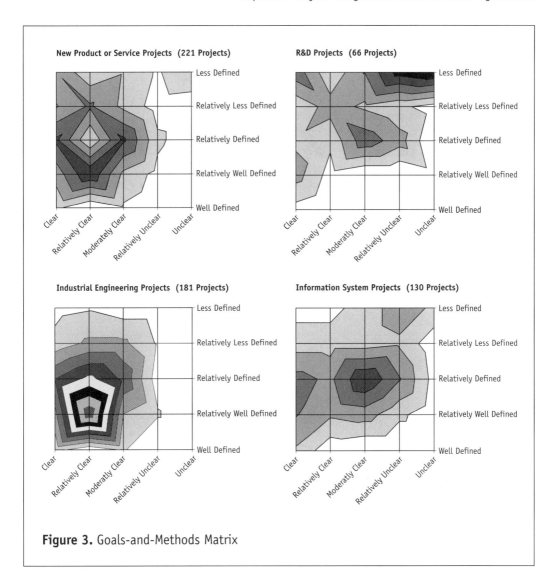

Figure 3. Goals-and-Methods Matrix

cent more. Although we don't have enough space to show all the results for the different types of projects, we can confirm the discriminating power of the two variables used by Turner and Cochrane.

What About the Key Success Factors?

We used the general frame of the famous "Ten-Factors Model" (Slevin and Pinto 1988) but in a simple way, asking for the ordering of the ten factors from one to ten. An explanation of the meaning of every factor was provided in the questionnaire in order to avoid misunderstandings. The general results (Figure 4) indicate very clearly that the project mission is considered the most important success factor, followed by top management support and by client consultation. Then with the same score come the next four factors: project schedule and plans, personnel,

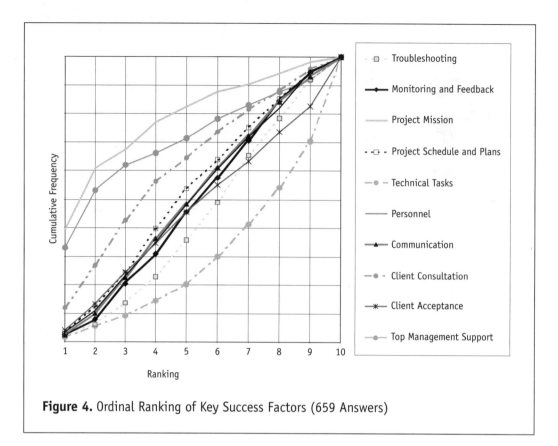

Figure 4. Ordinal Ranking of Key Success Factors (659 Answers)

communication, and monitoring and feedback. Client acceptance and troubleshooting are considered relatively less—and the very backbench is for technical tasks.

Calculations were also realized in introducing filters such as job function of the respondent, size of his company, nature of the status of the company, project orientation of the company, degree of experience cumulated in internal or external project, degree of experience according to specific role played in projects, and so on.

According to the status of the company, there are few differences between the respective ranking for private or public sector except for the personnel factor classified in fourth position in public sector and in sixth position for private one. Also the communication factor placed respectively in fifth versus seventh position.

A significant variance has been found between project-oriented companies or those not project oriented.

On the contrary, the size of the company variable is significant for three factors essentially. Client consultation is set in first place by people working in very little companies (< 10 employees) but always put in third place for any other company of the sample. The communication factor is better appreciated by little companies: third for companies with less of fifty persons, fifth for companies with a manpower comprised between fifty and 500, and seventh for companies over 500 employees.

It is very interesting to compare the ranking of success factors taking into consideration the job function of each respondent. In every situation, the top management support and project mission factors are fighting for the first place. Client consultation is quite always situated at the third place except for people taking care of human resources or production (5th). Project schedule and plans is a very unstable factor: second position for R&D people, seventh position for logistics and computer facility people, even eighth for human relations staff. The monitoring and feedback factor is also relatively unsteady but it is privileged by people working as financial or human resources staff (4th) and by project management specialists, R&D, and commercial employees (5th). The personnel factor fluctuates from the fifth to the seventh place except for project management consultants (9th) and computerists (8th), but got a brilliant third place for people from the production department. The communication factor is very unstable, varying generally from fourth to sixth place, but it obtained a third place by manpower staff people against a eighth place by the top management. The troubleshooting factor varies between the seventh and the ninth places except for logisticians (5th), top management, and human relations staff (6th), and the last position for manufacturing people. Client acceptance has the same range of variation as the troubleshooting factor but it is placed in fourth position by computerists, in fifth by top management, in sixth by project management consultants, and a not so surprisingly in tenth by R&D employees. Finally, the technical tasks factor is always at the last rank except for production people who give it the seventh score.

Nonetheless, these preliminary results deserve further investigation in order to determine precisely which kind of variables are the most influential in determining the ranking of success factors by the respondents.

Project Management Toolbox

The respondents were invited to clearly express, in a closed list of project management tools and methods, whether these are unknown to them, known but not used, used at least once, or systematically used. The global results are shown in Figure 5.

Although we don't have enough space to discuss the results here, our first investigations show a very important role of the job function in explaining the diversity of the real use of the project management toolbox (Figure 6). A preliminary hypothesis is that, taking into account the more recent diffusion of project management methods in France, the only emerging process of professional certification, and the extreme variety of our sample, people import into the project the tools they already know. This can partly explain the relative poor score obtained by traditional project control tools. No doubt that the use of specific tools is largely influenced by the particular way project management culture is implemented and fueled in each organization. This is another interesting study to perform in the future taking into account another type of data collected about project management culture.

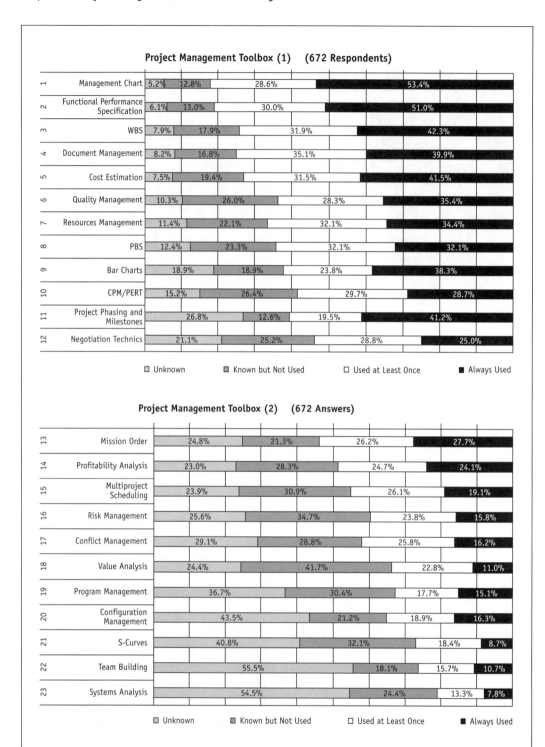

Project Management Toolbox (1)   (672 Respondents)

#		Unknown	Known but Not Used	Used at Least Once	Always Used
1	Management Chart	5.2%	12.8%	28.6%	53.4%
2	Functional Performance Specification	6.1%	13.0%	30.0%	51.0%
3	WBS	7.9%	17.9%	31.9%	42.3%
4	Document Management	8.2%	16.8%	35.1%	39.9%
5	Cost Estimation	7.5%	19.4%	31.5%	41.5%
6	Quality Management	10.3%	26.0%	28.3%	35.4%
7	Resources Management	11.4%	22.1%	32.1%	34.4%
8	PBS	12.4%	23.3%	32.1%	32.1%
9	Bar Charts	18.9%	18.9%	23.8%	38.3%
10	CPM/PERT	15.2%	26.4%	29.7%	28.7%
11	Project Phasing and Milestones	26.8%	12.6%	19.5%	41.2%
12	Negotiation Technics	21.1%	25.2%	28.8%	25.0%

□ Unknown   ■ Known but Not Used   □ Used at Least Once   ■ Always Used

Project Management Toolbox (2)   (672 Answers)

#		Unknown	Known but Not Used	Used at Least Once	Always Used
13	Mission Order	24.8%	21.3%	26.2%	27.7%
14	Profitability Analysis	23.0%	28.3%	24.7%	24.1%
15	Multiproject Scheduling	23.9%	30.9%	26.1%	19.1%
16	Risk Management	25.6%	34.7%	23.8%	15.8%
17	Conflict Management	29.1%	28.8%	25.8%	16.2%
18	Value Analysis	24.4%	41.7%	22.8%	11.0%
19	Program Management	36.7%	30.4%	17.7%	15.1%
20	Configuration Management	43.5%	21.2%	18.9%	16.3%
21	S-Curves	40.8%	32.1%	18.4%	8.7%
22	Team Building	55.5%	18.1%	15.7%	10.7%
23	Systems Analysis	54.5%	24.4%	13.3%	7.8%

□ Unknown   ■ Known but Not Used   □ Used at Least Once   ■ Always Used

Figure 5. Project Management Toolbox

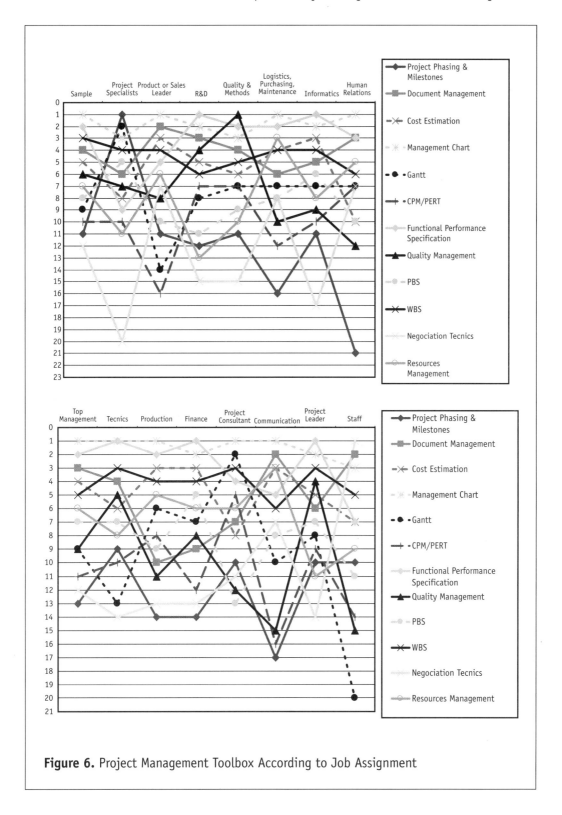

Figure 6. Project Management Toolbox According to Job Assignment

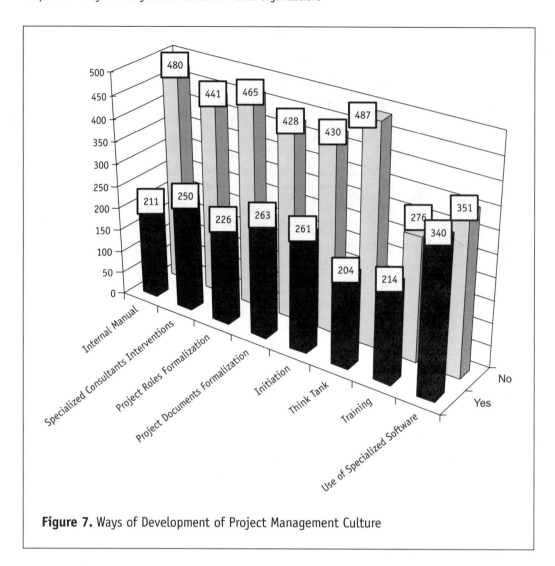

Figure 7. Ways of Development of Project Management Culture

Which Ways to Develop a Project Management Culture

Except for an open question to complete the internal project management landscape, eight dimensions have been proposed in the questionnaire to characterize the project management culture: use of specialized software, specific training programs, project management initiation program, formalization of projects roles, formalization of project documents, specific internal manual in project management, use of specialized consultants, and think tank. In Figure 7 are the general results for the sample.

Exploring more precisely the findings (Figure 8), we can say that the use of a specific manual in project management and the formalization of project roles are clearly growing in proportion with the size of the company. The very big companies are the champions of training programs in project management (57 percent). The public sector, although it is composed mainly of very big firms, seems to be

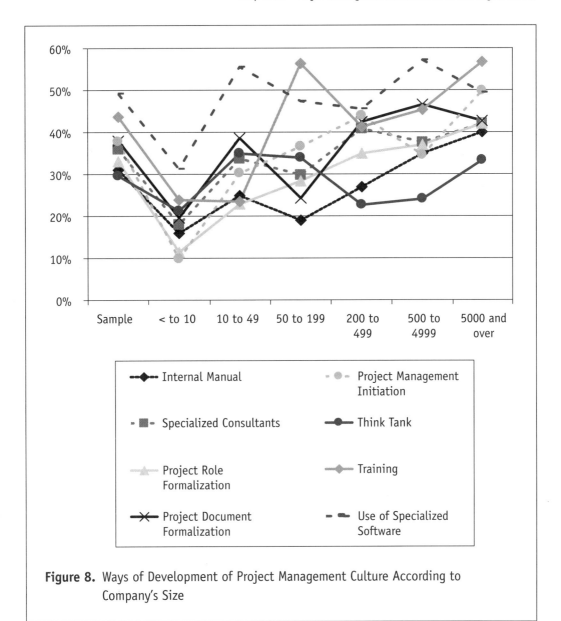

Figure 8. Ways of Development of Project Management Culture According to Company's Size

more active in comparison with the private sector: respectively 57 percent versus 40 percent for training program, 49 percent versus 33 percent for project management initiation, and 42 percent versus 30 percent for the formalization of the project roles. Evidently, the variable project-oriented company or department is very discriminative: 67 percent of project-oriented companies use specialized software against 42 percent, 34 percent have a specific manual versus 26 percent, 56 percent develop training program versus 39 percent, and 48 percent formalize the project documents versus 34 percent. Surprisingly, whether companies are project oriented or not, there are only 30 percent that animate a think tank in project management!

Conclusion

Undoubtedly, although the survey results presented here are in a preliminary stage and consequently very general, this statistical information leads to repeating the absolute necessity to more contextualize our knowledge in project management and to attempt to reinforce the external validity of project management research. This conclusion is reinforced when we pay attention to the organizational dimension of project management (project roles, dedication time to project activity, experience in project management, type of organizational structure, and so on). Nonetheless, this database in project management already has the sufficient size to offer a good overview of project management in France. The same questionnaire is going to be administrated in Quebec and soon in Australia, so international comparison can be realized. A benchmarking service on a website is proposed to French companies in the same spirit of Slevin and Pinto's "project implementation profile" and will permit us to continually fuel the database. The next step should be to use it as an analysis tool to verify the pertinence of causal hypotheses, of which there are numerous ones, as this chapter suggests.

References

Boutinet, J. P. 1992. *Anthropologie du projet*. 2nd ed. Paris: Presses Universitaires de France.

Leroy, Daniel. 1994. *Impact et fondements du management par projets*. Ph.D. thesis, Université des Sciences et Technologies de Lille.

Slevin D. P., and J. K. Pinto. 1988. Project Success: Definitions and Measurement Techniques. *Project Management Journal* 19 (3): 67–73.

Turner, Rodney J. 1993. *The Handbook of Project-Based Management*. England: McGraw-Hill.

Turner J. R., and R. A. Cochrane. 1993. Ill-defined Goals and/or Methods of Achieving Them. *International Journal of Project Management* 11 (2) (May): 93–102.

CHAPTER 11

A Framework for Analyzing the Development and Delivery of Large Capital Projects

Roger Miller, D.Sc., FCAE—University of Quebec at Montreal
Brian Hobbs, Ph.D., PMP—University of Quebec at Montreal

Introduction

The International Program on the Management of Large Engineering and Construction Projects (IMEC study) is based on sixty case studies of large capital projects on four continents. Projects studied were undertaken from the early 1980s to the present and were in the fields of electric power, urban transportation, roads, and tunnels. The analysis of the sixty projects has revealed the complexity of managing large capital projects and the corresponding richness of project management strategies that are required in order to initiate, develop, and deliver them successfully.

Projects experience difficulties not so much because engineers cannot cope with technical complications or side effects, but because sponsors cannot rise to the managerial challenges of coping with unforeseen turbulence, anchoring the projects in their social contexts, and developing strategic depth. Risks burst out as projects are being shaped and built. The longer the development time, the higher the likelihood it is that the project will be affected by emergent events. Turbulence can originate from exogenous events occurring outside of the control of management or from endogenous events arising within the project organization.

A logistic regression model has been built to help predict the performance of the sixty projects. The model, which predicts 87 percent of observed project performance, indicates two types of factors which significantly increase the probabilities of project success: 1) the completeness of the institutional arrangements and 2) the strategic abilities of sponsors as they steer and shape the project throughout trajectories.

Institutional Arrangements

The presence of coherent and well-developed institutional arrangements is, without a doubt, the most important determinant of project performance. Institutional arrangements are sets of laws, regulations, and established roles that form symbiotic relationships and provide effective practices for developing projects. Institutional arrangements provide the structure for contracts, binding agreements, and legal actions. They also provide legitimacy. Large capital projects require deals and agreements that will stand the test of time. By contrast, projects shaped in incomplete and shifting arrangements are at risk.

The main function of institutional arrangements is to help anchor projects in their social and economic contexts and ensure that investments will be repaid and social utility provided. Unless they are solidly legitimized, projects will be at the mercy of shifting interests, caprices, and opportunistic moves. The concept of project anchoring outlines three generic conditions to buttress large capital projects.

1. *Stabilization of the long-term future to enable investments*: Legal and regulatory frameworks, such as private monopoly regulation and concession frameworks, help to reduce risks by minimizing opportunities for clients, communities, or governments to attempt to capture revenues after the investment is sunk. The goal is to create the prospect of secure streams of funds in the long term.

2. *Flexibility to face turbulence*: During the front-end development of projects, when agreements are negotiated and commitments made, managers develop specific strategies to cope with foreseeable risks. They cannot, however, develop specific ways to cope with surprise events. Turbulence is likely to arise given the long time span required for development. Flexibility provided by elements of the institutional arrangements help many projects survive unforeseen events.

3. *Enhancing the legitimacy of projects*: Many projects face opposition from interest groups. Laws, regulations, and practices that create well-structured assessment frameworks enable sponsors and interest groups to air their views through public hearings and even to oppose decisions through legal appeal procedures. Public-bidding frameworks structure orderly selection and provide legitimacy. Practices such as inviting representatives of the public into planning and design meetings and proactively consulting conservationist groups and environmental regulators help to find credible solutions and reduce the likelihood of protest.

The Strategic Abilities of Sponsors

The strategic abilities of sponsors are revealed as they shape projects and steer them through to ramp-up. We have identified eight trajectories each with different probabilities of success. A trajectory is a sequence of moves by the sponsor and co-specialized organizations to shape a project through many episodes, often in response to turbulence, opportunities, or challenges.

Shaping efforts, over time, will roll the concept configuration forward, correct positive-feedback loops, and help a project move along the track desired by the sponsor. In this case, the trajectory is likely to lead to success. In contrast, sponsors may not be able to prevent and correct positive-feedback loops. Many moves may be right, but the inability to cope with a few unexpected events can create degenerative processes. Success requires most issues to be solved—adequately.

Why do sponsors enter into trajectories that lead to failure? The answer is that they lack the strategic knowledge and the abilities to identify what will be needed for the journey. The choice of a trajectory is determined by the interactions of three factors: the degree of development of institutional structures, the technical and social complexity of the projects, and the managerial competencies of the sponsors. We have structured the presentation around trajectories pursued by network operators, concessionaire/developers, and ad-hoc alliances.

Projects Sponsored by Network Operators

Projects sponsored by network operators have a high probability of success. Their sponsors usually have the resources and creditworthiness to carry the market, institutional, and completion risks. With a coherent and stable institutional structure, projects can be developed at the appropriate scale. Network operators have the expertise to shape projects, integrate them into their systems, and develop capabilities to interact with the community. In other words, technical, economic, social, and political issues can be integrated in a coherent manner. Financing is done through bond issues, with guarantees provided either by the government or by balance sheets. Unless the country has a bad credit rating, network operators backed by a government can get low-cost financing.

The negative side of sponsorship by network operators stems from the dominance of technical experts and the prevalence of organizational failures. Managers are often technical specialists who view projects as engineering challenges, fail to engage in relational interactions with communities, regulators, or suppliers, and build in technical features that add to costs. Organizational failures include adversarial relations, refusal to collaborate with suppliers, bureaucratic rigidities, and preference for known solutions.

Projects sponsored by network operators tend to be successful, as were nineteen out of twenty-five of these projects in the IMEC sample. Three trajectories in projects sponsored by large network operators were identified: 1) *push to meet demand*, 2) *network sponsorship and rational management*, and 3) *partners in technology*.

1. *Push to meet demand.* Six projects in the IMEC sample were designed as engineering solutions to meet growing demand in developing countries. These projects, sponsored by public utilities, were planned to be orderly and rational, but crises emerged, and projects were held up. Meeting demand rapidly, honoring contractual obligations, and respecting development plans were all good reasons for forging ahead without concerns about social integration. Because institutional structures did not force consideration of external effects and legitimacy, issues such as social acceptability, respect for the environment, and social disturbance were brushed aside.

The probability of success of projects following this trajectory turned out to be low, although most projects were eventually redesigned and restarted. Following a period of crisis, these projects were often redefined by teams that included engineers, social workers, and communications experts adopting systemic perspectives. The costs of making these projects socially acceptable could easily have been internalized in the first trial, because the opportunities they pursued were intrinsically rich. Most projects eventually rebounded.

2. *Network sponsorship and rational management.* Fourteen projects were shaped by network operators that worked under rational-system arrangements. Large sponsors, whether public or regulated private firms, undertook to make long-term forecasts, scrupulously meet environmental regulations, borrow on financial markets by providing guarantees, and honestly attempt to meet project opponents' objections in advance. Network sponsors engaged in productive relationships with regulators. The execution of the projects followed traditional patterns: internal design, detailed work packages, bidding, and owner control.

The traditional mode leads to both high and low performance, but a large majority of projects of this type in the IMEC sample were successful. Good risk analysis, adaptation to social and environmental needs, and an ability to face challenges by lenders, regulators, and constituents characterize high-performance projects.

3. *Partners in technology.* Five projects in the IMEC sample focused on the development of complex, technology-based solutions such as nuclear power plants and air-traffic-control systems. These projects were led by strong sponsors aiming to develop needed and highly complex technical solutions. Suppliers had the specialized expertise that the strong sponsors needed. A majority of these projects were successful. The development of long-term, collaborative relationships between owners and contractors and coherent institutional arrangements stressing the leadership role of the sponsors were determining factors. Two projects were failures because rigid contracting was used. In these cases, the sponsors insisted on using detailed specifications instead of relying on the suppliers' abilities to develop highly innovative technical solutions.

Whatever the trajectory, the competencies displayed by large network operators as they sponsor projects are creditworthiness, technical knowledge, and relational capabilities. Successful network operators put in place decision systems to ensure that technical, social, regulatory, and political aspects are embodied in selection processes. They also build a small, multidisciplinary core team that interacts with suppliers and contractors to innovate and build social expertise.

Projects Sponsored by International Concessionaire/Developers

Projects sponsored by concessionaire/developers usually take place in governance arrangements that favor foreign investments, deregulation, partnerships, and participatory engineering. Concessionaire/developers are domain specialists that promote risk allocation, build coalitions to help structure projects to face turbulence, and engage in discussions with regulators and government officials. The building of generative relationships with co-specialized firms such as investment banks and contractors is viewed as useful for developing innovative solutions, confronting viewpoints, and tapping otherwise dormant knowledge. Sharing the fruits of innovative ideas with these partners is seen as a wise move.

However, sponsorship of projects under governance arrangements is difficult because of the present incompleteness of institutional structures and the associated opportunistic behaviors of governments. Loopholes exist in laws, regulations, and responsibilities. Governments cause the downfall of projects by failing to honor agreements, creating legislative and regulatory risks, and shifting too much public infrastructure risk to private firms. Sponsors also put a great deal of faith in rigid power purchase agreements (PPA) and concessions. Undue optimism and assumptions about the superiority of private-sector management have often characterized such projects.

As governance arrangements are being adopted around the world, project concessionaire/developers have pursued three distinct trajectories: 1) *scrutiny-based projects*, 2) *institution breakers*, and 3) *engulfing illusions*.

1. *Scrutiny-based projects.* Scrutiny-based projects tend to be uncomplicated. Few negative external effects and little environmental opposition are involved. The sponsor builds strong partnerships with owners, and the institutional structures within which they are built are well developed. Examples of such projects include thermal-power plants with PPAs, short toll roads near large cities, and bridges that relieve traffic congestion. Such projects use standard technologies to meet real needs. Financial returns may be high for early sponsors, but as competitive entries arise, yields fall. As a result of their attractiveness, these projects are rapidly transformed into commoditized solutions.

Investment bankers, rating agencies, and regulators scrutinize these projects in detail. Rating agencies evaluate the sponsor's abilities to face risks. Bankers accept only the projects that meet the stringent criteria of non-recourse project financing. Project ratings are often necessary for the public issue of bonds. Most scrutiny-based projects are successful. Why are sponsors not confining themselves to such projects? Because the supply of such projects is limited and opportunities dwindle rapidly.

2. *Institution breakers.* Projects in this trajectory involve complicated technical tasks in incomplete or inadequate institutional arrangements. Project configurations need to be adjusted many times to meet the shifting expectations of bankers,

regional groups, and clients. Sponsors, however, are committed to shaping these projects well. They invest the resources necessary to ensure their survival and even their restructuring.

Shaping efforts focus first on correcting the shortcomings of the institutional framework. For this, sponsors seek the collaboration of governments, legal advisers, and international agencies. New laws need to be enacted to protect property rights, foster social acceptability, and promote environmental standards. In other words, such projects challenge the existing legal and regulatory structures. Concessionaire/developers invest resources to build sponsoring coalitions and make projects socially acceptable. The process of shaping is long, turbulent, and costly. Shaping costs for these projects are very high, ranging from 15 percent to 35 percent of total capital investment. Sponsors need to be able to keep their eye on the project's value in the face of difficulties. A majority of these projects in the IMEC sample were successful.

3. *Engulfing illusions.* Several urban infrastructure projects within the IMEC sample were projects promoted by private and public sponsors that naively accepted heroically optimistic assumptions concerning technical feasibility, market demand, and social acceptability. Engineering firms wishing to become international concessionaire/developers often sponsored these projects. Firms hungry for business opportunities created several of these projects, often in governance arrangements that were effervescent and shifting. Projects were sometimes promoted on the basis of the obvious superiority of the private sector. This superiority was so obvious that it precluded serious questioning of the project's viability.

When these heroic assumptions turn out to be false, crises emerge. On several projects, governments played opportunistic games, triggering processes of degradation. Incomplete institutional frameworks were unable to act as a bulwark. Problems were pushed toward private sponsors. As one government legal advisor put it, "The sovereign state is never a partner." Engulfing illusions often end in costly retreats or white elephants. In the IMEC sample, sponsors and bankers that engaged in such projects ended up losing a large part of their investment, even though the projects still had high social utility.

Sponsors of these projects failed to build long-lasting coalitions and agreements with regulators, government authorities, and clients. Key decisions were left uncovered because the sponsors had preferences for particular options. Furthermore, they did not allocate all of the effort needed to secure solid commitments from parties whose contributions are important. The physical project often survived, but only after painful restructuring. These projects highlight the primary dilemma of sponsorship: without non-recoverable, front-end expenditures, opportunities do not really exist. Without adequate investment in strategically positioning the project, the sponsor may get involved in costly illusions.

The competencies displayed by concessionaire/developers are 1) the ability to attract partners because of credibility and reputation, 2) the financial capacity to bear the cost of front-end strategic decisions, and 3) the knowledge of public policy issues and positive relationships with governments. Concessionaire/developers rapidly identify the value potential of projects that are worth shaping and reject others. They understand that projects are not selected in grand rational meetings but are shaped, negotiated, and redesigned over many episodes of risk analysis and strategy making. Sponsors know that front-end shaping costs can be high, as projects must pass many tests; accepting a bad project is viewed as worse than rejecting a good opportunity.

Projects Sponsored by Ad-Hoc Alliances

A dozen projects in the IMEC sample were sponsored by entrepreneurs or firms that formed ad-hoc alliances. The advantages of entrepreneurial sponsorship are many. First, many projects, even socially valuable ones, would never get completed without heroic entrepreneurs overlooking the inadequacies of institutional arrangements and substituting their strengths for institutional weaknesses. Second, entrepreneurs capture novel practices abroad, diffuse ideas, and shape daring projects. Third, entrepreneurs pursue opportunities that large sponsors would reject, such as power from coal piles or garbage dumps and impossible deadlines.

The negative side of entrepreneurial sponsorship is that socially suboptimal solutions are often pursued and deals are made without the benefit of public debate. Sponsors tend to reduce front-end shaping expenditures to the minimum and thus fail to build coalitions and governance structures to face future shocks. As a consequence, projects often end up in failure. Two trajectories were identified: 1) *entrepreneurial pioneers* and 2) *urgency-based projects*.

1. *Entrepreneurial pioneers.* Such projects consist of fitting standard technical solutions to viable opportunities in countries where demand is growing but the institutional arrangements are woefully underdeveloped. Eight projects in the IMEC sample fell into this category, but only four were successful. International and domestic firms that have advanced knowledge of the evolution of institutional structures seek these kinds of projects. Sponsors take high risks by supporting most front-end costs and even construction costs to move in rapidly. Solutions are developed rapidly to fit urgent needs. Entrepreneurs understand the dynamics of shaping and influencing institutional structures.

The danger is that weak institutional frameworks often allow unscrutinized and inefficient choices to be made. Institutions based on the rule of law and sector regulations are not well developed, and project anchoring is thus difficult. Political power is fractured into many simultaneously competing public agencies and concentrated at the political level. Pioneers have difficulty getting approval and must deal with ambiguity. They adopt innovations, such as concessions, turnkey contracts, and design-build-operate contracts, to appease bankers and international agencies.

2. *Urgency-based projects.* These projects are designed to meet real and urgent needs. Sponsors, domestic or international, agree to select socially inappropriate solutions because of the pressure for fast delivery and the absence of challenges by regulatory authorities. All parties, including regulators, sponsors, and clients, who sign purchase agreements, push for fast action. Early choices lock projects

on paths that cannot be modified. Such projects are inadequately shaped because political actors or institutional structures do not require extensive debates.

Most urgency-based projects in the IMEC sample did not perform well. One project, for example, concerned the building of a thermal-power plant in a South Asian country. The client, a publicly owned utility, was asked by political decision-makers to sign a PPA. In order to build fast, an international developer agreed to take on completion and operation risks by rapidly assembling components, erecting the plant in record time, and operating it at full capacity. The government assumed supply and currency risks by delivering fuel at guaranteed prices and using the United States (US) dollar as the currency for offshore accounting. The client assumed all market risks. The solution that was selected was outside the least-cost path, which would have taken more time to build. The client, the developer, and the bankers were all aware that a high-cost solution was being adopted.

The competencies to succeed in entrepreneurial projects, as we observed, are, first, persistent leadership, and second, political connections. Entrepreneurs make bold commitments, but they need to ensure that public decision-makers will eventually support them. The entrepreneurial sponsors in the IMEC sample were fearless. They made bold moves, and personal fortunes were at stake. To ensure that projects would eventually gain approval and permits, political connections were necessary.

A Framework for Managing Large Capital Projects

The primary issues involved in the management of large capital projects are presented in Figure 1. The framework highlights the role played by the institutional arrangement in each of four important phases of the projects: early front-end, strategic structuring, design and execution, and ramp-up. Throughout the project life cycle, the institutional framework can be a source of stability by anchoring projects, or a source of risk if the structure is ambiguous or if significant changes take place. During the very early project front-end activities of project identification, the institutional framework outlines the project opportunity and identifies the legitimate potential players and their roles. Changes in the institutional framework often create project opportunities as governments modify the framework to stimulate the initiation of projects and as promoters lobby for changes in order to create project opportunities. During the strategic structuring of the project, the sponsors investigate the institutional context to identify risks and lobby for legislative and regulatory changes to anchor the project.

During project design and execution, a stable institutional environment helps buttress the project against attacks by providing clear rules of engagement for project participants and for outside pressure groups, and by providing legitimacy. If the project gets into serious difficulty, the institutional framework can support the restructuring necessary to save the project. This is often quite critical at the ramp-up phase of projects when it becomes evident that market response is slow and the revenue stream is insufficient to support the project's financial obligations.

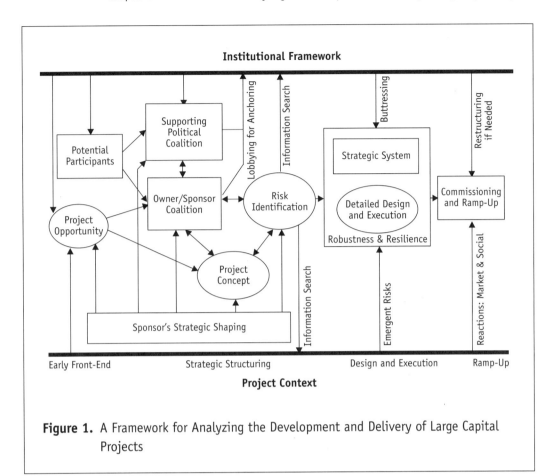

Figure 1. A Framework for Analyzing the Development and Delivery of Large Capital Projects

The project concept, the composition of the owner/sponsor coalition, and changes in the institutional framework are defined during a long and very interactive process. Though these activities, the project is modified several times before it takes its final form. We refer to this process as project shaping. To refer to this as a selection process misrepresents the reality of front-end development. There is, however, a selection process through which players decide to opt in and opt out of the project coalition.

Risk management plays an important role in the early phases of the project. Considerable attention is given to identifying sources of risk. This information has a profound impact on the way the project will be structured and on the strategic system that will be put in place to manage the project through the design and execution phase. Through shaping, the project is set up so as to minimize exposure to risk, both from the project environment and from opportunistic behavior on the part of project participants. A strategic system with a rich portfolio of responses is put in place. The richness of this portfolio we refer to as strategic depth.

Our investigation has shown that large capital projects are very often exposed to unforeseen or emergent risks. The projects in this study were exposed to an average of four unforeseen risks that threatened project viability. We refer to the ability to respond to or recover form these emergent risks as the project's resilience. Emergent risks pose a strategic dilemma, that of planning for the unforeseen. During strategic shaping, the project concept is elaborated, the project coalition is structured, and the strategic system is put in place. Project strategizing does not seem to explicitly address the question of the project's capacity to support emergent risks. However, in retrospect, it can be seen that some projects are more resilient than other. In many cases, the strategic system has the requisite variety to handle emergent risks. In other cases, the project sponsors are able to draw on extra resources to support the project in times of crisis. In extreme cases, the project will require restructuring in order to ensure its survival. Attempts to restructure projects have revealed another strategic paradox. In structuring the project to make it robust enough to withstand foreseen risks, the strategic actors sometimes introduce rigidities that hinder or prevent adequate responses to unforeseen risks.

Conclusion

Large capital projects are shaped through iterative processes involving project sponsors and participants in interaction with the institutional framework. The shaping of projects anchors them to the institutional framework and defines the trajectory. The adequacy and the stability of the institutional structure are the most important factors in determining the way in which the project will unfold. Throughout its life cycle, the project will be exposed to many different risks. These nearly inevitable but unforeseen risks constitute the most important challenges to project survival and success. Projects that have strong sponsors, are governed by rich portfolios of strategies, and have the flexibility to restructure in response to a crisis have shown themselves to be more resilient.

Notes

1. The IMEC project was supported by financial contributions from: the Project Management Institute (PMI®), Cofiroute, CAE, Électricité de France, the Electronic Commerce World Institute, the Export Development Corporation of Canada, the governments of Canada, France, and Quebec, Hydro-Québec, the Inter-American Development Bank, the Natural Sciences and Engineering Research Council/Social Sciences Research Council of Canada, Ontario-Hydro, and SNC-Lavalin.

2. MIT Press published a full account of the IMEC Research Program, *The Strategic Management of Large Engineering Projects: Shaping Institutions, Risks, and Governance*. Edited by Roger Miller and Donald Lessard, February 2001.

ORGANIZATIONAL AND TEAM RELATIONSHIPS—BEHAVIORAL PRACTICES

Introduction

Firms and other organizations that successfully manage their projects are almost always characterized by exhibiting superior human resource capabilities, leadership, team building, and "people-oriented" practices. Section III contains a set of papers from researchers who have explored a variety of the unique practices of these effective project-focused enterprises.

- Roland Gareis offers an update on his research looking at the behaviors and project management practices of successful companies. His work provides important guidelines for novice project-focused firms seeking to understand the scope of practices in which more experienced and effective project organizations routinely engage. Chapter 12—Competencies in the Project-Oriented Organization.

- Francis Hartman presents his model that integrates the dimensions of trust between project contractors and their key stakeholders. Trust is shown to be the lynchpin that cements the ties between project-focused firms and clients. Properly addressed and handled, the creation and maintenance of a trust-based relationship is a key element for long-term company success. Chapter 13—The Role of TRUST in Project Management.

- Edward Hoffman, Claire Kinlaw, and Dennis Kinlaw show their research into the characteristics of high performing project teams. Using six National Aeronautic and Space Administration (NASA) centers as survey sites, the authors polled 397 members of eleven projects to identify the key features that characterize effective project teams. Chapter 14—Developing Superior Project Teams: A Study of the Characteristics of High Performance in Project Teams.

- Rolf Lundin continues to explore the phenomenon of the temporary organization, best exemplified by project-focused firms and their unique characteristics. His essay captures the constantly shifting nature of modern organizations and some of the reasons why project-based work is fundamentally suited to these new environmental demands and opportunities. Chapter 15—Business in the World of Projects.

- Hans Thamhain looks at the characteristics of effective leadership of teams in technology-oriented firms. Based on his years of research and training, he offers some valuable insights into the current state of understanding of team behavior and leadership as it pertains to the challenges inherent in project management. Chapter 16—Criteria for Effective Leadership in Technology-Oriented Project Teams.

- J. Rodney Turner and Anne Keegan report on the results of their research and conceptual analysis of control structures and mechanisms in project-based organizations. In describing process models for operations management, they offer different control approaches based on an organization's key features: project size and number of customers. Chapter 17—Processes for Operational Control in the Project-Based Organization.

- Marko Arenius, Karlos Artto, Mika Lahti, and Jukka Meklin write on some important aspects of modern project management, citing several challenges to effective management, including managing multiple projects, recognizing the nature of "extended project success," and the nature of structural complexity as it affects project management. Their paper provides a framework for understanding some of these important dimensions and their impact on creating a "learning organization." Chapter 18—Project Companies and the Multi-Project Paradigm: A New Management Approach.

- Janice Thomas, Connie Delisle, Kam Jugdev, and Pamela Buckle address one of the key questions that is frequently cited as the most vexing among project managers in organizations; that is, the best method to "sell" project management to top management. Their paper takes an in-depth look at the process whereby uninformed top management can begin to recognize the unique benefits to be derived from moving to project-based work. Chapter 19—Selling Project Management to Senior Executives: What's the Hook?

CHAPTER 12

COMPETENCIES IN THE PROJECT-ORIENTED ORGANIZATION

Roland Gareis, Univ. Prof. Dkfm. Dr.—Vienna University of Economics and Business Administration

Introduction

In this chapter the model of the project-oriented organization (POO) is introduced. The advantages of "management by projects" as an organizational strategy are analyzed, the application of a new management paradigm in the POO is described, and specific organizational structures, such as expert pools, project portfolio groups, and a project management office, are described. A process model with processes, which are specific for the POO, is presented.

For the performance of these processes, specific competencies are required by individuals, teams, and the POO overall. It is the objective of this research and chapter to differentiate between the project management process and other specific processes of the POO, to operationalize the model of the POO, and to differentiate between individual, team, and organizational competencies in the POO.

The Model of the Project-Oriented Organization

A POO can be defined as an organization that:
- Defines "Management by Projects" as an organizational strategy.
- Applies temporary organizations for the performance of complex processes.

- Manages a project portfolio of different project types.
- Has specific permanent organization structures to provide integrative functions.
- Applies a "new management paradigm."
- Has an explicit project management culture.
- Perceives itself as being project-oriented.

The POO considers projects not only as tools to perform complex processes, but also as a strategic option for the organizational design of the company, the division, or the profit center. By applying management by projects the following organizational objectives are pursued:

- Organizational differentiation and decentralization of management responsibility
- Quality assurance by project work and holistic project definitions
- Goal orientation
- Organizational learning.

For processes of different complexities, different organizations are adequate. The POO perceives projects and programs as temporary organizations for the performance of complex processes. For unique processes of medium to high complexity and short to medium duration (three months to twelve months), projects are the appropriate organization form. Projects can be defined for contracts for external clients as well as for product developments, marketing campaigns, or reengineering activities for internal clients.

A program (of projects) is a temporary organization for the performance of a process of high complexity. The projects of a program are closely coupled by overall program objectives, overall strategies, and common processes and methods. A program has a time limit and is medium or long term (six months to thirty-six months) in duration.

Typical programs are the development of a "product family" (and not of a single product), the implementation of a comprehensive information technology (IT) solution (such as SAP software), the reorganization of a group of companies in a holding structure, and large investments, such as an oil platform.

The more different project types a POO holds in its project portfolio, the more differentiated it becomes and the higher its management complexity becomes. In order to support the successful performance of the single projects as well as to ensure the compliance of the project objectives with the overall strategies, specific integrative structures, such as expert pools, a project management office, and project portfolio groups, are required. Some of these permanent organizations might be virtual (Figure 1).

The POO is characterized by the existence of an explicit project management culture, i.e., by a set of project management-related values and norms. In the POO project management is considered as a business process, for which there exist specific procedures along with a common understanding of the project roles involved and the project management methods applied.

Further, in the POO the application of a new management paradigm is required. Traditional management approaches are emphasizing detailed planning

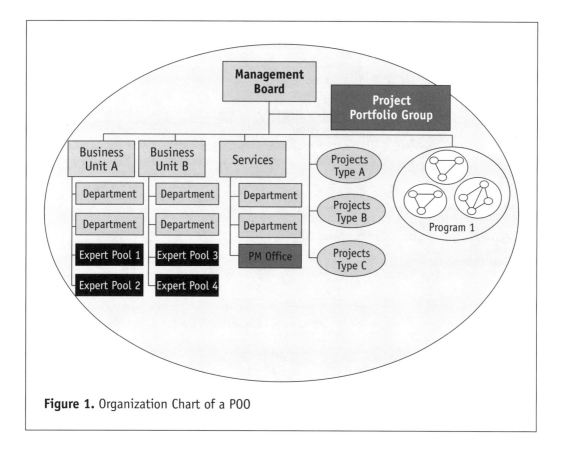

Figure 1. Organization Chart of a POO

methods, focusing on the assignment of clear defined work packages to individuals, relying on contractual agreements with clients and suppliers, and using the hierarchy as a central integration instrument. Compared with this traditional management approach the central features of the new management paradigm are:

- Consideration of the organization as competitive advantage
- Empowerment of employees
- Process orientation
- Teamwork in flat organizations
- Continuous and discontinuous organizational change
- Customer orientation
- Networking with clients and suppliers.

The POO has dynamic boundaries and contexts (Figure 2). On the one hand the number and the sizes of the projects and programs are constantly changing, permanent and temporary resources are employed, and cooperation is organized in virtual teams. On the other hand varying strategic alliances are established and relationships to the different social environments of the different projects and programs are managed.

In order to manage the dynamics of the POO, besides activities that reflect the corporate identity such as strategic controlling, clusters of projects such as

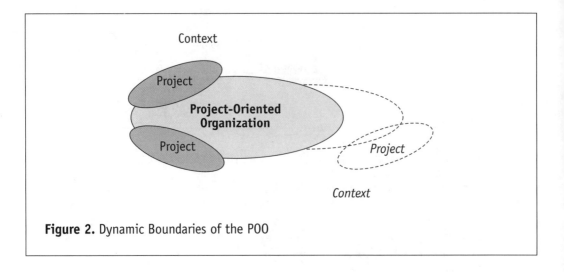

Figure 2. Dynamic Boundaries of the POO

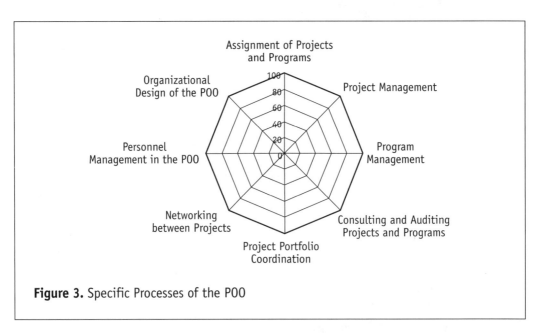

Figure 3. Specific Processes of the POO

chains of projects, a project portfolio, and networks of projects can be applied as new integrative structures.

Considering the timing in which sequential projects are performed, a chain of projects results. By relating a set of projects to each other according to a specific criterion, such as the technology applied or a geographic region, a network of projects results, and by considering all projects performed by an organization, the project portfolio results. A project portfolio is defined as a set of all projects the POO holds at a given point in time and the relationships between these projects. In comparison to a program a project portfolio is not an organization.

B 4.1) Which project organization documents result from the project start process?

Always = 1, Often = 2, Sometimes = 3, Seldom = 4, or Never = 5

Project Assignment	
Project Organization Chart	
Project Role Descriptions	
Project Responsibility Matrix	
Project Communication Structures	
Project-Related Incentive Systems	
Others (Please State: ....)	

Table 1. Example Question of Project Management Process

Processes of the Project-Oriented Organization

The POO is characterized by specific business processes. A process model of the POO can be visualized in a spider web (Figure 3). The axes represent the specific processes of the POO. These processes are briefly described.

Each process of the POO model is described in a POO questionnaire. In Table 1 an example of a question for the project management process is shown.

The questionnaire of the POO process model can be applied for assessing the maturity of the POO and for benchmarking it. Project management is the core business process of the POO. The project management process starts with the formal project assignment and ends with the project acceptance by the project owner. It consists of the subprocesses project start, project coordination, project controlling, project discontinuity management, and project close down (Figure 4). The project management process is performed in addition to the contents-related processes to achieve the project results. Examples for contents-related processes of an engineering project are engineering, procurement, logistics, and construction.

Objects of consideration in the project management process are the project objectives, the scope of work, the project schedule, and the project costs, as well as the project organization, the project culture, and the project context (project environment relationships, relationships to the company strategies, relationships to other projects, and so on).

Program management has to be performed in addition to the management of the single projects of a program. The program management methods are similar to the project management methods, i.e., there is a program work breakdown structure, a program bar chart, a program environment analysis, and so forth. The

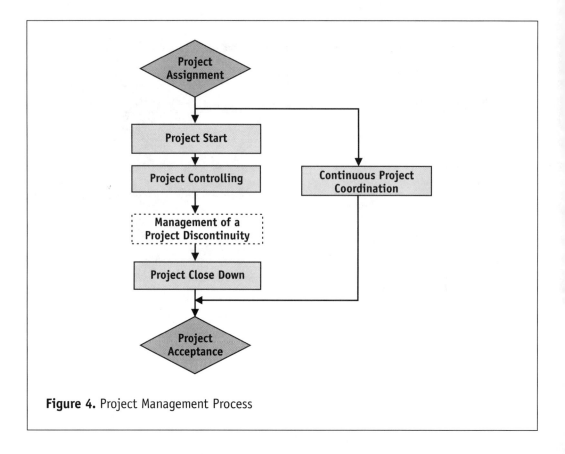

Figure 4. Project Management Process

program organization has to be designed in addition to the organizations of the single projects. Specific roles in a program are program owner, program manager, and program office (Figure 5).

The advantages of designing program organizations instead of defining a "mega-project" with several subprojects are as follows:
- A less hierarchal organization
- Clear structures and a clear terminology (a program manager and several project managers instead of one project manager and project managers of the subprojects)
- Empowerment of the projects of the program by allowing for specific project cultures, specific relationships to environments, specific project organizations, and so on
- Differentiation between program ownership and different ownerships for the projects.

Consulting and auditing of projects and programs are important instruments to ensure project and program quality.

The objectives of the project portfolio coordination are:
- Optimizing the results of the project portfolio (and not of the single projects)
- Selection of projects to be started

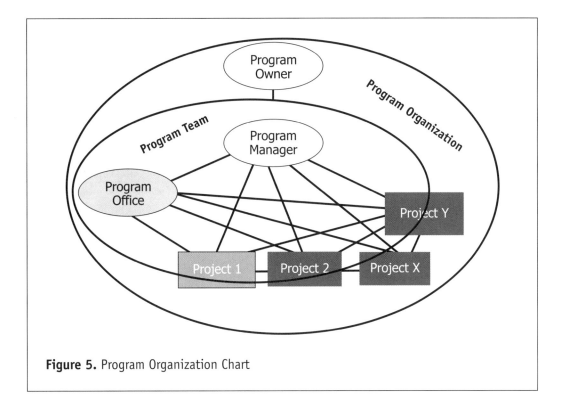

Figure 5. Program Organization Chart

- Definition of project priorities
- Coordination of internal and external resources
- Organization of learning of and between projects.

The basis for the coordination of the project portfolio is a project portfolio database, which allows the development of project portfolio reports. Typical project portfolio reports are the bar chart of projects, the projects profit versus risk graph, the progress chart of projects, and so forth.

Networking between projects occurs in an ad-hoc process, where a set of coupled projects cooperate, in order to create synergies. Personnel management processes in the POO are recruitment, disposition, and development of project personnel. In the POO a project management career path includes the roles junior project manager, project manager, and senior project manager (Figure 6).

The organizational design of a POO is characterized by specific integrative structures such as a project management office, a project portfolio group, and expert pools and specific tools, such as project management procedures and standard project plans.

Project Management Competencies in the Project-Oriented Organization

Competence can be defined as knowledge and experience for the performance of a business process. The specific competencies a POO requires relate to the performance of the previously described processes. Next the individual, team, and

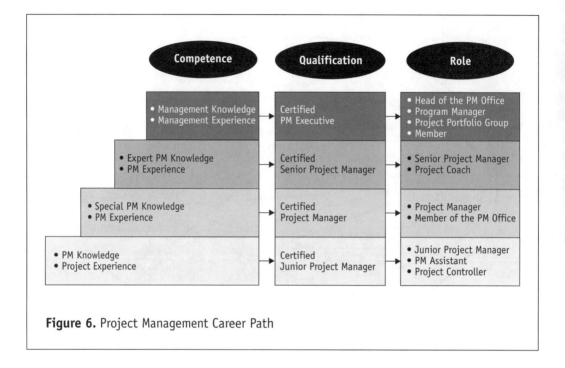

Figure 6. Project Management Career Path

organizational competencies to perform the project management process will be analyzed in detail.

Project Management Competencies of Individuals

The project management competencies required by individuals differ according to the project roles to be fulfilled. The following project roles can be performed by individuals: project owner, project manager, project management assistant, project team member, and project contributor. The specific project management functions to be performed by a project manager can be described in a role description.

From the role description (Table 2) it is obvious that the project manager requires knowledge and experience not just to apply project management methods, but also to creatively design the project management process.

This ability relates to:

■ The selection of the project management methods appropriate for a given project

■ The selection of the appropriate communication structures

■ The facilitation of the different workshops and meetings

■ The selection of the participants for the different workshops and meetings

■ The decision to involve a project consultant

■ The definition of the appropriate form for the project management documentations.

Functions in the project start process
■ Know-how transfer from the pre-project phase into the project
■ Development of adequate project plans
■ Design of an adequate project organization
■ Performance of risk management
■ Design of project-context-relations
■ etc.

Functions in the project controlling process
■ Determination of the project status
■ Redefinition of project objectives
■ Development of project progress reports
■ etc.

Functions in the project discontinuing management process
■ Analysis of the situation and definition of ad-hoc measures
■ Development of project scenarios
■ Definition of strategies and further measures
■ Communication of the project discontinuity to relevant project environments
■ etc.

Functions in the project close-down process
■ Coordination of the final contents work
■ Transfer of know-how into the base organization
■ Dissolution of project-environment relations
■ etc.

Table 2. Description of the Role of Project Manager

The project management competence of a project manager is the capability to fulfill all functions specified in the role description. Besides the project management knowledge and experience for a given project type, a project manager needs, to a certain degree, knowledge about the product and the organizations involved in the project. In international projects cultural awareness and language knowledge are prerequisites also.

Project Management Competencies of Project Teams

In order to perform a project successfully, a project team requires competencies. The competencies of a project team can be defined as the project management competencies of the project team members plus the social knowledge and experience of the team to commonly create the "big project picture," to produce synergies, to solve conflicts, and to ensure learning in the team.

A project team cooperates in workshops and meetings. The application of project plans, such as a work breakdown structure, a schedule, a project environment analysis, and so forth, have to be understood as tools to support the communication in the project team.

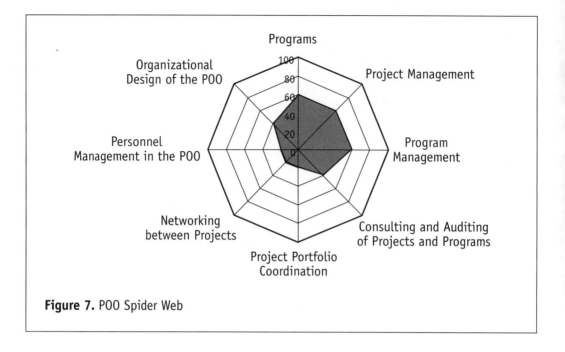

Figure 7. POO Spider Web

Project Management Competencies of the Project-Oriented Organization

Not just individuals, but also organizations have the capability to acquire knowledge and to experience and store it in a "collective mind" (Senge 1994; Weik and Roberts 1993). Willke (1998) describes organizational knowledge as hidden in organizational principles that define the way organizations work. Such organizational principles, which define the way projects are managed, are project management procedures, project management templates, and standard project plans.

Further, the organizational project management competence can be analyzed by observing the project management practices applied in specific projects. The project management documentations resulting from the project management sub-processes, the quality of project team meetings, the form of project marketing, and so on can be evaluated. Project management is subject to quality, too.

The project management competence of the POO can be described and assessed with a "project management competence" model (Gareis and Huemann 1998). The project management competence can be presented in the POO "spider web" model (Figure 7).

The overall competence of a POO is presented by the area resulting from the connection of the competence points at the spider web axes. The competence of a POO cannot only be shown in a spider web model but also a POO maturity ratio can be calculated. The POO ratio is the weighted sum of the competencies for the performance of the specific processes.

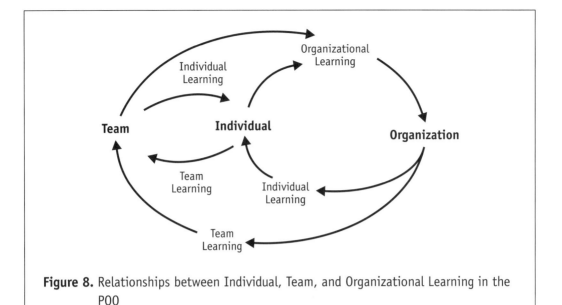

Figure 8. Relationships between Individual, Team, and Organizational Learning in the POO

Development of the Project Management Competence in the Project-Oriented Organization

Project management can be perceived as a core competence of the POO, as it creates a competitive advantage. To ensure this competitiveness, permanent further development of the project management competence is necessary. Project management competencies of organizations, teams, and individuals have to be developed.

The relationships between individual, team, and organizational learning in the POO are shown in Figure 8.

Instruments to develop the project management competencies of individuals are (self-) assessment, training (classroom and on the job), and coaching combined with training. Instruments to develop the project management competencies of teams are (self-) assessment, training and coaching, reflection, and supervision. Instruments to develop the project management competence of the POO are project management benchmarking and organizational development projects.

Conclusion

Even project management is an important business process competence, for the other specific processes of the POO have to be analyzed and further developed also. The spider web model of the POO, showing these processes, can be applied as a maturity model for the POO.

References

Gareis, R., and M. Huemann. 1988. A Process-Oriented PM-Approach. IRNOP III: *Conference of the International Research Network on Organizing by Projects*, July 6–8, University of Calgary.

Senge, P. 1994. *The Fifth Discipline Fieldbook: Strategies and Tools for Building a Learning Organization*. New York: Doubleday.

Weik, A., and K. Roberts. 1993. Collective Mind in Organizations Heedful Interrelating on Flight Decks. *Administrative Quaterly* 38: 357–381.

Willke, H. 1998. Systemisches Wissensmanagement (Systemic Knowledge Management). Stuttgart: Lucius & Lucius.

CHAPTER 13

THE ROLE OF **TRUST** IN PROJECT MANAGEMENT

Francis T. Hartman, Ph.D., PMP—University of Calgary

Introduction

A series of projects are being undertaken in a program intended to develop a theoretical model of the mechanics of trust and then to test that model. The initial studies identifying the need to better understand trust and that trust carries a price tag have been completed. The initial Trust model has been developed and the first two individual projects to test and further develop this Trust mechanics model are under way.

The research program has a general objective of enhancing project performance through a better understanding of the key underlying drivers for enhanced project delivery. The focus on trust was developed following a review of five years of research at the University of Calgary. Trust was a factor in all of the projects whether they studied alliances, distributed teams, team effectiveness, time to market, cost reduction, resource usage and allocation, progress reporting, or value engineering to mention a few. Trust is a commonly recurring theme in research reporting and recurs frequently in papers.

The research into trust in project management is intended to help understand the trust phenomenon, and to learn from this understanding how people and organizations need to work together in order to deliver projects more effectively.

The research program is using different approaches to test and develop a Trust model and to see how this model affects project management. Some examples of how this work will be undertaken are introduced and discussed.

Why is Trust Important to Project Management?

In 1994 the Natural Sciences and Engineering Research Council (NSERC) established a Chair in collaboration with the Social Sciences Research Council (SSHRC) of Canada and a number of industry partners. This Chair had a five-year mandate to identify better ways to manage projects. Working closely with industry, a research program was established and a number of research initiatives undertaken over this five-year period. These research initiatives studied such topics as contacting, team effectiveness, distributed project teams, value engineering, schedule acceleration, predictability of project outcomes in the early stages of project definition, project performance assessment, time to market, cost reduction, and incentive schemes for contracts. Other topics included research into risk identification and apportionment, dispute resolution, and the meaning of contract clauses. All of the research findings had one common factor.

The common factor in all of the findings in the first five years of research was trust. This in itself was an interesting discovery. It led to a review of the available literature and to an assessment of the potential impact of trust on the practice of project management. The potential implications appeared to be profound. Some of the potential areas of impact included better client relationships, accelerated time to market, reduced risk premiums in contracting—and thus, lower project costs and more effective communication. The last item alone made further exploration of the trust phenomenon worthwhile, as communication breakdowns account for most, if not all, project failures.

With some trepidation, the need for the study of trust was presented to industry sponsors of the research program as a potential next phase in the work of the Chair holder. The proposal was immediately accepted and a plan to apply for renewed funding from NSERC and SSHRC was made on this basis. The proposal for a second term of federal funding for the Chair was made and accepted. The potential impact and value of the research had been assessed and accepted.

The Research Program

The Color Trust Model

The extensive research conducted by others into trust has been done largely from the perspectives of disciplines such as family psychology, sociology, criminology, education, and anthropology. More recently, and generally only in North America, theorists in business studies have started to explore the trust phenomenon. So far, none of the models developed to explain trust have had general applicability. The ones that deal with specific situations could not address many of the situations that we identified in our research.

A review of the research findings identified two distinct situations where different trust types appeared to be needed in varying mixes. One of these was based on answering the question, "Can you do the job?" and the other was based on, "Will you take care of my interests in a predictable way?" A third element that was based on a more volatile, "Does this relationship feel right?" also needed consideration. From this review, three trust types, their behaviors, and their patterns were identified and a new model for explaining trust was developed. This model is the foundation of a new research stream of significant interest to industry sponsors.

The Trust model presented here was developed by Hartman with the assistance of Dr. Elke Romahn. Romahn was a research associate working for the author. To better understand the model that is presented in this chapter, it is useful to review whether we even need such a model. The argument that is put forward is that trust influences virtually every aspect of project management and is perhaps even more important in project management than in operations management. This added significance stems form the very nature of projects today. They are fast-paced and of short duration. They involve organizations, groups, and individuals who have never worked together. Worse, they involve groups that have worked together and who are still fighting over the last experience! We have little time and often little inclination to address the social niceties of getting along or even learning to trust one another. The consequence is that we end up with either difficult relations that lead to communication breakdown and hence to project failure, or we pay a price in additional work, churn, and premiums to offset the perceived risks.

The Need for a Trust Model

The trust phenomenon has moved from an item of curiosity in the management world to one that many organizations and senior managers are taking very seriously indeed. The driver for this is in two parts that are closely inter-linked. There is a continuing and increasingly challenging need to remain competitive. And technology is doubling every few years. With the growth in technology we see several things taking place. First, we see the need for increased specialization, leading to many corporations redefining core business. This has, in turn, led to outsourcing previously sacrosanct activities such as payroll, information systems (IS) and information technology (IT), training, and more.

Product development too, has been significantly affected by the need to specialize. All of today's manufacturing businesses are integrators of previously manufactured goods to add value and produce their "final" product. Any example will serve. Computers are composed of components manufactured by others. The central processing unit chip is assembled from materials produced and refined by others. Eventually we end up with sand from which the silica was produced. Even this was processed using manufactured goods (excavation equipment, screens, conveyors, computers, and so forth). So we come full cycle.

Trust Type	Color	Blend	Label
None	Black	—	Absence of Trust
Primary	Blue	—	Competence
Primary	Yellow (Gold)	—	Ethical
Primary	Red	—	Emotional
Secondary	Green	Blue and Yellow	Business
Secondary	Orange	Yellow and Red	Social
Secondary	Purple	Red and Blue	Sales
Comprehensive	White	Red, Yellow, and Blue	Balanced

Table 1. Colors of Trust (Hartman 1999)

The growth in technology has forced us into a position where we increasingly rely on our suppliers. This tightening relationship has led to situations that place a company in jeopardy if one or more of their suppliers are at risk. A common response has been to develop long-term relationships, often structured around and codified in an alliance agreement.

Trust Types

Trust in the literature seems to be defined in the context of a given relationship. This makes the efficacy and relevance of any definition dependent on the situation in which it is used. A further area of debate lies in the intrinsic complexity of trust as it has both an emotional (human?) and more analytical (clinical?) component to it. Consideration of where the elements of trust lie led to identification of three distinct types of trust. Rather than being black and white, it seems that trust has a spectrum of colors!

Three distinct but connected types of trust were identified for this model, each representing a specific dimension of what constitutes our personal perception of trust. Table 1 shows this basic construct. Also shown in this table is how the three primary trust types can be mixed—just like colors.

A particular challenge in a project environment lies in the temporary nature of the organization. The time available to build trust is severely limited by the window in which the project must be completed. It is further hampered by the fact that there is a high degree of randomness in the assembly of the organization, especially if we include all suppliers and contractors involved. Not only do we face the challenges of inter-company language and cultural differences, but also we probably have teams and groups of people who are involved for one reason only. They are available and have some or all of the necessary skills to complete the project.

This and other specific challenges of project delivery put special pressures on trust building that an operational environment does not necessarily have. The model is explained in more detail by Hartman (1999, 2000).

The Mechanics of Trust in a Project World

If the lack of time to develop trust in a project world is a significant problem, it certainly is not the only one. Conventional project management has developed a set of tools and processes that address integration management, scope management, scheduling and cost control, quality, communications, human resources, teams, procurement, and risk management (Project Management Institute 2000). There are many ways of describing this set of tools and processes.

Trust as Part of the Project Management Delivery Process

Trust (not specifically defined) has emerged as an ingredient in project success and business success research in various arenas. If we consider a few random elements of project management it is relatively easy to see the impact of trust on the effectiveness of the process. First, let's consider intuitive connections.

- Effective communication is easier and more likely to be complete between people who trust each other.
- Contract relationships, and as a result, contract administration, are easier if we can trust the contractor and the contractor can trust its client.
- Discovering and implementing cost-saving ideas will occur more readily if the participants can expect fair compensation and can be sure that their interests are being taken care of in the process.
- Teams work better together if the people in them can trust each other.
- Identifying client needs (the REAL ones) is easier if we have open communication, which is dependent on a high level of trust between the client and the supplier.
- Schedules and estimates are more likely to be accurate if the contributors feel that their honest opinion will be considered and valued (trusted).
- Progress reporting is more honest in a trust-based environment.
- We are more likely to be successful project managers if our team trusts us, and if our clients and suppliers do so also.
- We are more likely to be accepted as manager of a project (and have the resulting authority and influence on stakeholders) if others can trust us to do our jobs well.

These random examples are intended to illustrate the insidious nature of the trust phenomenon. To explore these in more detail, the first and last elements are considered specifically in the light of the Trust model described earlier.

The cost of trust was investigated in one project. Using the construction industry as the community to study, the cost of exculpatory clauses was investigated. About 150 companies across Canada participated. The cost of five well-known and broadly used exculpatory clauses was investigated. Specifically, the participants assessed the direct and indirect premium linked directly to these clauses. With surprising consistency, the cost of including these was seen to be an average of 9 percent in a buyer's market and 19 percent in a seller's market. The median of all situations was about 15 percent and the value was close to zero. These results were the costs as manifested in contracts and as identified through expert opinion and empirical data collected from practitioners (Master's Thesis by Mohammed Khan, Supervisor: Francis Hartman 1998).

This study was reworked to validate the findings—they appeared to show an inordinately high wastage of money. The new study confirmed the figures to within 1 percent (Master's Thesis by Ramy Mohammed, Supervisor: Francis Hartman—in progress).

The mechanics of trust were a clear focus for a study. The study involved development of the theoretical model outlined earlier (Principal Investigator Francis Hartman, Assistant: Elke Romahn). This theoretical model was developed—it was based on extensive literature review, and was then tested against "classic" models used to describe trust behaviors in the literature. The model continues to evolve. The next step is to develop and validate metrics for assessing both trusting and trustworthiness in the context of the three types of trust. This second phase is under way. Development of a model that will help us understand the mechanics of trust will then be developed (Ph.D. thesis by Dean Sheppard, Supervisor: Francis Hartman).

The impact of trust on contract relationships is being investigated as a follow on from earlier studies on the effectiveness of business relationships in a project context. This empirical study is using data collected from practitioners, based on cases and expert opinion (Ph.D. thesis by Ramy Mohammed, Supervisor: Francis Hartman—under way).

Another aspect of trust is the role it plays in *leadership and project management* in organizations exposed to rapid change. Increasingly, today's critical projects are happening in such an environment, and the demands on project managers as leaders are changing. Part of this study into the nature of leadership is also looking at trust and its part therein (Master's thesis by Scott Bartsch, Supervisor: Francis Hartman—under way).

It is likely that the *effective formation of distributed teams* will be affected by a number of factors. One important one is trust. The formation of these teams, spread geographically, is being studied—this study is primarily survey based (Ph.D. thesis by Connie Guss, Supervisor: Francis Hartman).

The impact of trust levels on perceptions of project success is also of interest. This project is in the planning stages (Potential researcher: Master's Thesis by Roch DeMaere, Supervisor: Francis Hartman).

The role of trust in accurate and useful progress reporting will also be studied (Master's thesis by Liwen Ren, Supervisor: Francis Hartman).

A number of other projects are in planning or under way that will investigate aspects of trust in project management processes and tools. Samples include:

- Measurable benefits of trust in: speed, innovation, cost, quality, team effectiveness, competitiveness, and sustainability of performance (in planning stages—a complex set of projects).
- Assessment of trust in a project context: inter- and intra-individual, team, management, group, and organizations. Likely based on Delphi method and grounded theory (in planning stages—again, a complex problem!).

Trust is at the headwater of business effectiveness. Projects are increasingly the business value delivery vehicle. Understanding how to work in different trust relationships will help us be more effective at balancing the conflicting issues that normally arise on projects. Significant financial support from industry to develop this research is also an indicator!

The rational behind one of the previously mentioned projects will be described further.

Trust and Communication

Open communication has been identified as an important ingredient in effective teams (Cahoon and Rowney 1995), as well as a factor in project success (Pinto and Slevin 1998). In order to communicate effectively with another person, we need to have the right level of comfort. This is largely situational. Consider the following:

1. Selecting a specific technical vendor: competence trust is needed here. We want to be sure that the engineering or other technical service will be completed competently and properly. If the specialist asks intelligent questions and we feel that we are communicating what we see to be the problem, then we are normally reassured that the future holds an appropriate technical solution for our project! How we behave in terms of contracting (cost plus fee, open-ended, or a stipulated price contract) will depend on the level of ethical trust we have, but will likely not affect our communication. This picture will be different if we have concerns over being charged for unnecessary work, in which case our communication will likely take on a different hue: we will communicate our concern and set up a defense system against the perceived risk.

2. In the situation of seeing a specialist consultant or advisor about business issues on our project, we certainly need both ethical and competence trust to be present. Depending on the nature of our issues and our relationship with the specialist, we may also need a degree of emotional trust. This latter element is sufficiently well understood since "desk-side manners" are taught in some business schools.

3. In a project environment, we see problems in defining the project properly and in many other arenas stemming from a number of causes that can be reassessed in the light of the Trust model. To communicate on technical matters, we need only have competence trust in place. This trust will likely evolve as the people who

are communicating gain a common language and understanding of the problem to be addressed. The completeness of the communication, elimination of defensive behavior (such as hoarding key information), and willingness to volunteer suggestions will only come as ethical trust is built. It is only then that such communication is seen as safe. If we add emotional trust—typically developed through socialization—we can reach an even higher plane of effectiveness in communication on a project between team members. With these three types of trust in place, and balanced, we have white trust and the potential for highly effective project teams to form and deliver a very successful outcome.

Conclusions and Observations

Trust has moved from an item of mild curiosity to one of being a business imperative. It needs to be managed. As what trust means is different for each of us, trying to define trust will forever be an exercise in futility. Studying it as a psychological phenomenon is undoubtedly both fascinating and necessary. But it is Pandora's research box!

The use of the color analogy and a mechanical model as opposed to psychological model for trust behavior allows the question of trust to be tackled in a more neutral and—arguably—a more depersonalized way.

The model described previously has been developed as a basis for a funded research program. It is based on an extensive review of the literature on this subject and a good amount of scholarship. It has been tested against trust situations drawn from the literature. In particular, it has been tested against the situations that other models have specifically failed to explain. Yet, an empirical research program needs to be completed to test this concept in a set of real situations. The author is looking for test sites and cases in the world of project management for this next phase in developing better ways to manage trust as part of the business of improving project management.

The Implications of the Trust Model on Project Management

The brief discussion of the project management related issues, previously, should have identified the nature of the implication of this model on project management as a whole. Let's now review the issues again at a higher level. For this chapter, just two critical issues are presented, followed by a brief update on the research since the paper underlying this chapter was initially written.

Re-Casting the Definition of Project Management

In a recent book, the author defined projects as anything that sustains or improves shareholder value (or its equivalent in the government sector). Any of these following activities delivers a step change that puts us back where we were—Y2K project, corporate reorganization that makes us as competitive as the competition, advertising campaign to maintain or regain market share, re-tooling for this year's model of car, ski, cell-phone, or other product. Or it helps us grow—new factory, new drug approved for manufacture and sale, new software package, oil discovered and recovered.

This definition of projects puts a new set of pressures on all of us in the business of managing them. We need to be faster, more accurate, better, and cheaper than the competition in delivering the needed results to our customers. The big driver is responsiveness and speed. Not new, it is however at the point where we need to redefine the success of projects in terms other than the traditional ones of "on time, within budget, and meets technical specifications." This definition needs to include perceptions of success. The perception of success is dependent in no small part on the trust we have in what we see and whom we deal with.

Research Update and Next Steps

The Trust model has evolved since the original version of this chapter was presented. A summary of the additions to the Trust model include the following:

- The three types of trust have been more carefully defined as follows:
  - Blue Trust is referred to as Competence Trust and it answers the question: Can you do the job (or the work)?
  - Yellow Trust has been labeled Integrity Trust and it answers the question: Will you consistently look after my interests?
  - Red Trust has been labeled Intuitive Trust. It answers a complex question: Does it feel right?
- The complexity of the question "Does it feel right?" has been investigated and two parts to this question have emerged. One is based on a raw emotional response and the other on something that is often referred to as "rapid processing," which is the effect of synapses connecting in the brain to harvest our knowledge and experience. It occurs typically at about 2,000 times the speed of logical thought. This latter part turns out to be of significant importance.
- Rapid processing is a critical ingredient in what is popularly referred to as "gut feeling." An informal pilot investigation into successful senior managers and executives suggests that virtually all decisions are based on an approximation of gut feeling that is probably a red trust reaction to a situation. The decision is then post-rationalized based on the other two types of trust in order to justify the decision and to protect the organization and the individuals for audit and accountability purposes.
- The first of the research projects described earlier is nearing completion. A prototype trust-based contract is being tested (now in its third year and delivering some interesting ideas regarding faster and lower cost contract formation and management). There is growing evidence of trust-based behaviors in management, including for example, a group of consultants in California who will not do business with clients or partners who require a formal contract. The principle appears to be that a trust-based relationship

will ensure a fair exchange of value through modified behavior rather than trying to get the "best deal" through a formal contract.

■ New projects addressing the validation of the Trust model in management practices and behaviors, cost and time saving opportunities, and testing of project management process improvements are being designed and will be launched in the next phase of this research program.

Research at the University of Calgary in the area of project management is not considered complete until it is converted into material and knowledge of direct application to the field of project management. Each of the above research projects has a pragmatic problem underlying the inquiry. If the learning from the research supports the hypothesis, then a potentially better solution to the problem may be generated. Those solutions are what industry and government supporters of the research are looking for. They also represent the added value that our students bring to the marketplace.

An ongoing research program will inevitably identify new areas for study and new questions to ask. The trust arena is a fertile area of study and one of increasing relevance to project management today.

References

Baier, Anette. 1985. Trust and Antitrust. *Ethics* 96: 231–260.

Barney, Jay B., and Mark H. Hansen. 1994. Trustworthiness as a Source of Competitive Advantage. *Strategic Management* 15 (Special Issue): 175–190.

Bies, Robert J., and Thomas M. Tripp. 1996. Beyond Distrust in Trust in Organizations. In *Trust in Organizations: Frontiers of Theory and Research* (246–260), edited by Roderick M. Kramer and T. R. Tyler. Thousand Oaks, CA: Sage Publications.

Bradach, J. L., and R. G. Eccles. 1989. Price Authority and Trust. From Ideal Types to Plural Forms. *Annual Review of Sociology* 15: 97–118.

Brenkert, George G. 1998. Trust, Morality and International Business. *Business Ethics Quarterly* 8 (2): 293–317.

Brien, Andrew. 1998. Professional Ethics and the Culture of Trust. *Journal of Business Ethics* 17 (4): 391–409.

Butler, John K., Jr. 1991. Towards Understanding and Measuring Conditions of Trust: Evolution of a Trust Condition Inventory. *Journal of Management* 17: 643–663.

Couch, Laurie L., and Warren H. Jones. 1997. Measuring Levels of Trust. *Journal of Research in Personality* 31: 319–336.

Coutu, Diane L. 1998. Organizations: Trust in Virtual Teams. *Harvard Business Review* 76 (3): 20–21.

Creed, W. E. Douglas, and Raymond E. Miles. Trust in Organizations: A Conceptual Framework Linking Organizational Forms, Managerial Philosophy, and the Opportunity Costs of Controls. In *Trust in Organizations: Frontiers of Theory and Research* (16–39), edited by Roderick M. Kramer and T. R. Tyler. Thousand Oaks, CA: Sage Publications.

Das, T. K., and B. S. Teng. 1998. *Academy of Management Review* 23 (3): 491–512.

Farries G., E. Senner, and D. Butterfield. 1973. Trust, Culture and Organizational Behaviour. *Industrial Relations* 12: 144–157.

Flores, Fernando, and Robert C. Soloman. 1998. Creating Trust. *Business Ethics* 8 (2): 205–232.

Fukuyama, F. 1995. *Trust: The Social Virtues and the Creation of Prosperity*. New York: McMillan.

Gabarro, J. J. 1978. The Development of Trust Influence and Expectations. In *Interpersonal Behavior: Communication and Understanding in Relationships* (290–303), edited by A. G. Athos and J. J. Gabarro. Englewood Cliffs, NJ: Prentice Hall.

Hartman F. 1999. The Role of Trust in Project Management. Proceedings: *Nordnet,* Helsinki, Finland.

———. 2000. *Don't Park Your Brain Outside: A Practical Guide to Improving Shareholder Value through SMART Management*. Newtown Square, PA: Project Management Institute.

Held, V. 1984. *Rights and Goods: Justifying Social Action*. New York and London: Free press.

Koehn, Daryl. 1996. Should We Trust in Trust. *American Business Law Journal* 34: 183–203.

Kipnis, David. 1996. Trust and Technology. In *Trust in Organizations: Frontiers of Theory and Research* (39–49), edited by Roderick M. Kramer and T. R. Tyler. Thousand Oaks, CA: Sage Publications.

Lewicki, Roy J., and Barbara Benedict Bunker. 1996. Developing and Maintaining Trust in Work Relationships. In *Trust in Organizations: Frontiers of Theory and Research* (114–139), edited by Roderick M. Kramer and T. R. Tyler. Thousand Oaks, CA: Sage Publications.

Mayer, Roger C., James H. Davis, and David F. Schoorman. 1995. An Integrative Model of Organizational Trust. *Academy of Management Review* 20: 709–734.

McAllister, D. J. 1995. Affect- and Cognition-Based Trust as Foundation of Interpersonal Cooperation in Organizations. *Academy of Management Journal* 38: 24–59.

McKnight, D. Harrison, Larry L. Cummings, and Norman L. Chervany. 1998. Initial Trust Formation in New Organizational Relationships. *Academy of Management Review* 23 (3): 473–490.

Meyerson, Debra, Karl E. Weick, and Roderick M. Kramer. 1996. Swift Trust and Temporary Groups. In *Trust in Organizations: Frontiers of Theory and Research* (166–195), edited by Roderick M. Kramer and T. R. Tyler. Thousand Oaks, CA: Sage Publications.

Mishra, Aneil. 1996. Organizational Responses to Crisis: The Centrality of Trust. In *Trust in Organizations: Frontiers of Theory and Research* (140–165), edited by Roderick M. Kramer and T. R. Tyler. Thousand Oaks, CA: Sage Publications.

Mishra, Aneil K., and Gretchen M. Spreitzer. 1998. Explaining How Survivors Respond to Downsizing: The Role of Trust, Empowerment, Justice, and Work Redesign. *Academy of Management Review* 23 (3): 567–588.

Project Management Institute. *A Guide to the Project Management Body of Knowledge (PMBOK® Guide)* – 2000 Edition. Newtown Square, PA: Project Management Institute.

Rotter, Julian B. 1967. A New Scale for the Measurement of Interpersonal Trust. *Journal of Personality* 35: 615–665.

Sheppard, Blair H., and Dana M. Sherman. 1998. The Grammar of Trust: A Model and General Implications. *Academy of Management Review* 23 (3): 422–437.

Zucker, L. G. 1986. Production of Trust: Institutional Sources of Economic Structure, 1840–1920. In *Research in Organizational Behavior* 8 (53–111), edited by B. W. Staw and L. L. Cummings.

CHAPTER 14

DEVELOPING SUPERIOR PROJECT TEAMS: A STUDY OF THE CHARACTERISTICS OF HIGH PERFORMANCE IN PROJECT TEAMS

Edward J. Hoffman, Ph.D.—US National Aeronautics and Space Administration
Claire S. Kinlaw, Ph.D.—Developmental Products, Inc.
Dennis C. Kinlaw, Ed.D.—Developmental Products, Inc.

Introduction

Project management is an approach being used by practitioners in a large variety of professions. The recent expansion in the project management method has led to an increased focus on project tools and techniques. The central importance of the team dimension has often been given minimal attention. In 1998, a research study commenced to explore the relationship between team development and performance in United States (US) National Aeronautics and Space Administration (NASA) projects. This chapter relates the findings of NASA's study. It identifies the characteristics of superior project teams and it indicates the behaviors associated with project managers of high performing teams. Sections in this chapter are:

- Rationale and Significance
- Literature Review
- Study Methodology and Data Collection
- Summary of Key Findings
- Applications and Next Steps.

Rationale and Significance

Although there is a plethora of general information about team formation, team development, and team performance, there is very little information that focuses on team development in projects. Most team effectiveness models are derived from research on non-project teams, and we do not know to what extent a project environment with its focus on time, cost, and customer requirements leads to a different dimension in team formation and maturation. There is widespread *belief* that the development of effective teams contributes to overall project success. However, the information that is available has, for the most part, not been derived from empirical studies. While much project methodology is derived from experience and scrutiny, rigorous definition and analysis of human variables have often been lacking. This lack has created a tendency to approach teams from a "guru of the month" philosophy. Often the latest trend is applied to a project team, as opposed to a well-designed team development strategy based on research and experience.

Many project management texts ignore the dimension of teams. A larger number of texts cover the topic by relying on traditional group dynamics theory originally based on functional work units. This is a mistake when we realize that many practitioners identify the human aspect (team cohesion, trust, communications, and so on) of project management to be the single most important determinant of project success. (Read some of the success stories of project managers in Laufer and Hoffman, 2000 for examples of this consideration.)

This study was intended to define the possibilities of a more project specific model of team development, to determine the characteristics associated with superior project teams, and to identify specific functions that are associated with leaders of successful project teams. In other words, when a project is starting up, what are the behaviors and actions that a project manager and other project leaders can take to promote effective team development? A final goal of the research was to serve as a catalyst to promote more research and exploration of the dimension of team in the broader context of project performance.

Literature Review

Prior to the formal research study, a literature review was conducted. The review concentrated on publications from 1994 through 1998. Despite this time frame, materials published earlier were also reviewed if they were particularly relevant to our interest.

Two conclusions became obvious about team development in projects. First, there is *not* a large body of published information that is concerned with team development in projects. Second, the books published on the general subject of project management give little space and attention to the subject of team development. When they do address the subject, they make small use of the information that is available on the subject. A typical example is Harold Kerzner's book,

Project Management: A Systems Approach to Planning, Scheduling, and Controlling (Kerzner 1995). This book is widely used and regularly revised and reprinted. The fifth edition of this book has 1,126 pages of text, and is one of the most comprehensive books published on project management. A total of *five* pages are devoted to team development. There are 284 entries in the bibliography of this fifth edition of the book. Of this number, *two* entries deal with team development in projects. One is from 1971 and the other is from 1974.

Although there is a lack of published information on team development in projects and not much space given to the subject by authors of books on project management, we cannot interpret this to mean that there is a lack of belief that team development in projects is important. Most papers and books on the general subject of project management typically acknowledge the importance of developing the project team and note that the project manager should give attention to this development (Baker and Baker 1992; Kerzner 1995; Kezsbom 1989; Lock 1996).

Some authors have drawn attention to possible dangers and limitations of teams, but no one has suggested that team development is not a desirable characteristic of projects and the groups within projects (Fleming and Koppleman 1997; Williams 1997). Most information reported about projects generally supports the notion that the better the project develops itself as a team, the better will be the performance of the project.

This position is fully congruent with the information reported generally about team development in organizations, i.e., that organizations which go to a team-centered structure improve their performance (Kerzner 1995; Rosenau and Moran 1993; Frame 1995). The success of production teams, process improvement teams, marketing teams, sales teams, research teams, cross-functional teams, supplier-customer teams, self-managed teams, and a host of other kinds of teams have been incontrovertibly established. There are no traditional functions like planning, research, product development, design, production, marketing, and selling that are not being done more and more by teams (Katzenbach and Smith 1993; Kinlaw 1998).

Much has been written about the benefits of teams for improving performance. An analysis of the role that teams have in continuous improvement (Frangos 1993; Katzenbach and Smith 1993; Kinlaw 1998; Romig 1996; Wellins et al. 1994) has underscored the potential power of team approaches. Teams have been cited as being the best resource for creating new knowledge and ideas, fully utilizing the competencies of people, ensuring broad influence of the most competent people, building commitment, and managing uncertainty and change.

Teams are clearly the *organizing principle* for improvement. Work is done through systems or processes that cannot be understood or improved so long as people are encouraged to think that they perform independent functions. The traditional "wire diagram" of organizations does not describe how work is accomplished. The growth of the use of cross-functional teams in projects is a clear testimony to this fact (Fleming and Kopplemant 1997; Hauptman and Hirgi 1996; Kezxbom 1989). Furthermore, continuous improvement in organizations, as well as in projects, is best supported when customers partner with suppliers and form teams (Catledge and Potts 1996; Larson 1997).

Song, Souder, and Dyer (1997) studied sixty-five Japanese projects and found that team skills in a project were a predictor of the technical proficiency demonstrated in the project. Larson (1997) examined 291 construction projects and found that partnering (i.e., creating customer-supplier teams) had a positive affect on meeting schedule, controlling costs, technical performance, meeting customer needs, avoiding litigation, and overall results. McMichael (1994) described the dramatic results achieved by partnering and the creation of Boeing's Spares Distribution Center as a world-class facility.

There is without question, a clear belief in the importance of teams and team development. There is however ambiguity about the specific details of exactly what team and team development mean. Of greater concern, there are few specific guidelines or references for project managers to use when forming a project. The majority of team models are borrowed from traditional organizations without any modification for project structures. In addition, there is little research to determine how to optimize performance in project teams.

Most writers use the term *project team* in reference to the group of people assigned to a project (Catledge and Potts 1996; Kerzner 1995; Kinney and Panko 1996; Lock 1996). Rosenau and Moran (1993) define the project team in this sense: "The project team is people who work on the project and report administratively to the project manager." We found no cases in which the project *as a team* was differentiated from the project *as a group*. The qualitative differences that exist between groups, teams, and superior teams were not addressed (Kinlaw 1981, 1989). We can conclude that the term, *project team*, is used almost wholly to denote collectively the people in a project and not to denote the qualitative aspects of a project group.

Team as a term is rarely defined in the literature on project management. The case might be that there already exists a consensus among its users about what it means and, therefore, it does not need to be defined further. A more likely possibility is that the full importance of defining the specific characteristics of a team has not been realized.

There are few research studies that try to identify the characteristics of successful teams in projects. Various authors list characteristics that they associate with superior teams. However, one of the problems in defining the characteristics of successful teams is that most authors do not make a clear distinction between team development and team performance. Having clear goals and understanding priorities is regularly identified as a characteristic of successful teams in and out of projects. But, is having clear goals a result of other conditions that exist in a team, and should having clear goals be considered a characteristic of performance or a characteristic of team development? It is of course probable that having clear goals and priorities can be used to measure both team development and team performance. However, the greater clarity that we can bring to the meaning of team development and its characteristics, the greater precision we can have in defining how teams develop and what can be done to develop them.

Study Methodology and Data Collection

The research was conducted in three phases. Data was collected in the three phases of the study by:

1. Structured interviews of individuals that were taped and transcribed
2. Structured interviews of groups that were taped and transcribed
3. Survey of project members and leaders (using the Project Team Development Survey [PTDS] or a later modification, the NASA Project Team Development Survey [NPTDS])
4. Assessment of project team performance based on customer perceptions and independent analysis
5. Structured observation of project meetings.

Protocols for conducting the structured interviews and for conducting the structured observation of meetings are found in the *Handbook for Study Field Representatives* (available by contacting the authors). Data collection resulted from conducting 129 interviews and surveying 397 members of eleven projects (188 NASA and 209 contractor members) in six NASA centers (Langley Research Center, Marshall Space Flight Center, Kennedy Space Center, Ames Research Center, Goddard Space Flight Center, and the Jet Propulsion Lab).

Protocols were developed for the content analysis of the interviews from the combined studies. The study researchers independently abstracted all statements from interviewees that denoted the characteristic of a best or superior project team. A working list of team characteristics was developed. All statements were next placed on cards and sent to two independent experts on project management and team development. These researchers were asked to place the cards in logical categories. The research team resolved the few differences that resulted from the sorts. The data was analyzed using statistical methods based on analysis of variance, multiple regression analysis, correlation analysis, discriminant analysis, and factor analysis.

The first phase consisted of the pilot study. The intent of the pilot phase was to determine the viability of the original research hypothesis and to establish an initial set of characteristics associated with superior project team performance. During this phase the primary data collection consisted of interviews with the key management personnel of six projects located at three NASA field centers. Using information from the interviews, literature review, and from a factor analysis of 2,012 respondents to the *Superior Team Development Inventory* (Kinlaw 1998), the PTDS was designed and used to survey members of the project teams. This stage of the research included fifty-four interviews and fifty-three project member responses to the PTDS.

The second phase of the research study was modified somewhat and data collection was expanded to an additional five projects, located at three additional

NASA field centers. The interview protocol was modified to test the validity of the characteristics of the best performing project teams and to obtain more concrete information about the characteristics of the most valued project team leaders and leadership functions developed in the pilot study. Based on the findings from the pilot phase, the team survey instrument was modified and renamed the NASA Project Team Development Survey (NPTDS). This second phase of the research included seventy-five interviews, 278 project member responses to the PTDS, and a further 119 project member responses to the NPTDS. Phase II findings were fully congruent with the findings from Phase I and added additional support to these findings.

By introducing the use of the NPTDS into a four-hour session in NASA's Advanced Project Management Program, and by making the survey tool widely available to NASA projects over the web (http://www.appl.nasa.gov; Leadership Place; TeamMates Tool), the collection of data has become a continuing process.

Summary of Key Findings

The findings briefly described below are arranged around seven questions that formed the basic purpose of the study. For each of the findings described there is more supporting evidence from the study than is included in this summary.

Question 1. How do project leaders and members understand team development?

Findings: Team development and project performance are often so closely associated and not conceptualized as separate processes that project managers and members often do not identify actions that focus on team development.

Discussion: Several interview questions produced responses that gave clear indications of how project leaders and members conceptualize and understand team development. Team development is not conceptualized as a process that starts on one level and proceeds to a higher level. Team development for leaders and members largely means putting groups of people to work on some common task. Interviewees demonstrated little or no awareness of the qualitative meaning of team development. They did not, for instance, describe any actions taken to strengthen the characteristics that they associated with the best or superior project teams, e.g., interdependence, cohesion, or commitment.

Question 2. In what way, if any, is team development related to project performance?

Findings: Measured perceptions of team development variables predict measured perceptions of project performance.

Discussion: The PTDS and the later modification, the NPTDS, have two sections. The first section (items 1–25, PTDS, or items 1–50, NPTDS) measures perceptions of team development. The second section (items 26–29, PTDS, or items 51–60, NPTDS) measures perceptions of project performance. Three statistics were used to compare responses to the team development items with responses to the performance items: regression analysis, step-wise regression analysis, and discriminant analysis. All three statistics produced strong indications that, if we know the way team members perceive team development, we can predict the way they will perceive project performance, i.e., the more positive they are about one, the more positive they will be about the other; the more negative they are about the one the more negative they will be about the other. For example, if we know how a person responds to a team development item like, "In my project we make sure that no member fails," we can predict better than 74 percent of the time how that person will respond to a performance item like, "In my project we will meet all technical requirements within our budget baseline."

Question 3. How do the perceptions of project members and leaders about a project's performance compare to the perceptions of key project stakeholders?

Findings: The assessment of project performance by customers and external evaluators are positively correlated with the perceptions of the project team.

Discussion: In the pilot study, project members were asked to rate the performance of their projects using a fever chart. Four variables were included on these charts: technical requirements, cost, schedule, and customer satisfaction. Interviewees were requested to rate each variable as follows:

- *Green* means the project is in good shape.
- *Yellow* means that you have concerns, but that these will be resolved within budget/schedule baseline.
- *Red* means there are concerns, and you are not sure that these will be resolved within budget/schedule baseline.

Numerical values of three for green, two for yellow, and one for red were assigned to responses and responses were compared by a two-way analysis of variance. Using a 0.05 level of significance, no differences were found to exist between the way project members, project managers, and project stakeholders and external evaluators perceived project performance. The data indicates that we can obtain reliable information about how well a project is doing by asking its members. Their candid assessments appear to be as objective as those of project stakeholders, e.g., principle investigators and external evaluators.

Question 4. What is the role of project managers in team development?

Findings: There is almost total agreement among the project members and leaders interviewed that the role of the project manager (and similarly placed leaders) determines how well projects develop as teams. In addition, there is a direct relationship between the number of team development actions that interviewees associated with their project leaders, and the average rating given to the items on the pilot phase PTDS that measured team development.

Discussion: Interviewees were asked the following question that yielded information about the specific team development actions undertaken by project leaders: "What are the most important things that the project manager has done to help your project become a team?" In addition, the mean response for items 1–25 in the PTDS was computed for each of the projects in the pilot study. The average number of team development actions mentioned by project members that were taken by their project manager were computed for each project and these means were placed in rank order. A Spearman Rank Order Correlation was computed. At the confidence level of 0.05 we can affirm that the number of project team development actions taken by project leaders correlates well with how project members perceive the development of their project teams.

Question 5. What are the characteristics of the best or superior project teams?

Findings: There is general agreement across projects about the characteristics that are associated with superior project teams.

Discussion: Protocols were developed for content analysis of the interviews from the combined studies. A working list of team characteristics was developed. All statements were next placed on cards and sent to two independent experts on project management and team development. These researchers were tasked to place the cards in logical categories. The primary researchers resolved the few differences that resulted from the sorts. The key characteristics of the best or superior project teams are:

- *Team Focus*—Members see beyond their individual wants to what the project needs. Problems are worked with a clear understanding of the project's requirements. Members stay clear about the difference between "nice to have" and "must have" and focus on what constitutes project success.
- *Communication*—Everyone, from top to bottom is committed to sharing information that may be preliminary, but is always honest and open.
- *Empowerment*—Members can influence everything that goes on in a project. Influence is balanced with competence. Empowered team members are members who influence through competence and who have the freedom to influence through competence. Continuous learning is stressed.
- *Competence*—Members have the knowledge and skill to perform technical tasks; the willingness or motivation to perform; and the ability to fit their own competency into the larger needs of the project.
- *Interdependence*—Members make full use of each other's competencies, understand how what they do affects the work of others, are fully confident that other members will do what they say they will do, and believe the information given by other members.
- *Cohesion*—Members exhibit strong team identity. Members typically enjoy each other's company and socialize. They exhibit intense loyalty to the project and to each other. There is a strong sense of inclusion and there are no second-class citizens.
- *Commitment*—Problems are worked until they are solved. People refuse to fail. They put the project first and make personal sacrifices to ensure the success of each project task.
- *Diversity*—Teams are characterized by diversity of gender, culture, and age. Members represent a broad range of experience and technical competence. Differences are accepted and made powerful positive assets.
- *Structure*—Individuals and teams know the boundaries of their jobs and how jobs are connected. They know the process for making changes that affect schedules, requirements, and interfaces. Their team focus, however, keeps them from becoming rigid. Responsibilities are fixed, but the work of the

project is everyone's work. People have complete freedom in contacting any person or team within the project when they need help. The only important distinctions have to do with competence rather than position.

- *Recognition*—The project assumes responsibility to recognize its own success and the contributions of individuals and teams within the project. A portion of most meeting time is used to draw attention to the achievements and contributions of members. Best project teams celebrate with project outings and social events.

Question 6. What are the key team development functions that project managers (and other leaders) typically perform?

Findings: There is general agreement across projects about the key specific functions performed by project leaders in developing the project into a superior team.

Discussion: The same process described above in question 5 was followed in identifying the key team development functions that project managers (and other leaders) perform. The most valued team development functions performed by project managers and leaders are:

- *Provides Resources*—Obtains the personnel with the skills and knowledge needed to accomplish the project goals. Secures a budget and schedule adequate for the project objectives.
- *Shields*—Protects project members from outside distractions that are not focused on the accomplishment of the projects primary goals.
- *Models Team Work*—Through personal behavior the leader models use of feedback from team members on personal team performance. Stimulates shared learning. Demonstrates openness and trust.
- *Builds Cohesion*—Includes everyone in the project as equal members of the team. Supports and encourages efforts of members. Consistently shows respect in interactions with members. Demonstrates concern for team members—on and off the job. Encourages team social activities.
- *Builds Commitment*—Ensures clarity regarding norms, tasks, responsibilities, and relationships. Involves members in setting performance expectations and schedules. Stimulates developing new competencies. Rewards and celebrates individual and team successes.
- *Coaches*—Practices high level of interpersonal competency. Responds to problems. Plays the role of a teacher, coach, and mentor. Challenges members to higher and higher levels of performance.
- *Plans Team Development*—Develops expectations for team development. Allocates time and resources for planning team development.
- *Initiates Team Development*—Communicates team development expectations/vision for the project. Involves the team in developing team development, performance requirements, and strategies.
- *Integrates Project Team Development and Project Performance*—Involves the team in all key project tasks. Supports key team development practices like making decision by consensus. Includes team development as variable in project reviews.

■ *Illustrates with Concrete Examples*—Communicates key concepts and strategies through the use of stories that illustrate premises. Can effectively lead through stories that reinforce project management guidelines and demonstrate personal experience and tacit knowledge.

Applications and Next Steps

The findings have many applications for improving project performance and for initiatives designed to develop project management competencies. A number of these applications are already being made to the various undertakings of NASA's Academy of Program and Project Leadership (APPL).

Findings from the combined studies are being applied to modify NASA's project management training and development initiatives managed by APPL. A training module on project team development leadership functions has been introduced into the training curriculum. The NPTDS has been made available to all NASA projects through a website (http://appl.nasa.gov; Leadership Place; TeamMates Tool). This website will provide projects with an empirically valid and statistically sound tool for assessing key variables in their project's development and performance. The team assessment tool is also being included in a NASA Assessment Center program for project managers, Project Mirror, that mentors and develops new project leaders by identifying specific leadership skills that individuals need and providing them with development opportunities to acquire these needed skills.

This study into superior project team performance is considered an initial step in placing a far greater spotlight into the importance of the team variable. Future studies are needed to generalize these findings to other project disciplines and environments. Further study is needed to determine the nature of team development and group process within the unique and changing world of a project. Most important, project management practitioners and researchers need to take a closer look into the central importance of the team dimension for project success. Project success is dependent on many variables and a high level of professionalism and preparation. The team variable is the foundation for ultimate success.

References

Alter, A. 1996. F.Y.I.: Systems Development Surprise. *Computerworld* 30 (7): 68–69.

Ayas, K. 1996. Professional Project Management: A Shift towards Learning and a Knowledge Creating Structure. *International Journal of Project Management* 14 (3): 131–136.

Baker, S., and K. Baker. 1992. *On Time/On Budget*. Englewood Cliffs, NJ: Prentice Hall.

Catledge, L., and C. Potts. 1996. Collaboration During Conceptual Design. *IEEE Proceedings of ICRE*: 182–189.

Egginton, B. 1996. The Project Start-Up Process, Getting It to Work Better. *Engineering Management Journal* (April): 88–92.

Fleming, Q., and J. Koppleman. 1997. Integrated Project Development Teams: Another Fad ... or Permanent Change. *Project Management Journal* (March): 4–11.

Frame, J. 1995. *Managing Projects in Organizations*. San Francisco: Jossey-Bass Publishers.

Garvin, D. 1991. Building a Learning Organization. *Harvard Business Review* (July–August): 78–91.

Hauptman, O., and K. Hirji. 1996. The Influence of Process Concurrency on Project Outcomes in Product Development: An Empirical Study of Cross-Functional Teams. *IEE Transactions on Engineering* 43 (2): 153–164.

Katzenbach, J., and D. Smith. 1993. *The Wisdom of Teams*. Boston: Harvard Business School Press.

Kerzner, H. 1995. *Project Management: A Systems Approach to Planning, Scheduling, and Controlling*. 5th ed. New York: Van Nostrand Reinhold.

Kezsbom, D. 1994. Self-Directed Teams and the Changing Role of the Project Manager. *Proceedings of the Internet 12th World Congress on Project Management*, Oslo: 589–593.

Kezsbom, D., D. Schilling, and K. Edward. 1989. *Dynamic Project Management: A Practical Guide for Managers and Engineers*. New York: John Wiley & Sons, Inc.

Kinlaw, D. 1991. *Developing Superior Work Teams*. New York: Lexington Books.

———. 1998. *Superior Teams: What They Are and How to Build Them*. London: Gower Publishing Company Limited.

Kinney, S., and R. Panko. 1996. Project Teams: Profiles and Member Perceptions as Indications of Group Support System Research and Products. *Proceedings of the 29th Annual Hawaii International Conference on System Sciences*: 128–137.

Kliem, R., and H. Anderson. 1996. Teambuilding Styles and Their Impact on Project Management Results. *Project Management Journal* (March): 41–50.

Larson, E. 1997. Partnering in Construction Projects: A Study of the Relationship between Partnering Activities and Project Success. *Transactions on Engineering Management* 44 (2): 188–195.

Laufer, A., and E. Hoffman. 2000. *Project Management Success Stories: Lessons of Project Leaders*. New York: John Wiley & Sons. Inc.

Leim, R., and I. Ludin. 1992. *The People Side of Project Management*. London: Gower Publishing Company Limited.

Lewis, J. 1998. *Team-Based Project Management*. New York: AMACOM.

Lock, D. 1996. *The Essentials of Project Management*. London: Gower Publishing Company Limited.

McMichael, J. 1994. Boeing Spares Distribution Center: A World-Class Facility Achieved through Partnering. *Project Management Network* 8 (9): 9–19.

Reiss, G. 1992. *Project Management Demystified*. New York: E and FN Spon.

Robert, D. 1997. Creating an Environment for Project Success. *Information Systems Management* (Winter): 73–79.

Rosenau, M., and J. Moran. 1993. *Managing the Development of New Products*. New York: Van Nostrand Reinhold.

Song, X., W. Souder, and B. Dyer. 1997. A Causal Model of the Impact of Skills, Synergy, and Design Sensitivity on New Product Performance. *Journal of Product Innovation Management* 14: 88–101.

Wilemon, D., and H. Thamhain. 1979. Team Building in Project Management. *1979 Proceedings of the Project Management Institute*: 373–380.

———. 1983. Model for Developing High Performance Project Teams. *1983 Proceedings of the Project Management Institute*: iii-H-1 to ii-H-11.

Williams, T. 1997. Empowerment vs. Risk Management? *International Journal of Project Management* 15 (4): 219–222.

CHAPTER 15

BUSINESSES IN THE WORLD OF PROJECTS

Rolf A. Lundin, Ph.D.—Jönköping International Business School

Novelties in Organization

When Jim March of Stanford University, in the beginning of the '90s, first mentioned and described the notion of "Disposable Organizations," my initial thought was, "Nice idea, but very marginal in practice!" His observation was that in the Silicon Valley area some young, talented engineers, recently graduated from the university, often started small businesses on their own, sometimes together with a few friends around some business idea related to computers and information technology (IT). They did so with the intention to sell off their business at the first opportunity, making a nice profit in virtually no time at all (March 1995). That seemingly odd phenomenon has become an everyday occurrence since then. The brave new economic rally at the turn of the millennium with an IT rally (including volatility of share prices) in the stock exchanges all over the world seems to have strengthened the tendency he described. The hunt is on, not only for young talent—especially in IT related areas—but also for small entrepreneurial companies with promising ventures. A new breed of very young and very well-educated entrepreneurs has arrived to the center stage of the economy in many countries. Making money fast while your talent is "hot" is a different and possibly also a new motive for starting a business. At least it is different if your comparison is with some kind of traditional entrepreneurs often starting companies because they are fed up with their present jobs or in connection with a situation when they have experienced some kind of turbulence in life (like a divorce).

These two types of entrepreneurs obviously have completely different intentions with their activities. For the traditional entrepreneur, the company in a sense is a goal in itself. Traditionally, that kind of entrepreneur has been found to stay with the newly created business for the rest of the life of the entrepreneur. That implicates two things: first, a lifelong engagement for the entrepreneur and second, the company is expected to have a life that might extend well beyond the lifetime of the original entrepreneur. For the other type of entrepreneur, the making money fast type, the company is merely a vehicle, not an end in itself. The effort is time limited in the sense that there seems to be a time limit beyond which the entrepreneur and the partners are not willing to put more energy into the venture at hand but move on to something else. It also has some other definite project characteristics with a stress on the task at hand inducing not only high motivation but also a definite preoccupation with success where the entrepreneur is willing to sacrifice what is considered as normal life for the sake of the success of the venture.

The point is that we are witnessing a marked drift in the way an enterprise is perceived. The new kind of entrepreneur is likely to think of the enterprise in a project-like manner or at least as a temporary organization. This is in sharp contrast to the traditional entrepreneur who is solidly rooted in the bureaucratic type of organization likely to be the basic organization type of previous jobs. Most people who grew up during the heydays of industrial success in the post-war era are also likely to think of industrial organizations as ever-lasting entities. Furthermore, the permanency character of those organizations is likely to have been strengthened by at least some of their experiences of working life. In a sense we see some kind of victims of traditions in that generation. Youngsters who come directly from universities are not bound to have become infected by those same traditions. Instead they at times become one with the observed projectization tendency in society (Lundin and Midler 1998). Their mere existence and their way of life lead to an organizational novelty. The explanation to that appears to be too simple. Since most of the experiences of youngsters from schooling are project like, they tend to think in terms of time-limited ventures when setting up what they want to do. A side comment is that one important and significant corollary of this statement is that the much criticized tendency to use youngsters from the university system in experiments concerning industry and industrial practices might become increasingly relevant for the society with heavy projectization and with an increase of the disposable organization phenomena.

The death rate among entrepreneurial companies in the emerging industries has been very high (at least if you adhere to the traditional notion that death occurs when the company disappears as an entity that is legally independent). For Sweden it has been estimated that at the turn of the millennium when bankruptcies overall are relatively low not to say rare, the survival rate as legal entity for the type of companies we are discussing is still considerably less than one out of ten during their first year of existence. It is tempting to think of the death rate in the new industries in Schumpeter (1943, 1996) terms, that is to account for the death rate as a company failure where death is a form of "creative destruction" that leads to a better use of resources tied up in an ailing company. Another view, the one suggested here, is that the companies in question should be thought of as projects where death is always natural. Possibly the outcome is approximately the same, that is the resources become available in a wider context. This remark concludes our discussion about companies becoming project-like. The next section will bring us over to an introduction about notions concerning the roles that traditional organizations have for projects.

Who Needs Traditional Organizations?

Those of us who have been studying projects and temporary organizations tend to set our mind accordingly. We open our eyes more widely toward those kinds of phenomena leaving very little and very limited room for traditional thinking about organizations as permanent entities. In our view, most of the important economic activities can be regarded as projects. Wherever we look, we see projects, projects, and projects. This is not to say that we do not see other organized activities as well. On the contrary, we see a lot of organization, but the organization we see is designed to get things done in a project-like manner. As already indicated, projects appear to be of main importance for profit generation, but they are far from being organized as traditional organizations.

This leaves us with projects as a matter of utmost interest and a notion of traditional organizations with a decided stress on "traditional." Together with the example of "making money fast" entrepreneurial activities mentioned under the first heading, this places a special emphasis to the question in the headline: "Who needs traditional organizations?" Part of the answer that is of interest in the present context is that these organizations often function as "mothers" to projects and that they are needed as hosts for projects. (The mother organization is where a project is conceived and the host organization is where a project is carried through. In the majority of real-world cases the mother and the host are the same organization, but there are of course exceptions.) Out of the twenty-five major projects used as illustrations by Ekstedt et al. (1999), twenty-one were hosted by one and only one organization. (This proportion does not at all reflect proportions in the project populations. The reason is that most projects hosted by a single organization are close to invisible to the outside world. At least there are very few statistics available to the general public concerning such projects.) These twenty-one cases covered projects of a wide variety: building construction, theater and opera, product development, and organizational renewal to mention a few. The remaining four projects were inter-organizational, meaning that they could be described as joint ventures with several important stakeholders involved. One feature of projects hosted by a single organization is that they are more or less totally under the control of that organization. Conversely, this means that the organization is responsible for how the project is handled.

Leaving the fairly trivial questions about hosts and mothers aside, there are two other types of answers to the previous question, why traditional organizations are needed after all. The discussion to ensue in the following sections is based on empirical work presented in Ekstedt et al. (1999) and by Pettigrew and his associates (Whittington et al. 1999), respectively. Essentially the arguments are of two types. The arguments based on the work presented in Ekstedt et al. center on learning in project work and how learning aspects relate to the organization of a traditional kind serving as hosts for the project in question. The Pettigrew material concerns how traditional and typically permanent organizations are changing character to become atypical and how new organizational forms for ventures also might alter the character of the host organizations. I will commence my discussion with the latter example.

Ventures and Organizations

Businesses are no longer what they used to be. This statement covers not only the "disposable organization" phenomenon mentioned previously, but also holds true for more traditional companies. We have tended to think of them as some kind of permanent entities providing a high degree of stability for our economies with extensive employment in personnel and with heavy investments in machinery and in real estate. No longer so, at least not in a traditional sense! Recent empirical results indicate that the ongoing transformation of businesses is very fast indeed. Activities mentioned in current literature as well as in material from professional associations on organization in an industrial context, like outsourcing, insourcing, strategic alliances, joint ventures, mergers, acquisitions, and movements concerning efficiency in terms of "back to core competencies" have become increasingly more prevalent over the last decade or so.

The examples in this enumeration are by no means unequivocal. A fairly simple and straightforward joint advertising campaign has been labeled "strategic alliance" even though it is time delimited, but at the same time the strategic alliance denomination is also used for very far-reaching cooperation. However, this is a nuance only. The main point is that there is a definite movement among business organizations. Sometimes elements of that movement related to the activities enumerated previously are about projects or can be described as projects. A "joint venture" is probably the most obvious example of that type, but several of the others also have definite project-like components. The popular trends include a fair amount of projectization.

A study under the auspices of the University of Warwick, England, considering major changes in industrial organizations in the United States (US), Japan, and Western Europe seems to confirm these tendencies observed in the literature by revealing and characterizing the major changes in the way these industrial organizations have organized their activities through empirical investigations. The Western Europe material has been presented in an article by Whittington et al. (1999). In the home page of the research group at Warwick (http://www.wbs.warwick.ac.uk/HotTopics/HT6.html) it is said that over a four-year period, outsourcing was increased by 65 percent of the companies. At the same time IT-related investments have increased in more than 80 percent of the same set of organizations. To top everything else off, project-based organization is up by 175 percent. Generally, the activities described in the article have one thing in common, i.e., the supposedly permanent organization focus is generally involved in activities of a kind seemingly leading to a destabilization of self. (Among other things it is this destabilization that makes the denomination "permanent organization" inappropriate. Possibly that choice of words refers to a situation long since passed, but even though there could be no such thing as a permanent organization anyway, the denomination will be used at times. The reader should remember though that "permanent" essentially means more permanent than others.)

One measure that supports the projectization notion is that temporary employment is increasing, at least in the European Union. In 1995 approximately 11 percent of the total workforce in the Union had temporary employment (SOU 1999, 27). There were substantial regional variations with Spain on top with 35 percent having temporary employment. However, the general share has been increasing over the preceding fifteen years and even though no statistics are available concerning the last years of the previous millennium, there is no reason to believe that the share has decreased lately. (It should be emphasized that "temporary employment" and "project employment" are two different things. The latter should be regarded as a subgroup of the former, but the former includes such things as seasonal variation in employment needs as well. Furthermore, it should be noted that the measure says nothing about people working in projects.)

Traditional organizations are the birthplaces for new ventures. The organizations become necessary conditions for the changes taking place no matter the origin of the changes, per se. Some people would probably argue that the tendencies described should be understood in terms of institutional change or fads penetrating the organizational world. The movements concerning quality and environmental concerns, just to mention a couple of obvious examples, could most probably be understood and described in terms of institutions or fads. No matter the origins of the changes, the traditional organizations are necessary conditions for the developments.

If projects are action oriented it is probably fair to say that traditional organizations, especially business organizations are decision oriented. At least many theories on business organizations have decisions as a fundamental mechanism. The implication of the decision orientation is that these organizations have the facilities to deliberate upon decisions and generate alternative outcomes in a decision situation. Such facilities are needed when it comes to generating new project ventures. Traditional organizations are properly endowed to give birth to projects.

We will now leave the discussion concerning how the business world as such is changing in an overall pattern and focus the relationships between projects and their hosts from a different angle. The question concerns how knowledge generated in project action is handled and can be handled.

Action, Learning, and Project Organizations

Projects are designed for action. In particular, getting things done by fulfilling an explicit and predetermined task is the main justification for the project itself. In normal projects such efforts are concerned with the orchestrated, concerted action of a group of people, the team. That team is entrusted with the project and the obligation of the members of the team is to get the project done. The function of the project manager is to see to it that measures are taken and that results are achieved in such a way that the task is fulfilled. In the popular view among professionals in the area, the only thing that counts is the project and the fulfillment of the task. Efficiency in working with the project at hand is of utmost importance.

Defining a project as a project points to the need for action. An implication of this is that the project as a work form comes in handy when a need for action is recognized. "Something has to happen" is a phrase often used in connection with unique projects. A project is called for when there is a need to focus a particular task and when it comes to intra-organizational projects, the task is related to the host organization itself.

A project does have one built-in weakness as an organization, though. It does not have an infrastructure of its own handy. The reason for that is simple. A project is a time-limited venture that eventually will evaporate or be dissolved. Thus, the team members and other resources made available for the project manager are the means to fulfill the task at hand. Whatever aptitudes and knowledge not possessed by the team members and needed to fulfill the task have to be fetched from somewhere else. The knowledge needed has to be stored in a readily retrievable way. Conversely, there is no readily available infrastructure to take care of knowledge generated in action over the lifetime of the project. One classical, not to say eternal, problem in any projectized company concerns how to distill knowledge generated in a project and how to store those experiences so that they can be put into use in future projects. Otherwise a lot of useful experiences might be wasted.

A traditional organization—to be thought of as permanent for the purposes at hand in the present context—has advantages over projects when it comes to transforming learning to knowledge and storing the results of the transformation in a retrievable system. This means that traditional organizations and projects might be thought of as complements to each other. Project action generates learning and a set of experiences in a knowledge formation process and the knowledge can be stored in a permanent organization.

It should be observed that knowledge in this case is not necessarily abstract and free of context. Rather, knowledge should be thought of as embedded knowledge. Ekstedt et al. (1999, 128) have analyzed notions of different forms of knowledge embeddedness. One form is when knowledge is embedded in physical equipment. This is capital-embedded knowledge. Another form is when knowledge is embedded in the organization (organization-embedded knowledge). A third, related form is when knowledge is embedded in institutions and "rules" of importance for more than one organization (institution-embedded knowledge). Individual-embedded knowledge is the traditional case when knowledge is associated with the individual only.

The notion of embeddedness is important since many of the renewal projects carried out for industrial firms are aimed at renewing the embedded knowledge. For that case the storing of the knowledge generated in a permanent organization is more or less natural since it is so well connected to the aim of the work. All the twenty-five renewal cases alluded to by Ekstedt et al. (1999) are good examples of how knowledge created in projects is stored in the organization. The renewal program of ABB Sweden, the T50 (meaning that all lead-times in the production should be slashed by 50 percent) has definitely resulted in a renewed set of embedded knowledge for most of the subsidiaries participating in the renewal program.

Storing knowledge generated for a customer outside the organization is more difficult. To mention one example, the habit in architectural firms is to store solutions to architectural problems from finalized projects in such a way that they are retrievable. (Such storage and retrieval is easier now than in old days with the extensive use of computer-aided design, IT, and electronic storage.) These solutions might be used for future projects. Storing knowledge related to how the project process, per se, is run is probably the most difficult case. In most project-organized activities in businesses, projects are evaluated in terms of the project process in the sense that evaluation reports are written to document what was good and what was bad. This is a regular habit when it comes to product development projects in industry. In practice it seems difficult to transform those experiences for future use in a systematic way, though.

This concludes our discussion concerning the implications of combining action prone projects and decision-oriented organizations. Suffice it to say at this point that this is a major task for what has been called "neo-industrial management" (Ekstedt et al. 1999). There are some good examples for how that can be handled.

Projects, Organizations, and the New Modernity

Thus far in the chapter—our treatise of businesses in the world of projects—we have tried to outline the roles that businesses might play in such a world. In the process we have covered different types of relations between projects and businesses. Thus, we have discussed instances where companies have come to be regarded and treated as projects. We have also alluded to the case where some aspects of business life have become projectized or transformed into project-like phenomena. We have also covered the case when projects and businesses seem to complement each other in terms of action and learning. This last section is supposed to take us a bit further but along a different type of avenue that will take us to grounds where historical developments play a definite role.

One way to analyze what seems to be going on when it comes to the development of projects and general organizations in thinking and in practice is to relate that development to changes in thinking of society and societal changes on a grand scale. One particular line of thinking appears relevant here, the sequence Modernism, Post-Modernism, and Neo-Modernism (or New Modernity). There is not space to develop in any detail at all for what these societal models stand. At that, such a task is very difficult since the views on these models or phenomena differ radically. I will refrain from delving into the details and try to outline the main characteristics only in order to back up the claims I want to make.

If you try to relate project thinking during the past century to the sequence mentioned above, you will find that the general notions of project management were formulated in the 1950s in the US (Engwall 1995) when Modernism is regarded as the dominating line of thinking. People were not necessarily discussing societal developments in those terms at the time. Rather the Modernism characterization was a label used in the subsequent era to form the contrast for whatever was to be seen as new. Anyway, the notions of project management were mainly formed in the defense industry and in the Department of Defense in the US. (One might even say that projects in the meaning of that time are a product of the so-called military-industrial complex.) The projects at that time had a technical character and were all representing major efforts on a grand scale with almost no resource constraints but with very seriously meant time limits. The cold war fostered such attitudes and the projects went well with the general characteristics of Modernism. They represented major efforts concerning control of the world, also encompassing social engineering efforts on a grand scale. In a general sense they were also like dreams of rationalization. Careful planning reassured the actors that the project adhered to the rationality norms of the era.

Subsequently, the character of projects changed. Initially, the techniques and the organization spread to other technical areas outside the military applications. However, the techniques for planning and follow-up still favored major projects involving extraordinary personnel and a lot of monetary resources. Over time, however, project management found applications in areas where it never had been used before. Over time notions of project management have also become integral parts of a variety of professions. At the same time the tendency has been that the size of projects (in terms of personnel and money) has decreased (Engwall 1999, 549). Small projects appeared in a wide variety of contexts and the projects themselves, as well as their contexts, gave a fragmented impression. In that sense the projects of the '80s and the '90s go well with the notions of the Post-Modern era. The ideas of social engineering on a grand scale have given way to the notions that control is very difficult, if not impossible. Problems are rather solved in a patchwork fashion, where the fragmented views of the world become very apparent. The spreading of project ideas to a diversity of new application areas is another sign of fragmentation.

In the '90s Neo-Modernism has appeared as a leading theme for the development of societies. Rationality is back as a key word for how societal problems are attacked. Efforts to that effect lead to a "risk society" according to Beck (1992). The notions of this new modernity (or Neo-Modernism) are that the introduction of rationalization efforts carries risks with it. The entire societal development might be regarded as a host of efforts to form rational institutions and at the same time trying to ameliorate dysfunction resulting from these efforts.

On a macro level, the focus of this essay has been on concomitant changes in the life of businesses and in the way projects seem to function. Possibly, both of them are examples of rationalization. Projects are governed so as to promote action rationality. Businesses are adapted in the same vein according to notions of how profitability arises and in accordance with the needs for rational projects.

To conclude this chapter with one notion of what the future might have in readiness for us, there is a need to illustrate how the discussion above has one fundamental weakness. The discussion about storing knowledge generated in projects ends up in the solution that the task of a permanent organization is to have a natural storage and retrieval system at hand. At the same time the argument is that businesses are on the move as well. In other words, businesses are not permanent organizations that can be used as fix points for the knowledge created in the temporary projects. Most likely, the storage problem alluded to has to be solved in another way in the long run. This might be regarded as one of the risks to which Beck (1992) alludes. It will give rise to new forms of storing and retrieving knowledge through reflexive modernization? Is there a need for institutional reflexivity carried by individuals to handle the unforeseen under these circumstances? Will there be a new role for universities in storing and retrieving knowledge?

References

Beck, Ulrich. 1992. *Risk Society—Towards a New Modernity*. London: Sage.

Ekstedt, Eskil et al. 1999. *Neo-Industrial Organizing—Action, Knowledge Formation and Renewal in a Project-Intensive Economy*. London: Routledge.

Engwall, Mats. 1995. *Jakten på det effektiva projektet* (*In Search of the Effective Project*, in Swedish). Stockholm: Nerenius and Santérus.

———. 1999. Multiproject Management: Effects, Issues and Propositions for Future Research. *Nordnet '99 Conference*, September, Helsinki, Finland.

Lundin, Rolf A., and Christophe Midler, eds. 1998. *Projects as Arenas for Renewal and Learning Processes*. Norwell, MA: Kluwer Academic Publishers.

March, James G. 1995. The Future, Disposable Organizations and the Rigidities of Imagination. *Organization* 2: 427–440.

Schumpeter, Joseph A. 1966, 1943. *Capitalism, Socialism and Democracy*. London: Allen & Unwin.

SOU. 1999. Statens Offentliga Utredningar: 27 DELTA—Utredningen om deltidsarbete, tillfälliga jobb och arbetslöshetsersättningen (The Official Investigations of the Swedish Government, No. 27 DELTA—Investigating Part Time Work, Occasional Work and Unemployment Compensation, in Swedish), Stockholm.

Whittington, Richard et al. 1999. Change and Complementarities in the New Competitive Landscape: A European Panel Study, 1992–1996. *Organization Science* 5: 583–600.

CHAPTER 16

CRITERIA FOR EFFECTIVE LEADERSHIP IN TECHNOLOGY-ORIENTED PROJECT TEAMS

Hans J. Thamhain, Ph.D., PMP—Bentley College

Introduction

Teamwork is the frontier in today's competitive business world. More than 70 percent of managers in our organizations consider effective cross-functional teamwork a key determinant of business performance and success. Virtually all managers recognize the critical importance of effective teamwork and strive for continuous improvement of team performance in their organizations. Yet, only one in ten of these managers have a specific metric for actually measuring team performance. Obviously, this creates some tough challenges, especially in project-based environments where teamwork is crucial to business success. In these organizational environments, work teams must successfully integrate multidisciplinary activities, unify different business processes, and deal with cross-functional issues, such as innovation, quality, speed, producability, sourcing, and service. Managerial principals and practices have changed dramatically. Not too long ago, project management was to a large degree considered "management science." Project leaders *could* ensure successful integration for most of their project by focusing on properly defining the work, timing, and resources, and by following established procedures for project tracking and control. Today, these factors are still crucial. However, they have become threshold competencies, critically important, but unlikely to guarantee by themselves project success. Today's complex business world requires *project teams* who are fast and flexible, and can dynamically and creatively work toward established objectives in a changing environment (Cusumano and Yoffie 1998; Engel 1997; Thamhain 1998, 1999, 2000). This requires effective networking and cooperation among people from different organizations, support groups, subcontractors, vendors, government agencies, and customer communities. It also requires the ability to deal with uncertainties and risks introduced by technological, economic, political, social, and regulatory factors. In addition, project leaders have to organize and manage their teams across organizational lines, dealing often with resource personnel over whom they have little or no formal authority. Resource sharing, multiple reporting relationships, and broadly based alliances are as common in today's business environment as email, flex time, and home offices. Managing project teams effectively in such dynamic environments, requires task leaders to understand the *interaction of organizational and behavioral variables*. These project leaders must develop their multidisciplinary task groups into unified teams, and foster a climate conducive to involvement, commitment, and conflict resolution, in spite of these organizational challenges.

What We Know About Teamwork in Project Organizations

Concept and Process

Teamwork is not a new idea. The basic concepts of organizing and managing teams go back in history to biblical times. In fact, work teams have long been considered an effective device to enhance organizational effectiveness. Since the discovery of important social phenomena in the classic Hawthorne studies (Roethlingsberger and Dickinson 1939), management theorists and practitioners have tried to enhance group identity and cohesion in the workplace (Dyer 1977). Indeed, much of the *human relations movement* that followed Hawthorne, is based on the group concept. McGregor's (1960) theory Y, for example, spells out the criteria for an effective work group, and Likert (1961) called his highest form of management the participating group or system 4. However, the process of team building becomes more complex and requires more specialized management skills as bureaucratic hierarchies decline and horizontally oriented teams and work units evolve.

Redefining the Process

In today's more complex multinational and technologically sophisticated environment, the group has reemerged in importance as the *project team* (Wellins, Byham, and Wilson 1991; Fisher 1993; Nurick 1993; Shonk 1996; Thamhain and Wilemon 1999). *Team building can be defined* as the process of taking a collection of individuals with different needs, backgrounds, and expertise and transforming them into an integrated, effective work unit. In this transformation process, the goals and energies of individual contributors merge and focus on specific objectives. When describing an effective project team, managers stress con-

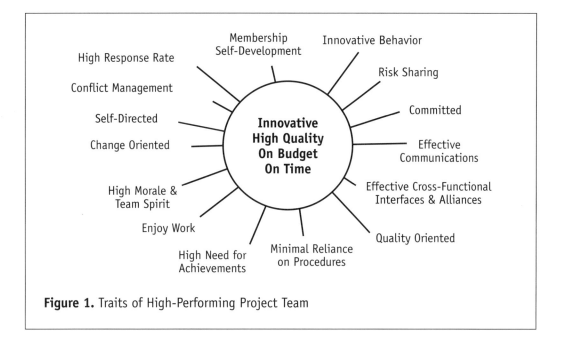

Figure 1. Traits of High-Performing Project Team

sistently that high-performance, although ultimately reflected by producing desired results, on time and within budget, is a derivative of many factors which are graphically shown in Figure 1. Team building is an ongoing process that requires leadership skills and an understanding of the organization, its interfaces, authority, power structures, and motivational factors. This process is particularly crucial in environments where complex multidisciplinary or transnational activities require the skillful integration of many functional specialties and support groups with diverse organizational cultures, values, and intricacies (Oderwald 1996). Typical examples of such multidisciplinary activities requiring unified teamwork for successful integration include:

- Establishing a new program
- Transferring technology
- Improving project-client relationships
- Organizing for a bid proposal
- Integrating new project personnel
- Resolving inter-functional problems
- Working toward major milestones
- Reorganizing mergers and acquisitions
- Transitioning the project into a new activity phase
- Revitalizing an organization.

Because of their potential for producing economic advantages, work teams and their development have been researched by many. Starting with the evolution of formal project organizations in the l960s, managers in various organizational settings have expressed increasing concern with and interest in the concepts and practices of multidisciplinary team building. As a result, many field studies have been

Definition: A group of people chartered with specific responsibilities for managing them-selves and their work, with minimal reliance on group-external supervision, bureaucracy, and control. Team structure, task responsibilities, work plans, and team leadership often evolve based on needs and situational dynamics.

Benefits: Ability to handle complex assignments, requiring evolving and innovative solutions that cannot be easily directed via top-down supervision. Widely shared goals, values, infor-mation, and risks. Flexibility toward needed changes. Capacity for conflict resolution, team building, and self-development. Effective cross-functional communications and work inte-gration. High degree of self-control, accountability, ownership, and commitment toward established objectives.

Challenges: A unified, mature team does not just happen, but must be carefully organized and developed by management. A high degree of self-motivation and sufficient job, admin-istrative, and people skills must exist among the team members. Empowerment and self-control might lead to unintended results and consequences. Self-directed teams are not necessary self-managed, they often require more sophisticated external guidance and lead-ership than conventionally structured teams.

Table 1. Characteristics of Self-Directed Teams

conducted, investigating work group dynamics and criteria for building effective, high-performing project teams. These studies have contributed to the theoretical and practical understanding of team building and form the fundamental concepts discussed in this chapter. Prior to 1980, most of these studies focused just on the behavior of the team members, with limited attention given to the organizational environment and team leadership. While the qualities of the individuals and their interaction within the team are crucial elements in the teamwork process, they represent only part of the overall organization and management system which influences team performance, as was recognized by Bennis and Shepard as early as 1956. Since 1980 an increasing number of studies have broadened the under-standing of the teamwork process (Tichy and Urlich 1984; Walton 1985; Dumaine 1991). These more recent studies show the enormous breadth and depth of subsystems and variables involved in the organization, development, and man-agement of a high-performing work team (Gupta and Wilemon 1996). These vari-ables include planning, organizing, training, organizational structure, nature and complexity of task, senior management support, leadership, and socioeconomic variables, just to name the most popular ones (Shaw, Fisher, and Randolph 1991; Thamhain and Wilemon 1983, 1987, 1991, 1993). Even further, researchers such as Dumaine (1991), Drucker (1996), Peters and Waterman (1987, 1997), Moss Kanter (1989), and Thamhain (1990, 1993) have emphasized the nonlinear, intri-cate, often chaotic, and random nature of teamwork, which involves all facets of the organization, its members, and environment. These teams became the con-

Definition: A group of project team members, linked via the Internet or media channels to each other and various project partners, such as contractors, customers, and regulators. Although physically separated, technology links these individuals so they can share information and operate as a unified project team. The number of elements in a virtual team and their permanency can vary, depending on need and feasibility. An example of a virtual team is a project review conducted among the team members, contractors, and customer over an Internet website.

Benefits: Ability to share information and communicate among team members and organizational entities of geographically dispersed projects. Ability to share and communicate information in a synchronous and asynchronous mode (application: communication across time-zones, holidays, and shared work spaces). Creating unified visibility of project status and performance. Virtual teams, to some degree, bridge and neutralize the culture and value differences that exist among different task teams of project organizations.

Challenges: The effectiveness of the virtual team depends on the team members' ability to work with the given technology. Information flow and access is not necessarily equal for all team members. Information may not be processed uniformly throughout the team. The virtual team concept does not fit the culture and value system of all members and organizations. Project tracking, performance assessment, and managerial control of project activities are often very difficult. Risks, contingencies, and problems are difficult to detect and assess. Virtual organizations often do not provide effective methods for dealing with conflict, power, candor, feedback, and resource issues. Because of the many limitations, more traditional team processes and communications are often needed to augment virtual teams.

Table 2. Characteristics of Virtual Teams

duit for transferring information, technology, and work concepts across functional lines quickly, predictably, and within given resource restraints.

Toward Self-Direction and Virtual Teams

Especially with the evolution of contemporary organizations, such as the matrix, traditional bureaucratic hierarchies have declined and horizontally oriented teams and work units became increasingly important to effective project management (Fisher 1993; Marshall 1995); the role of supervisor has been diminished in favor of more *empowerment and self-direction* of the team, as defined in Table 1. In addition, advances in information technology made it feasible and effective to link team members over the Internet or other media, creating a *virtual team* environment, as described in Table 2. *Virtual teams* and *virtual project organizations* are powerful managerial tools, especially for companies with geographically dispersed project operations, including contractors, customers, and regulators.

Teams of this contemporary nature exist in virtually all of our organizations, ranging from dedicated venture groups, often called *skunk works*, to product development teams, process action teams, and focus groups. These team concepts are being applied to different forms of project activities in areas of products, services, acquisition efforts, political election campaigns, and foreign assistance programs. For these kinds of highly multifunctional and nonlinear processes, researchers stress the need for strong integration and orchestration of cross-functional activities, linking the various work groups into a unified project team that focuses energy and integrates all subtasks toward desired results. Further, the life cycle of these teams often spans across the complete project, not just the phase of primary engagement. For example, the primary mission of the product development team may focus on the engineering phase, but the team also supports activities ranging from recognition of an opportunity, feasibility analysis, bid proposals, licensing, subcontracting, and transferring technology to manufacturing, distribution, and field service. While these realities hold for most team efforts in today's work environment, they are especially pronounced for efforts that are associated with risk, uncertainty, creativity, and team diversity such as high technology and/or multinational projects. These are also the work environments that first departed from traditional hierarchical team structures and tried more self-directed and network-based virtual concepts (Fisher 1993; Ouchi 1993).

Scope, Objective, and Method

This chapter reports selected parts of ongoing field research into best-in-class project management practices, investigating the way project leaders work with their teams in complex, mostly technology-intensive project situations. The objective of these studies was to examine team leadership methods and organizational criteria that are effective in complex project settings. This chapter draws on research from five field studies conducted over the last twelve years, which include surveys of over 900 project professionals in twenty-four companies. Specifically, these studies include data from 655 engineers, scientists, and technicians, 31 managers from functional support groups, 138 project team leaders, 69 project managers, 14 directors of research and development, 9 directors of marketing, and 10 general management executives. Together, the data covered over 180 projects in the area of product/service development with budgets averaging $1,200,000 (US) each. The host companies were large technology-based multinational companies of the "Fortune-1000" category. Specifically, data were collected between 1987 and 1999 by questionnaires and two qualitative methods: *participant observation* and *in-depth retrospective interviewing*. The purpose of this combined data collection method was to cast the broadest possible information-gathering net to identify the tools, techniques, and practices used for managing technical projects today, and to gain insight into applications, methods, and effectiveness.

A Model for Measuring Project Performance

"A castle is only as strong as the people who defend it." This Japanese proverb also applies to organizations. They are only as effective as their unified team efforts. Although team performance is difficult to measure, research agrees on specific metrics for characterizing winning teams, as graphically shown in Figure 1. More specifically, Table 3 breaks these characteristics of high performing project teams is into four categories: 1) work and team structure, 2) communications and control, 3) team leadership, and 4) attitude and values. These broad measures can provide a framework for benchmarking and a simple model for organizing and analyzing the variables that influence the team's characteristics and its ultimate performance. Teams that score high on these characteristics are also seen by upper management as most favorable in dealing with cost, quality, creativity, schedules, and customer satisfaction. They also receive favorable ratings on the more subtle measures of high team performance, such as flexibility, change orientation, innovative performance, high morale, and team spirit.

Influences of Team Environment on Leadership

Many observations from best practices and formal field studies are pointing at an interesting, professionally stimulating work environment, high on recognition and accomplishments, as conducive to effective team leadership and high project performance. These conditions seem to affect motivation and commitment of individual team members, cross-functional communications, and many components that ultimately influence the team characteristics favorably (Figure 1) and produce high project performance. However, more rigorous statistical tests had to be performed before conclusions could be drawn. Table 4 summarizes the results of a Kendall Tau analysis, measuring the association between the work environment and leadership effectiveness. The results show indeed that those conditions that are conducive to a *professionally stimulating work environment*, also lead to higher levels of 1) trust, 2) respect, 3) credibility, 4) ability to influence decisions, and ultimately 5) overall team leadership effectiveness.

The strength of the organizational and leadership variables was measured on a five-point scale as a perception of project team members, except for overall team leadership effectiveness, which was measured as a perception of both team members and senior management. As indicated by the strong positive correlation shown in Table 4, factors that fulfill professional esteem needs seem to have a particularly strong influence on overall team leadership effectiveness. The three most significant associations are: 1) professionally stimulating and challenging work environments [$\tau = 0.41$], 2) recognition of accomplishments [$\tau = 0.39$], and 3) the ability to resolve conflict and problems [$\tau = 0.37$]. Many of these factors that correlate favorably to team leadership effectiveness, appear to deal favorably with the integration of the personal goals and needs of team member with the project and organizational goals. In this context, these more subtle factors seem to become

Project Performance Metrics
1. Agreed-on results and performance
2. Innovative, creative solutions
3. Concern for quality
4. On-time and within budget delivery

Work and Team Structure
- Team participates in project definition, work plans evolve dynamically
- Team structure and responsibilities evolve and change as needed
- Broad information sharing
- Team leadership evolves based on expertise, trust, respect
- Minimal dependence on bureaucracy, procedures, politics

Communication and Control
- Effective cross-functional channels, linkages
- Ability to seek out and process information
- Effective group decision-making and consensus
- Clear sense of purpose and direction
- Self-control, accountability, and ownership
- Control is stimulated by visibility, recognition, accomplishments, autonomy

Team Leadership
- Minimal hierarchy in member status and position
- Internal team leadership based on situational expertise, trust, and need
- Clear management goals, direction, and support
- Inspires and encourages

Attitudes and Values
- Members are committed to established objectives and plans
- Shared goals, values, and project ownership
- High involvement, energy, work interest, need for achievement, pride, self-motivated
- Capacity for conflict resolution and resource sharing
- Team building and self-development
- Risk sharing, mutual trust, and support
- Innovative behavior
- Flexibility and willingness to change
- High morale and team spirit
- High commitment to established project goals
- Continuous improvement of work process, efficiency, quality
- Ability to stretch beyond agreed-on objectives

Table 3. Benchmarking Your Team Performance

catalysts for cross-functional communications, information sharing, and ultimate integration of the project team with focus on desired results. All associations are significant at p = 0.1 or better. The implications and lessons learned from the broader context of this field study are summarized next.

Characteristics of Team Environment*	Perceived Team Leader Characteristics# (Kendall's Tau Correlation)				
	Trust of Leader* τ_1	Respect of Leader* τ_2	Credibility of Leader* τ_3	Leader's* Ability to Influence Decisions τ_4	Overall# Leader Effectiveness τ_5
Interesting, Stimulating Work	.32	.38	.43	.36	.41
Recognition & Accomplishment	.39	.42	.40	.41	.39
Conflict & Problem Resolution	.30	.27	.35	.33	.37
Clear Understanding of Project Objectives & Plan	.46	.37	.25	.24	.36
Clear Understanding of Organizational Interfaces	.42	.22	.21	.22	.35
Direction & Leadership	.40	.37	.34	.32	.33
Effective Communications	.33	.33	.31	.28	.30
Job Skills & Expertise	.21	.28	.30	.24	.28
Low Interpersonal Conflict	.28	.25	.26	.26	.27
Top Management Involvement & Support	.33	.41	.28	.38	.25
Good Team Spirit and Morale	.31	.42	.26	.37	.22

@Kendall's Tau Rank-Order Correlation; Statistical Significance: $p = .10$ ($\tau > .20$), $p = .05$ ($\tau > .31$), $p = .01$ ($\tau > .36$).

*As perceived by project team members on a five-point scale 1) strongly disagree, 2) disagree, 3) neutral, 4) agree, and 5) strongly agree.

#As perceived by senior management on a four-point scale 1) poor, 2) marginal, 3) good, and 4) excellent.

Table 4. Influences of the Work Environment on Team Leadership Effectiveness

Building High-Performing Teams

What does all this mean to managers in today's work environment with high demands on efficiency, speed, and quality? The increasing technical complexities, cross-functional dependencies, and the need for innovative performance prompt enormous managerial challenges for directing, coordinating, and controlling teamwork. Especially with the expansion of self-directed team concepts, additional managerial tools and skills are required to handle the burgeoning dynamics and infrastructure. Effective teamwork is a critical determinant of project success and the organization's ability to learn from its experiences and position itself for future growth (Senge 1990). To be effective in organizing and directing a project team, the leader must not only recognize the potential drivers and barriers to high-performance teamwork, but also know when in the life cycle of the project they are most likely to occur. The effective project leader takes preventive actions early in the project life cycle and fosters a work environment that is conducive to team building as an ongoing process. The new business realities force managers to focus also on cross-boundary relations, delegation, and commitment, in addition to establishing the more traditional formal command and control systems.

The effective team leader is usually a social architect who understands the interaction of organizational and behavioral variables and can foster a climate of active participation and minimal dysfunctional conflict. This requires carefully developed skills in leadership, administration, organization, and technical expertise. It further requires the project leader's ability to involve top management to ensure organizational visibility, resource availability, and overall support for the new project throughout its life cycle. Moreover, project leaders and their management must understand the interaction of organizational and behavioral variables, so they can facilitate a climate of active participation, minimal dysfunctional conflict, and effective communication. They must also foster an ambiance conducive to change, commitment, and self-direction. Four major conditions must be present for building effective project teams: 1) professionally stimulating work environment, 2) good project leadership, 3) qualified personnel, and 4) stable work environment. Building effective project teams involves the whole spectrum of management skills and company resources, and is the shared responsibility between functional managers and the project leader. By understanding the criteria and organizational dynamics that drive people toward effective team performance, managers can examine and fine-tune their leadership style, actions, and resource allocations toward continuous organizational improvement.

References

Bennis, Warren G., and Herbert A. Shepard. 1956. A Theory of Group Development. *Human Relations* (9): 415–437.

Drucker, Peter F. 1996. *The Executive in Action: Managing for Results, Innovation and Entrepreneurship*. New York: Harper.

Dumaine, Brian. 1991. The Bureaucracy Buster. *Fortune* (June).

Dyer, W. G. 1977. *Team Building: Issues and Alternatives*. Reading, MA: Addison-Wesley.

Engel, Michael V. 1997. The New Non-Manager Manager. *Management Quarterly* 38 (2): 22–29.

Fisher, Kimball. 1993. *Leading Self-Directed Work Teams*. New York: McGraw-Hill.

Gray, Clifford F., and Erik W. Larson. 2000. *Project Management*. New York: Irwin McGraw-Hill.

Gupta, A. K., and D. L. Wilemon. 1996. Changing Patterns in Industrial R&D Management. *Journal of Product Innovation Management* 13 (6): 497–511.

Hersey, Paul, and Kenneth H. Blanchard. 1996. *Management of Organizational Behavior.* Upper Saddle River, NJ: Prentice Hall.

Likert, R. 1961. *New Patterns of Management.* New York: McGraw-Hill.

McGregor, D. 1960. *The Human Side of Enterprise.* New York: McGraw-Hill.

Moss Kanter, Rosabeth. 1989. The New Managerial Work. *Harvard Business Review* (November–December).

Nurick, A. J., and H. J. Thamhain. 1993. Project Team Development in Multinational Environments. In *Global Project Management Handbook.* Edited by D. Cleland. New York: McGraw-Hill.

Ouchi, William G. 1993. *Theory Z.* Avon Books.

Peters, Thomas J., and Robert H. Waterman. 1997. *In Search of Excellence.* New York: Harper & Row.

Roethlingsberger, F., and W. Dickerson. 1939. *Management and the Worker.* Cambridge, MA: Harvard University Press.

Senge, Peter. 1994. *The Fifth Discipline: The Art and Practice of the Learning Organization.* New York: Doubleday/Currency.

Shaw, J., C. Fisher, and A. Randolph. 1991. From Maternalism to Accountability. *Academy of Management Executive* 5 (1): 7–20.

Shonk, J. H. 1996. *Team-Based Organizations.* Homewood, IL: Irwin.

Thamhain, H. J. 1990. Managing Technologically Innovative Team Efforts towards New Product Success. *Journal of Product Innovation Management* 7 (1): 5–18.

———. 1990. Managing Technology: The People Factor. *Technical and Skill Training* (August/September).

———. 1998. Managing people. In *Mechanical Engineer's Handbook.* Edited by M. Kutz. New York: John Wiley & Sons, Inc.

———. 1998. Working with Project Teams. In *Project Management* by David I. Cleland. New York: Van Nostrand Reinhold.

Thamhain, H. J., and D. L. Wilemon. 1987. Leadership, Conflict and Project Management Effectiveness. *Executive Bookshelf on Generating Technological Innovations, Sloan Management Review* (Fall).

———. 1997. Building High Performing Engineering Project Teams. In *The Human Side of Managing Technological Innovation.* Edited by R. Katz. New York: Oxford Press.

———. 1999. Building Effective Teams in Complex Project Environments. *Technology Management* 5 (2).

Tichy, Noel, and David Ulrich. 1984. The Leadership Challenge—Call for the Transformational Leader. *Sloan Management Review* (Fall): 59–69.

Walton, Richard. 1985. From Control to Commitment in the Workplace. *Harvard Business Review* (March-April).

Wellins, Richard S., William C. Byham, and Jeanne M. Wiloson. 1991. *Empowered Teams.* San Francisco: Jossey Bass.

Zenger, John H. et al. 1994. *Leading Teams.* Homewood, IL: Business One Irwin.

CHAPTER 17

PROCESSES FOR OPERATIONAL CONTROL IN THE PROJECT-BASED ORGANIZATION

J. Rodney Turner, Ph.D.—Erasmus University

Anne Keegan, Ph.D.—Erasmus University

Project-based organizations require a different approach to their management than functional, hierarchical, line management approaches common in the 20th century. The latter works well where products are stable. During the latter half of the century, the nature of work changed so now every product is different, and markets and technologies change continuously. Classical management theories developed to manage mass production no longer apply; the new organization needs new theories for its management. We are researching the management of project-based organizations, to identify practices adopted internationally. Here, we report our findings about operations management practices adopted. We describe a process model for operations management, and show different approaches are used in its implementation depending on the size of projects undertaken and the number of customers. We describe different approaches in each of the four scenarios: large projects-few customers; large projects-many customers; small projects-few customers; and small projects-many customers.

Introduction

During the latter part of the 20th century, there was an evolution in the nature of organizations, their work, and their management, from the functional organization universally adopted in the first half of the century to the project-based organization (Drucker 1980; Hasting 1993; Turner 1999a). This was caused by the changing nature of work from mass production, with essentially stable customer requirements and slowly changing technology, to a situation where almost every product supplied could be against a bespoke design, and technology and markets change continuously and rapidly. Whereas the design of the functional organization is underpinned by a strong theoretical base, that is, classical management theory developed in the 19th and early 20th centuries (Mintzberg 1979; Huczynski 1996; Morgan 1997), the design of the project-based organization has no such theoretical base. The project-based organization requires new theories for its management. With the aim of developing such a theory, we at Erasmus University Rotterdam are conducting an international research project to determine how project-based organizations are managed (Turner and Keegan 1999). In this chapter we present our findings on practices and processes adopted for the management of operations within the project-based organization.

We define the project-based organization (PBO), and show it requires different approaches to its management than those used successfully in functional, hierarchical, line management organizations. We describe a model for the management of the PBO, and show how the size and nature of customers and the projects undertaken lead to four different approaches to the structuring and management of operations. We describe how PBOs manage their operations in each of the scenarios of:

- Large projects—few customers
- Large projects—many customers
- Small projects—few customers
- Small projects—many customers.

To create customer-focused processes, organizations strive to maintain a one-to-one relationship between project teams and customers. This exists perforce in the first scenario. In the second scenario, an internal sales or marketing department manages the interface with the many customers, and acts internally as a few customers for the few large projects. In the third scenario, the organizations group projects into a few large programs of projects for their few customers. In the fourth scenario, many different approaches are adopted to manage the interface between the projects and the customers. These include:

- The assignment of specific project roles to coordinate the network undertaking the projects.
- The creation of an internal market to manage the interface between projects and customers.
- The grouping of projects into programs, where each program has a few customers.
- The use of matrix management.

The Project-Based Organization and Classical Management Theory

We define a PBO as one in which:

> the majority of products made or services offered are against bespoke designs.

The PBO may be stand-alone, making products for external customers, or a subsidiary of a larger firm, making products for internal or external customers. It may even be a consortium of firms that collaborate to make products for third parties (Katzy and Schuh 1998). (Throughout the rest of the chapter, we use the word "product" to mean "product or service" for simplicity.) We previously described why classical management theory, developed as the basis for the management of the functional, hierarchical, line management organization, is inappropriate for the project-based organization (Turner and Keegan 1999). Classical management (Mintzberg 1979; Huczynski 1996; Morgan 1997) is based on the work of Smith (1776), Taylor (1913), Fayol (1949), Weber (1947), and Williamson (1975):

1. Smith proposed that economic improvement comes from a constant drive for greater efficiency. This striving for greater efficiency still pervades management thinking. We have previously called it the Economic Orthodoxy (Turner and Keegan 1999).

2. Taylor developed concepts of job design. Based on his scientific management thinking, the jobs of the organization are precisely defined, the competencies required to do the job described, and people found to fill the roles. This standard approach of assigning the person to the previously defined job, and not vice versa, we call the Human Resourcing Orthodoxy.

3. Fayol and his followers (Urwick 1943) designed organizations with administrative routines and command structures through which work could be planned, organized, and controlled. From this comes the concept of the organization structure, a single model of the organization and its functions, which is used for multiple purposes, including its governance, operational control, and knowledge and people management. The focus on a single model for the organization we call the Organization Structure Orthodoxy.

4. Weber (1947) said unfortunately this led to the creation of dehumanizing bureaucracies. The subsequent developments of human relations and neo-human relations (Huczynski 1996) merely put a humanistic gloss on the dehumanizing nature of the bureaucratic organization identified by Weber.

5. Williamson (1975) invoked transaction cost economics to explain the nature of the firm. He showed that two different types of customer-supplier relationship are adopted, hierarchies or markets, depending on whether the production machinery is designed specifically for the task at hand or can be used more generally. Hierarchies are adopted for products made for internal customers and markets for external ones.

Classical management theory works well, where the work of the organization is stable (Mintzberg 1979; Morgan 1997) and the customers' requirements and the technology used are slow to change. Job roles can be identified independently

Customer-Focused Processes	Cross Discipline Teams Deliver Results to Customer Requirements Guided by Precedent	Process Management (Military Approach)	Project-Based Management
Management Focus Internally-Focused Discrete Functions	Specialist Functions Do Work to Defined Systems Following Rules	Functional Hierarchical Line Management	Conventional Project Management
		Routine	Novel
		Nature of Product or Service	

Figure 1. Customer-Focused Processes versus Internally-Focused Functions (Turner and Peymai 1995)

of people doing them, stable command and control structures can be put in place, and the whole structure can make itself more and more efficient through habitual incremental improvement (Turner 1999). Stable functions can be defined because both the work of the functions and the intermediate products that pass between them are well defined and unchanging, leading to the functional approach to work. Such organizations work like machines (Burns and Stalker 1961; Mintzberg 1979; Morgan 1997).

The ideas of Smith, Fayol, and Taylor, and the associated orthodoxies, are at best inappropriate for the PBO, and sometimes positively damaging.

1. Because every customer's requirement is different, a unique, novel, and transient project must be undertaken to deliver every product or service (Turner 1999). This means the work of each function changes for every order, as does the intermediate products passing between them. This in turn means different customer-focused processes must be adopted for the completion of every order, see Figure 1 (Turner and Peymai 1995; International Organization for Standardization 10006 1996; CCTA 1996; Turner 1999). Figure 2 shows a version of customer-focused processes recommended by Projects in Controlled Environments (PRINCE) 2 (CCTA 1996). It is therefore not possible to define a single model for the organization to cover all circumstances. A different model must be developed for governance, the control of different operations, and for the development of the knowledge and people. Thus the Organization Structure Orthodoxy does not apply to the PBO.

2. Because work is always changing, it is not possible to define job roles precisely, nor independently of the person fulfilling the role. People with a different type of competence must be found; those who are familiar with the technology and knowledge of the firm but are able to work in unfamiliar, unstructured situations (Keegan et al. 1999). The individuals determine what job roles are required

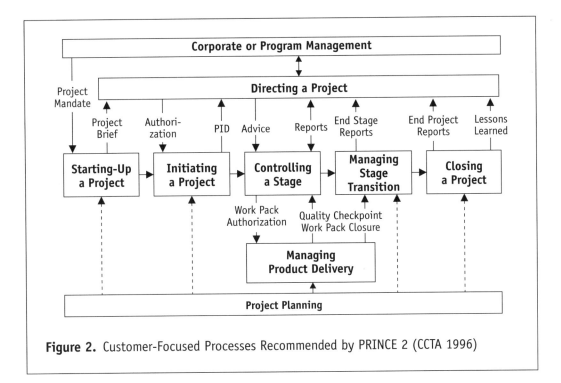

Figure 2. Customer-Focused Processes Recommended by PRINCE 2 (CCTA 1996)

by the task and adapt their work accordingly. This requires different approaches to people development, and means the Human Resourcing Orthodoxy is inappropriate for the PBO.

3. It is therefore not possible to aim for efficiency. Indeed, efficiency works against effective project management. A drive for efficiency reduces the ability to flexibly respond to risk and the uncertain, changing nature of projects (Turner and Keegan 1999; Turner 1999). The Economic Orthodoxy can be positively damaging for the PBO.

4. In some PBOs, the nature of the projects and customers are such that new command and control structures need to be created for every project, and sometimes even at each stage of a project. Some PBOs can have stable command and control structures, but others, particularly those undertaking large projects for a few customers, cannot. This requires organizations to adopt several models for their governance and control, several organization structures.

5. More recently (Turner and Keegan 2001) we have shown from a transaction cost perspective that PBOs adopt wholly different approaches to their governance than classically managed ones. Hybrid structures are adopted regardless of whether the product is being made for an internal or external customer. In order to manage the uncertainty in the bespoke product and the bespoke production process, a direct relationship must be maintained between the project team and the customer.

Thus, we need to find new theories for the management of the PBO to replace those of Smith, Taylor, and Fayol.

Our Research Project

To identify practices and processes adopted in the management of PBOs, we have undertaken an international research project in which we interviewed twenty firms from nine countries from three continents (Turner and Keegan 1999). Firms included:

- Design and construction contractors from the heavy and light engineering industries
- Building contractors
- Contractors and consultants from the information systems industry
- Design and construction contractors and operators from the telecommunications industry
- Design and delivery contractors from the electronics industry
- A supplier of data products.

In the functional, hierarchical, line management organization, the functions fulfill five roles, which must also be fulfilled in the PBO:

1. Governance
2. Operational control
3. Management of human resources (people and competence)
4. Management of knowledge, learning, and innovation
5. Management of customers.

Elsewhere we have written about governance and customer relationships in the PBO (Turner and Keegan 2001), the management of human resources (Keegan and Turner 2000a), learning (Keegan and Turner 2001a; Turner, Keegan, and Crawford 2000), and innovation (Keegan and Turner 2000b; Keegan and Turner 2001b).

In this chapter we report our findings about how the PBO undertakes one of those findings—the management of operations. We identify that different operational models are adopted for different project types, and that this identification is influenced by the nature of the customers and projects undertaken for them.

Operations Management in the Project-Based Organization

There are six essential steps in the operations management process in the PBO.

1. *Winning the customer's order*: In order to win the order the firm must identify potential customers, define their requirements, and demonstrate a superior ability to deliver them. This will often involve preparing a competitive tender, or bid, for the work.

2. *Designing the product and the process for its delivery*: The unique product and novel process required to deliver the client's requirement is designed. This includes the functionality of the product, its components and how they are configured to deliver the functionality, and the process by which they will be produced.

3. *Producing the components of the product*: Components of the product may be sourced from a number of different places, internal or external to the organization. The chain or network of supply needs to be designed and managed.

4. *Configuring the components of the product*: The individual components must then be configured into the eventual product to deliver the required functionality.

5. *Commissioning the product and delivering to the customer*: Not only must the product deliver the required functionality; it must work to meet the customer's requirement. The commissioning may be done by the customer or the PBO, or both working together. The firm may also need to provide ongoing support to the customer and continue to manage the relationship to win future work.

6. *Maintaining customer support after delivery*: After delivery of the product the customer may require ongoing maintenance or other support. This will also be an essential part of maintaining links with the customer to obtain leads for potential future work.

The Influence of Customers and Their Projects or Products

Different organizations adopt different approaches to the realization of this process dependent on the nature of their customers and the projects undertaken for them. Most organizations undertake a portfolio of projects for a range of customers, but we find that the operational processes adopted depend on whether the organization undertakes a few large projects or many small projects, and whether they have a few large customers or many small ones, see Figure 3. In reality most organizations operate in two or three quadrants from Figure 3. However, we find them adopting appropriate processes depending on the different quadrants. For instance, Reuters' back office operates in the bottom right quadrant for the delivery of new financial data products, but the top right for the delivery of data networks to distribute those data products over. Ericsson operates in the top right quadrant for the delivery of telephone networks to telephone operators, but bottom right for the delivery of telephone exchanges to organizations such as schools, hospitals, universities, and companies. Figure 3 also shows a typical firm from our sample in each quadrant. Names given to managers of each step in the operational management process by typical firms in each quadrant are given in Table 1.

Size of projects: We define a large project as one that is a significant proportion of the firm's turnover, and a small one that is a small proportion. Simple arithmetic says that if an organization is undertaking large projects it can only do a few of them, whereas if it is doing small projects it must be doing many of them to make up the turnover. The emphasis here is on the size of the projects as it is that dimension which determines the operational management approaches adopted.

Number of customers: Some organizations work for a few dominant customers, whereas others have a large number of customers. Again, simple arithmetic says that if there are a few customers, each must provide the firm with a significant proportion of its turnover (hence the reason they tend to be dominant). On the

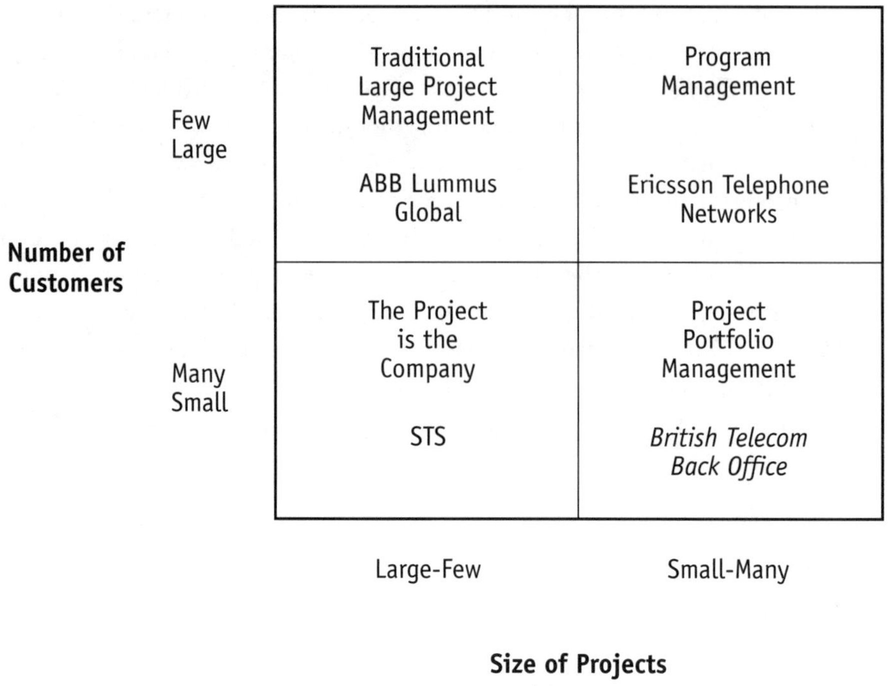

		Large-Few	Small-Many
Number of Customers	Few Large	Traditional Large Project Management ABB Lummus Global	Program Management Ericsson Telephone Networks
	Many Small	The Project is the Company STS	Project Portfolio Management *British Telecom Back Office*

Size of Projects

Key: Firms in italics are departments servicing other departments of the same organization.

Figure 3. Our Sample Size by Size of Project and Number of Customers

other hand, if there are many customers, each will provide the firm with a smaller proportion of its business, and the firm will be less reliant on any one customer. The emphasis here is on the number of customers as it is that dimension which determines the operational management approaches adopted.

Large Projects—Few Customers

Firms undertaking large projects for a few customers tend to be from the construction or heavy engineering industries. As the projects are large, dedicated teams are created to deliver them, and these are inevitably large, being almost small organizations in their own right. The project organizations adopted have what Frame (1995) describes as an isomorphic structure; the structure of the project organization reflects the nature of the task being done, with different team structures being adopted at each step of the operations process above.

Winning the order: This is the responsibility of the contracts or bid management department. The bid team is a task force, led by the bid or contracts manager. However, the structure of the task force may be one of two types described by Frame (1995), either a *surgical team* or an *egoless team*. In the surgical team the preparation of the bid is clearly managed by the bid or contracts manager, who

Process	Big Projects– Few Customers	Big Projects– Many Customers	Small Projects– Few Customers	Small Project– Many Customers	Small Projects– Many Customers	Small Projects– Many Customers	Small Projects– Many Customers
Example	ABB Lummus Global	STS	Ericsson	Virtuell Fabrik (Katzy & Schuh)	BT Back Office	Reuters Product Development	Consultancy
Win Customers	Contract Management	Marketing Director	Account Manager	Broker	Account Manager	Marketing Manager	Director
Design Product &/or Process	Lead Engineers	Research Director	Solutions & Projects Managers	Network Coach	Solutions Manager	Product Manager	Managing Consultant
Make Components	Construction Supervisors	Suppliers	Project Managers	Factory Manager	Project Manager	Project Manager	Consultant
Configure Components	Project Engineers	Marketing Director	Solutions Manager	Project Manager	Project Manager	Project Manager	Consultant
Deliver Product	Project Director	Marketing Director	Account Manager	Project Manager	Solutions Manager	Product Manager	Managing Consultant
Maintain Customer Support	Contracts or Commercial Department	Marketing Director	Account Manager	Broker	Account Manager	Front-Line Business Unit Manager	Director

Table 1. Names of Managers Responsible for the Operations Process

draws on the expertise of others as required. In the egoless team, the group preparing the bid works together as a team of equal players, and the bid or contracts manager facilitates the process, perhaps even working as a junior member of the team. Most of the organizations in our study adopted the surgical team. In one company, ABB Lummus Global, bid management is viewed as a core competence and attempts are made to continuously identify and spread best practice in bid management.

Designing the product: At the design stage, a matrix approach is adopted (Frame 1995). That is, teams of engineers and designers work in their specialist functions, doing the design work for that function or discipline for all areas of the plant. A lead engineer will be responsible for the input of a given engineering discipline. They work closely with the project engineers who are responsible for coordinating the design of a given area of the plant and configuring the components of the product. This is matrix working at the project team level; it is not matrix management since the designers are working for one manager only, the lead engineer, and the project engineers must work through them to obtain the design input to their part of the plant.

Construct components of the product: The construction is managed by the project engineers and specialist construction supervisors. The team structure adopted is a task hierarchy (Frame 1995). Multidisciplinary teams do all the work to complete an area of the plant.

Configure the components of the product: The delivery of each area is managed by a project engineer, who ensures the plant is delivered in accordance with the design. They are responsible for link up and commissioning of the plant. During this stage, the team type moves from the task hierarchy adopted during construction, back to the surgical type as the final product is configured and commissioned for the customer. Multidisciplinary task forces work under the lead of a specialist to ensure work is completed quickly and efficiently.

Deliver the product to the customer: The project is managed by a project manager or, if of sufficient size and complexity, by a project director. Reflecting the importance of this role, one firm we interviewed assigned it, for a strategic project critical to the firm's future, to the director of the previous project; he went from a governance role on the board to an operational role. However, the new role was of such risk and significance to the firm's future and to the client that it was viewed as a development for the individual concerned. In all of the companies in our sample, project management is considered as a key source of value added both to the company and the client.

Maintain customer support: After commissioning, the project team will be disbanded. Ongoing customer support, which may include maintenance, the supply of spares, or the design of plant upgrades or new products, should be maintained. The maintenance of customer support is essential for the winning of new business. The work at this stage will be handed back to the functional organization to be undertaken by appropriate departments. However, it may be managed by a commercial or contracts department, on a matrix working basis again.

There are two further points of interest:

1. Organizations adopting this approach create a command and control structure for each project. Further, projects are often remote from the head office. Until recently, communications were such that project managers had to be empowered to make decisions without reference to the head office. Communications are now instantaneous, but project directors still expect to operate as the head of their autonomous command structure. We interviewed a project director from a company that had recently been taken over by a company from the defense electronics industry, which does many projects for a few customers (see discussion in a later section). More stable command structures are adopted by this type of firm, and our interviewee found it difficult working for a master that would not empower him to the extent he was used to. (He left and is now a general manager with a competitor, and his previous company is now in liquidation having been destroyed through the application of inappropriate governance structures for the business they were in.)

2. The overall project structure adopted is isomorphic, so as a project progresses the nature of the team varies, reflecting a changing need of the process and a changing emphasis on the customer and product. It starts as a surgical team of experts led by a specialist, focusing on the customers' requirements. For design, a matrix structure is adopted to manage the simultaneous input of several resources into several of components of the product. For construction, a task hierarchy is adopted to manage the input of the resources into the construction of discrete components. For commissioning, the focus changes back to the customer's requirements and so a surgical team is readopted. For ongoing support a matrix structure is adopted again, with specialists performing work on all areas of the plant as required.

In this scenario, there is a direct, one-to-one relationship between the project and the customer. We find in all the other scenarios a broker linking the project team to the customer is created in one form or another.

Large Projects—Many Customers

Only one organization from our sample could be said to be undertaking large projects for many customers. That is a research company, established to develop an idea of the entrepreneurial managing director. It really only has one project which is the entire business. Indeed, one of their customers is viewed as being the main potential user for this product once developed. However, there are many other potential users for whom different variants of the product will be made. Hence, although one is funding much of the development work, and obtaining patent rights as a result, they are seeking many other related (but different) applications for the product, and so are talking to several customers. However, as far as the internal project team is concerned, there is only one external customer, the marketing director. Hence the organization has created an artifice whereby the project team appears to be undertaking a large project for a single dominant customer. The marketing director is the broker between the project team and all the external customers. The firm also adopts an isomorphic approach for the project structure. Effectively at this moment the project team is only working on the design of the product, and different members of the team are developing different components of the product. The firm is considering setting up a manufacturing unit to make the product, which would just extend the isomorphic structure, but they are also considering contracting out the manufacture.

Small Projects—Few Customers

These organizations effectively undertake a program of work for each of the few clients. Each program is large in itself, so is a significant proportion of the firm's turnover, but each program is made up of several small projects. The difference with the scenario of the large project with few customers is that the large project leads to a single deliverable, and when the result is delivered the project is over. The programs undertaken here can carry on indefinitely, and the eventual outcome is always being updated. Each individual small project is well defined, but technology is continuously developing. Although the clients know the general

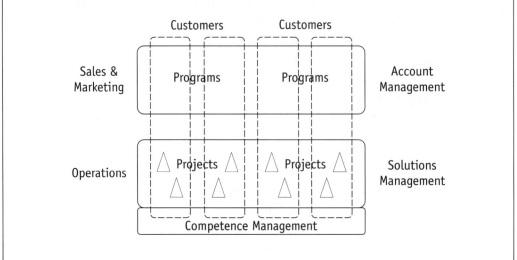

Figure 4. The Relationship between Sales and Operations in a Project-Based Organization Undertaking Many Projects for Few Customers

scope of what they want, the actual scope evolves as the technology develops. One organization we interviewed from this category was Ericsson in the Netherlands. They are developing telecommunications networks for several of the operators in the Netherlands. The networks evolve with time, but there are clearly identifiable projects to deliver individual components of the network.

Because these organizations have a long-term relationship with their customers, they tend to adopt functional approaches to the management of the early and later steps of the process, see Figure 4. A sales and marketing division with account managers, manages the relationship with the clients and draws on the skills of an operations division to undertake the work. However, within the operations division are solutions managers who have a long-term relationship with the client, working with them on the evolution of the program. They identify with the client a need for individual components to be delivered, and only then are individual project managers assigned, from the operations division, to deliver the individual project. This leads to an overall structure of the program that has not been previously identified in the project management literature, which may be described as a fishbone approach, see Figure 5. The backbone represents the ongoing development of the program, with project teams consecutively contributing individual components. The individual project teams tend to adopt a specialist or surgical structure (Frame 1995). Thus the operations process works as follows:

Win the order. This is a continuous (functional) process undertaken by accounts managers within the sales and marketing department. They win the order for the overall program and work with the client to maintain the relationship. The account managers and solutions managers are constantly working with the clients on the developments of the programs and the identification of new projects.

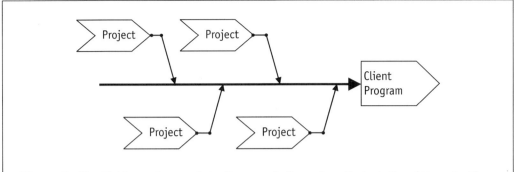

Figure 5. The Fishbone Approach to Program Delivery in a Project-Based Organization Undertaking Many Projects for Few Customers

Design the product and deliver individual components: One surgical project team is responsible for design and delivery of each project. The project managers and their specialist teams design individual components of the program delivered by the projects. Each project delivers a single product, a component of the overall program. The project managers and their specialist surgical teams deliver the individual project components.

Configure the components: The solutions managers work with the project managers to configure the individual project components into the overall program. Though each component is in itself unique and novel, this does tend to be an ongoing, repetitive development task.

Deliver the product to the customer and maintain customer support: Hence the delivery of the final product to the customer and the ongoing support is also a repetitive development task, undertaken by the solutions managers and the account managers.

We see a different approach here for the adoption of command and control structures and team types than we did with the companies undertaking few projects for few customers:

1. Stable command and control structures, linked to the overall structure of the business are adopted in this scenario. This is possible because there is a long-term relationship with the client based on programs of development. Individual projects, though unique, novel, and transient, deliver only a small component of the overall product. Although the project managers may be empowered within the context of their project, their scope for flexibility is limited by the size of their project and the constraints imposed by the program. You can imagine the tension that arose when a firm used to this way of working applied their standard control techniques to the project director of a half a billion-dollar (US) project (see previous mention).

2. Again the team structure changes between the interface with the customer and the project delivery, the emphasis shifting from customer focus to product focus. In this scenario, the team approach adopted at the customer interface is a

functional approach, sales and operations. The team structure adopted for projects is a surgical team, a team of specialists led by an expert, delivering a component of the product.

Small Projects—Many Customers

The most significant observation in this scenario is how organizations reduce the number of interfaces between project teams and their customers. The project teams here need to focus on completing the projects, managing the process, and delivering the product, not managing the relationship with a large number of customers. Just like in the one large project-many customers scenario, it is necessary to create an internal customer so that the project team can deal with that one customer. The project teams just do not have the capacity to manage an interface with a large number of external customers, and so an internal customer, or broker, must do it on their behalf. We have now given a transaction cost perspective of this governance structure (Turner and Keegan 2001). However, there are several ways of achieving this.

The Virtual Factory

The virtual factory was created by the University of St. Galen and involves a consortium of manufacturing companies around Lake Constance (Katzy and Schuh 1998). Bespoke products are delivered to clients which are beyond the capabilities of any one of the companies working on their own, either because they do not have the technical capability, or because they do not have the capacity. They deliver products to clients by forming a network in which individual companies fulfill different roles in the operational process. Effectively an isomorphic network is created project by project to meet the individual customer requirements for the product and process required to deliver it. This is most like the large projects-few customers scenario, with isomorphic project team structures created with bespoke command and control structures. Katzy and Schuh (1998) identify that companies in the consortium must undertake certain specialist roles on the project team, corresponding to some of the managerial roles associated with the operational process. These are listed in Table 1. Particularly, the broker acts as the customer interface, shielding the rest of the project team from the need to deal with several customers.

British Telecom's Back Office

British Telecom's (BT) back office suffers because the front office is constantly changing. Since 1990, the operating divisions have gone from three (domestic, business, and international) to sixteen and rising, recognizing growing telephone usage, market segmentation, and demographic changes. If the back office were to constantly adjust itself to deal with the changes in the front office, it would become chaotic. It has solved this problem by creating an internal market between itself and the front office. The internal market changes its structure to reflect the changing operating divisions. Effectively this works by the internal market maintaining a series of account managers, corresponding to the operating divisions in the front office, passing their requirements back to solutions managers, who place the orders for systems solutions on the back office. The arrangement is very similar to that illustrated in Figure 4. The individual projects so generated are of such a size and nature that the steps two to five in the operations process tend to be undertaken by specialist surgical teams.

Programs of Development

A variation of this approach used by many firms for their internal development work is to recognize that the projects can be grouped into development programs. A program manager is assigned to coordinate the projects, while a promoter or champion takes responsibility of dealing with the many internal customers who will use the development product and feeds their requirements into the project teams through the program manager.

Matrix Approach

This approach tends to be adopted by firms of consultants doing work for external customers. There are solutions managers working with customers and drawing on central resource pools to create teams of consultants to work for the clients. However, we interviewed one consultancy in the Netherlands that had grown so successfully that the application of this approach was leading to a growing feeling of isolation of the consultants from their resource leaders and from their clients. They solved the problem by changing their organization. They have created multi-disciplinary teams doing work for categories of clients. These strategic business units may service:

- A dominant client
- A geographic region
- An industry
- A collection of similar clients.

Effectively they have created several suborganizations, each a PBO. Some do large projects for large clients, some small projects for large clients, and some small projects for small clients. In this structure, the strategic business unit for which they work manages an individual's career development and work assignment. Their competence development is managed by the functional group to which they are assigned. The functional groups also develop new products for the strategic business units. So they too are PBOs servicing internal clients.

The Need for Different Approaches

The need to have different approaches for these different scenarios is recognized by some organizations and not by others. We interviewed one organization in the Netherlands from the engineering construction industry; an organization undertaking large projects for a few customers, with an American parent from the defense electronics industry, an organization undertaking many projects from one client. The American parent tried to manage the subsidiary in the close way required by their industry, rather than the empowering way required by the engineering construction industry, creating serious tensions.

On the other hand, this contrasts with ABB, an international company, with high project orientation. They recognize that not only do projects from the construction industry require an isomorphic structure to reflect the nature of the task, but also the culture of the different divisions needs to reflect the culturely different businesses they operate in and the customers within those businesses.

Summary

Project-based organizations (PBOs), undertaking unique, novel, and transient work to deliver bespoke products or services to their customers, require a different approach to their management than the functional, hierarchical, line management approach that has been successfully adopted by organizations with stable products and technologies. The functional organization can adopt an internally focused, discrete approach with:

- Well-defined job roles, designed to meet the internal needs of the organization
- Stable command and control structures
- A focus on increasing efficiency.

The PBO needs to adopt versatile, customer-focused processes to do the work required to meet the customers' bespoke requirements. We have observed that, within these constraints, PBOs adopt different strategies for their management approach, dependent upon the size and number of projects undertaken and the size and number of clients they service. They also adopt different tactical approaches, particularly the type of team structures used, for different stages in the project life cycle.

Organizations undertaking a few large projects tend to adopt traditional project management approaches, whereas organizations undertaking many smaller projects tend to group the projects into larger programs of work and adopt emergent program management techniques. Because the large projects truly are transient, bespoke command and control structures are adopted project by project. It is also appropriate to adopt isomorphic team structures appropriate to the stage of the project. Organizations undertaking programs of small projects find the programs are more continuous in their existence, and so they can adopt more stable command and control structures. They tend to use specialist, surgical teams to deliver the individual projects.

Organizations with a few customers tend to have a one-to-one relationship between the projects or programs and their customers. This becomes inappropriate where there are many customers, because the number of interfaces is the product of the number of customers and number of projects or programs. To avoid this, organizations create an "internal market," so the projects or programs supply the internal market, and that supplies the customers. This reduces the number of interfaces to the sum of the number of customers and the number of projects or programs. We speculate that some form of transactional analysis (economy of transaction and organization) would determine when it was appropriate to make the switch from one-to-one relationships to the internal market.

Organizations undertaking many projects for many customers tend to operate this internal market in many ways, depending on whether the size of project or number of customers dominates.

- The virtual factory adopts the isomorphic structures of the firms (in a versatile network) undertaking a few large projects for a few dominant customers, but using the broker rather than the project manager to manage the interface with the client.
- Companies undertaking many related internal development projects to be used by many internal departments create large programs working for those many customers, with a program director managing the program and a promoter (champion) managing the interface with the many users.
- One company undertaking many less-related development projects, created an internal market so that the projects had just one customer for whom to work. They deliver the product to that customer, and the customer passes it on to the front office.
- Matrix management tries to design a solution specific to this scenario, but when the operation becomes large, the need to maintain customer focus means that individual project teams need to be limited to doing a few projects for a few customers.

One consistent message coming from the firms we have studied and projects we have observed is organizations need to recognize different approaches and when they are appropriate. They should adopt different approaches for different businesses within a larger group, and try not to adopt a one-size-fits-all approach.

Elsewhere (Turner and Keegan 2001), we have given a transaction cost perspective of the governance structures adopted to manage these different scenarios. We now plan to investigate appropriate project contract types associated with these governance structures, and identify learning strategies adopted by clients and contractors to carried forward learning from unique, novel, and transient projects to long-term relationships, especially those associated with partnering and alliances.

References

Burns, T., and G. Stalker. 1961. *The Management of Innovation*. London: Tavistock.

Central Computer and Telecommunications and Agency. 1996. *PRINCE 2: Project Management for Business*. London: The Stationery Office.

Drucker, Peter. 1980. *Managing in Turbulent Times*. London: Butterworth-Heinemann.

Fayol, Henri. 1949. *General and Industrial Management*. London: Pitman.

Frame, J. Davidson. 1995. *Managing Projects in Organizations,* revised edition. San Francisco: Jossey-Bass.

International Organization for Standardization 10006. 1996. *Quality Management: Guidelines to Quality in Project Management*. Geneva: International Standards Organization.

Hastings, Colin. 1993. *The New Organization*. London: McGraw-Hill.

Huczynski, Andrzej A. 1996. *Management Gurus: What Makes Them and How to Become One*. London: International Thomson Business Press.

Katzy, Bernhard R., and G. Schuh. 1998. The Virtual Enterprise. In *The Handbook of Life-cycle Engineering: Concepts, Tools and Techniques*, edited by A. M. Gutierrez, J. M. Sanchez, and A. Kusiak.

Keegan, Anne, and J. Rodney Turner. 2000a. Managing Human Resources in the Project-Based Organization. In *The Gower Handbook of Project Management*, edited by J. Rodney Turner and Stephen J. Simister. Aldershot: Gower.

———. 2000b. The Management of Innovation in Project-Based Firms. *ERIM Report Series*, ERS-2000-57-ORG. Rotterdam, NL: Erasmus Research Institute of Management.

———. 2001a. Quantity versus Quality in Project-Based Learning Practices. *Management Learning* (special issue on project-based learning) 32 (1): 77–98.

———. 2001b. The Organic Management of Innovation Projects. *Comportamento Organizacional e Gestao* 7 (1): 57–70.

Keegan, Anne, J. Rodney Turner, and Jaap Paauwe. 1999. People Management in Project-Based Organizations. *RIBES Working Paper Series, 9924*. Rotterdam, NL: Rotterdam Institute of Business Economic Studies, Erasmus University Rotterdam.

Mintzberg, Henry. 1979. *The Structuring of Organizations*. Englewood Cliffs, NJ: Prentice Hall.

Morgan, Gareth. 1997. *Images of Organization*. 2nd ed. Thousand Oaks, CA: Sage Publications.

Smith, Adam. 1776. *The Wealth of Nations*. London: Stratton and Cadell.

Taylor, Frederick W. 1913. *The Principles of Scientific Management*. New York: Harper & Row.

Turner, J. Rodney. 1999. *The Handbook of Project-Based Management*. 2nd ed. London: McGraw-Hill.

Turner, J. Rodney, and Anne Keegan. 1999. The Versatile Project-Based Organization: Governance and Operational Control. *The European Management Journal* 17 (3): 296–309.

———. 2001. Mechanisms of Governance in the Project-Based Organization: A Transaction Cost Perspective. *The European Management Journal* 19 (3): to appear.

Turner, J. Rodney, Anne Keegan, and Lynn Crawford. 2000. Learning by Experience in the Project-Based Organization. In *Proceedings of PMI Research Conference 2000*, Paris, Edited by Lew Gedansky. Newtown Square, PA: Project Management Institute.

Turner, J. Rodney, and Reza Peymai. 1995. Process Management: The Versatile Approach to Achieving Quality in Project-Based Organizations. *Journal of General Management* 21 (1): 47–61.

Urwick, L. 1943. *The Elements of Administration*. New York: Harper and Row.

Weber, Max. 1947. *The Theory of Social and Economic Organization*. Oxford: Oxford University Press.

Willimason, Oliver E. 1975. *Markets and Hierarchies: Analysis and Antitrust Iimplications*. New York: Free Press.

CHAPTER 18

PROJECT COMPANIES AND THE MULTI-PROJECT PARADIGM: A NEW MANAGEMENT APPROACH

Marko Arenius—Helsinki Institute of Physics

Karlos A. Artto, Ph.D.—Helsinki University of Technology

Mika Lahti, M.Sc.—Nokia

Jukka Meklin, M.Sc.—Jippii Group Oyj

Introduction

The business environment of equipment and system suppliers has changed over the recent years. Project orientation has increased significantly in their businesses. Earlier, many of today's project-oriented companies delivered products that belonged to a single product or product family. The final project products were customized only to a limited extent to meet the requirements of specific customers. However, over the course of time companies have been forced to take even wider responsibility. For example, instead of simply selling a diesel engine to a power plant project, new customer demands may require that the diesel engine manufacturer take the responsibility for delivering the whole power plant. As projects serve as important vehicles for the whole business, mastering the management of manufacturing of single projects or products does not suffice. Today's management focus must cover the management of project-oriented business as a whole.

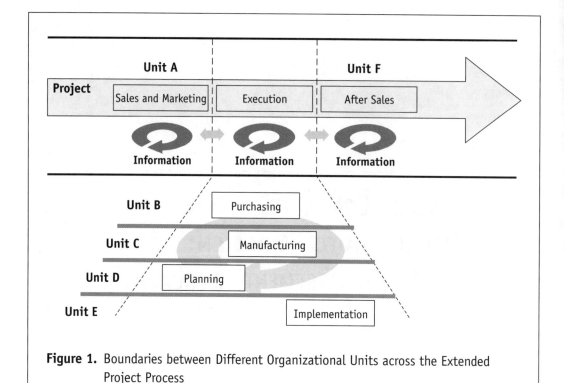

Figure 1. Boundaries between Different Organizational Units across the Extended Project Process

Kujala and Artto (2000) introduce the concept of extended project process. The extended project process is a result of extending the project process horizontally with pre-project and post-project phases. This is a key to integrating project management into managing corporate business. The extended project process divides delivery projects into three main phases: sales and marketing, execution, and after-sales phases. Names of these phases vary by companies, but a similar main phase structure can be found in many project supplier companies. In many cases each phase is organized to have responsible organizational units as their owners. The execution phase can be further divided into many subphases such as planning, manufacturing, purchasing, and so forth. These subphases, or works, are usually carried out by different lower-level organizational units. The phases of the overall extended process of a delivery project, with decision-making points included as phases, are (adapted from Artto et al. 2000; Cova 1998; and Holstius 1987): search, inquiry, bid preparation, bidding, contract (with contract negotiations), start-up, execution, commissioning, closeout, and after-sales.

The complicated organizational structure and the wide variety of organizational units involved in the project execution causes problems, as the divisional boundaries hamper information flows (see Figure 1). The results from previous empirical studies indicated that current organizational structures and practices do not correspond with the challenges of present-day project companies (Meklin et al. 1999; Artto et al. 1998). Learning from experiences and continuous improvement

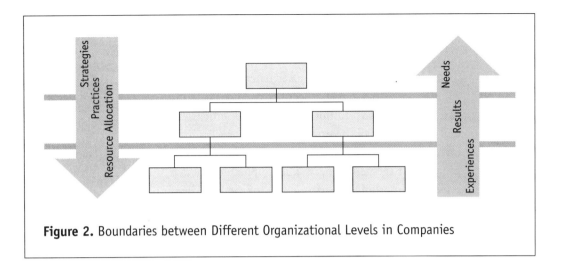

Figure 2. Boundaries between Different Organizational Levels in Companies

are important to all companies (Artto et al. 2001). However, in companies where activities are based on projects, effective learning schemes are particularly challenging to implement (Meklin et al. 1999).

The phenomenon of parallel projects serves as another challenge that renders knowledge management and business development in project companies. Most project companies are seeking means to control and manage an increasing number of parallel projects with overlapping contents and dependencies. This means not only that the company has to solve the resource allocation problem in a multiproject environment, but the company must also be capable of transferring information from one project to another in an effective manner. Furthermore, companies are implementing product development activities and they should be able to transfer new subcomponents and subsystems into practice to ongoing delivery projects. At the same time new product and process development operations need information and experiences from the project level. This requires that different organizational levels should receive and deliver information from each other according to a well-designed plan (Figure 2). However, concerning information transfer across organizational levels, a finding reported in Meklin et al. (1999) was that communication flows between the organizational levels are not always arranged in a systematic way. A challenge for the future studies and empirical applications of project management is the requirement for them to provide fine-grained knowledge on the information content at the various management levels in the overall organizational management framework.

Based on the previous discussion, project companies face two major challenges. First, management of organizational responsibilities, project structures, and knowledge sharing in the context of management of one single project, and second, organizing for responsibilities and knowledge sharing in the overall multiproject management system with integration of projects to the company business. Research, education, and business practices in project management have mainly focused on the management of one single project and have left many important organizational features of the multiproject paradigm without adequate attention. When a project takes place in a project company, the projects have not only external targets set by the customer but also internal targets set by the business requirements of the company. New management practices and tools have to be developed to cope with both targets. Another problem is that project management literature and standards do not define project processes that would provide a wide enough coverage of the extended project process with sales and after-sales aspects included. Instead, the implicit suggestion in project management literature is that project management processes are applied in the execution phase of the project only (International Organization for Standardization 10006 1997; Project Management Institute 1996).

This study contributes to the project management research by developing a three level approach to the management of a project company. Results of the conducted research demonstrated that there is a need to divide the management in the company into three levels: 1) business development, 2) business management, and 3) project management levels. These levels form a hierarchical structure with each level having a different managerial scope. This study puts forward practical recommendations on how to structure project-oriented companies in accordance with the proposed three level management approach. The results and recommendations were drawn from case studies conducted in Finnish project companies. The case studies were done during the research project "FIT-PRO—a product-oriented approach to industrial project management" (Meklin et al. 1999). The FIT-PRO research was carried out during 1998–1999. The case companies delivered industrial investment goods that were customized to meet the requirements of each individual operating environment and customer. The scope of the delivery projects in the case companies varied from the delivery of a single machine to the delivery of a turnkey project. The research data was collected mainly by interviewing project personnel of the case companies, but the interviews were supplemented with analyses and observations of delivered projects.

Typology of Project Companies

Many organizations develop either their project level activities to boost their temporary efforts, or "management by projects" related issues at the level of management of the whole organization. Management by projects refers to an organization's way to conduct its work and tasks in a project form (Turner 1993; Gareis 1994, 1996). A project company (or a project-oriented company) uses either internal [investment] or external [delivery] projects for its business purposes. Internal projects comprise investment projects that may have a nature of investment in systems or facilities, internal development projects, change and reengineering, management of technology and innovation, or research and development (R&D) management. External projects include delivery projects to [external] customers, e.g., deliveries of customer-specific systems or services (Artto 2001). In this study, however, when discussing project companies and their business operations, a project

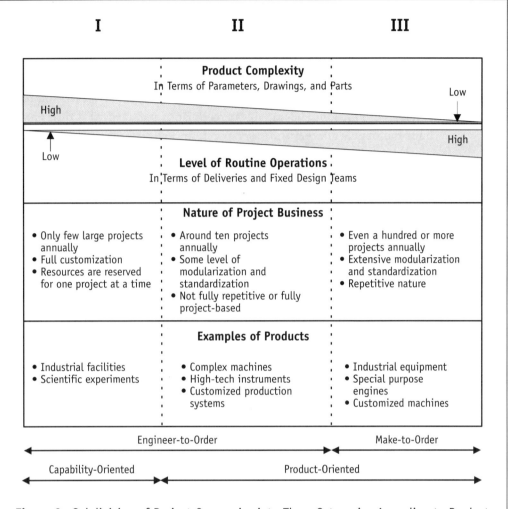

Figure 3. Subdivision of Project Companies into Three Categories According to Product Complexity and Level of Routine Operations (adapted from Hameri et al. 1998)

company is described as a mere project supplier company that has [external] delivery projects for its customers in its production line (Artto et al. 1998). Project supplier companies can be considered as analogous organizational entities to any project-oriented organization. The similarity of project-based operations with both external and internal customers is demonstrated by Turner and Keegan (1999), who provided a definition that the project-based organization may be stand-alone, making products for external customers, or a subsidiary of a larger firm, making products for internal or external customers.

In Figure 3, three different categories of project companies are presented. The categorization is based on product complexity and level of routine operations. Companies in the first category (I) produce truly one-of-a-kind products. They develop a unique design each time and deliver the product according to strict customer requirements, i.e., their products are fully customized. Companies in the second category (II) deliver technologically complex products but they are able to modularize and standardize their products to some extent. When some parts of the products can be modularized and standardized, the need for customer-specific engineering is reduced and the design cycles are shortened. The business practices of the companies of the third category (III) are closest to mass customization and mass production. They are able to modularize and standardize their products quite thoroughly but they still have to perform some customer-specific engineering within each delivery. These companies are characterized by the repetitive nature of their deliveries.

Companies in the first category can be classified as *product-oriented, make-to-order* companies, companies in the second category are *product-oriented, engineer-to-order* companies, and companies in the third category are *capability-oriented, engineer-to-order* companies (Figure 3). It is obvious that companies in the three different categories have a different project scope in their deliveries. Companies in different categories should also have a different stance toward project business. In categories two and three, the resources may not be allocated full-time for a particular project and they must mediate with multiple ongoing projects. Companies in the first category have only a few large projects per year and the resources are usually reserved only for one project at a time. As products are complex and the degree of modularization and standardization is low, the level of project scope is high.

Organizational Viewpoints in Project Companies: Project Portfolios and the Maturity of Project Operations

Organizational integration was given trust in the 1960s as the matrix organization form was introduced to manage complex and unique efforts that required a cross-functional and cross-disciplinary approach to resources. Ever since, the management of multiproject environments has focused on rather operative schemes. For example, many companies focus their management efforts on resource sharing among multiple projects at a detailed operative level.

Project offices (or project support offices) belong to the often-suggested organizational solutions to support project operations in multiproject environments. Project offices adopt either a project follow-up or supporting function, and the office is designed to serve in a staff role between the responsible company management and project management parties, serving as a link between lines and projects. Furthermore, a project office may be a center of excellence and a home base for project managers, methodologies, tools, and support (Block 1999; Hobbs et al. 1999; Knutson 1999; Lullen and Sylvia 1999). Project maturity models aim at supportive managerial help in organizations that conduct similar projects in a repetitive manner. Maturity models enable standardization of project activities in a company. There are several maturity models designed for different types of environments, such as software engineering, product development, R&D, and software acquisition. All maturity models include five levels. At the lowest levels, some form of systematic project management is implemented in projects. As we move toward higher levels, the project management practices become standardized across projects in the organization. The high end of the maturity continuum includes definition of measures for projects as a whole, implementation of systematic measuring, and performance improvements based on the measured data (Fincher and Levin 1997; Goldsmith 1997; Cusick 1999). Furthermore, many project management software packages include multiproject functionalities that support standardized project operations in an effective manner.

Our conclusion is that the current project office, project maturity, and software solutions in industry represent support for activities conducted mainly at the operative level. A tighter and more direct management link between the company management and the projects is needed to integrate projects into the strategic business management of the company. Strategic project management and project portfolio management practices should be introduced to supplement the current monitoring- and supporting-oriented procedures (Dobson 1999; Dye and Pennypacker 1999b; Jacob 1999). The objectives of project portfolio management are maximizing the value of the portfolio, balancing the portfolio, and linking projects with strategy (Dye and Pennypacker 1999a; Cooper et al. 1999). The fundamental questions will be the problems of how to organize the whole corporation with a relevant responsibility scheme and how to organize decision-making and objective setting concerning projects. Many important considerations of the future development of project management relate to the wider organizational context, and more specifically to these questions (Artto 2001):

- What are the project's interrelations with other organizational structures such as other projects and the line organization?
- What is the project's role in fulfilling the strategic objectives set in the company management, and what are the appropriate procedures to manage projects toward profit?

These issues relate also to questions of relevant information content, information sharing, decision-making, and aspects of learning in the project company.

Project Business in the Case Study Companies

The case study companies sell and deliver industrial goods. The scope of the delivery varies from delivery of a single machine to delivery of a whole industrial plant, such as a power plant. As the product and the delivery process have to be customized according to requirements set by the customer and environment, the product delivery process takes the form of a project. Although the case companies can be considered as project companies, they have their roots in machining workshops and equipment deliveries rather than in traditional project business. The companies have manufacturing units that are responsible for the production of the core products of the project. Previously, the companies concentrated on selling and manufacturing investment goods rather than delivering projects. The projects were seen as an inevitable means to carry out the delivery of the goods sold.

Over the years the case study companies have gained significant knowledge in certain application areas, which has enabled growth and globalization in their narrow market niches. The scope of an average delivery has become wider as the companies do not deliver a single product but a whole solution including the main product with several additional products and services. As the scope of a typical delivery has increased from the delivery of a single machine to even a delivery of a turnkey project, such as a paper mill or power plant, the whole business paradigm has changed. Good project management has become crucial, as companies are responsible for coordinating not just the production of their own products, but also the purchasing of several external services and components, and the delivering of the final end product composed of many complex parts and activities with responsibilities in many different organizational units. Delivering turnkey projects requires different know-how, infrastructure, and processes than delivering customized products.

The different nature of project business in three case study companies is analyzed in the following. A detailed analysis of these and a few other companies is reported in the book of the FIT-PRO research (Meklin et al. 1999).

Case Study Company 1: A Telecommunications Supplier

The first case study company is a telecommunications supplier. The size and the scope of its projects have expanded recently. In the present business environment the company could not concentrate only on the deliveries of network equipment, but it also had to be able to manage tasks from network planning to management of entire turnkey deliveries of telecommunication networks. The new situation was caused by a change in the customer base. Previously, customers had been state-controlled operators that had in-house knowledge of network planning and implementation. These companies ordered only the required equipment from the case study company. The de-regulation of the telecom markets brought along customers that adopted more a role of a financier and these new customer companies had selected a strategy of outsourcing the planning and implementation of the telecommunication network. These new customers wanted to buy an operating network solution. Thus, the telecom supplier company had to be able to manage the whole rollout process of an entire telecommunication network. Because of the various backgrounds of the customers, the case company had to offer service packages to satisfy the needs of these different customers. These service packages included those tasks that were needed to construct and implement a telecommunication network, and also additional tasks that the customer required to be carried out by the supplier.

At the time of the empirical study, the company had approximately 150 projects per year and twenty of these projects could be classified as large projects. New operators were in a hurry to get to the markets before the existing operators got all the potential subscribers. The most challenging projects were those that included the project management of the entire rollout process. In these delivery packages the company had to manage the complex entirety formed by the numerous geographically distributed sites.

Case Study Company 2: A Paper Machinery Supplier

The second case study company is a paper machinery supplier. The size of a project in the company varied from 2 to 200 million dollars with a more typical range of 10 to 100 million. There were three different scopes for the projects: delivery of an entire production line, delivery of one or several machines for the production line, and renewals of old production lines. The common characteristic of the different deliveries was that they required the cooperation of three to fifteen units inside the case study company to carry out the project. In addition to these units, the contribution of numerous subcontractors and consultants was also required.

Compared to the challenge in the telecom supplier company's projects, which was the management of the entirety formed by geographically distributed sites, the paper machinery supplier had one single complex site that it needed to manage. The demand for deliveries of entire production lines was forecasted to increase further. These deliveries required special efforts in the management and cooperation between different units. As the demand was expected to increase, the importance and need for developing management practices was emphasized.

Case Study Company 3: An Azimuthing Thruster and Deck Machinery Supplier

The third case study company is an azimuthing thruster and deck machinery supplier. It carries out approximately 100 projects per year. The size of the projects varied from 0.5 to five million dollars with an average duration of six months. The projects had a repetitive, make-to-order nature. This had been enabled by the development of pre-designed product architectures that were the basis for each delivered product. Only some parts of the products needed to be designed specifically to meet the individual customer's requirements. However, some of the larger deliveries include products that require special designing and development. These could be, for example, thrusters of new size and performance capabilities.

Results of the Study: Organizing the Company for Projects

The findings of the research project revealed that there is a need to divide the management of a project company into three different levels: business development, business management, and project management levels (Figure 4). The two upper levels include company level project management, and the lowest level of project management includes all activities that concern the management of individual projects. The empirical case studies indicated that business development level is usually relatively well organized in project companies. Also, at the lowest management level, the management of individual projects is taken good care of. However, the business management level in the middle often lacks systematic and well-organized management schemes.

The business development level at the top of the management pyramid (Figure 4) contains strategy development and strategic management of the company. For example, decisions concerning product strategy and market areas are made at

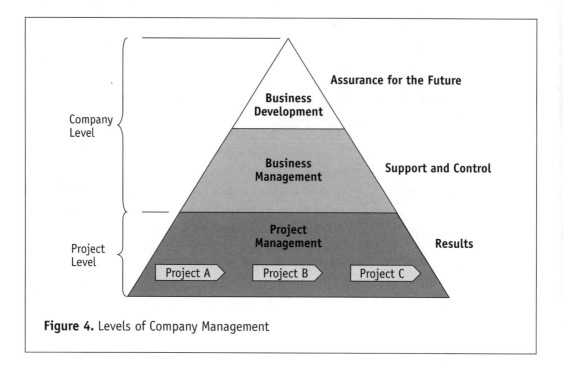

Figure 4. Levels of Company Management

that level. Also, decisions on where the company wants to be in the future and how the goal can be achieved are carried out at this management level. The top management defines the strategy and the vision of the company and communicates it down to lower levels.

The project management level at the bottom of the pyramid (Figure 4) must be emphasized as an important part of the management system. At the project level, important decisions and activities occur that finally ensure the achievement of business objectives. The project personnel have to cope with changes, problems, and even faults no matter how well the project is prepared and how much support and instructions the company level management has offered. The point is that the projects are in all circumstances so challenging that the company management has to use every opportunity to lessen this challenge by their activities.

The business management level in the middle of the pyramid (Figure 4) integrates projects and their management to the overall business context and to the business purpose by simultaneously instructing the way the projects are managed. The business management level serves as a link between the strategic business development and operative project management levels. This level includes project portfolio management content, which emphasizes management of the multiproject environment with strategic alignment of projects to business objectives, and on management of complex interactions between projects and between subsets of the whole corporate-level portfolio. Furthermore, the purpose of this middle level management is to organize the reporting and follow-up systems to ensure that relevant information, such as changes in markets, technologies, or customer environment, are reported to upper level. The business management level includes also the responsibility for arranging standard product structures and standard operating procedures for the company, defining clear sales policies, and ensuring that instructions are in place and that they are followed.

There are two major requirement categories posed to the business management level. The first set of requirements concerns the definition of operating policies, instructions, and structures for engineers, managers, and sales people. The operating policies define how projects are carried out in the different phases. Fulfilling these requirements forms the basis for the company to work effectively. The second set of requirements concerns supervising the projects into the right direction and following developments of the projects. This contains tasks such as making go/no-go decisions in the sales and marketing phase, evaluating risk, allocating resources to projects, and reviewing and reprioritizing objectives of the projects if necessary. In practice this means regularly organized meetings and follow-up mechanisms, which also facilitate informal information distribution. The main objectives of the business management level include processes and practices development and implementation, project portfolio management including market analysis, organizational learning and information sharing arrangements, and continuous customer care.

Furthermore, the business management level in the middle should help sales and marketing, planning, and project management to work efficiently, to ensure that learning occurs and that experiences are disseminated in the organization. Artto (1999) introduces the learning, innovation, and creativity loop in the management of a project company. The loop emphasizes the crucial importance of the ability to foster self-regulating and innovative aspects of the project company's activities. Instead of depending on rigid management methods, the company must employ knowledge intensive and flexible business practices that ensure adaptation to new situations. There must be sufficient room for innovative and creative solutions. The learning loop should encourage exploitation of experiences and business practices that facilitate learning in the organization. To fulfill these requirements the middle level should introduce tools, training, and reporting systems, develop competencies of the employees, take care of the long-term customer relations, and arrange structures and models for product and project processes.

Organizing for networking is essential at the business management level. Projects are in a pivotal position in customer relations and management of customer-related information. For a project supplier, cooperation and networking are natural parts of activities. Project suppliers facilitate concentration on core activities and development of their expertise and knowledge concerning also their customers' businesses. Thus, the learning, innovation, and creativity loop in project-supplier organizations should be understood as a wide enough concept. The loop in question must cover sales and marketing, execution, and after-sales stages. In all of these stages experiences are gained and applied, learning occurs accordingly, and new innovations and creative solutions are put in use. From the perspective of the business as a whole, of key importance are contacts with customers, understanding and support of the customers' businesses, as well as receiving customers' feedback in order to develop the project company's own operations. The business interactions of multiple projects across different corporations combine the individual projects to entities of whole networks of interacting projects and corporations. In the future, companies start measuring their success and business potential even more as a share of the overall success in entire project networks by measuring their customers, suppliers, and competitors (Artto et al. 2001). Priorities in project networks may be negotiated in the form of project delivery chains, as a content of business transactions. Project delivery chains are composed of external projects, the final customer's internal project being the ultimate downstream end point of the delivery chain, and the contractor as producer. They are manufacturing-oriented vehicles initiated for delivering the end product that fulfils the final customer's business need (Ollus et al. 1998a, 1998b; Poskela 2001; Siniharju 2000; Suominen 2001; Uzzi 1997).

The business management level must cover managerial issues organized for all phases across the extended project process. In the case of external delivery-centered projects, strategic project management, and the most important project portfolio management, decisions take place at least in pre-project (sales) and post-project (after sales) phases. In these stages it is possible to make real fundamental strategic decisions (e.g., no-go decisions) that concern even the justification of the existence of the whole project and the existence of the business relationship with the customer. The actual project phase (or project execution phase) is often regulated by a binding delivery contract between the supplier and the customer, which implies that the actual project execution occurs in the manufacturing mode without possibilities for the supplier to set any new fundamental directions at the strategic level. The go and no-go decisions, with a wide business perspective, are typically made in the pre-project and post-project phases of the extended project process. This emphasizes not only the strategic business importance of project sales and marketing, but also the importance of the after-sales activities with continuous customer care. Concerning the future development efforts in the project portfolio management field, Artto et al. (2001) raised not only the importance of defining portfolios and their boundaries with appropriate responsibilities in organizations, but also the importance of managing the interaction across boundaries between the portfolio and its projects, between single projects, between different portfolios, and between different corporations in business networks.

Company Level Project Management

A project company has to have strong company level management above the management of individual projects. The company level management is responsible for managing the whole delivery process and other processes to support project management in an effective manner. In the case study companies of the FIT-PRO research, three specific company level project management areas in need of improvements were identified:

- Sales management
- Structures and standard models for projects
- Learning between projects.

In the following, these areas are discussed in more detail. The discussion is based on empirical findings from the case study companies.

Sales Management

The success of the sales phase determines the success of the whole project. If the sales phase is poorly managed, project management has no chance of executing the project successfully. During the sales negotiation phase, the commercial aspects of the contract tend to dominate while the technical aspects are clarified often even after the contract has been already signed. Clarifying all the technical details would require a large amount of engineering work during the sales phase. In many cases, the required engineering work would consume too much resources and time. Thus, the company has to have a clear sales policy, which determines the preferred solutions and excludes the impossible solutions already during the sales phase.

The completeness of the sales specification is one of the important factors that predict the success of the project. Open questions include risks that may endanger the profitability of the project. Only part of these questions are related to customers' decision-making with the rest depending on the project company's internal processes. Typically, the technical solution includes many assumptions and many features that are yet unknown. This emphasizes the importance of risk management in the sales phase.

Standard Structures and Standard Models for Projects

The project company must have predefined structures and models both for its products and processes. In project deliveries, the delivered product is always somehow unique and it is, in practice, tailored to match the customer's requirements. The project company also has to tailor the delivery process case by case to match the requirements of the customer (see Figure 5). Application of standard structures and models enable:

- Faster project start-up and implementation
- Better project plans and budgets
- Reduced risks
- Distributed operations and effective use of sub-suppliers.

The first step toward better-managed projects is a modular project plan, which includes predefined project phases. The phases and their contents must enable several potential variations that each correspond to different business cases. The content descriptions for phases should determine the required tasks as well as the resources and tools that are needed to accomplish them. The ISO 9000 standard and other quality standards are basically used to fulfill the same needs, but their current empirical applications are often not detailed enough for daily use in project management. Many project companies have

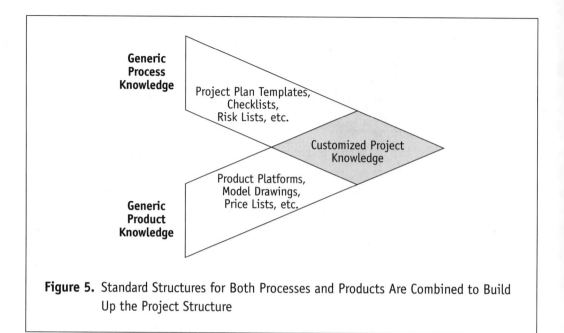

Figure 5. Standard Structures for Both Processes and Products Are Combined to Build Up the Project Structure

defined standard operating procedures that are used for implementing standardized and modularized product-related and process-related practices.

An analogy of successful management mechanisms concerning structures in management procedures is introduced by Brown and Eisenhardt (1997). They have studied the management of multiple-product innovation projects in six firms in the computer industry. According to the study, successful management principles blend limited structure around responsibilities and priorities with extensive communication and design freedom to create improvisation within current projects. In the management of companies with successful projects, rather than just communicate, managers combined limited structure or "semi-structures" (e.g., priorities, clear responsibilities, formal meetings) with extensive freedom to improvise current products. The semi-structures balance between order and disorder. Successful companies had clear priorities and responsibilities.

Learning between Projects

Disseminating experiences between projects is necessary for a project company in order to ensure its long-term success. In a project company the learning process takes place on several different levels. On the lowest level an individual working on a project learns. This individual gains experience in a project and carries this experience to his future projects. This type of learning is quite random if not organized properly. Furthermore, its usefulness is limited as the experience is tied up with the individual. In a project company, systematic learning schemes should be in place that ensure distributing experiences among project personnel. Learning among the project personnel may take place as social communication between group members and through different explicit information channels such as project documents (Figure 6).

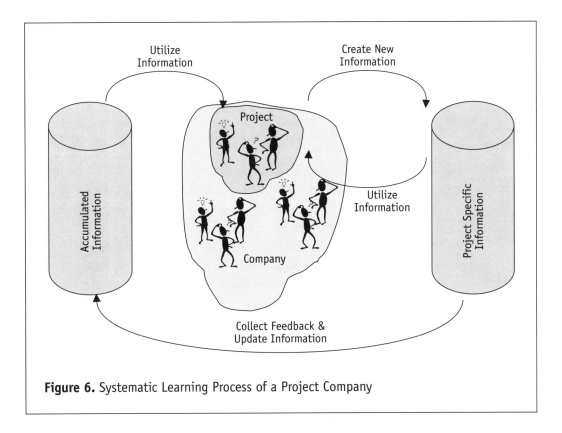

Figure 6. Systematic Learning Process of a Project Company

Tight schedules and geographical dispersion of projects have reduced the amount of social communication taking place during projects. When this social communication is missing, the project must develop specific means to increase communication. Such means may include, for example, project databases, document archives, and project portfolio databases that ensure effective information sharing and transparency of project information across projects. However, the technical tools cannot replace social communication completely. Meetings are still needed to guarantee possibilities for open discussion, e.g., project kickoff, review meetings, project closeout workshops, or portfolio review meetings. The empirical study with the case study companies indicated that from the viewpoint of other projects it is important to report and transform information of a single project in a predetermined format and in a formal way. Adequate technical support of appropriate information systems and databases is essential. Information sharing and learning across projects and across organizational units occur via a combination of transfer of both explicit and tacit knowledge and the situation in which the knowledge is shared. In this respect, the elements of a knowledge-creation model proposed by Nonaka et al. (2000) are most relevant. The model includes; the socialization-externalization-combination-internalization process for knowledge creation through the conversion of tacit and explicit knowledge; the shared context for knowledge creation ("Ba"); and knowledge assets, the inputs, outputs, and moderators of the knowledge-creating process.

Conclusions

Project management research and development have mainly focused on developing project management practices for single projects. Business management, and especially special requirements of the management of a project-based industry, needs more attention.

Due to the growth of the companies and the changes in their markets, project companies are struggling to find the appropriate ways of doing business. In this environment, there is a need for development and recurrence. The most important issue of development is to shift the managerial focus from the problems of one individual project, to the management layer above the projects, to the management of the project business as a whole.

This study is based on empirical investigations conducted in case study companies that delivered customized industrial investment goods to meet the requirements of each individual operating environment and customer. The case study companies included a telecommunications supplier, a paper machinery supplier, and an azimuthing thruster and deck machinery supplier. Results of the empirical study with case study companies demonstrate that companies should have a strong business management level above the project level in the organizational hierarchy. The study introduced a subdivision of company management into three different levels: business development, business management, and project management levels.

The business development level at the top of the management pyramid includes strategy development and definition of the vision to be communicated down to lower levels. The business management level in the middle acts as a link between the strategic business development and operative project management levels. Business management integrates projects and their management to the overall business context. It includes managerial processes that ensure organizational learning. The business management level also includes project portfolio management content with alignment of projects to business objectives. The project management level at the bottom of the management pyramid has responsibility to manage single projects. At the project level, important decisions and activities occur that finally ensure the achievement of business objectives.

The empirical study pointed out specific company level management areas that required improvements in the case study companies. These areas were sales management, structures and standard models for projects, and learning between projects.

The business management level must be organized to cover appropriate management for project sales and marketing. The management activities at the company level must cover the extended project process properly. An extended project process with pre-project (sales) and post-project (after sales) phases is a key to integrating project management into managing corporate business. This also emphasizes the importance of continuous customer care.

Project portfolio management covers the management of the multiproject environment with the strategic alignment of projects to business objectives and the management of complex interactions between projects and project portfolios. The managerial focus is on the projects' role in fulfilling the strategic business objectives and on the interrelation of projects with other projects, portfolios, and the line organization. The portfolio view becomes more complicated if multiple portfolios interact across different corporations and business networks. With project suppliers, for example, projects are significant vehicles for the management of customer relations and the management of customer-related information. Cooperation, networking, and learning from customers' businesses, as well as receiving customer feedback, are important issues.

The business management level also includes the responsibility for arranging processes and practices development and implementation, standard product structures and standard operating procedures, clear sales policies, and instructions for project-related activities. As far as standard product structures are concerned, the company has to have a clear sales policy, which determines the preferred product solutions and excludes the impossible solutions already in the sales phase. The project company must have predefined structures and models both for its products and processes. The first step toward better-managed projects is a modular project plan, which includes predefined project phases. The phases and their contents must be modular with several variations for different business cases. Many project companies have defined standard operating procedures that are used for implementing standardized and modularized product-related and process-related practices.

In the project-oriented corporation organizational and individual learning are significant success factors. Learning and adoption of innovative solutions must be fostered at all levels of activity (business and project levels). A real challenge for successful project business management, in any project company, is to define the relevant information content for decision-making purposes. Particularly it is important to pay attention to collaboration between the projects and the management levels, and to collaboration between the customer and suppliers in the whole business network. A management approach must be in place that focuses on decision-making, target setting, cross-project communication, and communication with the external environment. More research is needed to develop new tools and methods to support decision-making processes and information sharing.

In the organizational model of a project-oriented corporation, project structures must be linked to organizational structures by taking into account the ownership of projects and resources. It is important that clear responsibilities are in place in the overall management system. The management system must also involve clear priorities for clarity in business operations, successful project portfolio, and appropriate allocation of resources. A fundamental question and a relevant area for further project portfolio management research is the problem of how to organize the whole corporation's responsibilities, decision-making, and objective setting concerning projects. These issues relate also to the definition of relevant information content, information sharing, and organizational learning in the whole multiproject organization.

References

Artto, K. A. et al. 1998. *Global Project Business and the Dynamics of Change*. Helsinki, Finland: Technology Development Centre Finland and Project Management Association Finland.

Artto, K. A. 1999. Development of World-Class Practices in Project Companies. In *The Future of Project Management, Project Management Institute Research Series* (127–137). Newtown Square, PA: Project Management Institute.

———. 2001. Management of Project-Oriented Organization—Conceptual Analysis, In *Project Portfolio Management: Strategic Business Management Through Projects*, edited by K. A. Artto, M. Martinsuo, and T. Aalto. Helsinki, Finland: Project Management Association Finland.

Artto, K., K. Kähkönen, and P. Pitkänen. 2000. *Unknown Soldier Revisited: A Story of Risk Management*. Helsinki, Finland: Project Management Association Finland.

Artto, K. A., M. Martinsuo, and T. Aalto, eds. 2001. *Project Portfolio Management: Strategic Business Management Through Projects*. Helsinki, Finland: Project Management Association Finland.

Block, T. R. 1999. The Seven Secrets of a Successful Project Office. *PM Network* (April): 43–48.

Brown, S. L., and K. M. Eisendardt. 1997. The Art of Continuous Change: Linking Complexity Theory and Time-Paced Evolution in Relentlessly Shifting Organizations. *Administrative Science Quarterly* 42: 1–34.

Cooper, R. G., S. J. Edgett, and E. J. Kleinschmidt. 1999. Portfolio Management in New Product Development: Lessons from the Leaders, Phase II. In *Project Portfolio Management: Selecting and Prioritizing Projects for Competitive Advantage* (23–37), edited by L. D. Dye and J. S. Pennypacker. West Chester, PA: Center for Business Practices.

Cova, B. 1998. Holstius' Project Marketing Cycle: A Basis for Theory Building in Project Marketing. In *Marketing and International Business, Publications of the Turku School of Economics and Business Administration, Series A-2* (63–84), edited by H. Tikkanen. Turku, Finland.

Cusick, K. 1999. How to Use Capability Maturity Models to Help Manage Projects Effectively. *Project Management Institute Annual Seminars & Symposium*. Philadelphia, PA.

Dobson, M. S. 1999. *The Juggler's Guide to Managing Multiple Projects*. Newtown Square, PA: Project Management Institute.

Dye, L. D., and J. S. Pennypacker. 1999a. An Introduction to Project Portfolio Management. In *Project Portfolio Management: Selecting and Prioritizing Projects for Competitive Advantage* (xi–xvi), edited by L. D. Dye and J. S. Pennypacker. West Chester, PA: Center for Business Practices.

———. 1999b. *Project Portfolio Management: Selecting and Prioritizing Projects for Competitive Advantage*. West Chester, PA: Center for Business Practices.

Fincher, A., and G. Levin. 1997. Project Management Maturity Model. *Proceedings of Project Management Institute Annual Seminars & Symposium*. Chicago, IL.

Goldsmith, L. 1997. Approaches Towards Effective Project Management. *Proceedings of Project Management Institute Annual Seminars & Symposium*. Chicago, IL.

Gareis, R. 1994. Management by Projects: Specific Starategies, Structures, and Cultures of Project-Oriented Companies. In *Global Project Management Handbook*, edited by D. I. Cleland and R. Gareis. New York: McGraw-Hill.

———. 1996. The Application of the "New Management Paradigm" in the Project Oriented Company. *Proceedings of the IPMA International Project Management Association '96 World Congress*, June 24–26, Paris.

Hameri, A. P. et al. 1998. Product Data Management—Exploratory Study on State-of-the-Art in One-of-a-Kind Industry. *Computers in Industry* 35 (3).

Hobbs, B. et al. 1999. A Project Office Maturity Model. *Proceedings of Project Management Institute Annual Seminars & Symposium*. Philadelphia, PA.

Holstius, K. 1987. *Project Export*. Research Paper 1, Lappeenranta University of Technology, Finland.

International Organization for Standardization (ISO) 10006. 1997. *Quality Management—Guidelines to Quality in Project Management*. Switzerland: International Organization for Standardization.

Jacob, K. 1999. Executing Projects with Portfolio Management in Large Multi-Business, Multi-Functional Organizations. *Proceedings of Project Management Institute Annual Seminars & Symposium*. Philadelphia, PA.

Knutson, J. 1999. Project Office: An Evolutionary Implementation Plan. *Proceedings of Project Management Institute Annual Seminars & Symposium*. Philadelphia, PA.

Kujala, J., and K. A. Artto. 2000. Criteria for Project Performance in Business Context. *Project Management* 6 (1): 46–53.

Lullen, J. J., and R. Sylvia. 1999. Getting Organized: Implementing the Project Office. *PM Network* (April): 51–55.

Meklin, M. et al. 1999. *FIT-PRO—A Product-Oriented Approach to Industrial Project Management*. Helsinki, Finland: Project Management Association Finland.

Nonaka, I., R. Toyama, and N. Konno. 2000. SECI, Ba and Leadership: A Unified Model of Dynamic Knowledge Creation. *Long Range Planning* 33: 5–34.

Project Management Institute. 1996. *A Guide to the Project Management Body of Knowledge (PMBOK® Guide)*. Upper Darby, PA: Project Management Institute.

Ollus, M., J. Ranta, and P. Ylä-Anttila. 1998a. *Revolution of Networks: Management of Network Company*. Helsinki, Finland: Taloustieto Oy.

———. 1998b. *Company Networks—Competing with Knowledge, Speed, and Flexibility*. Helsinki, Finland: Taloustieto Oy.

Poskela, J. 2001. *Success and Relevant Measures in a Project Delivery Chain*. Master's Thesis, Department of Industrial Engineering and Management, Helsinki University of Technology.

Siniharju, M. 2000. *Collaboration in Project Delivery Chain*. Working Paper, Department of Industrial Engineering and Management, Helsinki University of Technology.

Suominen, V. 2001. *In Search for A Project Delivery Chain*. Master's Thesis, Department of Industrial Engineering and Management, Tampere University of Technology.

Turner, J. R. 1993. *The Handbook of Project-Based Management—Improving the Processes for Achieving Strategic Objectives*. 1st Edition. London, UK: McGraw-Hill.

Turner, J. R., and A. Keegan. 1999. The Management of Operations in the Project-Based Organization. In *Managing Business by Projects* 1 (57–85), edited by K. A. Artto, K. Kähkönen, and K. Koskinen. Project Management Association Finland and Nordnet.

Uzzi, B. 1997. Social Structure and Competition in Inter-Firm Networks: The Paradox of Embeddedness. *Administrative Science Quarterly* 42 (March): 35–67.

CHAPTER 19

SELLING PROJECT MANAGEMENT TO SENIOR EXECUTIVES: WHAT'S THE HOOK?

Janice Thomas, Ph.D.—Athabasca University and University of Calgary

Connie L. Delisle, Ph.D.—Athabasca University

Kam Jugdev, PMP, MEng, M.H.S.A.—University of Calgary

Pamela Buckle, MBA—University of Calgary

Introduction

Worldwide, project management continues to gain acceptance in many industry sectors. Increasingly, companies espouse project management as a key competency. On the one hand, we note a growing interest in using different elements of project management in virtually every segment of every industry. On the other hand, over 30 percent of projects end up being cancelled in midstream and over half of projects run as high as 190 percent over budget and 220 percent over the original time estimate (KPMG 1997; Standish Group 1995). Despite the pervasive high failure rate of projects and advocacy of project management by practitioners, the serious, long-term investment in project management remains a tough sell at the executive level. At the same time, KPMG's (1997) survey of over 1,400 senior organizations found the lack of top management commitment to be a key factor in failed projects. Clearly something needs to be done about this disconnect.

Over the last ten years, the topic of "selling" project management has generated a significant amount of interest within the Project Management Institute (PMI®) as evidenced by papers presented at PMI conferences (for example; Block

1991, 1992). Recently, PMI (1999) sponsored a research study to investigate the challenges of selling project management to senior executives. The authors of this chapter were awarded the research grant. This chapter presents the findings of Phase I of our two-phased study. In Phase I we investigate the root causes of the issue. A brief summary of Phase II that is currently under way is provided in the section entitled Future Research. By exploring situations where project management has been successfully or unsuccessfully introduced into organizations, this research seeks to:

- Identify the compelling arguments of how project management benefits the organizations.
- Articulate the practical and political approaches for selling at the executive level.

We set out to understand how the very people who best understand project management within particular organizations seem to have the hardest time selling it to their executives. At the same time we know that consultants and project management experts make a living selling project management to executives. Understanding this paradox provides a firm footing to better identify best practices necessary to build senior management awareness of the values and benefits of project management needed to sell the concept. Phase I was designed to be a small-scale exploratory study to build a framework for more extensive research. The research team interviewed three groups of experienced practitioners familiar with selling and purchasing project management—internal project managers, project management consultants/experts, and senior executives with project management purchasing power. A grounded theory approach identified trends or themes related to successful and unsuccessful sales strategies as they emerged from the data. The researchers paid particular attention to the similarities and differences in how the sample groups understood project management and its benefits.

This chapter provides a summary of Phase I of the research. The background literature sets the foundation for understanding the gaps in the knowledge this study aims to fill. The theoretical foundation provides a way to validate preliminary results and sets the boundaries for the field of investigation for the second phase of the research. In the next section, we summarize the most important findings and conclusions about marketing and selling of aspects of project management to senior executives.

Background Literature

We set out to explore the project management, marketing, and organizational literature to provide a framework for understanding the issues around selling project management to executives. We tackled this vast body of literature by focusing on a number of questions we found most pertinent to this study, namely:

- How are selling, marketing, and project management related?
- What are senior executives looking for?
- How do sellers and buyers interact?

- Why do you need to align values in the sales process?
- How do you use strategy to trigger sales?

The following section summarizes the results of this literature review and shows how it frames this piece of research. The section concludes by introducing the specific research questions Phase I was designed to answer.

How Are Selling, Marketing, and Project Management Related?

According to the Webster's dictionary selling means to "promote the sale, acceptance or adoption of" (1984, 628). Generally, companies sell project management methodologies to increase their market share and customers buy it as an aid to improve their bottom line and competitive position. Project management is typically sold as a service to customers or as a component of business solutions.

In contrast, marketing involves organizations determining "the needs, wants, and interests" of target audiences and delivering to that level of satisfaction "more effectively and efficiently than competitors" (Kotler 1994). This definition connotes expectations management. The essence of marketing is to apply strategies including market intelligence work to increase/maintain market share by securing new/repeat business with a customer (Daft 1987).

The terms selling and project management seem disconnected in the eyes and minds of most project managers. Typically, project managers view themselves as practitioners and do not consider the "marketing and sales" work as either their role or responsibility. A review of the project management practitioner literature shows that project managers *do* promote and advocate elements of project management in the course of their work. They generally promote it by describing the features of tools and techniques and inherent project benefits related to the priority triangle of time, cost, and scope. Project managers infrequently tie project management outcomes to corporate business outcomes as part of their sales strategies. Frost (1999) takes the abstract concept of values and frames it as continuum that builds on the Gardner, Bistritz, and Klompmaker (1996) model in Figure 1.

This value continuum portrays foundation values of efficiency (e.g., return on investment, cost reductions, revenue generation, increased market share) and effectiveness (e.g., organizational effectiveness, customer satisfaction) at the far left of the continuum. At the other end, innovation values (market expansion, advantage creation) dominate. Frost's model portrays the promise-centric values (rather than product-centric) as critical to managers and defines value as key to understanding the relationship between buying and selling project management in tactical, strategic, and competitive selling. Tactical selling involves both the vendor and customer being focused on the features of project management in short-term, quick-fix relationships. Strategic selling involves a longer-term relationship between the vendor and buyer, whereas strategic solutions are sold to address business problems. Lastly, competitive selling involves a business-to-business partnership that is more encompassing in terms of its focus on both organizations. Sellers generally craft their messages based on their experiences; but successful messages reflect the buyer's needs, as the buyer understands them.

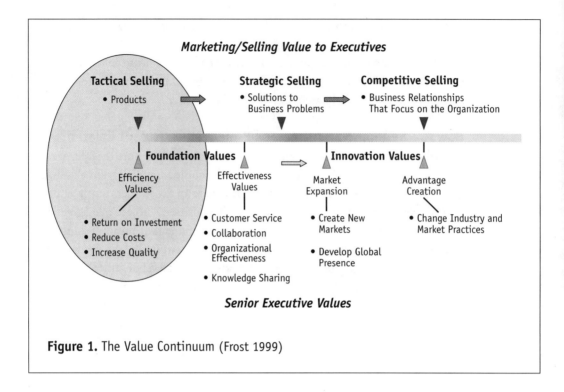

Figure 1. The Value Continuum (Frost 1999)

What Are Senior Executives Looking For?

Senior executives represent the highest level of management in organizations. Traditionally, senior executives look for information to help them make sound business decisions as well as position themselves favorably in terms of their personal and professional growth. The type of information they seek fits within their own construct of truth, and any new knowledge flows through their self-defined filters. During business crises or in time-pressured situations, senior executives will turn to known consultants with whom they have had past experiences rather than seek out new, unknown ones. Most executives are focused on foundation values as noted by their search for ways to measure and increase the return on their organization's investments and reduce expenditures (Dinsmore 1996; McElroy 1996). As well, outcomes seem more tied to corporate strategy not individual project outcomes. At times, they look for ways to measure and increase the return on investment and reduce costs without recognizing the cumulative effects and co-dependencies of the actions taken on failed and successful projects alike (Dinsmore 1996; McElroy 1996).

Heidrick & Stuggles, a leading executive search firm reports that over half of chief executive officer (CEO) and chief financial officer (CFO) respondents held their positions for five years or less. With this type of turnaround at the decision-maker level, those selling project management services must strive to make more immediate and responsive connections with these individuals in terms of their existing and future business challenges. In marketing terms, this is often referred to as relationship marketing.

The connection between the selling intention and the business direction may be a prerequisite for using project management to substantially maximize shareholder value and move the buyer-seller relationship along the continuum toward the innovation values side. The initial step in raising awareness about project management requires the identification of best practices that in turn can help senior executives understand how to use this knowledge. Part of the difficulty in raising awareness is that conventional definitions and treatment of value have a less direct connection to business strategy than what we assume to be the case.

How Do Sellers and Buyers Interact?

Marketing literature tells us that sellers and buyers act either tactically or strategically. Over the past thirty years there has been a noticeable shift in the sales proficiency toward strategic and competitive selling. A key issue appears to be that project management is rarely sold in isolation; it is generally sold as part of a solution or as a service to manage projects. Too often, tactical selling focuses on promoting the features of project management that will "save" time and money to increase efficiency. The challenge of selling project management services then becomes one of identifying, articulating, and achieving deliverables that are directly linked to business objectives.

Another issue making project management a tough sell relates to trust between the seller and buyer. Gardner, Bistritz, and Klompmaker (1996) researched factors that help salespeople develop trust and credibility with senior executives. They found understanding the customer's goals/objectives and being responsive to requests to be the most effective ways of establishing trust/credibility with executives. "The worst impression a salesperson can leave is wasted time" (Gardner, Bistritz, and Klompmaker 1996, 7). The relationship between the buyer and seller appears critical in selling services. Selling services involves the use of soft skills. Since selling services does not end once the sale has been made, the external project management team must demonstrate effective project management and strong interpersonal/communication skills with management to ensure the success of the project sold. Senior executives seem less interested in tactical approaches or "flavor of the month quick fixes," and more interested in seeking meaningful business relationships that help them personally and professionally (Gardner, Bistritz, and Klompmaker 1996). Gardner, Bistritz, and Klompmaker (1998) found that executives are willing to value salespeople whom they truly believed would help them solve the business problems they were facing.

Why Do You Need to Align Values in the Sales Process?

Part of developing a relationship with customers involves understanding and conveying the merits (benefits) of project management and bridging the connection to the buyer's values. Although the practical benefits of project management seem like common sense, Thomas (2000) found that even experienced project managers do not fully understand project management concepts. Organizations selling project management services fail to recognize the need to prepare the client for the sale by jointly working together to frame the problem instead of jumping directly into problem-solving mode. They continue to convey project management's business value as "efficiency," often promoting industrial-age tools and traditional financial metrics including tactical selling approaches, whereas senior executives may be open to considering very different value dimensions that are further along the value continuum. It seems important to ensure that those trying to market project management communicate values and benefits that remain consistent with and aligned to the indicators senior managers use to evaluate such offerings.

How Do You Use Strategy to Trigger Sales?

Successful selling strategies include an approach to trigger a need in the buyer, a prepared response that situates the product or service as the best solution coupled with evidence supporting the argument (Don 2000). Sometimes the need is triggered by events or circumstances external to the sales effort (e.g., a crisis) but these type of triggers are not as conducive to strategic selling, as the seller has little or no control over their timing or occurrence. Successful salespeople attempt to develop selling strategies that speak to internal triggers (e.g., what keeps senior management up at night) as a way of selling their products. This type of selling uses the needs of the buyer to intuitively frame the problem, and works closely with the buyer to address it with a solution.

Thus, part of the difficulty in selling project management stems from a misalignment of perception between buyers and sellers (executives, project managers, and consultants) around project management values. In turn, this impacts the intentions around selling and buying behaviors. Senior executives often receive mixed messages with respect to the benefits of project management, leading them to disconnect their understanding (cognitive) and feeling (affect) about the values used to sell and those used to buy project management. Based on this review, we set out to confirm the magnitude of this hypothesis and gain some practical insights into the nature of the problem by exploring the following two questions.

- How do sellers and buyers understand project management's functions and value?
- How is project management sold in organizations?

The Study

Phase I consisted of twenty-three face-to-face interviews. Initially, participants from the Project Management Advisory Council (PMAC—companies that advise the Project Management Specialization at the University of Calgary) served as lead contacts. These contacts allowed us to use the "snowball technique" to identify additional interviewees. Where possible, paired participants were interviewed, e.g., a project manager and executive from the same company and at times, a consultant who had sold project management services to that firm. Interviewees fit into one of three categories:

Senior Managers (Executives, CEOs, chief information officers (CIO), or Vice Presidents): The influential group of individuals making decisions to purchase or not purchase project management (n = 10).

Project Managers/Practitioners (Project Management Office Managers, Project Managers, or Directors of Project Management): Those championing/selling project management largely in the context of their own organizations (n = 6).

External Project Management Consultants/Experts (smaller and larger independent sellers): Experts whose experiences included both successful and unsuccessful attempts to sell project management to organizations (n = 9).

The qualitative, semi-structured interviews required that participants answer between 30–35 semi-structured questions. Questions were of the form: "What is project management?" "What is the value of project management to your organization?" "If you needed to sell project management to your manager, colleague, or peer, how would you do it?" The complete interview protocol is available from the authors of this chapter. We pre-tested the questions on a panel of project management practitioners to ensure that they were meaningful and capable of extracting the information needed to address the research questions. Two researchers were present for almost all the interviews for validation purposes. Each interview was taped and transcribed. The transcriptions comprised the data we analyzed in this chapter.

A grounded theory approach served to make sense of the Phase I findings. Results are "inductively derived from the study of the phenomenon it represents … it does not begin with a theory and then prove it but begins with an area of study to allow what is relevant to that area to emerge" (Strauss and Corbin 1990, 23). The analysis focused on identifying trends or themes related to successful implementation strategies. Grounded theory allows for the analysis of interview transcripts concurrently so that patterns become clearer during data collection. As anticipated, recurring patterns appeared by the fifteenth interview. Common themes and shared perceptions about selling project management appeared, and very little new information emerged after this point.

Data analysis consisted of five steps. First, all four researchers read the transcripts and identified key themes and processes. Second, we met as a group and came to consensus on the meaning and importance of the various themes identified. Third, these themes were summarized for each important question and for each participant in a Microsoft® Excel® spreadsheet that allowed us to compare themes across questions and participants. Fourth, we met as a team to brainstorm the linkages and relationships between the themes identified and the underlying processes. Finally, we drew linkages from discussions with relevant academic and practitioner resources to support and verify the validity of these preliminary findings. Rigorous analysis using the ATLAS computer-assisted qualitative analysis tool occurred into April 2000.

Participants represented a diverse set of organizations producing various products and services, including oil and gas, healthcare, new product development, and information technology. In terms of age, fourteen (61 percent) were between 36–46 years and nine (39 percent) were between 46–55 years. At the time of this research, two participants had their Project Management Professional (PMP®) certification and two were in the process of certification. In general, the participants represented an experienced and educated group of executives, project managers, and consultants.

Phase I is an exploratory phase subject to the limitations of the sample size of a distinct population subset. A few of the limitations of the study were that our sample size was localized to Calgary, Alberta; Canada and we had a small number of female participants. During Phase I we identified questions that will be relevant to ask in Phase II, e.g., project management's brand. The results of this study should be interpreted cautiously and within this framework.

Findings

This section presents our key findings and discussion on the two research questions identified above. First, we explore the participant's understandings of project management and identify any gaps that may exist. Then we look at the process of selling project management and the interaction patterns between the buyer and seller.

Understandings of Project Management and Its Value

Initially, when we asked the participants to describe project management and brainstorm words around it, they described it as a linear type of activity, much like the definition provided in *A Guide to the Project Management Body of Knowledge (PMBOK® Guide)* – 1996 Edition. "A project is a temporary endeavor undertaken to create a unique product or service" (Project Management Institute 1996, 167). "Project management is the application of knowledge, skills, tools, and techniques to project activities in order to meet or exceed stakeholder needs and expectations from a project" (Project Management Institute 1996, 167). These definitions are tactical in that they address tools, techniques, and skills. They also refer to a simple value statement of either meeting or exceeding expectations. The participants we interviewed described project management in tactical terms so it is understandable that as we asked them questions on selling project management, their approaches were tactical. None of the participants initially described project management as a philosophy and none referred to specific project management methodologies. In general, senior executives hold a fairly consistent, albeit basic, understanding of project management.

Although this initial definition gave the impression that project management principles were well understood in terms of the *PMBOK® Guide*, further questioning revealed a diverse understanding of project management. Some participants viewed it as a tool or technique and others viewed it as a lifestyle, something that was ingrained in them they believed. Some described it as "part of their makeup" or an innate potential. It was described in religious terms on more than a few occasions and practitioners indicated they had "found the religion of project management" and described themselves as "converts." However, the majority of executives provided less passionate or detailed depictions. They tended to describe project management as either a very high conceptual issue or as a tactical toolbox for getting things done. The consultants were the only group that described project management in strategic terms such as "a core understanding or belief, scalable, flexible, and related to shareholder value."

Looking at the understandings of project management expressed by our participants in another way, we explored the tactical versus strategic understandings held by the buyers (senior executives, CEOs, CIOs) versus sellers (consultants, project manager practitioners) group. When project managers were asked to comment on the value of project management, their feedback reflected its importance and worth relative to projects, e.g., use a proven, structured methodology to show project results. One described it as an "insurance policy." Another described it as having the right people do the right thing at the right time. Many related the value to the project management priority triangle of "on time, cost, and scope."

The value of project management varied widely across our participant groups. To project managers, its value related to being more efficient and effective and helped them with their track records and career paths. As such, they focused on tactical strategies in selling project management (features, attributes) because these were the values of importance to them. To many in this category, the value of project management was so obvious it almost didn't bear explaining. The value of project management to large-scale consultants rested in increasing revenue through sales and establishing their presence on accounts. They preferred to focus on strategic level outcomes and to sell project management at that level; however, they were willing to focus on whatever benefits the client wanted to buy. Small-scale consultants were also interested in revenue but tended to sell project management benefits relative to their individual skills and expertise. The value of project management to executives related to being more efficient and effective in their business capacities and ultimately with their careers. They wanted to buy services that were aligned to their strategic business and personal goals. They were far more interested in buying tools or techniques that impacted strategic outcomes than those aimed at improving or sustaining innovative business operations.

In all the interviews conducted, only those at one projectized firm consistently described project management as providing strategic benefits; all others interviewed described it as a corporate tactic. The rationale given was that business priorities lay elsewhere. Consultants confirmed these views based on experience with the same clients.

Summarizing these findings on the understanding and value of project management, we noted that the participants used efficiency and effectiveness values in different combinations that seemed to relate to their overall strategic or tactical understanding of project management. We depicted these relationships in Figure 2.

Figure 2 depicts the understandings and value of project management as viewed by the buyers and sellers. In quadrant 1 (Q1), project management is understood in tactical terms and purchased for efficiency values such as return on investment, reduced costs, and increased quality. Project management consists of tools

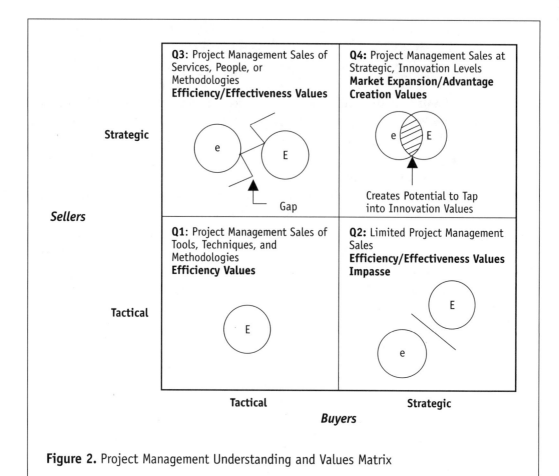

Figure 2. Project Management Understanding and Values Matrix

and techniques. Most project management sales relationships in the past have predominated in this quadrant. Some may purchase project management in quadrant 2 (Q2) when buyers are strategic and sellers are tactical, but not many. Instead, the buyers will seek out sellers that are aligned to their values. In quadrant 3 (Q3) where buyers are tactical and sellers strategic, executives that purchase these project management services may come to realize the added value of doing so but possibly at the risk of staff resistance to change as project management is introduced at a more advanced level. Those selling strategically to tactical buyers and those selling tactically to strategic buyers (Q2, Q3) will soon find that they are not aligned and either adapt their sales strategies or be given even less access to senior management. Those selling strategic solutions will be aligned with buyers seeking effectiveness values (customer satisfaction, collaboration, organizational effectiveness, and knowledge sharing). This point may be viewed at the intersection of the quadrants. Quadrant 4 (Q4) is similar to Q1 in that there is alignment. The seller and buyer (Q4) understand the need to use project management for long-term success from an organizational and business standpoint. Buyers are seeking innovation values of market expansion (creating new markets, developing a global presence) and advantage creation (changing industry and market practices) (Frost 1999). Sellers are selling relationships at the business-to-business level. We observed that this advanced case existed at only one firm where we interviewed projectized staff.

Barriers to Selling Project Management

The feedback on barriers to successful project management experiences indicated that project managers and executives do not view project management as useful for more than a control mechanism. This limited view leads to the dismissal of project management as expensive overhead that has little connection to business value creation.

Some executives see project management as "easy and something anyone can do." Others cite resistance to purchasing project management as a lack of alignment between stakeholders as well as a lack of willingness to "put some skin on the table" and share in the project risk. Still others indicated that some executives lacked a clear understanding of project management, and that they viewed it as expensive overkill. One practitioner stated that, "These people don't know project management, they don't trust it, and they think it is make-work." The results showed that within the buyer's domain, there is a significant range of diverse opinions and attitudes toward project management.

Similarly, consultants believed that senior management did not understand project management or its true value potential. Some consultants indicated that executives did not understand what it takes to do projects well, nor did they appreciate the detail involved in project management. They saw the major barrier as a matter of changing mindsets and organizations at a cultural level. One interviewee noted that, "People have to feel the value to change, not see it."

Other examples of executive resistance to project management as cited by project managers included comments such as "Don't tell me how it's done, just show me the results." One key issue appears to be a mismatch between need and expectations. That is, project managers do not always use the right arguments to convince management that project management can address a particular management need. Thus, disconnects occur between the project managers who tactically sell the features and attributes (merits) of specific tools and techniques for *project success* to management. Instead, executives want results and benefits at the *business* level. Therefore, project managers need to convince executives of the value of project management by going well beyond the traditional metrics of delivering on time, on budget, and within scope. This will require project managers to first understand what they do to add value to business objectives before expecting executives to change the way they see things.

These barriers to selling project management were common themes in the course of extracting meaning from the interviews. The barriers reflect a resistance to change and a desire to maintain the status quo. The barriers at the executive level related to their understanding of project management and, frequently, their lack of experience with it to appreciate its merits. On the basis of the differing viewpoints, it becomes clearer why a difficulty exists in understanding the value of project management. In particular, the disconnect looms large when the intentions of the seller and buyer diverge significantly.

How is Project Management Successfully Sold?

To answer this question, we asked each participant to tell us the story of a time when they were involved in the "purchase" or "sale" of project management within an organization. A synthesis of the stories resulted in the needs-based decision-making process depicted in Figure 3.

Not one interviewee mentioned that project management was successfully sold proactively, as a strategic investment. Block (1991, 1992) supports the difficulty of proactively selling project management. In organizations not rife with crises, the executives seem disinterested in spending money on project management due to the perception that it is overhead and expensive. This explains some of the frustrations and challenges internal project managers faced in their efforts to sell project management proactively.

The interviewees indicated that the *triggers* to buy project management were related to a combination of external and internal factors as reactions to specific needs. Externally, the decision to buy project management was primarily related to competition and market share issues amplified by the following driving environmental forces facing today's organizations including: time compression, blurring of industrial and organizational boundaries, knowledge intensity, increasing returns to scale, and increasing information technology (IT) intensity (Saway et al. 1999). These external forces influence the value creation process and in turn, the very core of how a business functions. Internally (personally and organizationally), the decision to buy project management primarily relates to an extremely troubled or failing/failed project or the advent of mega/complex projects. The impact of these internal and external contexts left the companies feeling that they were in *crisis* situations.

Specifically, crisis situations forced executives to consider the merits of project management in terms of the business problem. *Recognition* that the firm needed to improve the project management processes was usually based on the "insurance policy" value of project management in reducing risk and buying them certainty or its contribution to their personal success. Senior management's willingness to pay (WTP) for project management is associated with their perception of the payoff—total revenue must exceed total cost. They tend to avoid buying project management because the tangible benefits seem disconnected to the individual's WTP, especially on a larger project that takes a long time. Conversely, willingness to accept (WTA) the loss of project management as an option/strategy in the future becomes much more of a compensation issue that places the loss on a grander economic scale. For example, senior executives may be WTP for project management for $100,000 as an initial capital investment. However, the numbers may skyrocket when asked what they are willing to accept in terms of economic compensation for the loss of the opportunity to purchase this same opportunity in

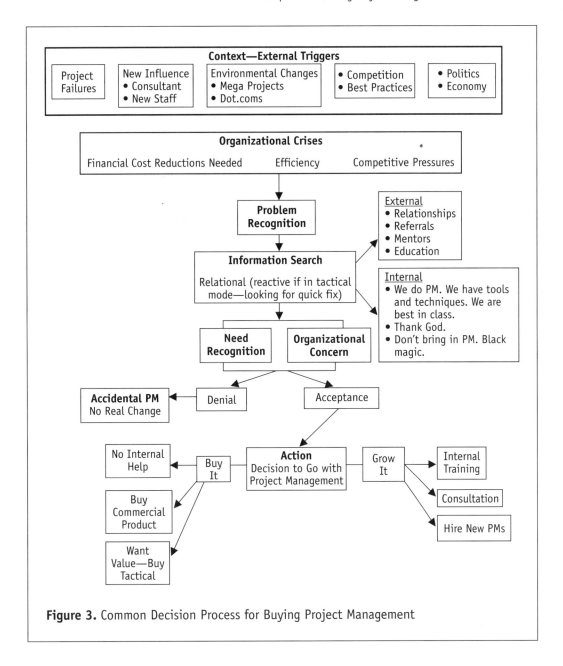

Figure 3. Common Decision Process for Buying Project Management

the future. In either case, the risk decision may rest on only one variable (typically cost), without reference to future opportunities over time, which acts to underestimate or overestimate the value of project management.

Decisions to buy project management are often triggered by "crisis situations." Thus, when executives begin searching for *information* externally, they reach out to specific project management consultants on the basis of prior relationships or referrals, e.g., those that were "top of mind" for specific services or skills. Rarely did the executives seek out new relationships with consultants or establish stronger ties with internal advocates of project management.

The results show three reasons internal sources of information are not culti-vated. First, executives tended to view consultants with a different degree of cred-ibility than their own project managers. In many cases the organizational crisis was in response to internal poor performance on projects. Project managers were usually the ones blamed or fingered when projects were in trouble and senior managers failed to appreciate the element of shared responsibility (Jugdev and Hartman 1998). This tended to reduce the credibility of project management proponents within the organization at the very time when executives might be ready to listen. Second, another challenge that internal project proponents faced in selling to their executives related to position power and language. Typically, project management proponents were not at a similar level in the hierarchy and so did not have access to resources, influence, or coalition and sometimes, more importantly, did not share a common language with the executives. When the project managers focused on project minutiae, executives further disconnected in terms of both receiving the message and listening. Finally, executives often received very mixed messages from their internal resources, messages often in direct conflict with those being offered by the consultants. Generally, senior exec-utives got responses to queries about the state of project management in the organization that range as follows:

- "We do project management and we do it well, so we don't need help." This reaction reflects a resistance to change and exemplifies denial in terms of project management improvements.
- "We don't need project management. We have managed to do projects 'the old way for years' and do not need to change our practices or learn new ways." This reaction reflects a resistance to change as well as a lack of aware-ness of project management.
- "We need help with project management. Thank goodness we are receiving help and our concerns are finally being heard." This level indicates a height-ened level of awareness that improvements are possible.

Executives receiving the first two types of responses are likely to be either con-fused or angry where they have recognized the organizational problems and out-comes related to suboptimal project management practices. Executives receiving the third type of response are not likely to turn to this group for advice.

Those seeking to promote project management are severely handicapped by the tendency of executives to be triggered to explore project management only in cri-sis situations. Clearly, this group needs to develop better ways of gaining access and promoting interest in proactive project management in support of business objectives.

Buying-Selling Process

Once the need was recognized and heightened awareness of project management achieved, it usually led to *acceptance* of project management as a potential solu-tion. Then, executives took *action* by either buying project management externally

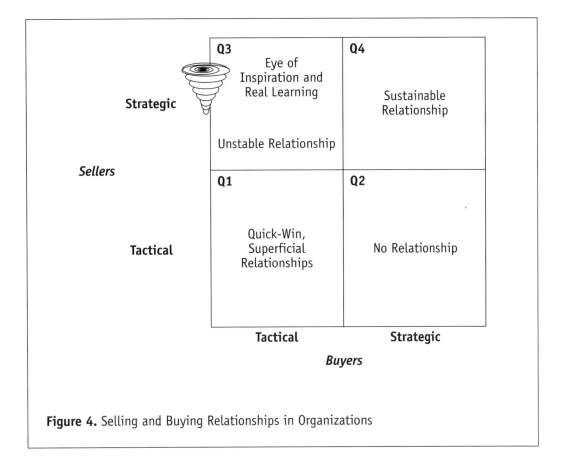

Figure 4. Selling and Buying Relationships in Organizations

from consultants or growing it internally by training their staff, hiring project managers, and augmenting this strategy with some consulting services. These two choices differ in that buying project management services reflects an organizational culture that views it as a commodity. On the other hand, those companies that grow it internally are more likely to support it as a core competency. These companies indicated that it took years to grow project management internally and that the progress was incremental.

In the cases where the need for project management continued to be denied at this stage, the practitioners believed that there would be no change. In these organizations, project management was simply something anyone could do when the need arose. In such companies, project managers were often promoted up the technical ranks and awarded the title "project manager" although they did not necessarily have the experience or training to fill the role effectively. One interviewee used the term "*accidental project manager*" to describe these individuals.

Based on the participant information and literature, we developed a model that describes the way project management is sold/bought in organizations (Figure 4).

Traditionally, project management sales relationships follow the trend shown in Q1, where the tactical relationships focus on selling features of a business solution. Buying occurs at a reflexive level or involuntarily such that no real learning takes place. If the seller does not "elicit" the desired response, then no relationship can be maintained (Q2). If the seller does elicit the desired response, a dysfunctional relationship can be established such that no new behaviors are learned; instead, associations are developed through pairing previous experiences with associations that are made in response to the belief that one has control over the external trigger events.

Currently, practitioners are selling tactically and demanding strategic respect. This puts us into a situation whereby actions and behaviors contradict and change feels chaotic, like the whirl of a tornado (Q3). Ultimately, to thread into the eye of the chaos to the level of true learning, sellers must sell strategically with the purchaser buying strategically. In terms of affecting change that resonates at a personal and organizational level, strategic selling must occur (Q4). As an intermediary step, sellers may initially reach buyers at a tactical level (Q3). The responsibility for where the relationship goes from here rests with the seller and buyer being honest about the benefits of the relationship rather than pushing the features of the project management solution. The seller as a strategist moves the buyer into an area of trust that nurtures a mutual proactive response to making a personal change. The seller can begin to identify how the business solution relates to internal issues (things that keep the executive up at night) as trigger events. Buyers can begin to see the futility of reacting reflexively and trying to control external trigger events such as market stability and politics as a way to affect change that resonates through an organizational system.

Q4 shows a healthy, sustainable relationship whereby new behaviors are learned. Sellers and buyers do not act out of past associations from failed or successful experience. Rather they jointly tell a story that makes sense because it resonates with each party. Both parties learn the desired behaviors instead of reflecting on what they perceive each other to want. This becomes more than a process of generalization and discrimination of the features that each perceives to be of value in sustaining and growing the relationship. Rather, the benefits of a mutual relationship emerge and grow stronger because each focuses only on what they can guide internally for themselves—what is true from them instead of exercising perceived control over external trigger events.

To summarize, our Phase I research indicates that:

- Project management continues to be sold from a foundation values perspective and has not evolved to the innovation values end of the continuum.
- There are a number of disconnects that relate to the understanding of project management and its perceived value in business terms. There is a lot of work to be done to improve how it is understood and valued by executives.
- Sellers of project management (including project managers) need to use effective marketing strategies and communication skills in presenting it to executives in a business, not project, context.
- Sellers need to be mindful of the dynamics around change management and ensure that they adjust their sales strategies accordingly. Company cultures are ingrained and change can be painfully slow. Recommending small-scale

project management initiatives and "quick-win" strategies will go farther than more dramatic changes.

■ Organizations are evolving in terms of their project management maturity. This relates to the 2 x 2 matrices presented and sellers need to be aware of this as they develop their strategies of selling project management.

■ Effective relationships between buyers and sellers built on trust and past experiences with each other are critical to future working relationships and potential sales. These relationships cannot be built over the course of a few meetings. Sellers need to ensure that they cultivate these relationships and develop their credibility with executives.

The preliminary findings from Phase I reveal common trends or relationships that bear further research and elaboration. Positioning and branding of project management appear to be central issues in establishing project management as a strategic capability. Both areas warrant further research with respect to the complex topic of selling project management. We will be researching aspects of these two topics in Phase II.

Conclusions

Our findings suggest that disconnects exist between what sellers promote and what buyers want to hear regarding project management. A naiveté appears around the belief that project management should be valued for its own sake. Thus, senior executives fail to see project management's value connection with the goals of the organization. In addition, the sale of project management at present appears to be the response to internal crises or changes in the environment instead of occurring as a proactive business decision. Those interested in being more effective at selling project management will benefit from learning and applying the basics of marketing strategies, listening to their target audience, and ensuring that they align the sale of project management to match the executive's degree of receptiveness on the value continuum.

Selling project management to senior executives requires project managers to learn different skills and overcome a discomfort with acting in a "sales" capacity. Project managers' experience with project management means that they best understand its value and benefit within their company. They appreciate its value and benefit when it is used effectively on projects and they appreciate its need when projects do not go well. Project managers are excellent ambassadors to promote project management in business terms to executives. They can develop skills in putting forth the arguments of how project management benefits organizations by applying best practices and heightening senior management awareness of the value and benefits of project management to realizing their business imperatives.

As with any project, the attempt to sell project management at the executive level benefits from careful planning and preparation. The results of Phase I provide some insights into the process necessary to sell project management and some of the arguments that others have found to be successful.

Contributions

Our preliminary research findings suggest that the difficulty in selling project management at the executive level often results from cognitive gaps in the marketing relationships. For example, project managers sell features and attributes when executives want to hear about results and benefits. At times project managers and consultants are guilty of selling before the need has been identified let alone agreed to by executives (Houle 1998). These disconnects could be viewed as misalignments between values and expectations. Those involved in selling project management to executives can benefit from understanding and applying some basic tenets from marketing and communication (e.g., improving their listening skills in terms to learn how to frame the problem executives want answered). This will enable them to make the right connections about what executives are receptive to hearing in business terms. We suggest using a three-point approach of triggers, responses, and proof to explain project management benefits.

Trigger: Understand what the triggers to buy are for executives. Currently, the strongest triggers for the need for project management at the executive level appear to be an external crisis or negative project activity. Buying occurs at a reflexive or involuntary level associated with current problems and no real learning takes place. This relegates project management to a reactive fast fix. This cycle perpetuates itself on the underlying belief that project management will help control and diffuse external trigger events. From a sales perspective this means that sales will always be reactive. However, until we determine how best to sell project management at the strategic level, project management proponents need to be ready to respond to external triggers.

To increase the potential for proactive sales, project managers can initiate the trigger by focusing on questions like: What are the top five things the executive is trying to do for the company? What are their priorities? What keeps them up at night? Listen for cues and insights into these areas. Once these are understood, project management can be fit into the appropriate context and sold more proactively.

Response: Sellers need to move away from selling project management by focusing on specific features and learn to reframe the information in terms of benefits and their connection to values relative to the executive's priorities. One way of doing this is by drawing analogies about the impact project failures have on the business strategy and discussing lessons learned. The goal is to stimulate deep learning on both sides, as opposed to making uninformed associations about the negative value of project management based on a fear of repeating past mistakes.

Proof: It helps to provide anecdotal information or proof of the value proposition in the context that executives will relate to. For example, restate the value of project management in terms that support the business objective and corporate strategies. This requires a tight, yet responsive to change, alignment between business goals and project management.

Worldwide, PMI has listened to the needs of its constituency to research this body of knowledge. In this chapter, we have presented preliminary findings on how project management is sold to executives and the barriers to doing so. Project management is a tough sell in a competitive environment characterized by a lack of boundaries and innovative partnering strategies. Credibility and trust are important advantages to have and contribute to successful services selling. The insights provided in this chapter enable sellers to create value-based propositions better aligned with executives' requirements. Helping practitioners and executives to better understand the value of project management improves project management's alignment with corporate strategies, which in turn facilitates the company's advancement from operations based on foundation values to those based in innovation values.

Future Research

Following Phase I, which was completed in the fall of 2000, the authors initiated the second phase of the study. It involved an online international survey with a response rate of 1,867. The study found that 71 percent of respondents agreed that selling project management was an important issue. 82 percent agreed that project management was used to deliver successful projects. Yet in another question, 60 percent disagreed that projects were completed on schedule or on budget. In keeping with the findings of Phase I, 77 percent agreed that executives were more interested in project management when there was an internal crisis or failure. Another finding that related to Phase I was that approximately one-third disagreed that emphasizing the detailed features, tools, or techniques were helpful ways of describing project management when selling to executives.

Briefly, the demographics for Phase II showed that 53 percent were project management personnel, 26 percent consultants, and 20 percent executives. 70 percent were male and 71 percent between the ages of thirty-one and fifty. The majority of participants were from North America.

At the time of this publication, the authors were in the process of conducting descriptive statistics on the data using SPSS® and qualitative software on the open-ended questions. Phase II research publications are forthcoming through PMI as a book in 2002.

Acknowledgments

The authors of this study would like to acknowledge the Project Management Institute for visionary directions toward this research initiative. In particular, we are indebted to Dr. Lewis Gedansky, PMI Research Manager and Mr. Paul Shaltry, volunteer on the PMI Research Program Member Advisory Group for their leadership and support. The authors would also like to thank the following organizations for their generous support:

- Project Management Institute Southern Alberta Chapter
- University of Calgary
- Athabasca University

- Computers in Information Processing Society—Calgary, Alberta Chapter
- IBM Canada Ltd.; Calgary, Alberta.

The authors would like to acknowledge the valuable insights contributed by the study participants.

References

Block, T. R. 1991. Selling Project Management to Senior Executives. *Project Management Institute Seminars & Symposium*. Dallas, Texas.

———. 1992. Selling Project Management to Senior Executives—The Sequel. *Project Management Institute Seminars & Symposium*. Pittsburgh, PA.

Daft, R. L. 1987. *Organizational Theory and Design*. 3rd Edition. St Paul, MN: West Publishing Company.

Dinsmore, P. 1996. Toward Corporate Project Management. *PM Network* (June).

Don, C. 2000. Personal interview. March 17, 2000.

Frost, J. 1999. *Assessing the Strategic Value of IT*. Intelligence Unit for UKP425. IBM Global Services.

Gardner, A., S. Bistritz, and J. Klompmaker. 1998. Selling to Senior Executives, Part 1. *American Marketing Association* (Summer).

———. 1998. Selling to Senior Executives, Part 2. *American Marketing Association* (Fall).

Heidrick and Stuggles. 1998. Unpublished research papers. URL: http://www.heidrick.com.

Houle, D. 1998. *Video Transcriptions: Persuading the Customer to Buy (Part One)*. URL: http://www.goldratt.com/juk13t-1.htm.

Jacobs, P. 1999. Recovering from Project Failure. *Infoworld Publications Inc.* 21 (39): 103–107.

Jugdev, K., and F. Hartman. 1998. Project Manager Fears and Frustrations. *Project Management Institute Seminars & Symposium*. Long Beach, California.

Kotler, P. 1994. Marketing Management: Analysis, Planning, Implementation and Control. 8th ed. Prentice-Hall.

KPMG. 1997. *What Went Wrong? Unsuccessful Information Technology Projects*. URL: http://audit.kpmg.ca/vl/surveys/it_wrong.htm.

McElroy, W. 1996. Implementing Strategic Change Through Projects. *International Journal of Project Management* 14 (6).

Project Management Institute. 1996. *A Guide to the Project Management Body of Knowledge (PMBOK® Guide)*. Upper Darby, PA: Project Management Institute.

Sawy, O. et al. 1999. IT-Intensive Value Innovation in the Electronic Economy: Insights from Marshall Industries. *MIS Quarterly*.

Strauss, A., and J. Corbin. 1990. *Basics of Qualitative Research: Grounded Theory Procedures and Techniques*. London: Sage.

Thomas, J. 1997. *It's Time to Make Sense of Project Management*. Unpublished manuscript, The University of Calgary, Project Management Specialization/Faculty of Management. Email: jthomas@mgmt.ucalgary.ca.

Webster's II New Riverside Dictionary. 1984. *Webster's II New Riverside Dictionary*. New York: Berkley Books.

Section IV

Project Management Techniques

Introduction

The final section of the book offers a variety of current, state-of-the-art project management techniques. In this section, issues of both a behavioral and technical nature are examined. They offer some important guidelines for improving project management practice.

- Timothy Lowe and Richard Wendell have developed a decision model for minimizing the risks associated with a variety of project management decisions. Their decision tree model, employing a variety of branching options, offers both research directions and practical applications for scientists and practitioners. Chapter 20—Managing Risks in Projects with Decision Technologies.

- M. Alquier, E. Cagno, F. Caron, V. Leopoulos, and M. A. Ridao also address the nature of risk management, focusing particularly on risk identification and analysis during the early and late phases of project development. Using the Project Risk Management (PRIMA) model, they offer guidelines for developing risk-driven approaches for risk analysis and management. Chapter 21—Analysis of External and Internal Risks in Project Early Phase.

- Stuart Anderson, Shekhar Patil, and G. Edward Gibson, Jr. present a new methodology for examining the owner-contractor work relationship, the Owner-Contractor Work Structure (OCWS) model. Their paper discusses the development and validation of the model, and its variety of uses and benefits in practice. Chapter 22—Improved Owner-Contractor Work Relationships Based on Capital Project Competencies.

- Graham M. Winch and Sten Bonke identify a process for stakeholder identification and management, the Stakeholder Mapping methodology. Through detailed conceptual development, they highlight the need for detailed stakeholder identification using a mapping model similar to the one they espouse. Chapter 23—Project Stakeholder Mapping: Analyzing the Interests of Project Stakeholders.

- Chris Chapman and Stephen Ward apply their expertise in project risk management to an essay on the general movement from risk management to the more generalized paradigm of uncertainty management. Their work is an important reconceptualization of an important topic as risk/uncertainty management continues to play a key role in modern project work. Chapter 24—Project Risk Management: The Required Transformations to Become Project Uncertainty Management.

- Van Gray, Joe Felan, Elizabeth Umble, and Michael Umble focus on an important and timely topic: the diffusion of Critical Chain project scheduling techniques in a number of project organizations. Through a comparison of Critical Chain and Drum-Buffer-Rope techniques, they identify and consider the unique and value-adding features underlying the Theory of Constraints as it is applied to project scheduling and control. Chapter 25—A Comparison of Drum-Buffer-Rope (DBR) and Critical Chain (CC) Buffering Techniques.

- H. Murat Gunaydin and David Arditi apply their research to the specific domain of construction project management as they consider the vital role that information technologies play in project management. Applying a multiple methodology research design, they uncover a number of important effects resulting from the use of information technologies in the design phase of building projects. Chapter 26—Cross-Impact Analysis of Information Technologies on Project Management Knowledge Areas in the Building Design Process.

- Bob Mills, Alan Langdon, Chris Kirk, and Janis Swan present their recent development, the Time-Block Innovation Project System or TIPS, as a technique that focuses on project portfolio management using sequenced blocks of time, rather than blocks of activities. Using results from research with twenty-five projects and project managers, the authors demonstrate the efficacy of their approach for better monitoring and control in technological innovation projects. Chapter 27—Managing Technological Innovation Projects: The Quest for a Universal Language.

- Suhrita Sen advances the theory and practice of project control through the development and application of earned value analysis. Her research reports on applications of her methodology to the problems of accurately assessing budgeted cost of work scheduled (BCWS) analyses. Chapter 28—Deriving the 2nd and 3rd Dimensions of the BCWS.

CHAPTER 20

MANAGING RISKS IN PROJECTS WITH DECISION TECHNOLOGIES

Timothy J. Lowe, Ph.D.—University of Iowa
Richard E. Wendell, Ph.D.—University of Pittsburgh

Introduction

Chapman and Ward (1997) define project risk as a "threat to [the] success" of the project. They investigate the roots of uncertainty through the systematic analysis of their *Project Definition Process*—providing answers to the following six questions: 1) Who are the parties involved? 2) What do the parties want to achieve? 3) What is it the parties are interested in? 4) How is it to be done? 5) What resources are required? 6) When does it have to be done? Further, they state that the *purpose* of risk management is to improve project performance via a systematic identification, appraisal, and management of project-related risk.

Alternatively, Kangari and Boyer (1989) define risk management as a systematic approach to risk identification, goal description, risk sharing and allocation, risk evaluation, and risk minimization and response planning. In a recent paper, Huchzermeier and Loch (2001) define five different types of uncertainty (leading to risk) in research and development (R&D) projects, and study the value of options when these uncertainties are present. The uncertainties considered are variability in market payoff, budget, performance, market requirement, and project schedule.

Thus, under these broad definitions of risk and quite general descriptions of risk management, it is clear that risk avoidance/risk mitigation programs must be multidimensional. These programs often include good management practice and leadership and human resource issues, as well as scheduling, contingency planning, and buffer management (buffer sizing and placement). The focus of this chapter is this latter set of programs in that we analyze the way that a project team can utilize quantitative planning tools to contain project risk and to hedge against its impact on success. We are mostly concerned with *schedule risk*—the uncertainty of project completion time. We wish to point out early on that our work in this area has just begun, but it appears to be a fruitful area for future research.

Hulett (1995) outlines seven sources of schedule risk:

1. Lack of a realistic schedule developed to a level of detail that accurately reflects how the work will be done, with fully developed work scopes and sequential logic.

2. Inherent uncertainty of the work, arising from advanced technology, design and manufacturing challenges, and external factors including labor relations and such.

3. Complexity of projects, which requires coordination of many contractors, suppliers, government entities, and so forth.

4. Estimates prepared in early stages of a project with inadequate definition of the work to be performed and inaccuracies or optimistic bias in estimating activity durations.

5. Overuse of directed (constraint) dates, perhaps in response to competitive pressures to develop aggressive, unrealistic schedules.

6. Project management strategies favoring late start scheduling or fast track implementation.

7. Lack of adequate float or management reserve.

Hulett argues that the key to risk management is the quantification of risk and the use of software tools to reduce the impact of risk on project schedules. We agree! Indeed, with the increasing power of the computer, better and easier-to-use software, more and better data available, and increasing pressures to manage projects effectively; we believe that using decision technologies to manage risk in projects is now an important part of project risk management. Accordingly, it is the focus of this chapter.

Background

Probably dating back to the first use of the critical path method (CPM) for project scheduling, project managers have realized the shortcomings of CPM for dealing with uncertainties that are inherent in any plan. As pointed out by Hulett (1995, 2000) the project duration calculated by CPM is accurate only if everything goes according to plan. This is rare in real projects. Furthermore, given uncertain activity duration times, the completion date provided by CPM is often not even the most likely project completion date, and the path using traditional CPM techniques may not be the one that will be most likely to delay the project and need management attention. The reasons for this phenomenon are well known and include the facts that CPM uses only point estimates of duration times (thereby ignoring duration variances) and only the longest path in the project network (using these point estimates) is used to compute the project length.

To circumvent the above difficulties with CPM, several methods have been investigated to obtain more realistic estimates of project completion time. Bendell et al. (1995) give a nice review of some of these methods. Probably the earliest attempt is what has become known as the program evaluation and review technique (PERT) method, whereby three duration estimates (optimistic, most likely, and pessimistic) are used for each activity. The critical path is then found using the most-likely duration values. The probability distribution of project completion time is taken to be the distribution provided by the distribution of the sum of random variables describing the durations of activities on the critical path. Difficulties with this approach include the assumption that activity durations are *independent* variables, and that durations of non-critical activities (even if their durations have a large variance) are ignored. In spite of these difficulties, the PERT method seems to be widely adopted and is a feature included in most project management software systems.

Another approach, often referred to as the *analytical approach*, involves the computation of the cumulative distribution function (CDF) of project completion time as a multiple integral distribution (Ringer 1969). Due to the complexity of the computations, this approach is feasible only if the network is small and the probability density functions of the activities are in analytical form. When exact methods are impractical, Ringer has proposed computer-based *numerical integration* methods to approximate the completion time CDF.

Another approximation method, called the *moments method*, is proposed by Sculli (1983) and it depends on being able to compute the first four central moments of the distribution of the sum and maximum of activity times. In this method, the project network is progressively reduced to a single arc, by collapsing serial and parallel arcs. Davis and Stephens (1983) have developed computer software to support this approach. Bendell et al. (1995) developed the moments method in the special case where activity times are Erlang distributed. Gong and Hugsted (1993) proposed a method they call *backward-forward uncertainty estimation* as a means to include non-critical activity time uncertainties in the risk analysis of a project network.

Other methods have also been proposed in the literature for managing risk. These include managerial approaches such as the *Planned Contingency Allowance* (PCA) technique proposed by Eichhorn (1997), using "unders" to offset "overs" as proposed by Ruskin (2000), or the application of the *Theory of Constraints* (TOC) to project management proposed by Goldratt (1997); as well as more analytical approaches such as those proposed by Gong and Rowlings (1997) and Gong (1997).

Computer simulation is another approach that is becoming even more popular as desktop computing power increases and special simulation software becomes available at an affordable price. Early simulation approaches include those of Van Slyke (1963), Gray and Reiman (1969), and Burt and Garman (1971a, 1971b). In this approach, each iteration of the activity time distribution of each activity is sampled, and the resulting values are used to compute the longest path in the network. This exercise is repeated a large number of times and a distribution of project completion times is then developed. In addition, other useful information such as the fraction of times a given activity appears in the critical path is gathered. Clearly, for the technological reasons mentioned above, this approach to estimating the distribution of project completion time will continue to become more popular (for example, see Levine 1996; Gump 1997). For a further discussion of simulation in project risk management see Grey (1995).

Simister (1994), whose paper provides a nice overview of various project risk analysis and management techniques, reported on the results of a mail survey of various methods that expert practitioners use to manage project risk. Although the number of respondents to his survey was quite modest, he concluded that computer applications, e.g., packages such as @RISK (@Risk, Inc.), are used by the majority of practitioners. He also concluded that one of the simplest of all possible techniques (checklists) was the most favored of all techniques suggested in his survey instrument. We remark that the results of that survey may be quite different now (in the year 2000) than in the year of his survey (1994).

Indeed, recent advances in such software have made them even more relevant and user-friendly. As an example, the @RISK add-on for Microsoft® Project 98 now allows "conditional branching" in the simulation analysis of project schedules. By conditional branching we mean that specific branches of the decision tree are "sampled" only if certain conditions are met. However, the user must specify the branching rules *prior* to the simulation run.

Specifying branching rules is a not easy. Yet it is a fundamental problem that must be faced. In this chapter we investigate the use of decision theory (Jones 2000; Johnson and Schou 1990) to make such decisions. Specifically, the problem with which we are concerned involves contracting opportunities to reduce task times on various project activities. These contracts involve financial commitments and in some cases lead-times to accept contract terms. Also, task times are uncertain but have known probability distributions. Thus, we are concerned with the decision process of crashing activities with the overall objective of minimizing expected project cost. A part of the planning process is to determine if, and when, to elect the crashing option for various tasks. Thus, the setting is ripe for the use of decision theory.

In the next three sections we consider a relatively simple (core) project with the characteristics mentioned previously. We show that when crash-decision lead-times are zero, the problem is quite easily solved. However, when lead-times are positive, the problem becomes much more challenging. We use the core project to demonstrate the relationship of (optimal) expected project cost to various prob-

		Task A		Task B		Task C	
	Probability	Normal	Crash	Normal	Crash	Normal	Crash
Short Duration	0.5	10	5	2	1	3	1
Long Duration	0.5	20	15	13	7	10	2
Crash Cost		$100		$50		$75	
Days Lead-Time		0		0		0	

Figure 1. Simple Serial Project with Zero Lead-Times

lem parameters. Our analysis allows us to gain insight into such problems, but clearly only scratches the surface of possible research efforts. In the section "Research Issues and Practical Considerations in Utilizing Decision Analysis," we discuss research issues as well as practical issues in utilizing this approach. In the last section of the chapter, we give some concluding observations and discuss other risk containment strategies that are possible to use in this problem environment.

A Tree Characterization of Crashing Options in a Serial Project

Consider a serial project where the durations of each task are either short or long, each occurring with a given probability. In addition to these normal durations, suppose that we have the option to crash each task. In particular, suppose that the crash decision for each task is simple—to crash it or not to crash it. Crashing a task costs a given amount of money, called its crash cost, above and beyond the normal cost of the task. As with normal durations, the durations of a task under crashing are either short or long. For simplicity of presentation, we assume that the probabilities of long and short durations under crashing are the same as in the normal case. However, under crashing, the duration of a task in a "crash mode" is generally smaller than its respective duration in a "normal mode." A decision to crash a task must be made in advance of the start of the task by a minimum amount of time, called its lead-time. Figure 1 illustrates such a situation when lead-times are zero.

A serial project having three tasks is depicted in Figure 1. To interpret the figure, consider task B. This task will take either two or thirteen days to complete in the normal mode, each with a probability of 0.5. In a crash mode, under which an additional $50 crash cost is incurred, it will take either one or seven days, each again with a probability of 0.5. Since B has a lead-time of zero, a decision to crash B can be made when task B begins.

Figure 2 depicts a decision tree for this example. (Actually because of size constraints, Figure 2 only gives the top half of the tree corresponding to not crashing

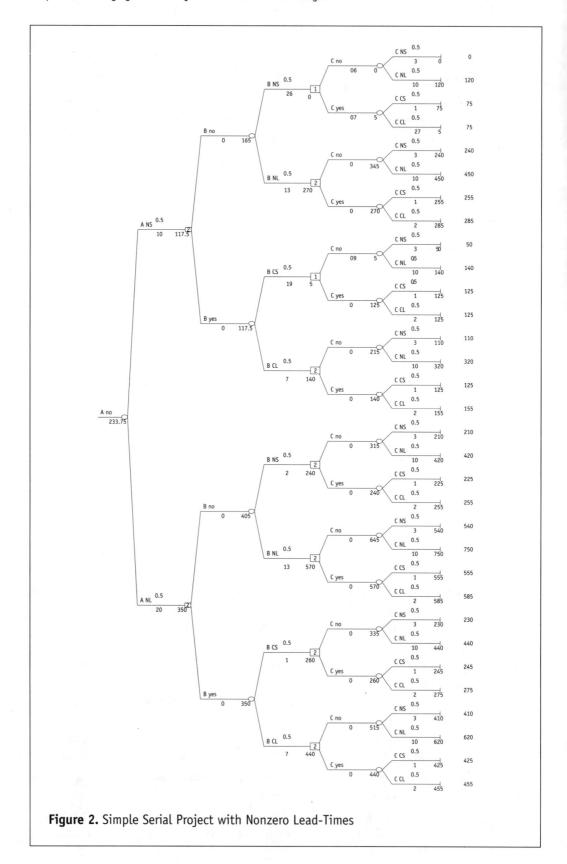

Figure 2. Simple Serial Project with Nonzero Lead-Times

task A. The bottom half, corresponding to crashing A, is similar.) We illustrate the notation in this tree for task B (with the notation for other tasks being analogous): "B no" designates a decision not to crash B and "B yes" means to crash it; "B NS" designates a normal, short duration and "B NL" designates a normal, long duration; "B CS" designates a short duration under crashing, while "B CL" means a long duration under crashing.

Suppose that the project in Figure 1 has a finishing target time of eighteen days and that a project duration exceeding this target will incur a penalty cost of $30 per day. Further, suppose that there are no other relevant costs and that the objective is to make crash decisions so as to minimize expected total cost. Using standard decision analysis, it can be verified that the optimal solution is to crash task B under all conditions, and only (as a contingency plan) to crash C in the following situations: when the duration of task A is long; or when the duration of task A is short but the duration of task B is long.

Note that each path in the decision tree in Figure 2 has one decision node at the start of every task—namely whether or not to crash it. We now add the possibility of a lead-time requirement that changes this characteristic.

Let everything be the same as in Figure 1 except that the lead-time of task B, as well as task C, is six days. Thus, if a decision to crash C is made at the start of task C then a six-day delay will occur before task C can begin. On the other hand, if you decided to crash C at the beginning of the project, then there might be little or no lead-time delay, but short durations for A and B could make crashing C unnecessary or uneconomical.

As evident from this example, a crashing decision under a lead-time is not just "whether to crash or not to crash," but also "when to crash." Making this decision requires knowing when information is available to the decision-maker about task durations.

In our analysis of such a problem, we assume that the decision-maker does not know which of the two possible task times (long or short) will occur until the short task time of the respective task has elapsed. (However, our modeling approach is valid under other scenarios regarding points in time when it is known which task times will apply.) Under the previous assumption, we have the following result regarding points in time when crash decisions are to be considered.

Sufficiency Result

For each task j, it is sufficient to consider the decision to crash the task at the beginning of the project, and at those points in time represented by the end of short duration completions of each task i preceding task j. Furthermore, crashing task j at a predecessor task i would only be considered if the duration of task i was not short.

This result follows from the fact that new information relevant to a crash decision will occur at only those points in time identified in the result. If the duration of a predecessor task i was short, then this result cannot motivate crashing task j since a short duration is the best outcome that could have occurred. As an illustration, in Figure 2 it will be sufficient to consider the decision to crash task C at the beginning of the project, at the point in time representing a short duration of task A if it happens that the duration of task A is long, and at the point representing a short duration of task B if it happens that the duration of task B is long.

Using the above sufficiency result, we can characterize the set of crashing decisions as a decision tree. Figure 3 denotes a decision tree for a simpler version of Figure 2—an example using only tasks A and B. In addition to the previous notation, we let "B LTD" designate the lead-time delay in the start time of B due to B's lead-time. (We will define the concept of a lead-time delay shortly, but for the moment it is convenient to think of it as a potential delay in project length due to the fact that the crashing decision has a positive lead-time.) Further, we sometimes break a long duration of a task into two components, where the duration of the first component equals the short duration of the task and where the duration of the second component equals the difference between its long and short durations. For example, "A1 CL" is the first component of A under a crash mode and its duration equals five, whereas "A2 CL" is the second component whose duration equals ten (i.e., 15 − 5). Finally, note that the durations of the "tasks" need to be computed in a tree corresponding to lead-time delays of tasks. We address this issue in the next section of the chapter.

Observe that Figure 3 is a *general tree* for two-activity serial projects (under our assumptions) since it includes all the logical possibilities that can occur. Indeed, this general tree includes all possible choices for probabilities, costs, lead-times, and so on. Furthermore, the pattern of such a general tree is clear for any serial project. At the beginning of the project, crash decisions are made (either to crash or not to crash at this time) for each task in the project. Then, we have the first activity duration. If this duration is short, it is immediately followed by the second activity duration. If the first activity duration is long, this fact will be known only at the point in time representing an early duration. At this point, we reconsider crashing decisions for all future tasks for which we have not decided earlier to crash. We let T denote this general tree.

Not surprisingly the general tree for the three tasks in Figure 2 is much larger and, therefore, is difficult to display in a figure. Figure 4 gives a *section* of this tree corresponding to when no tasks are crashed at the beginning of the project. Since we can choose to either crash or not to crash each of three tasks at the beginning of the project, observe that Figure 4 represents just one of eight (= 2^3) sections of the decision tree for Figure 2.

The tree in Figure 2 can be viewed as a special case of the general tree when lead-times are zero. Further, other choices of lead-times can yield other trees that are special cases of the general tree. In this chapter, we focus on the general tree since it is applicable to any serial problem.

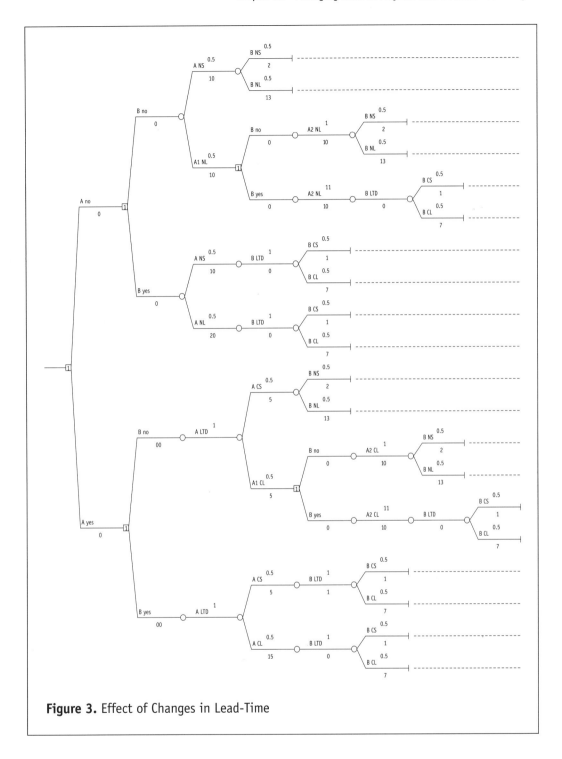

Figure 3. Effect of Changes in Lead-Time

Analysis of the Decision Tree

First, we have some notation. With T as the general decision tree for a project, let P denote a path in T, where a path is a sequence of edges of T, from the root of

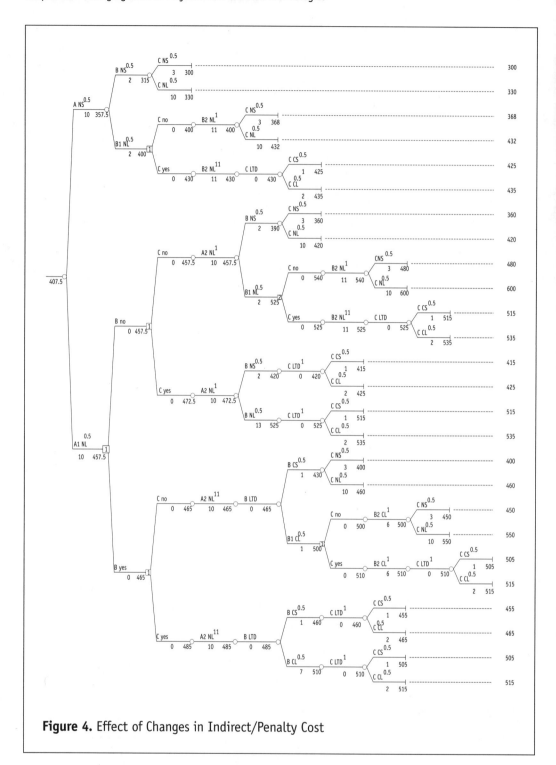

Figure 4. Effect of Changes in Indirect/Penalty Cost

T to a tip (terminal point) of T. What is the duration of the path P? Clearly this will be the sum of the durations of the tasks plus any lead-time delays along the path. Determining the delays requires some calculations, which we consider next.

Observe that lead-time delays can only occur for tasks that are crashed. Along a path P in T we start with task A and then iteratively consider B, and then C, and so forth. Suppose that A is crashed along P. If the lead-time for task A is positive, then A's lead-time delay equals its lead-time (since we assume that the project starts as soon as possible). Otherwise, A's lead-time delay is zero. In general, for any crashed task j on path P we compute the elapsed time along P from the point where the crash decision is made until the time that the predecessor tasks of j are completed. This elapsed time is, of course, simply the sum of the durations of the events (including any lead-time delays) along the path from the point of the crash decision to (and including) the immediate predecessors of task j. If the lead-time of task j is greater than this elapsed time, then the lead-time delay equals the difference "lead-time – elapsed time." Otherwise, we say that the lead-time delay is zero. In Figure 4, observe that the lead-time delay of task B on path nineteen (the 19th path from the top) is one. Here the corresponding elapsed time is five and the lead-time of B is six, so that the lead-time delay is $6 - 5 = 1$.

We now consider a companion concept of lead-time delay. Again, as above, for each crashed task j along P we iteratively compute the difference between elapsed time and lead-time. However, if the lead-time is less than the elapsed time, the difference (elapsed lead-time) is called the lead-time slack of j along P. If the lead-time slack is not less than the elapsed time, then we define the lead-time slack as zero. For a task not crashed along P we say that its lead-time slack along P is ∇. Let $S(j,P)$ denote the *lead-time slack* of task j along P. As an illustration, observe that the lead-time slack of task C along path five in Figure 4 is five since the elapsed time is eleven and the lead-time is six. Also note that for any task j, at most one of lead-time delay and lead-time slack in positive.

For given lead-times, the duration at each terminal point on the tree is simply the sum of the durations of the tasks along the corresponding path. This duration may result is some indirect or penalty cost, which can be added to the total cost of crashing tasks along the corresponding path. Then, the expected cost of the project can be determined by doing the standard backward folding of the decision tree T, yielding optimal decisions at the decision nodes. (Of course, some decision nodes may have alternative optimal decisions.)

Consider an optimal solution to the decision problem where exactly one branch out of each decision node is specified. Let T^* denote a *strategy subtree* consisting of those paths P where all decision branches on each such path correspond to this optimal solution. Observe that T^* specifies the optimal decision to be selected at each decision point that can be attained with a positive probability. To illustrate, consider the following example.

Suppose that indirect costs are related to project duration as given in Figure 5. It can be shown that the optimal solution in this situation is A no, B no, and C no at all decision points, except for the case where both A NL and B NL occur. In that case, we choose C yes. The optimal strategy subtree T^* for this is the union of paths 1, 2, 3, 4, 7, 8, 11, and 12 in Figure 4. The expected cost of this strategy is $407.50.

Days	7	8	9	10	11	12	13	14	15	16
$	200	260	286	288	290	292	296	298	300	304

Days	17	18	19	20	21	22	23	24	25	26
$	316	320	324	326	328	330	340	350	360	368

Days	27	28	29	30	31	32	33	34	35	36
$	374	380	390	400	410	420	432	440	460	480

Days	37	38	39	40	41	42	43			
$	500	580	582	584	586	588	600			

Table 1. Indirect Cost Table

Consider some path $P\lambda T^*$. We now define the *minimum lead-time slack of task j*, denoted S(j), as:

$$S(j) = Min\{S(j,P) \text{ for } P\lambda T^*\}$$

Note that S(j) gives the *upper limit of increase* in the lead-time in task j before any increase in the cost of the project will be incurred. In Figure 2 for task C the minimum lead-time slack is five since only two paths in T^* have a crashed duration for C (paths eleven and twelve in Figure 4) and the slack there is five. Thus, the cost impact of an increase in the lead-time of task C is zero up to an increase of five.

Impact of Changes in Lead-Time and Indirect Cost

For an increase in lead-time of a task beyond its slack, we can expect the project cost to increase. What is the nature of this increase? Of course, with the indirect cost table given in Table 1, the expected cost will be a nondecreasing, nonconvex, piecewise-linear function of lead-time. However, even if indirect cost increases as a linear function of project duration, the following figure illustrates that expected project cost is still a nondecreasing, nonconvex, piecewise-linear function of lead-time.

Consider a modification of the second example where the indirect cost is $30 per day multiplied by project duration. The solution (strategy) that minimizes expected cost is to crash A, B, and C at the beginning of the project, corresponding to an expected cost of $705. This cost is derived as follows. The cost of crashing all three tasks is $225. Since tasks A and B are crashed, if they both realize short durations, task C still cannot start until time six since C's lead-time is six. With this fact, it can be verified that the expected project duration for this strategy is sixteen days, leading to an indirect cost of $480. For this strategy, activity C has a lead-time slack of one, which is evident since activity B's lead-time of six

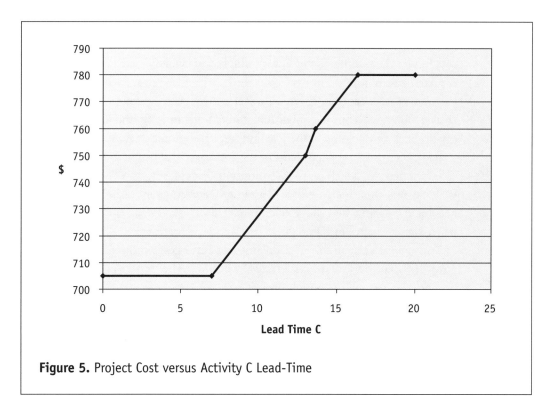

Figure 5. Project Cost versus Activity C Lead-Time

means that C cannot start until day seven at the earliest and since the lead-time of C is six. For increases in C's lead-time beyond seven, cost will increase, as depicted in Figure 5.

The shape of this cost curve can be readily understood. With a lead-time of six for C, tasks A, B, and C are all crashed in a minimum-cost solution. Beyond seven, increases in the lead-time of C will result in an increased project duration in the case when A has a duration of five and B has a duration of one. But this case occurs with a probability of 0.25 and so expected cost will increase at a rate of 0.25($30) = $7.50 per day. Cost will continue increasing at this rate until the lead-time of C is thirteen, at which point the expected cost is $750. At this point delay will occur when B takes on either a long or a short duration, so the cost will begin to increase at 0.5($30) or $15 per day. At the point when lead-time is 13.67 the optimal solution changes to one where only B and C are crashed. Now, with A not crashed, the project length will increase only when the durations of A and B are both short. This occurs with probability of 0.25, and so the rate of increase in expected project cost is again $7.50 per day. This rate will continue until the lead-time is 16 1/3, at which point we have an alternative optimal solution of crashing A and B, but not C. Above this point, C will remain "uncrashed" and so further increases in C's lead-time will not affect the expected project cost. Thus, the expected project cost stays constant at $780, starting at day 16 1/3.

In general, the shape of the expected cost curve, as in Figure 5, can be explained as follows. Consider any path P in some strategy subtree. As the lead-time of an activity j on the path increases, the length of the path will remain constant until its lead-time slack, $S(j,P)$, becomes zero. Then the path length, and hence the cost (under the assumption of linear indirect cost) will increase linearly. Since the expected cost of a solution strategy is the expected cost over each of the paths in its strategy subtree, the expected project cost of each strategy will be a nondecreasing, piecewise-linear, convex function of lead-time. To find an optimal strategy the backward folding of the tree finds the minimum cost solution over all such strategies. Thus, the general shape of the cost curve will be the minimum of these convex functions, which is generally nonconvex. Typically, it will be flat until slack is exhausted, then increase in a piecewise-linear, nonconvex fashion, and then become flat again when the selected task is not crashed in an optimal strategy—hence the "S-shape" in Figure 5.

We now turn our attention to the impact of changes in project indirect/penalty costs. In what follows, we systematically examine the impact of changes in the cost-per-day rate on the overall project cost.

Consider a modification of the second example where crashing costs and lead-times are fixed, but project indirect cost is simply proportional to the project duration, namely it equals an indirect cost rate multiplied by duration. If this rate equals zero, then obviously the optimal solution is to crash nothing and to incur a project cost of zero. As the indirect cost rate increases, crashing of tasks may be optimal. Figure 6 illustrates how expected project cost changes as this indirect cost rate changes. Observe that it is an increasing, concave, piecewise-linear function.

The rationale for the shape of Figure 6 is readily apparent. As the indirect cost rate increases from zero, expected project cost will increase with a slope equal to the average project length of twenty-nine under regular, i.e., noncrashed, durations for the tasks. This continues until the indirect rate reaches $14.28 at which point we have an *alternative* optimal solution, which involves crashing task B. Since under this solution the expected project duration is 25.5, this becomes the slope of the expected project cost until indirect cost reaches $15. Then a new solution of the crashing of tasks B and C becomes optimal with an expected project duration of 20.5, which becomes the new slope until the indirect rate reaches $22.22. After this, the optimal solution is to crash all tasks and the expected project duration, or slope, is 16.

In general, the shape of this cost curve is not surprising. For each strategy the expected cost increases as a linear function. Since the folding back process effectively finds the minimum over all strategy subtrees, it involves taking the minimum of a collection of linear functions—which is an increasing, piecewise-linear, concave function.

Research Issues and Practical Considerations in Utilizing Decision Analysis

Herein we showed how the problem of choosing among speedup options in a serial project can be characterized and solved using decision analysis. To do this we considered a core problem having two events for each task and two crash options

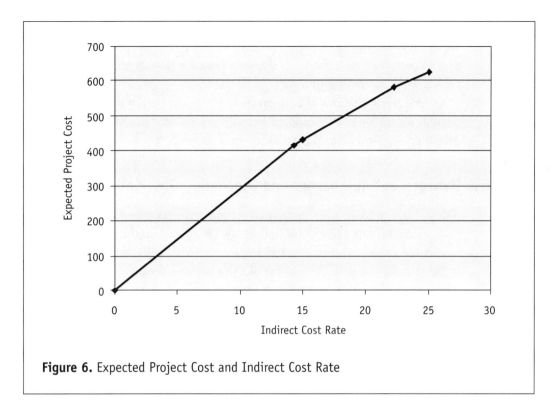

Figure 6. Expected Project Cost and Indirect Cost Rate

for each decision. We saw that the problem with lead-times is significantly more complex than the one without lead-times in that the decisions expand from "speedup/don't speedup" to "when to make such decisions." The problem has some fundamental properties that we discussed, including lead-time slack and the cost impact of changes in lead-time, as well as indirect costs. The purpose of the chapter is not only to consider a solution of the serial problem, but also to lay a foundation for future work in this area.

As for future work, much needs to be done. While the core problem and the corresponding decision analysis can be readily extended to situations with more than two events for each task and with more than two options for each decision, the corresponding complexity of the decision tree increases quickly. Also, as the number of tasks increase, the size of the tree grows exponentially. Thus, decision analysis can quickly become unwieldy for even modest-sized problems.

One avenue of future research is to find methods for reducing the size of the decision tree prior to analysis. It may be possible to do some form of decision tree reduction by developing domination conditions (conditions that eliminate segments of the decision tree).

Of course, in practice other issues may mandate generalizing the problem to incorporate other aspects such as stochastic lead-times, resources, and risk aversion. And finally there is the question of how to deal with nonserial projects (having parallel paths). Here again we can, in concept, utilize the decision analysis approach, but the complexity of the analysis may make this prohibitive. On this latter point, one possible approach is to reduce a project to a serial path using an approach analogous to classical PERT. However, just as in classical PERT, such an approach may yield suboptimal answers since it ignores other paths that are critical with a nonzero probability.

Given such limitations of decision analysis, future research should include the possible utilization of other approaches such as stochastic optimization, dynamic programming, and heuristic methods.

Other Risk Management Approaches and Concluding Observations

While this chapter focuses on decision technologies in dealing with risk, we recognize that it is just one tool for dealing with it. Indeed, in the development and delivery of project management training for research and development personnel at Bandag, Inc., one of the authors of this chapter helped to develop a Project Management Planning Guide for the management of schedule risk in the development of new products and services. The guide is a very simple document (two pages) with the purpose of instilling a common project planning discipline in the company. The guide is a dynamic document in that action items are triggered throughout the life of the project. Also, several steps of the guide are intended to reduce project schedule risk, e.g., involving the project sponsor early on in the development process (to avoid surprises later), ensuring that the project team is involved throughout the planning process, scheduling regular review meetings, and so forth. Bandag found this disciplined approach to project planning useful and has embedded the guide in its corporate product development process.

We believe that much can be learned by studying the risk analysis techniques currently used in finance. Motivated in large part by financial risk management we suggest a variety of strategies including: diversifying risks, transferring risks to contractors, purchasing insurance, building in slack (buffers), obtaining more information about uncertainties, controlling the outcome (e.g., through project design), and building in redundancy.

Consider, in particular, the use of diversification in portfolio composition. The notion is to spread the risk among several investments. To carry this concept over to project management, the natural thought is to diversify by selecting more than one "doer" (contractor) when there is uncertainty in task completion times. However, we now show by simple example that diversification is not always the best thing to do.

Let A, B, and C denote three tasks, where the task completion time for each task is either two or four days, with a probability of 0.5 for each event. We assume that if the tasks are done by a single contractor, the completion time distributions are perfectly correlated. However, if done by different contractors the distributions on task times are independent.

If the project involves doing the tasks in series, i.e., A then B then C, it is optimal to diversify (assign each task to a different contractor) since in that case, there is a 12.5 percent chance—$(0.5)^3$ each—that the project is completed in either six or twelve days and a 37.5 percent chance each that the completion time is either eight or ten days. By assigning each task to a single contractor, we note that the completion time would be (because of perfect correlation) either six or twelve days with a probability of 0.5 for each event. In this example, note that the *expected* completion time is the same (nine days), but diversification gives rise to a (desirable) lower variance of completion time. The analogy to finance portfolio theory is that in this project with serial tasks, total project time is the *sum* of task times.

Alternatively, suppose the tasks are done in parallel, i.e., A and B and C, and can begin at the same time. Thus, project completion time is the *maximum* of the completion time of the three tasks. In this case, it is optimal to assign all three tasks to a single contractor. This follows since project completion time is either two or four days with a probability of 0.5 for each event, while if independent contractors are chosen, project completion time distribution is 4 days at 87.5 percent and 2 days at 12.5 percent. Thus, non-diversification (sole-sourcing) reduces the expected completion time: three days versus 3.75 days.

The intent of the above example is to show that diversification is not always the best thing to do. Its choice depends upon project task dependencies as well as other factors such as independence of completion time distributions among contractors and so on. As with other risk strategies, the decision of what to do is not easy.

In this chapter we have advocated the use of readily available decision technologies to manage schedule risk in projects. Although our focus has been somewhat narrow, i.e., confined to schedule, we believe that the use of modern decision technology tools can be useful to a project team as it plans and executes a project. In conclusion, we hope that this chapter stimulates research in utilizing the advances in both computer hardware (the ability to solve larger problems more quickly) and decision technology software (algorithms for solving large, complex optimization problems) to assist project planners in dealing with risk.

References

Bendell, A., D. Solomon, and J. M. Carter. 1995. Evaluating Project Completion Times When Activity Times Are Erlang Distributed. *Journal of the Operational Research Society* 46: 867–882.

Burt, J. M., and M. B. Garman. 1971a. Monte Carlo Techniques for Stochastic PERT Network Analysis. *INFOR* 9: 248–262.

———. 1971b. Conditional Monte Carlo: A Simulation Technique for Stochastic Network Analysis. *Management Science* 19: 207–217.

Chapman, C., and S. Ward. 1997. *Project Risk Management: Processes, Techniques, and Insights*. New York: John Wiley & Sons, Inc.

Davis, C. S., and M. Stephens. 1983. Approximate Percentage Points Using Pearson Curves. Algorithm AS1. *Applied Statistics* 32: 322–327.

Eichhorn, B. 1997. Manage Contingencies, Reduce Risk: The PCA Technique. *PM Network* (October): 47–49.

Goldratt, E. 1997. *Critical Chain*. Great Barrington, MA: North River Press.

Gong, D. 1997. Optimization of Float Use in Risk Analysis-Based Network Scheduling. *International Journal of Project Management* 15: 187–192.

Gong, D., and R. Hugsted. 1993. Time-Uncertainty Analysis in Project Networks with a New Merge-Event Time-Estimation Technique. *International Journal of Project Management* 11 (August): 165–173.

Gong, D., and J. E. Rowlings. 1997. Calculation of Safe Float Use in Risk-Analysis-Oriented Network Scheduling. *International Journal of Project Management* 13: 187–194.

Gray, C. F., and R. E. Reiman. 1969. PERT Simulation: A Dynamic Approach to the PERT Technique. *Journal of Systems Management* (March): 18–23.

Grey, Stephen. 1995. *Practical Risk Assessment for Project Management*. West Sussex, England: John Wiley & Sons, Inc.

Gump, A. 1997. Scheduling High-Tech Projects. *PM Network* (July): 15–17.

Huchzermeier, A., and C. H. Loch. 2001. Project Management Under Risk: Using the Real Options Approach to Evaluate Flexibility in R&D. *Management Science* 47: 85–101.

Hulett, David T. 1995. Project Schedule Risk Assessment. *Project Management Journal* (March): 21–31.

———. 1996. Schedule Risk Analysis Simplified. *PM Network* (July): 23–30.

———. 2000. Project Schedule Risk Analysis: Monte Carlo Simulation or PERT? *PM Network* (February): 43–47.

Johnson, G. A., and C. D. Schou. 1990. Expediting Projects in PERT with Stochastic Time Estimates. *Project Management Journal* 2 (June): 29–33.

Jones, E. F. 2000. Risk Management—Why? *PM Network* 14 (February): 39–42.

Kangari, R., and L. T. Boyer. 1989. Risk Management by Expert Systems. *Project Management Journal* (March): 40–48.

Levine, H. A. 1996. Risk Management for Dummies, Part 2. *PM Network* (April): 11–14.

Ringer, L. J. 1969. Numerical Operators for Statistical PERT Path Analysis. *Management Science* 16: B136–B143.

Ruskin, A. M. 2000. Using Unders to Offset Overs. *PM Network* 14 (February): 31–37.

Sculli, D. 1983. The Completion Time of PERT Networks. *Journal of the Operational Research Society* 34: 155–158.

Simister, S. J. 1994. Usage and Benefits of Project Risk Analysis and Management. *International Journal of Project Management* 12: 5–8.

Van Slyke, R. M. 1963. Monte Carlo Methods, The PERT Problem. *Operations Research* 11: 839–860.

CHAPTER 21

ANALYSIS OF EXTERNAL AND INTERNAL RISKS IN PROJECT EARLY PHASE

Anne Marie Alquier, Ph.D.—Université des Sciences Sociales de Toulouse
Enrico Cagno, Ph.D.—Politecnico di Milano
Franco Caron—Politecnico di Milano
V. Leopoulos—NTUA
M. A. Ridao—University of Seville

Introduction

During the early "conceptual" phase of a project life cycle—considering for instance a competitive bidding process when a request for bidding has been received by an engineering and contracting company and the decision to bid has been made—the main objective of the proposal manager is to achieve an effective trade-off between the bid competitive value on the side of the client expectations and the project baseline in terms of time/cost/performance constraints on the side of the utilization of the internal resources. Since the project's final performance depends primarily on project risk analysis and management, a "risk-driven approach" to project management appears to be necessary, particularly during the early phase when only scarce information is available and contractual obligations are to be established. In this context, both "internal" risk (e.g., probability of cost overrun) and "external" risk (e.g., probability of winning) must be taken into account.

The chapter presents the PRIMA (Project RIsk MAnagement—The European Commission Information Society Technologies [IST] Community Research Project Number 1999-10193) research project aimed at implementing a risk-driven approach to project management through the development of a risk management corporate memory (RMCM) and a decision support system (DDS), allowing for collecting, storing, sharing, and using company knowledge both in terms of data records and expert knowledge in order to improve the company capability of project risk analysis and management.

The most critical phase in the project life cycle is the conceptual phase or bidding process, since only scarce information is available and nevertheless a project baseline has to be determined, a baseline that more or less becomes a constraint for the project in terms of time, cost, and product performance. In other words, the proposal manager faces an obvious, but not easy to loose, trade-off: the more competitive the bid in terms of offered price and non-price factors, the greater may be the probability of winning, but, conversely, the higher may be the probability of deviation from the planned project baseline.

Three main problems should be addressed:

- How to estimate the competitive value of the bid and measure the probability of winning?
- How to estimate the project baseline and measure the probability of meeting the related constraints?
- How to integrate both estimates, trading off bid competitive value and project baseline constraints with the related uncertainty levels?

Knowledge Structuring

The competitive value of a bid is estimated using competitive factors (such as price, delivery time, technical assistance, process safety, training service, plant dependability, and so on), which have to be defined following a top-down approach. Since these factors may be either qualitative or quantitative it is necessary to use, together with the limited set of factors available, a suitable ranking model. The ranking is related to the influence of each competitive factor on the overall bid competitive value. Obviously, the point of view of the owner is quite different from the point of view of the contractor (in the latter case all the data should be estimated through educated guesses).

Competitive factors may be structured in different ways, depending on the availability of external information (client, competitor, market) and the possibility to identify the cognitive process of experts on the domain as a:

- Simple list
- Hierarchical structure and a taxonomy of factors
- Semantic network
- Database or knowledge base
- Variety of other approaches.

A global performance indicator for the bid competitive value is calculated using the competitive factors as parametric variables. The calculation algorithm can depend on the number of parameters, the type of ranking, or the knowledge structure complexity. This problem may be effectively approached by a multi-attribute, decision-making model, such as Saaty's Analytic Hierarchy Process, which is in fact a prioritization technique.

On the other side, when estimating the overall project baseline, a breakdown approach may be applied by choosing an appropriate level of detail and by taking into account that the more detailed the analysis the greater the amount of information required. Baseline factors may be structured in such a way to make possible a detailed knowledge capitalization and an appropriate working method to build technical solutions using information stemming from previous projects. A traditional way to estimate a project baseline is based on an analytical approach. It requires a breaking down of the project in terms of products, processes, resources, and related costs. The overall project cost is therefore estimated by summing up all the detailed cost items. A quicker way of achieving a project baseline estimate—more suitable for the bid/no bid early phase during the bid process—may be to use a parametric approach based on the identification of the main cost, time, and performance drivers and the use of rates and adjustment factors corresponding to the specific case considered.

Specific models are generally required in order to evaluate overall project main performance parameters: cost (e.g., cost breakdown structure), duration (e.g., project network), and product performance (e.g., value and functional analysis).

Obviously, maintaining a memory of the information concerning previous projects, considering both bid competitive value and project baseline, makes more efficient and effective the process of proposal preparation, since an intelligent reuse of recurrent information items can be organized. Such information can be qualitative and quantitative and should consider product/service performance, client evaluation criteria, competitors behavior, project context, and so forth.

The main information sources for the bid competitive value and project baseline estimate are data records and expert knowledge. Information sources may be internal or external to the company involved in the competitive bidding process.

Knowledge Processing

Classically, the bid process focuses on cost estimations as a final point of the technical solutions building process and a comparison with the possible price is made (DECIDE [Decision Support Optimal Bidding in a Competitive Business Environment] Project, ESPRIT [The European Union Information Technologies Program] n.22298). As previously mentioned, the early phase of the project is characterised by a high level of uncertainty, affecting both competitive factors and cost/time/performance parameters. But risk is *the* prime management factor.

In this context, a risk-driven approach to project management appears to be necessary, since project final performance depends primarily on project risk analysis and management along the overall project life cycle. As a consequence, project risk analysis and management tends, more and more, to become an essential requirement for project management quality.

From the contractor point of view a competitive bidding process poses two kinds of relevant decisions:

- The problem of bidding (bid/no bid decision), i.e., the choice whether to take part in the auction or not, which primarily depends on a preliminary evaluation of the contractor strengths and weaknesses and must be viewed in the light of a project portfolio strategy and some assumptions about the competitors' behavior.
- The bidding problem, i.e., the choice of the bid profile, pursuing the objective of winning the competition without overbidding.

During the bidding phase the contractor has to decide whether to accept an *external risk* (described by the *probability of winning*) on the basis of the presumable judgment given by the client on his bid compared to those prepared by competitors, simultaneously incurring an *internal risk* (described by the probability of deviation from the project baseline representing a constraint for the project). Such a decision can be supported by the above mentioned knowledge organization. But a new way to define and take into account risk should be applied at the project management level.

The concept of risk is normally associated with an adverse event and described in terms of probability of occurrence and severity of consequences. But for managers, risk is a threat as well as an opportunity, which could affect adversely or favorably the achievement of project objectives.

Risk sources may be considered classically, as internal sources (i.e., related to industrial risk subject to company control) or external sources (i.e., related to market risk not subject to company control). For example, current company overall workload causing a possible slippage in project completion date, or currency fluctuation causing a possible financial loss.

The knowledge process organization needs an identification of risks as soon as possible during the proposal preparation process. For each project, it is possible to identify a list of "risk sources" from which a set of "risk events" may stem. For instance, an increase in the purchase price for an equipment item may stem from current market conditions and a loss of competitive value of the bid may stem from local safety rules and standards that have not been correctly considered.

PRIMA Proposal Preparation Process

A PRIMA model of the proposal preparation process has been developed in order to point out the main decision steps where risk aspects should be taken into account.

Normally, the first step of the proposal preparation process is the preliminary analysis of the request for proposal (RFP), leading to a bid/no bid decision. In the case of a bid decision, a corresponding bid strategy should be determined. The second step should include the startup and planning of the proposal preparation process.

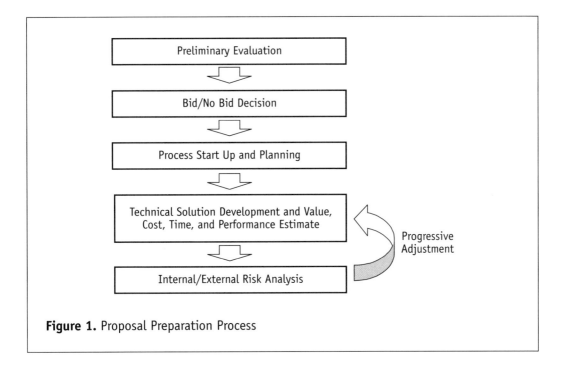

Figure 1. Proposal Preparation Process

The actual development of the technical solution suitable for the client's require-ments and the corresponding cost estimate involves different contributions com-ing from each functional department, with all contributions to be integrated by the proposal team. In PRIMA (IST-1999-10193), the analysis of internal and external risk is developed during the bidding process. Each alternative technical solution, corresponding to a bid profile and a project baseline, should be evalu-ated in terms of internal and external risk (Figure 1). An iterative adjustment process may be requested in order to obtain an effective trade-off between inter-nal and external risk. At each iteration possible risk mitigation actions can be con-sidered—modifying the bid profile and the project baseline—or further information can be requested. In both cases the degree of confidence on the value and cost of the bid should be estimated as a result of the risk analysis. The process ends with the final approval and the closeout step, in which lessons learned should be gathered.

As a follow-up step, data about each bid should be collected and maintained in a RMCM. The project actual values should be recorded and compared to base-line expected values in terms of time, cost, and product performance for each successful bid; in any case, estimated deviations of the bid profile from other com-petitors' bid profile, particularly from the winner's bid profile in case of unsuc-cessful bid, should be analyzed and recorded.

Principles of the PRIMA Project

As a consequence of the previous considerations about the proposal preparation process, objectives of the PRIMA project are to define, develop, and disseminate a management by risk method and the associated software tools: a RMCM and a DSS for bidding.

The PRIMA method and toolkit organizes:

- Risk knowledge capture, storage, and reuse during the early phase—e.g., bidding process—of programs, projects, products, or services life cycle
- A risk reference system with a precise definition of internal risk (affecting products, processes, resources, costs) and external risk (stemming from clients, customers, market, competitors, strategic position, regulation, environment, and so on), structured for business decision-making
- Projects and enterprise performance estimators.

The RMCM is designed to be:

- Knowledge-constructive, as it supports adjustment to new cases when reusing knowledge, restructuring ontology, and adding cases, either from the bid process itself or from other sources.
- Knowledge-emergent, as it allows tacit knowledge capture from senior proposal managers, encourages learning from experience for young employees, and supports best practices.

The DSS:

- Supports bid construction. Bids can be arranged through the provided analytical organization of products and processes, allowing for better precision and quickness; blueprints, sketches, bid/no bid decisions, essays and simulation, risk drivers estimation, and work distribution and refinement.
- Provides bid pricing and evaluation by risk, with internal and external risk analysis.
- Helps organize cooperative work during the process of bid construction. The risk breakdown structure is the basis for *group ware* as it provides a cooperative language used by the proposal team to acquire, share, make coherent, and value distributed knowledge about risks.

The research project starts with a review of as-is methods and practices. Benchmarking techniques are used. Information is gathered through interview techniques and used to support the initial expression of needs. In parallel, a research overview is performed in order to determine the state of the art of scientific developments and new research areas in the field of DSS and knowledge capture. The conceptual modelling will then be adapted to the bidding phase. The results of these tasks are then combined to define the global system architecture making the best use of functional analysis results and existing tools, modules, and methods available within the PRIMA consortium.

The toolkit production makes use of prototyping methods. The detailed specifications and architecture of the software tools are established and the generation of module specifications is shared among the PRIMA partners. After being tested the modules will be integrated and the complete tool will be validated. During the last part of the development phase the users' representatives will undertake an evaluation phase to examine the capability of the product to satisfy the customer needs.

The initial needs expression will be reviewed and improvements implemented. The documentation (user's guide and tutorial) will be updated and released.

The experimentation phase follows to evaluate the efficiency of the approach. This phase is prepared in the early months of the project in parallel with the global architecture definition by identifying the type of test schemes and input data, the database organization, and the performance indicators. Once the tool is eventually available, simulations will allow for evaluating the overall system performance.

Dissemination will be conducted along the project life cycle together with the preparation of the exploitation plan. It starts with a marketing study; the customization strategy in each country is defined and industrial associations are kept informed. Once the product is available, the methodology is disseminated by means of publications, workshops, Internet sites, and so on; and the tools are disseminated toward industries (especially small- and medium-sized companies) through the industrial partners.

The composition of the consortium in charge of the PRIMA research project includes important research and industrial partners, specifically: ALCATEL Space Industries, Université Toulouse1—Department Sciences Sociales Pour l'Ingénieur (UT1), CR2A-DI (software house specialized in the use of IC technologies for scientific and technical applications), Andalusian Association for Research and Industrial Cooperation (AICIA), Sociedad Anónima de Instalaciones de Control (SAINCO), National Technical University of Athens (NTUA)—Division of Mechanical Design and Control Systems and Industrial Management & Operations Research Sector, Hellenic Company for Space Applications S.A. (HCSA), Politecnico di Milano Dipartimento di Meccanica, and Snamprogetti, S.p.A.

External Risk

Assuming that the decision to take part in the bid auction has already been made, the bidding strategy, i.e., defining the bid profile in terms of technical, financial, service-related, and contractual aspects, can be driven by different objectives. For instance, a period of crisis due to a work under-load could force the contractor to submit a bid in order to maximize the *probability of winning* (P_{WIN}) even if the resulting profitability could be low or even negative. When a significant workload is available, on the other hand, the objective could be maximizing the monetary value that is expected in submitting the bid. The latter is widely assessed as the *expected profit contribution* (EPC), i.e., the product of the probability of winning (P_{WIN}) and the profit contribution if the bid is won, which is equal to the difference between the *price offered* and the *expected cost*, $(P - C)$:

$$EPC = P_{WIN} (P - C)$$

The bid profile, in terms of technical, financial, service-related, and contractual aspects, determines both the project baseline and the competitive value of the bid (Figure 2), which may be evaluated considering both the owner set of evaluation criteria and the competitors' bid profiles. The contractor faces an obvious

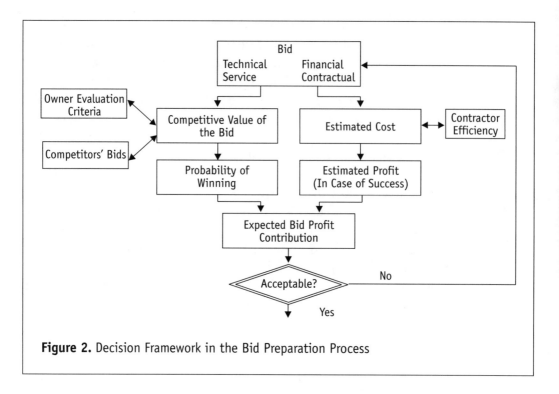

Figure 2. Decision Framework in the Bid Preparation Process

trade-off: the more competitive the bid in terms of price and non-price factors, the greater may be the probability of winning, but, conversely, the lower may be the profit contribution because of price reductions and/or cost increases. The bidding problem is generally a question of choosing the bid profile that maximizes the EPC. However, in order to enter a new market or when there is a work underload the contractor could accept a lower EPC, trading off a lower profit contribution with a greater probability of winning.

Since competitive bidding is a one-of-a-kind process, the proposal manager has to face it with *uncertainty* concerning his judgments, due to imprecise and vague knowledge of the competing context and the project baseline as well. The degree of uncertainty is generally high at the beginning of the bid preparation process and reduces as new pieces of information become available.

Both the problem of an accurate project baseline estimate and a quantitative evaluation of bid competitive value are well recognized as fundamental issues in the bid preparation process (Kotler 1987; Churchman 1957; King 1990; Ward 1988). This section focuses on the latter issue, since fewer results are available, especially in decision contexts in which multiple, quantitative, and qualitative factors have to be considered.

The assessment of the bid competitive value is characterised by at least two relevant sources of uncertainty:

■ The appraisal scheme of the owner, i.e., owner evaluation criteria and their relative importance
■ The profile of competitors' bids.

Assuming the point of view of the owner, the bid appraisal is, in general, a *multi-criteria decision problem* where both economical and technical elements must be considered. In fact, due to the complexity of the offered "product," bids may conform differently to the specific requirements and be non-homogeneous in their technical, financial, service-related, and contractual aspects. Moreover, the growing level of competition together with increasing customer expectations have broadened the number of service and financial aspects that are used to differentiate competing bids. In addition, competitive bidding is usually a *group decision-making process* in which different points of view should synthesise into a common decision.

It becomes necessary to develop a model allowing the contractor to estimate the bid competitive value on the basis of the information currently available concerning the owner, the competitors, and the profile of his own bid.

Models so far developed to assess the probability of winning are mainly based on the assumption that the competitive value of the bid primarily depends on the price offered. Various methods of calculating P_{WIN} as a function of the price offered have been suggested (King 1990; Friedman 1956; Vickrey 1961; Gates 1967; Rothkopf 1991; McAfee 1987). In most cases, the computation of P_{WIN} is a hard task due to the necessity, on one hand, to consider the relationships of dependence among the competitive value of competing bids and, on the other hand, to refer to historical data on competitors' past performances. These difficulties have the effect of reducing the user's confidence in the results of the techniques mentioned previously. Moreover, making decisions based just upon price is getting less and less important. The only way to design a useful decisional support tool is to take into account non-price competitive factors as well.

The importance of non-price factors is well recognized in the literature (Ward 1988; Simmonds 1968; King 1985, 1988; Seydel 1990). Table 1 provides a tentative overview of the main competitive factors describing the profile of a bid concerning the engineering and contracting sector. Even though some papers also suggest to correct P_{WIN} with non-price elements (Ward 1988; Simmonds 1968; King 1985, 1988), little work has been done on this issue and no analytical means are provided to implement these suggestions.

A model for the evaluation of the bid competitive value should present the following characteristics:

- Multi-attribute structure, allowing the integration of quantitative and qualitative factors in the assessment of the bid competitive value
- Allowance for uncertainty in individual judgments
- Integration in a rigorous way of the information becoming available during the decision-making process
- Support to group decision-making
- Flexibility, i.e., easy adaptability to decisional contexts which may be extremely different and characterized by one of a kind conditions
- Robustness, i.e., reduction of the possible uncertainty effects of the overall estimate.

Delivery Time	Time interval between the coming into force of the contract and the plant start up.
Technical Assistance	Maintenance service offered to the owner after plant start up.
Technology Transfer	Training service to help operators and managers effectively run the plant.
Process Technology	Process features influencing plant performance (quality, efficiency, etc.).
Dependability	Plant performance in terms of reliability, maintainability, availability, and supportability.
Safety	Plant performance in terms of operators safety and environmental impact.
Price	Monetary value of the offered plant.
Terms of Payment	Time profile for the owner expenditures.
Financial Package	Capacity of proposing convenient financial sources to the owner.
Utilization of Local Vendors	Share of local goods and services within the bid scope of work.
Contractors Cooperation	Measure of the overall financial solidity and technical capacity provided by cooperation forms (consortium, joint-venture, etc.).
Conformity to Tender Documents	Measure of the accomplishment of contract clauses specified in tender documents.
Liquidated Damages Clause	Fine the contractor commits to pay in case of damages for the owner due to delay in delivery time.

Table 1. Relevant Factors in Process Plant Design and Construction

Multi-attribute decision-making techniques in general and analytic hierarchy process in particular, appear to be suitable for competitive bidding problems, particularly using a probabilistic version based on Monte Carlo simulation. This way not only a rank order of the competing bids may be obtained, but also an evaluation of the probability of winning.

Internal Risk

In the case of internal risk, the first problem to be addressed is which element of the project is affected by a given risk driver. In order to carry out a systematic analysis, a work breakdown structure (WBS) is requested, considering for instance; deliverables, functional systems, components, integration make and buy processes, resources, and costs (Figure 3).

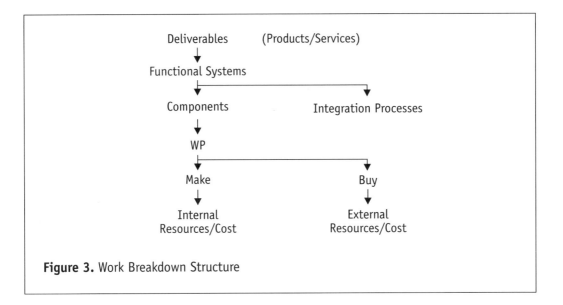

Figure 3. Work Breakdown Structure

At this point a very critical decision has to be made about the detail level of the risk analysis: the more detailed the breakdown of the project, the higher the amount of information to be collected and maintained. As a second problem, it is necessary to identify the links between risk sources (identified by the risk breakdown structure [RBS]) and project elements (identified by the WBS) in order to estimate the major effects of a given risk source on different project elements (obviously, effects stemming from the same risk source are correlated). In this context, risk events correspond, for each project element, to possible deviations of actual values from expected values in terms of cost, time, and product performance (Figure 4).

The RBS allows for an identification of the major risk types: policy, sales, contractual and legal, procurement, management, technical, safety, financial, and so forth. For instance, "management risk" could be broken down into different sources, such as WBS badly defined, project schedule inconsistent, lack of circulation of useful information, resources inadequate or unavailable, and so on.

Note that a given risk source (e.g., currency fluctuation) may affect both the internal and external risk parameters (i.e., estimated project budget and price offered).

Considering the probability of incurring a risk event, the magnitude of the possible deviation allows for a quantification of the risk. Obviously different models of the project are required if different types of risk are to be analyzed: a cost breakdown structure (CBS) model for cost risk, a network model for time risk, a functional model of the product for performance risk, a cash flow model for financial risk, and so forth.

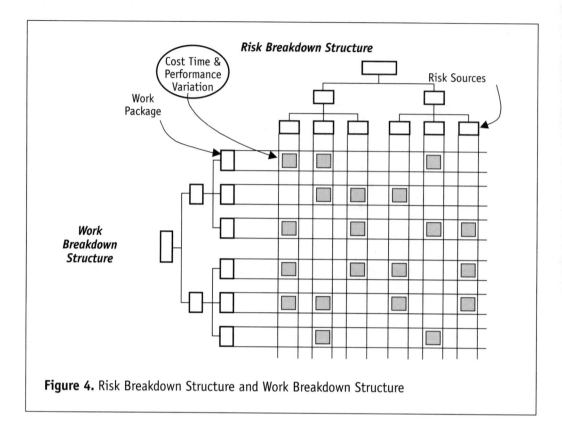

Figure 4. Risk Breakdown Structure and Work Breakdown Structure

PRIMA Decision Support System

A DSS is an interactive, flexible, and adaptable computer-based information system (CBIS) that utilizes decision rules and models coupled with a comprehensive database and the decision-maker's own insights, leading to specific decisions in solving problems that would not be amenable to management science optimization models, per se. Thus, a DSS supports complex decision-making and increases its effectiveness.

A DSS is composed of the following parts:

■ Data management. It includes the database(s), which contains relevant data and it is managed by software called database management systems (DBMS).

■ Model management. A software package that includes financial, statistical, management science, or other quantitative models that provide the system's analytical capabilities and an appropriate software management.

■ Communication. Interface with user.

The architecture of PRIMA DSS is described in Figure 5. The main modules composing the DSS are:

■ Estimate module (allowing for cost, time, and performance point estimates based on drivers, coefficients, and factors)

■ Statistical module (allowing for a measure of the forecasting capability of the company based on data records and expert judgment)

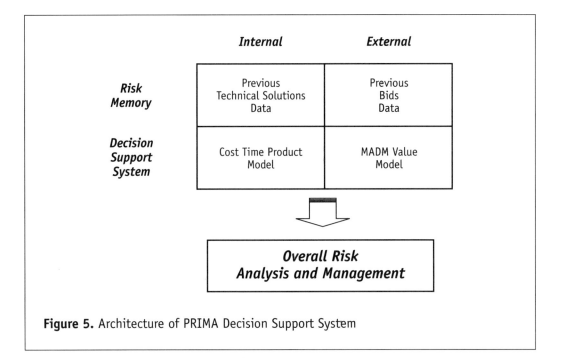

Figure 5. Architecture of PRIMA Decision Support System

- Risk breakdown structure (allowing for an identification and classification of the major risk sources)
- Work breakdown structure (allowing, through cross analysis with RBS and at a given level of detail, the identification of the major risk events, their probability, and consequence in terms of deviations from expected values of cost, time, and product performance)
- Simulation models (value, cost, time, and product models which allow, through simulation, the assessment of the overall risk in terms of time, cost, and product performance using input data coming from the statistical module for each risk event)
- Risk evaluation module (allowing for a tradeoff between external risk and internal risk, identifying possible actions to reduce overall risk level).

The increasing complexity of projects and products leads to the analysis of huge amounts of data. Moreover, the bidding process requires the involvement of different skills and resources in a very short period of time, based on knowledge sharing, both over space and time. A formal process of knowledge acquisition, structuring, accumulation, sharing, reuse, and adaptation to new cases makes a cooperative approach to work and a learning process at company level possible.

The PRIMA DSS focuses on trading off external risk analysis (i.e., analysis of uncertainty about bid competitive value following a top-down approach) and internal risk (i.e., analysis of uncertainty about possible deviations from project baseline following a bottom-up approach). The trade-off between these two sides of project risk is normally obtained by an iterative process allowing for a progressive adjustment of the bid profile, taking into account the several aspects involved.

In the case of the PRIMA RMCM the main information sources are data records and expert knowledge. The relative weight of these two types of sources may change: the more non-repetitive a project element is, the more important the expert judgment during the assessment phase is. On the contrary for repetitive elements, data records may exercise a greater influence in the assessment. The integration between available data records—generally limited by project "one-of-a-kind" features—and subjective judgments elicited by experts on the basis of previous experience about similar projects is an inherent issue of the knowledge engineering process.

The approach to cope with the quantitative aspect of the proposal preparation process is often deterministic, since only "point estimate" values are used for the input parameters of the models applied to estimate both the bid competitive value and the project baseline respectively (e.g., activities' budget and duration). But, as previously mentioned, the early phase of the project is characterised by a high level of uncertainty, affecting both competitive factors and cost/time/performance parameters. As a consequence, during the risk quantitative assessment phase—following the risk identification phase and anticipating the risk response development and risk response control phases—in order to safeguard contractor's uncertainty and nevertheless assess the risk implied in the project, an approach based on "distribution estimate"—and not on "point estimate"—should be applied when estimating parameters related to bid competitive value and project baseline. Distribution estimates can represent both the uncertainty of an individual involved in the decision process and the dispersion of judgments in a group decision-making process.

Such a distribution estimate allows for a greater information content to be used in the early phase of the project and for an answer to new questions—impossible to answer with the traditional deterministic approach—such as: How probable is the success of our bid? How confident are we about the possibility to comply with given constraints in terms of budget and duration? Is it worth carrying out research to reduce uncertainty through gathering further information?

Only the availability of a RMCM allows for an implementation of a distribution estimate approach and, as a consequence, an evaluation of the likelihood of a given budget or completion date estimates. Considering for instance data records, the shift from an "expected value" (point estimate) approach to a "distribution estimate" approach should imply an evaluation of the company forecasting capability. Distributions of forecasting errors—i.e., deviations of actual values about time/cost/performance from the expected values—stemming from data records and adjusted by experts opinion, may be used to obtain a distribution estimate for each relevant project element, considering both competitive factors and project baseline parameters. Since the main information sources are data records and expert knowledge, a distribution estimate should stem from a rigorous integration of both sources, based for instance on a Bayesian approach.

Conclusions

The PRIMA method and toolkit represent a modular approach to risk analysis and management during the early phase of a project. The traditional approach, based on a point estimate of cost and value of the bid, leading to a final trade-off between these two aspects, is enriched by the analysis of the internal and external risks associated to the technical solution developed during the proposal preparation process, eventually arriving at a trade-off between the two aspects of risk. Such a trade-off process allows for a progressive joint adjustment of the bid profile and the project baseline constraints, respectively. This objective may be achieved by obtaining further information or implementing suitable risk mitigation policies. The availability of a RMCM, allowing for gathering, storing, and reusing information stemming from previous bids and projects, makes it possible first, to estimate and improve the forecasting capability of the company and second, to estimate and improve the degree of confidence on given target values of the project in terms of cost, time, and product performance. The feedback of experience consists of recording the risks, the methods used to deal with them, and their effectiveness.

References

Armacost, R. L. et al. 1994. An AHP Framework for Prioritizing Customer Requirement in QFD: An Industrialized Housing Application. *IIE Transactions* 26: 72–79.

Cagno, E. et al. 1998. On the Use of a Robust Methodology for the Assessment of the Probability of Failure in an Urban Gas Pipe Network. *Safety and Reliability* 2: 913–919.

Capen, E. C. 1976. The Difficulty of Assessing Uncertainty. *Journal of Petroleum Technology*: 843–850.

Churchman, C. W., R. L. Ackoff, and E. L. Arnoff. 1957. *Bidding Models. Introduction to Operations Research*. New York: John Wiley & Sons, Inc.

Friedman, L. 1956. A Competitive Bidding Strategy. *Operations Research* 4: 104–112.

Gates, M. 1967. Bidding Strategies and Probabilities. *Journal of the Construction Division* 93: 75–103.

Hauser, D., and P. Tadikamalla. 1996. The Analytic Hierarchy Process in an Uncertain Environment: A Simulation Approach. *European Journal of Operational Research* 91: 27–37.

King, M., and A. Mercer. 1985. Problems in Determining Bidding Strategies. *Journal of the Operational Research Society* 36: 915–923.

———. 1988. Recurrent Competitive Bidding. *European Journal of Operational Research* 33: 2–16.

———. 1990. The Optimum Mark-Up When Bidding with Uncertain Costs. *European Journal of Operational Research* 47: 348–363.

Kotler, P. 1987. *Marketing Decision Making: A Model Building Approach*. London: Holt, Rinehart, and Winston.

Levary, R. R., and K. Wan. 1998. A Simulation Approach for Handling Uncertainty in the Analytic Hierarchy Process. *European Journal of Operational Research* 106: 116–122.

McAfee, R. P., and J. McMillan. 1987. Auctions and Bidding. *Journal of Economic Literature* 25: 699–738.

Min, H. 1992. Selection of Software: The Analytic Hierarchy Process. *International Journal of Physical & Logistics Management* 22: 42–52.

Montgomery, D. C. 1991. *Introduction to Statistical Quality Control*. New York: John Wiley & Sons, Inc.

Mustafa, M. A., and J. F. Al-Bahar. 1991. Project Risk Assessment Using the Analytic Hierarchy Process. *IEEE Transactions on Engineering Management* 38: 46–52.

Paulson, D., and S. Zahir. 1995. Consequences of Uncertainty in the Analytic Hierarchy Process: A Simulation Approach. *European Journal of Operational Research* 87: 45–56.

Project Management Institute Standards Committee. 1996. *A Guide to the Project Management Body of Knowledge (PMBOK® Guide)*. Upper Darby, PA: Project Management Institute.

Ramanathan, R., and L. S. Ganesh. 1994. Group Preference Aggregation Methods Employed in AHP: An Evaluation and an Intrinsic Process for Deriving Members' Weightages. *European Journal of Operational Research* 79: 249–265.

Rosenbloom, E. S. 1996. A Probabilistic Interpretation of the Final Rankings in AHP. *European Journal of Operational Research* 96: 371–378.

Rothkopf, M. H. 1991. On Auctions with Withdrawable Winning Bids. *Marketing Science* 10: 40–57.

Saaty, T. L., and L. G. Vargas. 1987. Uncertainty and Rank Order in the Analytic Hierarchy Process. *European Journal of Operational Research* 32: 107–117.

Saaty, T. L. 1980. *The Analytic Hierarchy Process*. New York: McGraw-Hill.

———. 1994. *Fundamentals of Decision Making and Priority Theory with the Analytic Hierarchy Process*. Pittsburgh, PA: RWS Publications.

Seydel, J., and D. L. Olson. 1990. Bids Considering Multiple Criteria. *Journal of the Construction Engineering and Management* 116: 609–623.

Simmonds, K. 1968. Competitive Bidding: Deciding the Best Combination of Non-Price Features. *Operational Research Quarterly* 19: 5–15.

Titolo, M. 1994. *Competitive Bidding*. Milan: Etaslibri.

Vickrey, W. 1961. Counterspeculation, Auctions, and Competitive Sealed Tenders. *Journal of Finance* 16: 8–37.

Ward, S. C., and C. B. Chapman. 1988. Developing Competitive Bids: A Framework For Information Processing. *Journal of the Operational Research Society* 39: 123–134.

CHAPTER 22

IMPROVED OWNER-CONTRACTOR WORK RELATIONSHIPS BASED ON CAPITAL PROJECT COMPETENCIES

Stuart D. Anderson, Ph.D.—Texas A&M University

Shekhar S. Patil, Ph.D.—Independent Project Analysis, Inc.

G. Edward Gibson, Jr., Ph.D.—University of Texas at Austin

Introduction

This chapter presents a decision process that assists owner companies in creating and sustaining properly aligned owner-contractor work relationships for the development and execution of capital projects. The objective of the research that led to the development of this decision process was to answer questions about how owner-contractor work relationship decisions are made in owner organizations. The decision process defines "work relationships" based on the stakeholders' technical and organizational capabilities, identified in terms of project competencies. The concept of a competency is widely used in management literature on organizational strategy. In this research, it is extended to the development and execution of capital projects. A relationship continuum is devised for assigning an appropriate work relationship for each project competency. An existing decision process developed by the Construction Industry Institute (CII) was evaluated and modified as a result of three successful applications of that process. The improved process was then validated using a Delphi approach. The Delphi validation involved experienced personnel from thirty-two owner companies in North America. The Delphi rounds were conducted by providing each participant with a summary of the process and a structured assessment protocol. The validated process constitutes a systematic approach for owner companies to evaluate their in-house capital project competencies and make rational decisions about creating well-aligned owner-contractor work relationships on capital projects.

Organizations respond to the changing business environment by adapting to the demands of that environment. Particularly, in the case of owner organizations, any attempts to reduce costs and maintain profitability while delivering quality products and services are frequently accompanied by downsizing or reducing capital projects organizations, shifting capital project responsibilities to business units or operating facilities, or outsourcing more project work to contractors. Concurrent with this phenomenon is the gradual attrition, through retirement, of a whole generation of experienced managers and engineers. The combined effect of these changes has left many owners inadequately equipped to develop and execute capital projects effectively (Sullivan et al. 1997; Gibson et al. 1998). Therefore, owners are seeking ways to realign their relationships with contractors, while leveraging contractor manpower and expertise where necessary. A recent research effort attempted to provide a solution to this problem by developing a decision process to assist owner companies in creating and sustaining properly aligned owner-contractor work relationships. The decision process was termed the "Owner-Contractor Work Structure (OCWS) process," and was published by CII in 1997 (Construction Industry Institute 1997).

OCWS Process Overview

The OCWS process involves identification of key capital project competencies, determination of competencies that are core and non-core to the owner, and evaluation of the sourcing approach for each competency. The sourcing approach is described in terms of a qualitative definition of the work relationship between an owner and a contractor, depending on the extent of their individual involvement in performing a competency for a project or a capital program.

The term "owner-contractor work structure," which was coined in the CII research, implies a set of competencies and corresponding work relationships. The term "contractor" may represent a design or construction contractor, a consultant, a supplier, or an entity that provides services to the owner organization. The process was developed from an owner's perspective. A project-focused and a corporate process were developed, depending on whether sourcing decisions are made for a specific project or for a capital program. The key terms of the OCWS process are as follows:

- *Owner/Contractor Work Structure*: the strategic distribution of roles and responsibilities between the primary project participants, based on key project competencies, measured on the continuum level of involvement of the owner and the contractor.

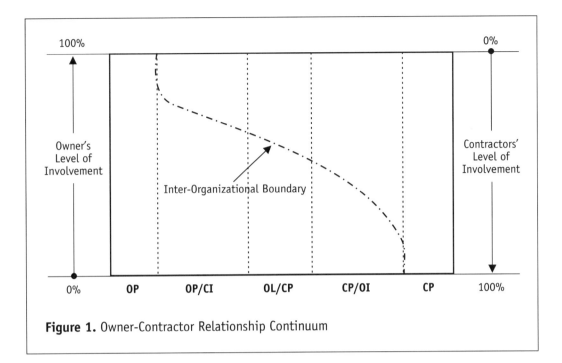

Figure 1. Owner-Contractor Relationship Continuum

- *Competency*: a project work process that is comprised of functions and associated critical capabilities needed to develop and execute a capital project.
- *Functions*: activities and tasks that describe the work involved in performing a competency.
- *Critical capabilities*: the knowledge, abilities, skills, and experience that are necessary to perform competency functions.
- *Core competency*: a competency that must be performed in-house by the owner and is critical to the success of capital projects.
- *Non-core competency*: a competency that could either be outsourced or performed in-house by the owner, depending on the project circumstances.
- *Work relationship*: a relationship that defines the extent of involvement of the owner and the contractor in performing, leading, and/or providing input with respect to a competency.

It is important to review the definitions of each of these terms as well as the concept of a work relationship in order to understand how the OCWS process works. The OCWS is characterized in terms of three types of work relationships between the owner and the contractor, and two other possibilities wherein either the owner or the contractor are fully responsible for performing the work. The work relationship typology used to describe roles and responsibilities in the work structure is illustrated in Figure 1.

The definition of each work relationship is as follows:

- OP: Owner performs all functions involved in the competency using owner resources and the owner's work process.

- OP/CI: Owner performs most functions using the owner's work process with contractor input. The majority of the work is performed using owner resources. Contractor provides input or acts as a consultant.

- OL/CP: Owner leads overall function performance with contractor performing detailed work using owner's work process. Owner leads by setting guidelines, directing, reviewing, and approving work. Contractor performs most of the competency work functions according to owner's work process.

- CP/OI: Contractor performs most functions using contractor's work process with input from the owner. The majority of work is performed using contractor resources.

- CP: Contractor(s) performs all functions involved in the competency using contractor resources and the contractor's work process. The owner can still supply input and guidance by performing a project management oversight competency.

The OCWS process includes detailed flow charts illustrating the inputs, actions, decisions, and outputs of the process and a set of worksheets that are used to document decisions and the rationale behind the decisions. Depending on whether the process is used for a specific capital project or for a capital program level application, the steps in the process are somewhat different.

A limitation in the development of the CII OCWS process was that the process was not fully validated. Therefore, there was minimal information available on how the industry would implement the process and how useful owner companies found the OCWS process when managing a capital program or a specific project. Concerns regarding the lack of validation of the OCWS process provided a premise for undertaking follow-up research.

Research Methodology

The Center for Construction Industry Studies (CCIS), jointly funded by CII and the Alfred P. Sloan Foundation, performed follow-up research with the objective of testing, validating, and improving the OCWS process. Due to the subjectivity inherent in an assessment of owner-contractor work relationships, with the help of the OCWS process, the nature of this research was qualitative. Also, given the limited existing knowledge base on the determination of owner-contractor work structures, investigations in this area were exploratory in nature, making it difficult to construct hypotheses based on quantifiable parameters. Therefore, the research methodology relied on an owner survey, case studies, and the Delphi method (Arditi and Ferreira 1996; Linstone and Turoff 1975). Three research phases were conducted.

Phase I—Owner Survey

Phase I of the research covered a survey of owner companies in North America, the formulation of a research methodology, and the development and testing of instruments and proposals for the case studies that followed in Phase II. As part of Phase I of the research, owner companies were contacted in the summer of 1998 to study the use of the OCWS process developed by CII. The results of this survey established the premise for subsequent phases of this research (Anderson et al. 2000). Out of the total of sixty-two owner companies contacted, twenty-three responded to the survey. Of the twenty-three companies, only three had used the OCWS process and eleven had reviewed the process but not used it. The remaining nine owner companies had not reviewed the OCWS process even though they had acquired a copy of the publication from CII. The relatively low use of the OCWS process and concerns regarding practicality and ease of use, as expressed by respondents, established the premise to undertake more in-depth, exploratory research through case studies.

Phase II—Case Studies

The case studies in Phase II involved a combination of interviews and process applications for gathering data. To initiate the case studies, company-specific proposals were developed with the objective of addressing each company's particular problem through the implementation of the OCWS process. Two owner companies in North America accepted the proposal to implement the OCWS process. The OCWS process implementation in one company involved the development of a new proposed alliance with a large contractor. In this case, the owner was a large refining company. The second implementation effort involved the restructuring of the owner company's capital projects organization based on a business model approved by top management. In this case, the owner was a large power company. A third company agreed to participate in an interview to evaluate a recent application of the process for developing an OCWS for an overseas chemical plant project.

The conceptual framework of the OCWS process was explained to participants in the case studies with the help of an owner-contractor work relationship continuum, as shown in Figure 1. The case studies provided valuable insight into the OCWS approach for developing owner-contractor work structures, and identified several weak areas in the existing process (Anderson et al. 2000). As a result, the OCWS process was modified and improved upon. The modifications in the OCWS process provided the necessary elements to help owner companies accomplish the following four key objectives:

1. Forming optimal work relationships with designers, constructors, suppliers, and consultants.

2. "Rightsizing" in-house capital project development and execution capabilities.

3. Addressing the problem of loss of expertise due to attrition of experienced personnel.

4. Forming potentially successful strategic alliances.

The steps and associated worksheets in the improved OCWS process are illustrated in Figure 2. The worksheets provide a mechanism to document decisions and create a common language that can be used throughout the life cycle of capital projects.

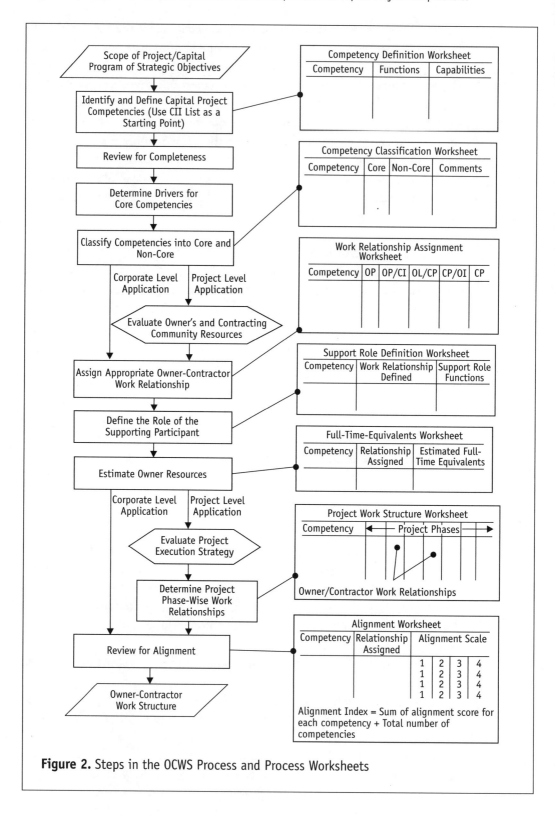

Figure 2. Steps in the OCWS Process and Process Worksheets

Phase III—Delphi Validation of OCWS Process

Validating the OCWS process posed a unique problem. Unlike most research problems that involve the study of organizational phenomenon based on some available data or surveys/interviews of personnel, validating the OCWS process involved having the research participants assess various aspects of the process. The participants' assessment of the process was based on their experiences with forming effective owner-contractor work relationships. Since the reliability of this approach was a function of how well the participants understood the process, it was inappropriate to conduct the validation in a single administration. A Delphi approach that involves multiple iterations of data collection was considered most suitable for testing the validity of the OCWS process that resulted from Phase II. The three key characteristics of a Delphi study are: 1) Anonymous response; 2) Iteration and controlled feedback; and 3) Statistical group response (Dalkey 1969).

Prior to beginning the Delphi validation the participants were first selected from a wide range of organizations, based on the extent of their experience in the area of capital project development and execution. Each participant was provided with an overview of the modified OCWS process, including Figure 2, and a structured response protocol. Ordinal Likert scales were used for soliciting responses from the participants, by having each of them rate various aspects of the OCWS process on a one to seven, strongly disagree to strongly agree scale. The responses were based on the participants' knowledge of capital project development and execution, and the relevance of the process described in the overview. Reliability and validity issues were addressed by computing appropriate indices.

Two types of reliability were critical in the study. The first, known as test-retest reliability, measured the consistency of results on repeated trials. In this procedure, each person's scores on the first administration of the test are related to his scores on a second administration, to provide a reliability coefficient (Tuckman 1999). The test-retest reliability was measured on a pilot basis prior to conducting the Delphi process. The second type of reliability measure that was relevant to this study was internal or inter-item consistency. The internal consistency was measured after each Delphi round.

Internal consistency was one of the two separate indicators that were used to draw inferences regarding the outcome of each Delphi round and determine the need for a subsequent round. It was measured by computing the intraclass correlation coefficient (ICC), which is a function of the true score variance and the error variance based on an analysis of variance (McGraw and Wong 1996; Nunnally and Bernstein 1994; Kastein et al. 1993; Kozlowski and Hattrup 1992; Bravo and Potvin 1991; Shrout and Fleiss 1979). The ICC measures the degree of consistency for measurements that are averages of the k independent measurements on randomly selected participants. In this research, the ICC was based on a two-way random effects analysis of variance, which is mathematically the same as Cronbach's alpha in psychometrics (McGraw and Wong 1996; Cohen and Swerdlik 1999).

The other indicator that was used to draw inferences regarding the outcome of each Delphi round was an Agreement Index (AI) (James, Demaree, and Wolf 1984, 1993; Kozlowski and Hattrup 1992). The AI is a function of the ratio of observed or sample variance and the random measurement variance, based on a uniform distribution. Since high inter-observer agreement is not sufficient to insure the *quality* of the data collected, evidence of the reliability of the data was also necessary (Mitchell 1979). Therefore, both the ICC and the AI were used to evaluate the data. It is important to note that the two measures are not related mathematically or otherwise.

The Delphi method served as an approach for testing the validity of the OCWS process. The ICC, used to estimate internal consistency, also provided evidence of construct validity (Cohen and Swerdlik 1999). The multi-round process of Delphi enabled the identification of problems related to judgments of the participants, as well as possible biases involved in their opinions (Arditi and Ferreira Martins 1996). The Delphi rounds were also very effective in resolving differences among the participants and addressing various issues that surfaced through participants' comments during each administration.

Limitations

The decision to involve participants from owner companies only and exclude any contractor companies from the research was based on the following considerations:

1. The objectives of the OCWS process are primarily geared towards fulfilling the needs of the owner. Therefore, this process is owner driven.

2. Contractors have an incentive to influence the owner into transferring as many competencies to the contractor as possible.

Notwithstanding these reasons, the fact that contractors were not involved in the validation effort is an important limitation of this research.

Another limitation was the absence of data that would establish a correlation between the use of the OCWS process and capital project outcomes. Collection of such data was not possible due to the limited use of the process at the time of conducting this research. These limitations are further addressed under future research.

Validation of OCWS Process

It was important to involve experienced project managers and executives in the validation effort. Invitation letters were sent to member companies of CII as well as non-CII companies that attended the 1999 CII Annual Conference. This group of companies represented a cross-section of the North American construction industry and provided a source for experienced project managers and executives. In addition to these individuals, participants in the case studies that were conducted prior to the Delphi study were also contacted. Out of the ninety individuals who were invited to participate, forty-seven participated in the study.

The design of the Delphi study was based on a series of discussions with experienced researchers and past research that used similar approaches for developing consensus (Arditi and Ferreira Martins 1996; Hartman and Baldwin 1995; Martorella 1991; Zinn 1998; Kastein et al. 1993; Raskin 1994). The design involved having each of the participants rate various aspects of the OCWS process over successive administrations or rounds of the study. The degree of agreement among the participants and the reliability of their ratings were computed at the end of each round of the study. The agreement and the reliability that were achieved at the end of the second round, and the fact that no new issues emerged at that point, suggested that a third round would not add any further value to the results.

Design of the Delphi Protocol

The first and foremost question to be addressed before commencing validation was *what* the participants needed to validate. This question was answered by developing research propositions, termed as themes, which described what the OCWS process was designed to accomplish. The themes were defined as follows:

- Theme I: The owner-contractor work relationship framework, illustrated in Figure 1, will enable project management to create optimal owner-contractor work relationships, given that all other conditions remain unchanged.
- Theme II: Steps in the OCWS process and the associated worksheets, illustrated in Figure 2, will assist owners and contractors in the creation of optimal work relationships, given that all other conditions remain unchanged.
- Theme III: Owner-contractor work relationships based on this process will contribute positively to capital project performance, given that all other conditions remain unchanged.
- Theme IV: The knowledge-base created by using this process, that is, the core/non-core classification of competencies and corresponding owner-contractor work relationships, will help owner companies to mitigate the effect of knowledge lost by way of retiring experts and the loss of experienced personnel to other companies, given that all other conditions remain unchanged.
- Theme V: This process will be useful for creating and sustaining a potentially successful strategic alliance between two firms, given that all other conditions remain unchanged.

A second question to be answered was *how* to conduct the validation. It was answered by constructing multiple statements that corroborated the proposition of each theme, and then having the participants rate each statement on a one- to seven-point Likert scale, where one represented the option strongly disagree and seven represented strongly agree.

Test-Retest Reliability of the Delphi Protocol

The response protocol for Delphi validation was tested for consistency of responses over time by conducting two administrations within a gap of three weeks to measure the test-retest reliability of the participant response protocol. Four individuals, including two graduate students and two faculty members at Texas A&M University participated in this exercise. Three of these individuals had more than five years of experience in the planning and development of capital projects. The fourth individual had no such experience. Each person's scores on the first administration of the test were related to the person's score on the second administration to provide a reliability coefficient. The Spearman rank correlation coefficient was used to measure the test-retest reliability and compare the measured values with estimated critical values at a 5 percent significance level (Tuckman 1999). The test-retest reliability measurement helped identify unreliable statements that had to be modified or deleted from the response protocol.

Delphi Validation of the OCWS Process

A key characteristic of the Delphi approach is the iterative feedback from participants in the study. At the time of commencing the Delphi study, all participants were informed that they would be required to provide input over a minimum of two and a maximum of three iterations. The upper limit of three iterations was set considering both time and effort required by the participants, and past research which suggested that two to three iterations were sufficient for achieving satisfactory results in a Delphi study (Zinn 1998; Martorella 1991). The AI and the ICC, explained earlier, were used to draw inferences regarding the outcome of each Delphi iteration and determine the need for a subsequent iteration.

Background of Participants

From the fifty-two professionals who had initially agreed to participate in the Delphi validation, forty-seven professionals representing thirty-two owner companies and two consulting companies from North America participated in the first round. The participants had an average of twenty-one years of experience in the development and execution of capital projects, with a standard deviation of eight years. The composition of the participants' expertise at various levels in the owner organization is shown in Figure 3. The terms executive management, project management, plant operations, and other were used, based on a universally recognized distinction between levels of involvement in capital project work.

The data on the participants' level of experience provided an important basis to split the participants into two subgroups; those working at the level of executive management, and those working closer to the level at which work is accomplished. Since individuals working at the latter level should be expected to have a substantially different perspective on using contract services (Gibson et al. 1998), splitting the data accordingly was considered very important. Moreover, the OCWS process has a two-level focus, one involving a project application and the other involving a corporate or capital program application. Depending on their

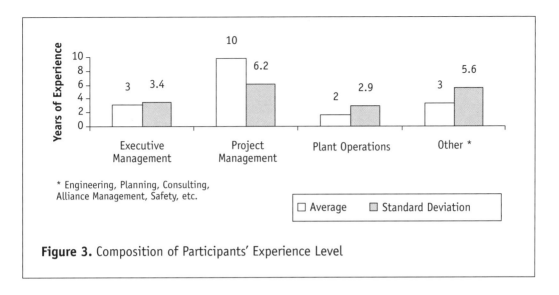

Figure 3. Composition of Participants' Experience Level

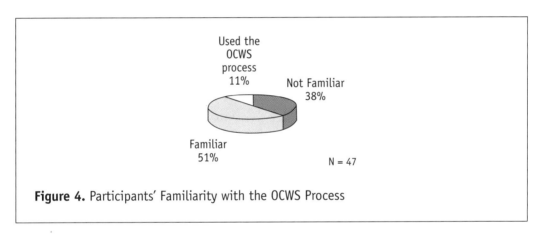

Figure 4. Participants' Familiarity with the OCWS Process

level of experience, the participants could respond differently to questions pertaining to the process. The information about participants' level of experience was used to assess whether or not differences existed in the perceptions of these two groups regarding various aspects of the OCWS process.

Another aspect of the participant characteristics that was particularly important in this research was their familiarity with the CII OCWS process. As shown in Figure 4, slightly more than half the participants indicated that they had some prior knowledge of the OCWS process, published by the CII in 1997, under the title *Owner-Contractor Work Structure Process Handbook* (Construction Industry Institute 1997). This information was used to assess whether or not there were differences in the perceptions of those that were familiar with or had used the OCWS process, and those who had no prior knowledge of the process. This background was considered very important since it served to assess if there was any bias involved in the participants' responses due to their prior knowledge of the OCWS process.

Theme Number	Mean	Standard Deviation	Agreement Index	ICC	P Value for ICC
I	5.8	0.93	0.95	0.46	0.12
II	5.6	1.02	0.97	0.88	≈ 0
III	6.0	0.84	0.95	0.96	≈ 0
IV	5.7	0.97	0.94	0.47	0.11
V	5.4	1.12	0.87	-0.17	0.43

Table 1. Summary of Round 1 Results

Analysis of Round 1 Data

A summary of data obtained from the first administration of Delphi is shown in Table 1. Each theme included between three and eleven statements that were rated by each of the forty-seven participants. The AI and ICC were used to measure participant agreement and reliability of the data, respectively. The results showed general agreement among the participants for all the themes. However, a low ICC for Themes I and IV and a negative ICC for Theme V indicated that the results lacked consistency between the participants.

The descriptive statistics suggested moderate to general agreement based on the Likert scale. The mean ratings for all themes were between five and six. The variability in terms of the standard deviation of participants' responses ranged from 0.84 to 1.12. The standard deviation for individual statements under each theme helped in identifying the statements that showed a relatively high degree of variance among the participants.

The AI ranged from 0.87 to 0.97, clearly suggesting that there was substantial agreement among the participants on the five themes. For the Themes I, IV, and V, the ICC values were unsatisfactory given a level of significance of 0.05. Also, since this was the participants' first opportunity to evaluate the OCWS process, it was possible that they had different perspectives with regard to the process and what it could accomplish. To help resolve the differences in the participants' perspectives to some extent, and to provide them with an opportunity to reconsider their first round ratings in light of the knowledge they could gain from the ratings and comments made by other participants in Round 1, another round of Delphi was used.

The second round was conducted using the same response protocol in Round 1, except the addition of one statement under Theme II. The addition of the statement was based on comments made by some participants that indicated that the strategic basis for core/non-core competency decisions had to be emphasized. In

Theme Number	Mean	Standard Deviation	Agreement Index	ICC	P Value for ICC
I	5.82	0.85	0.96	0.49	0.10
II	5.65	0.96	0.98	0.86	≈ 0
III	6.07	0.76	0.96	0.96	≈ 0
IV	5.69	0.80	0.96	0.05	0.38
V	5.46	1.08	0.88	-0.18	0.43

Table 2. Summary of Delphi Round 2 Results

addition to the response protocol, each participant was provided with an assessment of the findings of Round 1 and a comparison of his responses with the group response.

Analysis of Round 2 Data

Some attrition of the participant pool is expected in a Delphi study, due to the limited time frame in which the participants are expected to read and understand Round 1 results and complete the Round 2 response protocol. In this study, the number of participants in Round 2 dropped to forty-two.

Round 2 of the Delphi validation showed an improvement in the rating of various elements of the process by the Delphi panel. The results of Round 2 are summarized in Table 2. These results suggested that the participants in the Delphi study changed their earlier response in Round 1 to some extent, based on the knowledge they gained from Round 1 results. The mean ratings did, however, indicate that on a one to seven scale, the mean was above 6.0 only in the case of Theme III. On all other themes the mean ratings were between five and six, suggesting that the agreement was conditional. This was not a cause of concern though, since each user organization is very likely to adapt the OCWS process to fit within its own business approach.

The mean ratings for all themes increased marginally, while the standard deviations decreased in Round 2. These data suggest that the panelists rated the process more favorably in the second round, while moving closer to each other on the rating scale. The ICCs improved in Round 2 over the values in Round 1, with the exception of Theme IV. This theme dealt with the value and the utility of the information created by using the OCWS process for future projects. On this theme, some participants expressed their skepticism about the value of such information for future projects since, in their opinion, it constitutes an initial plan only. Moreover, this knowledge may not be useful since staffing and training decisions

Theme Number	Familiar with or Used the OCWS Process			Not Familiar with the OCWS Process			D.O.F.	t Statistic ($t_{0.025}$ = 1.645)
	N	μ	σ^2	N	μ	σ^2		
I	140	5.86	0.58	70	5.74	0.92	114	0.92 **
II	336	5.65	1.02	168	5.66	0.68	400	0.11 **
III	84	6.02	0.75	42	6.17	0.29	118	1.14 **
IV	140	5.71	0.67	70	5.64	0.64	141	0.54 **
V	84	5.55	1.26	42	5.29	0.89	96	1.38 **

* N = (Number of Statements under the Theme) * (Number of Participants)
** H_0 Cannot be Rejected, where H_0: Means Equal and H_1: Means Not Equal

Table 3. Statistical Comparison of Means

are driven by factors that may change over time. This realization may have persuaded the participants to change their response in the second round, leading to an increased inconsistency in responses to Theme IV.

The reliability of the results of Round 2, measured in terms of the ICC, improved in comparison with that of Round 1 for Themes I and V, stayed the same for Theme III, reduced marginally for Theme II, and reduced substantially for Theme IV. Theme II focuses on the steps in the OCWS process and the associated tools. Theme III focuses on the contribution that using the OCWS process makes to improving capital project performance. Although both agreement and reliability were satisfactory for Themes II and III, the reliability indicated by the ICC for Themes I, IV, and V was not satisfactory. Theme I focused on the owner-contractor work relationship framework, Theme IV considered the utility of knowledge base created by using the OCWS process, and Theme V dealt with the applicability of the OCWS process for creating alliances. The low reliability for Themes I, IV, and V indicated that the participants remained inconsistent in their responses to these themes despite having two opportunities to make their decision.

Additional analysis of Themes I, IV, and V concentrated on participants' familiarity with the OCWS process prior to this study, and the extent of their executive management experience. In order to assess if the participants' familiarity with the process influenced their ratings, the participants were segregated by the criteria of familiarity with the OCWS process. A statistical comparison of the means for each of these two subgroups, presented in Table 3, indicated that the means were statistically not different, suggesting that participants' familiarity with the OCWS process did not influence their rating of the process. This was an important finding since participant familiarity with the process could have biased the results.

Theme Number	With Executive Management Experience			Without Executive Management Experience			D.O.F.	t Statistic ($t_{0.025}$ = 1.645)
	N	μ	σ^2	N	μ	σ^2		
I	110	5.83	1.06	100	5.82	0.29	168	0.06
II	264	5.70	0.84	240	5.60	0.98	488	1.13
III	66	6.09	0.67	60	6.05	0.52	124	0.30
IV	110	5.82	0.63	100	5.54	0.65	205	2.52 **
V	66	5.62	1.41	60	5.28	0.82	120	1.81 **

* N = (Number of Statements under the Theme) * (Number of Participants)
** H_0 Cannot be Rejected, where H_0: Means Equal and H_1: Means Not Equal

Table 4. Statistical Comparison of Means

The possible influence of the participants' level of management experience was evaluated by stratifying the participants into two subgroups. The first group included twenty-two participants with more than two years of executive management experience. The second group included twenty participants with no executive management experience. These individuals were primarily involved in engineering, project management, and plant operations. Individuals in both groups did, however, have an average of ten years of project management experience. Table 4 provides a statistical comparison of mean ratings of the two subgroups.

Since the t-statistic for Themes IV and V was higher than the t-statistic at a significance level of 0.05 for a two-tailed analysis, the means were significantly different between the two subgroups, for these themes. This result suggests that the level of participants' experience had some influence on their ratings for these themes. A likely explanation for this difference was that individuals without executive management experience were relatively more concerned about the influence of project circumstances and conditions on decisions about capital projects. Since differences in mean ratings for the two subgroups were found to be statistically significant as shown in Table 4, further analysis was deemed necessary to test the reliability of responses *within* each subgroup for Themes I, IV, and V. The results of this analysis are shown in Table 5.

The ICCs indicated that the reliability was reasonably high for the first subgroup in Theme I, and for both subgroups in Theme V. The p-values were also satisfactory for the first subgroup under Theme I and the second subgroup under Theme V, suggesting that the probability (on repeated trials) of obtaining ICC values at least as high as 0.62 and 0.74, respectively, was higher than the significance level of 95 percent. This probability was 93 percent for the first subgroup under Theme

Theme Number	Subgroup	Agreement Index	ICC	p-Value
I	With Executive Management Experience	0.93	0.62	0.04
	Without Executive Management Experience	0.98	-0.39	0.58
IV	With Executive Management Experience	0.96	0.45	0.13
	Without Executive Management Experience	0.96	0.04	0.39
V	With Executive Management Experience	0.85	0.64	0.07
	Without Executive Management Experience	0.93	0.74	0.03

Table 5. Results of Delphi Round 2—Analysis by Subgroup for Themes I, IV, and V

V, which was marginally lower than the significance level of 95 percent that is typically used in scientific research. The reliability coefficient for the first subgroup in Theme IV was fairly low, while the reliability coefficients for the second subgroup in Theme I and the second subgroup in Theme IV were very low.

Based on these computations, the data suggested that the executive managers were consistent in their response to Theme I, while those without any executive management experience were not consistent. One possible explanation for this finding relates to the broader perspective of executive managers, placing them in a better position to understand the conceptual framework of the OCWS. In the case of Theme IV, the two subgroups, as well as the whole group are not consistent in their responses. This finding is indicative of an inherent flaw in the proposition of Theme IV; that the knowledge base created by using the OCWS process will help owner companies mitigate the effect of knowledge lost by way of retiring experts and the loss of experienced personnel to other companies.

Each of the two subgroups provided consistent responses to Theme V. However, the responses were not at all consistent when the entire participant pool was evaluated together. One possible explanation for this inconsistency could be that the two groups viewed alliances differently, given that the term "alliance" was not defined in the response protocols. The participants' comments did not offer other explanations for the inconsistent overall response to Theme V.

In summary, the data provided evidence to suggest that based on reliability considerations, Theme IV could not be considered valid. Also, Themes I and IV evoked a different response from those with executive management experience and those without such experience.

Results of the Delphi Study

The Delphi rounds suggested that some propositions or themes about the applicability and usefulness of the process were valid, while others were not entirely valid. Although this observation is based on the assumption that the statements under each theme were accurate measures for the respective themes, no attempt was made to introduce new statements for two reasons: 1) Comments made by the participants in support of their numeric ratings did not suggest the need for introducing new statements; and 2) The AIs were reasonably high for all themes, including the ones with low or negative ICCs. The following results provided the evidence regarding validity of the five themes:

- The mean ratings for each theme ranged from 5.46 to 6.07, suggesting that the participants were in moderate to complete agreement with the themes.
- AIs for the five themes were between 0.96 and 0.98, with the exception of Theme V, which had an agreement index of 0.88, which is also very high.
- The ICC was 0.86 and 0.96 for Themes II and III, respectively. Although the ICC was low and unacceptable for Themes I, IV, and V, additional analyses identified satisfactory ICCs for one subgroup under Theme I and both subgroups under Theme V. Theme IV, however, failed the reliability criteria.
- No new issues that would lead to changes in the OCWS process steps or tools emerged in the Delphi rounds. This suggested that the participants did not envisage further changes to the OCWS process.

These results eliminated the need for conducting another Delphi round or for making any changes in the OCWS process steps and tools. Therefore, it was concluded that with the exception of Theme IV, the OCWS process constituted a valid approach for creating and sustaining well-aligned owner-contractor work relationships.

Conclusions

The Delphi approach for validating the OCWS process led to the following conclusions:

- Theme II was validated. The steps and tools in the OCWS process can assist owner companies in the formation of optimal work relationships with designers, contractors, suppliers, and consultants.
- Theme III was validated. Using the OCWS process is likely to contribute positively to capital project performance.
- Non-executive managers were not consistent in their response to Theme I. This suggests that it may be more difficult for this group to relate to the OCWS conceptual framework, since they may not have a top management perspective.
- Theme IV could not be validated. Therefore, the OCWS process may not help owner companies mitigate the effect of knowledge lost due to retiring experts and the loss of experienced personnel to other companies.

■ Theme V evoked consistent responses from executive managers and others. However, the two groups were not consistent when combined together. Therefore, executive managers and non-executive managers differ in their perspective on the use of OCWS for structuring alliances. Their comments did not identify the specific issues that might have caused the ICCs to be different for the two subgroups.

In summary, the OCWS process constitutes a valid approach to encourage discussion, consensus, definition, and decisions while developing owner-contractor work relationships for capital projects. It may not, however, help owner companies mitigate the effect of knowledge lost by way of retiring experts and the loss of experienced personnel to other companies. In terms of its suitability as a process for creating and sustaining potentially successful alliances, executive managers and project managers differed in their perspectives, suggesting that the proposition was conditional and hence, could not be validated conclusively. Given the problems with understanding the implications of an outsourcing relationship, it is evident that an approach such as the OCWS process would improve the development and execution of capital projects.

Future Research

As identified previously, when discussing the limitations of the OCWS process approach, future research in this area should focus on the perceptions of contractor organizations with regard to owner-contractor work relationships. A separate research investigation at CCIS is currently targeting this topic. Most capital projects involve multiple contractors with different and possibly conflicting motivations. Although the OCWS process was conceived as an owner-driven process, complete validation of the process would require that the contractors' perceptions be fully addressed. Aligning owners' and contractors' perceptions, with regard to the approach for developing better work relationships, should, therefore, be the focus of future research in this area.

Measuring the effectiveness of the OCWS process is another area of future research. Establishing a correlation between the use of the OCWS process and capital project outcomes would provide a measure of what the owners and contractors stand to gain from using the OCWS process. In order to accomplish this objective, it would be necessary to identify measurable characteristics of owner-contractor work relationships as well as capital project outcomes. The OCWS framework provides such characteristics of the owner-contractor work relationships in the form of the five relationship types namely OP, OP/CI, OL/CP, CP/OI, and CP. Capital project outcomes can be characterized by four widely used measures in the industry; safety, cost, schedule, and operational performance. Benchmarking projects from an owner-contractor work relationship perspective would provide valuable insights into how these relationships evolve over time and the influence they have on capital project effectiveness. Relationship measures and capital project effectiveness are currently under investigation in two ongoing investigations at CCIS.

Another area of study should be focused on demographic changes within the industry. This is currently being investigated through a human resource survey and United States Census data evaluation at CCIS. Significant changes in the demographic makeup of the industry will drive changes in the OCWS framework.

A final area of future research would involve an assessment of the relationship between the general contractor and subcontractors. Although the OCWS framework can be theoretically extended to this relationship, the effectiveness and validity of that approach must be assessed before using it for that purpose.

References

Anderson, Stuart D., Shekhar S. Patil, and G. Edward Gibson, Jr. 2000. *Developing Optimal Owner-Contractor Work Structures—Case Studies*. Austin, TX: Center for Construction Industry Studies, University of Texas at Austin.

Arditi, D., and E. A. Ferreira Martins. 1996. Acquisition, Representation and Validation of Subjective Knowledge. *Microcomputers in Civil Engineering* 11 (4): 239–248.

Bravo, Gina, and Louise Potvin. 1991. Estimating the Reliability of Continuous Measures with Cronbach's Alpha or the Intraclass Correlation Coefficient: Toward the Integration of Two Traditions. *Journal of Clinical Epidemiology* 44 (4/5): 381–390.

Cohen, Ronald J., and Mark E. Swerdlik. 1999. *Psychological Testing and Assessment*. Mountain View, California: Mayfield Publishing Company.

Construction Industry Institute (CII). 1997. *Owner/Contractor Work Structure Process Handbook*. (Implementation Resource 111–2). Austin, TX: University of Texas at Austin.

Dalkey, Norman C. 1969. *The Delphi Method: An Experimental Study of Group Opinion* (RM-5888-PR). The Rand Corporation.

Dalkey, N. C., and O. Helmer. 1963. An Experimental Application of the Delphi Method to the Use of Experts. *Management Science* 9 (3): 458–67.

Gibson, G. Edward, Jr. et al. 1998. *Owner/Contractor Organizational Changes—Phase I Report*. Austin, TX: Sloan Program for the Construction Industry, University of Texas at Austin.

Hartman, Francis T., and Andrew Baldwin. 1995. Using Technology to Improve Delphi Method. *Journal of Computing in Civil Engineering* 9 (4): 244–249.

James, Lawrence R., Robert G. Demaree, and Gerrti Wolf. 1984. Estimating Within-Group Interrater Reliability with and without Response Bias. *Journal of Applied Psychology* 69 (1): 85–98.

———. 1993. RWG: An Assessment of Within-Group Interrater Agreement. *Journal of Applied Psychology* 78 (2): 306–309.

Kastein, Marcel R. et al. 1993. Delphi, the Issue of Reliability. A Qualitative Delphi Study in Primary Health Care in the Netherlands. *Technological Forecasting and Social Change* 44: 315–323.

Kozlowski, Steve W. J., and Keith Hattrup. 1992. A Disagreement About Within-Group Agreement: Disentangling Issues of Consistency versus Consensus. *Journal of Applied Psychology* 77 (2): 161–167.

Linstone, Harold A., and Murray Turoff, eds. 1975. *The Delphi Method: Techniques and Applications*. Massachusetts: Addison Wesley Publishing Company.

McGraw, Kenneth O., and S. P. Wong. 1996. Forming Inferences About Some Intraclass Correlation Coefficients. *Psychological Methods* 1 (1): 30–46.

Martorella, Peter H. 1991. Consensus Building among Social Educators: A Delphi Study. *Theory and Research in Social Education* XIX (Winter): 83–94.

Mitchell, Sandra K. 1979. Interobserver Agreement, Reliability, and Generalizability of Data Collected in Observational Studies. *Psychological Bulletin* 86 (2): 376–390.

Nunnally, Jum C., and Ira H. Bernstein. 1994. *Psychometric Theory*. New York: McGraw-Hill.

Raskin, Miriam S. 1994. The Delphi Study in Field Instruction Revisited: Expert Consensus on Issues and Research Priorities. *Journal of Social Work Education* 30 (Winter): 75–89.

Shrout, Patrick E., and Joseph L. Fleiss. 1979. Intraclass Correlations: Uses in Assessing Interrater Reliability. *Psychological Bulletin* 86 (2): 420–428.

Sullivan, George R., Miguel A. Yupari, and Stuart D. Anderson. 1997. *Owner/Contractor Work Structure: A Process Approach*. (Research Report 111-11). Austin, TX: University of Texas at Austin/The Construction Industry Institute.

Tuckman, Bruce W. 1999. *Conducting Educational Research*. 5th ed. Fort Worth: Harcourt Brace College Publishers.

Zinn, Jacqueline. 1998. Use of the Delphi Panel Method to Develop Consensus on Laboratory Performance Indicators. *Clinical Laboratory Management Review* 12 (2): 97–105.

CHAPTER 23

PROJECT STAKEHOLDER MAPPING: ANALYZING THE INTERESTS OF PROJECT STAKEHOLDERS[1]

Graham M. Winch, Ph.D.—UMIST
Sten Bonke, Ph.D., M.A.—Technical University of Denmark

Introduction

This chapter draws on theories of the social construction of technology to present a methodology aimed at enabling the better understanding, and hence management, of the definition of the project mission that explicitly addresses the inherently politicized nature of decision-making at this stage of the project life cycle. It therefore offers a complement to the better-known capital budgeting and cost-benefit analysis techniques that are frequently deployed to aid project scope definition. Through the presentation of three case studies of major construction projects, it presents two tools—the stakeholder map and the power/interest matrix—as tools for facilitating the more rigorous analysis of potential threats to the project arising from stakeholder activities. The three case studies are the development of farming in southern Egypt, the rebuilding of the Beirut, Lebanon central district following fifteen years of civil war, and the rebuilding of Montserrat in the West Indies following a devastating volcanic eruption.

The management of project stakeholders is a task of growing importance for project managers (Calvert 1995). Understanding their interests and relative power is vital for the effective management of the inception stages of many projects as the scope is defined. This chapter will build on research that developed an innovative stakeholder mapping approach to understand the management of Denmark's Storebælt project, which linked Zealand to the European mainland for the first time. The model maps stakeholders in terms of problems, solutions, and artifacts and then locates them on the power/interest matrix.

The approach, which regards technologies as socially constructed, concentrates on mapping the different stakeholders, what their interests are, and the likely compromises on scope definition that they would accept to allow the project to go forward. Thus, the roles of different national government ministries; politicians; clients; environmental groups; local winners and losers; and other project actors can all be mapped as a way of understanding how different project options are evaluated and a compromise is reached. Failure to achieve compromise typically leads to the cancellation of the project. After introducing the approach, the chapter will go on to apply it to the three projects—the Toshka project in the south of Egypt; the rebuilding of Beirut by SOLIDERE; and the housing program launched on the island of Montserrat following the devastating volcanic eruption of 1997.

Defining the Project Mission

The identification of a clear mission for the project is widely considered to be essential for the effective management of projects—indeed it can be considered one of the five principal project management processes (Winch 2000). However, the complexity of client organizations and the social, economic, and regulatory environments in which they operate, coupled with the absence of adequate quantitative project appraisal tools, means that the strategic definition of the project mission is inevitably politicized, and many project missions are the outcomes of complex negotiations and trade-offs (Winch 2002). The case studies by Hall (1980) show how decision-making around public sector projects is a complex trade-off between political, social, and economic interests, while Law and Callon (1992) pun the description of the TSR2 aircraft as a "variable geometry" aircraft due to the way in which it meant different things to different stakeholders. More recently, such a trade-off has become even more difficult with the emergence of principled opposition on environmental grounds and the consequent placing of the legitimacy of existing fora for handling such decisions in question. In such cases the trade-off process itself can be a major project management exercise in its own right, as the planning inquiry into London Heathrow's Terminal 5 shows.

These problems are, perhaps, most severe in the realm of the provision of public assets, because no clear economic criteria for the supply and distribution of such assets exist (Hall 1980, 189). Some projects, such as Mitterand's *grands projets*, appear to be entirely politically driven (Chaslin 1985). A recent development has been to privatize such projects through the development of concession contracting, which in turn has led to the recent rapid increase in the project finance market. The effect of this is that financiers become direct stakeholders in the management of the project, and the allocation of risks associated with the project, a matter for complex negotiation (Beidleman, Fletcher, and Veshosky 1990).

Purely private sector projects face similar problems. The context of the Eagle technology project was politicized within Data General, as the company moved its research and development functions from Boston to North Carolina (Kidder 1982). Kodak's Factory of the Future project was abandoned as a coherent vision that met the interests of all the stakeholders but could not be articulated (Bowen et al. 1994). The London Stock Exchange's Taurus project threatened the very existence of the registrars who keep records of share deals by proposing a central register. A compromise reached in 1989 provided for a decentralized system, but at the cost of a much higher level of complexity. Regulatory demands for high levels of security and opposition from small stockbrokers who feared the system would reinforce the dominance of the large banks led to its abandonment (Drummond 1996). As the former chief executive of the Stock Exchange stated, "Taurus meant an awful lot of different things to different people, it was the absolute lack of clarity as to its definition at the front that I think was its Achilles' heel" (*Financial Times* 3/7/95).

The purpose of this chapter is to present a methodology aimed at enabling the better understanding, and hence management, of the definition of a project's mission that explicitly addresses the inherently politicized nature of decision-making at this stage of the project life cycle. It therefore offers a complement to the better-known capital budgeting and cost-benefit analysis techniques that are frequently deployed to aid project definition. In essence, it addresses the generation of alternative definitions of the project mission, rather than the formal evaluation of the merits of alternatives. It is proposed that the methodology is most appropriately used at project inception. The use case is likely to be a small group-brainstorming session led by the client's project manager, organized with the objective of identifying possible opponents to the project who might be in a position to disrupt progress, thereby generating program and budget variances. The stakeholder map and power/interest matrix are proposed as tools for increasing the effectiveness of such sessions and facilitating the more rigorous analysis of the potential threats to the project.

An Approach to Stakeholder Mapping

The conceptual framework of stakeholder mapping demonstrated in this chapter is inspired by theories of social constructivism, typically known as the Social Construction of Technology (SCOT), developed and applied by Bijker and Pinch (1987), among others, in a considerable number of technology analyses. In relation to large construction projects, the mapping method was tentatively applied in an attempt to comprehend the peculiarities of technology solutions on the Storebælt fixed link project in Denmark (Bonke 1996).

Theories regarding technology as being socially constructed basically see technological development as arising from negotiations between different social actors, organized in "relevant social groups," each having their own comprehension of the problems to be solved and of the solutions available. Contrary to the linear projection of conventional technology models, this approach is multidimensional, making it possible to consider the development of a technological project as an alternation between *variation* and *selection*. Thus, as experienced in practice by most project managers, the unruly process of fixing and maintaining definite and consistent project objectives is at the very core of social constructivism. Rational technical arguments do not by themselves carry weight in the project definition process—only in the hands of a relevant, dedicated, and powerful stakeholder does rationality achieve the meaning of "universal importance" which governs the project through its life cycle.

SCOT theory's main conceptual relations are covered by the terms *artifact*, *relevant social group*, and *technological frame*. The artifact is the technological object, be it material or immaterial, toward which the actors in a SCOT analysis are orientated. In this context the artifact equals the *project mission*. Correspondingly the relevant social group represents a *project stakeholder*. Finally, technological frame defines the scope of a social group's actions and articulates the preferred technological solutions in terms of *problems* and preferred *solutions*.

Obviously, identifying the complete set of stakeholders is of great importance to the validity and usefulness of the mapping method. During this process all stakeholders must be identified, not on the basis of *a priori* distinctions between, for instance, technicians and economists, professionals and lay people, but rather from the perspective that any actor who possesses an interest in the project and the solutions to its problems should be considered a relevant stakeholder.

The technological frame of a stakeholder originates in the predominant practices, theories, tactics, political and economic goals, and means that characterize and are shared by specific stakeholders. It is then crucial for the manager of a project to realize that each stakeholder will be interpreting the project differently—that the artifact is constituted by as many meanings as there are relevant social groups. And this *interpretative flexibility* can be revealed by tracing the different meanings attributed to the project by the different stakeholders.

Normally, the interpretative flexibility of a project is easily demonstrated by its deconstruction into several alternative projects, each of which can be associated with the specific stakeholders. For instance, the construction of a fixed link across a sound, simultaneously represents turnover and profit for contractors, and increased pollution for environmentalist groups. This flexibility exists until consensus concerning the meaning of a project between different stakeholders occurs. The pluralism of the project then disappears into a *closure* as the project mission is defined (Haugbølle Hansen 1993).

Whether and when closure takes place will depend, in part, upon the degree of *stability* within each stakeholder's comprehension of the project. For instance, if stability is low and confronted by powerful actors, the closure may be of a purely rhetorical nature. Closure may also be achieved through a redefinition of the problems and solutions linked to the project, for instance through favoring public transport on a fixed link project (Bonke 1998). As demonstrated in technology studies, closure mechanisms will often occur through technological and organizational innovations, under constraint, through negotiations based on convincing or well-founded argumentation, or via loss of interest by one of the stakeholders (Misa 1992).

Closure and stability consequently should be regarded as two aspects of the same question. The concept of closure focuses on the different meanings that relevant stakeholders associate with the project. Stability focuses on the development of a specific stakeholders' comprehension of the project. As indicated above, the implication of closure is that interpretative flexibility disappears—that one comprehension becomes dominant while others vanish. In the dynamic project perspective the dominant comprehension then gradually pervades other stakeholders' interpretation of the project, thereby letting the project definition process progress. While in principle, it is possible to reopen negotiations about the meaning of a project at any stage; in practice closure is an almost irreversible process.

Analyzing the Stakeholder Map

Once the stakeholder map is prepared, it can be analyzed using a power/interest matrix (Johnson and Scholes 1999, 2002). There are two dimensions to the matrix—the level of interest of the stakeholder in the project and the stakeholder's power to influence the definition of the project mission. These yield the four basic categorizations of stakeholders shown in Figure 1.

Those in category A require minimal effort, but should still be watched in case their power or interest rises as circumstances change. Those in category B need to be kept informed of progress and, because many of those who hold alternative definitions of the project mission may be in this category, be treated with diplomacy. Again, signs that stakeholders here may gain power need to be watched for. Those in category C need to be kept satisfied. Often this group will include second-tier financiers who treat the project simply as another investment opportunity—their power over the project is considerable, but their interest may be fairly low, as they would simply remove their finance if not satisfied. Into this category also go those hired by the client to execute the project. While such stakeholders—particularly designers and financial advisors—may have considerable influence over the project mission, they are likely to be treating the project as one of many on which they are involved. They are also often insured against major project failures, or—more frequently in the case of contractors—will be using portfolio techniques to spread risks associated with the project. The final group (D) are the key players—those committed totally to the project, such as the client; the first-tier financiers; and those on the supply side who are betting their company on the project for one reason or another.

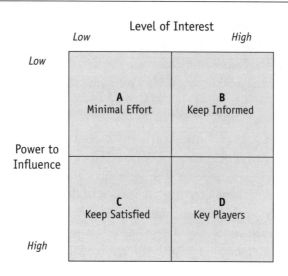

Figure 1. Categorization of Stakeholders
(Johnson and Scholes 1999, 2002—Reprinted with Permission from Pearson Education Limited)

The degree of *integration* of the stakeholder map will make a large difference in its manageability. If the stakeholders are at the far corners of Figure 1, then the definition process is likely to be turbulent and the process map unstable. If the stakeholders are clustered near the center of Figure 1, then the map will appear as relatively stable. The dispersion of the different stakeholders in the power/interest matrix will indicate the options of maneuverability in the project manager's decision and planning processes and the ability to broker compromise by renegotiating the project mission.

The Case Studies

Our argument now turns to illustrating the use of the stakeholder mapping methodology through three case illustrations. Two are major development projects with profound importance for the future of the two countries concerned. They are taken from the work of Hobballah (1998) and El-Missiri (1999), respectively. The third is much smaller in scale, but one in which the stakes are no less high for that country. It is taken from the work of Weekes (1999). These research reports were updated using The Financial Times Limited website (http://www.ft.com). Figure 2 provides the code to the stakeholder maps. The *internal* stakeholders are those who are members of the project coalition or providing finance; the *external* ones are those others affected by the project in a significant way (Calvert 1995).

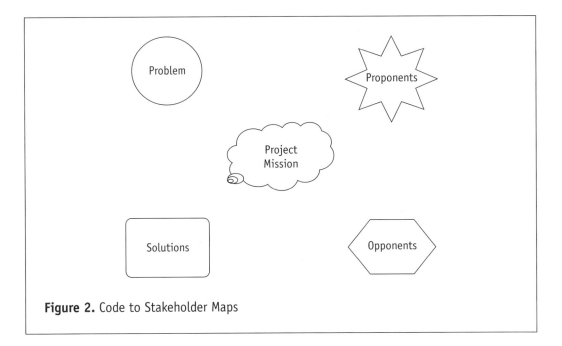

Figure 2. Code to Stakeholder Maps

SOLIDERE: Redeveloping Beirut's Central District

By 1991, over fifteen years of civil war had left the central district of Beirut in ruins. Formerly the most cosmopolitan commercial and cultural district in the Middle East, Beirut's Central District (BCD) was to be redeveloped with the aim of regaining its former role in the regional economic and social life. The master plan was developed by the Egyptian firm of consulting engineers, Dar Al-Handasah, with a scope including:

■ Responsibility for a total area of 1.8 million square meters of prime real estate

■ Reclamation of 608,000 square meters of unofficial landfill on the coast—the Reclaimed Land

■ Provision of a modern urban infrastructure of roads, parks, and telecommunications

■ Restoration of those existing buildings that were not beyond saving and were of historical value—the Retained Buildings

■ Extension of the *corniche* and the provision of two marinas

■ Reconstruction and expansion of the traditional *souks*.

There were two main problems that influenced the choice of organization for the project. First, the financial and managerial resources of Lebanon at the end of the war were completely inadequate to the challenges of delivering this master plan. Second, Lebanese property rights meant that the former tenants of the ruined buildings had the right to take up their tenancies again at the pre-war levels of rent. A further, but less intractable, problem was that many of the surviving buildings were "squatted" by those dislocated by the war, those to whom the country had a moral obligation. For these reasons, a private company was incorporated in 1994—the Société Libanaise pour le Développement et la Reconstruction du Centre Ville de Beyrouth (SOLIDERE)—as concessionaire for the redevelopment works. Essentially a form of public/private partnership, SOLIDERE had the right to:

- Expropriate land and buildings in return for A-class shares in its equity
- Raise equity capital through the sale of B-class shares to Lebanese nationals and firms, and some other categories of Middle Eastern investors—the Eligible Persons
- Raise loan capital on the international markets
- Make profits on the sale and rental of its assets
- Be exempt from taxes on its profits for ten years, while its shareholders are exempt from taxes on their dividends and capital gains for the same period.

The scale of the project is indicated by the fact that the final capitalization of SOLIDERE is equivalent to roughly one third of the total gross domestic product (GDP) of Lebanon. It is broken down into three main phases:

1. 1994–9—stabilization of the landfill, completion of infrastructure works in the traditional central district, and restoration of the Retained Buildings.

2. 2000–9—infrastructure work on the Reclaimed Land and further development of traditional central district.

3. 2010–19—development of the Reclaimed Land.

The first phase of the project is over both program and budget, but within the bounds of available finance. The main program slippages are due to the extent of the archaeological program and problems with the stabilization of the landfill, while the principal sources of budget variances are the squatter relocation program and the restoration of the Retained Buildings.

The stakeholder map for the project is shown in Figure 3. The principal *internal* stakeholders are:

- Class A shareholders, who are angry at the expropriation of their property and its alleged undervaluation by the Appraisal Committee.
- Class B shareholders, whose principal aim is a return on their capital.
- The project sponsor—the Lebanese government. Allied to this group are the former President Hariri, who is himself the largest B-class shareholder and an owner of construction firms, and pro-government political groups. The concern of this stakeholder is the revival of Beirut as an international commercial center and the economic benefits that entail. Hariri played a crucial champion role in the incorporation of SOLIDERE.

The principal *external* stakeholders are:

- The international community, in the shape of many Western leaders and the United Nations (UN) who are openly backing the project as a major contribution to political stability in the region.
- International merchant banks, providing loan capital.
- The Lebanese Order of Engineers (LOE), voicing concerns over the lack of accountability of SOLIDERE.

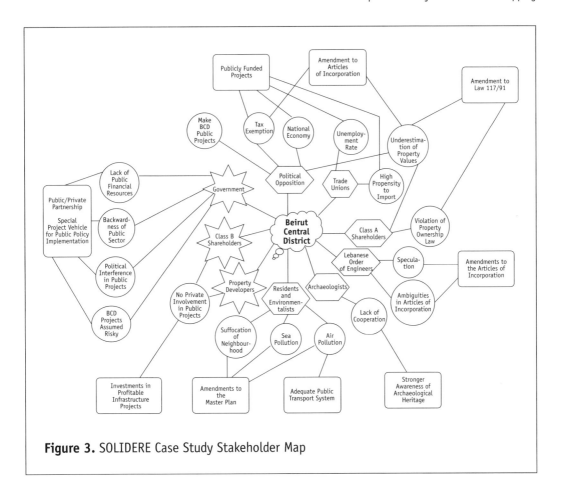

Figure 3. SOLIDERE Case Study Stakeholder Map

- Local banks, which are financing individual property developments.
- The national and international archaeological community, concerned about capturing the heritage of the area.
- Residents and environmentalists, particularly concerned with the land reclamation aspects of the project and the lack of mass transport in the scheme.
- Property developers.
- The political opposition, consisting of various left-wing, religious, and nationalist parties, voicing concerns about the use of a public-private partnership, tax holidays, and the up-market character of the developments.
- Trade unions, concerned about the use of cheap foreign workers in the construction.

Figure 4 shows the power/interest matrix for the BCD project. It shows how the key players are the class B shareholders, the Lebanese government itself, and the property developers who will carry out the individual developments once the infrastructure is provided. President Hariri lost a vote of confidence in December 1998, and since then there have been worries about government support for SOLIDERE. The class B shareholders and property developers dissatisfaction with the progress of the project recently led to the share-price of SOLIDERE dropping

	Level of Interest	
	Low	High
Low	Local Banks, International Community	Class A Shareholders, Trade Unions, LOE, Political Opposition, Archaeologists, Residents, Environmentalists
Power to Influence		
High	International Banks	Class B Shareholders, Lebanese Government, Property Developers

Figure 4. SOLIDERE Case Study Power/Interest Matrix

to a nadir by September 1999 on low profits due to an economic slowdown and continuing tension with Israel. International property developers such as Prince Alwaleed have engaged in protracted negotiations before agreeing to invest.

The international banks are happy so long as their loans are secure. A number of groups have a high interest, but the political balance of power nullifies the ability of the trade unions, the political opposition, and the LOE to lobby for stronger government control over SOLIDERE, and the class A shareholders to obtain relief for their grievances. The government of Salim el-Hoss has so far not attempted to alter the structure of SOLIDERE. The archaeological community has received concessions, but little has been offered to environmentalists and residents. However, the failure by SOLIDERE to protect some of the retained buildings is presently the subject of litigation. While the international community wishes the project well, supported by high-profile visits from the likes of Jacques Chirac and Kofi Annan, they have relatively little interest in the project as such. The local banks would in any case find investments for their funds without the intervention of SOLIDERE.

Toshka: Greening Al-Sae'ed

The Nile River is fundamental to the economy of Egypt and its lower valley is one of the most intensively farmed regions of the world. Yet only 5.5 percent of Egypt's total area is inhabited—most is desert—and some 40 percent of the population is crammed into the two principal cities of Cairo and Alexandria. For centuries the people of Egypt have lived by the rhythm of the river. Attempts by the Egyptians to manage the river more proactively began with the completion of the

Aswan Dam in 1901, and the Aswan High Dam in 1971; the latter also providing 2.1 million kilowatts of hydroelectric power generation capacity. The massive lake behind Aswan High Dam is known as Lake Nasser in Egypt and Lake Nubia in the Sudan. In 1978, a 22 km overflow canal—the Makhar Toshka—was completed, and used for the first time in the floods of 1996 by dumping millions of litres of water into the Monkhafad Toshka, a depression in the Western Desert to the northwest of Lake Nasser.

In the sixties and seventies, feasibility studies showed that the Monkhafad Toshka area was suitable for reclamation for agricultural use, and proposals were developed for the provision of the irrigation that would be required there, in one of the most inhospitable environments in Africa. However, Egypt was unable to obtain financing for such a project without the security of peace with Israel, which was secured in 1979. The main features of the Toshka irrigation project that would deliver 5.5 billion cubic meters of irrigation water each year to 226,700 hectares are:

- A 70 km main canal—the Sheikh Zayed Canal
- A massive pumping station located 8 km north of the Makhar Toshka— the Mubarak Pumping Station—to pump water from Lake Nasser into the main canal
- Four branch canals totalling 199 km
- Road infrastructure.

Construction work started at the beginning of 1997, with completion due at the end of 2001—the total budget is in the region of £770m, and the project is broadly on program. It is financed by the Egyptian government through internal resources and Arab development funds. Once the irrigation and infrastructure systems are completed, private Egyptian and foreign Arab investors have been offered a variety of incentives to make the agricultural investments, ranging from tax breaks to subsidised power. The World Bank is providing a further $200 million for land reclamation. Irrigation water will be provided to the farms free of charge. The project is strongly championed by President Mubarak. The irrigation project is the cornerstone of the £53.1 bn South Valley Development Project, which is expected to lead to 3 million people transferring to the region by 2017. It is one of five current megaprojects aimed at developing Egypt.

As shown in Figure 5, the principal *internal* stakeholders are:

- The Government of Egypt, which sees the project as the solution to Egypt's problems of population growth and overcrowding in the Nile River Valley. These include high levels of unemployment, massive imports of major foodstuffs, and the rise of fundamentalist politics amongst the urban *lumpenproletariat*.
- The agricultural investors. Principal amongst these is Prince Alwaleed, the nephew of King Faud of Saudi Arabia and the world's richest businessmen. Other major investors include the governments of the United Arab Emirates and Qatar—the main canal is named after the head of state of the former— and two private groups of Egyptian businessmen.

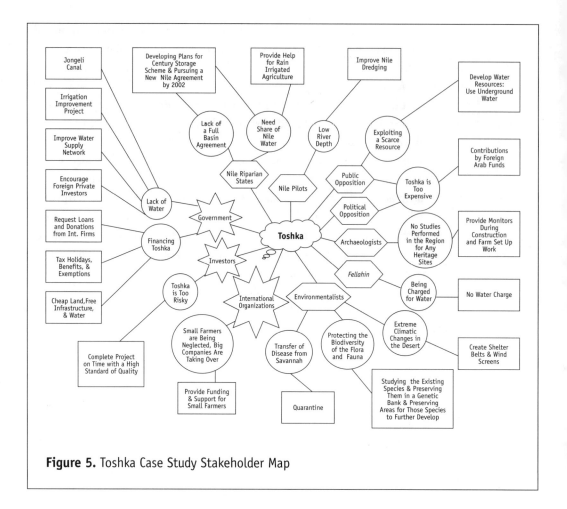

Figure 5. Toshka Case Study Stakeholder Map

The principal *external* stakeholders are:

■ The principal Nile riparian states. The treaties of 1929 and 1959 govern the sharing of the waters of the Nile between the riparian states. However, these are, in essence, agreements between Egypt and the Sudan, and have never been recognised by Ethiopia. Yet Ethiopia accounts for 85 percent of all water flowing into the Nile down the Blue Nile. One attempt to counter this problem was the construction of the 360 km Jongeli Canal through the Sudd swamps in southern Sudan where 90 percent of the volume of the White Nile is lost to evaporation, which started in 1976. However, the civil war in the Sudan led to its abandonment in 1984 after 267 km had been completed.

■ The other riparian states—Burundi, Tanzania, Uganda, and Eritrea—have their own plans for hydroelectric developments, but these are presently disrupted by wars and other problems.

■ Egyptian political opposition groups, principally the New Wafd Party, argue that the resources invested could have been put to much better use elsewhere in the country. However, the ruling National Democratic Party of Mubarak holds 95 percent of the seats in the legislature.

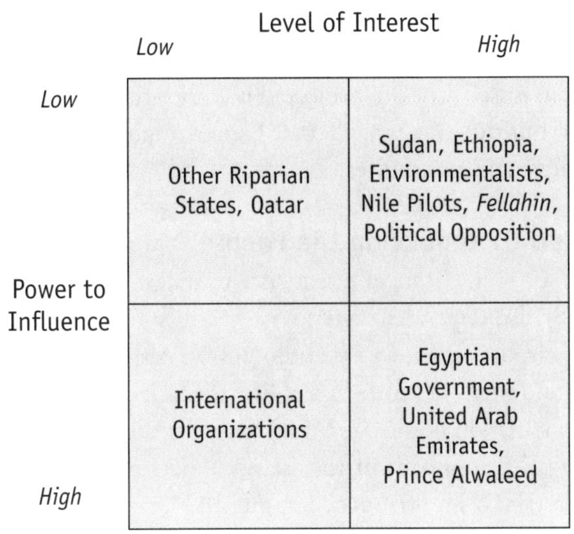

Figure 6. Toshka Case Study Power/Interest Matrix

- The Nile River pilots fear that the loss of 10 percent of the flow due to its diversion for irrigation will lead to navigation problems. These could be reduced by dredging.
- The *fellahin*—farmers of the lower Nile valley—fear that their own agriculture will be damaged and that they will be charged for water.
- International agencies, particularly Japanese and Arab development funds and the United Nations Food and Agriculture Organization, are supporting the development, providing both aid and advice.
- The environmentalists' principle fear is that the removal of the desert barrier will create a route for parasites and diseases from tropical Africa to move north to the Mediterranean coast. They have some support in the Egyptian Environment Ministry. These problems could be met by introducing a quarantine regime to control the movement of organic products, but this runs counter to the assurances given to the agricultural investors regarding their freedom to exploit the new farmland.

Figure 6 shows the power/interest matrix for the Toshka project. The key players are the Egyptian government and the principal agricultural investors, although Qatar's power is lower than the others due to its history of poor diplomatic relations with Egypt. Government support for the project remains strong. The political dominance of the governing party neutralizes the power of the opponents of the project within Egypt. Environmentalists have at this point voiced little concern regarding the project, while the archaeological dimension is unknown and has not been raised. The political tension between Egypt, the Sudan, and Ethiopia remains acute. There are also military and political issues among the primary countries. A significant change in the political situation could place either Sudan or Ethiopia in the high power category and/or frighten off investors. International aid agencies are central to the finance of the project and need to be kept satisfied regarding mission of the project. The other riparian states presently show little interest, but there are worries that Eritrea might become more proactive once its political situation stabilizes.

Montserrat: Rehousing the People

In June 1997, the start of a sequence of major volcanic eruptions left two thirds of the British dependent territory of Montserrat uninhabitable—including the capital, airport, and docks (Patullo 2000). Although the eruption had been predicted, and there was little loss of life, the lack of contingency planning left most of the population homeless. Many went abroad; the rest lived in tents and public buildings in the north of the island. The Immediate Housing Development Program (IHDP) was launched in July 1997, with the appointment of Brown and Root as construction managers, to house 1,000 people as soon as possible. As of August 1999, the IHDP was well behind time and over budget, and as late as March 2000, there were still few people living in temporary accommodation.

The IHPD was organized into three phases:

- Davy Hill—fifty prefabricated houses provided by International Building Systems (IBS) of the United States (US)
- Lookout Phase 1—fifty blockhouses designed by a local architect and built by local contractors
- Lookout Phase 2—fifty blockhouses and 100 Force-10 prefabricated houses sourced from Australia.

The IBS houses proved to be completely unsuitable for the Montserrat environment because the sealants melted in the heat and the houses therefore leaked when it rained. The use of local contractors for the first phase of blockhouses caused many problems due to their lack of skills in managing the building process, especially when all materials had to be imported. The decision by Brown and Root to strip all topsoil instead of using strip foundations led to extensive erosion of the steeply sloping site during heavy rains. The Force-10 houses were poorly adapted to the sloping site, leaving only one door usable, and instilling worries about uplift during the inevitable hurricanes. More generally, the houses were well below the standards expected by the population, and tended to be one-bedroom when the overwhelming requirement was for two-bedroom properties. None conformed to local building regulations. Waste was discharged from the sites into the sea within the tidal area at one of the only two beaches with the potential for tourist development.

The stakeholders on the IHPD project, mapped in Figure 7, are:

- The Department for International Development (DfID), the responsible UK ministry, which financed the project to fulfill its responsibilities to the UK dependent territory.

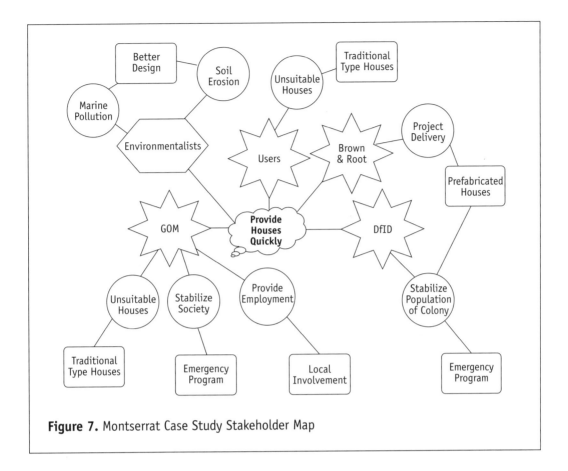

Figure 7. Montserrat Case Study Stakeholder Map

- Brown and Root, appointed as construction managers in July 1997 on a New Engineering Contract type 5 for an initial budget of £6.5m.
- The Government of Montserrat (GoM), with the overriding need to rebuild the country.
- The users, i.e., the homeless population, very dissatisfied with the quality of the houses provided and delays in provision.
- Environmentalists, concerned about the inappropriate construction techniques and treatment of waste.

The power/interest matrix for the project is illustrated in Figure 8. The research revealed considerable confusion amongst representatives of the project coalition as to who the client for the project was—DfID or GoM. Different interpretations of the role of Brown and Root were also reported, particularly whether they bore any of the risks associated with the project. This matter is presently the subject of litigation. However, analysis shows that the key player is DfID—the GoM was simply informed that Brown and Root had been appointed. Brown and Root has high power but low interest—this is simply another construction project for them. The other stakeholders fall into the high interest/low power category. Even the GoM has little say in what goes on. Their pressure to localize construction led to the second phase being awarded to local construction firms, but this proved to

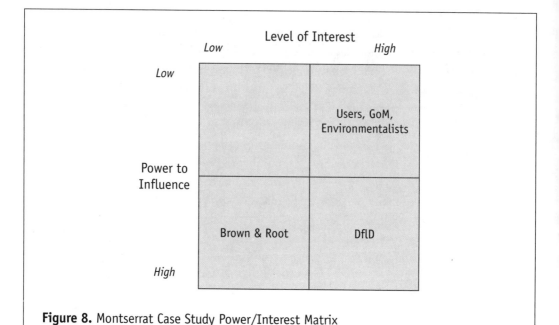

Figure 8. Montserrat Case Study Power/Interest Matrix

cause serious problems in progress, and even the design by the local architect was criticized. In the third phase, the local industry reverted to its role as a source of labor only. The long-suffering people of Montserrat—the users—are those with the highest interest, but least power.

Discussion

These are three very different projects, but the stakeholder analysis approach that we have developed yields insights into the dynamics of each project. Two of the projects might be called TINA projects ("there is no alternative," in Mrs. Thatcher's famous words)—BCD and IHDP. There is, therefore, no opposition to the project mission as such, but to the details of its implementation. In these cases it is clear that those who have lost the most—the residents of the areas devastated by the "horsemen of the apocalypse"—have the least say in the development and implementation of the project mission. Those who provide the redevelopment capital—be they the public or private sectors—are the key players.

The Toshka project is different in that it is the result of a clear political choice, and there is opposition to the very idea of the project—on an opportunity cost basis within the country and a geo-political basis from other riparian states. To date, the strength, internally and externally, of the Egyptian government has allowed the project to proceed smoothly, but there can be no guarantee that it will not meet the same fate as the Jongeli Canal in the future. What none of these projects have faced is the problem of local loser opposition. This can consist of either those who will directly lose out as a result of the project, such as the towns of Halsskov and Dover with the Storebælt and Channel fixed links (Bonke 1998;

Winch 1996); or NIMBY ("not in my back yard") opposition, where the mission is not contested in principle, but its local effects are opposed. Strong environmentalist attention has not been attracted to any of these projects. This is probably due to the TINA nature of two of them, but this is more surprising in the case of Toshka. This may well be a function of the lack of local losers. As so often, at least in Europe, failure to effectively manage the archaeological aspects of the project have led to delays in rebuilding BCD.

Both local losers and environmentalist opponents of projects have demonstrated the organizational capacity on a number of projects to shift themselves from the low power to high power categories, and have enforced the renegotiation of the mission of many projects. Their roles as stakeholders are increasingly institutionalized through the regulatory system in the shape of land use policies and procedures and environmental impact assessments.

The supply side of the project coalition—designers and contractors—has only been included in the stakeholder mapping for Montserrat. This is because, on our evidence, they only played an independent role in defining the project mission on that project, where Brown and Root were responsible for selecting the prefabricated housing types. On our evidence, they played no such role for Toshka and BCD. However, it seems unlikely that the presence of Hitachi in the consortium for the Mubarak Pumping Station is independent of Japanese aid funding; in other words, stakeholder analysis must take into account the possibility of alliances and dependencies between internal and external stakeholders.

Conclusions

Although the stakeholder mapping approach presented here has been developed in the context of major building and civil engineering projects, its application is much wider. Compromising the interests of powerful stakeholders is essential for the effective definition of any project mission, and this tool has a role to play in achieving that definition. The recent experience in the United Kingdom (UK) of major information technology projects in the private and public sectors shows that the failure to manage stakeholders leads to unclear definition of the project mission, abandonment of the project, and a large waste of resources. The stakeholder mapping approach presented here provides the basis for an effective stakeholder management strategy, as it identifies what sort of communications strategies different stakeholders might accept, and the sorts of compromises that would have to be made to ensure their commitment to the project.

Our analysis has been unable to do full justice to the richness of the maps due to length considerations. For the further development of this stakeholder mapping methodology, we would suggest that research should focus on the following areas:

- Further research is required into methods for manipulating the power/interest matrix in favor of any particular stakeholder—Johnson and Scholes (1999, 2002) provide some indications of ways of doing this. This will typically be done by the project manager acting for one of the key players, but the mapping technique is equally open to use by opponents of the project.

- A stakeholder approach implies that the criteria for project success are themselves contestable. What is considered success for one stakeholder may be failure for another. For instance, the banks and the contractors (Transmanche-Link) had very different views of price on the Channel fixed link (Winch 1996), stemming from their different business cultures. Banks bid high and trim their margins; contractors bid low and recoup their costs. The 69 percent budget overrun on the project shows that the contractors' view of price prevailed in the long term—the project was a success from their point of view, but not from that of the banks. Better understanding of these dynamics is required.

- Greater understanding is required of the shifting nature of the stakeholder map through time. This is particularly important if projects are phased and stakeholders learn from their experiences in the earlier phases. Changes in stakeholders—such as takeovers of client firms or changes in government—can also lead to changes in the project mission, or even outright cancellation. One of the most important tasks of the project manager is to sink in enough assets so that any shift in the power/interest matrix does not lead to project cancellation due to sheer momentum—"getting the concrete on the table," in the words of the project manager of the Storebælt project (Bonke 1998). SOLIDERE appears to have achieved this, with the new prime minister shifting towards a more conciliatory approach with the realization that changing its mission would be too disruptive at this stage. On Montserrat, stakeholder dissatisfaction with the outcome of each stage led to redefinition of the artifact within the overall mission.

Notes

[1] This chapter was prepared while the first-named author was Velux Visiting Professor at the Department of Civil Engineering, Technical University of Denmark. We are both grateful to the Villum Kann Rasmussen Fonden for supporting the preparation of both the *Project Management Insitute Research Conference 2000* paper and this chapter.

References

Beidleman, C. R., D. Fletcher, and D. Veshosky. 1990. On Allocating Risk: The Essence of Project Finance. *Sloan Management Review* 47.

Bijker, W. E., and J. Law, eds. 1992. *Shaping Technology/Building Society*. Cambridge: MIT Press.

Bijker, W. E. 1987. The Social Construction of Bakelite: Toward a Theory of Invention. In *The Social Construction of Technological Systems: New Directions in the Sociology and History of Technology*, edited by W. E. Bijker, T. P. Hughes, and T. Pinch. Cambridge: MIT Press.

Bonke, S. 1996. *Technology Management on Large Construction Projects*. London: Le Groupe Bagnolet. Working Paper 4.

———. 1998. *The Storebælt Fixed Link: The Fixing of Multiplicity*. London: Le Groupe Bagnolet. Working Paper 14.

Bowen, H. K. et al. 1994. *The Perpetual Enterprise Machine*. New York: Oxford University Press.

Calvert, S. 1995. Managing Stakeholders. In *The Commercial Project Manager*, edited by J. R. Turner. London: McGraw-Hill.

Chaslin, F. 1985. *Les Paris de François Mitterand*. Paris: Gallimard.

Drummond, H. 1996. *Escalation in Decision-Making: The Tragedy of Taurus*. Oxford: Oxford University Press.

El Missiri, I. M. 1999. *Developing Egypt's South: A Study of the Toshka Project (1997–2017)*. MSc Construction Economics and Management Report, University College London.

Hall, P. 1980. *Great Planning Disasters*. London: Weidenfield and Nicholson.

Haugbølle Hansen, K. 1993. *Genanvendelse af byggematerialer*. MSc Construction Management Report, Department of Planning, Technical University of Denmark.

Hobballah, K. 1998. *The Redevelopment of Beirut Central District through Public/Private Partnership: A Study of SOLIDERE*. MSc Construction Economics and Management Report, University College London.

Johnson, J., and K. Scholes. 1999. *Exploring Corporate Strategy*. 5th ed. London: Prentice-Hall.

———. 2002. *Exploring Corporate Strategy: Text and Cases*. 6th ed. London: Financial Time Prentice Hall.

Kidder, T. 1982. *The Soul of a New Machine*. Harmondsworth: Penguin.

Law, J., and M. Callon. 1992. *The Life and Death of an Aircraft: A Network Analysis of Technical Change*. Edited by Bijker and Law.

Misa, T. 1992. *Controversy and Closure in Technological Change: Constructing Steel*. Edited by Bijker and Law.

Patullo, P. 2000. *Fire from the Mountain: The Story of the Montserrat Volcano*. London: Constable.

Weekes, D. 1999. *The Redevelopment of Montserrat: The Immediate Housing Development Project*. MSc Construction Economics and Management Report, University College London.

Winch, G. M. 1996. *The Channel Tunnel; le Projet du Siècle*. London: Le Groupe Bagnolet. Working Paper 11.

———. 2000. The Management of Projects as a Generic Business Process. In *Projects as Guiding Motives for Business* (117–130), edited by R. A. Lundin and F. Hartman. Dordrecht: Kluwer.

———. 2002. *Managing Construction Projects: An Information Processing Approach*. Oxford: Blackwell Science.

CHAPTER 24

PROJECT RISK MANAGEMENT: THE REQUIRED TRANSFORMATIONS TO BECOME PROJECT UNCERTAINTY MANAGEMENT

Chris Chapman, Ph.D.—University of Southampton

Stephen Ward, Ph.D.—University of Southampton

Introduction

Project risk management is an essential part of project management, aimed at improving project performance via systematic identification, appraisal, and management of project-related risk. This aim, improving performance, implies a wide perspective that seeks to manage both threats, which if they occur have a negative effect on project performance, and opportunities, which if they occur have a positive effect on project performance (Project Management Institute 2000, 127; Simon, Hillson, and Newland 1997). In practice, the emphasis is often on managing threats or "down-side" risk. This emphasis might reflect a difficulty in throwing off the commonly understood meaning of "risk" or an underlying view that it is more important to manage threats than opportunities. A focus on threat management is reasonable, and very useful in the face of a general tendency to set challenging objectives. If a "tight" budget for a project is set, then by definition this implies a preponderance of threats to keeping to budget rather than opportunities for coming in below budget. Nevertheless, if the potential for opportunities is never explored, opportunities will not be discovered and exploited.

The importance of project opportunity management in project risk management has been understood for some time, and interest in project opportunity management has been growing steadily. For example, the approach to project risk management adopted worldwide by British Petroleum (BP) International in the mid-1970s (Chapman 1979) was built around the concept of risk efficiency (a minimum level of risk for a given level of expected profit or cost). This is a very basic objective for both opportunity and threat management. BP's approach also reflected a linked key objective for opportunity management: an aggressive approach to expected profit, so long as the risk/expected cost trade-off did not expose the organization to potentially catastrophic losses at a higher level of risk than other aspects of its operations. In addition, BP's approach recognized the importance of managing good luck as well as bad luck, and the need for corporate culture changes that would empower more explicit opportunity management. The IBM United Kingdom (UK) Forum 2 program in the late 1980s was built on these ideas to engineer a culture change involving less bureaucracy, faster responses, and more aggressive risk taking. The NatWest Bank internal project risk management process of the early 1990s transformed itself into a program benefit management process by the mid-1990s, which linked all project risk management to achieving the benefits of the program (portfolio of projects) as a whole; as defined in terms of the business case used to approve the program. These developments are all reflected in *Project Risk Management: Processes, Techniques and Insights* (Chapman and Ward 1997). And the opportunity management emphasis of that book has generated further interest in project opportunity management.

To emphasize the need for an even-handed approach to opportunities and threats, Ingemund Jordanger (1998) of Statoil recently adopted the term "project uncertainty management," instead of project risk management. This was a bold and seminal step. However, if the term project uncertainty management is to achieve the full potential that this term facilitates, it has to embrace more than a change in emphasis with respect to opportunities and threats as events that may or may not occur. What is needed is attention to uncertainty in terms of variability and ambiguity arising from a lack of knowledge, not readily attributable to a particular set of events or conditions, and therefore not readily treated as risk in the project risk management process. This chapter briefly explores four specific areas of ambiguity that need to be addressed and incorporated in an uncertainty management paradigm.

Uncertainty in Estimates of Risk Event Probability and Impact

Estimation and evaluation of uncertainty are core tasks in any process involving the management of uncertainty in projects. These tasks involve a number of important objectives addressed in the following, which contribute to a key aim of cost effective risk assessment.

1. *Understand uncertainty in general terms.* Understanding uncertainty needs to go beyond variability and available data. It needs to address ambiguity and

incorporate structure and knowledge, with a focus on making the best decisions possible given the available data, information, knowledge, and understanding of structure.

2. *Understand sources of uncertainty.* One important aspect of structure is the need to understand uncertainty in terms of sources of uncertainty, because some (not all) appropriate ways of managing uncertainty are specific to its source.

3. *Determine what to quantify.* It is very important to distinguish between what is usefully quantified and what is best treated as a condition or assumption in terms of decision-making effectiveness.

4. *Iterative processes.* To facilitate insight and learning, uncertainty has to be addressed in terms of an iterative process, with process objectives that change on successive passes. An iterative approach is essential to optimize the use of time and other resources during the uncertainty management process, because initially where uncertainty lies, whether or not it matters or how best to respond to it are unknown. At the outset the process is concerned with sizing risk to discover what matters. Subsequent passes are concerned with refining assessments in order to effectively manage what matters. Final passes may be concerned with convincing others that what matters is being properly managed. The way successive iterations are used needs to be addressed in a systematic manner. A simple one-shot, linear approach is hopelessly inefficient.

5. *A minimalist first pass at estimation and evaluation.* In order to "optimize" the overall process, a "minimalist" approach to the first pass at estimation and evaluation is critical. A minimalist first pass approach to estimation should be so easy to use that the usual resistance to appropriate quantification—based on lack of data and lack of comfort with subjective probabilities—is overcome.

6. *Avoid optimistic bias.* Most approaches to estimation and evaluation induce optimistic bias, which leads to systematic underestimation of uncertainty. This needs direct and explicit attention to manage expectations. If successive estimates associated with managing risk do not narrow perceived variability and improve the perceived expected cost or profit on average, then the earlier analysis process is flawed. Very few organizations have processes that meet this test. They are failing to manage expectations. In general, the more sophisticated the process used, the more optimistic bias damages the credibility of estimation and evaluation processes.

7. *Simplicity with constructive complexity.* Simplicity is an important virtue in its own right, not just with respect to the efficiency of a minimalist first pass approach, but because it can amplify clarity and deepen insight. However, appropriate "constructive complexity" is also important, for the same reasons. Getting the best balance is partly a question of structure and process, and partly a question of skills that can be learned via a process that is engineered to enhance learning.

The authors are not aware of any current approaches that explicitly address this set of objectives as a whole. Evidence of this is the sustained, widespread promotion and use of first pass approaches to estimation and evaluation employing a probability-impact matrix (PIM). This was deliberately accommodated, although not promoted, in the *Project Risk Analysis and Management (PRAM) Guide* (Simon, Hillson, and Newland 1997; Chapman 1997) because of differences of opinion amongst the working group. The PIM approach typically defines low, medium, and high bands for possible probabilities and impacts associated with identified sources of uncertainty (usually risks involving adverse impacts). These bands may be defined as quantified ranges or left wholly subjective. In either case assessment of probabilities and impacts is a relatively crude process whereby each source of uncertainty is assigned to a particular probability band and a particular impact band. This limited information about each source of uncertainty is often diluted by using "risk indices" with common values for different probability band and impact band combinations. Information about uncertainty is sometimes still further obscured by the practice of adding individual risk indices together to calculate spurious "project risk indices." The PIM approach seems to offer a rapid first pass assessment of the relative importance of identified sources of uncertainty, but it delivers very little useful information and even less real insight (Chapman and Ward 1997; Ward 1999).

Even with the availability of proprietary software products such as @Risk for quantifying, displaying, and combining uncertain parameters, the use of PIM has persisted (further encouraged by PIM software). This is surprising, but it suggests a gap between simple direct prioritization of sources of risk and quantification requiring the use of specialist software. In any event, none of these PIM approaches deals directly with the complete set of objectives set out above for estimation and evaluation.

To address this gap, Chapman and Ward (2000) describe a minimalist first pass approach to estimation and evaluation of uncertainty, set in the context of an approach that addresses all seven objectives. The minimalist approach defines uncertainty ranges for probability and impact associated with each source of uncertainty. Subsequent calculations preserve expected value and measures of variability, while explicitly managing associated optimistic bias.

The minimalist approach involves the following steps in a first pass attempt to estimate and evaluate uncertainty:

1. Identify the parameters to be quantified.
2. Estimate crude but credible ranges for probability of occurrence and impact.
3. Calculate expected values and ranges for composite parameters.
4. Present results graphically (optional).
5. Summarize results.

In step 1 a clear distinction is made between sources of uncertainty that are useful to quantify and sources that are best treated as conditions, following project risk management (Chapman and Ward 1997) in this respect. For example, suppose an oil company project team wants to estimate the duration and the cost of the design of an offshore pipeline using the organization's design department. Current common best practice would require a list of sources of uncertainty (a risk list or risk log), which might include entries like "change of route," "demand for design effort from other projects," "loss of staff," and "morale problems." Change of route would probably be regarded as a source of uncertainty best treated as a condition by the project manager and the head of the design department. Subsequent steps apply only to those sources of uncertainty that are usefully quantified.

In step 2 the "probability" of a threat occurring is associated with an approximate order of magnitude minimum and maximum plausible probability, assuming a uniform distribution (and a mid-point expected value). This captures the users feel for a "low, medium, or high" probability class in a flexible manner, captures information about uncertainty associated with the probability, and yields a conservative (pessimistic) expected value. For trained users it should be easier than designing appropriate standard classes for all risks and putting a tick in an appropriate box.

Similarly, the "impact" of a threat that occurs is associated with an approximate order of magnitude minimum and maximum plausible value (duration and cost), also assuming a uniform duration. This captures the user's feel for a "low, medium, or high" impact class in a flexible manner, captures information about the uncertainty associated with the impact, and yields a conservative (pessimistic) expected value.

In step 4 the expected values and associated uncertainties for all quantified sources of uncertainty are shown graphically in a way that displays the contribution of each to the total in expected value and range terms. This clearly indicates what matters and what does not, and is used as a basis for managing subsequent passes of the project risk management process in terms of data acquisition to confirm important probability and impact assessment, refinement of response strategies, and key decision choices.

Although simple, the minimalist approach is sophisticated in the sense that it builds in pessimistic bias. This minimizes the risk of dismissing as unimportant risks what more information might reveal as important. Also, it is set in the context of an iterative approach, which leads to more refined estimates wherever potentially important risks are revealed. Sophistication does not require complexity. It requires "constructive" simplicity, increasing complexity only when it is useful to do so.

The concern of the minimalist first pass approach is not a defensible quantitative assessment. The concern is to develop a clear understanding of what seems to matter, based on the views of those able to shed some light on the issues. This is an attempt to resolve the ambiguity associated with the size of uncertainty about the impact of risk events and the size of uncertainty about the probability of risk events occurring, the latter often dominating the former. A first pass may lead to the conclusion "there is no significant uncertainty, and no need for further effort." This is one of the reasons why the approach must have a conservative bias. Another reason is the need to manage expectations, with subsequent refinements of estimates indicating less uncertainty or increased uncertainty providing an explicit indication that the earlier process failed. An estimator should be confident that more work on refining the analysis is at least as likely to decrease the expected value estimate as to increase it. A tendency for cost estimates to drift upwards as more analysis is undertaken indicates a failure of earlier analysis. The minimalist approach is designed to help manage the expectations of those the estimator reports to in terms of expected values. Preserving credibility should be an important concern.

The minimalist approach departs from the first pass use of probability density histograms or convenient probability distribution assumptions, which the authors and many others have used for years in similar contexts. Readers who are used to first pass approaches that attempt considerable precision, may feel uncomfortable with the deliberate lack of precision incorporated in the minimalist approach. However, more precise modelling is frequently accompanied by questionable underlying assumptions like independence and lack of attention to uncertainty in original estimates. The minimalist approach forces explicit consideration of these issues. It may be a step back in terms of taking a simple view of the "big picture," but it should facilitate more precise modelling of uncertainty where it matters, and confidence that precision is not spurious.

Chapman and Ward (2000) use a specific context to illustrate the minimalist approach, but there is considerable scope for applying the approach in other contexts and in various stages of the project life cycle (PLC). The minimalist approach was deliberately designed for simple manual processing and no supporting software requirements. However, relatively simple hardware and inexpensive commercially available software (like @Risk) could be used to minimize the input demands of such analysis, make the outputs easy to interpret and rich, and make the movement on to second and further passes relatively straightforward. In general, application specific software should be developed once it is clear what analysis is required, after significant experience of the most appropriate forms of analysis for first and subsequent passes has been acquired.

Uncertainty About the Conditional Nature of Estimates

A large proportion of those using probabilistic project risk management processes often fail to address the conditional nature of probabilities and associated measures used for decision-making and control. The key outputs of the estimation and evaluation phases of the project risk management process are estimates of expected values for project parameters and measures of plausible variations on the high and low side. Interpretations of expected values or plausible extremes, like a 95 percent confidence value, have to be conditional on the assumptions made to estimate these values. For example, a sales estimate may be conditional on a whole set of assumed trading conditions, such as a particular promotion campaign and no new competitors. Invariably estimates ignore, or assume away, the existence of uncertainty that relates to three basic sources: known unknowns, unknown unknowns, and bias. These sources of uncertainty can have a very substantial impact on estimates that needs to be recognized and managed.

Known unknowns are of two types: explicit, extreme events (triple Es) and scope adjustment provisions (SAPs). Triple Es are "force majeure" events, like a change in legislation that would influence an oil company's pipeline design criteria in a fundamental way. SAPs are conditions or assumptions that may not hold, which are explicit, like the assumed operating pressure and flow value for an oil pipeline, given the assumed oil recovery rate.

Unknown unknowns are the unidentified triple Es or SAPs that should be factored into the project risk management process. We know that the realization of some unknown unknowns is usually inevitable. They do not include issues like "the world may end tomorrow" because it is sensible for most practical decision-making to assume we will still be here tomorrow, but the boundary between this extreme and what should be included is usually ill-defined.

Bias may be conscious or unconscious, pessimistic or optimistic, and clues, if not data, about the extent of bias may be available or not.

The impact of these three basic sources of uncertainty can be considered via the use of three scaling factors:

F_k = known unknowns
F_u = unknown unknowns
F_b = bias

For example, an F_k scaling factor might be defined in relation to an estimated expected cost in the form:

F_k = 1.0	Probability of F_k = 0.1
1.1	0.7
1.2	0.1
1.3	0.1

This example involves a mean F_k = 1.12. In simple, crude terms, this would imply that an uplift in the estimated cost of the order of 30 percent is plausible for a pessimistic scenario value, like a 95 percentile, and an uplift of 12 percent is an appropriate expectation. In practice F_k values could be much higher than in this example.

Combining these three scaling factors provides a single "cube" (KUUB) factor, F^3, defined by:

$$F^3 = F_k \times F_u \times F_b$$

This is then applied as a scaling factor to conditional estimates. This KUUB factor, F^3, can be estimated in probability terms directly or via these three components to clarify the conditional nature of the output of any quantitative risk analysis. This avoids the very difficult mental gymnastics associated with trying to interpret a quantitative risk analysis result that is conditional on exclusions and scope assumptions (which may be explicit or implicit) and no bias, without underestimating the importance of the conditions.

The key value of the explicit quantification of F^3 is forcing those involved to think about the implications of the factors that drive the expected size and variability of F^3. Such factors may be far more important than the factors captured in the prior conventional quantitative risk analysis. There is a natural tendency to forget about conditions and assumptions and focus on the numbers. Attempting to explicitly size F^3 makes it possible to avoid this. Even if different parties emerge with different views of an appropriate F^3, the process of discussion is beneficial.

If an organization refuses to estimate F³ explicitly, the issues involved do not go away. They simply become unmanaged risks. Many of them will be betting certainties.

An important source of ambiguity concerns the extent to which different project parties need to be concerned about particular F factors. For example, continuing the example of the last section, say the oil company project manager decides to contract out pipeline design. In estimating design costs the design company will not scale its estimates to allow for known unknowns if it can negotiate a contract to avoid bearing any risk associated with known unknowns. Similarly, it will not be appropriate for the project manager to scale the project design budget to incorporate an allowance for these known unknowns, unless they are wholly under the control of the project manager. For example, certain scope adjustments may come in this category. The potential impact of other unknown unknowns needs to be recognized in the oil company at some level above the project manager, where there is an ability to bear the consequences of any unknown unknown occurring. Thus, a KUUB factor needs to be estimated for the board of the oil company to adjust the design company's expected cost. A similar KUUB would need estimation if the oil company's design department undertook the work, but the risk allocation issues would be more complicated. Much post-project litigation arises because of a failure to appreciate or acknowledge exposure to KUUB factors, and a failure to resolve ambiguity about responsibility for KUUB factors earlier in the project.

Uncertainty About Commitments and Targets

An important reason for quantifying uncertainty is that it forces management to articulate beliefs about uncertainty and related assumptions. In addition, it forces an appreciation of the significance of differences between *target, expected values*, and *commitments*, with respect to costs, durations, and other performance measures. This in turn forces management to clarify the distinction between *provisions* and *contingency allowances*.

In cost terms, expected values are our best estimate of what costs should be realized on average. Setting aside a contingency fund to meet costs that may arise in excess of the expected cost defines a "level of commitment" (probability of being able to meet the commitment). The contingency allowance provides an uplift from the expected value, which is not required on average if it is properly determined. Determining this level of commitment should involve an assessment of perceived threats and the extent to which these may be covered by a contingency fund, together with an assessment of the implications of both over and underachievement in relation to the commitment.

Targets set at a level below expected cost, with provisions accounting for the difference, need to reflect the opportunity aspect of risk. Targets need to be realistic to be credible, but they also need to be lean to stretch people.

Sometimes differences between targets, expectations, and commitments are kept confidential, or left implicit. We argue that they need to be explicit, and a clear rationale for the difference needs to be understood by all, leading to an effective process of managing the evolution from targets to realized values. The ability to manage the gaps between targets, expected values, and contingency levels, and setting those values appropriately in the first place, is a central concern of project risk management.

This approach to quantifying uncertainty is useful if there is concern with aggregate performance on a single criterion such as cost or time. However, this approach is less helpful if applied to quantifying uncertainty about each activity individually in a chain or collection of activities. For example, setting commitment levels for the duration of each task in a chain of tasks may be counter productive. In *Critical Chain*, Goldratt (1997) describes the problem in the following terms: "we are accustomed to believing that the only way to protect the whole is through protecting the completion date of each step," as a result "we pad each step with a lot of safety time." Goldratt argues that this threat protection perspective induces three behaviors that, when combined, waste most of the safety time:

1. The student syndrome (leaving things to the last minute).
2. Multitasking (chopping and changing between different jobs).
3. Delays accumulate; advances do not (good luck is not passed on).

The challenge, and opportunity, is to manage the uncertainty about performance for each link in the chain in a way that avoids these effects and ensures that good luck is not only captured, but also shared for the benefit of the whole project. Joint management of the good luck, efficiency, and effectiveness of each project-related activity is needed. This implies some form of incentive agreement between the project manager and those carrying out project activities that encourages the generation and delivery of good luck, efficiency, and effectiveness, with the minimum of uncertainty. This agreement needs to recognize interdependency between performance measures. Duration, cost, quality, and time are not independent, and all four are functions of the motivation and priorities of those involved. For example, uncertainty about the duration of an activity is usually driven by ambiguity about quality, cost, and inefficient working practices. This needs to be managed, to reduce uncertainty and to capture the benefits of managing good luck, in the sense of the scope for low duration, high quality, and low cost.

To illustrate these ideas briefly, consider an extension of the earlier example of pipeline construction. If the activity of "pipeline design" is followed by "order pipe," "deliver the pipe," and so on, and if the internal design department is involved, do we need to set a commitment date for design completion? The simple answer is we do not. Rather we need a target duration and an expected duration for design that becomes firm as early as possible, in order to manage the good luck as well as the bad luck associated with variations in the duration of the design activity. We also need an agreement with the design department that recognizes that the design department can make and share their luck to a significant extent if they are motivated to do so. As the design department is part of the project-owning organization, a legal contract is not appropriate. However, a "contract" is still needed in the form of a "memorandum of understanding," to formalize the agreement. Failure to formalize an "internal contract" in a context like this implies "psychological contracts" between project parties that are unlikely to be effective. The ambiguity inherent in such contracts can only generate uncertainty, which is highly divisive and quite unnecessary.

Most internal design departments have a "cost-per-design hour" rate based on an historic accounting cost. A "design hours" estimate multiplied by this rate yields a "design cost" estimate. Design actual cost is based on realized design hours. The internal contract is "cost plus." The duration agreed to by the design department is a "commitment" date with a low chance of excedence, bearing in mind all the risks noted earlier. To address the problems that this arrangement induces, some form of incentive agreement is required which recognizes the potential for trade-offs between different measures of performance. What is needed is a fixed "nominal cost" based on the appropriate expected number of design hours, with a premium payment scale for completion earlier than an appropriate "trigger duration," and a penalty deduction scale for later completion. Additionally, a premium could be introduced for the correct prediction of the design completion date to facilitate more efficient preparation of following activities. The trigger duration might be something like an 80 percentile value, comparable to a "commitment duration." The target should be very ambitious, reflecting a plausible date if all goes as well as possible. Other performance objectives could be treated in the same way, with premium and penalty payments relative to cost and quality level triggers as possible options. However premiums and penalties need to be designed to ensure that appropriate trade-offs are encouraged.

Uncertainty About Objectives at Operational Levels

Careful attention to formal project risk management is usually motivated by the large scale use of new and untried technology while executing major projects, and other obvious sources of significant risk. A threat perspective encourages a focus on these initial motivating risks. However, key issues are often unrelated to the motivating risks and are usually related to sources of ambiguity introduced by the existence of multiple parties and the project management infrastructure. Such issues need to be addressed very early in the project and throughout the PLC, and should be informed by a broad appreciation of the underlying "root" uncertainties. A decade ago most project management professionals would have seen this in terms of a suitable high level activity structure summary and a related cost item structure. It is now clear that an activity structure is only one of six aspects, the "six Ws," which need consideration (Chapman and Ward 1997), the:

- Who (parties or players involved)
- Why (motives, aims, and objectives of the parties)
- What (design of the deliverable)

- Which way (activities to achieve the deliverable)
- Wherewithal (resource)
- When (time frame).

All six aspects are interconnected and need joint consideration in the pursuit of project performance (Chapman and Ward 1997). Much more critical than understanding the detailed activities proposed in a project is the need to appreciate the relationships between key parties to the project, their various objectives and motives, and the trade-offs parties are prepared to make between their objectives. The six Ws constitute a core framework for managing trade-offs between time, cost, and other performance criteria, different trade-offs for different project parties, and trade-offs that change over time.

A very common, specific context is projects that involve a buyer and supplier(s). In such contexts it is important to the buyer that the supplier be motivated to perform in the best interests of the buyer, via suitably formulated contractual arrangements. This means that the buyer must first resolve uncertainty about their own objectives and performance criteria for the product or service they seek. Specifically, the buyer needs to:

1. Identify pertinent performance criteria.

2. Develop a measure of the level of performance for each criterion.

3. Identify the most preferred (optimum) feasible combination of performance levels on each criterion.

4. Identify alternative combinations of performance levels on each criterion that would be acceptable instead of the optimum.

5. Identify the trade-offs between performance criteria implied by these preferences.

Adopting an iterative process and using a minimalist approach on the first pass may be the most effective way to complete these steps. The information gathered from these steps can then be used to formulate appropriate incentive contracts by selecting some or all of the performance criteria for inclusion in the contract, developing payment scales which reflect the acceptable trade-offs, and—with the supplier—negotiating acceptable "risk sharing" ratios for each contract performance criterion.

Clearly, steps 1–5 are not only applicable to buyers contemplating contractual arrangements with external suppliers. These steps should be undertaken by any project owner, particularly in the early conception and design stages of a project. Undertaking these steps should be part of the process of understanding the relationships between the six Ws of the project and managing uncertainty about project performance. The process of identifying and considering possible trade-offs between performance criteria is an opportunity to improve performance. It should enable a degree of optimization with respect to each performance measure, and it is an opportunity that needs to be seized. As a minimum, this process involves consideration of appropriate and effective trade-offs between cost, time, and quality—where "quality" involves performance measures other than capital cost and time, like operating cost (including maintenance and periodic refurbishment) and costs over the life cycle of the delivered product. Simultaneous improvement in all three areas of cost, time, and quality is rarely achievable, particularly in managing project risk, and it is important to be clear what appropriate degrees of freedom are available. In the face of a realized threat, any attempt to preserve performance in all three areas usually results in uncontrolled degradation of all three. In a deterministic context (no uncertainty), we can focus on what is most important. For project risk management purposes, it is vital to understand priorities, to know what is least important and what can be sacrificed.

This has important implications for performance measurement and the management of trade-offs within a single organization. For example, carrying on with the earlier example: how much is it worth to a project to be able to complete the design faster? If a trigger-based incentive contract with an internal design department is used, fewer hours may be required because the incentive structure will reduce multitasking. If multitasking is reduced, will the efficiency of the design department improve enough to eliminate the rumour of selling off the design function (outsourcing all design), which might be underpinning risks related to loss of staff and low morale? If these downside risks are eliminated, can the "upside risks" or opportunities associated with easy hiring and low turnover of good staff, high morale, and high efficiency be managed explicitly via a "virtuous circle?" Generalizing in other ways, would a flexible pipeline (laid by reel barge) be better than a rigid pipeline, and is a pipeline the best way to bring the oil to market?

Conclusion

Project risk management can make an important contribution to effective project management. However, there is substantial scope for improving project performance by developing a project uncertainty management paradigm that extends the scope of current project risk management. First, reduce reliance on PIMs and encourage an iterative learning approach to understanding uncertainty, more emphasis is needed on quantitative approaches that do not obscure variability. Second, more attention needs to be given to the identification and treatment of assumed operating conditions when developing estimates. KUUB uncertainties need to be allowed for at some level in the organization, as it is not efficient for KUUB factors to be considered only at project level. Third, we need to develop methods for articulating and comparing performance objectives and perceived trade-offs between them. Ambiguity in this area is a significant source of uncertainty and a major barrier to improving project performance. Explicit consideration of objectives and acceptable trade-offs are needed as a preliminary action to designing incentive schemes that encourage the generation and delivery of good luck, efficiency, and effectiveness, with the minimum of uncertainty.

The authors hope some of the uncertainty assessment ideas outlined here will stimulate others to put them to the test in practical applications and so contribute to the evolution of the paradigm as a whole.

References

Chapman, Chris B. 1979. Large Engineering Project Risk Analysis. *IEEE Transactions on Engineering Management* EM 26: 78–86.

Chapman, Chris B., and Stephen C. Ward. 1997. *Project Risk Management: Processes, Techniques and Insights*. Chichester, UK: John Wiley & Sons, Inc.

———. 2000. Estimation and Evaluation of Uncertainty: A Minimalist First Pass Approach. *International Journal of Project Management* 18: 369–383.

Goldratt, Eliyahu M. 1997. *Critical Chain*. Great Barrington, MA: The North River Press.

Jordanger, Ingemund. 1998. Value Orientated Management of Project Uncertainties. *Proceedings of the 14th World Congress on Project Management* 2 (821–821), June 10–13. Ljubljana, Slovenia.

Project Management Institute. 2000. *A Guide to the Project Management Body of Knowledge (PMBOK® Guide)* – 2000 Edition. Newtown, Square, PA: Project Management Institute.

Simon, Peter, David Hillson, and Ken Newland. 1997. *Project Risk Analysis and Management (PRAM) Guide*. Norwich, UK: The Association for Project Managers.

Ward, Stephen C. 1999. Assessing and Managing Important Risks. *International Journal of Project Management* 17: 331–336.

A COMPARISON OF DRUM-BUFFER-ROPE (DBR) AND CRITICAL CHAIN (CC) BUFFERING TECHNIQUES

Van Gray, Ph.D.—Baylor University

Joe Felan, Ph.D.—Baylor University

Elisabeth Umble—Baylor University

Michael Umble, Ph.D.—Baylor University

Introduction

Project-based management has long been the business style associated with the construction industry, United States (US) defense contractors, large consulting firms, and even Hollywood. Today, project management is spreading to all sectors of work. Accordingly, the membership in the Project Management Institute (PMI®), a professional organization for the project management specialist, quadrupled between 1993 and 1997. PMI membership is growing by some 1,200 members per month and is expected to break the 100,000-member mark by 2002. Clearly, the trend indicates that there will be an increase in the importance and role that projects and their successful management contribute to the strategic direction of the firm. David Cleland, an established project management scholar, has declared that this is the "Age of Project Management" (Cleland 1990).

At the same time that project management methods have become common practice, the pressures associated with global competition, increased customer focus, shortened manufacturing lead-times, and corporate downsizing have created many new challenges for traditional project management. Among these challenges are the issues of sharing resources and prioritizing those resources across a portfolio of concurrently implemented projects. Resolving the conflicts that arise during this resource sharing and prioritization is what really converts the project network into a project schedule.

Historically, the project management literature has made very little connection between the management of manufacturing activities necessary to create a variety of finished goods and the management of activities required to successfully complete a project. Despite the fact that every organization undertakes projects, manufacturing-based organizations and project-based organizations are generally perceived as being dramatically different. In fact, project managers have traditionally viewed the repetitive tasks of manufacturing a tangible item and the typically one-time, non-repetitive tasks associated with a project as being so different that a completely different set of tools is required to plan, schedule, and control the activities. Manufacturing activities are best coordinated and controlled using one of the many best practices of the day in combination with some variation of a material requirements planning (MRP) system, manufacturing resource planning (MRP II) system, or enterprise resource planning (ERP) system. But conventional wisdom suggests that project activities are best coordinated and controlled using variations of the critical path method (CPM) or program review and evaluation technique (PERT).

However, upon closer examination, it becomes obvious that both manufacturing-based and project-based organizations share a common set of objectives. Both must meet the expectations of their clients with on-time delivery, while adhering to budget limitations necessary to achieve levels of profitability acceptable to their stakeholders.

It is not unreasonable to believe that a general body of knowledge already exists that could be utilized to achieve the common objectives of both organizational types. The authors of this chapter suggest that such knowledge does, in fact, exist. The body of knowledge is broadly referred to as Theory of Constraints (TOC) or Constraint Management (CM). This approach, developed by Dr. Eli Goldratt, was first described in his now classic book, *The Goal* (Goldratt 1984, 1986, 1992). In this business novel, Dr. Goldratt provides the basic decision framework to solve numerous business problems. Those who are familiar with the book will remember the basic framework as the five focusing steps. We now describe in detail how these five steps provide the framework for coordinating and controlling activities in both manufacturing and project environments.

The Five Focusing Steps: The Basic Decision Framework of TOC

The five focusing steps can be summarized as:

- *Step 1: Identify the constraint.* A constraint is any element that limits the performance of a system, where performance is measured relative to the system's goal. Constraint identification must be the first step in any system-wide improvement process.

- *Step 2: Exploit the constraint.* Exploitation is the development of a plan of action for the system constraint.
- *Step 3: Subordinate everything else to the plan.* Subordination is the development of a plan of action for the system's non-constraints, in coordination with the previously developed constraint plan.
- *Step 4: Elevate the constraint.* Elevation is the analysis and development of a plan to increase the performance of the system by improving the performance or the capabilities of the current system constraint.
- *Step 5: Go back to step one.* In any system, actions may occur that cause the constraint to shift. If that happens, it is necessary to go back to Step 1 and repeat the process.

The basic assumption of constraint theory is that all systems have a limiting factor; the probability of the system being constrained is one. This is a critical assumption, and one that places the decision-maker in a decision environment under conditions of certainty, rather than the environment of risk. Initially ignoring the uncertainty that exists in a set of dependent tasks is a key trait of constraint theory. As will be explained later, the uncertainty in the system is accounted for and the effects of uncertainty are moderated through the use of strategically designed protection devices known as buffers.

While *The Goal* outlined the basic constructs of the TOC decision framework, it did not describe the numerous specific details necessary to apply the prescribed approach. This first occurred in two additional books by Dr. Goldratt. In *The Haystack Syndrome* (Goldratt 1990), the details of a scheduling application of the theory in traditional manufacturing operations were described. This methodology, which has experienced overwhelming success in manufacturing environments, is now widely known as the Drum-Buffer-Rope (DBR) scheduling technique. For an extended discussion of DBR and its application to a variety of manufacturing environments see Srikanth and Umble, 1997, and Umble and Srikanth, 1997. In *Critical Chain* (Goldratt 1997), the basic concepts are developed for applying the TOC approach to typical project management environments. The TOC-based project management scheduling method shares the name of the book in which it was first described—*Critical Chain. Project Management in the Fast Lane* (Newbold 1998) provides an excellent extended discussion of the critical chain approach.

In both manufacturing and project management environments, the recommended constraint theory approach to resolving problems is developed using the same five focusing steps described above. Both environments are treated as scheduling problems and solutions are developed using the same management constructs. It is important to understand the true underlying logical patterns of flow that exist in each environment. Thus, both environments are viewed from the perspective of "flow." In manufacturing environments, creating a logically correct product flow diagram (a combination of the bill of materials and the routing for each product) is essential. In project environments, developing a logically correct

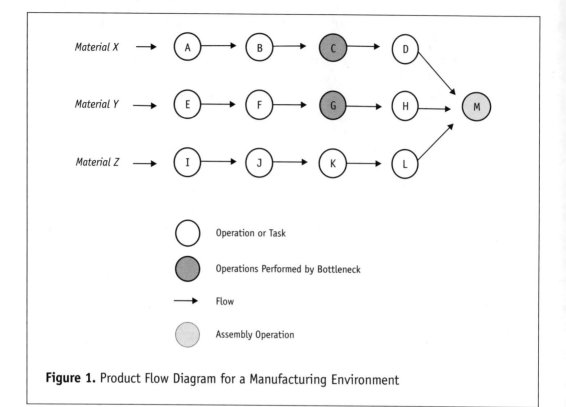

Figure 1. Product Flow Diagram for a Manufacturing Environment

network diagram that considers both the precedence relationships and the resource dependencies is essential to successful critical chain scheduling.

We now describe how each of the five focusing steps applies to both manufacturing and project environments. This allows us to highlight the key similarities of the DBR and the CC methodologies.

Identify the Constraint

The most fundamental element of the TOC approach to improving system performance is to identify the constraint of the system. Generally, the system constraint is the one element that most limits the performance of the whole system.

Manufacturing Environments

For purposes of this discussion, consider a manufacturing plant that has insufficient capacity to meet all of the demand generated by the marketplace. In such a system, the constraint is the single resource (worker, machine, team, department, and so on) whose capacity is the most limited, relative to the workload placed on that resource. (In common terms, this constraint resource is often called the bottleneck.) This constraint resource determines the throughput capability for the entire system.

Figure 1 illustrates a basic product flow diagram for a simple manufactured product. The figure shows a process requiring that three materials (X, Y, and Z)

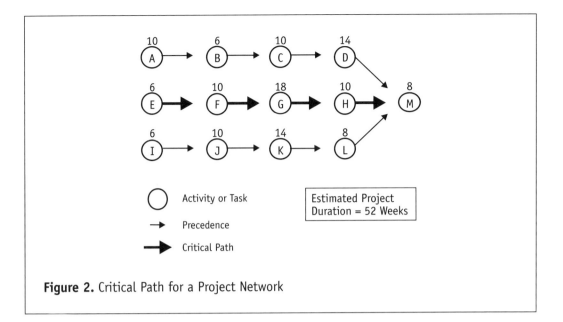

Figure 2. Critical Path for a Project Network

be processed through four operations each. Upon completing processing, the components are assembled into the final product in a final assembly operation—identified in the figure as operation M. The figure also indicates that operations C and G are performed by the constraint resource.

Project Environments

But how should we identify the constraint for a project? Our working definition of constraint is the element that limits the performance of the system. In projects, the constraint cannot simply be a bottleneck resource because the key measure of project performance is project duration. Since the longest sequence of dependent tasks in a project network determines project duration, this longest sequence of dependent activities can be considered to be the project's constraint. We have avoided using the term "critical path" here because the common usage of critical path includes only precedence requirements between activities. However, in most project environments, there is significant resource contention. (Resource contention occurs when a resource is scheduled to perform two or more tasks during the same window of time.) In such cases, this contention for resources must also be included in the determination of the longest sequence of dependent activities. In general, when resource contention is taken into account, the longest sequence will be composed of activities that are both path dependent and resource dependent. That is, the longest sequence will consist of activities on multiple paths, connected by common resources. This more realistic concept of the longest dependent sequence of activities is called the "critical chain."

The distinction between critical path and critical chain can be illustrated with a relatively straightforward example. Consider a simplified diagram of a product development project network as illustrated in Figures 2 and 3. Figure 2 shows that

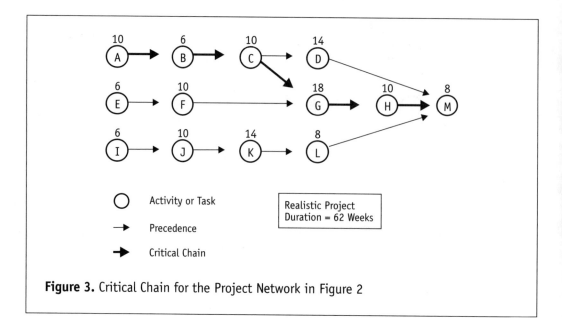

Figure 3. Critical Chain for the Project Network in Figure 2

the network consists of three paths. The figure also indicates that path EFGHM is the critical path, taking fifty-two weeks to complete.

Figure 3 introduces a resource contention problem—activities C and G are performed by the same resource and cannot be performed simultaneously. Following critical path logic, since activity G is on the critical path, it should be performed before activity C. Accordingly, path EFGHM is finished in fifty-two weeks. However, the start of activity C will be delayed by eighteen weeks while G is being completed. This delays path ABCDM so that it takes sixty-six weeks to complete. In essence, the "critical" sequence of dependent activities is EF(G)CDM. That is, G cannot start until E and F are completed, C cannot start until G is completed, and M and D follow C.

However, suppose that, contrary to critical path priorities, activity C is performed before G. Path ABCDM still takes forty-eight weeks. Moreover, since activity G is delayed ten weeks while C is being performed, this lengthens path EFGHM to a total of sixty-two weeks. This sequence of dependent activities is AB(C)GHM.

The resource contention problem between activities C and G clearly results in a realistic project duration that is much longer than the original critical path estimate of fifty-two weeks. Using the given activity times, the shortest realistic project duration is sixty-two weeks. The sequence of activities that yields this shortest realistic duration is the critical chain. Note that if the critical path priority of G before C is followed, the project duration is needlessly extended by four weeks to a sixty-six week completion time.

Exploit the Constraint

Once the constraint has been identified, the next step is to develop a plan that fully exploits the constraint. This plan should be one that squeezes the highest possible level of performance from the constraint, and thus, the system as a whole.

Manufacturing Environments

In DBR systems, the derived plan that fully exploits the constraint is called "the drum." This plan sets the production schedule for the entire plant and therefore determines the throughput for the plant. The drum includes a schedule for the constraint resource that maximizes the possible throughput. The prime directive for the plant is that none of the valuable constraint resource time should be wasted. This directive is implemented by enforcing key aspects of shop control such as:

- The constraint is never starved for work.
- The constraint should never work on defective materials.
- The constraint receives top priority on items such as repairs and setups.

In traditional production scheduling systems such as MRP, production lead-times are significantly inflated because they allow for inefficiencies such as queue time and wait time at each operation. In DBR scheduling plans all excess "safety time" for each operation is eliminated. This allows the products to flow through the system as quickly as possible. How the system is protected from variability and disruptions is the topic of Step 3.

Project Environments

The idea of excess safety time in production environments also extends to project environments. Goldratt defines safety time for an individual activity as the difference between the actual time estimate and the expected median completion time. Goldratt further argues that the time estimates for individual activities in a typical project contain a large amount of safety time, often as much as 200 to 300 percent of the median completion time. There are many reasons for the existence of this amount of safety time—multitasking, procrastination, Parkinson's Law, and so forth. The problem is that the use of safety time is an attempt to protect each individual activity and keep each activity "on schedule." The hope is that by keeping each activity on schedule, the project can be completed on schedule. However, despite all of the protection time afforded each individual activity, projects still tend to finish late, over budget, and/or with compromised specifications.

The basic TOC approach, which is very effective in DBR production scheduling applications, is to shift the focus away from trying to achieve local optimization at each activity and focus on the optimization of the whole system. This approach to project environments is applied by stripping all of the safety time from individual activities. If you don't know how much safety time is included in a time estimate, that makes it difficult to strip away the safety time. For such instances, Goldratt has developed a practical rule of thumb—assume that half of the time estimate is safety time.

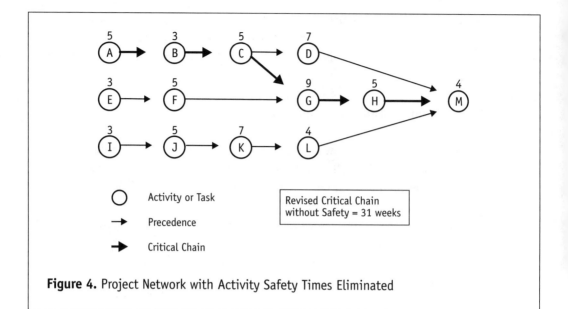

Figure 4. Project Network with Activity Safety Times Eliminated

We apply this rule to the project network shown in Figure 3. The result is a new project network, shown in Figure 4, with revised activity times. The revised critical chain for this network is thirty-one weeks, instead of the previous sixty-two weeks.

If the safety time for an individual activity is stripped away, what is left is the expected median completion time. This clearly implies that each individual activity has only a 50 percent chance of on-time completion. But remember, the objective of a project is not to finish an individual activity on time. The objective is to complete the project on time. How the project completion time is protected is the topic for Step 3, subordinate everything else to the plan.

Subordinate Everything Else to the Plan

The resulting plans that are developed using the constraint theory approach (in either environment) are initially ideal in nature and are not yet realistic. The development of a realistic manufacturing or project schedule is achieved through a series of actions designed to ensure that the impact of variability and disruption is minimized and that the non-constraining elements of the system do not interfere with the expected performance of the system constraint. In both manufacturing and project environments, this is achieved through the establishment of a variety of strategically designed and implemented "buffers."

Manufacturing Environments

If it were not for uncertainty, ideal schedules could be used. However, uncertainty does exist and must not be ignored. But even in the midst of uncertainty, the plant still has the commitment to meet the customer's delivery date. In constraint theory, buffers are established in order to develop a realistic schedule and protect

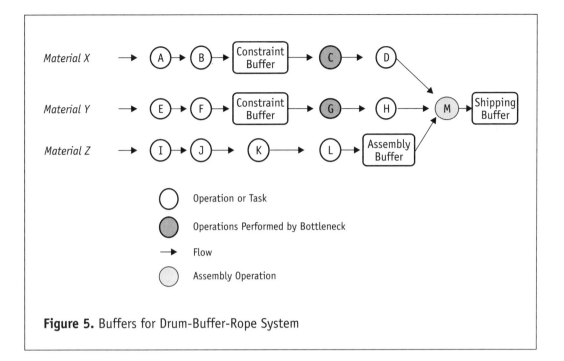

Figure 5. Buffers for Drum-Buffer-Rope System

the commitments that have been made to the customer. There are several types of buffers, but the buffers that are most critical to DBR applications are "time buffers." A brief description of the types of buffers utilized in DBR applications follows.

In DBR methodology, time buffers, space buffers, and stock buffers are all used to protect the decisions or actions that are required to meet customer expectations. Stock buffers are traditional and need no further explanation here. Space buffers are simply the planned allotment or dedication of sufficient manufacturing floor space to physically hold the preplanned arrival of a certain number of parts, semi-finished components, or materials. Constraint theory time buffers are established to ensure that timely product flow through critical resources is achieved, thereby protecting the ability of the system to meet customer expectations. Parts are planned to arrive at predetermined critical locations a certain amount of time earlier than needed. In one sense, TOC time buffers are a mechanism to facilitate parts arriving at key locations "just-before-their-time." The exact amount of buffer time is based on the level of protection that those managing the system are willing to authorize.

In order to not overly pad the length of time required to complete customer orders, time buffers are only established at critical locations. These significant locations give the time buffers their names—constraint buffer, assembly buffer, and shipping buffer. Figure 5 illustrates the placement of these three categories of buffers in our manufacturing environment.

A constraint buffer is the authorized early arrival of parts to the system constraint. The idea here is to insure that the system constraint is never left "waiting" for parts on which to work. Since the system constraint is what governs the ability to meet customer expectations, any time wasted at the constraint will translate into a lost opportunity to meet customer expectations. The constraint buffer protects the environment from disruptions (uncertainties) that can exist in activities prior to the constraint activity. Any non-productive time at the constraint always translates into lost system throughput. Obviously, such lost time should be kept to a minimum. If no capacity constraint resource exists, then it is not necessary to establish a constraint buffer.

An assembly buffer is the authorized early arrival of parts (or purchased items) that are to be combined with parts that have been previously processed through the constraint operation. This type of buffer is necessary to insure that no constraint-processed parts are stranded and not available to be assembled with other necessary, but not as critical, components on their journey toward the customer. The assembly buffer protects the environment from disruptions (uncertainties) that can exist in operations prior to the combination of non-constraint content parts with parts processed through the constraint. Depending on the network structure, assembly buffers may or may not be required.

A shipping buffer is the authorized early arrival of finished goods at the shipping area of the facility. This buffer is required to guard against uncertainties that can exist in the operations required of the non-constraint resources used subsequent to the constraint resource. A shipping buffer should always be established. In the case where no constraint resource exists, the constraint of the system is said to exist in the market because lack of demand is blocking the system from achieving higher performance. In this case, there is no constraint buffer and the shipping buffer must be sufficient to absorb all process disruptions.

When establishing buffers in DBR scheduling, the question of buffer length usually arises. The established duration of the buffers is based upon the amount of protection that the managers of the system are willing to authorize. There are rules of thumb, but the authors' experience indicates that buffer duration decisions are usually based on achieving a stable system.

Project Environments

Buffers are a key component of the CC approach to developing a realistic project schedule. The CC approach recommends removing all individual safety time and reallocating a portion of the stripped safety time to time buffers. This increases the level of protection against the uncertainties of the project, while also allowing for shorter project completion times than traditional project approaches can achieve.

We now consider the protection that the CC method provides to individual projects through the establishment of project, feeding, resource, and bottleneck buffers. The time blocks used in project and feeding buffers come from using a portion of the safety time that is removed from individual activities. The buffers are strategically located for maximum impact, just like in the DBR scheduling approach. Figure 6 illustrates the placement of project and feeding buffers in our ongoing project network example.

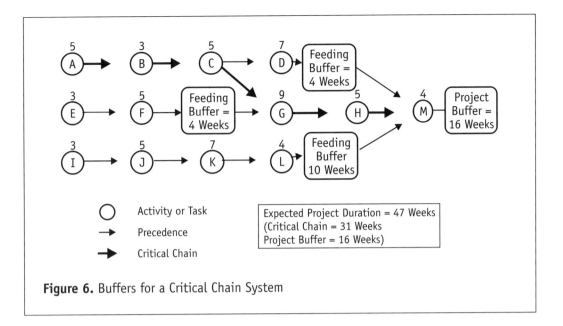

Figure 6. Buffers for a Critical Chain System

A project buffer is safety time added to the end of the critical chain in order to protect the completion date of the project. These buffers are similar in function to the DBR shipping buffer and offer protection for the project as a whole.

Stripping safety time from the individual critical chain activities frees up more than sufficient time to establish the project buffer. Each critical chain activity is started and finished as soon as possible. While some critical chain activities will take more than their median times, other critical chain activities will take less. The delays will be at least partially offset by the early completions. Any delays that are not offset by early completions will be absorbed by the project buffer. Stripping safety time from activities usually reduces the critical chain to a fraction of its previous length. Even with adding the project buffer, the expected project deadline is still less than what it otherwise would have been.

To establish the project buffer, Goldratt suggests adding back half of the safety time that was stripped from the critical chain activities. In our example in Figure 6, the stripped safety time was thirty-one weeks. Thus, we add back half of this stripped time (sixteen weeks) as a project buffer. The realistic expected project duration is now forty-seven weeks. If the entire project buffer is not needed, then the project is completed earlier than scheduled.

Feeding buffers protect the critical chain from delays that occur on non-critical paths. Feeding buffers are inserted at the point where a non-critical feeding path merges with the critical chain. This is logistically implemented by scheduling all non-critical paths to be completed before the corresponding critical chain activity is scheduled to begin. These feeding buffers are similar to the DBR constraint and assembly buffers. They help ensure that non-critical chain activities are completed in a timely manner so as not to delay the start of critical chain activities.

The appropriate location and size of feeding buffers are illustrated in Figure 6. Three feeding buffers are needed to protect the critical chain. Half of the safety time that was stripped from the non-critical path segments that feed into a critical chain activity is added back as a feeding buffer for that segment of activities. It is important to note that the feeding buffers do not add any time to the project duration. Their only purpose is to help insure the timely completion of the critical chain and the project. It should also be noted that if a feeding buffer is insufficient to protect the timely start of a critical chain activity, then the resulting delay will be absorbed by the project buffer.

Resource buffers are used to ensure that resources are available to perform critical chain activities when needed. This means making sure that necessary resources are kept properly informed as the activity start time nears. Whenever a resource contention arises, the critical chain activity receives top priority. Resource buffers represent additional buffer time created at a resource that is scheduled to begin work on a critical chain task. It protects against the case where a resource may not be instantly available to start on a critical chain task. Resource buffers generally do not change the elapsed time on a project. These buffers aid in priority setting and further enhance the reliability of the critical chain schedule.

Bottleneck buffers may be necessary when there is a true constraint resource in the project environment. In a single project environment, this problem can often be handled without much ado. However, in multiple project environments, the resource contention problem becomes more complicated. In such cases, the constraint resource can wreak havoc with attempts to synchronize the use of resources across different projects. If the constraint resource is not carefully managed and protected with buffers, the eventual result will be wasted constraint capacity. This will adversely affect project completion dates and reduce the number of projects that can be delivered.

This constraint resource in a project environment is very similar to the constraint resource in a manufacturing environment. To fully exploit the constraint, it must be carefully scheduled according to the completion dates of the various projects. The bottleneck buffer is designed to ensure that all prerequisite activities are completed before the constraint is scheduled to begin work. The bottleneck buffer does not increase the duration of a project, it is designed to protect it.

Elevate the Constraint

Since the system's constraint is what limits the performance of the entire system, the only way to increase the performance of the system is to increase the performance of the constraint. In many respects, elevation is a focused cost/benefit analysis, where the analysis is focused upon those initiatives that involve the current constraint of the system. In both of our environments, elevating the constraint means undertaking actions that increase the capabilities or the performance level of the constraint.

Manufacturing Environments

In DBR manufacturing systems, depending on the nature of the constraint, elevating the constraint may encompass a large variety of actions. If the constraint is a physical resource, then elevation might include constraint-focused actions such as assigning overtime, providing additional training to increase productivity, hiring additional workers, purchasing additional equipment, or replacing older, slower equipment with faster models. If it is determined that the constraint is insufficient demand (there are no significant resource constraints), then constraint elevation translates into implementing initiatives that generate additional orders. Such initiatives might include improving customer relations, shortening delivery lead-times, or improving product quality.

Project Environments

In project environments, TOC treats the critical chain as the system's constraint. Thus, all actions intended to elevate the constraint must involve the critical chain. If it becomes necessary to shrink project duration, then this provides a clear focus for project managers on where to apply stricter control and resources to "crash" the project. Typical elevation initiatives include hiring new people, moving people from other projects, hiring consultants, purchasing additional equipment or software, or assigning overtime. Critical chain activities are usually different from traditional critical path activities. If you attempt to add resources to enhance non-critical chain activities, you may be wasting those resources.

Go Back to Step One

Sometimes actions taken or independent developments within a system cause the limiting factor of the system to change. When this occurs, we say that the constraint has been broken. This also means that something different is now the constraint. Now the system must be reanalyzed according to the first four focusing steps.

Manufacturing Environments

In DBR systems, managers often proactively implement changes in order to elevate the constraint and increase system performance. Thus, breaking a constraint is usually a sign of improved performance. In DBR systems, the five focusing steps act as a systematic procedure to achieve an ongoing process of improvement, where each iteration through the five steps yields improved performance.

Project Environments

In project environments, breaking a constraint could be a sign of improvement, but it may also signal a problem. If actions taken to elevate the constraint significantly reduce the length of the critical chain, a different chain of activities may become the critical chain. This also reduces the project duration. However, if excessive variability or disruption occur on certain non-critical activities, then a formerly non-critical sequence of activities may become the new de facto critical chain. Whenever feasible, the recommended response is to initiate corrective elevation measures to force the new critical chain to revert to non-critical status. In cases where a new and longer critical chain emerges, project duration has increased. In such cases, the focusing steps should be repeated, even though this requires significant revision of established plans and priorities.

Suggestions for Resolving Conflicts

We have seen how the basic decision framework provided by TOC can be applied to scheduling practices in both manufacturing and project environments. Both constraint theory applications share the common elements of identifying the constraint, eliminating excess safety time, establishing protection through the creation of appropriate time buffers, and the resulting coordination of all tasks.

A complicating issue in most product and project environments has to do with the conflict that arises when managers are faced with the necessity to sequence multiple products or multiple projects. The conflict is between starting new products or projects in the midst of trying to make sure that existing products or projects flow through the system. The existing products or projects must flow through without interference from the new products or projects entering the system. Otherwise, the new orders or projects may cause the existing items in the system to become late. We can recommend three strategies for managing the conflicts that exist in both manufacturing and project environments.

1. Conflicts may be greatly reduced by "metering," or allowing into the system only those orders or projects that the organization has the capacity to fulfill. However, we realize it is difficult to turn down new orders or reject seemingly worthwhile new projects.

2. Resource contention problems may be significantly reduced by staggering individual orders or projects according to their relative priority and according to the available capacity of the firm. However, in dynamic environments, even the successful resolution of resource contention may be short-lived.

3. To promote stability and establish proper priorities, select what appears to be the most heavily loaded resources and declare that resource to be the bottleneck or constraint resource for the organization. Then develop a schedule for that resource based on the strategic priorities of the organization. If necessary, follow this approach for a second constrained resource. Release new orders or new projects only according to the available capacity of these constraint resources.

Project managers might employ one or more of the above suggestions to achieve higher performance and better control of their environment.

Future Research Opportunities

A critical aspect of the TOC approach is the accurate identification and elimination of safety time from individual tasks and the subsequent reallocation of a portion of that time into the appropriate project and feeding buffers. Thus, project managers need to be able to accurately identify individual task safety time. In addition, all personnel must buy into the concept that the project and not each individual task should be buffered. To encourage the required behaviors to make the TOC approach work, appropriate individual and group-related performance measures should be established. Additional theoretical and field research in all of the above mentioned areas are needed.

The authors also believe that additional research efforts are desperately needed in the area of effective conflict resolution, especially in multiproject environments. Three suggestions have been offered in the above section. These may be used as a starting point to guide future research efforts.

References

Cleland, David I. 1996. The Strategic Pathway of Project Management. *Proceedings of the 28th Annual PMI Seminars & Symposium*: 519–523.

Goldratt, Eliyahu M. 1984. *The Goal*. 1st ed. Croton-on-Hudson, NY: North River Press.

———. 1986. *The Goal*. 2nd ed. Croton-on-Hudson, NY: North River Press.

———. 1992. *The Goal*. 2nd revised ed. Croton-on-Hudson, NY: North River Press.

———. 1990. *The Haystack Syndrome*. Croton-on-Hudson, NY: North River Press.

———. 1997. *Critical Chain*. Great Barrington, MA: North River Press.

Newbold, Robert C. 1998. *Project Management in the Fast Lane: Applying the Theory of Constraints*. Series on Constraints Management. St. Lucie Press/APICS.

Srikanth, M. L., and M. Michael Umble. 1997. *Synchronous Management: Profit-Based Manufacturing for the 21st Century, Volume One*. Guilford, CT: The Spectrum Publishing Company.

Umble, M. M., and M. L. Srikanth. 1997. *Synchronous Management: Profit-Based Manufacturing for the 21st Century, Volume One: Implementation Issues and Case Studies*. Guilford, CT: The Spectrum Publishing Company.

CHAPTER 26

CROSS-IMPACT ANALYSIS OF INFORMATION TECHNOLOGIES AND PROJECT MANAGEMENT KNOWLEDGE AREAS IN THE BUILDING DESIGN PROCESS

H. Murat Gunaydin, Ph.D.—Izmir Institute of Technology
David Arditi, Ph.D.—Illinois Institute of Technology

Introduction

The dynamic nature of the design process, the interdependence of various participating entities, the high expectations for high quality products, processes, and services, and the need for teamwork, flexibility, and a high degree of coordination suggest that information technology (IT) has great potential in the design phase of a building project. The objective of the study presented in this chapter is to assess the impact of information technologies on project management knowledge areas in the building design process in the next fifteen years.

There seems to be no doubt that the quality and productivity achieved in the building design process can be enhanced without additional cost via the application of the rapidly developing information technologies. But, how can executives readjust and, if necessary, realign the processes involved in building design to synchronize them with the requirements of new information technologies? A major part of the answer to this fundamental question relies on having a good idea of the potential impact that the application of information systems and technologies will have on project management knowledge areas used in the building design process in the coming ten to fifteen years.

Methodology

The computerized model that is the subject of this chapter forecasts the impact of major breakthrough developments in seven information technologies (virtual reality, computer-aided design/computer-aided manufacturing [CAD/CAM], artificial intelligence, geographical information systems/global positioning systems [GIS/GPS], Internet/intranet, project management software, and wireless communication technology) on the maturity levels of the nine project management knowledge areas defined by *A Guide to the Project Management Body of Knowledge* (*PMBOK® Guide*) (Project Management Institute 1996)—project integration management, project scope management, project time management, project cost management, project quality management, project human resources management, project communications management, project risk management, and project procurement management—of organizations involved in building design projects.

In the research reported in this chapter, a modified Delphi approach was used over the Internet to elicit expert opinion. Three types of information were collected. First, the forecasted (next fifteen years) maturity levels of the nine project management knowledge areas were obtained from building designers (for the conceptual and design phases). Second, the forecasted (next fifteen years) probabilities of occurrence of major breakthrough developments in the seven information technologies were obtained from information technologists. Third, the assessments of the cross impacts between the variables of the model were obtained from relevant respective parties. The data collected were subjected to a multi-level cross-impact analysis, which is a method typically used for long-term forecasting in financial markets. Cross-impact analysis was used for analyzing the interdependencies between the variables of the model by means of a simulation model built into the system.

Delphi Method

The objective of most Delphi applications is the reliable and creative exploration of ideas or the production of suitable information for decision-making. The Delphi method is based on a structured process for collecting and distilling knowledge from a group of experts by means of a series of questionnaires interspersed with controlled opinion feedback (Adler and Ziglio 1996). According to Helmer (1977) Delphi represents a useful communication device among a group of experts and, thus, facilitates the formation of a group judgment. Wissema (1982) underlines the importance of the Delphi method as a monovariable exploration technique for technology forecasting. He further states that the Delphi method has been developed in order to make discussion between experts possible, without permitting a certain social interactive behavior as happens during a normal group discussion and hampers opinion forming. Baldwin (1975) asserts that lacking full scientific knowledge, decision-makers have to rely on their own intuition or on expert opinion. The Delphi method has been widely used to generate forecasts in technology, education, and other fields (Cornish 1977; Gatewood and Gatewood 1983; Huss 1988). The Delphi method recognizes human judgment as legitimate and useful inputs in generating forecasts. Later, the notion of cross impacts was introduced to overcome the shortcomings of this simplistic approach (Helmer 1977).

In the original Delphi process, the key elements were 1) structuring of information flow, 2) feedback to the participants, and 3) anonymity for the participants. Clearly, these characteristics may offer distinct advantages over the conventional face-to-face conference as a communication tool. Goldschmidt (1975) agrees that there have been many poorly conducted Delphi projects. However, he warns that it is a fundamental mistake to equate the applications of the Delphi method with the Delphi method itself, as too many critics do. On the other hand, there have been several studies (Fowles 1978; Helmer 1981; Wissema 1982; Reuven and Dongchui 1995) supporting the Delphi method.

In general, the Delphi method is useful in answering one specific, single-dimension question. An improvement in forecasting reliability of the Delphi method was thought to be attainable by taking into consideration the possibility that the occurrence of one event may cause an increase or decrease in the probability of occurrence of other events included in the survey (Helmer 1977). Therefore cross-impact analysis has developed as an extension of Delphi method.

Cross-Impact Analysis

A basic limitation of many forecasting methods and the Delphi method is that they produce only isolated forecasts; that is, events and trends are projected one by one, without explicit reference to their possible influence on each other. Most events and developments, however, are in some way connected to each other. Interdependencies between these events and developments can be taken into consideration for more consistent and accurate forecasts. Cross-impact analysis addresses the Delphi method's lack of a mechanism for discovering mutually exclusive or conflicting outcomes. Thus, some outcomes forecasted by the Delphi method could be impossible to obtain simultaneously (Reuven and Dongchui 1995): for example full employment and a low rate of inflation. Cross-impact analysis addresses this problem directly by analyzing conditional probabilities—for example, the likelihood that inflation will be low if full employment is achieved. It examines the interactions of forecasted items (Gordon and Hayward 1968).

The cross-impact concept originated with Olaf Helmer and Theodore Gordon in conjunction with the design of a forecasting game for Kaiser-Aluminum (Helmer 1977). It represented an effort to extend the forecasting techniques of the Delphi method. In 1968 at the University of California at Los Angeles (UCLA), Gordon and Hayward developed a computer-based approach to cross-impact analysis and they published their findings in the paper titled *Initial Experiments with the Cross-Impact Matrix Method of Forecasting* (Gordon and

Hayward 1968). In this approach, events were recorded on an orthogonal matrix and at each matrix intersection the question was asked: If the event in the row were to occur, how would it affect the probability of occurrence of the event in the column? The judgments were entered in the matrix cells. Cornish (1977) states that most forecasting methods may not consider many reactions between forecasted events. Cross-impact analysis, however, attempts to reveal the conditional probability of an event given that various events have or have not occurred. Duval, Fontela, and Gabus (1975) claim that cross-impact analysis differs from both probability theory and mathematical statistics; a cross-impact analysis is concerned with the identification of possible outcomes rather than with an understanding of what is or what was. They define cross-impact analysis as a systematic way to examine possible future developments and their interactions.

Technology forecasting does not follow a fixed methodological pattern. However, the way in which the study is approached and the choice of methods depend on the individual researcher (Wissema 1982). Several versions of cross-impact analysis have been developed by researchers (Gordon and Hayward 1968; Duval, Fontela, and Gabus 1975; Helmer 1977; Sarin 1978; Novak and Lorant 1978; Wissema and Benes 1980; Hanson and Ramani 1988; Fargionne, 1997). The evaluation of the technique has not followed a single path, but has produced a variety of different methods for constructing, utilizing, and evaluating cross-impact matrices.

There are several methodologies for different applications. Gordon and Hayward (1968) define three modes of connection between variables. Assume event E1 occurs. A second event, E2, may be completely unaffected by E1; it may be enhanced by the occurrence of E1; or it may be inhibited by the occurrence of E1. Thus, E1 may affect E2 as follows:

- Unrelated
- Enhancing
- Inhibiting.

The impact of breakthrough developments in IT in the building construction process can be measured in terms of the deviations in the maturity levels of project management knowledge areas. The project management knowledge areas that are described in the *PMBOK® Guide* are used in this study. The reason for the selection of these knowledge areas is their clear definition in terms of processes and their wide acceptance among project management professionals. The life cycle of a building project consists of the conceptual, design, construction, and operation phases. This holistic approach may benefit all stakeholders in building projects including the suppliers, the processors, and finally the customers of the construction industry. In this research three modules are taken into consideration (Figure 1):

Module 1: Information technology module

Module 2: Building processes module

Module 3: Project management functions module

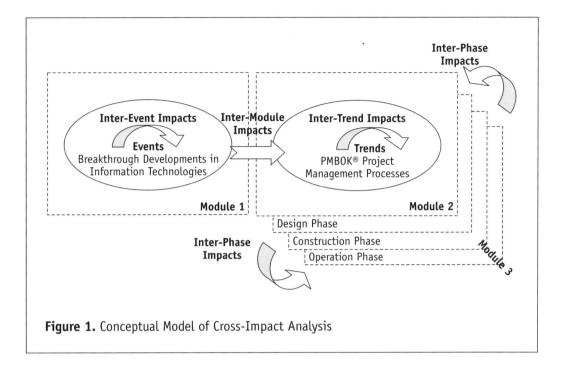

Figure 1. Conceptual Model of Cross-Impact Analysis

In these modules, events, trends, and phases are defined for causal cross-impact analysis. Module 1 defines the events; these are the breakthrough developments in information technologies. Module 2 identifies the trends; these are changes in the maturity level of the project management functions of the *PMBOK® Guide*. Module 3 covers the phases of a building project. Occurrence of the events in Module 1 has impacts on the trends in Module 2; these impacts are assessed within the framework of Module 3.

The modular design enhances the flexibility of the model. Therefore the model can be easily modified according to the needs of its user by adding or deleting modules. This multifunctional, multi-user, modular approach enables the model to develop without strict limitations and costly modifications.

Three five-year scenes are proposed for the years 2000–2005, 2005–2010, and 2010–2015 to define the time horizon in this study. The reasons for the selection of the time horizon of fifteen years and the three time intervals of five years each, namely scenes are as follows:

- They are easy to understand.
- They are long enough to allow experts not to make trend-based forecasting.
- They are not too long for practical and planning purposes.
- They are short enough that inter-event and inter-trend impacts in the same scene can be ignored.
- Time intervals are suitable for long-term forecasting.

Coefficient	Scale	Meaning
+3	SIG	Significantly High Impact
+2	MOD	Moderate Impact
+1	SLI	Slight Impact
0	NO	No Impact
-1	NEG	Negative Impact

Table 1. Scale Developed for Cross Impacts

Classifying the causal cross impacts into four groups makes the model easier to comprehend (Figure 1). These causal cross impacts between and within the modules are defined as:

1. Inter-module impacts
2. Inter-event impacts
3. Inter-trend impacts
4. Inter-phase impacts

Inter-event impacts assess the impacts of ITs on ITs. The occurrence of an IT may decrease or increase the probability of occurrence of the other ITs in the following scenes. These impacts are elicited from IT experts by means of a Delphi process.

Inter-trend impacts state the interdependencies between the project management knowledge areas. Fluctuation of the maturity level of any project management knowledge area may have impacts on the others in the next scene. These interdependencies are obtained from project management professionals.

Inter-phase impacts assess the impact of phases on each other. Any fluctuation of the maturity level of any project management knowledge area may not only have impacts on the same project management knowledge area in the next scene, but may also have impacts on the same project management knowledge area in the other phases of a building project. For example, any improvement in the project quality management knowledge area in the design phase may also affect the project quality management knowledge area in the construction phase in the following scene. In other words, project management knowledge areas may be impacted by other project management knowledge areas in other phases of the project.

The impacts are classified in terms of intuitive perceptions. The reason for this is to make use of experts in a most convenient way. The scale in Table 1 is developed to collect expert judgment. Actual cross-impact coefficients to be inserted in the matrix are also listed.

Information Technologies (1)	Scene 1 Years 2000–2005 (2)	Scene 2 Years 2005–2010 (3)	Scene 3 Years 2010–2015 (4)
Virtual Reality	0.6	0.7	0.7
CAD/CAM	0.7	0.8	0.8
Artificial Intelligence	0.6	0.8	0.8
GIS/GPS	0.8	0.8	0.8
Internet/Intranet	0.8	0.8	0.8
PM Software	0.5	0.6	0.7
Wireless Communication	0.8	0.8	0.9

Table 2. Forecasted Probability of Major Breakthrough Developments by Delphi Process

+3 and -1 are not absolute limits; occasionally, for extremely large impacts, numbers could be employed whose absolute value is in excess of 3 or less than -1. This flexible scale lets the experts judge their intuitive interpretations' effects on the model.

The modules and the causal relations between them are defined in the following sections. In this study, causal cross-impact analysis is inevitably conducted in a domain of what might be called "soft data" and "soft laws." As Helmer (1977) stated, dependence on intuitive judgment is not just a temporary expedient, but in fact a mandatory requirement. Therefore, instead of firm observational data, this model utilizes judgmental inputs; in place of well-confirmed empirical laws, the model makes use of intuitively perceived regularities. Therefore, reliance on expert opinion is essential. Even though the model can be used with data that are elicited from a single expert, a Delphi process is also included for added reliability.

In the Delphi method two types of data are elicited from the experts:

1. *Predictions for the future scenes*: event probabilities and trend values are elicited in respective scenes. These include:

   ■ Predictions of the probability of occurrence of major breakthrough developments in ITs in respective scenes (Table 2).
   ■ Predictions of the expected maturity levels of the *PMBOK® Guide* project management knowledge areas in the design phase in respective scenes (Table 3).

PM Knowledge Area (1)	Scene 0 Year 1997 (2)	Scene 1 Years 2000–2005 (3)	Scene 2 Years 2005–2010 (4)	Scene 3 Years 2010–2015 (5)	Total Change (%) (6)
Integration Management	3.3	3.4	3.7	3.9	18
Scope Management	3.5	3.6	3.7	3.8	9
Time Management	3.6	3.7	3.8	4.1	14
Cost Management	3.7	3.8	3.9	4.1	11
Quality Management	2.9	3.5	3.9	4.1	41
Human Resources Management	3.1	3.2	3.4	4	29
Communications Management	3.5	3.7	4	4.4	26
Risk Management	2.9	3.2	3.5	3.8	31
Procurement Management	3.3	3.4	3.6	3.9	18

1 = Zero Maturity, 2 = Low Maturity, 3 = Moderate Maturity, 4 = High Maturity, 5 = Complete Maturity

Table 3. Maturity Levels of Project Management Knowledge Areas in the Design Phase of a Building Project Forecasted by Delphi Process

2. *Assessments for the cross impacts*: impacts of the variables (events, trends, and phases) on each other are elicited by means of the intuitive scale described above. These include:

- Assessments of the cross impacts of ITs on project management knowledge areas in the design phase (Table 4).
- Assessments of the cross impacts of ITs on ITs.
- Assessments of the cross impacts of trends (project management knowledge areas) on trends.
- Assessments of cross impacts of building project phases (conceptual, design, construction, and operation phases) on phases.

Data elicitation for all cross impacts was obtained via Internet forms that were submitted to experts with required feedback for the Delphi process.

Information Technology Module

The IT module is basically a technology-forecasting module. From the beginning of this study, IT's rapid development led us to consider a model which does not strictly depend on specific ITs, but rather depends on a flexible technology module that can be changed and modified easily. This property of the model makes sure that the model will not be outdated because any development can be easily integrated into this modular model. Seven ITs are defined as events of the module. These ITs will be described later.

Impacting Information Technologies (1)	Integration Management (2)	Scope Management (3)	Time Management (4)	Cost Management (5)	Quality Management (6)	Human Resources Management (7)	Communications Management (8)	Risk Management (9)	Procurement Management (10)	Total Ratings (11)
Virtual Reality	1	3	1	1	2	1	2	1	1	13
CAD/CAM	1	3	1	1	1	0	1	1	1	10
Artificial Intelligence	3	3	3	1	1	1	2	3	3	20
GIS/GPS	0	0	1	0	0	0	0	1	0	2
Internet/Intranet	2	2	2	1	0	1	3	0	1	12
PM Software	3	2	3	2	1	2	2	1	2	18
Wireless Communication	1	0	1	0	1	1	1	0	0	5
Total Ratings	11	13	12	6	6	6	11	7	7	80

0 = No Impact, 1 = Slight Impact, 2 = Moderate Impact, 3 = Significant Impact

Table 4. Cross Impacts of Information Technologies on Project Management Knowledge Areas in the Design Phase

The IT module is the ignition point of the model (Figure 1). This module defines the likelihood of the occurrence of breakthrough developments in IT. When the model runs, it is this module that defines the scenarios based on the occurrence and nonoccurrence of the events in the respective scenes. Probabilities of the occurrence of breakthrough developments in these events are elicited from IT experts (Table 2). Each scenario consists of three scenes (years 2000–2005, 2005–2010, and 2010–2015) and the seven ITs defined in the following sections. Currently this scenario-generating module considers only the occurrence and nonoccurrence of the events in the defined time horizon; therefore 2^{21} (2,097,152) scenarios can be generated.

Project Management Knowledge Areas Module

The project management knowledge areas module defines and measures the trends in project management knowledge areas in the process of building projects (Figure 1). The maturity levels of project management knowledge areas are defined and measured by Kwak (1997) on a scale of 1–5 (1 being no conformity, 5 being complete conformity). Kwak (1997) reports on current maturity levels of project management knowledge areas in the United States (US) construction industry. Future trends in the maturity levels of project management knowledge areas are elicited from experts by means of a Delphi method (Table 3) in the design phase of a building project. The trends' cross impacts on each other are also elicited from experts. The nine *PMBOK® Guide* project management knowledge areas are used in this model and defined as trends.

Other trends throughout the building design process can also be simulated for different events. Modules such as productivity, safety, quality, and so on, can replace this module or be added to the model. This way, the effects of technological and environmental developments can be forecasted on several aspects of building projects. This modular design makes this methodology a generic forecasting frame for the construction industry.

Building Processes Module

The building processes module includes the phases of the life cycle of a building project. This module basically forms the backbone of the model (Figure 1). All project management knowledge areas and ITs are tested in the frame that is defined by this module. One can easily eliminate one or more phases or can easily add subphases. This brings the advantage of multipurpose use; one can focus on any phase or phases as this research focuses on the design phase of a building project. This module can be replaced by modules such as a management level module (strategic, tactical, and operational), a management hierarchy module (site or office practices), and so forth.

The building processes module also analyzes the relationships between the phases of a building project. Interdependencies between these phases are defined in terms of cross impacts of the maturity levels of project management knowledge areas. If one considers a construction project as a whole system, any development in any phase of the process may have an impact on the other phases. Departments responsible for the processes are in fact internal customers of the company, and they provide and get both services and products to and from other departments. Their sensitivity to the other departments of the company has to be analyzed for their efficiency, in addition to the efficiency of their relationships with external customers. This module therefore explicitly defines these interdependencies and helps professionals to understand their organization as a whole system.

Findings

The findings of this research are presented in two sections namely, Delphi survey results and cross-impact analysis. In the Delphi survey results, the data that are elicited from the experts are analyzed. In the second section, the multi-level cross-impact model is utilized in order to assess the impacts of IT on the maturity levels of the project management knowledge areas in the design process of a building project.

The multi-level cross-impact analysis model developed in this research demands data from experts in a variety of disciplines (i.e., designers, construction managers, property managers, and information technologists). Hence the model solely depends on the intuitive judgment of the experts and the model's output can be only as good as this input. Therefore, the selection of these experts is very important. To that end, a Delphi survey of the members of the Project Management Institute's (PMI®) Midwest Chapter in the United States (US) was conducted. The endorsement of the Chapter's Board of Directors was obtained. Volunteers were sought through an announcement in the Chapter's monthly newsletter. Later, members were invited via email to join the study. A total of thirty-four experts accepted the offer to participate. Data presented in Tables 1–3 were elicited from these experts.

Delphi Results

The results of the Delphi survey show the impacts of ITs on project management knowledge areas (Table 4) and the forecasted maturity levels of the project management knowledge areas (Table 3) in the design phase of a building project. First, the significant interdependencies between ITs and project management knowledge areas will be discussed. Then forecasted maturity levels of project management knowledge areas for each scene (i.e., years 2000–2005, 2005–2010, and 2010–2015) will be presented.

Table 4 is designed to exhibit the impacts of breakthrough developments in ITs on the maturity levels of project management knowledge areas. Each cell contains a rating between 0 and 3, where 0 is no impact, 1 is slight impact, 2 is moderate impact, and 3 is significant impact. The sum of the total impacts is recorded at the end of each row (i.e., impacting ITs) and column (i.e., impacted project management knowledge areas). The sum of the impacts at the end of a row indicates that particular IT's total impact on the project management knowledge areas, whereas, the sum of the impacts at the end of a column indicates the total impact coming from all the ITs to that particular project management knowledge area. For example, Table 4 shows that project scope management (column 3) is the most impacted project management knowledge area by ITs with a total impact rating of 13. On the other hand, artificial intelligence is the IT with the most impact on project management knowledge areas, with a total impact rating of 20 (column 11). The last row in Table 4 indicates that the most impacted project management knowledge areas by ITs are project scope management (rating = 13), project time management (rating = 12), project integration management (rating = 11), and project communications management (rating = 11). The least affected project management knowledge areas are project cost management (rating = 6), project quality management (rating = 6), and project human resources management (rating = 6). On the other hand, column 11 shows that the ITs with greatest impact on project management knowledge areas are artificial intelligence (rating = 20), project management software (rating = 18), and virtual reality (rating = 13), whereas the ITs with least impact are GIS/GPS (rating = 2) and wireless communication technologies (rating = 5).

The results of this Delphi survey indicate that the maturity levels of project management knowledge areas can be enhanced by the use of some ITs. Indeed virtual reality, CAD, and artificial intelligence technologies can actually help both the customer and designer to understand the actual building better before it is built. This ability can positively impact scope management activities in the design phase of a building project. Artificial intelligence and project management software can be utilized for more accurate project time management. On the other hand, project integration management is very important in the design phase because many problems related to the integration of the many disciplines and knowledge areas throughout the building process can be solved in the design phase. This may enhance the constructability and quality of the design. Project communications management in the design phase is significantly impacted by breakthrough developments in Internet/intranet technologies. The building design process highly depends on information from sources as diverse as material dealers, technology developers, equipment manufacturers, technical consultants, and so on. More and more business communications are done via the Internet/intranet. Blueprints and other information can be transferred between the parties by electronic means. Increasing integration of the software and hardware technologies makes this possible. This creates many opportunities for design firms. It eliminates to some extent the barrier of geography; design firms can work with other professionals with more flexible schedules and with fewer limitations. According to Buckley (1994), ITs also support concurrent engineering activities that can, if done correctly, reduce lead-times from concept to customer and increase quality performance. ITs with the most impact on project communication management are artificial intelligence, project management software, and Internet/intranet services.

The IT that has significant and moderate impact on all the four project management knowledge areas (project scope management, project time management, project integration management, and project communications management) appears to be artificial intelligence. Indeed artificial intelligence may help designers in a variety of ways; for example, artificial intelligence programs given the design constraints can generate design alternatives. Generation and evaluation of the design alternatives may enhance the designer's creativity to address potential design problems. Of course, the other advantage of artificial intelligence is the reduction of the time required for the decision-making process. Traditional sketch drawings may take days to generate a few alternatives, whereas, numerous alternatives can be generated and evaluated by the artificial intelligence technologies in matter of minutes.

One of the three project management knowledge areas that is least impacted by ITs is project cost management (total rating = 6). The IT that impacts project cost management the most is project management software technologies, which seems to have a relatively moderate impact on the maturity level of the project cost management knowledge area. This is because costs can be tracked and controlled in the design phase by cost control software. Project quality management, which also has the lowest rating of 6 is not impacted significantly by any of the ITs except for virtual reality, which has a moderate impact on it; it is either slightly or not impacted at all by the remaining ITs. The moderate impact of virtual reality on project quality management may come from the importance of virtual reality presentations in order to get more customer input and solve potential conflicts in the design phase before they actually occur. This may increase the quality of the building project. Project human resources management is the third knowledge area that is least impacted by ITs (total rating = 6). The strongest impact comes from project management software technologies that have a moderate impact on the maturity level of this knowledge area. While these knowledge areas do not receive direct impacts from ITs, they might be impacted by secondary impacts via other project management knowledge areas as discussed later.

On the other hand, artificial intelligence and project management software technologies significantly and moderately impact project procurement management, respectively. Indeed the processes required in acquiring goods and services from outside the performing organization and decision-making processes may benefit from both artificial intelligence and project management software technologies. Artificial intelligence, in this case, can help decision-makers in the selection process of sources or identifying the potential risk areas. Project management software technologies may help to keep track of procurement planning and contract administration.

Breakthrough developments in artificial intelligence have the highest impact (total rating = 20) on the maturity levels of project management knowledge areas in the design phase. Indeed the design process is an iterative process; therefore, artificial intelligence technologies may assist designers in their decision-making process. Developments in artificial intelligence may enhance the efficiency of CAD and virtual reality technologies.

The second part of the Delphi survey was designed to retrieve the forecasted values of the maturity levels of project management knowledge areas in the design phase. The results are presented in Table 3. The total change in the maturity level of each project management knowledge area is presented in column 6. The total change indicates the percentage increase in the maturity levels from scene 0 (i.e., year 1997) to scene 3 (i.e., years 2010–2015). The total changes show the experts' perceptions of potential improvement areas relative to each other. The highest increases can be seen in the maturity levels of project quality management (total change 41 percent) and project risk management (total change 31 percent); Kwak (1997) had measured the maturity levels of project quality management and project risk management as 2.9 in 1997, the lowest among the others. The maturity levels of project scope management and project cost management on the other hand show small increases of 9 percent and 11 percent, respectively. The predictions of the experts show that attaining full maturity in the industry (i.e., a maturity level of 5) is not reachable within the time horizon of this study. That is why companies that deal with the design of building projects can differentiate themselves from their competitors by enhancing their project management maturity levels.

Cross-Impact Analysis

A multi-level cross-impact analysis uses the data that were elicited from experts, as described in the preceding sections. A computer run of 10,000 replications of the model produced the results that consist of forecasted maturity levels of project management knowledge areas and the probabilities of major breakthrough developments in ITs in the given time horizon (i.e., years 2000–2005, 2005–2010, and 2010–2015). Hence the trigger actions of the model in the first scene can only affect the second scene (i.e., 2005–2010); the forecasted values for the first scene (i.e., 2000–2005) are limited to the Delphi survey results. The second and the third scenes (i.e., 2005–2010 and 2010–2015) have cross-impact analysis values along with the Delphi results. Because of the nature of the study, the relationships between the variables are all positive; therefore, the results of the Delphi survey are either positive (i.e., significant, moderate, and slight) impacts or no impacts. Lack of negative impacts naturally makes the model generate higher forecasts then the Delphi results. This is because the model generates new estimates based on the Delphi estimates and sums up all the negative and positive impacts around the Delphi results. Indeed, if there were negative impacts, the model might have generated lower values than the estimated Delphi results (in cases where the negative impacts overcame the positive impacts). For example, if we assume that the events (trigger actions) are not occurring at all, then the model should and actually does present the original Delphi estimates (i.e., forecasted maturity levels and forecasted probabilities), since there are no impacts either positive or negative on the estimated trend and event values. The model's performance depends on the Delphi estimates; indeed the results of the model can be as good as the inputs.

The results are presented in two sections. First, the results of the basic computer run are discussed. Then sensitivity analyses are conducted in order to determine the sensitivity of the project management knowledge areas in each phase to major breakthrough developments in ITs.

Results of the Basic Run

A basic computer run of the model consists of 10,000 replications. Computer runs of 1,000, 4,000, and 10,000 replications resulted in standard errors of 0.0038, 0.0019, and 0.0012, respectively, for the project integration management knowledge area with similar results in the other project management knowledge areas. For comparative policy analysis and scenario generating purposes, replications of 1,000 and above are reasonable given the low standard errors. The results consist of the forecasted maturity levels of project management knowledge areas in the design phase of a building project (Table 5) and the forecasted probabilities of the major breakthrough developments in ITs. Since the model produces values only for the second and the third scenes, the analysis will be conducted in the second (i.e., 2005–2010) and the third (i.e., 2010–2015) scenes. The values in

PM Knowledge Areas (1)	Scene 0 Year 1997 (2)	Scene 1 Years 2000–2005 (3)	Scene 2 Years 2005–2010 (4)	Scene 3 Years 2010–2015 (5)	Total Change (%) (6)
Integration Management	3.3	3.4	4.0	4.3	30
Scope Management	3.5	3.6	4.1	4.2	20
Time Management	3.6	3.7	4.1	4.4	22
Cost Management	3.7	3.8	4.1	4.3	16
Quality Management	2.9	3.7	4.1	4.3	48
Human Resources Management	3.1	3.2	3.6	4.2	35
Communications Management	3.5	3.7	4.2	4.5	29
Risk Management	2.9	3.2	3.8	4.1	41
Procurement Management	3.3	3.4	3.9	4.2	27

1 = Zero Maturity, 2 = Low Maturity, 3 = Moderate Maturity, 4 = High Maturity,
5 = Complete Maturity

Table 5. Maturity Levels of Project Management Knowledge Areas in the Design Phase of a Building Project Forecasted by the Model

the first scene (i.e., 2000–2005) are the Delphi forecasts. As discussed earlier, the model produces higher estimates than the Delphi forecasts in the last two scenes. A ranking of the mean values of the estimates or a ranking of the percentage increases are useful in this case.

In the design phase, Tables 3 and 5 are used for comparative analysis. The model forecasts more increases than the Delphi forecast for reasons discussed earlier. The differences can be calculated easily by subtracting the respective values of total change in column 6 of Table 3 from column 6 of Table 5. For example, while total change in project integration management is forecasted by experts as 18 percent, the model forecasts a 30 percent total change. The difference of 12 percent shows that experts' estimates are not consistent with the model's forecasts. The same situation can be observed in project scope management with an 11 percent higher increase forecasted by the model. In contrast, the forecasts generated by the model for project communications management (a difference of 3 percent) and project cost management (a difference of 5 percent) are much closer to the predictions made by experts. The mean of the differences of total changes between the Delphi forecasts and model forecasts is 8 percent in the design phase.

Sensitivity Analysis

Sensitivity of each project management knowledge area to an IT is important in order to understand the impacts of ITs on project management knowledge areas. The design of the model enables sensitivity analysis. For example, the sensitivity of the project management knowledge areas to major breakthrough developments in the Internet/intranet technologies can be observed by setting all the IT events' occurrence probabilities to 0 except for Internet/intranet technologies. Then running the model will show the impact of Internet/intranet technologies on the project management knowledge areas without the other ITs' interactions.

For each sensitivity run, the model starts at the same random number entry which guarantees that, at analogous, stochastic decision points, the likelihood of major breakthrough developments will be as "lucky" or "unlucky" as in the preceding basic run. Each basic run consists of 10,000 replications. The sensitivity analysis is conducted for each of the seven ITs defined in this study.

The deviations of the results (i.e., results of sensitivity runs) from the Delphi forecasts are used for sensitivity analysis. In order to accomplish the objective of this study, deviations from the Delphi estimates are calculated and summarized in terms of percentages for the design phase (Table 6). Table 6 shows the sensitivity (percent change) of each project management knowledge area to the given IT. For example, the maturity level of project integration management in the third scene of the design phase is 3.9 (Table 3). Considering breakthrough developments only in virtual reality, the maturity level of project integration management will be 4.0 in the third scene (result of the model). The difference is 0.1, which is a 2.6 percent increase from the Delphi estimate. The highest deviation in this study is found to be 5.7 percent. This result indicates that breakthrough developments in an IT taken individually do not impact the maturity level of any one project management knowledge area significantly, whereas they effect the maturity level of all project management knowledge areas through primary (tangible) and secondary (intangible) impacts. This finding can be used to maximize the benefits of IT deployment and, therefore, decreas the cost and failure rates at the initial phases of reengineering/restructuring efforts. The impact of an individual IT on the maturity level of all project management knowledge areas can be observed from the bottom row (total change percent) of Table 6.

The sensitivity analyses consider both primary and secondary impacts of IT. The primary impacts are the ones that affect the maturity level of a project management knowledge area directly. The secondary impacts are the impacts coming from the other knowledge areas and/or the impacts coming from the same knowledge area in the different phases. If only the primary impacts are considered, the results should and actually do reflect the Delphi results about the cross impacts of ITs on project management knowledge areas. However secondary impacts make

PM Knowledge Areas (1)	Virtual Reality (2)	CAD/CAM (3)	Artificial Intelligence (4)	GIS/GPS (5)	Internet/Intranet (6)	PM Software (7)	Wireless Communication (8)
Integration Management	2.6	2.6	2.6	0.0	2.6	5.1	0.0
Scope Management	5.3	2.6	5.3	0.0	2.6	5.3	0.0
Time Management	2.4	0.0	2.4	0.0	2.4	2.4	0.0
Cost Management	2.4	0.0	2.4	0.0	0.0	2.4	0.0
Quality Management	2.4	0.0	2.4	0.0	0.0	2.4	0.0
Human Resources Management	2.5	0.0	2.5	0.0	0.0	2.5	0.0
Communications Management	0.0	0.0	0.0	0.0	2.3	0.0	0.0
Risk Management	2.6	2.6	2.6	0.0	0.0	2.6	0.0
Procurement Management	2.6	2.6	2.6	0.0	0.0	2.6	0.0
Total Change (%)	22.8	10.4	22.8	0.0	9.9	25.3	0.0

Table 6. Sensitivity of the Maturity Level of Project Management Knowledge Areas to Major Breakthrough Developments in IT in the Design Phase of a Building Project in Terms of Percentage Change

this model more realistic because it considers the interdependencies between the variables.

The summary of the results for the design phase is presented in Table 6. Project management knowledge areas are sensitive to breakthrough developments in project management software (total change 25.3 percent), virtual reality (total change 22.8 percent), and artificial intelligence (total change 22.8 percent). The overall maturity level of project management knowledge areas in a design firm may be enhanced most by investing in these ITs. Focusing on one project management knowledge area will not help the organization to reach higher overall maturity levels. These results indicate that IT investments should be considered in a holistic environment. The secondary impacts of improvements will spread benefits of IT deployment throughout all project management knowledge areas.

Studies conducted by Alter (1996) and Callon (1996) conclude that IT investments are useless if the current business processes are not analyzed and redesigned to perform best with the new ITs. The different sensitivity of each project management knowledge area to an IT in the different phases of a project support this idea. Indeed, project management knowledge areas aim to achieve the same goals in each phase of a building project, but the tools to achieve these objectives should be and actually are different from each other. For example, project human resources management in the design phase has different procedures than project human resources management in the construction phase. While a relatively small number of employees dominate the process in a design firm, a large labor force may be typical in a construction company. To deal with these differences project management knowledge areas should utilize different ITs for their specific cases.

The modular design of the model allows the researcher to add other ITs in order to test the sensitivity of the maturity levels of project management knowledge areas in the process of a building project for those specific ITs. As the results of this study indicate, the pace of the developments in ITs is very fast. Change breeds change, and each change in IT brings different opportunities for the building design process. Further and more detailed studies in this area may help building construction professionals to redesign their processes for better performance in the light of the new ITs.

Conclusion

The results of the study show that the maturity levels of project management knowledge areas in the design process of the building project can be enhanced by major breakthrough developments in some ITs. In the time horizon of this study experts do not foresee the full maturity levels for project management knowledge areas in the design phase of a building project. However, steady increases are expected for the project management maturity levels. Increases are expected to be parallel to each other, which suggests strong interdependencies between the maturity levels of project management knowledge areas. Therefore, improvement efforts to project management knowledge areas have to consider not one or few, but all of the project management knowledge areas together. Likewise IT deployment should target not one, but all project management knowledge areas in order to increase overall project management maturity level.

Delphi results indicate an increasing pace of technological innovation in some ITs. The increasing rate of major breakthrough developments has the potential to change the processes in the design phase of a building project. This suggests that designers in the building construction industry have to be ready to face emerging challenges created by rapid major breakthrough developments in ITs.

Given the cross impacts between the variables, the model showed inconsistencies of the Delphi survey results (i.e., expert opinions) in some cases. For these cases experts may be asked again to consider their Delphi forecasts in the light of these findings. These inconsistencies are to be expected and probably the result of the multidimensional interdependencies (direct and secondary impacts) which cannot be judged by the experts. In this case, the model serves as a learning tool for professionals.

The maturity levels of project management knowledge areas are found to be sensitive to breakthrough developments in project management software, virtual reality, and artificial intelligence. Sensitivity analyses showed that developments in single ITs do not have significant impacts on the maturity levels of project management knowledge areas. On the other hand, major breakthrough developments in several ITs, with their direct and secondary impacts can enhance the project management maturity levels of a building design organization. Therefore, restructuring/reengineering efforts should address all aspects of process improvement. As the literature survey indicates, IT deployment without addressing the structural issues in the organization does nothing but create automation. This research showed that project management maturity levels in the building design process could be enhanced to some extent by the use of some ITs.

The model's scenario generating capability can be used effectively for planning and analysis purposes. The model can be used for comparative policy analysis. The testing of a variety of policies and their implementation through specific plans and appropriate budget allocations may identify several policies as potentially promising. The integrated approach used in this research, both in terms of disciplines and in terms of phases, helps professionals to develop robust strategies of IT deployment in their projects.

At a global level, this research developed a unique methodology for understanding ITs impact on the maturity levels of project management knowledge areas in the design phase of a building project by integrating expert, IT-specific, project management-specific, and process-specific knowledge and a mathematical structure. It is important to realize that "playing the model" is a learning experience. The greatest payoff may not be the determination of optimal strategies, but an increasing understanding of the insights of the subject and the gradual production of an improved model. This model might provide a conceptual framework within which to formulate forecasts, policies, and plans in areas where interdisciplinary approaches are essential and where reliable and comprehensive theories are absent.

References

Adler, M., and E. Ziglio. 1996. *Gazing into the Oracle.* Bristol, PA: Jessica Kingsley Publishers.

Alter, S. 1996. *Information Systems: A Management Perspective.* 2nd ed. New York: The Benjamin/Cummings Publishing Company, Inc.

Callon, J. D. 1996. *Competitive Advantage through Information Technology.* New York: McGraw-Hill.

Cornish, E. 1977. *The Study of the Future.* Washington, DC: World Future Society.

Duval, A., E. Fontela, and A. Gabus, eds. 1975. *Portraits of Complexity.* Edited by M. M. Baldwin. Columbus, OH: Battelle Memorial Institute.

Enzer, S., and S. Alter. 1978. Cross-Impact Analysis and Classical Probability: The Question of Consistency. *Futures* 10 (3): 227–239.

Fowles, J. 1978. *Handbook of Futures Research*. Connecticut: Greenwood Press.

Gatewood, R. D., and E. J. Gatewood. 1983. The Use of Expert Data in Human Resource Planning: Guidelines from Strategic Forecasting. *Human Resource Planning* 5 (1): 83–94.

Gordon, T. J., and H. Hayward. 1968. Initial Experiments with the Cross-Impact Matrix Method of Forecasting. *Futures* 1 (2): 100–116.

Hanson, W. H., and N. Ramani. 1988. Technology Forecasting: A Hydroelectric Company Experience. *Technology Management Publication* 1 (3): 266–270.

Helmer, O. 1977. Problems in Futures Research: Delphi and Causal Cross-Impact Analysis. *Futures* (February): 17–31.

———. 1981. Reassessment of Cross-Impact Analysis. *Futures* (October): 389–400.

Huss, W. R. 1988. A Move toward Scenario Analysis. *International Journal of Forecasting* 4: 377–388.

Kwak, Y. H. 1997. A Systematic Approach to Evaluate Quantitative Impacts of Project Management. Ph.D. dissertation, University of California, Berkeley.

Novak, E., and K. Lorant. 1978. A Method for the Analysis of Interrelationships between Mutually Connected Events: A Cross-Impact Method. *Technological Forecasting and Social Change* 12: 201–212.

Project Management Institute. 1996. *A Guide to the Project Management Body of Knowledge (PMBOK® Guide)*. Upper Darby, PA: Project Management Institute.

Reuven, L., and H. Dongchui. 1995. Choosing a Technological Forecasting Method. *Industrial Management* 37 (1): 14–22.

Sarin, R. K. 1978. A Sequential Approach to Cross-Impact Analysis. *Futures* (February): 53–62.

Wissema, J. G., and J. Benes. 1980. A Cross-Impact Case Study: The Dutch Construction Sector. *Futures* (October): 394–404.

CHAPTER 27

MANAGING TECHNOLOGICAL INNOVATION PROJECTS: THE QUEST FOR A UNIVERSAL LANGUAGE

Bob Mills, Ph.D.—University of Waikato

Alan Langdon, Ph.D.—University of Waikato

Chris Kirk, Ph.D.—Massey University

Janis Swan, Ph.D.—University of Waikato

Introduction

Innovation creates a benefit from an idea, a concept, an invention, or the application of a new technology. Technological innovation may involve "blue-skies" research, developing new products and new processes, and/or improvements to current products and processes.

Innovation projects are different than most other projects. Innovation projects will probably be stopped or fail, whereas practically all other projects are expected to be completed (Economist 1999). Success does not follow from compliance with predetermined objectives of cost, schedule, and quality, but instead from achieving profitable business outcomes. Further, the current value, health, and welfare of innovation projects cannot sensibly be judged against project prescriptions; they can only be assessed in relation to the remaining cost and effort and their updated predicted benefit. Innovation projects can expect continued support only if they maintain the promise of adequate return. Business purposes, therefore, overwhelm innovation project processes (Bartlett and Ghoshal 1994). Traditional project management tools, which make comparisons with plans and schedules, consequently appear to be largely irrelevant for monitoring and control.

The logic and simplicity of Gantt (bar) and program review and evaluation technique (PERT) network charts have made them enduring project management tools. However, in the 1970s and 1980s, "stage-gate" methods became popular for monitoring and controlling new product development (NPD) (Cooper 1993). More recently project portfolio appraisal systems provide a mechanism for regular and appropriate strategic decision-making by executive management (Cooper, Edgett, and Kleinschmidt 1998). Further, "Rapid Application Development" was introduced in the software industry in the 1990s (Mimno 1991). Traditional hierarchical and prescriptive innovation project management tools have therefore been perceived as ponderous in the context of today's organic business structures and are being challenged.

Other features of innovation projects also make the use of traditional tools impractical. For example, new technology and new market information may validly contribute to innovation project activities right up to the launch date, dramatically changing the shape of the project, making it difficult for documentation to keep pace. As well, individuals involved in the innovation process are often delegated high levels of responsibility and freedom. They might best be "self-managed" and monitored at regular intervals, rather than "directed" on the basis of a schedule of activities, and may also optimize resources better than specialist planners.

Technological innovation often changes "ownership" and focus within organizations and across them. For example, an innovation project can move from fundamental science and development in one company to production, sales, and marketing in another. While change of ownership may change scope and prospects, the essential idea may remain, as might the ultimate goal.

The traditional role of marketing, at the crossroad between the operational arm of organizational structure and the forces of disruption (research and development) and standardization (quality systems), is being diffused (Mintzberg 1979, 1989). Therefore, innovation project team members find themselves directly involved in ensuring their outputs profitably satisfy real and current customer need. Innovation program and project management must therefore be a transparent process to those responsible for setting the purpose of the organization, as well as for all the people involved in making it happen.

A widely understood process and format, more relevant to modern organizations is needed to meet the shortfalls of traditional project management. Bernaxo et al. (1999) and Englund and Graham (1999), however, warn of the many problems in implementing organizational change in the innovation project process. Intellectual support does not ensure change. A first requirement is for a universal language, integrative within and across organizations, and useful within and across functions. A second requirement is a means for successful implementation.

The innovation project management practices of twenty-five program and project managers from four research and development (R&D) purchasers, three R&D providers, and six successful New Zealand companies involved in the electronics, food, and forestry sectors were investigated. Without exception interviewees were actively seeking to improve monitoring and control processes. A new project and portfolio approach (called Time-Block Innovation Project System or TIPS) using sequenced blocks of time, rather than sequenced blocks of activities, was conceptualized to better meet managers needs.

TIPS uses a spreadsheet (Microsoft® Excel®) to regularly update forecasts of future cost, future benefits, and the likelihood of meeting customer needs by the scheduled date. At the end of each weekly, monthly, or quarterly time-block, past costs, schedules, and deliverables are replaced by revised projections arising from new technological and market knowledge gained in the preceding time-block.

The original interviewees reacted positively to the TIPS concept. A three-month TIPS pilot trial on six projects, three in each of two of the original trial companies, was therefore conducted. Iterative action research was used to simultaneously refine and implement TIPS, and a questionnaire was used to indicate its potential usefulness and value to the companies. Participant managers indicated that the project management information collected by TIPS was adequately comprehensive and very useful. Participants agreed that TIPS was better than existing arrangements at drawing early attention for corrective action. However, one third of the participants thought TIPS might be better implemented in dedicated software.

TIPS methodology was rated very highly by one of the companies, six project managers, and five technical managers. The second company rated the value of implementing TIPS as moderate. Respondents felt that TIPS could be implemented in their companies within twelve months. The pilot trial incidentally indicated potential improvements to the innovation processes in both companies.

TIPS may lead to a practical and more universal approach for monitoring and controlling small-scale innovation processes in wealth creating organizations.

Background to This Research

An initial study (Mills et al. 1996) was carried out with four representative purchasers and three providers of technological R&D services (n = 13) to assess the satisfaction of senior program and project managers with current practices by using in-depth, partially structured interviews. A second study (Mills et al. 1999) assessed six successful companies (two each from the electronics/manufacturing, food-processing, and forestry industries) (n = 12) by the same method as the initial study. Annual turnover, R&D expenditure, and number of respondents for each organization are shown in Table 1.

All organizations used Gantt charts and all companies and research providers used Microsoft Project software, but only for planning, as the costs and effort to maintain frequently changing schedules were too high. Three of the six companies had instituted stage-gate processes to some degree, which helped tie projects into

Organization Type	Code	Turnover (NZ$m)	R&D Expenditure (NZ$m)	Interviewees from Earlier Research	TIPS Survey Respondents
R&D Purchasers	P1	Not Applicable	259	2	1
	P2	Not Applicable	8	1	0
	P3	Not Applicable	3	1	1
	P4	Not Applicable	1	1	1
R&D Providers	R1	87	70	2	1
	R2	44	38	3	1
	R3	10	7	3	1
Electronics Companies	E1	50	2	2	2
	E2	20	1	2	2
Food Companies	F1	2500	5-30	2	2
	F2	1000	5-30	2	2
Forestry Companies	T1	3000	Not Available	2	1
	T2	480	10	2	1

Table 1. Organizational Profiles (At 1995 for R&D Purchasers and Providers; 1988 for Companies)

the organization. However, none of the stage-gate processes was fully functional. Formal monitoring and control were inconsistently applied to suit individual project and business reporting requirements, making project comparison within organizations for portfolio reviews difficult. A key finding in the two investigations was that only one of the twenty-five managers was satisfied with current practices; all desired improvement and were altering their organizational systems to better accommodate change introduced as a result of new information or knowledge.

Therefore, a new approach called TIPS was conceived and developed to accommodate the need to align individual projects with programs and business purposes, and to respond to increased individual accountability in the context of uncertainty in a rapidly changing environment. Figures 1 and 2 compare the tightly scoped array of traditional innovation projects against a typical innovation spectrum with the more universal scope of a TIPS innovation project.

Ten fundamental differences in philosophy between traditional and TIPS project management are:

1. Projects always start now and always finish when benefit (income) is received.

2. Project achievement goals are synchronized to the business calendar (weeks, months, quarters).

3. TIPS recognizes achievement, not activities, which helps create motivation and urgency.

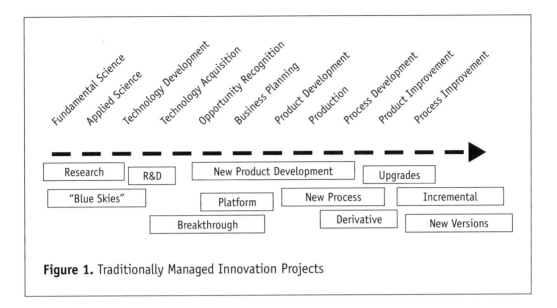

Figure 1. Traditionally Managed Innovation Projects

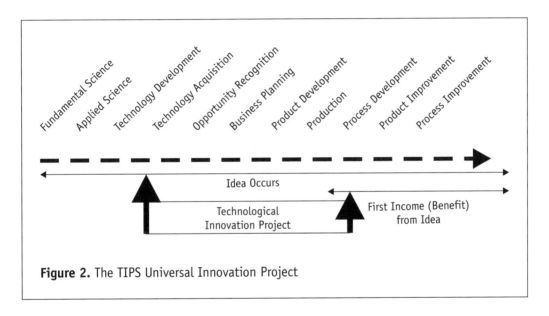

Figure 2. The TIPS Universal Innovation Project

4. Projects are monitored and controlled in relation to maximizing delivery of currently estimated future benefit and are not aligned with past plans and forecasts.

5. All past project cost and effort is considered as sunk, or in current terminology, invested in new knowledge.

6. TIPS projects are replanned from a zero base at the end of each time-block to incorporate new knowledge.

7. Each project is regularly reviewed in the context of project portfolios and assigned a unique priority rank within the organization.

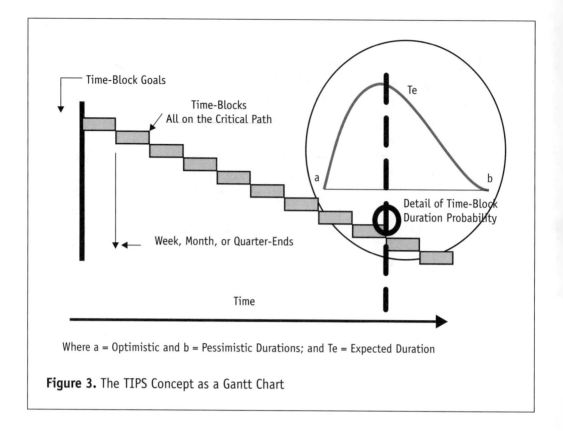

Where a = Optimistic and b = Pessimistic Durations; and Te = Expected Duration

Figure 3. The TIPS Concept as a Gantt Chart

8. Resource allocation is done on the basis of project priority ranking by empowered staff, rather than through the dictates of a central planning function.

9. TIPS acknowledges, quantifies, and standardizes risk estimates.

10. TIPS information is formatted for convenience and practical use.

In concept, TIPS can be considered as a Gantt chart where all project activities are allocated to sequential, equal-sized blocks of time (weeks, months, or quarters). Each time-block is allocated a description related to the focus of activity, goal, or milestone to be accomplished in that period (Figure 3). The nominal cost of each time-block and the probability that the time-block goal could actually be achieved are identified. The uncertainty of goal achievement by the end of the time-block is described using two duration estimates (optimistic and pessimistic).

By definition all time-blocks are on the critical path and the uncertainty of completion can therefore be readily calculated (we use a beta probability distribution after MacLeod and Petersen 1996). The latest estimated net present value (NPV) of the project benefit is transparently calculated and all key attributes for project and portfolio analysis and project ranking identified. Project rank disclosure enables individuals (in conjunction with their supervisors) to judge the best use of their time. Unlike a Gantt chart there is no need for or benefit from actually plotting activities against time. At the end of each time-block the project is

TIPS Week-block Project Sheet, Bob Mills, University of Waikato, 29 Sept 2000

SUMMARY	(Enter your data inside the double lined boxes)	COMPANY SPECIFIED DATA
	Company's Priority Rank Number for this project	
	Company's Strategic Category for this project	
	Target Market	
	Customer/Voice of Customer	
	End User	
	Project Output	
	Project Name	
	Project Sponsor	
	Project Manager	
	Interest Rate for using money (%)	
	Date Output is required	
Apr-01	Calculated Date First Sales Income receipt expected	
1.00	Calculated Probability that project is achievable	
Check Data	Calculated Probability that project is achievable on time	
0	Calculated Project Costs before sales income, NPC ($'000)	
0	Calculated Sales Income given project is achieved on time, NPV ($'000)	

(Transfer Summary and Company Specifed Data to Portfolio sheet automatically by pressing "Ctrl-w")

BEFORE FIRST INCOME

Block End Date	Block Manager	Block Goal (The final block goal is "First Income")	Probability Block Goal Achievable	Elapsed Time (Days) Optimistic<=7	Pessimistic=>7	Net PV Cost $ ('000)	Probability of finishing within 7 days
29-Sep-00			1.00				
6-Oct-00			1.00				
13-Oct-00			1.00				
20-Oct-00			1.00				
27-Oct-00			1.00				
3-Nov-00			1.00				
10-Nov-00			1.00				
17-Nov-00			1.00				
24-Nov-00			1.00				
1-Dec-00			1.00				
8-Dec-00			1.00				
15-Dec-00			1.00				
22-Dec-00			1.00				
29-Dec-00			1.00				
5-Jan-01			1.00				
12-Jan-01			1.00				
19-Jan-01			1.00				
26-Jan-01			1.00				
2-Feb-01			1.00				
9-Feb-01			1.00				
16-Feb-01			1.00				
23-Feb-01			1.00				
2-Mar-01			1.00				
9-Mar-01			1.00				
16-Mar-01			1.00				
23-Mar-01			1.00				
30-Mar-01			1.00				
6-Apr-01			1.00				
13-Apr-01		First Income	1.00				

(Update one time-block automatically by pressing "Ctrl-u")

AFTER FIRST INCOME

Net Sales NPV ($'000) Calculation

Year (from now)	Net Income
0	
1	
2	
3	
4	
5	
6	
7	
8	
9	
10	
11	
12	
13	
14	

Figure 4. TIPS Project Sheet for Weekly Time-Blocks

reviewed and may be completely revised. All costs are considered sunk and new knowledge gained incorporated into the improved plan.

The TIPS approach we have developed uses Microsoft Excel spreadsheet software to encapsulate key project dimensions for reporting and decision-making, shown in Figures 4 and 5.

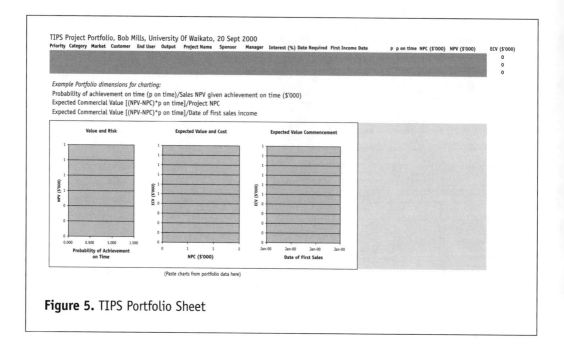

Figure 5. TIPS Portfolio Sheet

This chapter summarizes recent TIPS research, including the response of the original interviewees to this new and alternative approach and presents findings of pilot trials done late in the year 2000 (detailed in Mills et al. 2000 and Mills et al. 2001).

Method

Action research methodology involves direct researcher involvement and intervention to encourage the introduction of new systems and requisite behavioral and attitudinal changes. This approach has been used successfully in both education research (Cohen and Manion 1994) and when introducing new management systems (Koch et al. 1995). The approach overview developed is shown in Figure 6.

Survey of the TIPS Concept

The twenty-five interviewees from the initial study were sent a summary of the TIPS approach and asked (on a fax-ready reply form) to respond to two leading questions:

1. In what ways could TIPS potentially better meet the innovation project management needs of your organization?

2. What changes or modifications to TIPS are necessary before your organization could consider implementation?

The form of the questions was chosen to invoke comparison between TIPS and existing innovation project management arrangements (already acknowledged as unsatisfactory by the interviewees) and to provoke a considered response. Sixteen responses were acquired from twenty of the original twenty-five interviewees still with their organizations (Table 1).

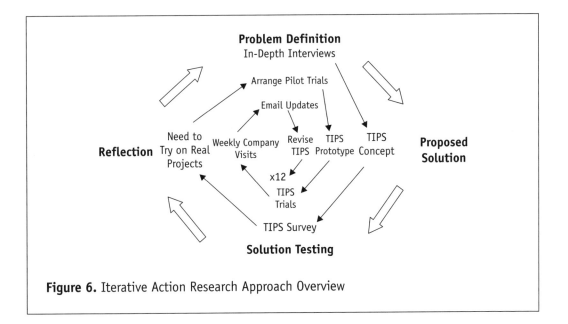

Figure 6. Iterative Action Research Approach Overview

TIPS Pilot Trials

The three research provider organizations and six successful companies from earlier research (Mills et al. 1999) were invited to consider trying TIPS on a sample of their current projects. Local (Hamilton, New Zealand) firms were particularly encouraged to respond so that direct researcher contact and support could be conveniently provided. After discussions an agricultural research company (R1) and an electronics/manufacturing company (E1) agreed to use TIPS on three projects in each company. The pilot trial took place between 12 July and 13 October 2000 and had eleven company participants. Formally allocated projects were managed by participants designated A, B, and C and X, Y, and Z, respectively, and overseen by one project portfolio manager from each firm (designated G and H, respectively). One participant (#6) working for R1 with C contributed to a joint survey response and another (#5) working for R1 in association with B also used TIPS on two informal projects and completed the final survey independently. A third participant (#7) was the engineering manager for E1. The functions of the managers, generically described as business/operations (O) or technical/scientific (T), were also identified. The designations, project responsibilities, and functions of the eleven participants are shown in Table 2 and brief descriptions of the six formal projects are shown in Table 3.

During initial discussions, the following three interrelated aspects of the trial emerged as being of particular significance for introducing TIPS:

1. Consolidating the type of information useful for managing innovation projects.

2. Formatting project information for convenient and practical use.

3. Encouraging the flow of project information across functional barriers and managerial levels.

Participant #	Company	Designation	Function
1	R1	G	O
2	R1	A	O
3	R1	B	O
4	R1	C	T
5	R1	-	T
6	R1	-	T
7	E1	-	O
8	E1	H	O
9	E1	X	T
10	E1	Y	T
11	E1	Z	T

Notes: R1 and E1 are an agricultural research company and an electronics/manufacturing company respectively, O represents business/operations, and T represents technician/scientist functions.

Table 2. Summary Descriptions of TIPS Pilot Trial Participants

Regular interaction between participants and the researcher (senior author of this chapter) developed in two ways—by visits and by weekly email updates. Each Friday during the three-month trial the project manager was visited at a convenient time (A, B, and C in the morning and X, Y, and Z in the afternoon), usually in the same sequence. The visit was used to assist project managers in updating the TIPS project spreadsheet and to discuss implementation problems and alternative solutions. Each Thursday email updates were sent to suggest solutions to common problems, to provide revised TIPS software, to motivate all participants, and to remind project managers of the Friday visit.

Research data was collected informally through notes made during the weekly visits and on reflection, and formally by a survey at the end of the trial. The survey was sent individually to the eleven participant managers, distributed, and collected through email using a protected Microsoft® Excel® spreadsheet.

The small number of respondents for the trial (nine) made definitive, statistical analysis by numerical rating alone impractical and unreliable. All answers requiring numerical rating were therefore supplemented with a request to write

Project Manager	Project Description
A	Development, approval, and launch of a new model of an existing animal remedy.
B	Development and launch of an existing production management software product for a different animal species.
C	Research, development, and commercialization of a novel animal-based drug production process.
X	Development and production of a new network security system.
Y	Fixing six specific faults in a recently launched new product and consequential upgrade of production line.
Z	Production and packaging for a new hardware/software security product for export.

Table 3. TIPS Pilot Trial Formal Project Descriptions

down the "reason for the rating." This approach allowed aggregate rating values to be verified and enhanced.

Survey formats and rating scales were based on examples provided by Bruner and Hensel (1994) and Aiken (1996) and standardized to five-point scales for consistency and convenience. Survey topics covered three aspects of project management: information content (twenty-seven measures), formatting (fifteen measures), and flow (seven measures). There was also a concluding section on organization-wide implementation requirements and prospects (eight measures).

TIPS Survey Findings and Discussion

R&D Purchasers

Executive managers for three R&D purchasers responded. The manager from P1 dealt with "public good" strategy policy issues and considered TIPS unhelpful for selecting strategy but it "looked useful for implementing it." The manager of P3 (from an accounting background) had a "hands-off," "sunk-cost" approach. The manager considered that judicious selection of a project, the credentials of the researcher, and receiving a completion report provided as much control as could be hoped for. Therefore, she considered TIPS irrelevant.

The manager of P4 operated at the business unit level. He felt that TIPS would provide "a simpler platform." Computer spreadsheets are more commonly used across organizational functions and levels than project Gantt charts.

R&D Providers

Two project managers and one executive manager responded. The project manager from R1 advised, "NPV (given success) still needs to be supplied." However, "It looks as if [TIPS] will deal better with [project] unpredictability ... which has been an issue for us." A "demonstration" of TIPS was desired.

Uncertainty and risk are quantified for each time-block, but the discounted cash flow and NPV calculation details were not included on the spreadsheet version of TIPS given to the interviewees, which created concern. Put another way, if R&D, engineering, and production are required to provide best estimates, so should marketing. Indeed, if TIPS is to be regarded as an organization-wide tool, calculating NPV should be done on the TIPS spreadsheet for each project.

The executive manager from R2 agreed that their organization needed a "structured approach like TIPS." Its staff was computer literate and would find TIPS "easy to pick up." He required that TIPS be made compatible for intranet use.

The project manager from R3, a very hierarchical organization, described the conceptual advantages of TIPS this way: "TIPS appears to allow [technological innovation] projects to 'morph' as they progress, in order to best achieve a successful outcome without being constrained to original 'guesstimates' as to cost, value, etc."

Electronics/Manufacturing Companies

Each of the respondents for the electronics companies originated from an engineering background, where detailed planning is common and manufacturing processes likely to be used are frequently well known. They generally had a strong desire for schedule prescription and compliance.

A program manager from E1 felt that TIPS has the advantage of summarizing a project for portfolio management and assigning priority in a scarce resource environment. However, he felt that TIPS provided nothing new or better for planning, tracking, or controlling projects. He contended that the main issues in project management were "keeping staff wound up and pointed in the right direction, accurately reporting progress, [and] correctly identifying and resolving big issues early to aid the prediction of the time/cost to completion." He consequently perceived time-blocks as an aid "for project reporting, rather than as a planning and control method."

A project manager in E1 envisaged TIPS as providing opportunity for project staff to develop leadership skills in the role of block manager and extend those skills by taking charge of blocks near the limits of their specialization and thus, providing the motivation and challenge desired by good staff. He also acknowledged that his company did not "really do a great deal" to account for risk and it had no formal method to "calculate or communicate the level of confidence in the project plan."

The project manager in E1 also considered the TIPS portfolio summary sheet with listed priority rankings to be useful. He commented that they try to avoid multitasking and said, "the best way to ensure project completion is to allow the design team to focus on one project and leave them to it." This suggests caution would be required when using TIPS. Project priorities should not be frequently or radically changed, nor should too many staff be expected to float across high priority projects.

The program and project managers of E2 sent in a combined survey response. They considered that TIPS would be a useful method for assessing and comparing "new technology/blue sky" projects, which in their company did not have a formal method for evaluation. E2 were also concerned about how to isolate critical tasks within time-blocks. Again, the desire to fully plan the schedule and tightly control resource allocation was evident, even though these features of existing systems were not used in any of the organizations.

Food Companies

The program manager of F1 felt that TIPS had the advantage of providing alignment with existing time-based requirements, and specifically cited "accounting and reporting processes." This program manager advised that multitasking on various projects was common and daily scheduling of personnel to specific projects was impractical, thereby validating the TIPS approach of delegating individuals to optimize the use of their own time.

A program manager from F2 concluded that TIPS combined several well-proven methodologies and should therefore be robust. He described it as "simple enough," which he regards as important because "many systems lose the plot as they become too complex (academic)." He suggested that meaningful feedback could only be achieved by trying the system and was looking for projects to do this. It should be noted that this manager was also the only interviewee originally satisfied with his current process!

A project manager for F2 felt that using TIPS had the advantage of formalizing the innovation process.

Forestry Companies

A project manager in T1 thought that intuitively "it looks like it frees up more time [to do] the project compared to managing the process." He reflected that "businesses are probably more interested in return on shareholder funds (ROI) these days than change in value (NPV)." This suggests that NPV measures, used for selecting and prioritizing projects, are less important to company executives when reporting to shareholders than the expenditure and income measures for the aggregate portfolio. Therefore, the TIPS approach, which does not track expenditure on individual projects, could be suitable.

A project manager at T2 felt that TIPS would best contribute to the innovation process by quantifying the probability of project completion alongside the remaining "net present cost" for completion. He considered that this feature alone would help provide a decision-base to abandon some projects "currently lingering." "At present, several specialist applications [software packages] are in use. Having TIPS in Excel makes it available for use to a far wider audience."

Survey Response Summary

The amount of information reported here comes from a very small sub-set of organizations and represents a "snapshot" of opinion only. Nevertheless, nearly all the survey respondents (fifteen out of sixteen) thought TIPS had several advantages over current systems. The remaining survey respondent did not feel qualified to comment since her organization had a "hands-off" approach to funding. The most frequently voiced advantages of TIPS can be distilled to "providing a simple, tangible, consistent, and transparent means to regularly compare innovation projects for inter-project ranking and compliance with organizational strategy." Transparency is aided because most managers use Excel spreadsheets, the proposed platform for TIPS. This platform interfaces well with the Internet (email and website access), which is useful for multiple-site projects.

Six of the sixteen respondents specifically requested demonstrations of TIPS on a "real" project before they would consider implementing TIPS in their organization.

TIPS Pilot Trial Findings and Discussion

Usefulness of the Action Research Approach in the TIPS Pilot Trial

During the first week of the pilot trial, participants were provided with a protected copy of the Excel spreadsheet template and the senior author introduced TIPS philosophy at a one-hour seminar on company premises. Project managers A and C used monthly time-blocks (project duration six months to two years) and B, X, Y, and Z used weekly time-blocks for their shorter projects as suggested. The Friday visits to project managers were particularly useful in encouraging regular project reviews. A copy of each project's updated TIPS file was made and retained by project managers at the end of each week, primarily for trial record and review.

Regular interaction during project reviews with project managers using TIPS was valuable because they confronted the senior author with problems, conflicts, frustrations, and insights first hand. The immediacy of the interaction also helped motivate four software upgrades during the trial (8 August, 7 September, 20 September, and 29 September). General issues identified at visits could be aired at subsequent visits and with other project managers, and were often discussed or resolved through the email updates. The action research approach therefore stimulated both progressive learning and TIPS system development.

TIPS Implementation During the Pilot Trial

While all project managers were well-intentioned, external commitments, work priorities, project complexity, the developmental status of TIPS, and the ready availability of data strongly influenced the rate at which the TIPS project sheet was initially completed. For example, at the first weekly meeting project manager Y was able to enter all data into all fields of the ten-week upgrade project within one hour. The two participants on project C (a two-year "blue-skies" research project) took

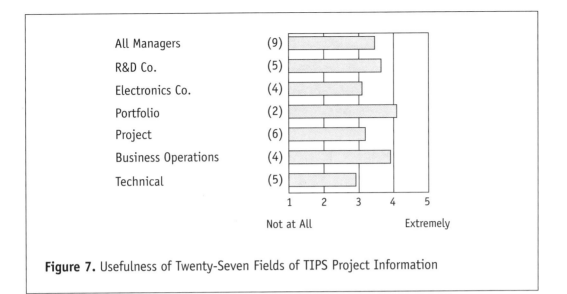

Figure 7. Usefulness of Twenty-Seven Fields of TIPS Project Information

the longest. They were unable to complete data entry until the last week of the trial when the data fields and TIPS software functionality had been developed to accommodate their reasonable requirements. They were further delayed by the time taken to extricate two auxiliary projects, initially co-scheduled for the purposes of arranging continuity of work for the research group staff.

The original intention was to send TIPS project and portfolio files to project portfolio managers G and H at the end of each time-block for progress reporting and to assign the updated project priority rank. However, the practice for most projects was that submission did not begin until the end of the trial period. Therefore, TIPS interaction between these management levels was not adequately tested.

TIPS Information Development
The final format for the pilot trial TIPS worksheets is shown in Figures 4 and 5. Calculating and expressing project risk was clarified by defining three types of probability:

1. The probability of ever achieving a block goal.

2. The probability of achieving a block goal on time (using optimistic and pessimistic elapsed time estimates for each block goal).

3. The probability of commercial success (incorporated into the dollar value of project "net income").

The ratings for overall "usefulness" of the project management information fields were assessed and counted at values between one and five, with 2.0 or less being "not useful at all" or worse, and equal to or above 4.0 being "extremely useful" (Figure 7).

Overall TIPS data fields were rated at an average of 3.4 or more than merely "useful." Company R1, which had a less structured existing innovation project management process, found more fields more useful than E1 (nine compared to

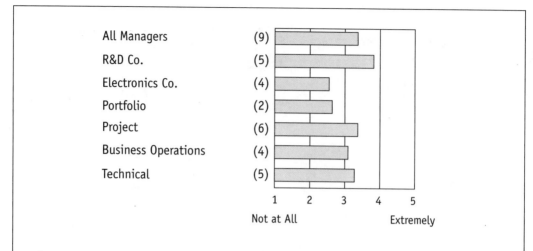

Figure 8. Usefulness of Fifteen Aspects of the TIPS Format.

one of the twenty-seven fields rating four or higher). Portfolio managers and business managers rated information fields as most useful (twenty-one and thirteen fields, respectively, rating four or higher). Technical managers were least impressed, rating four of the fields (priority rank, strategic category, project income, and company specified data) at two or less. Both company E1 and the project manager groups rated the priority rank and strategic category fields poorly. Technical managers thought that the field project income data was not useful, nor were company specified data fields (incorporated at the request of portfolio managers).

In a fully operational TIPS environment, it is envisaged that priority ranking will help empower staff to self-select day-to-day work and will strongly influence project funding and resource levels. The fields currently ranked poorly by the technical managers will consequently attract increasing attention.

TIPS Software Format

The usefulness of the TIPS format was surveyed and presented in Figure 8.

The overall rating of 3.3 indicates that the TIPS format is useful. Company R1 (mean 3.8) and the project managers (mean 3.4) were the most positive.

Company R1 and the technical managers group considered that familiarity with Excel across functions and levels was particularly useful (rating 4.0 and 3.6). Six of the nine respondents verified that Excel was useful as the platform for TIPS, whereas the other three had reservations especially about tidiness, flexibility, and robustness at the user interface.

Specifying achievements instead of activities and tying these into the calendar on a weekly, monthly, and quarterly basis was rated positively (3.4 and 3.2, respectively) with little variation across groups (range: 2.5–3.6). The Excel cell, comments feature, was found to be a useful (if cumbersome) facility for expanding descriptions, listing tasks, and allocating jobs.

Company R1 considered the probability of block goal achievement and the consistent approach to estimating schedule achievement as very useful. This was in sharp contrast to the views of E1 who rated both these features very poorly. Similarly, the presentation and transfer of project information and the convenience of updating TIPS was rated at 4.2 to 4.8 for R1, compared with only between 2.5 and 3 by E1. This may reflect the multi-site operation for R1 compared to the single-site operation of E1.

TIPS Project Information Flow

Useful project management information must be identified and then acted upon to effect good monitoring and control. Overall, respondents slightly agreed that TIPS could be expected to increase useful project management information compared to existing arrangements (3.4 compared to 2.6, where one represented strong disagreement and five strong agreement).

TIPS identified project information more effectively and earlier than did existing arrangements in both companies (3.8 mean).

R1 thought that existing information exchange between R&D and marketing functions was unsatisfactory (1.8 mean) where it was acknowledged that no formal arrangements were in place. However, E1 managers agreed they had satisfactory arrangements (4.0 mean). Similarly, project information exchange across management levels was rated as poorly in R1, at 1.8, and neutrally in E1, at 3.0.

R1 considered that the amount of useful project information exchanged would increase when using TIPS (3.5), but E1 did not (2.8). However, when asked if TIPS was expected to improve useful communications between R&D and marketing, R1 expected no change, while E1 expected a mild improvement (3.3).

TIPS Implementation

A better user interface, perhaps using icons, was urged by three of the nine respondents, suggesting also that TIPS should be linked to a company database. Respondents suggested that staff education was needed for upper management "buy-in" of TIPS. An organizational culture change was also needed to accommodate the philosophical differences with existing arrangements, for example, to celebrate achievement rather than finish activities, and to accept that past expenditure is an investment in new knowledge. Awareness of the TIPS approach would be required for all staff, with project manager and higher levels needing specific training, both in project management principles and TIPS software use.

The estimate for the time to establish an operational TIPS system ranged from "as long as it takes for you to write a specific program" to five years. The broad median consensus was twelve months, which is considerably shorter than the three to seven years expected (Englund and Graham 1999).

The Rated Value of Implementing TIPS

Company R1 project managers and technical managers rated the potential value of implementing TIPS, or a similar approach, for monitoring technological

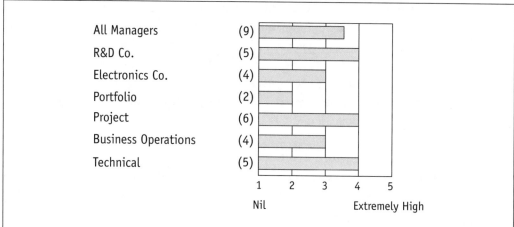

Figure 9. The Rated Value of Implementing TIPS (In Your Organization)

innovation projects as high (4.0) (Figure 9). The mean rating of all respondents was moderate to high (3.6). Only one respondent gave a value at less than moderate (3.0). If dedicated software was used, this respondent's rating increased dramatically from one to five! One advantage of TIPS is that it can be introduced even if the project has started. Also, retrospective information is not required.

The mean for probability of TIPS implementation was moderate and ranged from 2.7 to 3.1, perhaps reflecting the developmental nature of the pilot trial and the lack of information about its performance elsewhere. R1 perceived the most value (4.0) from implementing TIPS, having no consistent innovation project approach and projects operating from dispersed sites. Project managers placed the same high value on TIPS, which was encouraging, because they had the greatest interaction during the pilot trial and were potentially most affected. Likewise, technical managers rated TIPS highly, the survey data indicating positively their expectations of improved communication of project information, particularly to higher levels of management.

Summary and Conclusions

R&D purchasers, providers, and companies are all potentially important contributors to the innovation process in New Zealand and share common problems and concerns in managing the innovation process. A new management model called TIPS was conceptualized. TIPS could potentially integrate technological innovation project management into the operational fabric of these organizations. TIPS is intended to encourage a regular review of projects and programs, help prioritize projects within portfolios, and operate from a widely used platform (Microsoft® Excel®). A survey of project and program managers (interviewees from earlier research) produced an 80 percent response rate. The respondents had generally positive reactions to the novel simplification for managing a typically complex and uncertain process. Respondents intellectually supported TIPS and offered useful insights on how the process might be perceived and implemented.

Three of the nine responding participants in the TIPS pilot trial were very keen to see TIPS implemented in dedicated software. This would help improve the user interface. Two of these participants were software specialists and the third had seen company specific competitive advantage created by having better interfaces and increased robustness and security. It is therefore suggested that TIPS be further pursued and the feasibility of implementing TIPS in dedicated software should be investigated before full-scale implementation trials.

TIPS may provide a practical and more universal approach for monitoring and controlling small-scale innovation processes in wealth creating organizations.

References

Aiken, L. R. 1996. *Rating Scales and Checklists: Evaluating Behavior, Personality, and Attitudes*. New York: John Wiley & Sons, Inc.

Bartlett, C. A., and S. Ghoshal. 1994. Changing the Role of Top Management: Beyond Strategy to Purpose. *Harvard Business Review* 72 (6): 79–88.

Bernaxo, W. et al. 1999. Balanced Matrix Structure and New Product Development Process at Texas Instruments Materials and Controls Division. *R&D Management* 29 (2): 121–131.

Bruner, G. C., and P. J. Hensel. 1994. *Marketing Scales Handbook: A Compilation of Multi Item Measures*. Chicago, IL: American Marketing Association.

Cohen, L., and L. Manion. 1994. *Research Methods in Education*. 4th ed. London: Routledge.

Cooper, R. G. 1993. *Winning at New Products*. 2nd ed. Reading, MA: Addison Wesley.

Cooper, R. G., S. J. Edgett, and E. J. Kleinschmidt. 1998. *Portfolio Management for New Products*. Reading, MA: Addison Wesley.

Economist, The. 1999. Innovation in Industry Survey. *The Economist* (February): 5–24.

Englund, R. L., and R. J. Graham. 1999. From Experience: Linking Projects to Strategy. *Journal of Product Innovation Management* 16: 52–64.

Goldratt, E. 1997. *The Critical Chain*. Barrington, MA: North River Press.

Kaplan, R. B., and D. P. Norton. 1992. The Balanced Scorecard: Measures that Drive Performance. *Harvard Business Review* 70 (1): 71–80.

Koch, N. F., R. J. McQueen, and J. L. Scott. 1995. *A Methodology to IS Study in Organisations through multiple Action Research Cycles*. Research Report Series. Hamilton: The University of Waikato.

MacLeod, K. R., and P. F. Petersen. 1996. Estimating the Tradeoff between Resource Allocation and Probability of On-Time Completion in Project Management. *Project Management Journal* 27 (1): 26–33.

McKenna, R. 1991. Marketing is Everything. *Harvard Business Review* 69 (1): 65–79.

Mills, R. A., J. Dale, C. M. Kirk, and A. G. Langdon. 1996. Upfront with Uncertainty—A Planned Approach for Managing Innovation Project Duration. In *Proceedings of the Project Management Institute* (43–58), New Zealand Chapter Conference, Auckland.

Mills, R. A., A. G. Langdon, C. Fee, and C. M. Kirk. 1999. Innovation Project Management: A New Zealand Approach. In *Portland International Conference on the Management of Engineering and Technology Proceedings*, vol 2, CD-ROM, file 16_07.pdf. Portland, Oregon: Portland State University.

Mills, R. A., A. G. Langdon, C. M. Kirk, and J. E. Swan. 2000. Managing Technological Innovation Projects: The Quest for a Universal Language. *Proceedings of the Project Management Institute Research Conference* (375–384), Paris, France.

———. 2001. Managing Technological Innovation Projects: TIPS Pilot Trials. *Proceedings of the 2001 R&D Management Conference*, Wellington. CD-ROM.

Mimno, P. R. 1991. What is RAD? *American Programmer* (January): 28–37.

Mintzberg, H. 1979. *The Structuring of Organizations: A Synthesis of the Research*. Inglewood Cliffs, Illinois: Prentice-Hall.

Mintzberg, H. 1989. *Mintzberg on Management: Inside our Strange World of Organizations*. New York: Free Press.

CHAPTER 28

DERIVING THE 2ND AND 3RD DIMENSIONS OF THE BCWS

Suhrita Sen, B. Arch, MBEM, MSRED—"Nirh," New Delhi, India

Introduction

Project implementation requires a multidimensional understanding of the dynamics of management models. Any planning and monitoring exercise that is one-dimensional in representation is bound to falter in the real, three-dimensional world. Since every project is a process of inquiry, it should allow the project manager to analyze, experiment, and innovate within limits. This can only happen if we understand that performance management is not about precision in adherence—projects rarely keep variances to zero and schedule and cost performance indices hardly ever equal one! We need space to play; yet our boundaries have to be objectively apparent.

Acceptance of "managed non-conformance" integrates some valuable insensitivity from statistical process control into the project performance baseline. It is only then that we can manage the project such that it will have the highest probability of success.

This chapter delves into structuring a multidimensional performance management model out of the planned value and earned value parameters of time and cost control. All such comparisons between the planned and earned values can now be viewed in a three-dimensional perspective—the graphics are generated out of statistically quantified growth patterns in the 2nd and 3rd dimensions.

Here is a tool to record the experiences of variations and their management on multiple levels and at different scales—building and allowing the project life cycle to develop through iterative processes of modeling, quantifying, and visualizing.

The Background to Earned Value

Cost Schedule Control Systems Criteria

The earned value (EV) method of performance measurement had its origin in the Cost Schedule Control Systems Criteria (CSCSC) developed in the United States (US). As of today, it is the best industry standard tool for effectively integrating cost, schedule, and technical performance management. All work is planned, budgeted, and scheduled in time phased, "planned value" increments constituting a cost and schedule measurement baseline. There are two major objectives of an EV system: 1) to encourage contractors to use effective cost and schedule management control systems and 2) to permit the customer to be able to rely on timely data produced by those systems for determining the contract status.

Three basic indicators quantify the EV concept: they are the actual cost of work performed (ACWP), the budgeted cost of work performed (BCWP), and the budgeted cost of work scheduled (BCWS).

- ACWP—Represents the costs actually incurred in accomplishing the work performed within a given time period.
- BCWP—Is the EV. It signifies the value of completed work. BCWP is derived by determining the budget for all completed work, including the completed portions of in-progress work. In contrast to the traditional measurements of actual costs against the budget, earned value is the performance indicator of both cost and schedule. This dual characteristic of the BCWP provides the required integration. Instead of merely stating whether or not money is being spent as fast as it was planned, BCWP when compared to ACWP indicates whether the progress achieved is worth the money spent. In short, BCWP provides the required integration of physical progress, time, and cost.
- BCWS—Indicates where the project manager planned to be by a certain date. It is the indicator of planned progress—the performance measurement baseline.

These three values determined at each reporting period and plotted cumulatively, provide a very precise picture of the performance of the work package against the budget and the schedule. Figure 1 shows the relationship between these curves.

Inadequacy Defined

The present environment of Earned Value Management (EVM), as defined now in the profession, provides a very good and simplistic integration of cost and time. However, as our projects go through extensive mutation, rarely keeping variances to zero, inadequate robustness of the model becomes apparent. EVM only considers deviations from a one-dimensional BCWS. In order for the world to accept EVM as a separate management science in itself, the model needs to stretch into

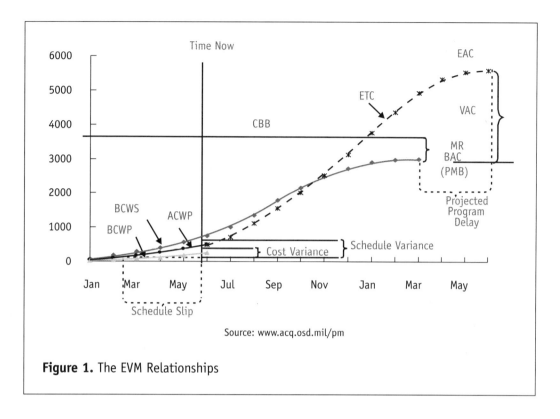

Figure 1. The EVM Relationships

newer dimensions and horizons. Success need not only be related to the deterministic approach in pursuing a numerical goal.

Toward a Sensible Solution

The model reads occurring deviations only—but does not tell us when corrective actions are required to get back on course. Corrective action should only be directed at significant or important variances. It will not be productive to attempt corrective actions on all variances that may be temporary trends. This chapter shows an evolution of the BCWS, from a one-dimensional line first, to a two-dimensional polyline, and then its transition to a three-dimensional polyline, as the EV model strives to integrate the missing dimensions.

The Second Dimension: Definition of Thresholds for BCWS

The definition of thresholds for BCWS should be statistically defined. The thresholds cannot be defined arbitrarily as some percentage of allowable variations, agreed to between parties in the contract. Only a quantitative evaluation of it will make the EVM process seamlessly applicable to all applications. So effectively, the process will have a built in "insensitivity." As long as the cost and schedule deviations are within the thresholds or tolerance lines, no specific corrective action is warranted. However, if a deviation crosses the threshold or tolerance lines, a full investigation is required.

Statistical Quality Control

Development of such threshold and tolerance lines can be derived from the basic principles of Statistical Quality Control (SQC) or the Statistical Control Chart theory in general. Control charts were developed as a technique for ensuring that a process remained in statistical control, but not necessarily for ensuring that every item produced was within the tolerance limits set by the specifications. Consider a process that produces items, one of whose dimensions are of primary importance. Statistical control is achieved if the items are produced with a constant mean and variance. The variance is said to be due to non-assignable causes. If the mean level of the dimension moves away from the original mean or if the variance alters by a significant amount, the process is said to have gone out of control. Investigation may also arise if a trend appears, if an unusually large number of observations are above or below the central value, or if several observations are near a control limit.

So the basic concept is that all processes, outputs, and systems exhibit variability. No two things are exactly the same. Schewart refers to the sources of variability as chance and assignable causes and Deming calls them common or special causes. What control charts do is separate the signal of variability due to assignable causes, from the background noise of variability due to chance causes. When chance causes are only playing, the variation follows known patterns of statistical distributions. If a set of data is analyzed and the pattern of variation of data is shown to conform to such statistical patterns that are produced by chance, we can assume that only chance or common cause is operating on the system. In such a situation, a process is said to be under statistical control (Levine et al. 1995). To construct a control chart, we require an estimate of central tendency—the mean—and an estimate of variability—the standard deviation.

According to schewart control charts, the means of each sample n are distributed normally with the mean m and

standard deviation $\dfrac{\overline{R}}{(dn\sqrt{n})}$, where

$\overline{R}$ = sample range
dn = constant for given sample size n
n = sample size.

Using the fact that a variable which is normally distributed has 99.8 percent of it's values lying less than 3.09 standard deviations from it's mean, it is expected that 99.8 percent of the sample means would lie between $m(\text{mean}) - 3.09s$ and $m(\text{mean}) + 3.09s$,

where $s = \dfrac{\overline{R}}{(dn\sqrt{n})}$

These are the lower and upper action limits. Again using the properties of the normal distribution, it may be expected that 95 percent of the sample means would lie between $m\,(\text{mean}) + 1.96s$ and $m\,(\text{mean}) - 1.96s$. These values are known as the lower and upper warning limits.

Application to Costs

When we try and apply this to costs, the first thing to understand is that cost as a standard for control cannot be a specific value, it has to take the form of a frequency diagram—from which the limits of variation can be determined. If we extend a similar analogy of the Schewart chart method to the various costs constituting a reporting period, we realize that there is a distinct difference. Unlike the Schewart chart methods in the production industry, the problem with cost distribution over a period of time is that what is monitored is not the mean of the costs of the different activities, but their sum total. Table 1, which is a small example of the calculation of various limits, illustrates the point. Hence the formula used for deriving the control limits in Schewart control charts needs to be modified.

In Table 1, the mean of the "l" observations is m, and each of these "l" observations is the mean of sample size n. The mean m has to be modified to form the sum of the "l" observations.

Adding such frequencies whose mean is m, the formula for control limits becomes:

$$= 1m \pm 3\sqrt{\text{Grand variance}}$$
$$= 1m \pm 3\sqrt{\text{Sum of variances}}$$

(Since variances and not standard deviations can be added up.)

$$= 1m \pm 3\sqrt{1(\text{st.dev})^2}$$

$$= 1m \pm 3\sqrt{1\left(\dfrac{\bar{R}}{dn\sqrt{n}}\right)}$$

Similarly, the warning limits get modified to:

$$= 1m \pm 2\sqrt{1\left(\dfrac{\bar{R}}{dn\sqrt{n}}\right)}$$

Since this method considers the ranges of the sample size n, it is important that the various ranges are of compatible order, so that the mean range of the n samples has a significance. This seems to be ideal when the constituent costs are from similar or homogeneous activities, indicating the same order of the quantity of work involved. Activities from the same or similar work package are good examples. Say RCC work in floors one to ten, when the floor sizes are similar. Let's call this Method 1. However, when dealing with non-homogeneous activities or when summing up through various work packages of dissimilar nature, it is better to add up the various variances rather than considering the mean range of samples.

So, the control limits will be:

$$= 1m \pm 3\sqrt{\text{Grand variance}}$$
$$= 1m \pm 3\sqrt{\text{All component variance}}$$

And the warning limits will be:

$$= 1m \pm 2\sqrt{\text{Grand variance}}$$
$$= 1m \pm 2\sqrt{\text{All component variance}}$$

Let's call this Method 2.

Schewart Chart Example Data

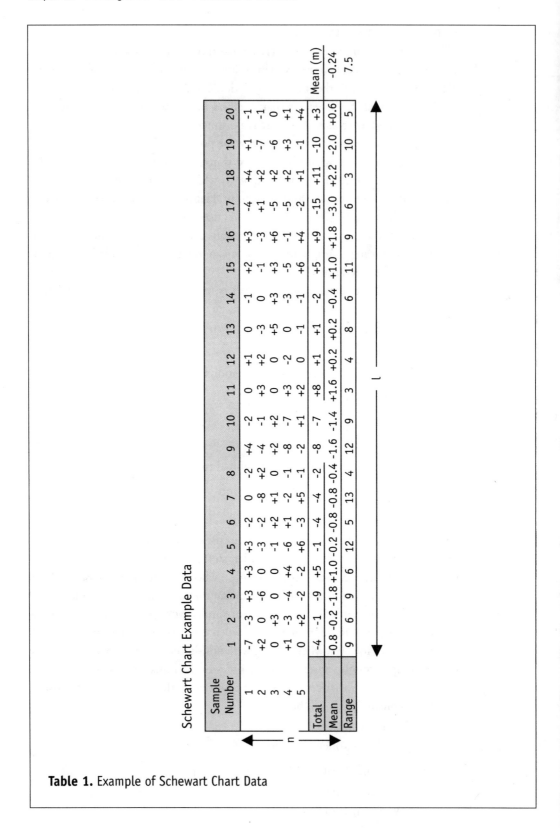

Sample Number	1	2	3	4	5	6	7	8	9	10	11	12	13	14	15	16	17	18	19	20	Mean (m)
1	-7	-3	+3	+3	+3	-2	0	-2	+4	-2	0	+1	0	-1	+2	+3	-4	+4	+1	-1	
2	+2	0	-6	0	-3	-2	-8	+2	-4	-1	+3	+2	-3	0	-1	-3	+1	+2	-7	-1	
3	0	+3	0	0	-1	+2	+1	0	+2	+2	0	0	+5	+3	+3	+6	-5	+2	-6	0	
4	+1	-3	-4	+4	-6	+1	-2	-1	-8	-7	+3	-2	0	-3	-5	-1	-5	+2	+3	+1	
5	0	+2	-2	-2	+6	-3	+5	-1	-2	+1	+2	0	-1	-1	+6	+4	-2	+1	-1	+4	
Total	-4	-1	-9	+5	-1	-4	-4	-2	-8	-7	+8	+1	+1	-2	+5	+9	-15	+11	-10	+3	
Mean	-0.8	-0.2	-1.8	+1.0	-0.2	-0.8	-0.8	-0.4	-1.6	-1.4	+1.6	+0.2	+0.2	-0.4	+1.0	+1.8	-3.0	+2.2	-2.0	+0.6	-0.24
Range	9	6	9	6	12	5	13	4	12	9	3	4	8	6	11	9	6	3	10	5	7.5

Table 1. Example of Schewart Chart Data

Example Project

The example project in Table 2 shows activities and their quantities and costs distributed monthly. The cumulative total of these costs when plotted on a time versus cost graph will constitute the initial BCWS. In order to find the threshold limits, each of these costs have to be distributed as a frequency. We need to make a frequency diagram of sample size n. We can consider normal distributions with a 95 percent level of confidence and start with a positive or negative 15 percent variation on either side of a mean—the point estimate. So each cost estimate is made into a sample size of three, with a lower and an upper limit estimated at 95 percent confidence (Table 3). So in our calculations n will be equal to three and "l" will be varying in different months. If a month has five activities in it, "l" will be equal to five, and if it has two, "l" will be equal to two.

Table 4 shows part of a worksheet that calculates the action limits for cumulative costs in different months. The cumulative mean range of a month is the mean of all component ranges from the beginning of the project until that month. This reflects Method 1.

Table 5 shows a part of a worksheet that calculates the action limits for cumulative costs in different months, by Method 2. The cumulative grand variance of a month adds all component variances from the beginning of the project until that month.

Figure 2, shows the graphical BCWS drawn as a cumulative S curve, obtained by the Method 1. Figure 3 shows the graphical BCWS curve, obtained by the Method 2. In our example project, both turned out more or less similar. The most important conclusion from this exercise emerged in the finding that although we started with a 15 percent allowance in variation of each of the component costs (with a 95 percent confidence), the final allowable variance in the total cost worked out at 4 percent only, for a 99 percent confidence interval.

This looks like too narrow a band for all practical purposes as shown in Figures 2 and 3. However, just the fact that the action limits are mostly like parallel curves on both sides of the BCWS indicates that it has maintained the same distance from a higher cumulative cost (at the end of the project) as from a lower cumulative cost (at the initial stages of the project). This means a lower percentage of variation for the higher costs than for the lower costs. This also brings us to the point where we need to optimize the allowable variations in the components and the total cost by using a sensitivity analysis. It turned out to be an iterative process, where we determined an end contingency and distributed it. The most important tool was the understanding that a 10 percent contingency to the total cost allowed us to have a much bigger contingency of the component costs.

Dealing with Contingency

Normally distribution of contingency is a subjective issue, in the hands of the project manager, but here it becomes part of the planning process—distinctively linked with the allowable threshold values to costs. This part of the contingency

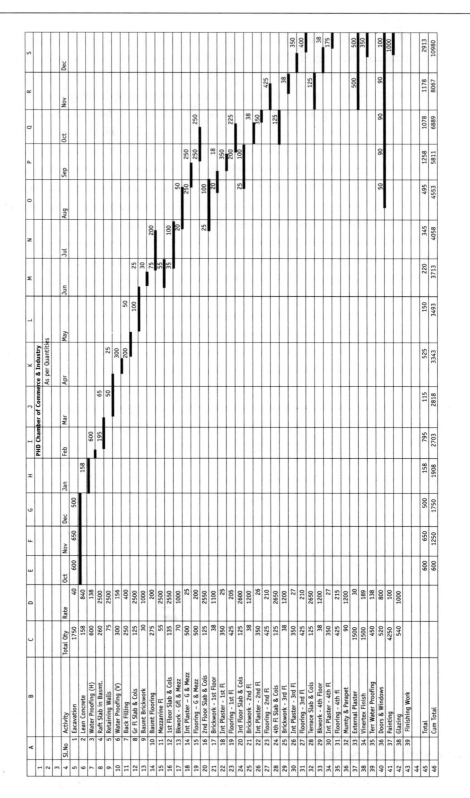

Table 2. Distribution of Quantities and Costs on Activity Schedule

Item	Rate								
Eacavation	40	20400	22100	17000					
		24000	26000	20000					
		27600	29900	23000					
Lean Concrete	840	112812							
		132720							
		152628							
Water Proofing (H)	138	70380							
		82800							
		95220							
Raft Slab in Basmt.	2500	414375	138125						
		487500	162500						
		560625	186875						
Retaining Walls	2500	106250	53125						
		125000	62500						
		143750	71875						
Water Proofing (V)	156	39780							
		46800							
		53820							
Back Filling	400	68000	17000						
		80000	20000						
		92000	23000						
Gr Fl Slab & Cols	2500	212500	53125						
		250000	62500						
		287500	71875		25500				
Basmt Brickwork	1000	30000	34000						
		34500	40000						
			46000						
Basmt Flooring	200	12750							
		15000							
		17250							
Mezzanine Fl	2500	116875							
		137500							
		158125							
1st Floor Slab & Cols	2550	75862.5	216750						
		89250	255000						
		102637.5	293250						
Bkwork - Gfl & Mezz	1000	17000							
		20000							
		23000							
Int Plaster – G & Mezz	25								
Flooring – G & Mezz	200								
2nd Floor Slab & Cols	2550	54187.5							
		63750							

Table 3. Making a Sample Size of n

Total + 3@l (s/@n)	839668.9	1019615	997364.7	579772.4	1306722	875223.8	60600.17	15000
Cum	5318615	6338230	7335595	7915367	9222090	10097313	10157914	
1a from Ranges - R1	1875	15000	26775	2835	1575	16200		15000
R2	15000	13837.5	13680	25200	1417.5	19845		
R3	5940	13680	99375	13680	27412.5	30000		
R4	2625	2730	4500	1417.5	16200	102000		
R5	12300	99375	21600	4500	4500	13200		
R6	78000	21600		19845	45360			
R7	21600			24000	18630			
R8				30000	24000			
R9					67500			
R10					60000			
Cum Values								
Cum Mean R	26818.89	26948.38	27626.38	25783.17	25920.09	26668.57	27060.75	
s=(Cumm R)/(1.693*@n)	9145.24	9189.397	9420.596	8792.06	8838.752	9093.981	9227.716	
3s @l	162145.1	176436.4	191614.9	193601.2	212130	224803.2	229770.1	
Cum + 3s @l	3291015	3859381	4427660	4834571	5741750	6238423	6293390	
Cum - 3s @l	2966725	3506509	4044430	4447369	5317490	5788817	5833850	

Note: All "@" Should Be Read as "sq root"

Table 4. Method 1

is something that the planning process foresees. Design and estimating variances, differences in site conditions, weather conditions, and probable delays and costs fall within the reasons of a foreseen contingency. The other type of contingency that should be kept is for unforeseen reasons.

Foreseen and Unforeseen Contingencies

When total foreseen contingency is fixed, it can be distributed equally between component activities or work packages or there could even be an uneven distri-

CV10 Grand Variance	435783740.6	684563895.7	704140228.1	170143934.8	225000000		14062500
For Cum Sigmas					760967599.2	758406501.6	
Cum Grand Variance	3574936580	4259500476	4963640704	5133784639	5894752238	6653158739	6667221239
Cum Std Dev (Sigma)	59790.77337	65264.8487	70453.10997	71650.43363	76777.28986	81566.89733	81653.05407
3 Sigma	179372.3201	195794.5461	211359.3299	214951.3009	230331.8696	244700.692	244959.1622
Cum Total +3 Sigma	3308242.32	3878739.546	4447404.33	4855921.301	5759951.87	6258320.692	6308579.162
Cum Total – 3 Sigma	2949497.68	3487150.454	4024685.67	4426018.699	5299288.13	5768919.308	5818660.838
2 Sigma	119581.5467	130529.6974	140906.2199	143300.8673	153554.5797	163133.7947	163306.1081
Cum Total + 2 Sigma	3248451.547	3813474.697	4376951.22	4784270.867	5683174.58	6176753.795	6226926.108
Cum Total - 2 Sigma	3009288.453	3552415.303	4095138.78	4497669.133	5376065.42	5850486.205	5900313.892

Table 5. Method 2

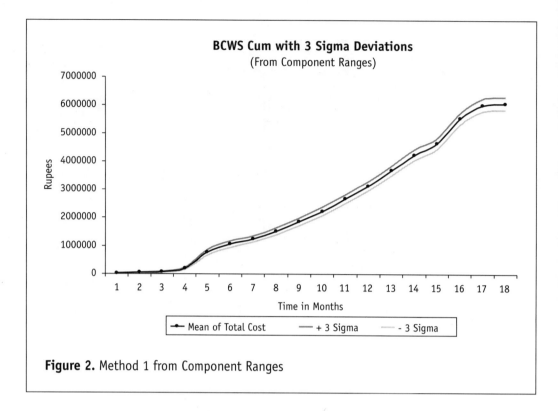

Figure 2. Method 1 from Component Ranges

bution for special reasons. The following is a statistically defined sensitivity analysis between end contingency and component contingencies. In case of even distribution of component contingencies,

$$\text{grand } \sigma = \sqrt{\sigma_1^2 + \sigma_2^2 + \sigma_3^2 + \ldots + \sigma_n^2}$$

$$= \sqrt{c^2\mu_1^2 + c^2\mu_2^2 + c^2\mu_3^2 + \ldots + c^2\mu_n^2}$$

$$= c\sqrt{\mu_1^2 + \mu_2^2 + \mu_3^2 + \ldots + \mu_n^2}$$

where c is a constant contingency allowed in each activity

$$\text{or } C\mu = c\sqrt{\mu_1^2 + \mu_2^2 + \mu_3^2 + \ldots + \mu_n^2}$$

where C is a contingency allowed on total cost and μ=mean of total cost.

$$c = \frac{C\mu}{\sqrt{\mu_1^2 + \mu_2^2 + \mu_3^2 + \ldots + \mu_n^2}}$$

For example: for a 10 percent contingency, a total cost with 99.8 percent confidence

$$c = \frac{0.03\mu}{\sqrt{\mu_1^2 + \mu_2^2 + \mu_3^2 + \ldots + \mu_n^2}} \quad \text{and at 95 percent confidence level}$$

$$c = \frac{0.05\mu}{\sqrt{\mu_1^2 + \mu_2^2 + \mu_3^2 + \ldots + \mu_n^2}}$$

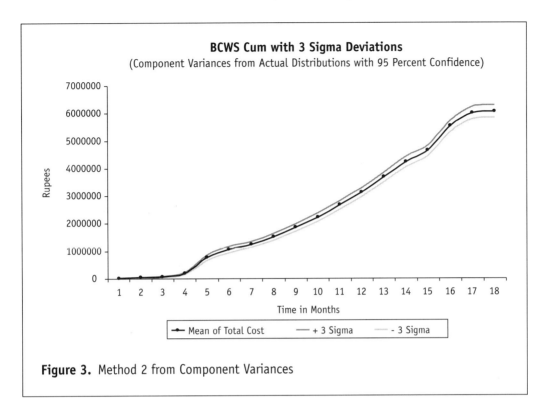

Figure 3. Method 2 from Component Variances

In case of unequal contingencies within work packages or activities,

$$\text{grand } \sigma = C_1^2 \mu_1^2 + c_2^2 \mu_2^2 + c_3^2 \mu_3^2 + \ldots + c_n^2 \mu_n^2$$

So, we need to do a sensitivity analysis for finding c_1, c_2, c_3, etc.—which are separate contingencies for separate activities.

There is a part of this foreseen contingency that needs to be dealt with using an understanding of probabilities. Suppose we see two possibilities in schedules beyond a certain time, say due to weather conditions. In our example project we were running into the monsoon (rainy) season during the middle of the program, which would affect some prime concreting activities and their curing times. So the barchart was loaded with both the first and second schedules at 50 percent probability levels. The second schedule is drawn on top of the first for activities where both are possible. This consideration of a foreseen vital variable and its probability brings us to a parallel yet concurrent consideration of two different schedules, as shown in Figure 4. Here, the delayed schedule is arrived at by reducing the respective costs by 50 percent wherever the two schedules overlap. The two schedules can be given two distinctly different probabilities also.

The selection of these kind of "vital few" variables and quantification of them in terms of their probabilistic effects on the project BCWS, takes care of uncertainty in terms of cost and schedule. Hence, the baseline should build in as much of the uncertainties and their consequences as is predictable. It helps us present our project life cycle like a walk through experience even before it has started.

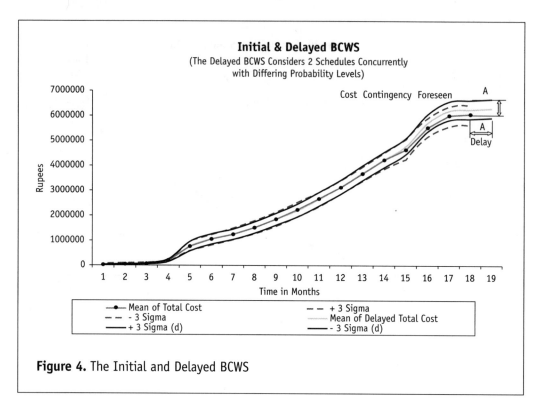

Figure 4. The Initial and Delayed BCWS

The "vital few" parameters, thus optimized, will convert the BCWS to a band or a polyline (a line with a thickness) so that the system now responds to deviant performance in a non-interacting way. Understanding the process of non-interacting and freely interacting variables is vital in separating the chaff from the variables of interest.

Apart from the foreseen contingency, which should be built into the schedule and planning, some amount of unforeseen contingency should be kept at hand on management reserve. Figure 5 shows the performance of the BCWP compared with the BCWS band made out of two schedules. The significance of the fall out of the contractor's performance is seen as the BCWP crossed the band and the second schedule actually took over. The project still had cost and time overruns. The schedule contingency was fully used up but some costs could be saved, thanks to a probabilistic understanding of the project and our robust process design, which had a built in insensitivity to surprises and deviations from standard operating conditions.

Lessons in "Non Conformance"—Do not Pursue the Nominal Value as Celebrated in the EVM Metrics—De-Emphasize Perfection

Performance measurement in a resource's constrained environment can no longer be "focussed on quality conformance" (Tapiero 1996), but should be focused on optimum performance. A good process control mechanism is more important than achieving the target on line, although it is highly likely to be achieved as a corollary, when such a system is in place. As Deming (1997) says, "A numerical

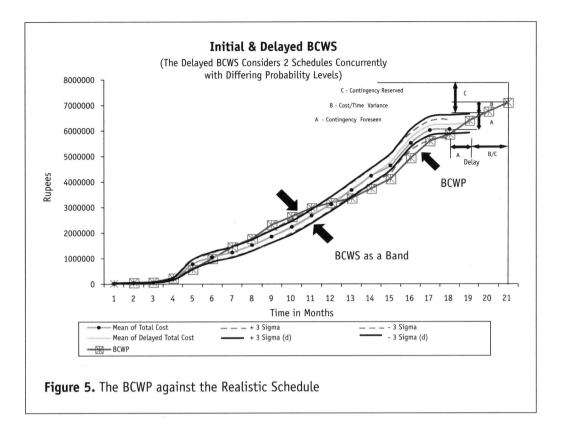

Figure 5. The BCWP against the Realistic Schedule

goal accomplishes nothing. Only the method is important, not the goal." As the construction management profession struggles to establish a credibility in a world of unmet targets, nothing can be more important than the importance of a innovative, honest, and well-meaning effort in improving the process, especially when the system is often incapable of meeting its goals due to various constraints. The author's experience with various projects has reinforced the fact that processes are often in statistical control, yet fail to deliver the time and cost objectives because the demand supply imbalance of various economic situations generate corruption and collusion. We do not operate in the perfect competitive markets. The resultant uncertainty and unpredictability of the process causes variations, which are way beyond acceptable control limits. However, the system expectation tends to ignore the unquantified effects of these uncertainties, focussing on narrow specification limits. In such cases, some basic optimization and a study of the process show the systems to be predictably faltering; which in itself is a state of statistical control. As Deming (1997) says "a process could be in statistical control yet 100 percent defective. To go about reduction of fires, treating every fire as if it arose from a special cause, an accident, is totally different from regarding it as a product of a stable process. This supposition that every fire is an accident may well block the road to reduction in the number of fires." The solution lies only in the improvement of the process. Thus, it seems vital for EVM to accept "non-conformance." The BCWS as a nominal value in terms of time and cost is rather

Figure 6. EVM is a Three-Dimensional Process

simplistic, and not worthwhile to pursue as an absolute number at the beginning of the process cycle. But it still remains relevant because, as the cycle matures and we make the system come near to its goal, we will be in a position to deliver the nominal value. And just as always, qualitative, quantitative, graphical, and statistical studies are required to provide insights and solutions, which cannot be detected just through visual and simplistic interpretation of data (Tapiero 1996).

The Third Dimension—Conflict of Interests

The traditional approach to EVM and statistical control, just explained, ignores the element of conflict. Although the owner normally thinks that the contract document resolves all conflicts, in reality it is only a beginning. Conflict is all-pervasive. Negotiations happen throughout the project duration and unless the basis for such negotiations is "best for everybody concerned" (Deming 1997), the conflict of financial interests is the third unquantified dimension in most contracts. Both owners and contractors expect "risk protection to ensure that they obtain what they expected at the time of the transactions." However, the project objective frequently changes for all or some of the project stakeholders during the course of the project. In construction programs, as part of real property investment, all stakeholders, in their positions as owners, contractors, developers, or equity partners, have an expectation of a fair return from a portfolio of multiple, interrelated projects which are being managed simultaneously for an aggregate return on investment. They all have some forecasts of expected cash flows. But the uncertainty inherent in the forecasting process carries with it a potential trap. It often

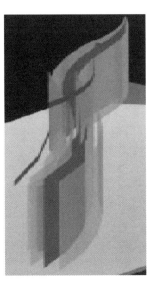

Figure 7. View of the BCWP and BCWS Band

creates gaps in expected and realized returns and the results and their effects are different for all the stakeholders as they manage their unique portfolios. Theoretically, the contract should protect all parties and reduce the uncertainty they face in order to stabilize their operating environments. In a practical sense, we need to at least accept the conflicts and understand the need to cooperate, coordinate activities, and reach a greater level of performance in a win-win relationship. Unmanaged conflicts have significance beyond the scope of a single current project, as they damage future project opportunities as well. The third dimension of the BCWS is an acceptance of this phenomenon. Figures 6, 7, and 8 show the BCWS extruded to the third dimension—the differing heights suggesting different conflict levels at various stages of the project.

Often times, the contractor operates in a multiproject environment and his profitability at any time is determined by how all the projects are doing. A detrimental effect in one could snowball to others if his rate of return on investment and working capital is affected. This induces a new negotiating and maximizing attitude in an otherwise "in control" project, ultimately jeopardizing its route to success. Shifting priorities often destroy the mutually compatible set of interests envisioned in the contract document. Suddenly there arise conflicting expectations, which ultimately deteriorate the trust between stakeholders. The mitigation and optimization of these conflicts within the contractual framework is the third dimension, which determines the success of project performance.

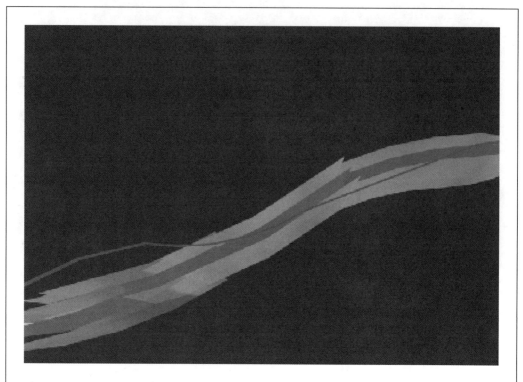

Figure 8. View of the BCWP and BCWS Band

The Project and the Portfolio

All the stakeholders in a project vie for the same fixed resources of all the others. It is the ability to manage these multiple projects in a comprehensive manner that defines the program management space of all the players. What happens to the single project in these multiple project scenarios is a very interesting issue. We need to interpret the residual significance of the time and cost constraint imposed on the individual project when all the players are actually in a dynamic environment, dictated by their levels of commitment at the program management level. In fact, the development of the theory of diversification through portfolio selection is an adequate acknowledgement of the issue. It is based on the concept of maximizing the utility of an investor's wealth under conditions of uncertainty. A portfolio achieves a maximum return for any given level of risk or a minimum level of risk for a given level of return. Hence the assumption of a guaranteed payoff is clearly unrealistic. We can only put forward our best forecast based on the information we have today. Whether it is time or cost or the future value of the property under construction, it is wiser to talk of expected financial returns over the life cycle of the property or over the holding period of the investment. So as we widen our horizon, the view of our project changes. We are not only trying to minimize the standard deviation of our project returns; we are also trying to simultaneously minimize the standard deviation of our portfolio risk. Changing market conditions put new constraints on resources and the priority of projects in a portfolio may change for one or more of the parties in a contract. With numerous stakeholders in complex projects, the situation is essentially going to be different for different stakeholders in a project. This intriguing relationship of the project to the portfolios of the various stakeholders can very well be the focus of further research, but for now, optimizing this conflict within this process envelope is the final challenge.

References

Deming, W. A. 1997. *The New Economics*. Massachusetts Institute of Technology: Center for Advanced Educational Services.

Ghose, Suhrita. 1989. *Development of an Integrated Approach to Project Monitoring*. New Delhi: School of Planning and Architecture.

Levine, David, P. Ramsay, and M. Berenson. 1995. *Business Statistics for Quality and Productivity*. Prentice Hall International.

Peters, Glen. 1981. *Project Management and Construction Control*. Construction.

Pilcher, Roy. 1985. *Project Cost Control in Construction*. London: Collin.

Tapiero, Charles S. 1996. *The Management of Quality and Its Control*. Chapman and Hall.

Wearne, Stephen. 1989. *Control of Engineering Projects*. P. Telford.

Editor and Author Contact Information

Co-Editors

Dennis P. Slevin, Ph.D.
   Professor
   Katz Graduate School of Business
   University of Pittsburgh
   dpslevin@katz.business.pitt.edu

David I. Cleland, Ph.D.
   Professor Emeritus
   Industrial Engineering Department
   School of Engineering
   University of Pittsburgh
   dic@engrng.pitt.edu

Jeffrey K. Pinto, Ph.D.
   Breene Fellow in Management & Professor
   School of Business
   Pennsylvania State University at Erie
   jkp4@psu.edu

SECTION I—A LOOK AT BACKGROUND RESEARCH IN THE FIELD

Chapter 1—Forty Years of Project Management Research: Trends, Interpretations, and Predictions

Primary Authors:

Timothy J. Kloppenborg, Ph.D., PMP
   Associate Professor
   Xavier University
   Tim_Kloppenborg@notes.xu.edu

Warren A. Opfer, MBA, PMP
   Principal
   The Dayton Group
   waopfer@thedaytongroup.com

Chapter 2—Research Trends in the 1990s: The Need Now to Focus on the Business Benefit of Project Management

Peter W. G. Morris, Ph.D.
Professor of Construction and Project Management
University College, London
Professor of Engineering Project Management
UMIST
Executive Director
INDECO Ltd.
pwmorris@netcomuk.co.uk

Chapter 3—Project Management Research: Experiences and Perspectives

David Wilemon, Ph.D.
Director, Innovation Management Program
School of Management
Syracuse University
dwilemon@som.syr.edu

Chapter 4—Proposition of a Systemic and Dynamic Model to Design Lifelong Learning Structure: The Quest of the Missing Link between Men, Team, and Organizational Learning

Christophe N. Bredillet, D.Sc.
Professor Chair of Project Management & Economics, Director of Program
UTS, ISGI Lille Graduate School of Management
cbredillet@nordnet.fr

Chapter 5—What the United States Defense Systems Management College Has Learned from Ten Years of Project Leadership Research

Owen C. Gadeken, D.Sci., PMP
Professor of Engineering Management
Defense Systems Management College
owen.gadeken@dau.mil

Chapter 6—United States Defense Acquisition Research Program: A New Look

Mark E. Nissen, Ph.D.
Assistant Professor
Graduate School of Business & Public Policy
Naval Postgraduate School
mnissen@nps.navy.mil

Keith F. Snider, Ph.D.
Assistant Professor
Graduate School of Business & Public Policy
Naval Postgraduate School
ksnider@nps.navy.mil

Ira Lewis, Ph.D.
Associate Professor
Graduate School of Business & Public Policy
Naval Postgraduate School
ialewis@nps.navy.mil

Chapter 7—Project Management for Intensive, Innovation-Based Strategies: New Challenges for the 21st Century

Christophe Midler
>   Directeur de Recherche
>   Centre de Recherche en Gestion
>   de l'École polytechnique
>   midler@poly.polytechnique.fr

SECTION II—EFFECTIVE PRACTICES & SUCCESS FACTORS

Chapter 8—Profiling the Competent Project Manager

Lynn Crawford, DBA
>   Project Management and Economics Program
>   University of Technology Sydney
>   Lynn.Crawford@uts.edu.au

Chapter 9—Measuring Project Management's Value: New Directions for Quantifying PM/ROI[SM]

C. William Ibbs, Ph.D., P.E.
>   Professor
>   Department of Civil and Environmental Engineering
>   University of California, Berkeley
>   ibbs@ce.berkeley.edu

Justin Reginato, P.E.
>   Graduate Student Researcher
>   Department of Civil and Environmental Engineering
>   University of California, Berkeley
>   jregi@uclink4.berkeley.edu

Chapter 10—Project Management Practices in French Organizations: A State of the Art

Daniel Leroy, Ph.D.
>   Directeur du DESS Gestion de Projet, Maitre de Conferences en Sciences de Gestions
>   Institut d'Ádministration de Enterprises de Lille
>   Université des Sciences et Technologies de Lille
>   dleroy@nordnet.fr

Chapter 11—A Framework for Analyzing the Development and Delivery of Large Capital Projects

Roger Miller, D.Sc., FCAE
>   University of Quebec at Montreal
>   miller.roger@uqam.ca

Brian Hobbs, Ph.D., PMP
>   Professor
>   Master's Program in Project Management
>   University of Quebec at Montreal
>   hobbs.brian@uqam.ca

SECTION III—ORGANIZATIONAL AND TEAM RELATIONSHIPS—
BEHAVIORAL PRACTICES

Chapter 12—Competencies in the Project-Oriented Organization
Roland Gareis, Univ. Prof. Dkfm. Dr.
Professor
Vienna University of Economics and Business Administration
Roland.Gareis@wu-wien.ac.at

Chapter 13—The Role of TRUST in Project Management
Francis T. Hartman, Ph.D., PMP
NSERC/SSHRC/Industry Chair in Project Management
Project Management Specialization
University of Calgary
fhartman@ucalgary.ca

Chapter 14—Developing Superior Project Teams: A Study of the Characteristics of High Performance in Project Teams
Edward J. Hoffman, Ph.D.
Director, Academy of Program Project Leadership
U.S. National Aeronautics and Space Administration
ed.hoffman@hq.nasa.gov

Claire S. Kinlaw, Ph.D.
Special Projects Manager
Developmental Products, Inc
clairek@team-zone.com

Dennis C. Kinlaw, Ed.D.
Founder
Developmental Products, Inc

Chapter 15—Businesses in the World of Projects
Rolf A. Lundin, Ph.D.
Dean, Professor of Business Administration
Jönköping International Business School
Rolf.A.Lundin@jibs.hj.se

Chapter 16—Criteria for Effective Leadership in Technology-Oriented Project Teams
Hans J. Thamhain, Ph.D., PMP
Professor of Management
Director of Project Management Programs
Department of Management
Bentley College
hthamhain@bentley.edu

Chapter 17—Processes for Operational Control in the Project-Based Organization

J. Rodney Turner, Ph.D.
  Professor of Project Management
  Faculty of Economics
  Erasmus University
  turner@few.eur.nl

Anne Keegan, Ph.D.
  Assistant Professor
  Faculty of Economics
  Erasmus University
  keegan@few.eur.nl

Chapter 18—Project Companies and the Multi-Project Paradigm: A New Management Approach

Marko Arenius
  Researcher
  European Organization for Nuclear Research
  Helsinki Institute of Physics
  Marko.Arenius@cern.ch

Karlos A. Artto, Ph.D.
  Professor, International Project Business
  Department of Industrial Engineering and Management
  Helsinki University of Technology
  karlos.artto@hut.fi

Mika Lahti, M.Sc.
  Senior Manager
  Nokia
  mika.s.lahti@nokia.com

Jukka Meklin, M.Sc.
  Product Manager
  Jippii Group Oyj
  jukka.meklin@jippiigroup.com

Chapter 19—Selling Project Management to Senior Executives: What's the Hook?

Janice Thomas, Ph.D.
  Associate Professor and Program Director
  Athabasca University and University of Calgary
  janicet@athabascau.ca

Connie L. Delisle, Ph.D.
  Athabasca University
  Connie_Delisle@mba.athabascau.ca

Kam Jugdev, PMP, MEng, M.H.S.A.
  PhD Candidate, Project Management Consultant
  University of Calgary
  kjugdev@shaw.ca

Pamela Buckle, MBA
   Ph.D. Student
   University of Calgary
   pmbuckle@home.com

SECTION IV—PROJECT MANAGEMENT TECHNIQUES

Chapter 20—Managing Risks in Projects with Decision Technologies

Timothy J. Lowe, Ph.D.
   C. Maxwell Stanley Professor of International Operations Management
   Tippie College of Business
   University of Iowa
   Timothy-Lowe@uiowa.edu

Richard E. Wendell, Ph.D.
   Professor of Business Administration
   Katz Graduate School of Business
   University of Pittsburgh
   WENDELL@katz.pitt.edu

Chapter 21—Analysis of External and Internal Risks in Project Early Phase

Anne Marie Alquier, Ph.D.
   Université des Sciences Sociales de Toulouse
   Alquier@univ-tlse1.fr

Enrico Cagno, Ph.D.
   Dipartimento di Ingegneria Gestionale
   Politecnico di Milano
   Enrico.Cagno@PoliMI.it

Franco Caron
   Associate Professor
   Dipartimento di Ingegneria Gestionale
   Politecnico di Milano
   Franco.Caron@PoliMI.it

V. Leopulos
   National Technical University of Athens
   vleo@hermes.central.ntua.gr

M. A. Riado
   University of Seville
   'ridao@cartuja.us.es

Chapter 22—Improved Owner-Contractor Work Relationships Based on Capital Project Competencies

Stuart D. Anderson, Ph.D.
   Associate Professor
   Department of Civil Engineering
   Texas A&M University
   s-anderson5@tamu.edu

Shekhar S. Patil, Ph.D.
   Project Analyst
   Independent Project Analysis, Inc.
   spatil@ipaglobal.com

G. Edward Gibson, Jr., Ph.D.
   Associate Professor
   Department of Civil Engineering
   University of Texas at Austin
   egibson@mail.utexas.edu

Chapter 23—Project Stakeholder Mapping: Analyzing the Interests of Project Stakeholders

Graham M. Winch, Ph.D.
   Head, Project Management Division; Professor
   Manchester Centre for Civil and Construction Engineering
   UMIST
   g.winch@ucl.ac.uk

Sten Bonke, Ph.D., M.A.
   Associate Professor, Construction Management
   Department of Civil Engineering
   Technical University of Denmark
   sb@byg.dtu.dk

Chapter 24—Project Risk Management: The Required Transformations to Become Project Uncertainty Management

Chris Chapman, Ph.D.
   Professor of Mangement Science
   School of Management
   University of Southampton
   cbc@socsci.soton.ac.uk

Stephen Ward, Ph.D.
   Senior Lecturer
   School of Management
   University of Southampton
   scw@socsci.soton.ac.uk

Chapter 25—A Comparison of Drum-Buffer-Rope (DBR) and Critical Chain (CC) Buffering Techniques

Van Gray, Ph.D.
   Associate Professor
   Baylor University
   Van_Gray@baylor.edu

Joe Felan, Ph.D.
   Assistant Professor
   Department of Management
   Baylor University
   Joe_Felan@baylor.edu

Elisabeth Umble
  Baylor University

Michael Umble, Ph.D.
  Professor
  Baylor University
  Mike_Umble@baylor.edu

Chapter 26—Cross-Impact Analysis of Information Technologies and Project Management Knowledge Areas in the Building Design Process

H. Murat Gunaydin, Ph.D.
  Assistant Professor
  Faculty of Architecture
  Izmir Institute of Technology
  gunaydin@likya.iyte.edu.tr

David Arditi, Ph.D.
  Professor
  Department of Civil and Architectural Engineering
  Illinois Institute of Technology
  arditi@iit.edu

Chapter 27—Managing Technological Innovation Projects: The Quest for a Universal Language

Bob Mills, Ph.D.
  Senior Lecturer
  Department of Materials and Process Engineering
  School of Science and Technology
  University of Waikato
  b.mills@waikato.ac.nz

Alan Langdon, Ph.D.
  Associate Professor
  Department of Materials and Process Engineering
  School of Science and Technology
  University of Waikato
  a.langdon@waikato.ac.nz

Chris Kirk, Ph.D.
  Director of Research Policy and Strategy
  Massey University
  C.Kirk@massey.ac.nz

Janis Swan, Ph.D.
  Associate Professor
  Department of Materials and Process Engineering
  School of Science and Technology
  University of Waikato
  j.swan@waikato.ac.nz

Chapter 28—Deriving the 2nd and 3rd Dimensions of the BCWS

Suhrita Sen, B. Arch, MBEM, MSRED
Principal Consultant
"Nirh," New Delhi, India
suhritasen@hotmail.com

Upgrade Your Project Management Knowledge

with First-Class Publications from PMI

A Guide to the Project Management Body of Knowledge (PMBOK® Guide) – 2000 Edition

PMI's *PMBOK® Guide* has become *the* essential sourcebook for the project management profession and its de facto global standard, with over 700,000 copies in circulation worldwide. It has been designated an American National Standard by the American National Standards Institute (ANSI) and is one of the major references used by candidates to study for the Project Management Professional (PMP®) Certification Examination. This new edition incorporates numerous recommendations and changes to the 1996 edition, including: progressive elaboration is given more emphasis; the role of the project office is acknowledged; the treatment of earned value is expanded in three chapters; the linkage between organizational strategy and project management is strengthened throughout; and the chapter on risk management has been rewritten with six processes instead of four. Newly added processes, tools, and techniques are aligned with the five project management processes and nine knowledge areas.

ISBN: 1-880410-23-0 (paperback)
ISBN: 1-880410-22-2 (hardcover)
ISBN: 1-880410-25-7 (CD-ROM)

PMI Project Management Salary Survey – 2000 Edition

This 2000 Edition updates information first published in 1996 and expands coverage to over forty industry affiliations in nearly fifty countries in seven major geographic regions around the world. Its purpose is to establish normative compensation and benefits data for the project management profession on a global basis. The study provides salary, bonus/overtime, and deferred compensation information for specific job titles/positions within the project management profession. It also contains normative data for a comprehensive list of benefits and an array of other relevant parameters. *The PMI Project Management Salary Survey – 2000 Edition* is a vital new research tool for managers and HR professionals looking to retain or recruit employees, current members of the profession or those interested in joining it, researchers, and academics.

ISBN: 1-880410-26-5 (paperback)

Project Management Research at the Turn of the Millennium: Proceedings of PMI Research Conference 2000

Project Management Institute
This state-of-the-art compilation includes the full text and graphics of the 46 papers presented at the first PMI project management research conference, held in Paris, France in June 2000. The conference's themes were professional needs assessment, the future of project management, inspiring project management research, project management information, and advancing the project management profession. Presenters included respected academics, researchers, and practitioners from around the globe. Their topics covered a span of 40 years of past, present, and future research efforts, and, by being gathered into this one volume, actually form one of the baseline documents for the modern project management profession.

ISBN: 1-880410-88-5 (paperback)

Selling Project Management to Senior Executives

Janice Thomas, Connie Delisle, and Kam Jugdev
Available in June 2002, this handbook presents new research findings about successful techniques to raise awareness of project management among senior executives. It also details ways to gain their support in implementing project management capabilities and practices throughout an organization.

ISBN: 1-880410-95-8 (paperback)

Quantifying the Value of Project Management

C. William Ibbs, Justin Reginato, and Peter W.G. Morris
Available in June 2002, this new guide covers current research documenting the financial and organizational returns that accrue to organizations that invest in focused or enterprise-wide project management capabilities.

ISBN: 1-880410-96-6 (paperback)

Best Practices of Project Management Groups in Large Functional Organizations

Frank Toney and Ray Powers
The best thinking of some of the world's leading project management practitioners is presented in this comprehensive study of current project management practice. In benchmarking project management, Toney and Powers provide specific key success factors and core best practices that practitioners can apply to their own workplace; information about the results of benchmark analysis; a detailed set of guidelines to enable others to replicate the benchmark process; and templates consisting of letters, agendas, ethical codes, and surveys for practitioners to use in the conduct of their own benchmark activities.

ISBN: 1-880410-05-2 (paperback)

The Benefits of Project Management: Financial and Organizational Rewards to Corporations

C. William Ibbs and Young-Hoon Kwak

This study documents the organizational and financial benefits that result from implementing project management tools, processes, and practices. In particular, it looks at the return on investment that organizations can realize by investing in all aspects of project management and provides tools for estimating the kind of return on investment they can expect from taking certain actions.

ISBN: 1-880410-32-X (paperback)

The PMI Project Management Fact Book, Second Edition

Project Management Institute

First published in 1999, this newly enlarged and updated "almanac" provides a single, accessible reference volume on global project management and PMI. Topics include the history, size, explosive growth, and the future of the project management profession; parameters of the typical project; a statistical profile of the individuals working in project management based on recent, global research; the organizational settings in which project management activities take place; and valuable information about the world's largest professional association serving project management, the Project Management Institute. Appendices offer an additional wealth of information: lists of universities with degree programs in project management and PMI Registered Educational Providers; PMI's Ethical Standards; professional awards; a glossary; and an extensive bibliography. This is *the* central reference for those working in project management and a career guide for those interested in entering the profession.

ISBN: 1-880410-73-7 (paperback)

Project Management Institute Practice Standard for Work Breakdown Structures

Project Management Institute

PMI's first practice standard to complement and elaborate on *A Guide to the Project Management Body of Knowledge* (PMBOK® Guide) - 2000 Edition, this new manual provides guidance and universal principles for the initial generation, subsequent development, and application of the Work Breakdown Structure (WBS). It introduces the WBS and its characteristics, discusses the benefits of using a WBS, and demonstrates how to build a WBS and determine its sufficiency for subsequent planning and control. A unique feature is the inclusion of 11 industry-specific examples that illustrate how to build a WBS, ranging from Process Improvement and Software Design to Refinery Turnaround and Service Industry Outsourcing.

ISBN 1-880410-81-8 (paperback)

People in Projects

Project Management Institute

This important new book focuses on one of the nine knowledge areas of the *PMBOK® Guide* and one of the most important aspects of every project—human resources management. It is a collection of the best articles relating to the people side of project management that PMI has produced in the last five years. The authors are acknowledged experts in their fields, and the wide-ranging topics include leadership, negotiation, relationship building, job evaluation and appraisal, worldwide teams, and managing change.

ISBN:1880410729 (paperback)

Project Management for the Technical Professional

Michael Singer Dobson

Dobson, project management expert, popular seminar leader, and personality theorist, understands "promotion grief." He counsels those who prefer logical relationships to people skills and shows technical professionals how to successfully make the transition into management. This is a witty, supportive management primer for any "techie" invited to hop on the first rung of the corporate ladder. It includes self-assessment exercises; a skillful translation of general management theory and practice into tools, techniques, and systems that technical professionals will understand and accept; helpful "how to do it" sidebars; and action plans. It's also an insightful guide for those who manage technical professionals.

"The exercises and case studies featured here, along with the hands-on advice, hammer home fundamental principles. An intriguing complement to more traditional IT management guides, this is suitable for all libraries." —*Library Journal*

ISBN: 1-880410-76-1 (paperback)

The Project Surgeon: A Troubleshooter's Guide to Business Crisis Management

Boris Hornjak

A veteran of business recovery, project turnarounds and crisis prevention, Hornjak shares his "lessons learned" in this best practice primer for operational managers. He writes with a dual purpose—first for the practical manager thrust into a crisis situation with a mission to turn things around, make tough decisions under fire, address problems when they occur, and prevent them from happening again. Then his emphasis turns to crisis *prevention*, so you can free your best and brightest to focus on opportunities, instead of on troubleshooting problems, and ultimately break the failure/recovery cycle.

ISBN: 1-880410-75-3 (paperback)

Risk and Decision Analysis in Projects
Second Edition

John R. Schuyler

Schuyler, a consultant in project risk and economic decision analysis, helps project management professionals improve their decision-making skills and integrate them into daily problem solving. In this heavily illustrated second edition, he explains and demystifies key concepts and techniques, including expected value, optimal decision policy, decision trees, the value of information, Monte Carlo simulation, probabilistic techniques, modeling techniques, judgments and biases, utility and multi-criteria decisions, and stochastic variance.

ISBN: 1-880410-28-1 (paperback)

Earned Value Project Management
Second Edition

Quentin W. Fleming and Joel M. Koppelman

Now a classic treatment of the subject, this second edition updates this straightforward presentation of earned value as a useful method to measure actual project performance against planned costs and schedules throughout a project's life cycle. The authors describe the earned value concept in a simple manner so that it can be applied to any project, of any size, and in any industry.

ISBN: 1880410-27-3 (paperback)

Project Management Experience and Knowledge Self-Assessment Manual

Based on the *Project Management Professional (PMP) Role Delineation Study*, this manual is designed to help individuals assess how proficiently they could complete a wide range of essential project management activities based on their current levels of knowledge and experience. Included are exercises and lists of suggested activities for readers to use in improving their performance in those areas they assessed as needing further training.

ISBN: 1-880410-24-9 (spiral paperback)

Project Management Professional (PMP) Role Delineation Study

In 1999, PMI® completed a role delineation study for the Project Management Professional (PMP®) Certification Examination. In addition to being used to establish the test specifications for the examination, the study describes the tasks (competencies) PMPs perform and the project management knowledge and skills PMPs use to complete each task. Each of the study's tasks is linked to a performance domain (e.g., planning the project). Each task has three components to it: what the task is, why the task is performed, and how the task is completed. The *Role Delineation Study* is an excellent resource for educators, trainers, administrators, practitioners, and individuals interested in pursuing PMP certification.

ISBN: 1-880410-29-X (spiral paperback)

PM 101 According to the Olde Curmudgeon

Francis M. Webster Jr.

Former editor-in-chief for PMI®, Francis M. Webster Jr. refers to himself as "the olde curmudgeon." The author, who has spent thirty years practicing, consulting on, writing about, and teaching project management, dispenses insider information to novice project managers with a friendly, arm-around-the-shoulder approach. He provides a history and description of all the components of modern project management; discusses the technical, administrative, and leadership skills needed by project managers; and details the basic knowledge and processes of project management, from scope management to work breakdown structure to project network diagrams. An excellent introduction for those interested in the profession themselves or in training others who are.

ISBN: 1-880410-55-9 (paperback)

The Project Sponsor Guide

Neil Love and Joan Brant-Love

This practical guide is intended for executives and middle managers who will be, or are, sponsors of a project, particularly cross-functional projects. It is also helpful reading for facilitators and project leaders.

ISBN: 1-880410-15-X (paperback)

Don't Park Your Brain Outside: A Practical Guide to Improving Shareholder Value with SMART Management

Francis T. Hartman

Hartman has assembled a cohesive and balanced approach to highly effective project management. It is deceptively simple. Called SMART™, this new approach is Strategically Managed, Aligned, Regenerative, and Transitional. It is based on research and best practices, tempered by hard-won experience. SMART has saved significant time and money on the hundreds of large and small, simple and complex projects on which it has been tested.

ISBN: 1-880410-48-6 (hardcover)

The EnterPrize Organization: Organizing Software Projects for Accountability and Success

Neal Whitten

Neal Whitten is a twenty-three-year veteran of IBM and now president of his own consulting firm. Here he provides a practical guide to addressing a serious problem that has plagued the software industry since its beginning: how to effectively organize software projects to significantly increase their success rate. He proposes the "Enterprize Organization" as a model that takes advantage of the strengths of the functional organization, projectized organization, and matrix organization, while reducing or eliminating their weaknesses. The book collects the experiences and wisdom of thousands of people and hundreds of projects, and reduces *lessons learned* to a simple format that can be applied immediately to your projects.

ISBN: 1-880410-79-6 (paperback)

Teaming for Quality

H. David Shuster

Shuster believes most attempts at corporate cultural change die because people fail to realize how addicted they are to the way things are, the root causes of their resistance to change, and the degree to which their willingness to change depends on the moral philosophy of management. His new book offers a stimulating synthesis of classical philosophy, metaphysics, behavioral science, management theory and processes, and two decades of personal teaming experience to explain how individuals can choose change for themselves. Its philosophy-to-practice approach will help people team in ways that promote exceptionally high levels of bonding, individual creative expression (innovation), and collective agreement (consensus). Shuster shows how personal work fulfillment and corporate goals *can* work in alignment.

ISBN: 1-880410-63-X (paperback)

The Juggler's Guide to Managing Multiple Projects

Michael S. Dobson

This comprehensive book introduces and explains task-oriented, independent, and interdependent levels of project portfolios. It says that you must first have a strong foundation in time management and priority setting, then introduces the concept of Portfolio Management to timeline multiple projects, determine their resource requirements, and handle emergencies.

ISBN: 1-880410-65-6 (paperback)

Recipes for Project Success

Al DeLucia and Jackie DeLucia

This book is destined to become "the" reference book for beginning project managers, particularly those who like to cook! Practical, logically developed project management concepts are offered in easily understood terms in a lighthearted manner. They are applied to the everyday task of cooking—from simple, single dishes, such as homemade tomato sauce for pasta, made from the bottom up, to increasingly complex dishes or meals for groups that in turn require an understanding of more complex project management terms and techniques. The transition between cooking and project management discussions is smooth, and tidbits of information provided with the recipes are interesting and humorous.

ISBN: 1-880410-58-3 (paperback)

Tools and Tips for Today's Project Manager

Ralph L. Kliem and Irwin S. Ludin

This guidebook is valuable for understanding project management and performing to quality standards. Includes project management concepts and terms—old and new—that are not only defined but also are explained in much greater detail than you would find in a typical glossary.

ISBN: 1-880410-61-3 (paperback)

The Future of Project Management

Developed by the 1998 PMI® Research Program Team and the futurist consultant firm of Coates and Jarratt, Inc., this guide to the future describes one hundred national and global trends and their implications for project management, both as a recognized profession and as a general management tool. It covers everything from knowbots, nanotechnology, and disintermediation to changing demography, information technology, social values, design, and markets.

ISBN: 1-880410-71-0 (paperback)

New Resources for PMP® Candidates

The following publications are recommended resources that candidates may study to prepare for the Project Management Professional (PMP) Certification Examination.

PMP Resource Package

The Cultural Dimension of International Business, Fourth Edition
by Gary P. Ferraro

Doing Business Internationally: The Guide to Cross-Cultural Success
by Terence Brake, Danielle Walker, Thomas Walker

Earned Value Project Management, Second Edition
by Quentin W. Fleming and Joel M. Koppelman

Effective Project Management
by Robert K. Wysocki, Robert Beck Jr., David B. Crane

Focus Groups: A Step-by-Step Guide
by Gloria E. Bader and Catherine A. Rossi

Global Literacies: Lessons on Business Leadership and National Cultures
by Robert Rosen (Editor), Patricia Digh, Carl Phillips

A Guide to the Project Management Body of Knowledge (PMBOK® Guide) – 2000 Edition
by Project Management Institute

How to Lead Work Teams: Facilitation Skills, Second Edition
by Fran Rees

Human Resource Skills for the Project Manager
by Vijay K. Verma

The New Project Management
by J. Davidson Frame

Organizational Architecture: Designs for Changing Organizations
by David A. Nader, Marc S. Gerstein, Robert Shaw, and Associates

Principles of Project Management
by John Adams, et al.

Project & Program Risk Management
by R. Max Wideman, Editor

Project Management Experience and Knowledge Self-Assessment Manual
by Project Management Institute

Project Management: A Managerial Approach, Fourth Edition
by Jack R. Meredith and Samuel J. Mantel Jr.

*Project Management: A Systems Approach to Planning, Scheduling, and Controlling,
Seventh Edition*
by Harold Kerzner

Visit PMI's Website at *www.pmi.org*

or Shop at Our Online Bookstore at *www.pmibookstore.org*

Also Available from PMI

Project Management for Managers
Mihály Görög, Nigel J. Smith
ISBN: 1-880410-54-0 (paperback)

Project Leadership: From Theory to Practice
Jeffrey K. Pinto, Peg Thoms, Jeffrey Trailer, Todd Palmer, Michele Govekar
ISBN: 1-880410-10-9 (paperback)

Annotated Bibliography of Project and Team Management
David I. Cleland, Gary Rafe, Jeffrey Mosher
ISBN: 1-880410-47-8 (paperback)
ISBN: 1-880410-57-5 (CD-ROM)

How to Turn Computer Problems into Competitive Advantage
Tom Ingram
ISBN: 1-880410-08-7 (paperback)

Achieving the Promise of Information Technology
Ralph B. Sackman
ISBN: 1-880410-03-6 (paperback)

Leadership Skills for Project Managers
Editors' Choice Series
Edited by Jeffrey K. Pinto, Jeffrey W. Trailer
ISBN: 1-880410-49-4 (paperback)

The Virtual Edge
Margery Mayer
ISBN: 1-880410-16-8 (paperback)

The ABCs of DPC
Edited by PMI's Design-Procurement-Construction Specific Interest Group
ISBN: 1-880410-07-9 (paperback)

Project Management Casebook
Edited by David I. Cleland, Karen M. Bursic, Richard Puerzer, A. Yaroslav Vlasak
ISBN: 1-880410-45-1 (paperback)

Project Management Casebook, Instructor's Manual
Edited by David I. Cleland, Karen M. Bursic, Richard Puerzer, A. Yaroslav Vlasak
ISBN: 1-880410-18-4 (paperback)

The PMI Book of Project Management Forms
ISBN: 1-880410-31-1 (paperback)
ISBN: 1-880410-50-8 (diskette)

Principles of Project Management
John Adams et al.
ISBN: 1-880410-30-3 (paperback)

Organizing Projects for Success
Human Aspects of Project Management Series, Volume One
Vijay K. Verma
ISBN: 1-880410-40-0 (paperback)

Human Resource Skills for the Project Manager
Human Aspects of Project Management Series, Volume Two
Vijay K. Verma
ISBN: 1-880410-41-9 (paperback)

Managing the Project Team
Human Aspects of Project Management Series, Volume Three
Vijay K. Verma
ISBN: 1-880410-42-7 (paperback)

Value Management Practice
Michel Thiry
ISBN: 1-880410-14-1 (paperback)

The World's Greatest Project
Russell W. Darnall
ISBN: 1-880410-46-X (paperback)

Power & Politics in Project Management
Jeffrey K. Pinto
ISBN: 1-880410-43-5 (paperback)

Best Practices of Project Management Groups in Large Functional Organizations
Frank Toney, Ray Powers
ISBN: 1-880410-05-2 (paperback)

Project Management in Russia
Vladimir I. Voropajev
ISBN: 1-880410-02-8 (paperback)

A Framework for Project and Program Management Integration
R. Max Wideman
ISBN: 1-880410-01-X (paperback)

Quality Management for Projects & Programs
Lewis R. Ireland
ISBN: 1-880410-11-7 (paperback)

Project & Program Risk Management
Edited by R. Max Wideman
ISBN: 1-880410-06-0 (paperback)

A Framework for Project Management
ISBN: 1-880410-82-6, Facilitator's Manual Set
(3-ring binder)
ISBN: 1-880410-80-X, Participants' Manual Set, (paperback)

Project Management Software Survey
ISBN: 1-880410-52-4 (paperback)
ISBN: 1-880410-59-1 (CD-ROM)

Order online at www.pmibookstore.org

Book Ordering Information
Phone: +412.741.6206
Fax: +412.741.0609
Email: pmiorders@abdintl.com

Mail: PMI Publications Fulfillment Center,
PO Box 1020, Sewickley, Pennsylvania 15143-1020 USA